The Lost Origins of the Essay

THE
Lost Origins
of the
Essay

Edited and introduced by

John D'Agata

Graywolf Press

Permission acknowledgments begin on page 691.

Publication of this volume is made possible in part by a grant provided by the Minnesota State Arts Board, through an appropriation by the Minnesota State Legislature; a grant from the Wells Fargo Foundation Minnesota; and a grant from the National Endowment for the Arts, which believes that a great nation deserves great art. Significant support has also been provided by the Bush Foundation; Target; the McKnight Foundation; and other generous contributions from foundations, corporations, and individuals. To these organizations and individuals we offer our heartfelt thanks.

Published by Graywolf Press
250 Third Avenue North, Suite 600
Minneapolis, Minnesota 55401
All rights reserved.

www.graywolfpress.org

Published in the United States of America

Printed in Canada

ISBN 978-1-55597-532-6

2   4   6   8   9   7   5   3

Library of Congress Control Number: 2008941982

Cover design: Christa Schoenbrodt, Studio Haus

What word is there to describe that kind of logic that sings?

PLUTARCH

◀▶

The word for it is new, but the thing itself is ancient.
BACON

◖◗

Oh, yes, dear reader: the essay is alive. There is no reason to despair.
WOOLF

◦◦

Contents

To the Reader

Six thousand years ago, in the middle of the desert, an industrious and lucky tribe lived where two rivers converged. This was a rare and verdant place: dark soil, lots of fish, thousands of birds on their way to the sea perching in large and shady palms to escape from the desert's sun. Many years later, European travelers would call this Mesopotamia, "the place between two rivers," but the ancient people who lived there simply called the place *kalam*—"the land"—for they hadn't ever known any home except this place, and because of this they assumed that they had been created for it. They believed, in fact, that they had come from those rivers, that their home was the place where the world itself was born, where the earliest piece of earth had first emerged above the waters, and where finally, out of that chaos, some intent had taken shape. The Sumerians are the people who invented civilization. They invented agriculture, kilns, alcohol, wheels, the first cities, the first government, the first legal codes. Their inventions became so numerous, and their prosperity so abundant, that the Sumerians actually needed to invent accounting, too, and so they produced a rudimentary series of small notches in clay that we recognize today as the first system of writing:

> From a cultivated field in the southern valley, Itta-bala has made a purchase of six talents of wheat from his neighbor, Tash-itum.

1

Their earliest written accounts are therefore records of trade and commerce:

> As to the gold ring in which an emerald has been set, Beli-akka guarantees that for twenty-five years that stone will not fall from the ring. If the stone should fall out within twenty-five years, the purchaser shall be paid ten more mannas of new silver.

There were even the occasional contracts to protect them from their contracts:

> I, Ra-immum, have taken for my wife Bash-atum, the daughter of my friend, Beli-nu. The bridal payment shall be ten shekels of gold. If, however, after receipt of this, Bash-atum ever says to me "You are not my husband!" she shall be strangled and cast into the river. If I, Ra-immum, ever say to Bash-atum "You are not my wife!" I will pay her father another ten shekels of gold.

Indeed, it's estimated that over 90 percent of what the Sumerians wrote down only served an administrative function. Writing, in other words, began as nonfiction. But unfortunately it was the worst kind of nonfiction there is: informational, literal, nothing about it mattering beyond the place it held for facts. Nevertheless, the efficiencies that writing introduced to their markets helped the Sumerian people become the richest in the world, their home slowly growing from an outpost of huts to a kingdom of broad boulevards and giant apartment blocks. The culture grew nonstop like this for almost five centuries, their tallies, receipts, and records the only literature they produced. And because of this success the gods began to notice Sumer, looking down and seeing those many marketplaces, those huge apartment blocks, the clanging carts on paved streets, the butchers and the potters and the prostitutes and the beggars—the ceaseless shapeless clattering of the *who-what-when-where-why*. The gods took note of Sumer because it'd never been so noisy. And scholars agree that this is what finally did Sumer in. The rivers surrounding Sumer started suddenly overflowing, and for seven days and seven nights they overcame their banks, coursed rapidly into Sumer, dissolved everything back to mud. The home of the Sumerians was rendered once again indistinguishable from the nothing that it had emerged from. As one version of the story has described the scene for us, "The windstorms rose . . . and then the waves rose . . . and after the gods were finished there was land but nothing else." It's embarrassing, of course, to think nonfiction destroyed the world, especially since some readers are still suspicious of the form: a genre that is merely a dispensary of data—not a true expression of one's dreams, ideas, or fears. But I think this misperception is prevalent today because we haven't yet laid claim to an alternative tradition. Do we read nonfiction in order to receive information, or do we read it to experience art? It's not very clear sometimes. So this is a book that will try to offer the reader a clear objective: I am here in search of art. I am here to track the origins of an alternative to commerce.

It begins in ancient Sumer, once the waters have receded, once a single survivor, named Ziusudra, washes onto the flattened muddy shore of this new world and begins to write a letter to its long and empty future. He's uncertain whether his letter will ever find a recipient, but he's compelled to write, and so he writes, cataloguing the problems that he had witnessed in the past by offering some advice about whatever's coming next. This list that Ziusudra makes is five thousand years old—half a millennium older than the earliest known poem, a full millennium older than the earliest known story. Scholars like to say, therefore, that Ziusudra started literature. But I think that Ziusudra did something much more important. I think his list is the beginning of an alternative to nonfiction, the beginning of a form that's not propelled by information, but one compelled instead by individual expression—by inquiry, by opinion, by wonder, by doubt. Ziusudra's list is the first essay in the world: it's a mind's inquisitive ramble through a place wiped clean of answers. It is trying to make a new shape where there previously was none.

The Lost Origins of the Essay

The List of Ziusudra

Back in those days—in those far remote days—back in those nights—in those far-away nights—back in those years—in those long ago years—back at that time when the wise ones were wise, the wisest of all of them had given up hope.

Friends, let me share with you the advice that those wise ones tried to offer. Let me give you these instructions, and please don't neglect them. Lessons from the past can still be useful for today, for any path that we may take in life is one that is treading the earth.

So first, don't ever buy a donkey that excessively brays, for this is the kind animal that will knock you on your ass.

Neither should you buy your prostitutes from the street, for they are the kind that will usually bite.

Also avoid the weekly sale of whores from the palace, for they are usually sold from the bottom of the barrel.

And do not ever hire a recently freed man, for you know that now he's tasted what you are not hiring for.

When there's a quarrel in progress, don't stand around watching it. Witnessing such things will only encourage more to happen. It goes without saying therefore that you shouldn't start a quarrel either, nor participate in one, nor bet on those who are fighting. Don't wait around the corner to hear from others about what happened. Do not listen to such nonsense.

Do not even want to care.

Stay away from quarrels altogether, in other words. These are the instructions I leave you.

You should not disgrace yourself, should not tell lies, should not boast, or gossip, or deliberate for too long.

You should not draw water from a well you can't reach, for this will make you suspicious to anyone nearby.

You should not go to work by only using your eyes, for possessions can't be multiplied if you only stare at them.

And don't ever shoo away a powerful man from your house, for this would be like tearing down the back wall of your home.

Instead, just as you'd grasp an ox in order to cross a mighty river, align yourself with a powerful man to lead you to success.

Understand, however, that it is easy for someone to share his bread while the dough is still in the oven.

The eyes of the slanderer always move like a spindle.

The garrulous man fills his grain bag while the haughty one brings his empty.

He who works with leather will eventually work his own.

And a weak wife will always be seized by fate.

For fate, dear friends, is like a wet bank. It is always going to make you slip.

—Ziusudra of Sumer, c. 2700 B.C.E.

(translated by Joshua Barnes)

1 5 0 0 B . C . E .

Babylonia

However, back then when writing was just taking off, the wise ones also told us that it would be a passing fad. The problem with writing, they said, is that you cannot ask it questions. When you try, it repeats itself. There is no give-and-take, no difference in what it says. But I think the essay is a antidote to the stagnancy of writing because the essay tries to replicate the activity of a mind. From the Middle French *essai*—"a test," "a trial," "an experiment"—the essay is the equivalent of a mind in rumination, performing as if improvisationally the reception of new ideas, the discovery of unknowns, the encounter with the "other." We see this in Susan Sontag's famous "Unguided Tour," a conversation that she holds within herself, about herself. We see it in Emerson, too, whenever he quotes another author, a technique that he employs not to support his working thesis but rather to introduce a new challenge to his claims. We even see this happening in the work of Thucydides, the world's first genuine practitioner of history, a writer who claimed that he didn't begin composing *The Peloponnesian War* until he had fought as a soldier on both sides of that conflict. The word for this comes from the Greek for "across"—*dia*—and "to think"—*logos*—emphasizing not the number of participants in such texts but rather the activity that those texts engage in: "to think through," "to investigate," "to wander." I think that this is an inherently human activity. And I think that when we're essaying we are in dialogue with the world.

9

Dialogue of Pessimism

One

"Slave! Come here!" "Yes, master, yes. I am always ready to serve you?"
"Go get my chariot and hitch up the horses. We're going to take a ride to the
palace." "Right away, sir. Excellent! The King's going to be very pleased to
have a visit from you." "Wait, wait. Hold on, slave. I'm changing my mind.
I don't want to ride all the way to the palace." "No, sir. Of course. That's
quite a distance to make at this hour. And the King's likely to send you
off on some errand for him. It'd be such an inconvenience, and for what?"

Two

"Slave, come back here." "Yes, master. At your service." "Get me some
water so that I can clean my hands. I'm ready to eat my supper." "Sounds
like a plan, sir. I always say that a well-fed man has a hearty spirit." "Hold
up there. On second thought, I'm really not that hungry. So forget it,
slave. Take the water away." "No problem, sir. It's good as gone. No reason
you should eat if you don't have an appetite. Drink and thirst, food and
hunger—it's not like they're going to go away!"

Three

"Slave!" "Yes, my master. You called?" "Maybe you should go to the stables
and hitch up the horses. Instead of going to the palace, let's just take a
ride." "Excellent idea, sir. A carefree mind always feeds a man's body. Or, as
my father often said: It's the stray dog that finds the bone. The wise ones say
that a migrating swallow will always build the best nest. And wild donkey

will find the freshest grass in the desert." "Huh? Forget it. I'm not going anywhere." "Well like I always say, sir: A wandering life is a dicey game. Stray dogs lose more teeth than domestics. The nests of migrating swallows fall easily out of trees. And the desert is the tomb of the donkey."

Four

"Slave! I'm calling you!" "Yes, master. I hear you!" "I feel like starting a family. I think I'd like to beget some children." "Then go to it, sir! You start a family. After all, he who has children secures his name in the future." "I don't actually like children, though." "Well then don't have any, sir. A family is like a broken door with squeaky hinges. Some of your kids are going to be healthy, but there will also be some who rack up huge bills. I always say that he who starts a family ends up ruining his house."

Five

"Slave, come here." "I'm at your service, sir." "I feel like causing some trouble, what do you say?" "I like the sound of that, sir. By all means, let's wreak some havoc! How else can you expect to get ahead in this world?" "But evildoing's not very proper, is it?" "Well, they either end up killed, or flayed alive and blinded. Or sometimes they're blinded and flayed alive and then thrown into a dungeon. My point is that, no, it's really not worth doing."

Six

"Slave!" "Yes, master, yes?" "I've decided: I am going to fall in love with a woman." "Way to go! Now you're talking! A man who's in love will forget his grief and sorrow." "But who am I kidding? I don't want to love a woman." "You know, I was going to say, sir. A woman is nothing but a snare. She's a pit, a trap. A dagger in the darkness that's ready to slit a man's throat."

Seven

"Slave? Where are you?" "Right here, sir. At your service." "I need some water to wash my hands. I'm going to make an offering to the gods." "Excellent idea, sir. He who makes offerings becomes rich in other ways." "Ah, forget it. Scratch that, slave. How many ways does a man really need to be rich? I'm going to keep my offerings for myself. That way I'll cut out the middleman." "Rightly so, sir. Rightly so. Are the gods really going to bow down to thank you? I mean, offerings come with rituals, sacrifice, obedience—who needs that song and dance?"

Eight

"Slave!" "Yes?" "I'm going to invest my fortune by offering some loans to the unfortunate." "Oh! You'll be helping so many people, sir, and the interest from all those loans will help you amass even more!" "But do I really want the hassle of chasing after all those payments?" "If you ask me, sir? No. Lending money to the poor is like begetting a rotten child. One way or another he'll end up eating up your profit."

Nine

"How about this?" "Yes, sir?" "I'm going to do a good deed for my country." "I like it, sir. Very good! I've heard it said that the names of those who serve their country are inscribed on gold rings that are worn by the gods." "You mean that's it?" "Sir?" "A gold ring? That's all? What's in it for me?" "You're reading my mind, sir. Take a walk among the ruins of any ancient city. The skulls of both commoners and noblemen fill up this earth. Do you know which belonged to the criminals and which to the greatest patrons?"

Ten

"Well, then . . . ay." "Sir?" "What's the point, slave? What's the point? Is there anything that's worth my time here on earth? Shall I hang myself now, throw myself into the river? If that's all that we're headed for, why not end it now?" "As the wise ones often say, sir: Who among us is so tall as to ascend to heaven alone? Who is so broad that he can reach around the world?" "You agree with me, then? Lower your neck for me, slave, and I'll put us both out of our miseries." "Yes, sir. Of course, sir. But may I first say, sir: I am not as miserable as you."

(translated by Emily Dimasi)

500 B.C.E.

Greece

The ancient Greeks are asking at some point this year what would happen if they were to break a piece of matter in half, and then what would happen if they took those halves and continued to break them repeatedly. Would they eventually reach a point beyond which nothing broke? Or would those halves keep splitting for as long as they were as broken? At stake is the kind of universe in which we're going to live: one that can be known, or one that never can. At this point in history, the Greeks decide that matter has a fundamental limit. They're imagining something so small at the bottom of the world that they're calling this thing *atoma*—"indivisible" in Greek—despite the fact that no evidence for such a thing yet exists. "Nothing exists," the Greeks explain, "except atoms and empty space." On the north shore of the Mediterranean Sea, however, the sole heir to the throne of ancient Ephesus, the wealthiest and most powerful city at the time, is abdicating his throne and declining his inheritance in pursuit of a life of the mind. "All things change to fire," he writes, "and fire, exhausted, falls back into things." After a lifetime spent observing the world around him, Heraclitus proposes that nothing in it is stable—that everything is in flux—and the more closely he looks inside it the more pieces of it he finds. He is living in a universe that is susceptible to change. Twenty-five hundred years before Albert Einstein, in fact, he is splitting the atom apart. "I am," writes Heraclitus, "as I am not." These

15

days his essays only exist for us in fragments, but it is still clear that he was a writer who relished instability: not only in ideas and things, but also in the words that we might use to represent them. Even in his own day, Heraclitus was referred to as "The Riddler," for his sentences sometimes use the exact same word to simultaneously signify both a subject and its object. "Heraclitus is a writer of the most splendid sort," Socrates once said about his predecessor. "But I think it would take a diver of the world's deepest seas to get to the bottom of him." It will take a hundred years for Socrates to be born. Another two hundred for China's *Tao Te Ching*. And it will take two millennia for Michel de Montaigne—the first modern exemplar of discursive human logic—to ask himself, What do I know? and then to invent a genre to help postpone the answer.

I Have Looked Diligently at My Own Mind

Those who wish to know about the world must learn about it in details.

◀ ▶

Knowledge is not intelligence.

◀ ▶

Men dig up and search through much earth in order to find gold.

◀ ▶

I have looked diligently at my own mind.

◀ ▶

It is natural for man to know his own mind and to be sane.

◀ ▶

Yet nature loves to hide.

◀ ▶

We share a world when we are awake.

◀ ▶

Awake, a dying world.

◀ ▶

Everything flows; nothing remains.

◀ ▶

One cannot step into the same river again.

◀ ▶

Change alone unchanges.

◀ ▶

History is a child building a sandcastle by the sea, and that child is the whole majesty of our power in the world.

◀ ▶

When Homer said that he wished war might disappear from the lives of humans, he forgot that without opposition all things would cease to exist.

◀ ▶

This world, which is always the same for all men, has always been, always is, and always shall be an everlasting fire rhythmically dying and flaring up again.

◀ ▶

Divides and rejoins, goes forward then backward.

◀ ▶

The first metamorphosis of fire is to become the sea, and half of the sea becomes the earth, half the flash of lightning.

◀ ▶

Lightning is the lord of everything.

◀ ▶

The life of fire comes from the death of earth. The life of air comes from the death of fire. The life of water comes from the death of air. The life of earth comes from the death of water.

◀ ▶

Fire, in time, catches up with everything.

◀ ▶

Not enough; too much.

◀ ▶

If every man had exactly what he wanted he would be no better than he is now.

◀ ▶

The stuff of the psyche is a smoke-like substance of fine particles that give rise to all other things, particles of less mass than any other substance and constantly in motion: only movement can know movement.

◀ ▶

The psyche rises as a mist from things that are wet.

◀ ▶

A dry psyche is most skilled in intelligence and is brightest in virtue.

◀ ▶

A drunk man, staggering and mindless, must be led home by his son, so wet is his psyche.

◀ ▶

Water brings death to the psyche, as earth brings death to water.

◀ ▶

The psyche lusts to be wet.

◀ ▶

All men are equally mystified by unaccountable evidence, even Homer, wisest of Greeks. He was mystified by children catching lice. He heard them say, *What we have found and caught we throw away; what we have not found and caught we still have.*

◀ ▶

We know health by illness, good by evil, satisfaction by hunger, leisure by fatigue.

◀ ▶

The same road goes both up and down.

◀ ▶

The beginning of a circle is also its end.

◀ ▶

The river we stepped into is not the river in which we stand.

◀ ▶

A bow is alive only when it kills.

◀ ▶

Dogs bark at strangers.

◀ ▶

Pigs wash in mud.

◀ ▶

Chickens in dust.

◀ ▶

Character is fate.

◀ ▶

There are gods here, too.

(translated by Guy Davenport)

100 B.C.E.

Greece

Contemporary accounts from ancient Athens tell us that the writer Tyrtamus was a particularly good dresser. They tell us that he was childless, unmarried, and that he only had sex once—at the age of forty-seven—with Aristotle's son. He was in fact Aristotle's favorite student, so cherished as a public lecturer that he was officially renamed "Theophrastus," literally "divine speaker," a title derived from the Greek words for "godly"—*theo*—and "explainer"—*phras*. Indeed, in more than two hundred books with titles like *On Weather, On Stones, On Water, On Wind, On Fire, On Senses,* and *On Wine and Oil,* it is clear that what best characterizes Theophrastus's writing is his tendency to generously note the opinions of different sources before quietly introducing his own point of view. In fact, a common refrain in Theophrastus's work is, "Where the truth actually lies is not the objective of this discourse." In this way, therefore, Theophrastus is really more of an encyclopedist than an essayist, far more interested in assembling information than in developing his own original body of work. And in this regard, at least, his diplomacy paid off. For upon Aristotle's death Theophrastus was named the new dean of the Lyceum, a position he held for the next forty years, overseeing a student body of two thousand students and inspiring the city of Athens to repeal its long-standing law that banned all philosophers from the city. So when a peculiar little manuscript entitled "These Are Them" is dug up from beneath a Turkish chicken coop this year, no one really believes that it could be by Theophrastus. Rediscovered two centuries after Theophrastus died, the essay is composed of clipped and snarky portraits of flawed societal types, dramatically contradicting the image of Theophrastus as the empathetic encyclopedist with room for everyone in his heart. The Athenian characters that populate this essay are described in short, distinctive, circumstantial vignettes that not only give us a glimpse of life in fourth-century Athens, but they also help us appreciate who Theophrastus really was: grumpy, natty, a tattler and a prude. Theophrastus was an essayist at heart.

These Are Them

This Is the Garrulous Man

This is the sort of man who sits down beside perfect strangers and begins to immediately rattle off his wife's good and bad points. Then he'll describe his dreams, what he ate for dinner, the condition of his crops, etc. He'll mention, by way of nothing, that people seem to act a lot worse today than they did in the days of yore, or that many foreigners are in town, some more rain wouldn't hurt, a friend of his has dedicated a beautiful new torch at the Olympic Games—do you know how many columns the largest temple there has?—oh life is difficult sometimes, I hate my new barber, do you have any more figs?

This Is the Boorish Man

This is the kind of guy who will walk up to people after eating garlic and ask them if they can guess what he had for dinner. His shoes are two sizes too big, his voice always too loud, his pants sometimes rolled up far above his knees because of his tendency to bathe in public fountains. He doesn't care about making a good impression, and in turn he's seldom impressed by anything else around him. However, should a cow or donkey or goat suddenly cross his path he will immediately stop where he is and stand there, gawking: the most spectacular thing he's seen. If someone were to give him a coin in order to repay him for something, this is the type of guy who'll say the coin is worn too thin. He often sings in the street. He once seduced the kitchen maid.

This Is the Talkative Man

During conversation, this man will respond to any remark with a claim to the contrary. He'll say he knows the whole story, that you've got it all wrong, just listen to him, etc. You might try to edge a comment of your own in there, but he'll immediately respond with something like "Hold on now, you've had your say" or "That reminds me of something else" or "You're an impatient one, huh?" Suppose somebody innocently asks this man what went on at a council meeting. Well, he'll do more than give a full report: somehow he'll work in mentioning some old Athenian battle, which inevitably will make him recall the Spartans' victory under Lysander, his memories of giving speeches while a minor public official, a rumor decades old, a joke that he's told you before. This is the guy, in other words, whom you do not want on a jury. When he goes to dinner parties he is called "the chattering parrot." Really the only people with any patience for this man are children nearing their bedtime. They beg him to tell them stories to help them fall quickly asleep.

This Is the Offensive Man

The offensive man is the kind who exposes himself when he passes married women on the street. At the theater he goes on clapping long after everyone else has stopped, or if there's a break in the dialogue he'll turn around in his seat and burp at someone behind him. At the market, at the busiest time of day, he'll stand beside the fruit cart, popping grapes into his mouth while chatting up the grape merchant about the high price of produce. He's rude to his mother, damns fortune-tellers, tells jokes under his breath during sacred temple blessings. At a formal dinner party, he spits olive pits across the table to get the host's attention. Or while others might be quietly listening to the performance of a young lyre player, he'll start whistling and clapping out of time just to draw attention. He's the kind of guy, while making an offering to the gods, who drops the libation cup—"accidentally"—and then laughs out loud at his own supposed cleverness.

This Is the Hapless Man

This is the guy who'll give a toast at a wedding by talking bitterly about his ex-girlfriend. He'll approach a man who's already badly in debt to ask him for a reference. He comes to court to offer his testimony a day after the case has closed. Shows up to his home after a long journey by foot and suggests taking a walk with his wife around town. Upon signing the papers for the sale of your house, he's likely to show up with the name of a friend who would have certainly paid you more. He likes offering his friends the kinds of favors that no friend would really want. He'll watch a slave being whipped in the city street and then walk up to him afterward to let the slave know that after a recent beating that one of his own slaves had got he found the man hanged in his quarters.

This Is the Absentminded Man

He hides presents and then can't find them. Sends get-well cards to men who've died. In the winter, he's the type that would complain about not having spring cucumbers. Suppose someone should ask him: "How many funerals do you suppose have gone through the sacred gates?" He is likely to respond: "You and I should have so many!" This man's soup is too salty.

This Is the Faultfinder

For example: his mistress is spontaneously and passionately kissing him for over an hour. The faultfinder asks her: "I wonder if you really love me as much as you claim you do." He quarrels with the weather. Finds a wallet on the street and then exclaims: "Aye, me! Always this . . . never a real find!" Suppose he purchases a new slave at the market after a long afternoon of bargaining. Just as he and the seller settle on a price, the faultfinder will ask, "I wonder if this slave is as good as you say. I mean, why would you sell him so cheap?" Someone congratulates him on the birth of his son, and the faultfinder will reply: "You might as well have told me that half of my estate is now gone!" Or if his friends raise a loan to help him out a jam, the first thing that will come out of the faultfinder's mouth is: "Great, now I have to pay all of you back, too!"

This Is the Man of Petty Ambition

The man who displays this trait is the kind who would bring his son all the way to Delphi in order to partake in a "coming-of-age" ceremony that he hired someone to invent. He takes pains to have only "Ethiopians" as servants. Pays bills with new coins. Invites himself to parties and then demands to sit near the host. After he kills a cow to feed his family for the month, he'd probably drape the horns with a wreath and then set them over his doorway so that everybody can see it: ooh, he killed a cow! He would probably buy a tiny ladder for his pet bird and a miniature brass shield for it to carry in its beak while it hops up and down in its cage. (Why?) Or, if his puppy were to die, this guy would erect a monument to the dog and inscribe it with the epitaph: "Here lies the scion of Greece's purest stock." He can't leave an offering at the temple without coming back every day in order to rub and polish it, setting it toward the front. And then maybe a week later he's likely to return with a wreath, on which would be written not a tribute to the gods but rather a tribute to the earlier offering he left.

(translated by the editor)

46

Greece

This is the year that Plutarch's born, and over the next eighty years he'll compose some of the most formally radical essays in the history of the genre. His day job is that of an administrative priest, which makes him responsible for interpreting the auguries of an oracle who presides over the Temple of Apollo at Delphi. From all over the ancient world, pilgrims come to this shrine with their worries and dreams. They give Plutarch a list of questions, make an offering to the god, and then wait as Plutarch confers with the oracle inside. By Plutarch's day, this is a ceremony that is already nine hundred years old, and because of the popularity of this ancient sacred rite, the city of Delphi comes to build the largest fortune in the world. It goes without saying, therefore, that Plutarch shares in this. Nevertheless, even though Plutarch manages the culture's most prestigious religious shrine, as a writer he doesn't give himself over to it fully. Plutarch's essays have survived for almost two thousand years because they subtly straddle both experience and faith: that which we can clearly see, and that which we just need. "On the Oracles of the Shrine" is one of his earliest essays, and in it Plutarch exposes the realities of his job. In the essay, he tells us that the oracle receives her messages from Apollo in a private stone chamber that is hidden underground. She emerges after a few minutes with inspired and garbled puzzles that Plutarch is then responsible for unscrambling for the pilgrims. But that chamber, he suspects, is often filled with what he describes as ethylene gas, a natural hallucinogen. Plutarch doesn't proceed to the obvious conclusion, however—that these oracles have been getting high for the past nine hundred years—rather, Plutarch simply just presents this information and moves on, reminding us that sometimes the longevity of a tradition is almost just as sacred as what it represents. He is not a journalist, therefore, but he is also not a prophet. He's an essayist who's in love with the myths that move us all, and simultaneously with the facts that underlie their power. "It is not history that I am writing," he says of his greatest work, a groundbreaking series of biographical portraits, "but simply people's lives." His is a spare and observational style that is stripped of the ornament of expository gesture, that tendency in essays to dilute a potent image by dissecting it, inspecting it, and explaining it away. Example: Among the seven dozen essays that Plutarch leaves behind is "Some Information about the Spartans," a sketch of Spartan culture that historians call the first work of cultural anthropology because this compilation of various Spartan sayings never has imposed on it the framework of a thesis. Plutarch provides a title, a selection of anecdotes, and then a space in which our own experiences of the text can accrete into our own interpretations of his meaning. "Sometimes it's the small thing," Plutarch wrote about his style, "—the trivial remark, the joke, the aside—that provides a better picture of one's subject than one's words."

Some Information
about the Spartans

Sources say that one evening, at a dinner party, an Athenian woman was showing off one of her new tapestries she'd woven. A Spartan mother who happened to be at that party overheard this woman's boasting, so she walked over to the tapestry to see what was the fuss. She lifted up the tapestry, put it back down, then called out for her four sons to join her inside.

The four Spartan boys rushed immediately to their mother, picked her up above their shoulders and carried her around the party.

Their mother looked back at the Athenian hostess, who stood in silence with the tapestry in her hands.

"It is a lovely wall hanging," said the Spartan to the Athenian. "But this is what a woman should really boast of having made!" *a woman's purpose is to produce sons, not art*

◦▸

Another mother in Sparta once said to her son: "I send you off to battle with this shield your father made. Through many years and many battles he kept this weapon safe. Let me suggest that you also keep it safe, for the terrors of the battlefield won't be anything compared to what will happen if you lose it." *heirlooms are very important*

◦▸

There is the story of the Spartan boy who complained to his mother that the sword she had given him was too small for battle.

His mother replied sternly: "A real man doesn't need a sword."

◦▸

One day, at the funeral of a Spartan boy who had been killed in a battle, an elderly woman approached the boy's mother.

"Oh, what a loss!" the elderly woman said.

"Loss?" replied the mother. "Old woman, you're crazy! This is a blessing from the gods. I gave that boy life that he might do something with it, and now he has died for Sparta!"

a man's purpose is to die honorably

When a battle veteran was describing to one Spartan mother the way that her son had died in battle, she said to the vet: "I wouldn't expect anything less from my boy."

Then paused for a moment.

"But I can't help noticing that you are still alive."

‹ ›

Another woman, upon hearing that her son had died in battle, said to those neighbors who offered their condolences, "Yes, thank you. He was my very good boy."

But later during the war, when her other son managed to survive a battle, that same mother turned her head away from the news, saying to her neighbors, "I do not know who you are talking about."

you are supposed to die in battle

It is said that when another woman's son arrived home from a battle with his left arm missing and the stump bleeding terribly in a long trail behind him, she said: "Turn around and follow that back to your courage."

‹ ›

One Spartan mother saw her son in the distance, panting and in tears as he returned home from battle.

She called out to the boy: "How did we do there, my son?"

The boy called back crying, "All my friends are dead, Mom!"

The mother picked up a stone and then hurled at her son.

He was struck in the head and died in the road.

"May they forgive you, then, for your treachery."

‹ ›

When another mother's son fled back home from a battle, she met him at the door with her dress over her head.

"Do you plan on crawling back inside here like an infant?"

◀ ▶

And while handing her only child his weapon before battle, another Spartan mother offered a last word of advice:

"Son," she told her boy, "either with this, or on it."

(translated by the editor)

105

Rome

This year, under the emperor Trajan, the Roman army constructs a four-thousand-foot-long bridge across the Danube, thus defeating the Dacians, the last rebellious holdouts in the new Roman Empire. For the next two hundred years the Mediterranean world experiences unprecedented peace, and as newly unearthed knowledge pours into Rome daily the historian Pliny fills thirty-seven volumes of his book *The Natural History.* He proclaims in the preface that his book offers readers twenty thousand new facts, two thousand different sources, four hundred quoted authors. Etc. This, then, is the true birth of the information age. And it's also why the Romans seldom produced great essays. Instead, it's through this culture's letters that its best essaying is revealed: its hypocrisy, its self-doubt, its humanity, its reality. For example: when Lucius Seneca was given the responsibility of tutoring the newly crowned teenaged emperor, he was already the empire's most famous Stoic philosopher, advocating a life of self-control and detachment. Nevertheless, for several years before the young Nero was ready to take full command, the world's most famous Stoic was secretly running the empire, secretly amassing a personal fortune that even rivaled the emperor's, and secretly engaging in so many affairs that his home was nicknamed *cubiculum* by children in the streets. (*Cubiculum* means: "the bedroom.") And yet privately, Seneca was writing letters that reveal a man so unsure of himself that he references suicide over three dozen times. "I cannot, after all, be expected—can I?—to continue drawing on my last breath forever." In Seneca's letters, we can feel his mind struggling against each new adversity, his syntax often yielding to new contradictory thoughts: *I cannot / after all / be expected / can I / to continue drawing on my last breath forever.* The sentence is simultaneously a statement and a question: hesitant, staccato, desperately trying to hide any suggestion of uncertainty while no less desperate to find a single reason to go on. Whether we read Seneca's letter as an exercise in self-delusion or a gorgeous demonstration of a struggle with faith, at its core it is a triumphant performance of logic. It is the best essay that Seneca wrote.

LUCIUS SENECA

Sick

I am sick.

True, I may not be so at this moment, but I am sick nonetheless.

What are you talking about? you ask.

I am talking about this illness which has singled me out for life. Which has been with me since my birth, hangs over my head, taunts me, threatens me, strikes suddenly at its will.

There's no reason to beat around the bush by calling it "asthma" like the Greeks.

does that make death more or less scary?

I am constantly at my last breath—I am "rehearsing death," as my doctor says—and sooner or later, without any doubt, this illness is going to permanently achieve what it's been practicing for years. I cannot, after all, be expected—can I?—to continue drawing on my last breath forever.

Sure, there are other ailments in the world—and trust me, I've had my share—but none of them, in my opinion, is more unpleasant than this. That's not surprising—is it?—since with any other kind of illness you're only that: you're ill. But with this sickness I am always at death's door, knocking.

what makes this one different? because it's incurable?

I imagine that you're thinking now, But surely as you write this you must be feeling better!

You're wrong. I don't. Because that's like thinking that I would be relieved because the latest attack has passed, ignoring the fact that soon enough another attack will come. The accused man doesn't believe that he's won his case, now, does he, just because he's gotten an extension of his trial?

Yet even as I fight for breath, day after day after day, sometimes I find comfort by reflecting on my state.

"So," I say to death, "you're having another go at me. Well, go ahead! Come and get me! I had my own go at you long ago."

35

suicide attempt?

You did? you ask.

I did. Back before I was born. Death, you see, is just a state of "unbeing." And we have all experienced that while waiting for life to start. Death, therefore, will be the same after our lives as it was beforehand. So if there's any heartache in the period that's to follow this one, surely there must have been some in the period preceding this. And yet, none of us can recall any distress from that time. I ask you, then: Isn't it stupid to believe that a lamp is suffering any more after it's been put out than it was before it was lit?

[handwritten: interesting]

[handwritten: very philosophical]

We are lit and put out. We are born and die. We suffer a little in the intermission, but on either side of life I know there is deep tranquility. I know that death doesn't follow only; I know it precedes as well. That is why it shouldn't matter to us whether we cease to be—or even never *be*—because the experience of both is simply nonexistence.

[handwritten: oh fuck. god damn]

This is how I talk to myself whenever I'm under attack. I do it quietly, of course, in spurts beneath quickened breaths. But then, little by little, the attack loosens its grip on me and my breathing returns to pants, and my thinking becomes more clear.

[handwritten: very strong idea]

My latest attack still lingers of course. I can feel its catch and release in my lungs even now. But let it do as it pleases. Just as long as my heart's still going you can be assured of this: I'm not afraid of my last hour. I'm prepared, but not planning.

It's the man who finds true joy in life—and who still doesn't feel remorse at having to leave what he has behind—who should be the most admired.

But you see: I wouldn't know. I'm not joyful. It would seem to me very hard for this man to approach death as I do. Leaving a life that one enjoys would feel like an expulsion.

I'm not being expelled, however.

I am merely departing.

A wise man cannot be evicted from a place he is not a part of.

(translated by the editor)

315

Ask a friend: what is an essay? An essay, I suspect, is something to which your friend might turn to watch a problem being solved, a proclamation made, the world recorded honestly. After all, no matter how playful Seneca, Plutarch, or Theophrastus make their essays, let's not kid ourselves about them: their essays are making arguments. We might read these arguments through the lens of emotion, or experience, or a boldly clever adventure into the limits of human logic, but once we emerge from reading them aren't we nevertheless changed? Haven't we been moved? Doesn't good art resist the intelligence only *almost* successfully? Or: is every essay an intelligence that inaugurates its own form? The question that I think we ought to ask our friends is whether there is room in this genre for its namesake, for *experiment.*

AZWINAKI TSHIPALA

Questions and Answers

QUESTION: What is the doorstep?
ANSWER: The doorstep is a woman.

QUESTION: And the crossbar over the door, what is that?
ANSWER: The crossbar is a man.

QUESTION: When the door is being installed, then, what's that?
ANSWER: That is when the man comes.

QUESTION: And the hingepin on the door?
ANSWER: His penis.

QUESTION: What is the ceiling of the hut and the floor beneath it?
ANSWER: A boy and a girl who are mating.

QUESTION: And the grass bundles above?
ANSWER: The python.

QUESTION: Then what is the beaten floor?
ANSWER: That is my cunt.

QUESTION: Who has been beating the floor?
ANSWER: A hand.

QUESTION: But what is the door?
ANSWER: The door is the crocodile.

QUESTION: And if the door is closed, what is that?
ANSWER: The crocodile stretching out.

QUESTION: What is the door from the outside?
ANSWER: The crocodile's back.

QUESTION: And if it is closed?
ANSWER: The woman being made pregnant.

QUESTION: Then what is a door that's open?
ANSWER: The woman afterward.

QUESTION: What are the two sides of the river?
ANSWER: A boy and a girl when they meet.

QUESTION: Which is the crocodile that bites?
ANSWER: That is the top one, the one below has no sense.

QUESTION: What is the wall in front of you?
ANSWER: A man that is virile.

QUESTION: And what is the wall behind?
ANSWER: A man who is impotent.

QUESTION: Then what is this housepost?
ANSWER: A man who has ripped open a girl.

QUESTION: And that one?
ANSWER: He is the striker of thighs, the crusher of little ribs.

(translated by N. J. van Warmelo)

4 2 7

China

Meanwhile, in China, there is a violent civil war. The golden age of writing under the great Han dynasty—a period that saw the development of the world's first paper, the world's first publishers, and the nation's greatest output of literary work—is gone. Barbarians are in power. Insurrections are erupting. A small elite ruling class has emerged out of nowhere, enslaving the nation's peasants and declaring itself divine. "I shall not break my back for five bushels of grain," says a poet and a farmer named T'ao Ch'ien this year. At thirty-nine years old, Ch'ien retires in seclusion to a small private hut that stands in a field of willows. There, for the remainder of his life, he drinks a special home brew of Chinese yellow wine. He drinks a lot, historians tells us, so much so that he achieves "a serene sense of clarity through which the world of artificially imposed restrictions and distinctions falls away to be replaced by the imposition of attention." Ch'ien, in other words, begins to compose essays. And what he achieves, according to some scholars, is the first true modern voice in all of Eastern prose: an unassuming surface of imagistic simplicity that veils a darker depth of personal heartbreak. Sometimes the essay is where we end up when everything that we know must change.

The Biography of Mr. Five-Willows

No one knows where he came from. And his given name is also a mystery. But we know there were five willows growing beside his house, which is why he used this name. At peace in idleness, rarely speaking, he had no longing for fame or fortune. He loved to read books, and yet never puzzled over their profound insights. But whenever he came upon some realization, he was so pleased that he forgot to eat.

He was a wine-lover by nature, but couldn't afford it often. Everyone knew this, so whenever they had wine they'd call him over. And when he drank, it was always bottoms-up. He'd be drunk in no time; then he'd go back home, alone and with no regrets over where things were going.

In the loneliness of his meager home, there was little shelter from wind and sun. His short coat was patched and sewn. And made from gourd and split bamboo, his cup and bowl were empty as often as Yen Hui's. But he kept writing to amuse himself, and his writing shows something of who he was. He went on like this, forgetting all gain and loss, until he came naturally to his end.

In appraisal we say: *Don't make yourself miserable agonizing over impoverished obscurity, and don't wear yourself out scrambling for money and honor.* Doesn't that describe this kind of man perfectly? He'd just get merrily drunk and write to cheer himself up. He must have lived in the most enlightened and ancient of times.

(translated by David Hinton)

7 9 0

China

Sometimes it's a journey that cannot ever end, to a place that might not exist.

HEAVEN)?

LI TSUNG-YUAN

Is There a God?

Just beyond our valley's edge, a road turns toward the north. Eventually, it separates. The lefthand path leads nowhere in particular, but if you follow the other one, which turns easterly for a quarter mile, you'll find that the path meets up with a stream that forks around a tall pile of boulders. The boulders look like an elegantly built look-out tower from a long-forgotten culture. But this is only what they look like. Below them, on the other side, there are more stones piled up that themselves look like a wall, in the middle of which could be a gate, through the opening of which is a kind of darkness that seems to go on for hours. I think that if you were to throw a stone in here it would land with a splash reminiscent of water, echoing for as long as you remained in this place. I stood there, a stone in hand. Surrounding the scene are two groves of straight trees, growing on either side of the tower and its gate and the wall in which darkness is, looking as if they were intentionally placed to frame what isn't there.

(translated by Lucy Willis)

858

China

And sometimes it's just a listing of those things we think we know.

Miscellany

Incongruities

A poor Persian.
  A sick physician.
  A Buddhist disciple not addicted to drink.
  Keepers of granaries coming to blows.
  A great fat bride.
  An illiterate teacher.
  A pork-butcher reciting sūtras.
  A village elder riding in an open chair.
  A grandfather visiting courtesans.

— contradictions of stereotypes

Shameful

A pregnant nun.
  Wrestlers with swollen faces.
  A rich man suddenly poor.
  A maid offending public opinion.
  A son in mourning getting drunk.

No Alternative

Drinking wine when ill.
  Attending meetings in hot weather.
  Beating children without explanation.
  Being ceremonious when sweating.
  Being cauterized when in pain.

Abusing one's concubine at the behest of one's wife.
Receiving visitors in hot weather.
Applying to resign on account of old age.
Entertaining guests in a miserable temple.

Resemblances

A metropolitan official, like a winter melon, grows in the dark.
A raven, like a hard-up scholar, croaks when hungry and cold.
A magistrate, like a tiger, is vicious when disturbed.
Nuns, like rats, go into deep holes.
Swallows, like nuns, always go in pairs.
A slave, like a cat, finding any warm corner, stays.

Vexations

Happening upon a tasty dish when one's liver is out of order.
Making a night of it, and then the drinks giving out.
For one's back to itch when calling upon a superior.
For the lights to fail just when the luck begins to favor one at cards.
Inability to get rid of a worthless poor relation.
A man cleaning out a well who has to go to the toilet in a hurry.

The Name Without the Reality

A student who does not study the appointed themes is not a real student.

A mourner who feels no grief when condoling with the bereaved is not a real mourner.

An old servant who neither tidies things away nor chatters about family affairs is not a real old servant.

A host who escorts a guest no farther than the door is not a real host.

A cook without an apron or knife and chopping block is not a real cook.

A teacher who does not correct his pupil's exercises and studies is not a real teacher.

Underlings who do not squabble and curse are not real underlings.

The head of a family who does not check his possessions regularly is not a real head.

A guest who sends his host no word of thanks after a feast is not a real guest.

Indications of Prosperity

Horses neighing.
    Candles guttering.
    Chestnut husks.
    Lichee shells.
    Flower petals.
    The twittering of orioles.
    The sound of reading aloud.
    Dropped hair ornaments.
    A flute being played in a lofty belvedere.
    The sound of pounding drugs and rolling tea.

Disheartening

No wine at blossom time.

Dismaying

To meet an enemy.
    To meet a creditor.
    To hear one's drunken remarks only after one gets sober.

Desecration of Scenery

To weep when looking at flowers.
    To spread a mat on moss.
    To cut down a weeping poplar.
    To dry small clothes amid flowers.
    To carry a load on a spring jaunt.
    To tether a horse to a decorative stone pillar.
    To bring a lamp into moonlight.

To plant cabbages in a fruit garden.
To keep poultry under a flower-stand.

Unbearable

The coarse talk of the marketplace.
Sounds from the threshing floor at a wayside inn in autumn.
A young wife mourning her husband.
An old man mourning his son.
The sound of music when in mourning.

Hard to Bear

Priests joking with courtesans.
Servants imitating the behavior of scholars.
Juniors behaving arrogantly.
Servants and concubines cutting into the conversation.
Soldiers and rustics trying to talk like scholars.

The Power of Suggestion

Wearing green in winter makes one feel cold.
Seeing red in summer makes one feel hot.
Heavy curtains suggest someone lurking.
Passing a butcher's gives a frowzy feeling.
Seeing water cools one.
Seeing plum trees makes one's mouth water.

Bad Form

To fall from one's polo pony.
To smoke in the presence of superiors.
To fall asleep in somebody's bed with one's boots on.
To preface remarks with a giggle.
To sing love songs in the presence of one's father- or mother-in-law.
To lay chopsticks across a soup-bowl.

Contemporary Crazes

Jealousy.
 Invoking the Spirits in one's cups.
 A son in mourning reciting ditties.
 A son in mourning going to cock-fights and dog-races.
 Adults flying kites.
 Women cursing in public.
 Mortgaging one's house and lands.

Things Gone Awry

Good parents lacking good sons.
 A good son lacking a good wife.
 A good daughter lacking a good husband.
 Having money and not being able to use it.
 Having fine clothes and not being able to wear them.
 A fine dwelling left unswept.
 Having silk and not making clothes.
 Having a beautiful color and not knowing how to match it.
 Looking at beautiful flowers and not reciting poetry.

Unlucky

To eat lying down.
 To sigh for nothing.
 To sing in bed.
 To eat bareheaded.
 To write bareheaded.
 To swear an oath involving one's parents.
 To sit on matting on which a corpse has previously lain.
 To go to the toilet or let down one's hair in the light of the sun or moon.
 To let one's hair down in the sun.
 To dip a spoon or chopsticks in the bowl before the meal begins.

(translated by E. D. Edwards)

996

Japan

So apparently, when Sei Shōnagon begins compiling her *Pillow Book* this year she is not really breaking new ground. At least not formally speaking. The book is an example of what is called *makura no sōshi*—"notes of the pillow"—a trend in Japanese culture of recording one's thoughts into a journal at night and then storing them in a drawer beneath the pillow of one's bed. Indeed, the best known writer of Sei Shōnagon's time, Murasaki Shikibu, the author of *The Tale of Genji*, described Shōnagon's writing as "full of commonness":

> Actually, she was dreadfully conceited, thinking her writing so clever. But if you examine the work closely it leaves a great deal to be desired. Those who think themselves superior to everyone else will inevitably suffer and come to a bad end, just as those who believe their experiences are so precious that they go out of their way to be sensitive in the most unpromising situations—trying to capture every moment, however slight it is—and end up looking ridiculous and utterly superficial. How can the future turn out well for a woman such as this?

In fact, things did not turn out well for her. Sei Shōnagon's book was so thoroughly suppressed following her death that despite Shōnagon's popularity with readers today we aren't entirely sure what her real name even was. It isn't completely clear when she died or where she's buried. And it's even hard determining the right order of her book. The oldest extant copy of Sei Shōnagon's masterpiece is a manuscript that dates from the late sixteenth century—half a millennium after *The Pillow Book* was written. So why was the book suppressed? It could be because *The Pillow Book* was written in Japanese, while serious books in medieval Japan were only composed in Chinese. It could also be because Sei Shōnagon was a single divorced mother, uncommonly educated, uncommonly sexual, uncommonly willing to address subjects that no one in the culture dared. It could be, in other words, because Sei Shōnagon was real. Compare the voice of *The Pillow Book* with that of *The Tale of Genji*. Four hundred characters in *Genji* promenade through its pages while reciting to each other long speeches about love, honor, loyalty, faith. Sei Shōnagon, on the other hand, is her book's only character. And she is gossipy, bitchy, snobby, fun. A complainer, a bragger, a tease, a sap. Hers is a directness that was perceived as uncouth, and her blunt syntactical structures were unsophisticatedly terse. Yet these lists that seem insignificant because of their brevity are actually demonstrations of a philosophical outlook: *mono no aware*—"beauty is precious because it is brief." Her lists set into motion the imaginations of her readers, encouraging us to fill the narrative vacuum that she's created with our own interpretations of how everything fits together. And yet, before we can do that, Sei Shōnagon moves on, creating another list, setting it into motion, letting it spin free. *Mono no aware*. Maybe her critics didn't care about her sexuality, in the end. Maybe she just reminded them about the imminence of death.

SEI SHŌNAGON

The Pillow Book

In spring, the dawn: when the slowly paling mountain rim is tinged with red, and wisps of faintly crimson-purple cloud float in the sky.

In summer, the night: moonlit nights, of course, but also at the dark of the moon, it's beautiful when fireflies are dancing everywhere in a mazy flight. And it's delightful too to see just one or two fly through the darkness, glowing softly. Rain falling on a summer night is also lovely.

In autumn, the evening: the blazing sun has sunk very close to the mountain rim, and now even the crows, in threes and fours or twos and threes, hurrying to their roost, are a moving sight. Still more enchanting is the sight of a string of wild geese in the distant sky, very tiny. And oh how inexpressible, when the sun has sunk, to hear in the growing darkness the wind, and the song of autumn insects.

In winter, the early morning: if snow is falling, of course, it's unutterably delightful, but it's perfect too if there's a pure white frost, or even just when it's very cold, and they hasten to build up the fires in the braziers and carry in fresh charcoal. But it's unpleasant, as the day draws on and the air grows warmer, how the brazier fire dies down to white ash.

Things people despise: A crumbling earth wall. People who have a reputation for being exceptionally good-natured.

connection? why just these 2 things? [handwritten annotation]

Things that make your heart beat fast: A sparrow with nestlings. Going past a place where tiny children are playing. Lighting some fine incense and then lying down alone to sleep. Looking into a Chinese mirror that's a little clouded. A fine gentleman pulls up in his carriage and sends in some request.

To wash your hair, apply your makeup, and put on clothes that are well-scented with incense. Even if you're somewhere where no one special will see you, you still feel a heady sense of pleasure inside. *yes!*

On a night when you're waiting for someone to come, there's a sudden gust of rain and something rattles in the wind, making your heart suddenly beat faster.

your heart can beat faster in many different ways, for many different reasons

The Emperor's cat had received the fifth rank, and was given the appropriate title-name "Myōbu." It was a charming creature, and the Emperor was
quite devoted to it.

One day its carer, Muma no Myōbu, found it lying basking on the ve-
randa. "How vulgar!" she scolded. "Back you come inside." But the cat
continued to lie there asleep in the sun, so she decided to give it a fright.
"Okinamaro!" she cried to the dog. "Here, boy! Come and get Myōbu!"
The foolish dog couldn't believe its ears, and came rushing over, whereupon the terrified cat fled inside through the blind.

The Emperor was at that time in the Breakfast Room, and he witnessed
this event with astonishment. He tucked the cat into the bosom of his robe,
and summoned his men. When the Chamberlains Tadataka and Narinaka
appeared, the Emperor ordered them "Give Okinamaro a thorough beating and banish him to Dog Island! Be quick about it!"

Everyone gathered and a noisy hunt ensued. The Emperor went on to
chastise Muma no Myōbu, declaring that he would replace her as Myōbu's
carer as she was completely untrustworthy, and thenceforth she no longer
appeared in his presence. Meanwhile, they rounded up the dog, and had
the guards drive it out.

We all pitied the poor thing. "Oh dear," we said, "and to think how he
used to swagger about the place as if he owned it."

"Remember how on the third of the third month the Secretary Con-
troller decked him out with a garland of willow and a peach-flower comb,
and tied a branch of cherry blossom on his back? Who'd have guessed then
that he'd meet with such a fate?"

"And the way he always attended Her Majesty at meal times. How we'll
miss him!"

Then around noon three or four days later, we heard a dog howling
dreadfully. What dog could be howling on and on like this? we wondered,
and as we listened dogs gathered from everywhere to see what was afoot.
One of the cleaning women came running in. "Oh, it's dreadful! Two of
the Chamberlains are beating the dog! It's bound to die! His Majesty ban-
ished it, but apparently it came back, so they're teaching it a lesson."

Alas, poor creature! It was Okinamaro. "It's Tadataka and Sanefusa
doing it," someone said.

of course it came back! this is its home.

We sent someone to stop them, but at that point the dog finally ceased its howling. "It's dead," came the report, "so they've thrown it outside the guardhouse."

That evening as we were sorrowing over poor Okinamaro, up staggered a miserable trembling creature, terribly swollen and looking quite wretched. Can if Okinamaro? we wondered. What other dog could be wandering around at this hour in such a state?

We called his name, but he didn't respond. "It's him," some of us declared, while others maintained that it wasn't, till Her Majesty said, "Send for Ukon. She would recognize him." We duly did so, and when she came Her Majesty showed her the dog and asked if it was indeed Okinamaro.

"There's certainly a likeness," replied Ukon, "but this dog looks simply revolting. And you only have to say his name and Okinamaro bounds happily up, but this dog doesn't respond at all. It must be a different dog. And they did say they'd killed him and thrown out the corpse, didn't they? How could he have survived after two men had beaten him like that?" This moved Her Majesty to fresh sorrow.

It grew dark. We gave the dog some food, but it didn't eat it, so we decided that it was indeed a different dog and left it at that.

The next morning, Her Majesty had performed her ablutions and had her hair combed, and I was holding the mirror for her to check that all was in order when I spied the dog, still there, crouching at the foot of a pillar. Seeing it I said aloud to myself, "Oh poor Okinamaro, what a terrible beating he got yesterday! It's so sad to think he must be dead. I wonder what he'll be reborn as next time. How dreadful he must have felt!"

At this the dog began to tremble, and tears simply poured from its eyes. How extraordinary! I realized it was indeed Okinamaro! It was pitiful to recall how he'd avoided revealing himself the night before, but at the same time the whole thing struck me as quite marvelous. I set down the mirror and said, "So you're Okinamaro, are you?" and he threw himself on the ground, whimpering and weeping.

Her Majesty laughed with relief, and sent for Ukon and told her the story. There was a great deal of laughter over it all, and the Emperor heard and came in to see what was happening. He laughed too, and observed, "Isn't it odd to think a dog would have such fine feelings." His gentlewomen also heard of it and gathered around, and this time when we called the dog he got up and came.

"His poor face is swollen!" I cried. "I do wish I could do something for it."

"Now you're wearing your heart on your sleeve," everyone teased me.

Tadataka heard from the Table Room, and sent saying, "Is it really him? I must come and have a look."

"Oh dear no, how awful!" I declared. "Tell him it's not Okinamaro at all!"

"He's bound to be found out sooner or later," came Tadataka's reply. "You can't go on hiding him forever."

Well, in due course Okinamaro was pardoned, and everything returned to normal. Now has there ever been such a delightful and moving moment as when Okinamaro began to tremble and weep at those pitying words of mine? Humans may cry when someone speaks to them sympathetically—but a dog?

dogs feel much more
than we give them credit for

Cats: Cats should be completely black except for the belly, which should be very white.

I wonder what inspired this thought. The Emperor's cat?

Young people and babies should be plump. Provincial Governors and such-like people who have some authority should also be on the portly side.

she says "should be" a lot, why? does she mean "tends to be"?

She uses very absolute language

Things that can't be compared: Summer and winter. Night and day. Rainy days and sunny days. Laughter and anger. Old age and youth. White and black. People you love and those you hate. The man you love and the same man once you've lost all feeling for him seem like two completely different people. Fire and water. Fat people and thin people. People with long hair and those with short hair.

The noisy commotion when crows roosting together are suddenly disturbed by something in the night. The way they tumble off their perches, and flap awkwardly about from branch to branch, squawking sleepily, makes them seem utterly different from daytime crows. *? how?*

Rare things: A son-in-law who's praised by his wife's father. Likewise, a wife who's loved by her mother-in-law.

A pair of silver tweezers that can actually pull out hairs properly.

A retainer who doesn't speak ill of his master.

A person who is without a single quirk. Someone who's superior in both appearance and character, and who's remained utterly blameless throughout his long dealings with the world.

You never find an instance of two people living together who continue to be overawed by each other's excellence and always treat each other with scrupulous care and respect, so such a relationship is obviously a great rarity.

Copying out a tale or a volume of poems without smearing any ink on the book you're copying from. If you're copying it from some beautiful bound book, you try to take immense care, but somehow you always manage to get ink on it.

Two women, let alone a man and a woman, who vow themselves to each other forever, and actually manage to remain on good terms to the end.

Things that create the appearance of deep emotion: The sound of your voice when you're constantly blowing your runny nose as you talk.
    Plucking your eyebrows.

ha.
tue tho,

Alarming-looking things: Thorny acorn husks. A hairy yam that's been baked. The prickly water lily. Water chestnuts. The sight of a man with a lot of hair, drying it after washing.

because he looks like a woman?

Things that look fresh and pure: Earthenware cups. Shiny new metal bowls. Rushes to be used for making mats. The transparent light in water as you pour it into something.

I think she'd write really good slam poetry.

Things with terrifying names: River deeps. Mountain caves. "Scale-board" walls. Iron. Clods. Thunder—not just the name, but the thing itself is extremely terrifying. Gales. Ominous clouds. Comets. "Arm-umbrella" rain. The wilds.

Robbery is terrifying in every way. Violent monks are very terrifying indeed. So are *kanamochi*. Living spirit possession. The snake berry. Devil fern. Devil vine. Thorn bushes. Chinese bamboo. Roasted charcoal. A bull-demon. Anchors—the sight of one is more terrifying than the name.

What do those words sound like in japanese?.

Things that look ordinary but become extraordinary when written: Straw-berries. The dew plant. The prickly water lily. Spiders. Chestnuts. Doctors of literature. Postgraduate students. Acting Master of the Empress Dowager's Palace. The arbutus tree.

People write the name "knotweed" with characters meaning "tiger's staff." A tiger doesn't look as though it would need a staff!

ha A priest who gives a sermon <u>should be</u> handsome. After all, you're most
aware of the profundity of his teaching if you're gazing at his face as he
speaks. If your eyes drift elsewhere you tend to forget what you've just
heard, so an unattractive face has the effect of making you feel quite sinful.
But I'll write no further on this subject. I may have written glibly enough
about sinful matters of this sort in my younger days, but at my age the
idea of sin has become quite frightening.

I must say, however, from my own sinful point of view, it seems quite
uncalled-for to go around as some do, vaunting their religious piety and
rushing to be the first to be seated wherever a sermon is being preached.

An ex-Chamberlain never used to take up the vanguard of imperial
processions, and once he retired from the post you'd no longer see him
about the palace. These days things are apparently different. The so-called
"Chamberlain fifth-ranker" is actually kept in reasonably busy service, but
privately he must nevertheless miss the prestige of his former post and feel
at a loss how to fill his days, so once he tries going to these places and hears
a few sermons he'll no doubt develop a taste for it and start to go along on a
regular basis.

You'll find him turning up there with his summer under-robe prominently displayed beneath his cloak even in baking summer weather, and the
hems of his pale lavender or blue-gray gathered trousers loose and trodden.
He has an abstinence tag attached to his lacquered cap, and he no doubt
intends to draw attention to the fact that although it's an abstinence day
and he shouldn't leave the house, this doesn't apply to him since his outing
is of a pious nature. He chats with the officiating priest, even goes so far
as to help oversee the positioning of the ladies' carriages, and is generally
completely at home in the situation. When some old crony of his whom he
hasn't seen recently turns up, he's consumed with curiosity. Over he goes,
and they settle down together and proceed to talk and nod and launch
into interesting stories, spreading out their fans and putting them to their
mouths when they laugh, groping at their ornately decorated rosaries and
fiddling with them as they talk, craning to look here and there, praising
and criticizing the carriages, discussing how other priests did things this
way or that in other Lotus Discourses and sutra dedication services they've
been to, and so on and so forth—and not listening to a word of the actual

sermon they're attending. Indeed they would have heard it all so often before that they'd gain nothing from it anyway.

And then there's another type. The preacher has already seated himself when after a while up rolls a carriage, accompanied by only a couple of outriders. It draws to a halt, and the passengers step out—three or four slender young men, dressed perhaps in hunting costume or in cloaks more delicately gauzy than a cicada's wing, gathered trousers and gossamer silk shifts, and accompanied by a similar number of attendants. Those already seated move themselves along a little to make way for them when they enter. They seat themselves by a pillar near the preacher's dais and set about softly rubbing their rosaries as they listen to the sermon, and the preacher, who no doubt feels rather honored to have them there, throws himself with fresh vigor into the task of putting his message across. The young men, however, far from casting themselves extravagantly to the floor as they listen, instead decide to leave after a decent amount of time has passed, and as they go they throw glances in the direction of the women's carriages and comment to each other, and you'd love to know what it was they were saying. It's funny how you find yourself watching them as they depart, interestedly identifying the ones you know, and speculating on the identity of those you don't.

Some people really take things to extremes, though. If someone mentions having been to a Lotus Discourse or other such event, another will say, "And was so and so there?" and the reply is always, "Of course. How could he not be?" Mind you, I'm not saying one should never show up at these places. After all, even women of low standing will apparently listen to sermons with great concentration. Actually, when I first started attending sermons, I never saw women going about here and there on foot to them. Occasionally you would find women in traveling attire, elegantly made up, but they were out as part of another excursion to some temple or shrine. You didn't often hear of women attending sermons and the like in this costume, though. If the ladies who went to sermons in those days had lived long enough to see the way things are today, I can just imagine how they would have criticized and condemned.

unkempt = repulsive?

Repulsive things: The back of a piece of sewing. Hairless baby mice tumbled out of their nest. The seams of a leather robe before the lining's been added. The inside of a cat's ear. A rather dirty place in darkness.

A very ordinary woman looking after lots of children. The way a man must feel when his wife, who he's not really very fond of, is ill for a long time.

ᄀ.

Things that look lovely but are horrible inside: <u>Screens decorated with Chinese paintings</u>. A limed wall. A heaped plate of food. The top of a cypress-bark roof. The prostitutes of Kōjiri.

auch.

Things that are near yet far: Relationships between siblings or relatives who don't like each other.

Things that are far yet near: Paradise.
   The course of a boat.
   Relations between men and women.

Dispiriting things: A dog howling in the middle of the day. The sight in spring of a trap for catching winter fish. Robes in the plum-pink combination, when it's now the third or fourth month. An ox keeper whose ox has died. A birthing hut where the baby has died. A square brazier or a hearth with no fire lit in it. A scholar whose wife has a string of daughters.

A household that doesn't treat you hospitably, though you're there because of a directional taboo—this is particularly dispiriting if it happens to be at one of the season changes.

A letter from the provinces that arrives without any accompanying gift. You might say the same for a letter sent from inside the capital, but this would contain plenty of things you wanted to hear about and interesting news, which makes it a very fine thing to receive in fact.

You've taken special care to send off a beautiful, carefully written letter, and you're eagerly awaiting the reply—time passes, it seems awfully long in coming, and then finally your own elegantly folded or knotted letter is brought back, now horribly soiled and crumpled and with no sign remaining of the brush stroke that sealed it. "There was no one in," you're told, or "They couldn't accept it on account of an abstinence." This is dreadfully dispiriting.

A carriage is sent off to fetch someone you're sure is going to come. You wait, and finally there's the sound of the carriage returning. "It must be her," you think, and everyone in the house goes out to see—but the driver is already dragging the carriage back into its shed. He drops the shafts with a noisy clatter. "What happened?" you ask. "She's going somewhere else today, so she won't be coming," he replies offhandedly, then he hauls out the harness and off he goes.

It's also very dispiriting when a man stops coming to visit his wife at her home. It's a great shame if he's gone off with a lady of good family who serves at court, and the wife sits moping at home, feeling ashamed and humiliated.

A little child's nurse has gone out, promising that she won't be long. You do your best to keep the child entertained and comforted, but when you send word saying "please hurry," back comes a message to the effect that she won't be able to return this evening. This is not just dispiriting, it's downright hateful.

It's even more dispiriting for a man when a woman fails to visit him. And when the night has grown late at his house and suddenly he hears a subdued knock at the gate, and with beating heart he sends to find out who it is, only to have the servant return and announce the name of some other, boring person, well the word "dispiriting" doesn't begin to cover it.

An exorcist priest comes to quell a spirit that has possessed a member of the household. With a confident air he hands the medium the rosary and the other paraphernalia to induce possession, and sets about his incantations in a high, strained, cicada-like chant. But there's no sign of the spirit shifting, and the medium fails to be possessed by the Guardian Deity. Everyone who's gathered to pray, men and women both, begins to find this rather odd. The exorcist chants on until the change of watch two hours later, when he finally stops, exhausted. "Get up," he says to the medium as he retrieves the rosary. "The spirit just won't budge," and running his hand back from his forehead over his bald head he declares, "Oh dear, the exorcism was quite futile." Whereupon he lets out a yawn, leans back against some nearby object and falls asleep. It's truly awful for him when someone not especially important comes over to him, though he's feeling dreadfully sleepy, and prods him awake and forces him into a conversation.

Then there's the house of a man who has failed to receive a post in the recent Appointments List. Word had it that he was certain to get one this year, and all his former retainers, who have scattered far and wide or are now living off in the country-side somewhere, have gathered at his house in anticipation. His courtyard is crammed with the coming and going of their carriages and the tangle of their shafts; if he sets off on an excursion they all jostle to accompany him; and they eat, drink and clamor their way through the days as they wait—but as the last day dawns, there's still no knock at the gate. "How odd," they think, and as they sit straining to catch the sound, they hear the cries of the outriders as the court nobles emerge from the palace at the close of the Appointments ceremonies. The underlings who have spent a chilly night shivering outside the palace waiting to hear the news come trudging back dejectedly, and no one can even bring himself to ask them what happened. When some outsider inquires, "What appointment did your master receive?" they always reply evasively, "Oh, he's the former Governor of So-and-So."

All those who really rely on him feel quite devastated. As morning comes, a few among the people who've been packed in together waiting begin to creep stealthily away. Those who've been many years in his service, however, can't bring themselves to leave his side so lightly. It's terribly touching to see them weaving solemnly about as they pace the room, hopefully counting on their fingers the Provincial Governorships due to come to the end of their term the following year.

There are also those times when you send someone a poem you're rather pleased with, and fail to receive one in reply. Of course there's no more to be done about it if it's to a man you care for. Even so, you do lose respect for someone who doesn't produce any response to your tasteful seasonal references. It also dampens the spirit when you're leading a heady life in the swim of things and you receive some boring little old-fashioned poem that reeks of the longueurs of the writer, whose time hangs heavy on her hands.

You have a particularly fine fan intended for some ceremonial event, and you hand this precious thing to a person who you trust will treat it well, but when the day arrives it comes back to you with something quite unforeseen painted on it.

A messenger delivers a congratulatory birth gift or a farewell present, and isn't given any gift in repayment. Messengers should always be given something, such as decorative herbal balls or New Year hare-mallets, even if they're only delivering some object of no permanent use. If he receives something when he's not expecting to, he will feel thoroughly pleased that he made the delivery. However, it's particularly dispiriting when he's come feeling sure he'll receive something for this errand, and his excited hopes are dashed.

A house where four or five years have passed since they brought in a husband but there's still been no joyous birth celebration is most depressing. A couple has already produced numerous children, all now adult, and indeed of an age at which there could even be grandchildren crawling about, yet the two parents are indulging in a "daytime nap." It's dispiriting for the children who witness this, with nowhere to turn while their parents are off behind closed doors.

The purificatory hot bath that you have to get up to take on New Year's Eve is not merely dispiriting, it's downright irritating.

Rain all day on New Year's Eve. Perhaps this is what's meant by the expression "a single day of purificatory abstinence."

Things that lose by being painted: Pinks. Sweet flag. Cherry blossom. <u>Men and women described in tales as looking "splendid."</u>

things always look better
in our heads.

Things that gain by being painted: Pine trees. Autumn fields. Mountain villages. Mountain paths.

Embarrassing things: The heart of a man.

A night-priest who's a light sleeper.

Who knows when there might not be a thief hiding in some secret place nearby and watching? Oblivious to him, someone chooses a moment under cover of darkness to steal something lying about. The thief would find it most amusing to witness another with the same urge as himself.

The night-priest is a rather embarrassing person in general, for he eagerly takes in all the things that the younger gentlewomen tend to say about other people when they get together—the gossip and the funny stories, the maligning and the carping. "Come come, that's quite enough!" the older ladies near Her Majesty will scold them, but they take no notice of this, and on and on they chatter, until at last they settle down to sleep in an unmannerly way. This is very embarrassing, when you consider the night-priest who overhears it all.

I must say I'm ashamed for any woman who's taken in by some man who is privately thinking, "How depressing! She's not at all what I hoped she'd be. She's full of irritating faults," but when he's with her will fawn and flatter and convince her to trust him. This is particularly true of someone who has a reputation for the dashing nature of his love affairs—such a lover will certainly never act in a way that would suggest to the woman that he's lacking in feelings for her. And then there's the man who doesn't keep his criticisms to himself, but will speak his mind about one woman's faults to another woman, and do the same about her when he's with the first, while she never suspects that he slanders her in the same way to the other, and assumes that his confiding these criticisms to her can only mean that she's the one he really loves. I must say, if ever I do come across a man who seems to feel for me at all, I immediately assume he's actually quite shallow-hearted, so I have no need to expose myself to potential embarrassment.

I really do find it astonishing the way a man will fail to be the slightest bit affected by the moving nature of a woman's deep unhappiness, when he considers abandoning her. Yet how glibly he'll criticize the actions of others! And then there's the man who takes advantage of a lady at court who has no one to protect her interests, wins her over, and when she falls pregnant, repudiates the affair completely.

It's towards the middle of the first month. Heavy black clouds are darkening the sky, but through them the sunlight flashes intensely. The barren field beside the house of some lowly folk is a tumble of untended earth, and in it stands a healthy young peach tree, thick with little branchlets. One side still holds its green leaves, while the other is covered in rich, glossy, rust-red leaves that shine in the sunlight, and in the tree is clambering a beautifully slender youth, hunting costume rather torn but hair well-kempt. A little boy, his hems hitched high and shins bare above his short boots, stands beneath the tree. "Cut me one for a bat!" he begs the lad.

Now three or four little girls with pretty hair come along, in ragged *akomé* gowns and limp skirted trousers but with nice robes beneath. "Cut us some sticks for good hare-mallets!" they cry. "Our mistress wants them." The boy cuts some sticks and throws them down, and the children under the tree all scramble for them, some pausing to look up and cry, "Lots for me!"

And now a man in black skirted trousers comes running up and asks the boy for sticks, and when he refuses the man shakes the tree dangerously, and the boy clings there like a monkey, protesting loudly. A charming scene!

Endearingly lovely things: A baby's face painted on a gourd. A sparrow coming fluttering down to the nest when her babies are cheeping for her.

A little child of two or three is crawling rapidly along when his keen eye suddenly notices some tiny worthless thing lying nearby. He picks it up in his pretty little fingers, and shows it to the adults, This is very endearing to see. It's also endearing when a child with a shoulder-length "nun's cut" hairstyle that's falling into her eyes doesn't brush it away but instead tilts her head to tip it aside as she examines something.

A very young son of a noble family walking about dressed up in ceremonial costume. An enchanting little child who falls asleep in your arms while you're holding and playing with it is terribly endearing.

Things children use in doll play. A tiny lotus leaf that's been picked from a pond. A tiny *aoi* leaf. In fact, absolutely anything that's tiny is endearing.

A very white, plump child of around two, who comes crawling out wearing a lavender silk-gauze robe with the sleeves hitched back, or a child walking about in a short robe that looks more long sleeves than robe. All these are endearing. And it's very endearing when a boy of eight or ten reads something aloud in his childish voice.

It's also enchanting to see a pretty little white chick, its lanky legs looking like legs poking out from under a short robe, cheeping loudly as it runs and pauses here and there around someone's feet. Likewise, all scenes of chicks running about with the mother hen. The eggs of a spot-billed duck. A green-glass pot.

Things that fall: Snow. Hail. Sleet is unpleasant, but it's lovely when it falls mingled with white snowflakes. *and you don't have to be in it*

Snow is splendid on a cypress bark roof, particularly when it's just on the point of melting. It's also delightful when just a little has fallen, and it lies nestled in all the joins between the roof titles, emphasizing their lovely black curves.

For autumn showers and hail, a shingle roof is best. Frost is also good on shingles, and in gardens.

Things that just keep passing by: A boat with its sail up.
   People's age.
   Spring. Summer. Autumn. Winter.

It's beautiful the way the water drops hang so thick and dripping on the garden plants after a night of rain in the ninth month, when the morning sun shines fresh and dazzling on them. Where the rain clings in the spider webs that hang in the open weave of a screening fence or draped on the eaves, it forms the most moving and beautiful strings of white pearly drops.

I also love the way, when the sun has risen higher, the bush clover, all bowed down beneath the weight of the drops, will shed its dew, and a branch will suddenly spring up though no hand has touched it. And I also find it fascinating that things like this can utterly fail to delight others.

(translated by Meredith McKinney)

1 2 8 1

Japan

At this point in time, the Mongols control the world—or at least the largest part of it: twelve million square miles, one hundred million people, nations as far west as Russia, Poland, and Austria, and as far east as the islands surrounding mainland Japan. They do not control Japan yet, but they desperately are trying to. The Mongols have sent a fleet of eight hundred warships packed with twenty thousand men to sit threateningly offshore until the Japanese surrender. They wait for four years, but the Japanese don't give in. The Mongols therefore develop a new diplomatic plan: they'll attack the eastern shore of Japan and wipe everybody on it out. They've got catapults, they've got cannons, they've got long-range proto-grenades. The Japanese, for their part, have finely engraved swords. So on the evening of October 18th, along the shores of Hakata Bay, both armies wait for the next day's sun and the battle that it will begin. Instead, however, when the 19th dawns, a typhoon mysteriously blows in from the east, whorling over the Mongolian fleet and ravaging it completely. The Japanese eventually name this storm "The Divine Wind"—*Kamakaze*—and celebrate their victory with a literary festival that lasts for eleven days. Many critics cite these constant threats on Japan as one of the strongest influences on its thirteenth-century literature, a period that saw the popularization of a form called *zuihitsu,* a kind of text that's best characterized by its associative, irregular, and incomplete nature. As one literary critic once wrote of this form: "The finished work is, in times and climates of anguish, a lie."

YOSHIDA KENKŌ

In all things I yearn for the past

In all things I yearn for the past. Modern fashions seem to keep on growing more and more debased. I find that even among the splendid pieces of furniture built by our master cabinetmakers, those in the old forms are the most pleasing. And as for writing letters, surviving scraps from the past reveal how superb the phrasing used to be. The ordinary spoken language had also steadily coarsened. People used to say "raise the carriage shafts" or "trim the lamp wick," but people today say "raise it" or "trim it." When they should say, "Let the men of the palace staff stand forth!" they say, "Torches! Let's have some light!" Instead of calling the place where the lectures on the Sutra of the Golden Light are delivered before the emperor "the Hall of the Imperial Lecture," they shorten it to "the Lecture Hall," a deplorable corruption, an old gentleman complained.

〈 〉

When I recall the months and years I spent as the intimate of someone whose affections have now faded like cherry blossoms scattering even before a wind blew, I still remember every word of hers that once so moved me; and when I realize that she, as happens in such cases, is steadily slipping away from my world, I feel a sadness greater even than that of separation from the dead. That is why, I am sure, a man once grieved that white thread should be dyed in different colors, and why another lamented that roads inevitably fork. Among the hundred verses presented to the Retired Emperor Horikawa one runs:

The fence round her house,
The woman I loved long ago,
Is ravaged and fallen;

93

Only violets remain
Mingled with the spring weeds.

◀ ▶

Nothing is more saddening than the year of imperial mourning. The very appearance of the temporary palace is forbidding: the wooden floor built close to the ground, the crudely fashioned reed-blinds, the coarse grey cloth hung above the blinds, the utensils of rough workmanship, and the attendants all wearing strangely drab costumes, sword scabbards, and sword knots.

◀ ▶

Kin'yo, an officer of the second rank, had a brother called the High Priest Ryōgaku, an extremely bad-tempered man. Next to his monastery grew a large nettle-tree which occasioned the nickname people gave him, the Nettle-tree High Priest. "That name is outrageous," said the high priest, and cut down the tree. The stump still being left, people referred to him now as the Stump High Priest. More furious than ever, Ryōgaku had the stump dug up and thrown away, but this left a big ditch. People now called him the Ditch High Priest.

◀ ▶

When the Princess Ensei was a small child she asked someone going to the cloistered emperor's palace to relay the following poem as a message from her:

The letter in two strokes,
The letter like an ox's horns,
The straight letter,
And the crooked letter too
All spell my love for you.

The poem means that she missed her father, the cloistered emperor.

◀ ▶

There was in Tsukushi a certain man, a constable of the peace it would seem, who for many years had eaten two broiled radishes each morning under the impression that radishes were a sovereign remedy for all ailments. Once some enemy forces attacked and surrounded his constabulary, choosing a moment when the place was deserted. Just then, two soldiers rushed out of the building, and engaged the enemy, fighting with no thought for their lives until they drove away all the enemy troops. The constable, greatly astonished, asked the two soldiers, "You have fought most gallantly, gentlemen, considering I have never seen you here before. Might I ask who you are?" "We are the radishes you have faithfully eaten every morning for so many years," they answered, and with these words they disappeared. So deep was his faith in radishes that even such a miracle could occur.

◀ ▶

Things which seem in poor taste: too many personal effects cluttering up the place where one is sitting; too many brushes in an ink-box; too many Buddhas in a family temple; too many stones and plants in a garden; too many children in a house; too many words on meeting someone; too many meritorious deeds recorded in a petition. Things which are not offensive, no matter how numerous: books in a book cart, rubbish in a rubbish heap.

◀ ▶

Otozurumaru, a boy in the service of the major counselor and high priest, was intimate with one Sir Yasura and constantly went to visit him. Once when the boy had returned after a visit, the high priest asked him, "Where have you been?" The boy answered, "To see Sir Yasura." The boy was asked, "Is this Sir Yasura a layman or a priest?" He respectfully brought his sleeves together and replied, "I am not sure. I have never seen his head." Why should he have been unable to see the man's head, I wonder.

◀ ▶

There are innumerable instances of things which attach themselves to something else, then waste and destroy it. The body has lice; a house has mice; a country has robbers; inferior men have riches; superior men have benevolence and righteousness; priests have the Buddhist law.

◀ ▶

The people of former times never made the least attempt to be ingenious when naming temples or other things, but bestowed quite casually whatever names suggested themselves. The names given recently sound as if they had been mulled over desperately in an attempt to display the bestower's cleverness, an unfortunate development. In giving a child a name, it is foolish to use unfamiliar characters. A craving for novelty in everything and a fondness for eccentric opinions are the marks of people of superficial knowledge.

〈 〉

Seven kinds of persons make bad friends. The first is the man of lofty position; the second, the young man; the third, the man of robust constitution who has never known a day's illness; the fourth, the man fond of liquor; the fifth, the fierce soldier; the sixth, the liar; the seventh, the miser.

Three kinds of men make desirable friends. First is the friend who gives you things; second, a doctor; and third, the friend with wisdom.

〈 〉

I feel sorry for the man who says that night dims the beauty of things. At night colors, ornaments, and the richness of materials show to their best advantage. By day you should wear simple, conservative clothes, but at night showy, flashy costumes are most attractive. This holds true of people's appearance too: lamplight makes a beautiful face seem even more beautiful, and a voice heard in the dark—a voice that betrays a fear of being overheard—is endearing. Perfumes and the sound of music too are best at night.

It is charming if, on a night which is not any special occasion, a visitor arriving at the palace after it has grown quite late appears in splendid attire. Young people, being observant of one another irrespective of the time of day, should always be dressed in their best, with no distinction of formal and informal attire, above all when they are most at their ease. How pleasant it is when a handsome man grooms his hair after dark, or a woman, late at night, slips from an audience chamber and, mirror in hand, touches up her make-up before she appears again.

〈 〉

Visits to shrines and temples are best made on days when others do not go, and by night.

〈 〉

When they were leveling the ground to build the Kameyama palace, they came on a mound where a huge number of large snakes were coiled together. They decided that these snakes were the gods of the place and reported this to His Majesty. He asked, "What should be done about it?" People all said, "These snakes have occupied the place since ancient times. It would be wrong to root them up recklessly." But the prime minister said, "What curse would creatures dwelling on imperial property place on the site of a new palace? Supernatural beings are without malice; they surely will not wreak any punishment. We should get rid of all the snakes." The workmen destroyed the mound and released the snakes into the Oi River. No curse whatsoever resulted.

( )

When I turned eight years old I asked my father, "What sort of thing is a Buddha?" My father said, "A Buddha is what a man becomes." I asked then, "How does a man become a Buddha?" My father replied, "By following the teachings of Buddha." "Then, who taught the Buddha to teach?" He again replied, "He followed the teachings of the Buddha before him." I asked again, "What kind of Buddha was the first Buddha who began to teach?" At this my father laughed and answered, "I suppose he fell from the sky or else he sprang up out of the earth."

My father told other people, "He drove me into a corner, and I was stuck for an answer." But he was amused.

(translated by Donald Keene)

1336

Italy

April 26th, 1336: the day that's commonly celebrated as the birth of Alpinism. It's the day on which the most popular writer in Europe at the time, Francesco Petrarch, climbed up a mountain in southern France simply because it was there. Or at least that's what he tells us. Petrarch was indeed a self-proclaimed traveler. He's credited with writing the world's first travel guide, *Petrarch's Guide to the Holy Land,* without actually having visited Jerusalem. It's worth asking, therefore, whether this means that his guide should be considered unreliable—but the answer would depend on what it is that we are reading his guide for. After all, this is a period that Petrarch saw as a transition toward something new. He coined the term "The Dark Ages" in order to describe what had come before him. And while he wasn't entirely sure what it was that was coming at him, the burgeoning Age of Exploration was opening up the old world, and Petrarch was enthusiastically volunteering to step inside it, christening himself Europe's first true humanist, and providing the world with answers before it had even come up with questions. "There is a peak higher than any other," he writes in his essay about climbing up the mountain, "which the people on the mountain call 'The Little Fellow'; why, I do not know, unless, as I suspect, this is meant, as things sometimes are, ironically; for it really seems to be the father of all the other mountains." His sentence is almost breathless in its halting fits and starts, its labored rumination. It's a great mimetic demonstration of a mind ascending something as the body does the same. But what if it is only Petrarch's mind that is doing the ascending? The real title of Petrarch's essay contains an extra word that seldom finds its way into English translations: *allegorico*. How much less significant is a journey of just the mind?

My Journey Up the Mountain

Today I climbed a mountain. What I wanted, I guess, was height. I've lived here all my life, as you know, and so the mountain's been in my line of sight every day since I was a child. I've wanted to do this for a while. But finally, after rereading that passage in Livy in which King Philip climbs Mount Haemus in Thessaly and looks out simultaneously over the Adriatic and Black seas, I was seized by a desire to go for it. To climb. Who would not want to experience the view from the top of the world? To be honest, nobody really knows if King Philip could actually see two seas from where he stood. The historical accounts of his journey are spectacularly varied. Nevertheless I decided that nothing was really stopping me from climbing a mountain of my own—no matter the veracity of Philip's ascent—and so I set my mind to it.

However, when it came time to find someone willing to help me with this journey, I found myself at a loss. It seemed that my interest in height was not as passionately shared others. One of my friends was too slow; another too hasty. One seemed too cautious, another absentminded. Some were gloomy, silly, stupid, drab. I was alarmed by one's incessant jabbering and another's utter silence. In one way or another they all seemed indifferent to this quest I felt I was on. True, none of these idiosyncrasies have bothered me till now. It was only planning for this trip that brought these limitations to my attention.

So, to make a long story short, I asked my brother to join me on this journey, and he was more than happy to come.

We left home in the morning and before nightfall reached the town of Malaucene, at the foot of the mountain. We had a good night's rest in the local inn, and then today—with quite a bit of difficulty, I might add—we did it. We climbed it.

Basically, the mountain is a steep mass of rocks, almost inaccessible. But as the ancients like to say, determination can overcome anything. What we had on our side was a good long day, pleasant weather, the agility of our bodies, the strength of our minds . . . indeed, the mountain itself was all that was in our way.

A hundred yards up the slope we went, meeting there an old shepherd who tried his darndest to dissuade us from proceeding any further. What's the problem? I asked him. He told us that fifty years earlier he had tried to climb the mountain himself, propelled by the same youthful vim that he saw in us that morning. The only thing he succeeded in achieving, however, was disappointment in his effort, his body and clothes torn apart by brambles, his mind worn down by failure.

He'd never heard of anyone trying to climb the mountain since.

We were determined, however. And I suppose we also felt challenged—our drive increasing only more so as the old man offered warnings.

When he realized that his efforts were in vain, though, the old shepherd joined us up the slope, pointing out the more treacherous paths, doling out advice, continuing to warn us even after we sped up ahead and past him.

All hindrances were now behind us.

Cheerfully we were climbing now. But, as it happens with such efforts, we eventually grew tired. We found ourselves stopped at a cliff face out of breath. We waited, rested, and soon started up again, more slowly, but still determined. I, a little slowly, while my brother more boldly. He chose a shortcut along the ridge, quickly reaching further heights. I, being weaker, tended toward the vertical paths that stretched out before me. Once, when he called back to me to point out a faster path, I replied that I was hoping to find an easier route than that. I didn't mind taking longer to reach the summit of the mountain if it meant that I could do it more gradually, and with ease.

But really, I was being lazy. In fact, by then my brother had reached the summit, while I was still wandering in circles trying to find that "easy" route. I never did, though. On the contrary: the path got longer, more ridiculous, even farther from the summit. Thoroughly annoyed with myself and seriously frustrated with my aimless wandering, I decided to go at it more directly: straight up, wearily, frightfully, but with more determination now. My brother called down to encourage me.

And then, soon enough, somehow—who knows?—I found myself nevertheless on the same path again.

What can I say?

To my brother's amusement, and to my annoyance, I kept stumbling straightaway on that same path for hours.

I'd been deluded like this before. I sat down for a minute on the slope in a ditch and began to reflect spiritually on what was physically before me. Rebuking myself, I started to think:

> What you have experienced today while climbing this mountain also happens when one nears blessedness. This, however, is not often recognized, for while the movements of the body are easily apparent, the activities of the mind are not. The blessed life is a great goal indeed, and narrow is the way that leads to it. But just as Horace wrote, wishing for it is not enough. Desire must come from a deep passion within. *Well, surely I have passion,* I thought to myself. So what's holding me back? I suspect that it's that gentle path, the one that hovers against the pleasures of the earth, seeming like the easier route while it is not. For when you consistently find yourself taking the wrong road in life, there comes a point when you either have to get up off your feet to try the path you've been putting off, or you resign yourself to sinking even more deeply in despair.

My goodness. What wonders such thoughts can inspire in the body!

Suffice it to say: I soon finished my journey. I reached the mountain's summit.

But, O! if I could only make that journey in my soul!

There's a peak up there on the mountain that's higher than any other, one that the local people call "The Little Fellow"; but why, I do not know, unless, as I suspect, this is meant, as such things are, ironically; for it really seems to be the better of all the other peaks. We were stopped there to rest before we started our way down, and there was a freshness in the air that I wasn't used to feeling. I stood gazing into the view as it opened out before me. There were clouds below my feet. There were towns and land for miles. Up there, it was easy for me to believe what I'd often heard about Mount Olympus.

I turned west to glimpse my homeland. Those frozen Alps, which were once crossed by that fiercest enemy of Rome, that man who broke up rocks with hammers, rope, and vinegar, seemed so near to me. But they were obviously very far. I have to admit, I was homesick. It's been a decade now since I graduated from Bologna. And, my goodness, how life has changed! As my teacher once wrote, "Let me recall the shames of my past, the carnal corruptions of my soul, not because I think fondly of them, but because I want to love You more honestly, God." I am still preoccupied with a lot that is troublesome. What I used to love, I no longer love. But on second thought, that isn't true. I think that I still love those things, I just love them a little less. No, I lie again! Of course I still love those things, and love them just as much. It's just now I love with guilt. And that at last is the truth. I love . . . but prefer not to love. I desire that which I desire to hate. Wretch that I am, I see myself in that famous line: "I shall hate if I can; and if not, I shall love despite myself." Fewer than three years ago that perverse desire that completely possessed me without any opposition began to be faced down by another kind of desire, one that was hostile to it. For some years now there's been a hard-fought battle between the two for control of my very soul.

I began to be concerned with what might happen in the future, saying to myself, What if I were to live for just another decade? And what if I pursue virtue at the same rate that I've retreated from obstinacy, could I not therefore meet death in my fortieth year happily? This is what I kept thinking about. And I was very proud of the progress I was making, lamenting my imperfections while bewailing life's mutability. But then I remembered where I was, and why. I looked up, and really saw for the first time what it was I had come to see. In the west, the boundary between France and Spain was imperceptible to me—not because there's something in the way of that boundary, but rather because our vision is too weak for such faint distinctions. I could see on my right the mountains of Lyons, and to the left the sea that laps Marseilles, the sea that beats Aigues-Mortes. I stood there admiring each of these places, thinking first of earthly matters and then finally raising my mind to higher things, just as my body itself had done. I turned to a book by Saint Augustine that I had brought with me up the mountain. Opening it randomly, I read whatever I chanced upon. And I swear to God that these are the words that struck my eyes that moment:

"And men go to the mountains to look out in amazement at the huge waves of the sea and the broad flow of the rivers and the tracts of the oceans and the stars in their courses, and they overlook themselves."

I was astonished, I must confess. My brother was sitting beside me and asked me to read more, but I told him to be quiet. I wanted to be alone. I closed the book, furious. There I was, marveling at all those earthly delights, when ancient philosophers from eons past had realized that nothing but the mind is wonderful.

Happy to have seen the mountain, and now having seen enough, I turned my eyes on myself. I didn't say anything again until we reached the ground, Saint Augustine's words still roiling through my mind. I couldn't believe that what I'd read was happened upon by chance. I knew that it was a sign. I remember how Saint Augustine once thought that the same thing had happened to him. He was reading the Gospel when he came across these words: "Not in reveling and drunkenness, not in debauchery and licentiousness, not in strife and jealousy, but in Jesus Christ alone." And just as Saint Augustine, upon reading that passage, did not need to read any further, so for me those few words were all that I really needed. Silently I reflected on what little sense we mortals have: spreading ourselves over so many things just to lose ourselves in vanity. We look outside for what's within. I turned around as we descended to look back upon the mountain. It now seemed so small. If I did not resent all the sweat and toil involved in bringing my body just a little nearer to heaven, what cross, what prison, what torture ought to deter my mind from treading beneath the swollen peak of arrogance to reach God? But how rare that person is who refuses to be diverted from this way because he is afraid of suffering, because he loves the easier way. If there is such a man, surely he is happy. As the ancient poet said, "Blessed is he who has come to an understanding of the causes of all things, and who has stomped down all his fears, all thoughts of unyielding fate, even the roaring of greedy Acheron!" How zealously we must all try to keep those fears at bay.

Somehow I've returned to that little inn now, unconscious of the stony path that brought me back to earth. The innkeepers are busy preparing supper, and here I am alone in a quiet corner of the inn, trying to write this essay without premeditation. There is nothing I want to keep hidden from you. What I offer are my thoughts. I can only hope that after wandering for so long in uncertainty, I may write a few sentences that may finally stand firm. That after being tossed pointlessly here and there for so many years in my youth I may now be directed toward what is good, what is true, what is certain, and what will last.

(translated by the editor)

1499

Spain

Thanks to the explorations of the Spanish in the New World, this is the year that Europeans are first tasting the pineapple. This is the first year that they are tasting nutmeg. And this is the first time that Europeans try chocolate, something that Mesoamericans have been enjoying for two millennia. When the Spanish writer Bernardino de Sahagún is born this year, five million people are living Mesoamerica. He'll visit them as a Franciscan monk in 1529, teaching the Aztec people Spanish and learning from them Nahuatl. With three of his native students, over the course of forty-five years, he'll eventually compile a twelve-volume study of the Aztec people called *A General History of the Things of New Spain,* a bilingual project of Spanish and Nahuatl that represents what some critics call the first work of oral ethnography. It is a book of definitions, histories, descriptions, and memories that are told in the voices of anonymous informants. The information is repetitive, contradictory, sometimes wrong, unbelievable. But it's unlikely that the book's point is the accuracy of its data. By the time that de Sahagún finishes his multivolume study, an estimated 70 percent of the Aztec people will have died of Old World diseases. I think the point of the book is song.

BERNARDINO DE SAHAGÚN

Definitions of Earthly Things

A Shellfish

It falls out on the ocean shore; it falls out like mud.

A Mushroom

It is round, large, like a severed head.

Seashell

It is white. One is large, one is small. It is spiraled, marvelous. It is that which can be blown, which resounds. I blow the seashell. I improve, I polish the seashell.

Little Blue Heron

It resembles the brown crane in color; it is ashen, grey. It smells like fish, rotten fish, stinking fish. It smells of fish, rotten fish.

Ruby-Throated Hummingbird

It is ashen, ash colored. At the top of its head and the throat, its feathers are flaming, like fire. They glisten, they glow.

A Water-Strider

It is like a fly, small and round. It has legs, it has wings; it is dry. It goes on the surface of the water; it is a flyer. It buzzes, it sings.

A Mountain

High, pointed; pointed on top, pointed at the summit, towering; wide, cylindrical, round; a round mountain, low, low-ridged; rocky, with many rocks; craggy with many crags; rough with rocks; of earth, with trees; grassy; with herbs; with shrubs; with water; dry; white; jagged; with a sloping plain, with gorges, with caves; precipitous, having gorges; canyon land, precipitous land with boulders.

I climb the mountain; I scale the mountain. I live on the mountain. I am born on the mountain. No one becomes a mountain—no one turns himself into a mountain. The mountain crumbles.

Another Mountain

It is wooded; it spreads green.

Forest

It is a place of verdure, of fresh green; of wind—windy places, in wind, windy; a place of cold: it becomes cold; there is much frost; it is a place which freezes. It is a place from which misery comes, where it exists; a place where there is affliction—a place of affliction, of lamentation, a place of affliction, of weeping; a place where there is sadness, a place of compassion, of sighing; a place which arouses sorrow, which spreads misery.

It is a place of gorges, gorge places; a place of crags, craggy places; a place of stony soil, stony-soiled places; in hard soil, in clayey soil, in moist and fertile soil. It is a place among moist and fertile lands, a place of moist and fertile soil, in yellow soil.

It is a place with cuestas, cuesta places; a place with peaks, peaked places; a place which is grassy, with grassy places; a place of forests, forested places; a place of thin forest, thinly forested places; a place of thick forest, thickly forested places; a place of jungle, of dry tree stumps, of underbrush, of dense forest.

It is a place of stony soil, stony-soiled places; a place of round stones, round-stoned places; a place of sharp stones, of rough stones; a place of crags, craggy places; a place of *tepetate;* a place with clearings, cleared places; a place of valleys, of coves, of places with coves, of cove places; a place of boulders, bouldered places; a place of hollows.

It is a disturbing place, fearful, frightful; home of the savage beast, a dwelling-place of the serpent, the rabbit, the deer; a place from which nothing departs, nothing leaves, nothing emerges. It is a place of dry rocks, of boulders; bouldered places; boulder land, a land of bouldered places. It is a place of caves, cave places, having caves—a place having caves.

It is a place of wild beasts; a place of wild beasts—of the ocelot, the *cuitlachtli*, the bobcat, the serpent, the spider, the rabbit, the deer; of stalks, grass, prickly shrubs: of the mesquite, of the pine. It is a place where wood is owned. Trees are felled. It is a place where trees are cut, where wood is gathered, where there is chopping, where there is logging: a place of beams.

It becomes verdant, a fresh green. It becomes cold, icy. Ice forms and spreads; ice lies forming a surface. There is wind, a crashing wind; the wind crashes, spreads whistling, forms whirlwinds. Ice is blown by the wind; the wind glides.

There is no one; there are no people. It is desolate; it lies desolate. There is nothing edible. Misery abounds, misery emerges, misery spreads. There is no joy, no pleasure. It lies sprouting; herbs lie sprouting; nothing lies emerging; the earth is pressed down. All die of thirst. The grasses lie sprouting. Nothing lies cast about. There is hunger; all hunger. It is the home of hunger; there is death from hunger. All die of cold; there is freezing; there is trembling; there is the clattering, the chattering of teeth. There are cramps, the stiffening of the body, the constant stiffening, the stretching out prone.

There is fright, there is constant fright. One is devoured; one is slain by stealth; one is abused; one is brutally put to death; one is tormented. Misery abounds. There is calm, constant calm, continuing calm.

Mirror Stone

Its name comes from nowhere. This can be excavated in mines; it can be broken off. Of these mirror stones, one is white, one black. The white one—this is a good one to look into: the mirror, the clear, transparent one. They named it mirror of the noblemen, the mirror of the ruler.

The black one—this one is not good. It is not to look into; it does not make one appear good. It is one (so they say) which contends with one's face. When someone uses such a mirror, from it is to be seen a distorted mouth, swollen eyelids, thick lips, a large mouth. They say it is an ugly mirror, a mirror which contends with one's face.

Of these mirrors, one is round; one is long: they call it *acaltezcatl*. These mirror stones can be excavated in mines, can be polished, can be worked.

I make a mirror. I work it. I shatter it. I form it. I grind it. I polish it with sand. I work it with fine abrasive sand. I apply to it a glue of bat shit. I prepare it. I polish it with a fine cane. I make it shiny. I regard myself in the mirror. I appear from there in my looking-mirror; from it I admire myself.

Secret Road

Its name is secret road, the one which few people know, which not all people are aware of, which few people go along. It is good, fine; a good place, a fine place. It is where one is harmed, a place of harm. It is known as a safe place; it is a difficult place, a dangerous place. One is frightened. It is a place of fear.

There are trees, crags, gorges, rivers, precipitous places, places of precipitous land, various places of precipitous land, various precipitous places, gorges, various gorges. It is a place of wild animals, a place of wild beasts, full of wild beasts. It is a place where one is put to death by stealth; a place where one is put to death in the jaws of the wild beasts of the land of the dead.

I take the secret road. I follow along, I encounter the secret road. He goes following along, he goes joining that which is bad, the corner, the darkness, the secret road. He goes to seek, to find, that which is bad.

The Cave

It becomes long, deep; it widens, extends, narrows. It is a constricted place, a narrowed place, one of the hollowed-out places. It forms hollowed-out places. There are roughened places; there are asperous places. It is frightening, a fearful place, a place of death. It is called a place of death because there is dying. It is a place of darkness; it darkens; it stands ever dark. It stands wide-mouthed, it is wide-mouthed. It is wide-mouthed; it is narrow-mouthed. It has mouths which pass through.

I place myself in the cave. I enter the cave.

(translated by Charles E. Dibble and Arthur J. O. Anderson)

1580

France

He grew up on an estate called Montaigne in Bordeaux, a name that literally means "mountain" in Old French—a fitting place therefore for a family that aspired to nobility, which is the only reason they bought it. According to French law in the sixteenth century, a family could claim itself officially noble after three consecutive generations of its patriarchs "lived the lives of gentlemen," which was defined by French convention at the time as "consistently refraining from engaging in commerce . . . or any other activities associated with commoners." So when Michel Eyquem turned fourteen years old, officially—but barely—becoming eligible for nobility, his parents encouraged him to assume the lifestyle of a noble, calling the boy from that day forward Michel de Montaigne. "In a time when it is so common to do evil," he later wrote, "it is practically praiseworthy to do what is useless." I really wish that he hadn't ever used the word "useless." While his life from the outside seems preposterously charmed, the leisure in which Montaigne was perpetually engaged afforded him the luxury of one vital risk—something that would change the face of world literature forever. "Know thyself," reads one of the seventy-seven quotes that he carved into the ceiling of his study. "I am human, and nothing that is human is foreign to me." "All is vanity." "What do I know?" Round, and stone, and three stories high, the tower in which Montaigne established his study was isolated from the rest of his rambling old chateau, standing free on the grounds, safely distant from the smell of the horses in the stables, the heat inside the vineyard, the daily grind of thirteen servants who worked to maintain his nobility. It is here where Montaigne wrote every day, removed from the busyness of the world below him, but situated with a view of it all. His tower was a place of deep meditation, and simultaneously a source for endless observations. "In most authors I see someone writing," one scholar wrote, "but in Montaigne I see someone thinking." Indeed, while he may not have invented this literary form, Montaigne was more importantly the first to call it *essai*—literally, an "attempt"—a term that conveys the tentative, the speculative, the nondefinitive, a term that turned inquiry officially inward, inspiring later essayists like Jean-Jacques Rousseau, Henry David Thoreau, Annie Dillard, Kamau Brathwaite, and David Foster Wallace, a term that finally freed this form from the argumentative posturing of political, religious, or scientific treatises, granting it the credentials to be recognized at last as what it's always been: art. I really do not care that Montaigne did this from a tower.

MICHEL DE MONTAIGNE

On Some Verses of Virgil

To the extent that useful thoughts are fuller and more solid, they are also more absorbing and more burdensome. Vice, death, poverty, disease, are grave subjects and grieve us. We should have our soul instructed in the means to sustain and combat evils, and in the rules for right living and right belief, and should often arouse it and exercise it in this fine study. But for a soul of the common sort this must be done with some respite and with moderation; it goes mad if it is too continually tense.

In my youth I needed to warn and urge myself to stick to my duty: blitheness and health do not go so well, they say, with these wise and serious reflections. At present I am in another state. The conditions of old age warn me, sober me, and preach to me only too much. From an excess of gaiety I have fallen into an excess of severity, which is more disagreeable. Wherefore at this point I deliberately let myself go a bit to license and sometimes occupy my soul with youthful wanton thoughts to give it a rest. Henceforth I shall be only too sedate, too heavy, and too mature. The years lecture me every day in coldness and temperance. This body of mine flees disorder and fears it. It is my body's turn to guide my mind toward reform. It dominates in turn, and more roughly and imperiously. It does not leave me a single hour, sleeping or waking, unoccupied with instruction about death, patience, and penitence. I defend myself against temperance as I once did against sensual pleasure; for it pulls me too far back, even to the point of insensibility.

Now I want to be master of myself in every direction. Wisdom has its excesses, and has no less need of moderation than does folly. Thus, for fear I may dry up, wither, and grow heavy with prudence, in the intervals that my ills grant me—

Lest my mind dwell too much upon its ills

OVID

—I very gently sidestep and avert my gaze from this stormy and cloudy sky that I have in front of me, which, thank God, I do indeed consider without fright, but not without effort and study, and I amuse myself in the remembrance of my past youth:

human nature

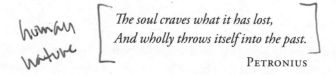

> *The soul craves what it has lost,*
> *And wholly throws itself into the past.*
>
> PETRONIUS

Let childhood look ahead, old age backward: was not this the meaning of the double face of Janus? Let the years drag me along if they will, but backward. As long as my eyes can discern that lovely season now expired, I turn them in that direction at intervals. If youth is escaping from my blood and my veins, at least I want not to uproot the picture of it from my memory:

appreciate the life you have had

Our lives are two
If we can relish our past life anew.

MARTIAL

Plato orders men to attend the exercises, dances, and games of youth, in order to rejoice in others at the suppleness and beauty of body that is no longer in themselves, and to call to mind the grace and charm of that flowering age; and he wants them to attribute the honor of victory in these sports to the young man who has most exhilarated and delighted the greatest number of them.

Extraordinary? = Unusual.

Once I used to mark the burdensome and gloomy days as extraordinary. Those are now my ordinary ones; the extraordinary are the fine serene ones. I am on my way to the point where I will leap for joy as at a novel favor when nothing pains me. Though I tickle myself, I can scarcely wring a poor laugh out of this wretched body any more. I am merry only in fancy and in dreams, to divert by trickery the gloom of old age. But indeed it would require another remedy than a dream: a feeble struggle, that of art against nature. It is great simplicity to lengthen and anticipate human discomforts, as everyone does. I would rather be old less long than be old before I am old. Even the slightest occasions of pleasure that I can come upon, I seize. I know indeed by hearsay several kinds of pleasures that are prudent, strong, and glorious; but opinion has not enough power over me to give me an appetite for them. I do not so much want them noble, magnificent, and ostentatious, as sweet, easy, and ready at hand. *We depart from nature; we give ourselves up to the people, who are not a good guide in anything* (Seneca).

My philosophy is in action, in natural and present practice, little in fancy. Would I might take pleasure in playing at cobnut or with a top!

> *He set not people's shouts before the public safety.*
>
> ENNIUS, QUOTED BY CICERO

Pleasure is a rather unambitious quality. It thinks itself rich enough in itself without adding the prize of reputation, and prefers to be in the shade. We should take the whip to a young man who spent his time discriminating between the taste of wines and sauces. There is nothing I ever knew less or valued less than this. At present I am learning it. I am much ashamed of it, but what should I do? I am still more ashamed and vexed at the circumstances that drive me to it. It is for us to trifle and play the fool, and for the young to stand on their reputation and in the best place. They are going toward the world, toward reputation; we are coming from it. *Let them have to themselves weapons, horses, spears, clubs, ball games, swimming, and races; let them leave to us old men, out of many sports, dice and knuckle-bones* (Cicero).

The laws themselves send us home. I can do no less, on behalf of this puny condition into which my age pushes me, than furnish it with toys and pastimes, like childhood: and into that indeed we are falling back. Both wisdom and folly will have all they can do to support me and help me by their alternate services in this calamity of old age:

> *Mingle a dash of folly with your wisdom.*
>
> HORACE

Likewise I flee the slightest pains; and those that formerly would not even have scratched me, now pierce me through and through: so easily is my habit of body beginning to apply itself to illness. *To a frail body every pain is intolerable* (Cicero).

> *And nothing that is hard can a sick mind endure.*
>
> OVID

I have always been sensitive and susceptible to pain; now I am still more tender, and exposed on all sides:

> *Anything cracked will shatter at a touch.*
>
> OVID

My judgment keeps me indeed from kicking and grumbling against the discomforts that nature orders me to suffer, but not from feeling them. I, who have no other aim but to live and be merry, would run from one end of the world to the other to seek out one good year of pleasant and cheerful tranquillity. A somber, dull tranquillity is easy enough to find for me, but it puts me to sleep and stupefies me; I am not content with it. If there are any persons, any good company, in country or city, in France or elsewhere, residing or traveling, who like my humors and whose humors I like, they have only to whistle in their palm and I will go furnish them with essays in flesh and bone.

Since it is the privilege of the mind to rescue itself from old age, I advise mine to do so as strongly as I can. Let it grow green, let it flourish meanwhile, if it can, like mistletoe on a dead tree. But I fear it is a traitor. It has such a tight brotherly bond with the body that it abandons me at every turn to follow the body in its need. I take it aside and flatter it, I work on it, all for nothing. In vain I try to turn it aside from this bond, I offer it Seneca and Catullus, and the ladies and the royal dances; if its companion has the colic, it seems to have it too. Even the activities that are peculiarly its own cannot then be aroused; they evidently smack of a cold in the head. There is no sprightliness in its productions if there is none in the body at the same time.

Our masters are wrong in that, seeking the causes of the extraordinary flights of our soul, they have attributed some to a divine ecstasy, to love, to warlike fierceness, to poetry, to wine, but have not assigned a proper share to health—an ebullient, vigorous, full, lazy health, such as in the past my green years and security supplied me with now and then. The blaze of gaiety kindles in the mind vivid, bright flashes beyond our natural capacity, and some of the lustiest, if not the most extravagant, enthusiasms.

Now then, it is no wonder if a contrary state weighs down my spirits, nails them down, and produces a contrary effect.

> *Drooping with the body, it rises to no task.*
>
> Maximianus

Moreover, my mind wants me to be grateful to it because, so it says, it concedes much less to this bond than is usual with most men. At least, while we have a truce, let us banish troubles and difficulties from our relations:

> *So while we may, let's banish wrinkle-fronted age;*
>
> Horace

gloomy things should be lighted with pleasantries (Sidonius Apolinaris).

I love a gay and sociable wisdom, and shun harshness and austerity in behavior, holding every surly countenance suspect:

> *The sullen arrogance of a gloomy face.*
>
> Buchanan

> *That sad group also has its sodomites.*
>
> Martial

I heartily agree with Plato when he says that an easy or a difficult humor is of great importance to the goodness or badness of the soul. Socrates had a settled expression, but serene and smiling, not settled like that of old Crassus, who was never seen to laugh. Virtue is a pleasant and gay quality.

I know well that very few people will frown at the license of my writings who do not have more to frown at in the license of their thoughts. I conform well to their hearts, but I offend their eyes. It is a well-ordered humor that criticizes Plato's writings and glides over his supposed relations with Phaedo, Dion, Stella, and Archeanassa. *Let us not be ashamed to say what we are not ashamed to think* (author unknown).

I hate a surly and gloomy spirit that slides over the pleasures of life and seizes and feeds upon its misfortunes: like flies, which cannot cling to a smooth and well-polished body, and attach themselves to and rest on rough and uneven places, and like leeches that suck and crave only bad blood.

Furthermore, I have ordered myself to dare to say all that I dare to do, and I dislike even thoughts that are unpublishable. The worst of my actions and conditions does not seem to me so ugly as the cowardice of not daring to avow it. Everyone is discreet in confession; people should be so in action. Boldness in sinning is somewhat compensated and bridled by boldness in confessing. Whoever would oblige himself to tell all, would oblige himself not to do anything about which we are constrained to keep silent. God grant that this excessive license of mine may encourage our men to attain freedom, rising above these cowardly and hypocritical virtues born of our imperfections; that at the expense of my immoderation I may draw them on to the point of reason. A man must see his vice and study it to tell about it. Those who hide it from others ordinarily hide it from themselves. And they do not consider it covered up enough if they themselves see it; they withdraw and disguise it from their own conscience. _Why does no one confess his vices? Because he is still in their grip now; it is only for a waking man to tell his dream_ (Seneca).

The diseases of the body become clearer as they increase. We find that what we were calling a cold or a sprain is the gout. The diseases of the soul grow more obscure as they grow stronger; the sickest man is least sensible of them. That is why they must be handled often in the light of day, with a pitiless hand, be opened up and torn from the hollow of our breast. As in the matter of good deeds, so in the matter of evil deeds, mere confession is sometimes reparation. Is there any ugliness in doing wrong that can dispense us from the duty of confessing it?

It is painful for me to dissemble, so much so that I avoid taking others' secrets into my keeping, not really having the heart to disavow what I know. I can keep silent about it, but deny it I cannot without effort and displeasure. To be really secret a man must be so by nature, not by obligation. In the service of princes it is a small thing to be secret if one is not a liar to boot. If the man who was asking Thales the Milesian whether he should solemnly deny having committed adultery had asked me, I would have answered him that he should not do it, for lying seems to me even worse than adultery. Thales advised him quite differently: to swear to his innocence, so as to shield the greater fault by the lesser. However, this advice was not so much a choice as a multiplication of vices.

Whereupon let us say this word in passing, that we offer a good bargain to a man of conscience when we propose to him some difficulty as a counterpoise to vice. But when we shut him up between two vices, we put him to a rough choice, as they did to Origen: that he should either worship an idol or endure being carnally enjoyed by a big ugly Ethiopian who was brought before him. He submitted to the first condition, and sinfully, it is said. On this basis those women would not be wrong who protest to us these days, according to their error, that they would rather burden their conscience with ten men than with one Mass.

If it is indiscretion to publish one's errors thus, there is no great danger that it will pass into an example and custom. For Aristo used to say that the words men fear most are those that uncover them. We must tuck up this stupid rag that covers our conduct. They send their conscience to the brothel and keep their countenance in good order. Even those who are traitors and assassins espouse the laws of ceremony and fix their duty there. Yet it is not for injustice to complain of indecorum, or malice of indiscretion. It is a pity that a wicked man is not also a fool, and that outward decency should palliate his vice. These decorative incrustations belong only to a good, healthy wall that deserves to be preserved or whitened.

In honor of the Huguenots, who condemn our private and auricular confession, I confess myself in public, religiously and purely. Saint Augustine, Origen, and Hippocrates have published the errors of their opinions; I, besides, those of my conduct. I am hungry to make myself known, and I care not to how many, provided it be truly. Or to put it better, I am hungry for nothing, but I have a mortal fear of being taken to be other than I am by those who come to know my name.

A man who does everything for honor and glory, what does he think to gain by presenting himself to the world in a mask, concealing his true being from public knowledge? Praise a hunchback for his handsome figure, and he is bound to take it as an insult. If you are a coward and people honor you as a valiant man, is it you they are talking about? They take you for another. I would just as soon have such a man find gratification in having people doff their hat to him, thinking that he is master of the troop, when he is one of the meanest of the retinue.

As Archelaus, king of Macedonia, was passing in the street, someone poured some water on him. Those with him said he should punish the man. "Yes," he said, "but he did not pour water on me, but on the man he thought I was." Socrates said to the man who informed him that people were speaking ill of him: "Not at all; there is nothing in me of what they say."

As for me, if someone praised me for being a good pilot, for being very modest, or for being very chaste, I would owe him no thanks. And similarly if someone called me traitor, robber, or drunkard, I would consider myself offended just as little. Those who have a false opinion of themselves can feed on false approbations; not I, who see myself and search myself to my very entrails, who know well what belongs to me. I am pleased to be less praised, provided I am better known. I might be considered wise with the kind of wisdom I consider folly.

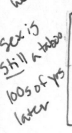

I am annoyed that my essays serve the ladies only as a public article of furniture, an article for the parlor. This chapter will put me in the boudoir. I like their society when it is somewhat private; when public, it is without favor or savor.

In farewells we exaggerate the warmth of our affection toward the things we are leaving. I am taking my last leave of the world's pastimes; here are our last embraces. But let us come to my theme.

What has the sexual act, so natural, so necessary, and so just, done to mankind, for us not to dare talk about it without shame and for us to exclude it from serious and decent conversation? We boldly pronounce the words "kill," "rob," "betray"; and this one we do not dare pronounce, except between our teeth. Does this mean that the less we breathe of it in words, the more we have the right to swell our thoughts with it?

For it is a good one that the words least in use, least written and most hushed up, are the best known and most generally familiar. No age, no type of character, is ignorant of them, any more than of the word "bread." They impress themselves on everyone without being expressed, without voice and without form. It is also a good one that this is an action that we have placed in the sanctuary of silence, from which it is a crime to drag it out even to accuse and judge it. Nor do we dare to chastise it except roundaboutly and figuratively. A great favor for a criminal, to be so execrable that justice deems it unjust to touch and see him: free and saved by virtue of the severity of his condemnation.

Is it not the same as in the matter of books, which become all the more marketable and public by being suppressed? For my part I am going to take Aristotle at his word when he says that bashfulness serves as an ornament to youth but a reproach to old age.

These verses are preached in the ancient school, a school I adhere to much more than to the modern; its virtues seem to me greater, its vices less:

> *Those who flee Venus too much sin no less*
> *Than those who do pursue her to excess.*
>
> PLUTARCH

> *Thou, goddess, thou alone rul'st over everything;*
> *Without thee nothing rises to the light of day;*
> *Nothing becomes, without thee, lovable or gay.*
>
> LUCRETIUS

I do not know who can have put Pallas and the Muses on bad terms with Venus and made them cold toward Love; but I know no deities better suited or more indebted to one another. Whoever takes away from the Muses their amorous fancies will rob them of the best subject they have and the noblest matter of their work. And whoever makes Love lose the communication and service of poetry will disarm him of his best weapons. In this way they charge the god of intimacy and affection, and the patron goddesses of humanity and justice, with the vice of ingratitude and lack of appreciation.

I have not been so long cashiered from the roll and retinue of this god as not to have a memory informed of his powers and merits:

> *I know the traces of the ancient flame.*
>
> VIRGIL

There is still some remnant of heat and emotion after the fever:

> *In wintry years, let me not lack this heat.*
>
> JOHANNES SECUNDUS

Dried out and weighed down as I am, I still feel some tepid remains of that past ardor:

> *As the Aegean, when those winds have died*
> *Which only lately made it churn and leap,*
> *Does not at once grow calm, or put aside*
> *The roar and violence of the raging deep.*
>
> TASSO

But from what I understand of it, the powers and worth of this god are more alive and animated in the painting of poetry than in their own reality,

> *And verses have their fingers to excite.*
>
> JUVENAL

Poetry reproduces an indefinable mood that is more amorous than love itself. Venus is not so beautiful all naked, alive, and panting, as she is here in Virgil:

> *The goddess ceased to speak, and snowy arms outflung*
> *Around him faltering, soft fondling as she clung.*
> *He quickly caught the wonted flame; the heat well-known*
> *Entered his marrow, ran through every trembling bone.*
> *Often a brilliant lightning flash, not otherwise,*
> *Split by a thunderclap, runs through the cloudy skies.*
> *He spoke,*
> *Gave the embraces that she craved; then on her breast,*
> *Outpoured at last, gave himself up to sleep and rest.*
>
> VIRGIL

What I find worth considering here is that he portrays her as a little too passionate for a marital Venus. In this sober contract the appetites are not so wanton; they are dull and more blunted. Love hates people to be attached to each other except by himself, and takes a laggard part in relations that are set up and maintained under another title, as marriage is. Connections and means have, with reason, as much weight in it as graces and beauty, or more. We do not marry for ourselves, whatever we say; we marry just as much or more for our posterity, for our family. The practice

interesting

and benefit of marriage concerns our race very far beyond us. Therefore I like this fashion of arranging it rather by a third hand than by our own, and by the sense of others rather than by our own. How opposite is all this to the conventions of love! And so it is a kind of incest to employ in this venerable and sacred alliance the efforts and extravagances of amorous license, as it seems to me I have said elsewhere. A man, says Aristotle, should touch his wife prudently and soberly, lest if he caresses her too lasciviously the pleasure should transport her outside the bounds of reason. What he says on account of conscience, the doctors say on account of health: that an excessively hot, voluptuous, and assiduous pleasure spoils the seed and hinders conception. They say, on the other hand, that for a languid encounter, as this one is by its nature, we should present ourselves rarely and at considerable intervals, to fill it with a just and fertile heat:

> *Athirst to take the member in and hide it deep.*
>
> VIRGIL

I see no marriages that sooner are troubled and fail than those that progress by means of beauty and amorous desires. It needs more solid and stable foundations, and we need to go at it circumspectly; this ebullient ardor is no good for it.

Those who think to honor marriage by joining love to it act, it seems to me, the same as those who, to favor virtue, hold that nobility is nothing else but virtue. These are things that have a certain relationship, but there is a great difference between them. There is no point in mixing up their names and titles; we wrong one or the other by confusing them. Nobility is a fine quality, and introduced with reason. But inasmuch as it is a quality dependent on others, and which can fall to a vicious and worthless man, it is well below virtue in esteem. It is a virtue, if indeed it is one, that is artificial and visible, dependent upon time and fortune. Varying in form according to countries, living and mortal, with no more source than the river Nile, genealogical and common to many, a matter of succession and resemblance, derived by inference, and a very weak inference at that. Knowledge, strength, goodness, beauty, riches, all other qualities, fall into the range of communication and association; this one is self-consuming, of no use in the service of others.

One of our kings was proposed the choice between two competitors for the same office, one of whom was a nobleman, the other was not. He ordered that they choose, without regard to this quality, the one who had the more merit; but that if the worth should be entirely equal, they should then take nobility into account. That was giving it exactly its proper place. Antigonus said to a young stranger who was asking him for the post of his father, a man of valor who had just died: "My friend, in such benefits I do not consider so much the nobility of my soldiers as I do their prowess." In truth, it should not go as it did with the functionaries of the kings of Sparta, trumpeters, minstrels, cooks, whose duties were inherited by their children, no matter how ignorant they were, in preference to the most experienced men in the trade.

The people of Calicut make of their nobles a superhuman species. Marriage is forbidden them, and every other occupation but war. Of concubines they may have their fill, and the women as many lovers, without jealousy toward one another; but it is a capital and unpardonable crime to mate with a person of another condition than their own. And they consider themselves polluted if they are so much as touched by them in passing, and, as their nobility is marvelously injured and damaged by this, they kill those who have merely approached a little too close to them; so that the ignoble are obliged to cry out as they walk, like the gondoliers in Venice at the street corners, to avoid collisions; and the nobles command them to move aside in the direction they want. Thereby the nobles avoid an ignominy that they consider perpetual; and the others, a certain death. No length of time, no princely favor, no office or virtue or riches can make a commoner become a noble. In which this custom helps, that marriages are forbidden between one trade and another. A girl from a shoemaker's family cannot marry a carpenter. And the parents are obliged to train their children exactly for the father's calling and not for any other; whereby the distinction and continuity of their fortune is maintained.

A good marriage, if such there be, rejects the company and conditions of love. It tries to reproduce those of friendship. It is a sweet association in life, full of constancy, trust, and an infinite number of useful and solid services and mutual obligations. No woman who savors the taste of it,

Whom the nuptial torch with welcome light has joined,

CATULLUS

would want to have the place of a mistress or paramour to her husband. If she is lodged in his affection as a wife, she is lodged there much more honorably and securely. When he dances ardent and eager attention elsewhere, still let anyone ask him then on whom he would rather have some shame fall, on his wife or his mistress; whose misfortune would afflict him more; for whom he wishes more honor. These questions admit of no doubt in a sound marriage.

The fact that we see so few good marriages is a sign of its price and its value. If you form it well and take it rightly, there is no finer relationship in our society. We cannot do without it, and yet we go about debasing it. The result is what is observed about cages: the birds outside despair of getting in, and those inside are equally anxious to get out. Socrates, when asked which was preferable, to take or not to take a wife, said: "Whichever a man does, he will repent it." It is a compact to which the saying is applied most appropriately, *man* is *to man* either *a god* or *a wolf* (Cecilius, quoted by Symmachus; and Plautus). Many qualities must come together to construct it. It is found nowadays better suited to simple plebeian souls, in which luxury, curiosity, and idleness do not disturb it so much. Men with unruly humors like me, who hate any sort of bond or obligation, are not so fit for it:

Sweeter it is to me to live with neck unyoked.

MAXIMIANUS

Of my own choice, I would have avoided marrying Wisdom herself, if she had wanted me. But say what we will, the custom and practice of ordinary life bears us along. Most of my actions are conducted by example, not by choice. At all events, I did not really bid myself to it, I was led to it, and borne by extraneous circumstances. For not only inconvenient things, but anything at all, however ugly and vicious and repulsive, can become acceptable through some condition or circumstance: so inane is our human posture. And I was borne to it certainly more ill-prepared and contrary than I am now after having tried it. And, licentious as I am thought to be, I have in truth observed the laws of marriage more strictly than I had either promised or expected. It is no longer time to kick when we have let ourselves be hobbled. A man must husband his freedom prudently; but once he has submitted to an obligation, he must keep to it under the laws of common duty, at least make an effort to. Those who make this bargain only to behave with hatred and contempt act unjustly and harmfully. And that fine rule that I see passing from hand to hand among the women like a sacred oracle,

he doesn't think he's cut out for marriage

> *Serve your husband as your master*
> *And guard against him as a traitor,*
>
> FRENCH; SOURCE UNKNOWN

which is to say "Behave toward him with a constrained, hostile, and distrustful reverence," a war cry and a challenge, is equally unjust and hard. I am too soft for such thorny plans. To tell the truth, I have not yet attained such perfection of cleverness and refinement of wit as to confound reason with injustice and cast into derision any order and rule that does not accord with my appetite. Because I hate superstition, I do not promptly throw myself into irreligion. If a man does not always do his duty, at least he must always love and acknowledge it. It is treachery to get married without getting wedded. Let us pass on.

Our poet represents a marriage full of harmony and well matched, in which, nevertheless, there is not much loyalty. Did he mean that it is not impossible to give in to the impact of love and nonetheless reserve some duty toward marriage, and that one may injure marriage without breaking it up completely? A servant may shoe his master's mule without hating him for all that. Beauty, opportunity, destiny (for destiny has a hand in it too)

> *There is a destiny that rules*
> *The parts our clothes conceal; for if the stars abhor you,*
> *Unheard-of length of member will do nothing for you*
>
> JUVENAL

—have attached her to a stranger; not so wholly, perhaps, that she may not have some tie left by which she still holds to her husband. Love and marriage are two intentions that go by separate and distinct roads. A woman may give herself to a man whom she would not at all want to have married; I do not mean because of the state of his fortune, but because of his personal qualities. Few men have married their mistresses who have not repented it—even in the other world: what a bad match Jupiter made with his wife, whom he had first frequented and enjoyed in love affairs! It is the old saying: "Shit in your hat and then put it on your head." ᴡᴀ †

I have seen in my time, in high place, love shamefully and dishonorably cured by marriage: the considerations are too different. We love, without conflict, two diverse and contrary things. Isocrates used to say that people liked Athens the way men like the ladies they serve for love. Everyone loved to come and wander around and pass his time there; no one loved it enough to marry it, that is to say, to reside and settle there. I have been vexed to see husbands hate their wives for the mere fact that they themselves are doing them wrong. At least we should not love them less for our own fault. Through repentance and compassion, at least, they should be dearer to us.

They are different ends, Isocrates says, and yet in some sort compatible. Marriage has for its share utility, justice, honor, and constancy: a flat pleasure, but more universal. Love is founded on pleasure alone, and in truth its pleasure is more stimulating, lively, and keen: a pleasure inflamed by difficulty. There must be a sting and a smart in it. It is no longer love if it is without arrows and without fire. The liberality of the ladies is too profuse in marriage, and blunts the point of affection and desire. Just see the pains that Lycurgus and Plato take in their laws to avoid this disadvantage.

Women are not wrong at all when they reject the rules of life that have been introduced into the world, inasmuch as it is the men who have made these without them. There is naturally strife and wrangling between them and us: the closest communion we have with them is still tumultuous and tempestuous.

In our author's opinion we treat them inconsiderately in the following way. We have discovered, he says, that they are incomparably more capable and ardent than we in the acts of love—and that priest of antiquity so testified, who had been once a man and then a woman,

> *To him in both aspects was Venus known.*
>
> Ovid

—and besides, we have learned from their own mouth the proof that was once given in different centuries by an emperor and an empress of Rome, master workmen and famous in this task: he indeed deflowered in one night ten captive Sarmatian virgins; but she actually in one night was good for twenty-five encounters, changing company according to her need and liking,

> *Her secret parts burning and tense with lust,*
> *And, tired by men, but far from sated, she withdrew.*
>
>   JUVENAL

We know about the dispute that occurred in Catalonia from a woman complaining of the too assiduous efforts of her husband: not so much, in my opinion, that she was bothered by them (for I believe in miracles only in matters of faith), as by way of a pretext to curtail and curb, in the very thing that is the fundamental act of marriage, the authority of husbands over their wives, and to show that the peevishness and malignity of wives extends beyond the nuptial bed and treads underfoot the very graces and sweets of Venus; to which complaint the husband, a truly brutish and perverted man, answered that even on fast days he could not do with less than ten. There intervened that notable sentence of the queen of Aragon, by which, after mature deliberation with her council, this good queen, to give for all time a rule and example of the moderation and modesty required in a just marriage, ordained as the legitimate and necessary limit the number of six a day, relinquishing and giving up much of the need and desire of her sex, in order, she said, to establish an easy and consequently permanent and immutable formula. At which the doctors cry out: "What must the feminine appetite and concupiscence be when their reason, their reformation, and their virtue are set at this rate?" Consider these varying judgments about our sexual needs, and then the fact that Solon, chief of the lawgiving school, assesses conjugal intercourse, in order to keep from failing, at only three times a month. After believing and preaching all this, we have gone and given women continence as the particular share, and upon utmost and extreme penalties.

There is no passion more pressing than this, which we want them alone to resist, not simply as a vice of its own size, but as an abomination and execration, more to be resisted than irreligion and parricide; and meanwhile we give in to it without blame or reproach. Even those of us who have tried to get the better of it have sufficiently admitted what difficulty, or rather impossibility, there was in subduing, weakening, and cooling off the body by material remedies. We, on the contrary, want them to be healthy, vigorous, plump, well-nourished, and chaste at the same: that is to say, both hot and cold. For marriage, which we say has the function of keeping them from burning, brings them but little cooling off, according to our ways. If they take a husband in whom the vigor of youth is still boiling, he will pride himself on expending it elsewhere:

> *Bassus, for shame, or we must go to law:*
> *I bought your penis at a heavy price;*
> *You've sold it, Bassus, it is yours no more.*

MARTIAL

... did she catch him jacking off?

The philosopher Polemon was justly brought to justice by his wife, for sowing in a sterile field the fruit that was due to the genital field. If they take one of those broken-down ones, there they are in full wedlock worse off than virgins or widows. We consider them well provided for because they have a man beside them, as the Romans considered Clodia Laeta, a Vestal, violated because Caligula had approached her, even though it was attested that he had only approached her. But on the contrary, their need is only increased thereby, inasmuch as the contact and company of any male whatever awakens their heat, which would remain quieter in solitude. And for the purpose, it is likely, of rendering their chastity more meritorious by this circumstance and consideration, Boleslaus and Kinge, his wife, the king and queen of Poland, by mutual agreement consecrated it by a vow, while lying together on their very wedding night, and maintained it in the face of marital opportunities.

We train them from childhood to the ways of love. Their grace, their dressing up, their knowledge, their language, all their instruction, has only this end in view. Their governesses imprint in them nothing else but the idea of love, if only by continually depicting it to them in order to disgust them with it. My daughter (she is the only child I have) is at the age at which the laws allow the most ardent of them to marry. She is of a backward constitution, slight and soft, and has been brought up by her mother accordingly, in a retired and private manner: so that she is now only just beginning to grow out of the naïveté of childhood.

She was reading a French book in my presence. The word *fouteau* occurred, the name of a familiar tree. The woman she has to train her stopped her short somewhat roughly and made her skip over that perilous passage. I let her go ahead in order not to disturb their rules, for I do not involve myself at all in directing her: the government of women has a mysterious way of proceeding; we must leave it to them. But if I am not mistaken, the company of twenty lackeys could not have imprinted in her imagination in six months the understanding and use and all the consequences of the sound of those wicked syllables as did this good old woman by her reprimand and interdict:

> *The ripened maid delights to learn*
> *In wanton Ionic dance to turn,*
> *And fondly dreams, when still a child,*
> *Of loves incestuous and wild.*
>
> > Horace

Let them dispense with ceremony a bit, let them speak freely; we are but children compared with them in this knowledge. Hear them describe our wooings and our conversations, and you will realize full well that we bring them nothing that they have not known and digested without us. Could it be as Plato says, that they were once dissipated boys? My ear one day happened to be in a place where without suspicion it could snatch some of the talk they were having among themselves. If only I might repeat it! By Our Lady, I said, we make fine use of our time by going off to study the phrases of Amadis and the stories of Boccaccio and Aretino so as to seem worldly-wise! There is not a word, not an example, not a trick that they do not know better than our books: it is a teaching that is born in their veins,

> *And Venus herself inspired them,*
>
> > Virgil

which those good schoolmasters, nature, youth, and health, continually breathe into their souls. They have no need to learn it, they breed it:

> *Nor any more delighted is a snow-white dove,*
> *Or if there be another thing more hot for love,*
> *To keep on plucking kisses with a biting bill,*
> *Than is a woman with her many-fancied will.*
>
> > Catullus

If this natural violence of their desire were not somewhat held in check by the fear and honor with which they have been provided, we would be shamed. The whole movement of the world resolves itself into and leads to this coupling. It is a matter infused throughout, it is a center to which all things look. We still see some of the ordinances of wise old Rome drawn up for the service of love, and the precepts of Socrates for the instruction of courtesans:

> *Nor do the Stoics' little volumes hate*
> *On silken cushions to lie in state.*
>
> Horace

Zeno, among his laws, also made rules for the splitting and battering operations required to deflower virgins. What was the point of the philosopher Strato's book "Of Carnal Conjunction"? And what did Theophrastus treat of in those he entitled, one "The Lover," the other "Of Love"? And Aristippus in his, "Of Ancient Delights"? What is the purpose of Plato's so extensive and vivid descriptions of the boldest amours of his time? And "The Book of the Lover" by Demetrius Phalereus? And "Clinias, or the Ravished Lover," by Heraclides Ponticus? And Antisthenes' book "Of Begetting Children, or of Weddings," and the other, "Of the Master or the Lover"? And Aristo's "On Amorous Exercises"? And Cleanthes', one "Of Love," the other "On the Art of Loving"? The "Dialogues on Love" of Sphaerus? And Chrysippus' fable of Jupiter and Juno, shameless beyond all endurance, and his fifty very lascivious Epistles? For I must leave aside the writings of the philosophers who followed the Epicurean sect.

Fifty deities were in times past assigned to this office, and there were nations where, to assuage the lust of those who came to their devotions, they kept girls and boys in the churches to be enjoyed, and it was a ceremonious act to use them before coming to service. *Doubtless incontinence is necessary for the sake of continence; a conflagration is extinguished by fire* (Tertullian).

In most parts of the world this part of our body was deified. In one and the same province some flayed off the skin in order to offer and consecrate a piece of it, the others offered and consecrated their seed. In another, the young men publicly pierced and opened it in various places between the flesh and the skin, and put skewers through these openings, the longest and thickest that they could endure; and of these skewers they afterward made a fire as an offering to their gods. They were considered deficient in vigor and chastity if they were upset by the power of this cruel pain. Elsewhere the most sacred magistrate was revered and recognized by those parts of him; and in many ceremonies an effigy of it was carried in pomp in honor of various divinities.

The Egyptian ladies, at the festival of the Bacchanals, wore a wooden one around their neck, exquisitely fashioned, big and heavy, according to each one's capacity; besides which the statue of their god displayed one which surpassed in size the rest of the body.

The married women hereabouts form a figure of one with their kerchiefs over their forehead to glory in the enjoyment they have of it; and when they come to be widows they put it down in back and hide it beneath their coifs.

The most modest matrons in Rome were honored to offer flowers and garlands to the god Priapus; and the virgins at the time of their nuptials were made to sit on his least seemly parts. And I know not but that I have seen some semblance of a like devotion in my time. What was the meaning of that ridiculous part of the breeches worn by our fathers, which is still seen on our Swiss? What is the point of the show we make even now of the shape of our pieces under our galligaskins, and what is worse, often by falsehood and imposture beyond their natural size?

I am tempted to believe that this sort of garment was invented in better and more conscientious ages so as not to deceive people, so that each man alike might publicly and gallantly render an account of his capacity. The simpler nations still have it somewhat corresponding to the real size. In those days the workman was taught the art, as is done in measuring the arm or the foot.

That good man who, when I was young, castrated so many beautiful ancient statues in his great city, so that the eye might not be corrupted, following the advice of that other ancient worthy—

> *Nude bodies shown in public lead to shameful acts*
> ENNIUS, QUOTED BY CICERO

—should have called to mind that nothing was gained unless he also had horses and asses castrated, and finally all nature, just as in the mysteries of the Bona Dea all semblance whatever of masculinity was excluded.

[handwritten margin note: Curious obsession w/ penises here]

Yes, everything on earth, the race of man and beast,
Fish of the sea, and flocks, and gaily painted birds,
Rush into passionate flame.

VIRGIL

So ... without sex or private parts go crazy?

The gods, says Plato, have furnished us with a disobedient and tyranni-cal member, which, like a furious animal, undertakes by the violence of its appetite to subject everything to itself. To women likewise they have given a gluttonous and voracious animal which, if denied its food in due season, goes mad, impatient of delay, and, breathing its rage into their bodies, stops up the passages, arrests the breathing, causing a thousand kinds of ills, until it has sucked in the fruit of the common thirst and therewith plentifully irrigated and fertilized the depth of the womb.

Now my legislator should also have called to mind that it is perhaps a more chaste and fruitful practice to let them know the living reality early than to leave them to guess it according to the freedom and heat of their imagination. In place of the real parts, through desire and hope, they sub-stitute others three times life-size. And a certain man of my acquaintance ruined his chances by exposing his in a place where he was not yet in a posi-tion to put them to their more serious use.

What mischief is not done by those enormous pictures that boys spread *penis envy* about the passages and staircases of palaces! From these, women acquire a cruel contempt for our natural capacity.

How do we know that Plato did not have this in mind when, imitating other well-constituted states, he ordained that men and women, young and old, should appear in one another's sight stark naked in gymnastics?

The Indian women, who see the men in the raw, have at least cooled their sense of sight. And although the women of the great kingdom of Pegu, who have nothing to cover them below the waist but a cloth slit in front and so narrow that whatever ceremonious modesty they seek to preserve, at each step they can be seen whole, may say that this is a device thought up in order to attract the men to them and divert them from their fondness for other males, to which that nation is altogether addicted, it might be said that they lose by it more than they gain and that a complete hunger is sharper than one that has been satisfied at least by the eyes.

Moreover, Livia used to say that to a good woman a naked man is no more than a statue.

The Lacedaemonian women, more virginal as wives than our women are as maidens, saw the young men of their city every day stripped at their exercises, and were not too careful themselves to cover their thighs in walking, considering themselves, as Plato says, sufficiently covered by their virtue without a farthingale.

But those men of whom Saint Augustine tells us attributed to nudity a wonderful power of temptation by doubting whether at the universal judgment women will rise again in their own sex and not rather in ours, lest they tempt us still in that holy state.

In short, we allure and flesh them by every means; we incessantly heat and excite their imagination; and then we bellyache. Let us confess the truth: there is hardly one of us who is not more afraid of the shame that comes to him for his wife's vices than for his own; who does not take better care (wonderful charity) of his good wife's conscience than of his own; who would not rather be a thief and sacrilegious and have his wife be a murderess and a heretic, than not to have her be more chaste than her husband.

And the women will gladly offer to go to the law courts to seek gain, and to war to seek a reputation, rather than be obliged to keep so difficult a guard in the midst of idleness and pleasures. Don't they see that there is not a merchant, or a lawyer, or a soldier who will not leave his business to run after this other—and the porter and the cobbler, all harassed and worn out as they are with work and hunger?

> *Would you give, for all Mygdonian Phrygia's gold,*
> *Or all the wealth Achaemenes possesses,*
> *Or what Arabia's full coffers hold,*
> *One of Licinnia's tresses,*
>
> *While to your kisses sweet her neck so white*
> *She bends, or, cruel, tenderly denies*
> *Those in which more than you she takes delight,*
> *And soon she'll snatch by surprise?*
>
> HORACE

Iniquitous appraisal of vices! Both we and they are capable of a thousand corruptions more harmful and unnatural than lasciviousness. But we create and weigh vices not according to nature but according to our interest, whereby they assume so many unequal shapes. The severity of our decrees makes women's addiction to this vice more exacerbated and vicious than its nature calls for, and involves it in consequences that are worse than their cause.

I do not know whether the exploits of Caesar and Alexander surpass in hardship the resoluteness of a beautiful young woman brought up in our fashion, in full view of and contact with the world, assailed by so many contrary examples, keeping herself entire in the midst of a thousand continual and powerful solicitations. There is no action more thorny, or more active, than this inaction. I find it much easier to bear a suit of armor all one's life than a virginity; and the vow of virginity is the most noble of all vows, as being the hardest: *The power of the Devil is in the loins,* says Saint Jerome.

Certainly we have resigned to the ladies the most arduous and vigorous of human duties, and we leave them the glory of it. That should serve them as a singular spur to persevere in it. This is a fine occasion for them to defy us and to trample underfoot that vain preeminence in valor and virtue that we claim over them. They will find, if they take note, that they will be not only very esteemed for this but also more loved. A gallant man does not abandon his pursuit for being refused, provided the refusal is dictated by chastity rather than choice. We can swear, threaten, and complain all we like: we lie, we love them the better for it. There is no allurement like a modesty that is not heartless and surly. It is stupidity and baseness to persevere against hatred and contempt, but against a virtuous and constant resolution mingled with a grateful good will, it is the exercise of a noble and generous soul. They may recognize our services up to a certain degree, and honorably make us feel that they do not disdain us.

For that law that commands them to abominate us because we adore them and to hate us because we love them is indeed cruel, if only for its difficulty. Why shall they not hear our offers and requests so long as they keep within the duty of modesty? Why do we go surmising that they have some more licentious idea within? A queen of our time used to say shrewdly that to refuse to hear these advances was a testimony of weakness and an accusation of one's own facility; and that a lady who had not been tempted could not boast of her chastity.

The limits of honor are by no means so curtailed. It has room to relax, it can allow itself some freedom without transgressing. At its frontier there is some space that is free, indifferent, and neutral. If a man has been able to hunt it down and bring it to bay by force right in its corner and stronghold, he is a fool if he is not satisfied with his fortune. The prize of victory is estimated by its difficulty. Do you want to know what impression your service and your merit have made on her heart? Measure it by her character. Some may grant more who do not grant so much. The obligation for the benefit is entirely relative to the will of the person who grants it. The other circumstances that enter into a benefit are dumb, dead, and fortuitous. It costs her more to give that little than it costs her companion to give her all. If in anything rarity is a value, it must be in this. Do not consider how little it is, but how few have it. The value of money changes according to the coinage and the place where it is minted.

Whatever the spite and indiscretion of some men may make them say in the excess of their discontent, virtue and truth always regain their advantage. I have known women whose reputation was long unjustly damaged to restore themselves to the universal esteem of men by their constancy alone, without any effort or artifice. Everyone repents and takes back what he had believed of them; after being slightly suspect girls, they hold the first rank among ladies of virtue and honor. Someone said to Plato: "Everyone is speaking ill of you." "Let them talk," he said. "I will live in such a fashion as to make them change their tune."

Besides the fear of God and the prize of so rare a glory, which should incite women to preserve themselves, the corruption of our time forces them to; and if I were in their place, there is nothing I would not do rather than entrust my reputation to such dangerous hands. In my time the pleasure of telling about it (a pleasure which yields little in sweetness to that of the thing itself) was permitted only to those who had some faithful and unique friend. Nowadays the ordinary conversation at gatherings and at table consist of boasts of the favors received and the secret liberality of the ladies. Truly one must be abject and base in heart beyond measure to allow these tender charms to be so cruelly persecuted, pawed over, and ransacked by such ungrateful, indiscreet, and fickle persons.

This immoderate and illegitimate exasperation of ours against this vice is born of the most vain and tempestuous malady that afflicts human souls, which is jealousy.

> *Who forbids taking a light from a flaming torch?*
>
> Ovid

> *Give all they will, yet thereby nothing's lost.*
>
> Priapea

Jealousy and her sister envy seem to me among the most foolish of the troop. Of the latter I can scarcely speak: this passion, which is painted as being so strong and powerful, has, by its good grace, no access to me. As for the other, I know it, at least by sight. The animals have a sense of it: when the shepherd Crastis fell in love with a goat, her mate out of jealousy came and butted his head as he was asleep and crushed it. We have raised this fever to an excessive pitch, after the example of same barbarian nations. The better disciplined ones have been touched by it, which is reasonable, but not carried away:

> *Never adulterer, by sword of husband slain,*
> *Did with his purple blood the Stygian waters stain.*
>
> Johannes Secundus

Lucullus, Caesar, Pompey, Antony, Cato, and other brave men were cuckolds and knew it without stirring up a tumult about it. In those days there was only one fool of a Lepidus who died in anguish over it.

> *Then you will suffer the adulterer's fate.*
> *They'll spread your legs, and cram your open gate*
> *With radishes and mullets.*
>
> Catullus

And the god of our poet, when he surprised one of his companions with his wife, contented himself with putting them to shame:

And one merry wag among the gods,
Wished that thus he might he disgraced;

OVID

and, for all that, he allows himself to be warmed by the sweet caresses she offers him, complaining that it was on this account she had come to mistrust his affection:

Why go seek causes from afar? Whither has gone,
Goddess, your faith in me?

VIRGIL

In fact she asks a favor of him for a bastard of hers—

I ask for arms, a mother for her son

VIRGIL

—which is liberally granted her; and Vulcan speaks honorably of Aeneas,

Arms for a warrior must be made,

VIRGIL

with a humanity truly more than human. And I will consent that this excess of goodness be left to the gods:

Nor is it fair to equal men with gods.

CATULLUS

As for the confusion of children, not only do the most serious legislators ordain and favor it in their republics, but furthermore it does not concern the women, in whom this passion of jealousy is, I know not how, still more firmly seated:

For often Juno, mistress of the gods,
Burns at her husband's daily escapades.

CATULLUS

When jealousy seizes these poor, weak, and unresisting souls, it is pitiful how cruelly it drags them about and tyrannizes over them. It insinuates itself into them under the title of friendship, but once it possesses them, the same causes that served as the foundation of good will serve as the foundation of mortal hatred. Of all the diseases of the mind it is the one which the **true** most things serve to feed and the fewest things to remedy. The virtue, the health, the merit, the reputation, of the husband are the firebrands of the wives' ill will and fury:

> *No hatreds are so keen as those of love.*
>
> PROPERTIUS

male vs. female jealousy?

This fever disfigures and corrupts all that is otherwise beautiful and good in them; and in a jealous woman, however chaste she may be and however good a housewife, there is no action that does not smack of bitterness and unpleasantness. It is a frenzied agitation, which tosses them to an extreme completely contrary to its cause. A good example was one Octavius in Rome. After he had slept with Pontia Posthumia, his affection was increased by the enjoyment, and he sought most urgently to marry her. When he was unable to persuade her, his extreme love threw him into the reactions of the most cruel and mortal hatred: he killed her. Likewise the ordinary symptoms of that other love malady are intestine hatreds, plots, conspiracies,

> *'Tis known what woman in a rage can do,*
>
> VIRGIL

and a rage which is all the more fretful for being constrained to justify itself under the pretext of good will.

Now the duty of chastity is very extensive. Is it their will that we want our women to curb? That is a very supple and active faculty; it has a lot of agility if we try to immobilize it. What if dreams sometimes involve them so far that they cannot deny them? It is not in them, nor perhaps in Chastity herself, since she is a female, to keep themselves from lust and desire. If their will alone concerns us, where are we? Imagine the great rush if a man had the privilege of being borne swift as a bird, without eyes to see or tongue to tell, into the arms of each woman who would accept him.

The Scythian women put out the eyes of all their slaves and prisoners of war to make use of them more freely and secretly.

Oh, what a terrific advantage is opportuneness! If someone asked me the first thing in love, I would answer that it is knowing how to seize the right time; the second likewise, and the third too; it is a point that can accomplish anything.

I have often lacked luck, but also sometimes enterprise: God keep from harm the man who can laugh at this. These days love calls for more temerity, which our young men excuse on the pretext of ardor; but if the women considered the matter closely, they would find that temerity comes rather from contempt. I used to be scrupulously afraid of giving offense, and I am inclined to respect what I love. Besides, in these negotiations, if you take away respect you rub out the glamor. In this I like to have a man somewhat play the child and the timid slave. If not altogether in this, in other situations I have something of the stupid bashfulness that Plutarch speaks of, and the course of my life has been harmed and blemished by it in various ways: a quality very ill-suited to my nature in general—and indeed what are we but sedition and discrepancy? My eyes are tender for enduring a refusal, as they are for refusing; and it troubles me so much to be troublesome to others that on the occasions when duty forces me to test out someone's will in a doubtful matter which may cost him some trouble, I do it halfheartedly and against the grain. But if the matter affects my personal interest, through Homer truly says that bashfulness is a stupid virtue in a needy man, I ordinarily commission a third person to blush in my place. And with the same difficulty I dismiss people who want to use me; so that it has happened to me sometimes to have the wish to refuse but not the strength. *does that make him stupid?*

Thus it is folly to try to bridle in women a desire that is so burning and so natural to them. And when I hear them boast of having such a virginal and cold disposition, I laugh at them: they are leaning over too far backward. If it is a toothless and decrepit old woman or a dry and consumptive young one, though it is not altogether credible, at least they have some semblance of truth in saying it. But those who still move and breathe make their position worse in this way, since ill-considered excuses serve as accusation. Like a gentleman, one of my neighbors, who was suspected of impotence,

[handwritten: lol poor thing]

> *Whose member, feebler than a tender beet,*
> *Never rose even up to middle height,*

[handwritten: he was "suspected of impotence" – is impotence a crime?] CATULLUS

who, three or four days after his wedding, to justify himself, went around boldly swearing that he had ridden twenty stages the night before; which was afterward used to convict him of pure ignorance and to annul his marriage. Besides, what these women say has no value, for there is neither continence nor virtue unless there is an urge to the contrary. "It is true," they should say, "but I am not ready to give myself up." The saints themselves talk that way. I mean those women who boast in good earnest of their coldness and insensibility and who, with a straight face, want to be believed. For when it is with an affected countenance, in which the eyes belie their words, and with the jargon of their profession which has its effect in reverse, I think that's fine. I am a great admirer of naturalness and freedom, but there is no help for it: unless it is completely simple and childlike, it is unbecoming to ladies and out of place in these dealings: it promptly slides into shamelessness. Their disguises and their faces deceive only fools. Lying holds an honorable place in love; it is a detour that leads us to truth by the back door.

If we cannot hold back their imagination, what do we expect of them? Deeds? There are enough of these that escape all outside communication, by which chastity may be corrupted:

> *That which he does unwitnessed, he does often.*

> MARTIAL

And the deeds that we fear the least are perhaps the most to be feared; silent sins are the worst: *[handwritten: because they're harder to catch?]*

> *A simpler prostitute offends me less.*

> MARTIAL

There are acts by which they can lose their chastity without unchastity, and, what is more, without their knowledge. *A midwife, for instance, making a manual examination of some virgin's integrity, whether through malice, un-skilfulness, or accident, by inspecting it has destroyed it* (Saint Augustine). Some have lost their maidenhead for having looked for it; some have destroyed it in sport.

We could not possibly circumscribe precisely for them the actions that we forbid them. We must formulate our rules in general and uncertain terms. The very idea that we form of their chastity is ridiculous; for among the extreme examples I know of is Fatua, wife of Faunus, who never let herself be seen by any man whatever after her wedding; and Hiero's wife, who never noticed her husband's stinking breath, thinking that this was a quality common to all men. They must become insensible and invisible in order to satisfy us.

Now let us confess that the crux in judging this duty lies principally in the will. There have been husbands who have suffered cuckoldry not only without reproach or sense of offense toward their wives but with singular obligation to and recommendation of their virtue. Some women, who loved their honor better than their life, have prostituted it to the frenzied appetite of a mortal enemy to save their husband's life, and done for him what they would not at all have done for themselves. This is not the place to extend these examples; they are too lofty and too rich to be displayed in this light; let us keep them for a nobler setting.

But for examples of more commonplace luster, are there not women every day who lend themselves for the mere profit of their husbands and by their express order and mediation? And in ancient times Phaulius of Argos offered his wife to King Philip out of ambition; just as out of civility a certain Galba, who had Maecenas to supper, seeing that his wife and his guest were beginning to conspire by glances and signs, let himself sink down on his cushion, acting like a man weighed down with sleep, to lend a hand to their understanding. And he admitted it with rather good grace; for when at this point a servant made bold to lay hands on the wine that was on the table, he shouted at him: "Don't you see, you rogue, that I am asleep only for Maecenas?"

One woman may be of loose conduct, and yet have a more reformed disposition than another who conducts herself in a more regular manner. As we see some who complain of having been vowed to chastity before the age of discretion, so I have seen some complain truthfully of having been vowed to debauchery before the age of discretion. The vice of the parents can be the cause of this, or the force of necessity, which is a rough counselor. In the East Indies, where chastity was in singular repute, nevertheless custom allowed a married woman to abandon herself to any man who presented her with an elephant, and that with some glory for having been valued at so high a price.

Phaedo the philosopher, a man of good family, after the capture of his country, Elis, made it his trade to prostitute the beauty of his youth as long as it lasted to anyone that wanted it for the price in money, so as to make a living. And Solon was the first in Greece, they say, who, by his laws, gave women the liberty to provide for the necessities of their life at the expense of their chastity, a custom which Herodotus says was accepted in many governments before his time.

And then what is the fruit of this painful anxiety? For whatever justice there may be in jealousy, it still remains to be seen whether its agitation is really useful. Is there someone who thinks to shackle women by his ingenuity?

holy mother of misogyny

> Put on a lock, confine her. But then who will guard
> The guards themselves? Your wife is shrewd; with them
> she'll start.
>
> JUVENAL

What occasion will not be enough for them in so knowing an age?

Curiosity is vicious in all things, but here it is pernicious. It is folly to want to be enlightened about a disease for which there is no medicine that does not make it worse and aggravate it; the shame of which is increased and made public principally by jealousy; revenge for which wounds our children more than it cures us. You dry up and die in quest of a proof so obscure.

How pitifully have those men reached their goal who in my time have succeeded in this quest! If the informer does not present at the same time the remedy and relief, the information he gives is injurious and be deserves a dagger-thrust more than does a man who gives you the lie. People make no less fun of the man who takes pains to do something about it than of the man who is unaware of it. The mark of cuckoldry is indelible; once a man is stamped with it he is stamped forever; the punishment makes it public more than the fault. It is a fine thing to see our private misfortunes torn out of the shadows and doubt to be trumpeted on the tragic stage, and especially misfortunes that pinch us only by the telling. For "a good wife" and "a good marriage" are said not about those that are so, but about those that are not talked about. We have to be ingenious to avoid this annoying and useless knowledge. And the Romans had the custom, when returning from a trip, of sending someone ahead to the house to make their arrival known to their wives, in order not to surprise them. And therefore a certain nation introduced the custom that the priest open the way to the bride on the wedding day, to rid the husband of doubt and of the curiosity of investigating in this first trial whether she comes to him a virgin or damaged by another's love.

"But people talk about it." I know a hundred honorable men who are cuckolded, honorably and not very discreditably. A gallant man is pitied for it, not disesteemed. Make your virtue stifle your misfortune, make good people curse the occasion of it, make the man who wrongs you tremble at the very thought of it. And then, who is not talked about in this sense, from the smallest to the greatest?

> *Who many legions did command, and was*
> *A better man than you, poor wretch, in many ways.*
>
>   LUCRETIUS

See how many honorable men are involved in this reproach in your presence? Don't think that you are spared any more elsewhere. "But even the ladies will laugh at it." And what are they fonder of laughing at these days than a peaceful and well-settled marriage? Each one of you has made someone a cuckold: now nature is all in similarities, in compensation and tit for tat. The frequency of this accident should by this time have moderated its bitterness; it will soon have become a custom.

Miserable passion, which has also this about it, that it is incommunicable,

> *E'en Fortune would not lend an ear to our laments.*
>
>   CATULLUS

For to what friend do you dare entrust your griefs, who, even if he does not laugh at them, will not use them as an approach and an instruction *why?*

to get a share in the quarry himself? The bitternesses of marriage, like the sweets, are kept secret by the wise. And among the other annoying conditions that are found in it, this, for a talkative man like myself, is one of the main ones: that custom makes it improper and prejudicial to communicate to anyone all that we know and feel about it.

To give women the same advice in order to disgust them with jealousy would be a waste of time. Their very essence is so steeped in suspicion, vanity, and curiosity, that one should not expect to cure them by any legitimate way. They often recover from this ailment by a form of health much more to be feared than the disease itself. For as there are enchantments that can take away the evil only by unloading it onto another, so they are apt to transfer this fever to their husbands when they lose it. *"them" = women*

However, to tell the truth, I do not know if a man can suffer anything worse from them than jealousy. It is the most dangerous of their conditions, as the head is of their members. Pittacus used to say that everyone had his weakness, and that his was his wife's bad temper: except for that, he would consider himself happy in every respect. It is a very grievous misfortune where a man so just, so wise, so valiant, feels the whole state of his life altered by it; what are we small fry to do? *really? jealousy is all it takes to defeat a man?*

The senate of Marseilles was right to grant the request of the man who asked permission to kill himself to deliver himself from his tempestuous wife; for this is a disease which never goes away without taking everything with it, and which has no effective solution but flight or endurance, though both are very hard.

That man knew what it was all about, it seems to me, who said that a good marriage was one made between a blind wife and a deaf husband.

Let us also see to it that the great and violent rigor of this obligation that we enjoin on them does not produce two effects contrary to our purpose: that is, that it does not make the pursuers keener and the wives more ready to surrender easily. For as for the first point, by increasing the value of the place, we increase the value and desire of the conquest. May it not have been Venus herself who thus shrewdly raised the price of her merchandise by making panders of the laws, knowing how insipid a pleasure it is unless it is given value by imagination and a high cost? In short, it is all hog's flesh that is given variety by the sauce, as Flamininus' host said. Cupid is a treacherous god; he makes it his sport to wrestle with piety and justice; he glories in the fact that his power clashes with every other power and that all other rules yield to his.

> *He seeks out matter for his sin.*
>
> OVID

And as for the second point, would we not be less cuckolded if we were less afraid to be, according to the nature of women? For prohibition incites and invites them:

> *You would, they won't; and when you won't, they will.*
>
> TERENCE

some good ol' fashioned sexism

> *They are ashamed to go by the permitted way.*
>
> LUCIAN

What better interpretation could we find for Messalina's behavior? In the beginning she made her husband a cuckold in secret, as people do; but carrying on her affairs too easily, through his stupidity, she soon disdained that practice. Now behold her making love openly, acknowledging her lovers, entertaining them and favoring them in the sight of one and all. She wanted him to feel it. When that animal could not be awakened for all that, and made her pleasures flat and insipid by the over-lax facility with which he seemed to authorize and legitimize them, what did she do? Wife of a healthy, live emperor, and in Rome, the theater of the world, at high noon, in a public festival and ceremony, and with Silius, whom she had been enjoying a long time beforehand, she got married one day when her husband was out of town.

Does it not seem as if she was on her way to becoming chaste through her husband's nonchalance, or seeking another husband who would whet her appetite by his jealousy, and who by opposing her would arouse her? But the first difficulty she encountered was also the last. The animal awoke with a start. One is often worse off with these deaf and unconscious people. I have found by experience that this extreme tolerance, when it comes apart, produces some of the harshest acts of vengeance; for the anger and fury, heaped up together, catching fire all of a sudden, explodes all its energy at the first attack,

> *And looses all the reins of wrath,*
>
> VIRGIL

He put her to death and also a great number of those who were intimate with her, even to some who could not help it and whom she had invited to her bed with scourges.

What Virgil says of Venus and Vulcan, Lucretius had said more appropriately of a stolen enjoyment between her and Mars:

> *He who rules the savage things*
> *Of war, the mighty Mars, oft on thy bosom flings*
> *Himself; the eternal wound of love drains all his powers;*
> *Wide-mouthed, with greedy eyes thy person he devours,*
> *Head back, his very soul upon thy lips suspended:*
> *Take him in thy embrace, goddess, let him be blended*
> *With thy holy body as he lies; let sweet words pour*
> *Out of thy mouth.*
>
> LUCRETIUS

When I ruminate that *rejicit* (flings), *pascit* (devours), *inhians* (wide-mouthed), *molli* (soft), *fovet* (fondles), *medullas* (marrow), *labefacta* (trembling), *pendet* (suspended), *percurrit* (runs through), and that noble *circumfusa* (blended), mother of the pretty *infusus* (outpoured), I despise those petty conceits and verbal tricks that have sprung up since. These good people needed no sharp and subtle play on words; their language is all full and copious with a natural and constant vigor. They are all epigram, not only the tail but the head, stomach, and feet. There is nothing forced, nothing dragging; the whole thing moves at the same pace. *Their whole contexture is manly; they are not concerned with pretty little flowers* (Seneca). This is not a soft and merely inoffensive eloquence; it is sinewy and solid, and does not so much please as fill and ravish; and it ravishes the strongest minds most. When I see these brave forms of expression, so alive, so profound, I do not say "This is well said," I say "This is well thought." It is the sprightliness of the imagination that elevates and swells the words. *It is the heart that makes a man eloquent* (Quintilian). Our people call judgment language and fine words full conceptions.

This painting is the result not so much of manual dexterity as of having the object more vividly imprinted in the soul. Gallus speaks simply, because he conceives simply. Horace is not content with a superficial expression; it would betray him. He sees more clearly and deeply into the thing. His mind unlocks and ransacks the whole storehouse of words and figures in order to express itself; and he needs them to be beyond the commonplace as his conception is beyond the commonplace. Plutarch says that he saw the Latin language through things. It is the same here: the sense illuminates and brings out the words, which are no longer wind, but flesh and bone. The words mean more than they say. Even the weak-minded feel some notion of this; for when I was in Italy I said whatever I pleased in ordinary talk, but for serious discourse I would not have dared trust myself to an idiom that I could neither bend nor turn out of its ordinary course. I want to be able to do something of my own with it.

Handling and use by able minds give value to a language, not so much by innovating as by filling it out with more vigorous and varied services, by stretching and bending it. They do not bring to it new words, but they enrich their own, give more weight and depth to their meaning and use; they teach the language unaccustomed movements, but prudently and shrewdly. And how little this gift is given to all is seen in so many French writers of our time. They are bold and disdainful enough not to follow the common road, but want of invention and of discretion ruins them. There is nothing to be seen in them but a wretched affectation of originality, cold and absurd disguises, which instead of elevating the substance bring it down. Provided they can strut gorgeously in their novelty, they care nothing about effectiveness. To seize a new word they abandon the ordinary one, which is often stronger and more sinewy.

In our language I find plenty of stuff but a little lack of fashioning. For there is nothing that might not be done with our jargon of hunting and war, which is a generous soil to borrow from. And forms of speech, like plants, improve and grow stronger by being transplanted. I find it sufficiently abundant, but not sufficiently pliable and vigorous. It ordinarily succumbs under a powerful conception. If your pace is tense, you often feel it growing limp and giving way under you, and that when it fails you Latin comes to your aid, and Greek to others.

Of some of those words that I have just picked out it is harder for us to perceive the energy, because the frequent use of them has somewhat debased and vulgarized their grace for us; as in our vernacular we encounter excellent phrases and metaphors whose beauty is withering with age and whose color has been tarnished by too common handling. But that takes away nothing of their savor to those who have a good nose, nor does it detract from the glory of those ancient authors who, as is likely, first brought these words into this luster.

Learning treats of things too subtly, in a mode too artificial and different from the common and natural one. My page makes love and understands it. Read him Leon Hebreo and Ficino: they talk about him, his thoughts and his actions, and yet he does not understand a thing in it. I do not recognize in Aristotle most of my ordinary actions: they have been covered and dressed up in another robe for the use of the school. God grant these men may be doing the right thing! If I were of the trade, I would naturalize art as much as they artify nature. Let us leave Bembo and Equicola alone.

When I write, I prefer to do without the company and remembrance of books, for fear they may interfere with my style. Also because, in truth, the good authors humble me and dishearten me too much. I am inclined to do the trick of that painter who, after painting a miserable picture of some cocks, forbade his boys to let any real cock come into his shop. And to give myself a little luster I would rather need the device of the musician Antinonides, who, when he had to make music, arranged that either before or after him the audience should be steeped in some other bad singers.

But it is harder for me to do without Plutarch. He is so universal and so full that on all occasions, and however eccentric the subject you have taken up, he makes his way into your work and offers you a liberal hand, inexhaustible in riches and embellishments. It vexes me that I am so greatly exposed to pillage by those who frequent him. I cannot be with him even a little without taking out a drumstick or a wing. he knows his writing is in- fluence of other

For this purpose of mine it is also appropriate for me to write at home, in a backward region, where no one helps me or corrects me, where I usually have no contact with any man who understands the Latin of his Paternoster and who does not know even less French. I would have done it better elsewhere, but the work would have been less my own; and its principal end and perfection is to be precisely my own. I would indeed correct an accidental error, and I am full of them, since I run on carelessly. But the imperfections that are ordinary and constant in me it would be treachery to remove.

When I have been told, or have told myself: "You are too thick in figures of speech. Here is a word of Gascon vintage. Here is a dangerous phrase." (I do not avoid any of those that are used in the streets of France; those who would combat usage with grammar make fools of themselves.) "This is ignorant reasoning. This is paradoxical reasoning. This one is too mad. You are often playful: people will think you are speaking in earnest when you are making believe." "Yes," I say, "but I correct the faults of inadvertence, not those of habit. Isn't this the way I speak everywhere? Don't I represent myself to the life? Enough, then. I have done what I wanted. Everyone recognizes me in my book, and my book in me."

Now I have an aping and imitative nature. When I used to dabble in composing verse (and I never did any but Latin), it clearly revealed the poet I had last been reading. And of my first essays, some smell a bit foreign. In Paris I speak a language somewhat different than at Montaigne. Anyone I regard with attention easily imprints on me something of himself. What I consider, I usurp: a foolish countenance, an unpleasant grimace, a ridiculous way of speaking. Vices even more: once they prick me, they stick to me and will not go away without shaking. I have been observed to swear more often by imitation than by nature.

A murderous imitation, like that of the horribly big and strong apes that King Alexander encountered in a certain region of the Indies. Otherwise it would have been hard to get the better of them, but they lent him the means of doing so by that inclination of theirs to imitate everything they saw done. For from this the hunters got the idea of putting on shoes in their sight with many knots in the laces, of rigging themselves out in headgear with running nooses, and of seeming to anoint their eyes with glue. Thus their apish nature brought these poor imprudent beasts to harm. They glued up their own eyes, hobbled their own feet, and strangled themselves.

That other faculty of ingeniously mimicking the gestures and words of another on purpose, which often brings pleasure and wonder, is not in me any more than in a stump.

When I swear in my own way, it is only "by God," which is the most straightforward of all oaths. They say that Socrates swore by the dog, Zeno by the same interjection that Italians use now, *cappari*, and Pythagoras by water and air.

I so easily receive these superficial impressions without thinking of them that when I have had "Sire" or "Highness" in my mouth for three days in a row, a week later they will slip out instead of "Excellency" or "Lordship."

And what I have begun to say in sport and in jest I will say seriously the next day. Wherefore in writing I am the more unwilling to accept the well-worn topics, for fear I may treat them at someone else's expense.

Any topic is equally fertile for me. A fly will serve my purpose; and God grant that this topic I have in hand now was not taken up at the command of so flighty a will! Let me begin with whatever subject I please, for all subjects are linked with one another.

But I am displeased with my mind for ordinarily producing its most profound and maddest fancies, and those I like the best, unexpectedly and when I am least looking for them; which suddenly vanish, having nothing to attach themselves to on the spot: on horseback, at table, in bed, but mostly on horseback, where my thoughts range most widely. In speech I am rather sensitively jealous of attention and silence if I am speaking in earnest: whoever interrupts me stops me. When I travel, the very necessity of the road cuts conversation short; besides, I most often travel without company fit for these protracted discussions, whereby I get full leisure to commune with myself.

It turns out as with my dreams. While dreaming I recommend them to my memory (for I am apt to dream that I am dreaming); but the next day I may well call to mind their coloring just as it was, whether gay, or sad, or strange; but as to what they were besides, the more I strain to find out, the more I plunge it into oblivion. So of these chance thoughts that drop into my mind there remains in my memory only a vain notion, only as much as I need to make me rack my brains and fret in quest of them to no purpose.

Now then, leaving books aside and speaking more materially and simply, I find after all that love is nothing else but the thirst for sexual enjoyment in a desired object, and Venus nothing else but the pleasure of discharging our vessels—a pleasure which becomes vicious either by immoderation or by indiscretion. For Socrates love is the appetite for generation by the mediation of beauty. And considering often the ridiculous titillation of this pleasure, the absurd, witless, and giddy motions with which it stirs up Zeno and Cratippus, that reckless frenzy, that face inflamed with fury and cruelty in the sweetest act of love, and then that grave, severe, and ecstatic countenance in so silly an action; and that our delights and our excrements have been lodged together pell-mell, and that the supreme sensual pleasure is attended, like pain, with faintness and moaning; I believe that what Plato says is true, that man is the plaything of the gods:

> *What savage jest is this!*
>
> Claudian

and that it was in mockery that nature left us the most confused of our actions to be the most common, in order thereby to make us all equal and to put on the same level the fools and the wise, and us and the beasts. The most contemplative and wisest of men, when I imagine him in that position, seems to me an impostor to put on wise and contemplative airs; here are the peacock's feet that humble his pride:

> *Against truth said in laughing*
> *Is there a law?*
>
> Horace

Those who will not allow serious ideas in the midst of games act, as someone says, like a man who is afraid to worship the statue of a saint if it is undraped.

We eat and drink as the animals do, but these are not actions that hinder the operations of our mind. In these we keep our advantage over them. But this other puts every other thought beneath its yoke and by its imperious authority brutifies and bestializes all the theology and philosophy there is in Plato; and yet he does not complain of it. In everything else you can keep some decorum; all other operations come under the rules of decency. This one cannot even be imagined other than vicious or ridiculous. Just to see this, try to find a wise and discreet way of doing it. Alexander used to say that he knew himself to be mortal chiefly by this action and by sleep. Sleep suffocates and suppresses the faculties of our mind; the sexual act likewise absorbs and dissipates them. Truly it is a mark not only of our original corruption but also of our inanity and deformity.

On the one hand Nature pushes us on to it, having attached to this desire the most noble, useful, and pleasant of all her operations; and on the other hand she lets us accuse and shun it as shameless and indecent, blush at it, and recommend abstinence. Are we not brutes to call brutish the operation that makes us?

The various nations in their religions have many conventions in common, such as sacrifices, lamps, burning incense, fasts, offerings, and, among other things, the condemnation of this action. All opinions come to this, besides the very widespread practice of cutting off the foreskin, which is a punishment of the act. Perhaps we are right to blame ourselves for making such a stupid production as man, to call the action shameful, and shameful the parts that are used for it. (At present mine are truly shameful and pitiful.)

The Essenes, of whom Pliny speaks, maintained their numbers for several centuries without nurses and without baby clothes, by the influx of foreigners who, following this fine humor, continually joined them: a whole nation risked exterminating itself rather than involve themselves in a woman's embrace, and forfeiting the continuation of mankind rather than create a man. They say that Zeno had to do with a woman only once in his life, and then out of civility, so as not to seem too obstinately to disdain the sex.

Everyone shuns to see a man born, everyone runs to see him die. For his destruction we seek a spacious field in broad daylight; for his construction we hide in a dark little corner. It is a duty to hide and blush in order to make him; and it is a glory and a source of many virtues to be able to unmake him. One is an offense, the other an act of grace; for Aristotle says that to benefit someone, in a certain phrase of his country, is to kill him. The Athenians, to put the disgrace of these two actions on the same level, when they had to purify the island of Delos and justify themselves to Apollo, forbade both any burial and any birth within its territory. *We are ashamed of our very selves* (Terence). We regard our being as vice.

There are nations that cover themselves when eating. I know a lady, and one of the greatest, who has this same opinion, that chewing is a disagreeable grimace which takes away much of women's grace and beauty; and she does not like to appear in public with an appetite. And I know a man who cannot bear to see anyone eat or to be seen eating, and who avoids any company even more when he is filling than when he is emptying himself.

In the empire of the Turk are found a great number of men who, to outdo others, never let themselves be seen when they have their meals; who have only one a week; who cut and mangle their face and limbs; who never speak to anyone: all of them people who think they honor their nature by denaturing themselves, who prize themselves for their contempt, and think to improve themselves by their impairment. What a monstrous animal to be a horror to himself, to be burdened by his pleasures, to regard himself as a misfortune!

There are some who conceal their lives—

They change for exile their sweet homes and hearths

VIRGIL

—and hide them from the sight of other men; who avoid health and cheerfulness as hostile and harmful qualities. Not only many sects but many nations curse their birth and bless their death. There are some nations in which the sun is abominated and the darkness adored.

We are ingenious only in maltreating ourselves; that is the true quarry of the power of our mind—a dangerous tool when out of control.

O wretched men, who hold their joys as crimes!

MAXIMIANUS

Alas, poor man! You have enough necessary ills without increasing them by your invention, and you are miserable enough by nature without being so by art. You have real and essential deformities enough without forging imaginary ones. Do you find that you are too much at your ease unless your ease strikes you as unpleasantness? Do you think you have fulfilled all the necessary duties to which nature obligates you, and that she is wanting and idle in you unless you take on new duties? You are not afraid to offend the universal and indubitable laws, and are proudly intent on your own laws, which are partial and fanciful: and the more particular, uncertain, and contradicted they are, the more you devote your effort to them The positive rules of your own invention possess and bind you, and the rules of your parish; those of God and the world leave you untouched. Just run through a few examples that would illustrate this idea; your life is all made up of them.

The verses of these two poets, treating of lasciviousness as reservedly and discreetly as they do, seem to me to reveal it and illuminate it more closely. The ladies cover their bosoms with a veil, the priests many sacred things; painters put shadows in their work to bring out the light more; and it is said that the sun and wind strike harder by reflection than direct. An

Egyptian made a wise answer to the man who asked him: "What are you carrying there hidden under your cloak?" "It is hidden under my cloak so that you won't know what it is." But there are certain other things that people hide only to show them.

Listen to this man, who is more open:

And pressed her naked body unto mine.

OVID

I feel that he is caponizing me. Let Martial turn up Venus' skirts as high as he pleases, he will not succeed in revealing her so completely. He who says everything satiates and disgusts us; he who is afraid to express himself leads us on to think more than there is. There is treachery in this sort of modesty, and especially in half opening to us, as these do, so fair a road to the imagination. Both the action and the picture of it should smack of theft.

I like the love-making of the Spaniards and Italians, more respectful and timid, more mannered and veiled. I don't know who it was in ancient times who wanted his throat as long as a crane's neck so as to relish longer what he swallowed. That wish is more appropriate in this quick and precipitate pleasure, especially for such natures as mine, for I have the failing of being too sudden. In order to arrest its flight and prolong it in preambles, everything among them serves as a favor and a recompense: a glance, a bow, a word, a sign. If a man could dine off the steam of a roast, wouldn't that be a fine saving? This is a passion that with very little solid essence mixes in much more vanity and feverish dreams: it should be satisfied and served accordingly. Let us teach the ladies to make the most of themselves, to respect themselves, to beguile and fool us. We make our ultimate attack the first one; the French impetuosity is always there. If the ladies spin out and spread out their favors in small amounts, each man, even to miserable old age, will find there some little scrap of pleasure, according to his worth and merit.

He who has no enjoyment except in enjoyment, who must win all or nothing, who loves the chase only in the capture, has no business mixing with our school. The more steps and degrees there are, the more height and honor there is in the topmost seat. We should take pleasure in being led there, as is done in magnificent palaces, by divers porticoes and passages, long and pleasant galleries, and many windings. This arrangement would redound to our advantage; we would stay there longer and love there longer. Without hope and without desire we no longer go at any worth-while gait.

Our mastery and entire possession is something for them to fear infinitely. Once they have wholly surrendered to the mercy of our fidelity and constancy, they are in a very hazardous position. Those are rare and difficult virtues. As soon as the ladies are ours, we are no longer theirs:

> *The lust of greedy mind once satisfied,*
> *We fear nor care for oaths once sworn, but now denied.*
>   CATULLUS

And Thrasonides, a young Greek, was so much in love with his love that having won his mistress' heart he refused to enjoy her, so as not to deaden, satiate, and weaken by enjoyment that restless ardor on which he prided and fed himself.

Dearness gives relish to the meat. See how much the form of salutation which is peculiar to our nation debases by its facility the charm of kisses, which Socrates says are so powerful and dangerous for stealing our hearts. It is a disagreeable custom, and unfair to the ladies, to have to lend their lips to any man who has three footmen at his heels, however unattractive he may be:

> *A bluish ice, from nostrils like a dog's,*
> *Comes banging down, his beard stiffens and clogs . . .*
> *A hundred times I'd rather kiss his ass.*
>   MARTIAL

And we ourselves do not gain much by it; for as the world is divided, for three beautiful women we have to kiss fifty ugly ones. And for a tender stomach, as men of my age have, one bad kiss is too high a price for one good one.

In Italy they play the part of timid suitors even with the women who are for sale, and they defend the practice thus: that there are degrees in enjoyment, and that by courting they want to obtain for themselves that which is most complete. These women sell only their bodies; the will cannot be put on sale, it is too free and too much its own master. Thus these men say that they are wooing their will; and they are right. It is the will that must be courted and solicited. I abhor the idea of a body void of affection being mine. And it seems to me that such frenzy is close to that of the boy who went and defiled out of love the beautiful statue of Venus that Praxiteles had made, or that of the frantic Egyptian hot after the carcass of a dead woman he was embalming and shrouding; which gave rise to the law that was made since then in Egypt, that the bodies of beautiful young women and of those of good family should be kept three days before being put in the hands of the undertakers. Periander behaved more monstrously when he extended his conjugal affection (more regular and legitimate) to the enjoyment of Melissa, his dead wife.

Doesn't it seem a lunatic humor in Luna, unable otherwise to enjoy her darling Endymion, to put him to sleep for several months, and take her satisfaction in enjoying a boy who stirred only in his dreams?

I say likewise that we love a body without soul or sentiment, when we love a body without its consent and desire. Not all enjoyments are alike. Some are meager and languid. A thousand causes other than good will may win us this concession from the ladies. It is not sufficient evidence of affection; there may be treachery in it as elsewhere; sometimes they go to it with only one buttock:

> *As cool as if preparing frankincense and wine . . .*
> *You'd think her absent or of marble.*
>
> Martial

I know some who would rather lend that than their coach, and who communicate only in that way. You must observe whether they like your company for yet some other purpose or for this alone, as they might that of some husky stable-boy; in what rank and at what value you are lodged there,

> *If to you alone*
> *She gives herself, and marks that day with a whiter stone,*
>
> Catullus

What if she eats your bread with the sauce of a more agreeable imagination?

'Tis you she holds, but sighs for other, absent loves.

TIBULLUS

What! have we not seen someone in our own time use this act for the purpose of a horrible vengeance, thereby to poison and kill, as he did, an honorable woman?

Those who know Italy will never find it strange if for this subject I do not seek examples elsewhere; for that nation may be called the teacher of the world in this. They have generally more beautiful women and fewer ugly ones than we; but in rare and outstanding beauties I think we are on a par. And I judge as much of their intellects. Of the ordinary sort they have many more, and obviously brutishness is incomparably rarer there; in unusual minds and minds of the highest stature, we concede them nothing. If I had to extend this comparison, it would seem to me I could say that on the contrary valor is more common and natural among us than among them; but in them we sometimes see it so full and vigorous that it surpasses the sturdiest examples that we have.

The marriages of that country are lame in this: their custom commonly imposes so harsh and so slavish a law on the wives that the most distant contact with a stranger is as capital an offense to them as the most intimate. The result of this law is that all approaches necessarily become substantial; and since it all comes to the same for them, they have a very easy choice. And once they have broken through these partitions, believe me, they are on fire: *Lust, like a wild beast, irritated by its chains, is then let loose* (Livy). We must give them a little more rein:

> *Lately I saw, rebellious to the bit, a colt*
> *With stubborn mouth run like a thunderbolt.*

OVID

The desire for company is weakened by giving it a little liberty.

We run about the same chance. They are too extreme in constraint, we in license. It is a fine practice of our nation that our sons are received into good families to be brought up and trained as pages, as in a school of nobility. And it is considered a discourtesy and an affront to refuse one of noble birth. I have perceived—for so many houses, so many different styles and forms—that the ladies who have tried to give the maidens in their retinue the most austere rules have not come out any better. Moderation is needed: a good part of their conduct must be left to their own discretion; for one way or another, there is no discipline that can curb them in all directions. But it is quite true that a girl who has escaped safe, bag and baggage, from a free schooling, inspires much more confidence than one who comes out safely from a severe, prisonlike school.

Our fathers trained their daughters' faces to bashfulness and timidity (hearts and desires were the same); we, to self-assurance: we don't know what we're doing. That is for the Sarmatian women, who may not lie with a man until with their own hands they have killed another in war.

For me, who have no rights in this except through the ears, it is enough that they retain me as counsel, according to the privilege of my age. So I counsel them abstinence, as I do to us; but if this generation is too hostile to it, at least discretion and modesty. For as the story tells about Aristippus, speaking to some young men who blushed to see him enter the house of a courtesan, "The vice is in not coming out, not in entering." If she will not keep her conscience clear, let her keep her name clear; if the substance is not worth much, let the appearance be preserved.

I commend gradation and delay in the dispensation of their favors. Plato shows that in every kind of love the defenders are forbidden to yield easily and promptly. It is a trait of greediness, which they must cover up with all their art, to surrender so heedlessly, completely, and impetuously. By conducting themselves with order and measure in granting their favors, they beguile our desire much better and conceal their own. Let them always flee before us, I mean even those who intend to let themselves be caught; they conquer us better in flight, like the Scythians. Indeed, according to the law that Nature gives them, it is not properly for them to will and desire; their role is to suffer, obey, consent. That is why Nature has given them a perpetual capacity, to us a rare and uncertain one. They have their hour always, so that they may be ready for ours: *born to be passive* (Seneca). And whereas Nature has willed that our appetites should show and declare themselves prominently, she has made theirs occult and internal, and has furnished them with parts unsuitable for show and simply for the defensive.

We must leave to Amazonian license actions like this one. When Alexander was passing through Hyrcania, Thalestris, queen of the Amazons, came to find him with three hundred warriors of her own sex, well mounted and well armed, having left the remainder of a large army that was following her beyond the neighboring mountains; and said to him, right out loud and in public, that the fame of his victories and valor had brought her there to see him, to offer him her resources and power in support of his enterprises; and that finding him so handsome, young, and vigorous, she, who was perfect in all his qualities, advised him that they should lie together, so that of the most valiant woman in the world and the most valiant man who was then alive there should be born something great and rare for the future. Alexander thanked her just the same for the rest; but to allow enough time for the accomplishment of her last request, he stopped in that place thirteen days, which he celebrated as lustily as he could in honor of so courageous a princess.

We are in almost all things unjust judges of their actions, as they are of ours. I admit the truth when it hurts me, just as when it serves me. It is an ugly aberration that pushes them so often to change and keeps them from fixing their affection on any object whatever, as we see of that goddess to whom are attributed so many changes and lovers. Yet the truth is that it is contrary to the nature of love if it is not violent, and contrary to the nature of violence if it is constant. And those who are astonished at this and exclaim against it and seek out the causes of this malady in women as if it were unnatural and incredible, why don't they see how often they accept it in themselves without being appalled and calling it a miracle? It would perhaps be more strange to see any stability in it. It is not simply a bodily passion. If there is no end to avarice and ambition, neither is there any to lechery. It still lives after satiety; no constant satisfaction or end can be prescribed to it, for it always goes beyond its possession.

And furthermore, inconstancy is perhaps somewhat more pardonable in them than in us. They can allege, as we can, the inclination to variety and novelty which is common to us both; and allege secondly, as we cannot, that they buy a cat in a bag (Joanna, queen of Naples, had Andreasso, her first husband, strangled at the bars of her window with a gold and silk cord woven by her own hand, when in matrimonial duties she found that neither his parts nor his efforts corresponded well enough with the expectations she had formed of them on seeing his build, his beauty, his youth and agility, whereby she had been caught and deceived); that action involves more effort than submission; and that consequently they are always able to satisfy our needs whereas it may be otherwise when it is up to us to satisfy theirs.

Plato for this reason wisely established in his laws that in order to decide on the suitability of a marriage the judges should see the young men who aspire to it stark naked, and the girls naked down to the girdle only. When they come to try us, they may not find us worthy of their choice:

> *Having explored his body, found his member limp*
> *As a wet thong, impossible by hand to primp,*
> *She leaves the dastard bed.*
>
> MARTIAL

It is not enough that a man's will should carry straight. Weakness and incapacity legitimately break up a marriage: *incapacity for what?.*

> *A stronger lover elsewhere must be found*
> *By whom her virgin zone may be unbound.*
>
> CATULLUS

Why not? And according to her standard, a more licentious and active amorous relationship,

> *If he cannot last out the pleasant task.*
>
> VIRGIL

But is it not a great impudence to bring our imperfections and weaknesses where we desire to please and leave a good opinion and recommendation of ourselves? For the little that I need nowadays,

> *Even for one*
> *Encounter, limp,*
>
> HORACE

I would not want to trouble a person whom I have to reverence and fear:

> *Nor ever fear*
> *A man whose life, alas, has tottered past*
> *His fiftieth year.*
>
> HORACE

Nature should have contented herself with making this age miserable, without making it also ridiculous. I hate to see it, for one inch of wretched vigor that heats it up three times a week, bustle about and swagger with the same fierceness as if it had some great and proper day's work in its belly: a real flash in the pan. And I marvel to see such a lively and frisky flame so sluggishly congealed and put out in a moment. This appetite should belong only to the flower of beauty and youth. Just rely on age, if you want to find out, to second that indefatigable, full, constant, and great-souled ardor that is in you: it will leave you nicely in the lurch! Rather pass it on boldly to some tender, dazed, and ignorant boy, still trembling under the rod and blushing at it,

> *Even as Indian ivory, stained with red,*
> *Or lilies mingled in the flower bed*
> *With roses.*
>
> VIRGIL

He who can await, the morning after, without dying of shame, the disdain of those fair eyes that have witnessed his limpness and impertinence,

> *Her silent looks made eloquent reproach,*
>
> OVID

has never felt the satisfaction and pride of having conquered them and put circles around them by the vigorous exercise of a busy and active night. When I have seen one of them grow weary of me, I have not promptly blamed her fickleness; I have wondered whether I did not have reason rather to blame Nature. Certainly she has treated me unfairly and unkindly—

> *But if the penis be not long or stout enough . . .*
> *Even the matrons—all too well they know—*
> *Look dimly on a man whose member's small.*
>
> PRIAPEA

—and done me the most enormous damage.

Each one of my parts makes me myself just as much as every other one. And no other makes me more properly a man than this one.

I owe a complete portrait of myself to the public. The wisdom of my lesson is wholly in truth, in freedom, in reality; disdaining, in the list of its real duties, those petty, feigned, customary, provincial rules; altogether natural, constant, and universal; of which propriety and ceremony are daughters, but bastard daughters.

We will readily take care of the vices of appearance when we have taken care of those of reality. When we have done with the latter, we will attack the others, if we find we need to attack them. For there is danger that we dream up new duties to excuse our negligence toward our natural duties and mix them up. As proof of this: we see that in places where faults are crimes, crimes are only faults; that in nations where the laws of propriety are rarer and looser, the primitive and common laws are better observed; for the innumerable multitude of so many duties smothers, weakens, and dissipates our concern. Application to trivial things draws us away from urgent ones. Oh what an easy and applauded route those superficial men take, compared with ours! These are shadows with which we comfort ourselves and pay one another off; but we do not really pay, we rather add to our debt to that great Judge who tucks up our rags and tatters from around our shameful parts and does not merely pretend to see us throughout, even to our inmost and most secret filth. Our virginal modesty would be a useful propriety if it could keep him from making this discovery.

In short, whoever would wean man of the folly of such a scrupulous verbal superstition would do the world no great harm. Our life is part folly, part wisdom. Whoever writes about it only reverently and according to the rules leaves out more than half of it. I am not making excuses to myself, and if I did, I would make excuses rather for my excuses than for any other part of me. I am making excuses to certain humors which I believe to be stronger in number than those that are on my side. In consideration of them I will further say this—for I wish to satisfy everyone, though it is a very difficult thing *for one single man to accommodate himself to so great a variety of ways, discourses, and wills* (Cicero)—that they should not properly blame me for what I quote from authorities accepted and approved for many centuries; and that it is not right that they should refuse me, because I lack rhyme, the dispensation that even churchmen, and some of the most proudly crested at that, enjoy in our time. Here are two of them:

> *May I die if your crack is more than a faint line.*
>
> BEZA

A friendly tool contents and treats her well.

SAINT-GELAIS

And what about the many others?

I like modesty, and it is not by judgment that I have chosen this scandalous way of speaking; it is nature that has chosen it for me. I do not commend it, any more than I do any forms that are contrary to accepted practice; but I excuse it, and by particular and general circumstances I make the accusation lighter. Let's get on.

Likewise whence can come that usurpation of sovereign authority that you assume over those women who grant you favors at their own expense—

If she gave you furtive favors in the black of night

CATULLUS

—so that you immediately put on the rights, the coldness, and the authority of a husband? It is a free compact; why do you not keep to it as you want to hold them to it? There is no power of prescription in voluntary things.

It is contrary to form, but still it is true that in my time I have handled this business, as far as the nature of it would permit, as conscientiously as any other business and with some air of justice; and that I swore to them only what I felt about my affection, and represented to them candidly its decadence, its vigor, and its birth, its fits and its lapses. One does not always go about it at the same pace. I have been so sparing in promising that I think I have carried out more than I promised or owed. They have found me faithful even to the point of serving their inconstancy—I mean an avowed and sometimes multiplied inconstancy. I have never broken with them as long as I held to them even by a bit of thread; and whatever occasions for it they have given me, I have never broken with them to the point of scorn or hatred. For such intimacies, even when acquired on the most shameful terms, still oblige me to some good will. Anger and somewhat heedless impatience I have sometimes shown them on the occasion of their ruses and evasions and our quarrels; for by my nature I am subject to sudden outbursts which, though slight and brief, often harm my affairs. If they wanted to test the freedom of my judgment, I did not shirk giving them sharp paternal advice and pinching them where they smarted. If I have left them with any reason to complain of me, it is rather for having found in me a love which, compared with modem usage, was stupidly conscientious. I have kept my word in things in which I might easily have been excused. In those days they sometimes surrendered with honor and on conditions that they readily suffered the conqueror to break. I have more than once, in the interest of their honor, made pleasure yield in its greatest stress; and when reason urged me, I have armed them against myself, so that they conducted themselves more safely and severely by my rules, when they freely relied on them, than they would have done by their own.

As much as I could, I have taken upon myself alone the risk of our assignations, to free them of it, and I have always arranged our meetings in the hardest and most unexpected ways, so that they might be less under suspicion and besides, in my opinion, more accessible. Meetings are chiefly exposed in the places people think are automatically enclosed. Things least feared are least guarded against and observed. You can more easily dare what no one thinks you will dare, which becomes easy by its difficulty.

Never was a man more impertinently genital in his approaches. This way of loving is more according to the rules; but who knows better than I how ridiculous it is to people nowadays, and how ineffectual? Yet I shall not repent of it; I have nothing more to lose there:

> *A votive tablet shows*
> *I hung my dedicated clothes,*
> *Dripping with brine,*
> *Here in the sea-god's shrine.*
>
> HORACE

It is time now to speak of it openly. But just as I might peradventure say to another: "My friend, you are dreaming; love in your time has little to do with faith and probity"—

> *If under reason's certain rule*
> *You seek to bring this, all you do is add*
> *This to your tasks: with reason to go mad*
>
> TERENCE

—so, on the contrary, if I were to begin over again, it would certainly be by the same method and the same procedure, however fruitless it might be for me. Ineptitude and stupidity are praiseworthy in a blameworthy action. The further I depart from their attitude in this, the nearer I approach my own.

For the rest, in this business I did not let myself go entirely; I took pleasure in it, but I did not forget myself; I preserved entire the little sense and discretion that nature has given me, for their service and mine: a little excitement, but no folly. My conscience was also involved in it to the point of licentiousness and dissoluteness; but to the point of ingratitude, treachery, malignity, and cruelty, no. I did not purchase the pleasure of this vice at all costs, but contented myself with its proper and simple cost: *No vice is self-contained* (Seneca).

I hate almost equally a stagnant and sleepy idleness and a thorny and painful busyness. The one pinches me, the other puts me to sleep. I like wounds as much as bruises, and cutting blows as much as dry ones. I found in this business, when I was more fit for it, a just moderation between these two extremes. Love is a sprightly, lively, and gay agitation; I was neither troubled nor afflicted by it, but I was heated and moreover made thirsty by it. A man should stop there; it is hurtful only to fools.

A young man asked the philosopher Panaetius whether it would be becoming to a wise man to be in love. "Let us leave aside the wise man," he replied, "but you and I, who are not, let us not get involved in a thing so excited and violent, which enslaves us to others and makes us contemptible to ourselves." He spoke truly, that we should not entrust a thing so precipitous in itself to a soul that has not the wherewithal to withstand its assaults and to disprove in practice the saying of Agesilaus, that wisdom and love cannot live together. It is a vain occupation, it is true, unbecoming, shameful, and illegitimate; but carried on in this fashion, I consider it healthy, proper to enliven a heavy body and soul; and as a physician, I would prescribe it to a man of my temperament and condition as readily as any other recipe to rouse him and keep him in vigor till he is well on in years, and to keep him from the clutches of old age. While we are only in its outskirts and the pulse still beats,

> *While hair is freshly gray, old age hale and erect,*
> *While Lachesis has thread to spin, and while I stand*
> *And walk on my own feet, no staff in my right hand.*
>
> JUVENAL

we need to be stimulated and tickled by some biting agitation such as this. See how much youth, vigor, and gaiety it gave back to the wise Anacreom. And Socrates, when older than I am, speaking of an object of his love said: "When I had leaned my shoulder against his and brought my head close to his, as we were looking into a book together, I suddenly felt, without prevarication, a stinging in my shoulder like some animal's bite, and I was more than five days with it prickling, and a continual itching flowed into my heart." A touch, and an accidental one, and by a shoulder, to inflame and alter a soul cooled and enervated by age, and the first of all human souls in reformation! Indeed, why not? Socrates was a man, and wanted neither to be nor to seem anything else.

Philosophy does not strive against natural pleasures, provided that measure goes with them; she preaches moderation in them, not flight. The power of her resistance is employed against alien and bastard pleasures. She says that the appetites of the body are not to be augmented by the mind, and warns us ingeniously not to try to arouse our hunger by satiety, not to stuff instead of filling the belly, to avoid all enjoyment that brings us want and all meat and drink that makes us thirsty and hungry; as, in the service of love, she orders us to take an object that simply satisfies the body's need, that does not stir the soul, which should not make this its business but simply follow and assist the body.

But am I not right to consider that these precepts, which by the way are in my opinion still a bit rigorous, concern a body that performs its function, and that for a run-down body, as for a broken down stomach, it is excusable to warm it up and support it by art, and by the mediation of fancy to restore appetite and blitheness to it, since by itself it has lost them?

May we not say that there is nothing in us during this earthly imprisonment that is purely either corporeal or spiritual, and that we do wrong to tear apart a living man, and that it seems somewhat reasonable that we should behave as favorably at least toward the use of pleasure as we do toward pain? Pain, for example, was vehement even to perfection in the souls of the saints, through penitence; the body naturally had a share in it by virtue of their union, and yet could have little share in the cause. Yet they were not content that it should simply follow and assist the afflicted soul; they afflicted the body itself with atrocious and appropriate torments, in order that, vying with each other, the soul and the body should plunge man into pain, the more salutary for its harshness.

In a similar case, that of bodily pleasures, is it not unjust to cool the soul toward them and say that she should be dragged to them as to some constrained and servile obligation and necessity? It is rather for her to hatch them and foment them, to offer and invite herself to them, since the authority of ruling belongs to her; as it is also for her, in my opinion, in the pleasures that are her own, to inspire and infuse into the body all the feeling their nature allows, and to strive to make them sweet and salutary to it. For it is indeed reasonable, as they say, that the body should not follow its appetites to the disadvantage of the mind; but why is it not also reasonable that the mind should not pursue its appetites to the disadvantage of the body?

I have no other passion to keep me in breath. What avarice, ambition, quarrels, lawsuits, do for others who, like me, have no assigned occupation, love would do more agreeably. It would restore to me vigilance, sobriety, grace, care for my person; would secure my countenance, so that the grimaces of old age, those deformed and pitiable grimaces, should not come to disfigure it; would take me back to sane and wise studies, whereby I might make myself more esteemed and more loved, ridding my mind of despair of itself and its employment, and reacquainting it with itself; would divert me from a thousand troublesome thoughts, a thousand melancholy moods, that idleness and the bad state of our health loads us with at such an age; would warm up again, at least in dreams, this blood that nature is abandoning; would hold up the chin and stretch out a little the muscles and the soul's vigor and blitheness for this poor man who is going full speed toward his ruin.

But I quite understand that love is a very hard commodity to recover. By weakness and long experience our taste has become more delicate and exquisite. We demand more when we bring less; we most want to choose when we least deserve to be accepted. Knowing ourselves for what we are, we are less bold and more distrustful; nothing can assure us of being loved, knowing our condition and theirs. I am ashamed to find myself amid this green and ardent youth,

> *Whose member firmer stands, in its undaunted pride,*
> *Than a young tree upon a mountainside.*
>
> HORACE

Why should we go offering our wretchedness amid this sprightliness?

> *That ardent youngsters may stand round and watch,*
> *Not without mocking shout,*
> *As into ashes our weak torch burns out?*

HORACE

They have strength and right on their side; let us make way for them, we have no hold left.

And this bud of nascent beauty does not let itself be handled by such stiff hands or be won over by purely material means. For as that ancient philosopher replied to one who mocked him for having been unable to win the good graces of a tender youth he was pursuing: "My friend, the hook will not bite into such fresh cheese."

Now this is a relationship that needs mutuality and reciprocity. The other pleasures that we receive may be acknowledged by recompenses of a different nature; but this one can be paid for only in the same kind of coin. In truth, in this delight the pleasure I give tickles my imagination more sweetly than that which I feel. Now there is no nobility in a man who can receive pleasure where he gives none; it is a mean soul that is willing to owe everything and takes pleasure in fostering relations with persons to whom he is a burden. There is neither beauty, nor grace, nor intimacy so exquisite that a gallant man should desire it at this price. If they can be kind to us only out of pity, I had much rather not live at all than live on alms. I would like to have the right to ask it of them in the style I have seen beggars use in Italy: *"Do good for your own sake"*; or in the manner in which Cyrus exhorted his soldiers: "Who loves himself, let him follow me."

Rally, someone will tell me, round women of your own condition, whom company in like fortune will make easier for you. Oh what a stupid and insipid compromise!

> *I will*
> *Not pluck at a dead lion's beard.*

MARTIAL

Xenophon uses it as an objection and an accusation against Meno that in his love affairs he made use of persons who had passed their flower. I find more sensual pleasure in merely seeing the just and sweet union of two young beauties, or in merely considering it in imagination, than in myself making the second in a sad and ill-formed union. I resign that fantastic appetite to the Emperor Galba, who was addicted only to tough old meat, and to this poor wretch:

> *Would God that as I dream of you I might behold you,*
> *And press sweet kisses on your altered locks,*
> *Take your worn body in my arms and thus enfold you!*
>
> OVID

And among the leading forms of ugliness I count artificial and forced beauties. Hemon, a young boy of Chios, thinking by fine attire to acquire the beauty that nature denied him, presented himself to the philosopher Arcesilaus and asked him whether a wise man could fall in love. "Yes indeed," he replied, "provided it is not with a bedecked and sophisticated beauty like yours." An avowed ugliness and old age is less old and less ugly to my taste than another that is painted and glossed over.

Shall I say it, provided no one takes me by the throat for it? Love does not seem to me properly and naturally in its season except in the age next to childhood:

> *If you should place him in a troop of girls,*
> *With his ambiguous face and flowing curls,*
> *A thousand sharp onlookers could be wrong*
> *And fail to pick him out amid the throng.*
>
> HORACE

Nor beauty either. For when Homer makes beauty last until the chin begins to show a shadow, Plato himself remarks that such a flower is rare. And it is well known why the sophist Dion so humorously called the downy hairs of adolescence Aristogeitons and Harmodiuses. In manhood I find it already out of place; not to speak of old age:

> *For pitiless past the withered oaks*
> *Love flies.*
>
> HORACE

And Margaret, queen of Navarre, like a woman, prolongs the advantage of women very far, ordaining that at thirty it is time for them to change the title of "beautiful" to "good."

The shorter the possession we give Love over our life, the better we are. Look at his bearing: he is a beardless boy. Who does not know how in his school they proceed contrary to all order? Study, exercise, practice, are ways leading to incapacity; the novices there give the lessons: *Love knows no rule* (Saint Jerome). Certainly Love's conduct has much more style when it is mingled with heedlessness and confusion; mistakes and misadventures give it point and grace. Provided it is sharp and hungry, it matters little whether it is prudent. See how he goes reeling, tripping, and wantonly playing; you put him in the stocks when you guide him by art and wisdom, and you constrain his divine freedom when you subject him to those hairy and callous hands.

Moreover, I often hear women portray this relationship as wholly spiritual and disdain to place in consideration the interest that the senses have in it. Everything contributes to it. But I may say that I have often seen us excuse the weakness of their minds in favor of their bodily beauties; but I have never yet seen that for the sake of our beauty of mind, however wise and mature that mind may be, they were willing to grant favors to a body that was slipping the least little bit into decline. Why is not one of them seized with desire for that noble Socratic exchange of body for soul, buying a philosophical and spiritual intelligence and generation at the price of her thighs, the highest price to which she can raise them? Plato ordains in his *Laws* that whoever has performed some signal and useful exploit in war, regardless of his ugliness or old age, may not for the war's duration be refused a kiss or other amorous favor from whomever he wants. What he finds so just in recommendation of military worth, may it not also be so in recommendation of some other kind of worth? And why is not one of them seized with desire to gain before her sisters the glory of this chaste love? And I do mean chaste,

> *For if it comes to love's encounter,*
> *Like fire in straw, mighty in size, with little power,*
> *They spend their rage in vain.*
>
> VIRGIL

The vices that are stifled in thought are not the worst.

To conclude this notable commentary, which has escaped from me in a flow of babble, a flow sometimes impetuous and harmful—

> *And as an apple, secret present from her love,*
> *Falls out from the chaste bosom of the maid,*
> *Where she has quite forgot it, hid beneath her robe,*
> *When at her mother's step she starts, afraid;*
> *As she rises it falls, rolls off at a swift pace;*
> *A guilty blush spreads o'er her downcast face*
>
>   CATULLUS

—I say that males and females are cast in the same mold; except for education and custom, the difference is not great. Plato invites both without discrimination to the fellowship of all studies, exercises, functions, warlike and peaceful occupations, in his commonwealth. And the philosopher Antisthenes eliminated any distinction between their virtue and ours. It is much easier to accuse one sex than to excuse the other. It is the old saying: The pot calls the kettle black.

                                    (translated by Donald M. Frame)

1623

England

After its conversion to Protestantism under Elizabeth I, England was transformed into a virtual police state, a society in which the wrong belief could easily get you killed. Note the spies that were everywhere. Heads displayed on pikes. As a Catholic member of Parliament at the age of twenty-nine, Francis Bacon was vulnerable in this kind of environment. When he publicly opposed a proposal that Elizabeth I had made requiring Catholics to pay their debts in half the time as others, Bacon was banned from being in the same room with her again. Blacklisted, voted out, and unable to secure further positions in any public office, Bacon was eventually arrested for debt as rumors spread he was a traitor. Some even said, a pederast. Three years later, when he eventually did gain back a minor public office, the House of Lords immediately accused him of corruption, a charge he was convicted of without any evidence, but for which he ended up spending seven months in jail. After that, Bacon retired $4 million in debt, dying shortly after with nothing to his name. And yet, what seems to have sustained the writer throughout all these uncertainties are the essays that he composed as testaments to control. His are arguments of precise and confident and startlingly clear thought, each of which is based upon a simple aphorism. Coming from the Greek roots for "from"—*apo*—and "boundary"—*horismos*—the word literally means to mark off, to demarcate, to define. An aphorism is in this way very much like a thesis, a declaration constricted by a limitation of space but whose implications are deepened by the confidence of its claim: "Love the sinner and not the sin;" "Some praise at morning what they blame at night;" "Life is short, art is long, opportunity fleeting, experimenting dangerous." Francis Bacon, the founder of the scientific method in Europe, considered the aphorism so fundamental that he believed that nothing smaller could make its own sense in the world. "There is nothing more exact," Francis Bacon once wrote, "nor more comforting to me, indeed."

FRANCIS BACON

Antitheses of Things

Youth

For	*Against*
First thoughts and young men's counsels have more of divineness.	Youth is the seedbed of repentance.
Old men are wiser for themselves, not so wise for others and for the commonwealth.	There is implanted in youth contempt for the authority of age; so every man must grow wise at his own cost.
Old age, if it could be seen, deforms the mind more than the body.	The counsels to which Time is not called, Time will not ratify.
Old men are afraid of everything, except the Gods.	In old men the Loves are changed into the Graces.

Health

For	*Against*
The care of health humiliates the mind and makes it the beggar of the body.	Often to recover health, is often to renew youth.
A healthy body is the soul's host, a sick body her gaoler.	Ill health is a good excuse for many things; which we are glad to use, even when well.
Nothing forwards the conclusion of business so much as good health; weak health on the contrary takes too many holidays.	Good health makes too close an alliance between the soul and the body.
	Great empires have been governed from bed, great armies commanded from the litter.

Wife and Children

For	*Against*
Love of his country begins in a man's own house.	He that has wife and children has given hostages to fortune.
A wife and children are a kind of discipline of humanity; whereas unmarried men are harsh and severe.	Man generates and has children; God creates and produces works.
To be without wife or children is good for a man only when he wants to run away.	The eternity of brutes is in offspring; of men, in fame, good deserts, and institutions.
He who begets not children, sacrifices to death.	Domestic considerations commonly overthrow public ones.
They that are fortunate in other things are commonly unfortunate in their children; lest men should come too near the condition of Gods.	Some persons have wished for Priam's fortune, who survived all his children.

Nature

For	*Against*
Custom advances in an arithmetical ratio, nature in a geometrical.	We think according to our nature, speak as we have been taught, but act as we have been accustomed.
As common laws are to customs in states, such is nature to custom in individuals.	Nature is a schoolmaster, custom a magistrate.
Custom against nature is a kind of tyranny, and is soon and upon slight occasions overthrown.	

Fortune

For	*Against*
Overt and apparent virtues bring forth praise; secret and hidden virtues bring forth fortune.	The folly of one man is the fortune of another.
Virtues of duty bring forth praise; virtues of ability bring forth fortune.	The best that can be said of fortune is that, as she uses no choice in her favors, so she does not care to uphold them.
Fortune is like the Milky Way; a cluster of obscure virtues without a name.	Great men, to decline the envy of their own virtues, turn worshippers of fortune.
Fortune is to be honored if it be but for her daughters, Confidence and Authority.	

Pride

For	*Against*
Pride is unsociable to vices among other things; an as poison by poison, so not a few vices are expelled by pride.	Pride is the ivy that winds about all virtues and all good things.
The good-natured man is subject to other men's vices as well as his own; the proud man to his own only.	Other vices do but thwart virtues; only pride infects them.
Let pride go a step higher, and from contempt of others rise to contempt of self, and it becomes philosophy.	Pride lacks the best condition of vice—concealment.
	The proud man while he despises others neglects himself.

Ingratitude

For	*Against*
The crime of ingratitude is nothing more than a clear in-sight into the cause of a benefit conferred.	The crime of ingratitude is not restrained by punishments, but given over to the Furies.
In our desire to show gratitude to certain persons we sacrifice both the justice we owe to others and the liberty we owe to ourselves.	The bonds of benefits are stricter than the bonds of duties; wherefore he that is ungrateful is unjust and every way bad.
Before we are called on to be grateful for a benefit, let us be sure as to the value of it.	This is the condition of human-ity: no man is born in so public a fortune but he must obey the private calls of both gratitude and revenge.

Unchastity

For	*Against*
It is owing to jealousy that chas-tity has been made a virtue.	Unchastity was the worst of Circe's transformations.
A man must be of a very sad disposition to think love a serious matter.	He that is unchaste is without all reverence for himself, which is the bridle of all vices.
Why make a virtue of that which is either a matter of diet, or a show of cleanliness, or the child of pride?	All who like Paris prefer beauty, quit like Paris wisdom and power.
Loves are like wildfowl; there is no property in them, but the right passes with possession.	It was no vulgar truth that Alexander lighted on, when he said that sleep and lust were earnests of death.

Cruelty

For	*Against*
None of the virtues has so many crimes to answer for as clemency.	To delight in blood one must be either a wild beast or a Fury.
Cruelty, if it proceeds from revenge, is justice; if from danger, prudence.	To a good man cruelty always seems fabulous, and some tragical fiction.
He that has mercy on his enemy has no mercy on himself.	
Bloodlettings are not oftener necessary in medicine than executions in states.	

Justice

For	*Against*
Kingdoms and governments are but accessories to justice; for there would be no need of them if justice could be carried on without.	If to be just be not to do that to another which you would not have another do to you, then is mercy justice.
It is owing to justice that man is a god to man, and not a wolf.	If everyone has a right to his own, surely humanity has a right to pardon.
Justice though it cannot extirpate vices, yet prevents them from doing hurt.	What tell you me of equal measure, when to the wise man all things are equal?
	Consider the condition of accused persons among the Romans, and conclude that justice is not for the good of the commonwealth.
	The ordinary justice of governments is but as a philosopher in the court—it merely conduces to the reverence of those who govern.

Fortitude

For	*Against*
Nothing is to be feared except fear itself. There is nothing either solid in pleasure, or secure in virtue, where fear intrudes.	A noble virtue, to be willing to die yourself in order to kill another!
	A noble virtue, which a man may acquire by getting drunk!
He that looks steadily at dangers that he may meet them, sees also how he may avoid them.	He that is prodigal of his own life is dangerous to other men's.
Other virtues free us from the domination of vice, fortitude only from the domination of fortune.	Fortitude is the virtue of the iron age.

Temperance

For	*Against*
The power of abstinence is not much other than the power of endurance.	I like not these negative virtues; for they show innocence and not merit.
Uniformity, concord, and measured motion, are attributes of heaven and characters of eternity.	The mind grows languid that has no excesses.
Temperance is like wholesome cold; it collects and braces the powers of the mind.	I like those virtues which induce excellence of action, not dullness of passion.
Exquisite and restless senses need narcotics; so do passions.	If you will have the motions of the mind all consonant, you must have them few—for it is a poor man that can count his stock.
	To abstain from the use of a thing that you may not feel the want of it, to shun the want that you may not fear the loss of it, are precautions of pusillanimity and cowardice.

Loquacity

For

He that is silent betrays want of confidence either in others or in himself.

All kinds of constraint are unhappy, that of silence is the most miserable of all.

Silence is the virtue of a fool. And therefore it was well said to a man that would not speak, "If you are wise you are a fool; if you are a fool, you are wise."

Silence, like night, is convenient for treacheries.

Thoughts are wholesomest when they are like running waters.

He that is silent lays himself out for opinion.

Silence neither casts off bad thoughts nor distributes good.

Against

Silence gives words both grace and authority.

Silence is the sleep which nourishes wisdom.

Silence is the fermentation of thought.

Silence is the style of wisdom.

Silence aspires after truth.

Learning

For

If books were written about small matters, there would be scarce any use of experience.

In reading a man converses with the wise, in action generally with fools.

Sciences which are of no use in themselves are not deemed useless, if they sharpen the wit and put the thoughts it order.

Against

In colleges men learn to believe. What art ever taught the seasonable use of art?

To be wise by rule and to be wise by experience are contrary proceedings; he that accustoms himself to the one unfits himself for the other.

Art is often put to a foolish use, that it may not be of no use at all.

Almost all scholars have this—when anything is presented to them, they will find in it that which they know, not learn from it that which they know not.

Love

For

See you not that all men seek themselves? But it is only the lover that finds himself.

There is nothing which better regulates the mind than the authority of some powerful passion.

If you are wise, seek something to desire; for to him who has not some special object of pursuit all things are distasteful and wearisome.

Why should not one be content with one?

Against

The stage is much beholden to love, life not at all.

Nothing has so many names as love; for it is a thing either so foolish that it does not know itself, or so foul that it hides itself with paint.

I hate those men of one thought.

Love is a very narrow contemplation.

1658

And yet, a thesis statement, like an aphorism, precludes real essaying. It denies a text the possibility for reflection, digression, discovery, or change. Instead, it is Sir Thomas Browne, not Francis Bacon, whom George Orwell will credit with officially introducing the essay into English. "It is Browne's introspection," he writes of his progenitor, "which shifted us from the outside world of rhetoric, to the inner and private world of mystery and wonder." We can pinpoint that shift precisely. It happens in "Urn Burial," in chapter V, the first sentence. It's the simple question that's posed after Browne's first colon—"what prince can promise such diuturnity unto his relicks . . . ?"—a question that Browne doesn't immediately answer because Browne does not believe in the efficacy of rhetoric. By this point in the essay, Browne's text has transformed itself into something that has probed so deeply into its subject that the author finds himself in unexpected terrain. It's a place no English essayist had yet visited till then: a place deep within himself. "In vain we hope to be known by open and visible conservatories," Browne later reflects on the question that he raised, "when to be known was the means of their continuation, and obscurity their protection."

THOMAS BROWNE

Hydriotaphia, Urn Burial; or, A Discourse of the Sepulchral Urns Lately Found in Norfolk

CHAPTER I

In the deep discovery of the subterranean world a shallow part would satisfy some inquirers; who, if two or three yards were open about the surface, would not care to rake the bowels of Potosi, and regions toward the centre. Nature hath furnished one part of the earth, and man another. The treasures of time lie high, in urns, coins, and monuments, scarce below the roots of some vegetables. Time hath endless rarities, and shows of all varieties; which reveals old things in heaven, makes new discoveries in earth, and even earth itself a discovery. That great antiquity America lay buried for thousands of years, and a large part of the earth is still in the urn unto us.

Though if Adam were made out of an extract of the earth, all parts might challenge a restitution, yet few have returned their bones far lower than they might receive them; not affecting the graves of giants, under hilly and heavy coverings, but content with less than their own depth, have wished their bones might lie soft, and the earth be light upon them. Even such as hope to rise again, would not be content with central interment, or so desperately to place their relicks as to lie beyond discovery; and in no way to be seen again; which happy contrivance hath made communication with our forefathers, and left unto our view some parts, which they never beheld themselves.

Though earth hath engrossed the name, yet water hath proved the smartest grave; which in forty days swallowed almost mankind, and the living creation; fishes not wholly escaping, except the salt ocean were handsomely contempered by a mixture of the fresh element.

Many have taken voluminous pains to determine the state of the soul upon disunion; but men have been most phantastical in the singular contrivances of their corporal dissolution: whilst the soberest nations have rested in two ways, of simple inhumation and burning.

That carnal interment or burying was of the elder date, the old examples of Abraham and the patriarchs are sufficient to illustrate; and were without competition, if it could be made out that Adam was buried near Damascus, or Mount Calvary, according to some tradition. God himself, that buried but one, was pleased to make choice of this way, collectible from Scripture expression, and the hot contest between Satan and the archangel about discovering the body of Moses. But the practice of burning was also of great antiquity, and of no slender extent. For (not to derive the same from Hercules) noble descriptions there are hereof in the Grecian funerals of Homer, in the formal obsequies of Patroclus and Achilles; and somewhat elder in the Theban war, and solemn combustion of Meneceus, and Archemorus, contemporary unto Jair the eighth judge of Israel. Confirmable also among the Trojans, from the funeral pyre of Hector, burnt before the gates of Troy: and the burning of Penthesilea the Amazonian queen: and long continuance of that practice, in the inward countries of Asia; while as low as the reign of Julian, we find that the king of Chionia burnt the body of his son, and interred the ashes in a silver urn.

The same practice extended also far west; and besides Herulians, Getes, and Thracians, was in use with most of the Celtæ, Sarmatians, Germans, Gauls, Danes, Swedes, Norwegians; not to omit some use thereof among Carthaginians and Americans. Of greater antiquity among the Romans than most opinion, or Pliny seems to allow: for (besides the old table laws of burning or burying within the city, of making the funeral fire with planed wood, or quenching the fire with wine), Manlius the consul burnt the body of his son: Numa, by special clause of his will, was not burnt but buried; and Remus was solemnly burned, according to the description of Ovid.

Cornelius Sylla was not the first whose body was burned in Rome, but the first of the Cornelian family; which being indifferently, not frequently used before; from that time spread, and became the prevalent practice. Not totally pursued in the highest run of cremation; for when even crows were funerally burnt, Poppæa the wife of Nero found a peculiar grave interment. Now as all customs were founded upon some bottom of reason, so there wanted not grounds for this; according to several apprehensions of the most rational dissolution. Some being of the opinion of Thales, that water was the original of all things, thought it most equal to submit unto the principle of putrefaction, and conclude in a moist relentment. Others conceived it most natural to end in fire, as due unto the master principle in the composition, according to the doctrine of Heraclitus; and therefore heaped up large piles, more actively to waft them toward that element, whereby they also declined a visible degeneration into worms, and left a lasting parcel of their composition.

Some apprehended a purifying virtue in fire, refining the grosser commixture, and firing out the æthereal particles so deeply immersed in it. And such as by tradition or rational conjecture held any hint of the final pyre of all things; or that this element at last must be too hard for all the rest; might conceive most naturally of the fiery dissolution. Others pretending no natural grounds, politickly declined the malice of enemies upon their buried bodies. Which consideration led Sylla unto this practice; who having thus served the body of Marius, could not but fear a retaliation upon his own; entertained after in the civil wars, and revengeful contentions of Rome.

But as many nations embraced, and many left it indifferent, so others too much affected, or strictly declined this practice. The Indian Brachmans seemed too great friends unto fire, who burnt themselves alive and thought it the noblest way to end their days in fire; according to the expression of the Indian, burning himself at Athens, in his last words upon the pyre unto the amazed spectators, "thus I make myself immortal."

But the Chaldeans, the great idolaters of fire, abhorred the burning of their carcases, as a pollution of that deity. The Persian magi declined it upon the like scruples, and being only solicitous about their bones, exposed their flesh to the prey of birds and dogs. And the Persees now in India, which expose their bodies unto vultures, and endure not so much as *feretra* or biers of wood, the proper fuel of fire, are led on with such niceties. But whether the ancient Germans, who burned their dead, held any such fear to pollute their deity of Herthus, or the earth, we have no authentic conjecture.

The Egyptians were afraid of fire, not as a deity, but a devouring element, mercilessly consuming their bodies, and leaving too little of them; and therefore by precious embalmments, depositure in dry earths, or handsome inclosure in glasses, contrived the notablest ways of integral conservation. And from such Egyptian scruples, imbibed by Pythagoras, it may be conjectured that Numa and the Pythagorical sect first waived the fiery solution.

The Scythians, who swore by wind and sword, that is, by life and death, were so far from burning their bodies, that they declined all interment, and made their graves in the air: and the Ichthyophagi, or fish-eating nations about Egypt, affected the sea for their grave; thereby declining visible corruption, and restoring the debt of their bodies. Whereas the old heroes, in Homer, dreaded nothing more than water or drowning; probably upon the old opinion of the fiery substance of the soul, only extinguishable by that element; and therefore the poet emphatically implieth the total destruction in this kind of death, which happened to Ajax Oileus.

The old Balearians had a peculiar mode, for they used great urns and much wood, but no fire in their burials, while they bruised the flesh and bones of the dead, crowded them into urns, and laid heaps of wood upon them. And the Chinese without cremation or urnal interment of their bodies, make use of trees and much burning, while they plant a pine-tree by their grave, and burn great numbers of printed draughts of slaves and horses over it, civilly content with their companies in *effigy*, which barbarous nations exact unto reality.

Christians abhorred this way of obsequies, and though they sticked not to give their bodies to be burnt in their lives, detested that mode after death: affecting rather a depositure than absumption, and properly submitting unto the sentence of God, to return not unto ashes but unto dust again, and conformable unto the practice of the patriarchs, the interment of our Saviour, of Peter, Paul, and the ancient martyrs. And so far at last declining promiscuous interment with Pagans, that some have suffered ecclesiastical censures, for making no scruple thereof.

The Mussulman believers will never admit this fiery resolution. For they hold a present trial from their black and white angels in the grave; which they must have made so hollow, that they may rise upon their knees.

The Jewish nation, though they entertained the old way of inhumation, yet sometimes admitted this practice. For the men of Jabesh burnt the body of Saul; and by no prohibited practice, to avoid contagion or pollution, in time of pestilence, burnt the bodies of their friends. And when they burnt not their dead bodies, yet sometimes used great burnings near and about them, deducible from the expressions concerning Jehoram, Zedechias, and the sumptuous pyre of Asa. And were so little averse from Pagan burning, that the Jews lamenting the death of Cæsar their friend, and revenger on Pompey, frequented the place where his body was burnt for many nights together. And as they raised noble monuments and mausoleums for their own nation, so they were not scrupulous in erecting some for others, according to the practice of Daniel, who left that lasting sepulchral pile in Ecbatana, for the Median and Persian kings.

But even in times of subjection and hottest use, they conformed not unto the Roman practice of burning; whereby the prophecy was secured concerning the body of Christ, that it should not see corruption, or a bone should not be broken; which we believe was also providentially prevented, from the soldier's spear and nails that passed by the little bones both in his hands and feet; not of ordinary contrivance, that it should not corrupt on the cross, according to the laws of Roman crucifixion, or an hair of his head perish, though observable in Jewish customs, to cut the hair of malefactors.

Nor in their long cohabitation with Egyptians, crept into a custom of their exact embalming, wherein deeply slashing the muscles, and taking out the brains and entrails, they had broken the subject of so entire a resurrection, nor fully answered the types of Enoch, Elijah, or Jonah, which yet to prevent or restore, was of equal facility unto that rising power able to break the fasciations and bands of death, to get clear out of the cerecloth, and an hundred pounds of ointment, and out of the sepulchre before the stone was rolled from it.

But though they embraced not this practice of burning, yet entertained they many ceremonies agreeable unto Greek and Roman obsequies. And he that observeth their funeral feasts, their lamentations at the grave, their music, and weeping mourners; how they closed the eyes of their friends, how they washed, anointed, and kissed the dead; may easily conclude these were not mere Pagan civilities. But whether that mournful burthen, and treble calling out after Absalom, had any reference unto the last conclamation, and triple valediction, used by other nations, we hold but a wavering conjecture.

Civilians make sepulture but of the law of nations, others do naturally found it and discover it also in animals. They that are so thick-skinned as still to credit the story of the Phoenix, may say something for animal burning. More serious conjectures find some examples of sepulture in elephants, cranes, the sepulchral cells of pismires, and practice of bees,—which civil society carrieth out their dead, and hath exequies, if not interments.

CHAPTER II

The solemnities, ceremonies, rites of their cremation or interment, so solemnly delivered by authors, we shall not disparage our reader to repeat. Only the last and lasting part in their urns, collected bones and ashes, we cannot wholly omit or decline that subject, which occasion lately presented, in some discovered among us.

In a field of Old Walsingham, not many months past, were digged up between forty and fifty urns, deposited in a dry and sandy soil, not a yard deep, nor far from one another.—Not all strictly of one figure, but most answering these described; some containing two pounds of bones, and teeth, with fresh impressions of their combustion; besides the extraneous substances, like pieces of small boxes, or combs handsomely wrought, handles of small brass instruments, brazen nippers, and in one some kind of opal.

Near the same plot of ground, for about six yards compass, were digged up coals and incinerated substances, which begat conjecture that this was the *ustrina* or place of burning their bodies, or some sacrificing place unto the *Manes*, which was properly below the surface of the ground, as the *aræ* and altars unto the gods and heroes above it.

That these were the urns of Romans from the common custom and place where they were found, is no obscure conjecture, not far from a Roman garrison, and but five miles from Brancaster, set down by ancient record under the name of Branodunum. And where the adjoining town, containing seven parishes, in no very different sound, but Saxon termination, still retains the name of Burnham, which being an early station, it is not improbable the neighbour parts were filled with habitations, either of Romans themselves, or Britons Romanized, which observed the Roman customs.

Nor is it improbable, that the Romans early possessed this country. For though we meet not with such strict particulars of these parts before the new institution of Constantine and military charge of the count of the Saxon shore, and that about the Saxon invasions, the Dalmatian horsemen were in the garrison of Brancaster; yet in the time of Claudius, Vespasian, and Severus, we find no less than three legions dispersed through the province of Britain. And as high as the reign of Claudius a great overthrow was given unto the Iceni, by the Roman lieutenant Ostorius. Not long after, the country was so molested, that, in hope of a better state, Prastaagus bequeathed his kingdom unto Nero and his daughters; and Boadicea, his queen, fought the last decisive battle with Paulinus. After which time, and conquest of Agricola, the lieutenant of Vespasian, probable it is, they wholly possessed this country; ordering it into garrisons or habitations best suitable with their securities. And so some Roman habitations not improbable in these parts, as high as the time of Vespasian, where the Saxons after seated, in whose thin-filled maps we yet find the name of Walsingham. Now if the Iceni were but Gammadims, Anconians, or men that lived in an angle, wedge, or elbow of Britain, according to the original etymology, this country will challenge the emphatical appellation, as most properly making the elbow or *iken* of Icenia.

That Britain was notably populous is undeniable, from that expression of Cæsar. That the Romans themselves were early in no small numbers— seventy thousand, with their associates, slain, by Boadicea, affords a sure account. And though not many Roman habitations are now known, yet some, by old works, rampiers, coins, and urns, do testify their possessions. Some urns have been found at Castor, some also about Southcreak, and, not many years past, no less than ten in a field at Buston, not near any recorded garrison. Nor is it strange to find Roman coins of copper and silver among us; of Vespasian, Trajan, Adrian, Commodus, Antoninus, Severus, &c.; but the greater number of Dioclesian, Constantine, Constans, Valens, with many of Victorinus Posthumius, Tetricus, and the thirty tyrants in the reign of Gallienus; and some as high as Adrianus have been found about Thetford, or Sitomagus, mentioned in the *Itinerary* of Antoninus, as the way from Venta or Castor unto London. But the most frequent discovery is made at the two Castors by Norwich and Yarmouth at Burghcastle, and Brancaster.

Besides the Norman, Saxon, and Danish pieces of Cuthred, Canutus, William, Matilda, and others, some British coins of gold have been dispersedly found, and no small number of silver pieces near Norwich, with a rude head upon the obverse, and an ill-formed horse on the reverse, with inscriptions *Ic. Duro. T.;* whether implying Iceni, Durotriges, Tascia, or Trinobantes, we leave to higher conjecture. Vulgar chronology will have Norwich Castle as old as Julius Cæsar; but his distance from these parts, and its Gothick form of structure, abridgeth such antiquity. The British coins afford conjecture of early habitation in these parts, though the city of Norwich arose from the ruins of Venta; and though, perhaps, not without some habitation before, was enlarged, builded, and nominated by the

Saxons. In what bulk or populosity it stood in the old East-Angle monarchy tradition and history are silent. Considerable it was in the Danish eruptions, when Sueno burnt Thetford and Norwich, and Ulfketel, the governor thereof, was able to make some resistance, and after endeavoured to burn the Danish navy.

How the Romans left so many coins in countries of their conquests seems of hard resolution; except we consider how they buried them under ground when, upon barbarous invasions, they were fain to desert their habitations in most part of their empire, and the strictness of their laws forbidding to transfer them to any other uses: wherein the Spartans were singular, who, to make their copper money useless, contempered it with vinegar. That the Britons left any, some wonder, since their money was iron and iron rings before Cæsar; and those of after-stamp by permission, and but small in bulk and bigness. That so few of the Saxons remain, because, overcome by succeeding conquerors upon the place, their coins, by degrees, passed into other stamps and the marks of after-ages.

Than the time of these urns deposited, or precise antiquity of these relicks, nothing of more uncertainty; for since the lieutenant of Claudius seems to have made the first progress into these parts, since Boadicea was overthrown by the forces of Nero, and Agricola put a full end to these conquests, it is not probable the country was fully garrisoned or planted before; and, therefore, however these urns might be of later date, not likely of higher antiquity.

And the succeeding emperors desisted not from their conquests in these and other parts, as testified by history and medal-inscription yet extant: the province of Britain, in so divided a distance from Rome, beholding the faces of many imperial persons, and in large account; no fewer than Cæsar, Claudius, Britannicus, Vespasian, Titus, Adrian, Severus, Commodus, Geta, and Caracalla.

A great obscurity herein, because no medal or emperor's coin enclosed, which might denote the date of their interments; observable in many urns, and found in those of Spitalfields, by London, which contained the coins of Claudius, Vespasian, Commodus, Antoninus, attended with lacrymatories, lamps, bottles of liquor, and other appurtenances of affectionate superstition, which in these rural interments were wanting.

Some uncertainty there is from the period or term of burning, or the cessation of that practice. Macrobius affirmeth it was disused in his days;

but most agree, though without authentic record, that it ceased with the Antonini,—most safely to be understood after the reign of those emperors which assumed the name of Antoninus, extending unto Heliogabalus. Not strictly after Marcus; for about fifty years later, we find the magnificent burning and consecration of Servus; and, if we so fix this period or cessation, these urns will challenge above thirteen hundred years.

But whether this practice was only then left by emperors and great persons, or generally about Rome, and not in other provinces, we hold no authentic account; for after Tertullian, in the days of Minucius, it was obviously objected upon Christians, that they condemned the practice of burning. And we find a passage in Sidonius, which asserteth that practice in France unto a lower account. And, perhaps, not fully disused till Christianity fully established, which gave the final extinction to these sepulchral bonfires.

Whether they were the bones of men, or women, or children, no authentic decision from ancient custom in distinct places of burial. Although not improbably conjectured, that the double sepulture, or burying-place of Abraham, had in it such intention. But from exility of bones, thinness of skulls, smallness of teeth, ribs, and thigh-bones, not improbable that many thereof were persons of minor age, or woman. Confirmable also from things contained in them. In most were found substances resembling combs, plates like boxes, fastened with iron pins, and handsomely overwrought like the necks or bridges of musical instruments; long brass plates overwrought like the handles of neat implements; brazen nippers, to pull away hair; and in one a kind of opal, yet maintaining a bluish colour.

Now that they accustomed to burn or bury with them, things wherein they excelled, delighted, or which were dear unto them, either as farewells unto all pleasure, or vain apprehension that they might use them in the other world, is testified by all antiquity, observable from the gem or beryl ring upon the finger of Cynthia, the mistress of Propertius, when after her funeral pyre her ghost appeared unto him; and notably illustrated from the contents of that Roman urn preserved by Cardinal Farnese, wherein besides great number of gems with heads of gods and goddesses, were found an ape of agath, a grasshopper, an elephant of amber, a crystal ball, three glasses, two spoons, and six nuts of crystal; and beyond the content of urns, in the monument of Childerek the first, and fourth king from Pharamond, casually discovered three years past at Tournay, restoring unto the world much gold richly adorning his sword, two hundred rubies, many hundred imperial coins, three hundred golden bees, the bones and horse-shoes of his horse interred with him, according to the barbarous magnificence of those days in their sepulchral obsequies. Although, if we steer by the conjecture of many a Septuagint expression, some trace thereof may be found even with the ancient Hebrews, not only from the sepulchral treasure of David, but the circumcision knives which Joshua also buried.

Some men, considering the contents of these urns, lasting pieces and toys included in them, and the custom of burning with many other nations, might somewhat doubt whether all urns found among us, were properly Roman relicks, or some not belonging unto our British, Saxon, or Danish forefathers.

In the form of burial among the ancient Britons, the large discourses of Cæsar, Tacitus, and Strabo are silent. For the discovery whereof, with other particulars, we much deplore the loss of that letter which Cicero expected or received from his brother Quintus, as a resolution of British customs; or the account which might have been made by Scribonius Largus, the physician, accompanying the Emperor Claudius, who might have also discovered that frugal bit of the old Britons, which in the bigness of a bean could satisfy their thirst and hunger.

But that the Druids and ruling priests used to burn and bury, is expressed by Pomponius; that Bellinus, the brother of Brennus, and King of the Britons, was burnt, is acknowledged by Polydorus, as also by Amandus Zierexensis in *Historia* and Pineda in his *Universa Historia* (Spanish). That they held that practice in Gallia, Cæsar expressly delivereth. Whether the Britons (probably descended from them, of like religion, language, and manners) did not sometimes make use of burning, or whether at least such as were after civilized unto the Roman life and manners, conformed not unto this practice, we have no historical assertion or denial. But since, from the account of Tacitus, the Romans early wrought so much civility upon the British stock, that they brought them to build temples, to wear the gown, and study the Roman laws and language, that they conformed also unto their religious rites and customs in burials, seems no improbable conjecture.

That burning the dead was used in Sarmatia is affirmed by Gaguinus; that the Sueons and Gathlanders used to burn their princes and great persons, is delivered by Saxo and Olaus; that this was the old German practice, is also asserted by Tacitus. And though we are bare in historical particulars of such obsequies in this island, or that the Saxons, Jutes, and Angles burnt their dead, yet came they from parts where 'twas of ancient practice; the Germans using it, from whom they were descended. And even in Jutland and Sleswick in Anglia Cymbrica, urns with bones were found not many years before us.

But the Danish and northern nations have raised an era or point of compute from their custom of burning their dead: some deriving it from Unguinus, some from Frotho the great, who ordained by law, that princes and chief commanders should be committed unto the fire, though the common sort had the common grave interment. So Starkatterus, that old hero, was burnt, and Ringo royally burnt the body of Harold the king slain by him.

What time this custom generally expired in that nation, we discern no assured period; whether it ceased before Christianity, or upon their conversion, by Ausgurius the Gaul, in the time of Ludovicus Pius, the son of Charles the Great, according to good computes; or whether it might not be used by some persons, while for an hundred and eighty years Paganism and Christianity were promiscuously embraced among them, there is no assured conclusion. About which times the Danes were busy in England, and particularly infested this country; where many castles and strongholds were built by them, or against them, and great number of names and families still derived from them. But since this custom was probably disused before their invasion or conquest, and the Romans confessedly practised the same since their possession of this island, the most assured account will fall upon the Romans, or Britons Romanized.

However, certain it is, that urns conceived of no Roman original, are often digged up both in Norway and Denmark, handsomely described, and graphically represented by the learned physician Wormius. And in some parts of Denmark in no ordinary number, as stands delivered by authors exactly describing those countries. And they contained not only bones, but many other substances in them, as knives, pieces of iron, brass, and wood, and one of Norway a brass gilded jew's-harp.

Nor were they confused or careless in disposing the noblest sort, while they placed large stones in circle about the urns or bodies which they interred: somewhat answerable unto the monument of Rollrich stones in England, or sepulchral monument probably erected by Rollo, who after

conquered Normandy; where 'tis not improbable somewhat might be discovered. Meanwhile to what nation or person belonged that large urn found
at Ashbury, containing mighty bones, and a buckler; what those large urns
found at Little Massingham; or why the Anglesea urns are placed with their
mouths downward, remains yet undiscovered.

CHAPTER III

Plaistered and whited sepulchres were anciently affected in cadaverous and
corrupted burials; and the rigid Jews were wont to garnish the sepulchres
of the righteous. Ulysses, in Hecuba, cared not how meanly he lived, so he
might find a noble tomb after death. Great princes affected great monuments; and the fair and larger urns contained no vulgar ashes, which makes
that disparity in those which time discovereth among us. The present urns
were not of one capacity, the largest containing above a gallon, some not
much above half that measure; nor all of one figure, wherein there is no
strict conformity in the same or different countries; observable from those
represented by Casalius, Bosio, and others, though all found in Italy; while
many have handles, ears, and long necks, but most imitate a circular figure,
in a spherical and round composure; whether from any mystery, best duration or capacity, were but a conjecture. But the common form with necks
was a proper figure, making our last bed like our first; nor much unlike the
urns of our nativity while we lay in the nether part of the earth, and inward
vault of our microcosm. Many urns are red, these but of a black colour
somewhat smooth, and dully sounding, which begat some doubt, whether
they were burnt, or only baked in oven or sun, according to the ancient
way, in many bricks, tiles, pots, and testaceous works; and, as the word
testa is properly to be taken, when occurring without addition and chiefly
intended by Pliny, when he commendeth bricks and tiles of two years old,
and to make them in the spring. Nor only these concealed pieces, but the
open magnificence of antiquity, ran much in the artifice of clay. Hereof
the house of Mausolus was built, thus old Jupiter stood in the Capitol, and
the statua of Hercules, made in the reign of Tarquinius Priscus, was extant
in Pliny's days. And such as declined burning or funeral urns, affected coffins of clay, according to the mode of Pythagoras, a way preferred by Varro.
But the spirit of great ones was above these circumscriptions, affecting copper, silver, gold, and porphyry urns, wherein Severus lay, after a serious

view and sentence on that which should contain him. Some of these urns were thought to have been silvered over, from sparklings in several pots, with small tinsel parcels; uncertain whether from the earth, or the first mixture in them.

Among these urns we could obtain no good account of their coverings; only one seemed arched over with some kind of brickwork. Of those found at Buxton, some were covered with flints, some, in other parts, with tiles; those at Yarmouth Caster were closed with Roman bricks, and some have proper earthen covers adapted and fitted to them. But in the Homerical urn of Patroclus, whatever was the solid tegument, we find the immediate covering to be a purple piece of silk: and such as had no covers might have the earth closely pressed into them, after which disposure were probably some of these, wherein we found the bones and ashes half mortared unto the sand and sides of the urn, and some long roots of quich, or dog's-grass, wreathed about the bones.

No Lamps, included liquors, lacrymatories, or tear bottles, attended these rural urns, either as sacred unto the *manes,* or passionate expressions of their surviving friends. While with rich flames, and hired tears, they solemnized their obsequies, and in the most lamented monuments made one part of their inscriptions. Some find sepulchral vessels containing liquors, which time hath incrassated into jellies. For, besides these lacrymatories, notable lamps, with vessels of oils, and aromatical liquors, attended noble ossuaries; and some yet retaining a vinosity and spirit in them, which, if any have tasted, they have far exceeded the palates of antiquity. Liquors not to be computed by years of annual magistrates, but by great conjunctions and the fatal periods of kingdoms. The draughts of consulary date were but crude unto these, and Opimian wine but in the must unto them.

In sundry graves and sepulchres we meet with rings, coins, and chalices. Ancient frugality was so severe, that they allowed no gold to attend the corpse, but only that they allowed no gold to attend the corpse, but only that which served to fasten their teeth. Whether the Opaline stone in this were burnt upon the finger of the dead, or cast into the fire by some affectionate friend, it will consist with either custom. But other incinerable substances were found so fresh, that they could feel no singe from fire. These, upon view, were judged to be wood; but, sinking in water, and tried by the fire, we found them to be bone or ivory. In their hardness and yellow colour they most resembled box, which, in old expressions, found the epithet of eternal, and perhaps in such conservatories might have passed uncorrupted.

That bay leaves were found green in the tomb of S. Humbert, after an hundred and fifty years, was looked upon as miraculous. Remarkable it was unto old spectators, that the cypress of the temple of Diana lasted so many hundred years. The wood of the ark, and olive-rod of Aaron, were older at the captivity; but the cypress of the ark of Noah was the greatest vegetable of antiquity, if Josephus were not deceived by some fragments of it in his days: to omit the moor logs and fir trees found underground in many parts of England; the undated ruins of winds, floods, or earthquakes, and which in Flanders still show from what quarter they fell, as generally lying in a north-east position.

But though we found not these pieces to be wood, according to first apprehensions, yet we missed not altogether of some woody substance; for the bones were not so clearly picked but some coals were found amongst them; a way to make wood perpetual, and a fit associate for metal, whereon was laid the foundation of the great Ephesian temple, and which were made the lasting tests of old boundaries and landmarks. Whilst we look on these, we admire not observations of coals found fresh after four hundred years. In a long-deserted habitation even egg-shells have been found fresh, not tending to corruption.

In the monument of King Childerick the iron relicks were found all rusty and crumbling into pieces; but our little iron pins, which fastened the ivory works, held well together, and lost not their magnetical quality, though wanting a tenacious moisture for the firmer union of parts; although it be hardly drawn into fusion, yet that metal soon submitteth unto rust and dissolution. In the brazen pieces we admired not the duration, but the freedom from rust, and ill savour, upon the hardest attrition; but now exposed unto the piercing atoms of air, in the space of a few months, they begin to spot and betray their green entrails. We conceive not these urns to have descended thus naked as they appear, or to have entered their graves without the old habit of flowers. The urn of Philopoemen was so laden with flowers and ribbons, that it afforded no sight of itself. The rigid Lycurgus allowed olive and myrtle. The Athenians might fairly except against the practice of Democritus, to be buried up in honey, as fearing to embezzle a great commodity of their country, and the best of that kind in Europe. But Plato seemed too frugally politick, who allowed no larger monument than would contain four heroick verses, and designed the most barren ground for sepulture: though we cannot commend the goodness of that sepulchral ground which was set at no higher rate than the mean salary of Judas. Though the earth had confounded the ashes of these ossuaries, yet the bones were so smartly burnt, that some thin plates of brass were found half melted among them. Whereby we apprehend they were not of the meanest caresses, perfunctorily fired, as sometimes in military, and commonly in pestilence, burnings; or after the manner of abject corpses, huddled forth and carelessly burnt, without the Esquiline Port at Rome; which was an affront continued upon Tiberius, while they but half burnt his body, and in the amphitheatre, according to the custom in notable malefactors; whereas Nero seemed not so much to fear his death as that his head should be cut off and his body not burnt entire.

Some, finding many fragments of skulls in these urns, suspected a mixture of bones; in none we searched was there cause of such conjecture, though sometimes they declined not that practice.—The ashes of Domitian were mingled with those of Julia; of Achilles with those of Patroclus. All urns contained not single ashes; without confused burnings they affectionately compounded their bones; passionately endeavouring to continue their living unions. And when distance of death denied such conjunctions, unsatisfied affections conceived some satisfaction to be neighbours in the grave, to lie urn by urn, and touch but in their manes. And many were so curious to continue their living relations, that they contrived large and family urns, wherein the ashes of their nearest friends and kindred might successively be received, at least some parcels thereof, while their collateral memorials lay in minor vessels about them.

Antiquity held too light thoughts from objects of mortality, while some drew provocatives of mirth from anatomies, and jugglers showed tricks with skeletons. When fiddlers made not so pleasant mirth as fencers, and men could sit with quiet stomachs, while hanging was played before them. Old considerations made few mementos by skulls and bones upon their monuments. In the Egyptian obelisks and hieroglyphical figures it is not easy to meet with bones. The sepulchral lamps speak nothing less than sepulture, and in their literal draughts prove often obscene and antick pieces. Where we find *D. M.* it is obvious to meet with sacrificing *pateras* and vessels of libation upon old sepulchral monuments. In the Jewish hypogæum and subterranean cell at Rome, was little observable beside the variety of lamps and frequent draughts of Anthony and Jerome we meet with thigh-bones and death's-heads; but the cemeterial cells of ancient Christians and martyrs were filled with draughts of Scripture stories; not declining the flourishes of cypress, palms, and olive, and the mystical figures of peacocks, doves, and cocks; but iterately affecting the portraits of Enoch, Lazarus, Jonas, and the vision of Ezekiel, as hopeful draughts, and hinting imagery of the resurrection, which is the life of the grave, and sweetens our habitations in the land of moles and pismires.

Gentle inscriptions precisely delivered the extent of men's lives, seldom the manner of their deaths, which history itself so often leaves obscure in the records of memorable persons. There is scarce any philosopher but dies twice or thrice in Lærtius; nor almost any life without two or three deaths in Plutarch; which makes the tragical ends of noble persons more favourably resented by compassionate readers who find some relief in the election of such differences.

The certainty of death is attended with uncertainties, in time, manner, places. The variety of monuments hath often obscured true graves; and cenotaphs confounded sepulchres. For beside their real tombs, many have found honorary and empty sepulchres. The variety of Homer's monuments made him of various countries. Euripides had his tomb in Africa, but his sepulture in Macedonia. And Severus found his real sepulchre in Rome, but his empty grave in Gallia.

He that lay in a golden urn eminently above the earth, was not like to find the quiet of his bones. Many of these urns were broke by a vulgar discoverer in hope of enclosed treasure. The ashes of Marcellus were lost above ground, upon the like account. Where profit hath prompted, no age hath wanted such miners. For which the most barbarous expilators found the most civil rhetorick. Gold once out of the earth is no more due unto it; what was unreasonably committed to the ground, is reasonably resumed from it; let monuments and rich fabricks, not riches, adorn men's ashes. The commerce of the living is not to be transferred unto the dead; it is not injustice to take that which none complains to lose, and no man is wronged where no man is possessor.

What virtue yet sleeps in this *terra damnata* and aged cinders, were petty magic to experiment. These crumbling relicks and long fired particles superannuate such expectations; bones, hairs, nails, and teeth of the dead, were the treasures of old sorcerers. In vain we revive such practices; present superstition too visibly perpetuates the folly of our forefathers, wherein unto old observation this island was so complete, that it might have instructed Persia.

Plato's historian of the other world lies twelve days incorrupted, while his soul was viewing the large stations of the dead. How to keep the corpse seven days from corruption by anointing and washing, without extenteration, were an hazardable piece of art, in our choicest practice. How they made distinct separation of bones and ashes from fiery admixture, hath found no historical solution; though they seemed to make a distinct collection and overlooked not Pyrrhus his toe. Some provision they might make by fictile vessels, coverings, tiles, or flat stones, upon and about the body (and in the same field, not far from these urns, many stones were found underground), as also by careful separation of extraneous matter composing and raking up the burnt bones with forks, observable in that notable lamp of Galvanus Martianus, who had the sight of the *vas ustrinum* or vessel wherein they burnt the dead, found in the Esquiline field at Rome, might have afforded clearer solution. But their insatisfaction herein begat that remarkable invention in the funeral pyres of some princes, by incombustible sheets made with a texture of asbestos, incremable flax, or salamander's wool, which preserved their bones and ashes incommixed.

How the bulk of a man should sink into so few pounds of bones and ashes, may seem strange unto any who considers not its constitution, and how slender a mass will remain upon an open and urging fire of the carnal composition. Even bones themselves, reduced into ashes, do abate a notable proportion. And consisting much of a volatile salt, when that is fired out, make a light kind of cinders. Although their bulk be disproportionable to their weight, when the heavy principle of salt is fired out, and the earth almost only remaineth; observable in sallow, which makes more ashes than oak, and discovers the common fraud of selling ashes by measure, and not by ponderation.

Some bones make best skeletons, some bodies quick and speediest ashes. Who would expect a quick flame from hydropical Heraclitus? The poisoned soldier when his belly brake, put out two pyres in Plutarch. But in the plague of Athens, one private pyre served two or three intruders; and the Saracens burnt in large heaps, by the king of Castile, showed how little fuel sufficeth. Though the funeral pyre of Patroclus took up an hundred foot, a piece of an old boat burnt Pompey; and if the burthen of Isaac were sufficient for an holocaust, a man may carry his own pyre.

From animals are drawn good burning lights, and good medicines against burning. Though the seminal humour seems of a contrary nature to fire, yet the body completed proves a combustible lump, wherein fire finds flame even from bones, and some fuel almost from all parts; though the metropolis of humidity seems least disposed unto it, which might render the skulls of these urns less burned than other bones. But all flies or sinks before fire almost in all bodies: when the common ligament is dissolved, the attenuable parts ascend, the rest subside in coal, calx, or ashes.

To burn the bones of the king of Edom for lime, seems no irrational ferity; but to drink of the ashes of dead relations, a passionate prodigality. He that hath the ashes of his friend, hath an everlasting treasure; where fire taketh leave, corruption slowly enters. In bones well burnt, fire makes a wall against itself; experimented in Copels, and tests of metals, which consist of such ingredients. What the sun compoundeth, fire analyzeth, not transmuteth. That devouring agent leaves almost always a morsel for the earth, whereof all things are but a colony; and which, if time permits, the mother element will have in their primitive mass again.

He that looks for urns and old sepulchral relicks, must not seek them in the ruins of temples, where no religion anciently placed them. These were found in a field, according to ancient custom, in noble or private burial; the old practice of the Canaanites, the family of Abraham, and the burying-place of Joshua, in the borders of his possessions; and also agreeable unto Roman practice to bury by highways, whereby their monuments were under eye:—memorials of themselves, and mementoes of mortality unto living passengers; whom the epitaphs of great ones were fain to beg to stay and look upon them,—a language though sometimes used, not so proper in church inscriptions. The sensible rhetorick of the dead, to exemplarity of good life, first admitted to the bones of pious men and martyrs within church walls, which in succeeding ages crept into promiscuous practice: while Constantine was peculiarly favoured to be admitted into the church porch, and the first thus buried in England, was in the days of Cuthred.

Christians dispute how their bodies should lie in the grave. In urnal interment they clearly escaped this controversy. Though we decline the religious consideration, yet in cemeterial and narrower burying-places, to avoid confusion and cross-position, a certain posture were to be admitted: which even Pagan civility observed. The Persians lay north and south; the Megarians and Phoenicians placed their heads to the east; the Athenians, some think, towards the west, which Christians still retain. And Beda will have it to be the posture of our Saviour. That he was crucified with his face toward the west, we will not contend with tradition and probable account; but we applaud not the hand of the painter, in exalting his cross so high above those on either side: since hereof we find no authentic account in history, and even the crosses found by Helena, pretend no such distinction from longitude or dimension.

To be knav'd out of our graves, to have our skulls made drinking-bowls, and our bones turned into pipes, to delight and sport our enemies, are tragical abominations escaped in burning burials.

Urnal interments and burnt relicks lie not in fear of worms, or to be an heritage for serpents. In carnal sepulture, corruptions seem peculiar unto parts; and some speak of snakes out of the spinal marrow. But while we suppose common worms in graves, 'tis not easy to find any there; few in churchyards above a foot deep, fewer or none in churches though in fresh-decayed bodies. Teeth, bones, and hair, give the most lasting defiance to corruption. In an hydropical body, ten years buried in the churchyard, we met with a fat concretion, where the nitre of the earth, and the salt and lixivious liquor of the body, had coagulated large lumps of fat into the consistence of the hardest Castile soap, whereof part remaineth with us. After a battle with the Persians, the Roman corpses decayed in few days, while the Persian bodies remained dry and uncorrupted. Bodies in the same ground do not uniformly dissolve, nor bones equally moulder; whereof in the opprobrious disease, we expect no long duration. The body of the Marquis of Dorset seemed sound and handsomely cereclothed, that after seventy-eight years was found uncorrupted. Common tombs preserve not beyond powder: a firmer consistence and compage of parts might be expected from arefaction, deep burial, or charcoal. The greatest antiquities of mortal bodies may remain in putrefied bones, whereof, though we take not in the pillar of Lot's wife, or metamorphosis of Ortelius, some may be older than pyramids, in the putrefied relicks of the general inundation. When Alexander opened the tomb of Cyrus, the remaining bones discovered his proportion, whereof urnal fragments afford but a bad conjecture, and have this disadvantage of grave interments, that they leave us ignorant of most personal discoveries. For since bones afford not only rectitude and stability but figure unto the body, it is no impossible physiognomy to conjecture at fleshy appendencies, and after what shape the muscles and carnous parts might hang in their full consistencies. A full-spread *cariola* shows a well-shaped horse behind; handsome formed skulls give some analogy of fleshy resemblance. A critical view of bones makes a good distinction of sexes. Even colour is not beyond conjecture, since it is hard to be deceived in the distinction of the Negroes' skulls. Dante's characters are to be found in skulls as well as faces. Hercules is not only known by his foot. Other parts make out their comproportions and inferences upon whole or parts. And since the dimensions of the head measure the whole body, and the figure thereof gives conjecture of the principal faculties: physiognomy outlives ourselves, and ends not in our graves.

Severe contemplators, observing these lasting relicks, may think them good monuments of persons past, little advantage to future beings; and, considering that power which subdueth all things unto itself, that can resume the scattered atoms, or identify out of anything, conceive it superfluous to expect a resurrection out of relicks: but the soul subsisting, other matter, clothed with due accidents, may salve the individuality. Yet the saints, we observe, arose from graves and monuments about the holy city. Some think the ancient patriarchs so earnestly desired to lay their bones in Canaan, as hoping to make a part of that resurrection; and, though thirty miles from Mount Calvary, at least to lie in that region which should produce the first-fruits of the dead. And if, according to learned conjecture, the bodies of men shall rise where their greatest relicks remain, many are not like to err in the topography of their resurrection, though their bones or bodies be after translated by angels into the field of Ezekiel's vision, or as some will order it, into the valley of judgment, or Jehosaphat.

CHAPTER IV

Christians have handsomely glossed the deformity of death by careful consideration of the body, and civil rites which take off brutal terminations: and though they conceived all reparable by a resurrection, cast not off all care of interment. And since the ashes of sacrifices burnt upon the altar of God were carefully carried out by the priests, and deposed in a clean field; since they acknowledged their bodies to be the lodging of Christ, and temples of the Holy Ghost, they devolved not all upon the sufficiency of soul-existence; and therefore with long services and full solemnities, concluded their last exequies, wherein to all distinctions the Greek devotion seems most pathetically ceremonious.

Christian invention hath chiefly driven at rites, which speak hopes of another life, and hints of a resurrection. And if the ancient Gentiles held not the immortality of their better part, and some subsistence after death, in several rites, customs, actions, and expressions, they contradicted their own opinions: wherein Democritus went high, even to the thought of a resurrection, as scoffingly recorded by Pliny. What can be more express than the expression of Phocylides? Or who would expect from Lucretius a sentence of Ecclesiastes? Before Plato could speak, the soul had wings in Homer, which fell not, but flew out of the body into the mansions of the dead; who also observed that handsome distinction of Demas and Soma, for the body conjoined to the soul, and body separated from it. Lucian spoke much truth in jest, when he said that part of Hercules which proceeded from Alcmena perished, that from Jupiter remained immortal. Thus Socrates was content that his friends should bury his body, so they would not think they buried Socrates; and, regarding only his immortal part, was indifferent to be burnt or buried. From such considerations, Diogenes might contemn sepulture, and, being satisfied that the soul could not perish, grow careless of corporal interment. The Stoicks, who thought the souls of wise men had their habitation about the moon, might make slight account of subterraneous deposition; whereas the Pythagoreans and transcorporating philosophers, who were to be often buried, held great care of their interment. And the Platonicks rejected not a due care of the grave, though they put their ashes to unreasonable expectations, in their tedious term of return and long set revolution.

Men have lost their reason in nothing so much as their religion, wherein stones and clouts make martyrs; and, since the religion of one seems madness unto another, to afford an account or rational of old rites requires no rigid reader. That they kindled the pyre aversely, or turning their face from it, was an handsome symbol of unwilling ministration. That they washed their bones with wine and milk; that the mother wrapped them in linen, and dried them in her bosom, the first fostering part and place of their nourishment; that they opened their eyes toward heaven before they kindled the fire, as the place of their hopes or original, were no improper ceremonies. Their last valediction, thrice uttered by the attendants, was also very solemn, and somewhat answered by Christians, who thought it too little, if they threw not the earth thrice upon the interred body. That, in strewing their tombs, the Romans affected the rose; the Greeks amaranthus and myrtle: that the funeral pyre consisted of sweet fuel, cypress, fir, larix, yew, and trees perpetually verdant, lay silent expressions of their surviving hopes. Wherein Christians, who deck their coffins with bays, have found a more elegant emblem; for that it, seeming dead, will restore itself from the root, and its dry and exsuccous leaves resume their verdure again; which, if we mistake not, we have also observed in furze. Whether the planting of yew in churchyards hold not its original from ancient funeral rites, or as an emblem of resurrection, from its perpetual verdure, may also admit conjecture.

They made use of musick to excite or quiet the affections of their friends, according to different harmonies. But the secret and symbolical hint was the harmonical nature of the soul; which, delivered from the body, went again to enjoy the primitive harmony of heaven, from whence it first descended; which, according to its progress traced by antiquity, came down by Cancer, and ascended by Capricornus.

They burnt not children before their teeth appeared, as apprehending their bodies too tender a morsel for fire, and that their gristly bones would scarce leave separable relicks after the pyral combustion. That they kindled not fire in their houses for some days after was a strict memorial of the late afflicting fire. And mourning without hope, they had an happy fraud against excessive lamentation, by a common opinion that deep sorrows disturb their ghosts.

That they buried their dead on their backs, or in a supine position, seems agreeable unto profound sleep, and common posture of dying; contrary to the most natural way of birth; nor unlike our pendulous posture, in the doubtful state of the womb. Diogenes was singular, who preferred a prone situation in the grave; and some Christians like neither, who decline the figure of rest, and make choice of an erect posture.

That they carried them out of the world with their feet forward, not inconsonant unto reason, as contrary unto the native posture of man, and his production first into it; and also agreeable unto their opinions, while they bid adieu unto the world, not to look again upon it; whereas Mahometans who think to return to a delightful life again, are carried forth with their heads forward, and looking toward their houses.

They closed their eyes, as parts which first die, or first discover the sad effects of death. But their iterated clamations to excitate their dying or dead friends, or revoke them unto life again, was a vanity of affection; as not presumably ignorant of the critical tests of death, by apposition of feathers, glasses, and reflection of figures, which dead eyes represent not: which, however not strictly verifiable in fresh and warm *cadavers,* could hardly elude the test, in corpses of four or five days.

That they sucked in the last breath of their expiring friends, was surely a practice of no medical institution, but a loose opinion that the soul passed out that way, and a fondness of affection, from some Pythagorical foundation, that the spirit of one body passed into another, which they wished might be their own.

That they poured oil upon the pyre, was a tolerable practice, while the intention rested in facilitating the ascension. But to place good omens in the quick and speedy burning, to sacrifice unto the winds for a despatch in this office, was a low form of superstition.

The archimime, or jester, attending the funeral train, and imitating the speeches, gesture, and manners of the deceased, was too light for such solemnities, contradicting their funeral orations and doleful rites of the grave.

That they buried a piece of money with them as a fee of the Elysian ferryman, was a practice full of folly. But the ancient custom of placing coins in considerable urns, and the present practice of burying medals in the noble foundations of Europe, are laudable ways of historical discoveries, in actions, persons, chronologies; and posterity will applaud them.

We examine not the old laws of sepulture, exempting certain persons from burial or burning. But hereby we apprehend that these were not the bones of persons planet-struck or burnt with fire from heaven; no relicks of traitors to their country, self-killers, or sacrilegious malefactors; persons in old apprehension unworthy of the earth; condemned unto the Tartarus of hell, and bottomless pit of Pluto, from whence there was no redemption.

Nor were only many customs questionable in order to their obsequies, but also sundry practices, fictions, and conceptions, discordant or obscure, of their state and future beings. Whether unto eight or ten bodies of men to add one of a woman, as being more inflammable and unctuously constituted for the better pyral combustion, were any rational practice; or whether the complaint of Periander's wife be tolerable, that wanting her funeral burning, she suffered intolerable cold in hell, according to the constitution of the infernal house of Pluto, wherein cold makes a great part of their tortures; it cannot pass without some question.

Why the female ghosts appear unto Ulysses, before the heroes and masculine spirits,—why the Psyche or soul of Tiresias is of the masculine gender, who, being blind on earth, sees more than all the rest in hell; why the funeral suppers consisted of eggs, beans, smallage, and lettuce, since the dead are made to eat asphodels about the Elysian meadows:—why, since there is no sacrifice acceptable, nor any propitiation for the covenant of the grave, men set up the deity of Morta, and fruitlessly adored divinities without ears, it cannot escape some doubt.

The dead seem all alive in the human Hades of Homer, yet cannot well speak, prophecy, or know the living, except they drink blood, wherein is the life of man. And therefore the souls of Penelope's paramours, conducted by Mercury, chirped like bats, and those which followed Hercules, made a noise but like a flock of birds.

The departed spirits know things past and to come; yet are ignorant of things present. Agamemnon foretells what should happen unto Ulysses; yet ignorantly inquires what is become of his own son. The ghosts are afraid of swords in Homer; yet Sibylla tells Æneas in Virgil, the thin habit of spirits was beyond the force of weapons. The spirits put off their malice with their bodies, and Cæsar and Pompey accord in Latin hell; yet Ajax, in Homer, endures not a conference with Ulysses; and Deiphobus appears all mangled in Virgil's ghosts, yet we meet with perfect shadows among the wounded ghosts of Homer.

Since Charon in Lucian applauds his condition among the dead, whether it be handsomely said of Achilles, that living contemner of death, that he had rather be a ploughman's servant, than emperor of the dead? How Hercules his soul is in hell, and yet in heaven; and Julius his soul in a star, yet seen by Æneas in hell?—except the ghosts were but images and shadows of the soul, received in higher mansions, according to the ancient division of body, soul, and image, or *simulachrum* of them both. The particulars of future beings must needs be dark unto ancient theories, which Christian philosophy yet determines but in a cloud of opinions. A dialogue between two infants in the womb concerning the state of this world, might handsomely illustrate our ignorance of the next, whereof methinks we yet discourse in Pluto's den, and are but embryo philosophers.

Pythagoras escapes in the fabulous hell of Dante, among that swarm of philosophers, wherein, whilst we meet with Plato and Socrates, Cato is to be found in no lower place than purgatory. Among all the set, Epicurus is most considerable, whom men make honest without an Elysium, who contemned life without encouragement of immortality, and making nothing after death, yet made nothing of the king of terrors.

Were the happiness of the next world as closely apprehended as the felicities of this, it were a martyrdom to live; and unto such as consider none hereafter, it must be more than death to die, which makes us amazed at those audacities that durst be nothing and return into their chaos again. Certainly such spirits as could contemn death, when they expected no better being after, would have scorned to live, had they known any. And therefore we applaud not the judgment of Machiavel, that Christianity makes men cowards, or that with the confidence of but half-dying, the despised virtues of patience and humility have abased the spirits of men, which Pagan principles exalted; but rather regulated the wildness of audacities in the attempts, grounds, and eternal sequels of death; wherein men of the boldest spirits are often prodigiously temerarious. Nor can we extenuate the valour of ancient martyrs, who contemned death in the uncomfortable scene of their lives, and in their decrepit martyrdoms did probably lose not many months of their days, or parted with life when it was scarce worth the living. For (beside that long time past holds no consideration unto a slender time to come) they had no small disadvantage from the constitution of old age, which naturally makes men fearful, and complexionally superannuated from the bold and courageous thoughts of youth and fervent years. But the contempt of death from corporal animosity, promoteth not our felicity. They may sit in the orchestra, and noblest seats of heaven, who have held up shaking hands in the fire, and humanly contended for glory.

Meanwhile Epicurus lies deep in Dante's hell, wherein we meet with tombs enclosing souls which denied their immortalities. But whether the virtuous heathen, who lived better than he spake, or erring in the principles of himself, yet lived above philosophers of more specious maxims, lie so deep as he is placed, at least so low as not to rise against Christians, who believing or knowing that truth, have lastingly denied it in their practice and conversation—were a query too sad to insist on.

But all or most apprehensions rested in opinions of some future being, which, ignorantly or coldly believed, begat those perverted conceptions, ceremonies, sayings, which Christians pity or laugh at. Happy are they

which live not in that disadvantage of time, when men could say little
for futurity, but from reason: whereby the noblest minds fell often upon
doubtful deaths, and melancholy dissolutions. With these hopes, Socrates
warmed his doubtful spirits against that cold potion; and Cato, before he
durst give the fatal stroke, spent part of the night in reading the Immortality
of Plato, thereby confirming his wavering hand unto the animosity of that
attempt.

It is the heaviest stone that melancholy can throw at a man, to tell him
he is at the end of his nature; or that there is no further state to come, unto
which this seems progressional, and otherwise made in vain. Without this
accomplishment, the natural expectation and desire of such a state, were
but a fallacy in nature; unsatisfied considerators would quarrel the justice of
their constitutions, and rest content that Adam had fallen lower; whereby,
by knowing no other original, and deeper ignorance of themselves, they
might have enjoyed the happiness of inferior creatures, who in tranquillity
possess their constitutions, as having not the apprehension to deplore their
own natures, and, being framed below the circumference of these hopes,
or cognition of better being, the wisdom of God hath necessitated their
contentment: but the superior ingredient and obscured part of ourselves,
whereto all present felicities afford no resting contentment, will be able at
last to tell us, we are more than our present selves, and evacuate such hopes
in the fruition of their own accomplishments.

CHAPTER V

Now since these dead bones have already outlasted the living ones of
Methuselah, and in a yard underground, and thin walls of clay, outworn
all the strong and specious buildings above it; and quietly rested under the
drums and tramplings of three conquests: what prince can promise such
diuturnity unto his relicks, or might not gladly say,

> *Sic ego componi versus in ossa velim?*

Time, which antiquates antiquities, and hath an art to make dust of all
things, hath yet spared these minor monuments.

In vain we hope to be known by open and visible conservatories, when
to be unknown was the means of their continuation, and obscurity their

protection. If they died by violent hands, and were thrust into their urns, these bones become considerable, and some old philosophers would honour them, whose souls they conceived most pure, which were thus snatched from their bodies, and to retain a stronger propension unto them; whereas they weariedly left a languishing corpse and with faint desires of re-union. If they fell by long and aged decay, yet wrapt up in the bundle of time, they fall into indistinction, and make but one blot with infants. If we begin to die when we live, and long life be but a prolongation of death, our life is a sad composition; we live with death, and die not in a moment. How many pulses made up the life of Methuselah, were work for Archimedes: common counters sum up the life of Moses his man. Our days become considerable, like petty sums, by minute accumulations: where numerous fractions make up but small round numbers; and our days of a span long, make not one little finger.

If the nearness of our last necessity brought a nearer conformity into it, there were a happiness in hoary hairs, and no calamity in half-senses. But the long habit of living indisposeth us for dying; when avarice makes us the sport of death, when even David grew politickly cruel, and Solomon could hardly be said to be the wisest of men. But many are too early old, and before the date of age. Adversity stretcheth our days, misery makes Alcmena's nights, and time hath no wings unto it. But the most tedious being is that which can unwish itself, content to be nothing, or never to have been, which was beyond the malcontent of Job, who cursed not the day of his life, but his nativity; content to have so far been, as to have a title to future being, although he had lived here but in an hidden state of life, and as it were an abortion.

What song the Syrens sang, or what name Achilles assumed when he hid himself among women, though puzzling questions, are not beyond all conjecture. What time the persons of these ossuaries entered the famous nations of the dead, and slept with princes and counsellors, might admit a wide solution. But who were the proprietaries of these bones, or what bodies these ashes made up, were a question above antiquarism; not to be resolved by man, nor easily perhaps by spirits, except we consult the provincial guardians, or tutelary observators. Had they made as good provision for their names, as they have done for their relicks, they had not so grossly erred in the art of perpetuation. But to subsist in bones, and be but pyramidally extant, is a fallacy in duration. Vain ashes which in the oblivion of names, persons, times, and sexes, have found unto themselves a fruitless continuation, and only arise unto late posterity, as emblems of mortal vanities, antidotes against pride, vain-glory, and madding vices. Pagan vain-glories which thought the world might last for ever, had encouragement for ambition; and, finding no *atropos* unto the immortality of their names, were never dampt with the necessity of oblivion. Even old ambitions had the advantage of ours, in the attempts of their vain-glories, who acting early, and before the probable meridian of time, have by this time found great accomplishment of their designs, whereby the ancient heroes have already outlasted their monuments and mechanical preservations. But in this latter scene of time, we cannot expect such mummies unto our memories, when ambition may fear the prophecy of Elias, and Charles the Fifth can never hope to live within two Methuselahs of Hector.

And therefore, restless inquietude for the diuturnity of our memories unto the present considerations seems a vanity almost out of date, and super-annuated piece of folly. We cannot hope to live so long in our names, as some have done in their persons. One face of Janus holds no proportion unto the other. 'Tis too late to be ambitious. The great mutations of the world are acted, or time may be too short for our designs. To extend our memories by monuments, whose death we daily pray for, and whose duration we cannot hope, without injury to our expectations in the advent of the last day, were a contradiction to our beliefs. We whose generations are ordained in this setting part of time, are providentially taken off from such imaginations; and, being necessitated to eye the remaining particle of futurity, are naturally constituted unto thoughts of the next world, and cannot excusably decline the consideration of that duration, which maketh pyramids pillars of snow, and all that's past a moment.

Circles and right lines limit and close all bodies, and the mortal right-lined circle must conclude and shut up all. There is no antidote against the opium of time, which temporally considereth all things: our fathers find their graves in our short memories, and sadly tell us how we may be buried in our survivors. Gravestones tell truth scarce forty years. Generations pass while some trees stand, and old families last not three oaks. To be read by bare inscriptions like many in Gruter, to hope for eternity by enigmatical epithets or first letters of our names, to be studied by antiquaries, who we were, and have new names given us like many of the mummies, are cold consolations unto the students of perpetuity, even by everlasting languages.

To be content that times to come should only know there was such a man, not caring whether they knew more of him, was a frigid ambition in Cardan; disparaging his horoscopal inclination and judgment of himself. Who cares to subsist like Hippocrates's patients, or Achilles's horses in Homer, under naked nominations, without deserts and noble acts, which are the balsam of our memories, the *entelechia* and soul of our subsistences? To be nameless in worthy deeds, exceeds an infamous history. The Canaanitish woman lives more happily without a name, than Herodias with one. And who had not rather have been the good thief, than Pilate?

But the iniquity of oblivion blindly scattereth her poppy, and deals with the memory of men without distinction to merit of perpetuity. Who can but pity the founder of the pyramids? Herostratus lives that burnt the temple of Diana, he is almost lost that built it. Time hath spared the epitaph of Adrian's horse, confounded that of himself. In vain we compute our felicities by the advantage of our good names, since bad have equal durations, and Thersites is like to live as long as Agamemnon without the favour of the everlasting register. Who knows whether the best of men be known, or whether there be not more remarkable persons forgot, than any that stand remembered in the known account of time? The first man had been as unknown as the last, and Methuselah's long life had been his only chronicle.

Oblivion is not to be hired. The greater part must be content to be as though they had not been, to be found in the register of God, not in the record of man. Twenty-seven names make up the first story and the recorded names ever since contain not one living century. The number of the dead long exceedeth all that shall live. The night of time far surpasseth the day, and who knows when was the equinox? Every hour adds unto that current arithmetick, which scarce stands one moment. And since death must be the *Lucina* of life, and even Pagans could doubt, whether thus to live were to die; since our longest sun sets at right descensions, and makes but winter arches, and therefore it cannot be long before we lie down in darkness, and have our light in ashes; since the brother of death daily haunts us with dying mementoes, and time that grows old in itself, bids us hope no long duration;—diuturnity is a dream and folly of expectation.

Darkness and light divide the course of time, and oblivion shares with memory a great part even of our living beings; we slightly remember our felicities, and the smartest strokes of affliction leave but short smart upon us. Sense endureth no extremities, and sorrows destroy us or themselves. To weep into stones are fables. Afflictions induce callosities; miseries are slippery, or fall like snow upon us, which notwithstanding is no unhappy stupidity. To be ignorant of evils to come, and forgetful of evils past, is a merciful provision in nature, whereby we digest the mixture of our few and evil days, and, our delivered senses not relapsing into cutting remembrances, our sorrows are not kept raw by the edge of repetitions. A great part of antiquity contented their hopes of subsistency with a transmigration of their souls,—a good way to continue their memories, while having the advantage of plural successions, they could not but act something remarkable in such variety of beings, and enjoying the fame of their passed selves, make accumulation of glory unto their last durations. Others, rather than be lost in the uncomfortable night of nothing, were content to recede into the common being, and make one particle of the public soul of all things, which was no more than to return into their unknown and divine original again. Egyptian ingenuity was more unsatisfied, contriving their bodies in sweet consistences, to attend the return of their souls. But all is vanity, feeding the wind, and folly. Egyptian mummies, which Cambyses or time hath spared, avarice now consumeth. Mummy is become merchandise, Mizraim, cures wounds, and Pharaoh is sold for balsams.

In vain do individuals hope for immortality, or any patent from oblivion, in preservations below the moon; men have been deceived even in their flatteries, above the sun, and studied conceits to perpetuate their names in heaven. The various cosmography of that part hath already varied the names of contrived constellations; Nimrod is lost in Orion, and Osyris in the Dog-star. While we look for incorruption in the heavens, we find that they are but like the earth;—durable in their main bodies, alterable in their parts; whereof, beside comets and new stars, perspectives begin to tell tales, and the spots that wander about the sun, with Phæton's favour, would make clear conviction.

There is nothing strictly immortal, but immortality. Whatever hath no beginning, may be confident of no end;—all others have a dependent being and within the reach of destruction;—which is the peculiar of that necessary essence that cannot destroy itself;—and the highest strain of omnipotency, to be so powerfully constituted as not to suffer even from the power of itself. But the sufficiency of Christian immortality frustrates all earthly glory, and the quality of either state after death, makes a folly of posthumous memory. God who can only destroy our souls, and hath assured our resurrection, either of our bodies or names hath directly promised no duration. Wherein there is so much of chance, that the boldest expectants have found unhappy frustration; and to hold long subsistence, seems but a scape in oblivion. But man is a noble animal, splendid in ashes, and pompous in the grave, solemnizing nativities and deaths with equal lustre, nor omitting ceremonies of bravery in the infamy of his nature.

Life is a pure flame, and we live by an invisible sun within us. A small fire sufficeth for life, great flames seemed too little after death, while men vainly affected precious pyres, and to burn like Sardanapalus; but the wisdom of funeral laws found the folly of prodigal blazes and reduced undoing fires unto the rule of sober obsequies, wherein few could be so mean as not to provide wood, pitch, a mourner, and an urn.

Five languages secured not the epitaph of Gordianus. The man of God lives longer without a tomb than any by one, invisibly interred by angels, and adjudged to obscurity, though not without some marks directing human discovery. Enoch and Elias, without either tomb or burial, in an anomalous state of being, are the great examples of perpetuity, in their long and living memory, in strict account being still on this side death, and having a late part yet to act upon this stage of earth. If in the decretory term of the world we shall not all die but be changed, according to received translation, the last day will make but few graves; at least quick resurrections will anticipate lasting sepultures. Some graves will be opened before they be quite closed, and Lazarus be no wonder. When many that feared to die, shall groan that they can die but once, the dismal state is the second and living death, when life puts despair on the damned; when men shall wish the coverings of mountains, not of monuments, and annihilations shall be courted.

While some have studied monuments, others have studiously declined them, and some have been so vainly boisterous, that they durst not acknowledge their graves; wherein Alaricus seems most subtle, who had a river turned to hide his bones at the bottom. Even Sylla, that thought himself safe in his urn, could not prevent revenging tongues, and stones thrown at his monument. Happy are they whom privacy makes innocent, who deal so with men in this world, that they are not afraid to meet them in the next; who, when they die, make no commotion among the dead, and are not touched with that poetical taunt of Isaiah.

Pyramids, arches, obelisks, were but the irregularities of vain-glory, and wild enormities of ancient magnanimity. But the most magnanimous resolution rests in the Christian religion, which trampleth upon pride and sits on the neck of ambition, humbly pursuing that infallible perpetuity, unto which all others must diminish their diameters, and be poorly seen in angles of contingency.

Pious spirits who passed their days in raptures of futurity, made little more of this world, than the world that was before it, while they lay obscure in the chaos of pre-ordination, and night of their fore-beings. And if any have been so happy as truly to understand Christian annihilation, ecstasies, exolution, liquefaction, transformation, the kiss of the spouse, gustation of God, and ingression into the divine shadow, they have already had an handsome anticipation of heaven; the glory of the world is surely over, and the earth in ashes unto them.

To subsist in lasting monuments, to live in their productions, to exist in their names and predicament of chimeras, was large satisfaction unto old expectations, and made one part of their Elysiums. But all this is nothing in the metaphysicks of true belief. To live indeed, is to be again ourselves, which being not only an hope but an evidence in noble believers, 'tis all one to lie in St Innocent's church-yard as in the sands of Egypt. Ready to be anything, in the ecstasy of being ever, and as content with six foot as the *moles* of Adrianus.

1 6 9 2

Japan

In English, the term *memoir* comes directly from the French for "memory," *mémoire,* a word that is derived from the Latin for the same, *memoria.* It is a word that seems to be so stable that when Julius Caesar's contemporaries refer to his first book as "the best memoirs available on how to live a moral life," we're pretty sure we know what they mean. Indeed, when used in reference to a book these days the term still suggests a document of instructional memory: remembrances of something that one has survived, overcome, and now can refer to confidently as evidence of one's triumphs. A contemporary memoir is not experience that is rendered anew—as in the lyric tradition—nor observed—as in the narrative tradition—but experience that's framed educationally, something so harmlessly distant that it is now merely an anecdote. And yet, more deeply rooted in the word *memoir* is a far less confident one. Embedded in Latin's *memoria* is the ancient Greek *mérmeros,* an offshoot of the Avestic Persian *mermara,* itself a derivative of the Indo-European for that which we think about but cannot grasp: *mer-mer,* "to vividly wonder," "to be anxious," "to exhaustingly ponder." In this darker light of human language, the term suggests a literary form that is much less confident than the effortlessly relayed experiences in today's novelistic memoirs. Instead, according to its roots, a memoir is an instinctual essaying of ideas, images, and feelings. It is, in its best sense, an impulsive exploration. It is not storytelling. It is not moralizing. It is not theorizing, learning, or knowing. Etymologically speaking, at the core of this form is a world of emotional doubt. This year, in America, twenty men and women are hanged for being witches. An earthquake submerges a quarter of Jamaica. And in a province beside the sea, on the east coast of Japan, a small grass hut mysteriously catches fire, from which there slowly emerges a forty-five-year-old man who immediately begins a five-year-long journey by foot, composing along the way a text that someone claims is "a memoir sung through the soul of Japan itself."

MATSUO BASHŌ

Narrow Road to the Interior

The moon and sun are eternal travelers. Even the years wander on. A lifetime adrift in a boat, or in old age leading a tired horse into the years, every day is a journey, and the journey itself is home. From the earliest times there have always been some who perished along the road. Still I have always been drawn by windblown clouds into dreams of a lifetime of wandering. Coming home from a year's walking tour of the coast last autumn, I swept the cobwebs from my hut on the banks of the Sumida just in time for New Year, but by the time spring mists began to rise from the fields, I longed to cross the Shirakawa Barrier into the Northern Interior. Drawn by the wanderer-spirit Dōsojin, I couldn't concentrate on things. Mending my cotton pants, sewing a new strap on my bamboo hat, I daydreamed. Rubbing moxa into my legs to strengthen them, I dreamed a bright moon rising over Matsushima. So I placed my house in another's hands and moved to my patron Mr. Sampū's summer house in preparation for my journey. And I left a verse by my door:

Even this grass hut
may be transformed
into a doll's house

◦ ◦

Very early on the twenty-seventh morning of the third moon, under a predawn haze, transparent moon still visible, Mount Fuji just a shadow, I set out under the cherry blossoms of Ueno and Yanaka. When would I see them again? A few old friends had gathered in the night and followed along far enough to see me off from the boat. Getting off at Senju, I felt three thousand miles rushing through my heart, the whole world only a dream. I saw it through farewell tears.

> *Spring passes*
> *and the birds cry out—*
> *tears in the eyes of fishes*

With these first words from my brush, I started. Those who remain behind watch the shadow of a traveler's back disappear.

◀ ▶

The second year of Genroku, I think of the long way leading into the Northern Interior under Go stone skies. My hair may turn white as frost before I return from those fabled places—or maybe I won't return at all. By nightfall, we come to Sōka, bony shoulders sore from heavy pack, grateful for warm night robe, cotton bathing gown, writing brush, ink stone, necessities. The pack made heavier by farewell gifts from friends. I couldn't leave them behind. *very strong sentimental value— represents his friends?*

◀ ▶

Continuing on to the shrine at Muro-no-Yashima, my companion Sora said, "This deity, Ko-no-hana Sakuya Hime, is Goddess of Blossoming Trees and also has a shrine at Fuji. She locked herself inside a fire to prove her son's divinity. Thus her son was called Prince Hohodemi—Born-of-Fire—here in Burning Cell. And that's why poets here write of smoke, and why the locals despise the splotched *konoshiro* fish that reeks like burning flesh. Everyone here knows the story."

◀ ▶

The last night of the third moon, an inn at the foot of Mount Nikkō. The innkeeper is called Hoteke Gozaemon—Joe Buddha. He says his honesty earned him the name and invites me to make myself at home. A merciful buddha like an ordinary man, he suddenly appeared to help a pilgrim along his way. His simplicity's a great gift, his sincerity unaffected. A model of Confucian rectitude, my host is a saint.

◀ ▶

On the first day of the fourth moon, climbed to visit the shrines on a mountain once called Two Wildernesses, renamed by Kūkai when he dedicated the shrine. Perhaps he saw a thousand years into the future, this shrine under sacred skies, his compassion endlessly scattered through the eight directions, falling equally, peaceably, on all four classes of people. The greater the glory, the less these words can say.

hard to condense the greatness of the story

> *Speechless before*
> *these budding green spring leaves*
> *in blazing sunlight*

◀ ▶

Mount Kurokami still clothed in snow, faint in the mist, Sora wrote:

> *Head shaven*
> *at Black Hair Mountain*
> *we change into summer clothes*

Sora was named Kawai Sōgorō; Sora's his nom de plume. At my old home—called Bashō (plantain tree)—he carried water and wood. Anticipating the pleasures of seeing Matsushima and Kisagata, we agreed to share the journey, pleasure and hardship alike. The morning we started, he put on Buddhist robes, shaved his head, and changed his name to Sogo, the Enlightened. So the "changing clothes" in his poem is pregnant with meaning.

A hundred yards uphill, the waterfall plunged a hundred feet from its cavern in the ridge, falling into a basin made by a thousand stones. Crouched in the cavern behind the falls, looking out, I understood why it's called Urami-no-Taki, "View-from-behind-Falls."

> *Stopped awhile*
> *inside a waterfall:*
> *the summer begins*

◀ ▶

A friend lives in Kurobane on the far side of the broad Nasu Moor. Tried a shortcut running straight through, but it began to rain in the early evening,

so we stopped for the night at a village farmhouse and continued again at
dawn. Out in the field, a horse, and nearby a man cutting grass. I stopped to
ask directions. Courteous, he thought awhile, then said, "Too many inter-
secting roads. It's easy to get lost. Best to take that old horse as far as he'll go.
He knows the road. When he stops, get off, and he'll come back alone."

Two small children danced along behind, one with the curious name of
Kasane, same as the pink flower. Sora wrote:

> With this kasane
> she's doubly pink
> a fitting name

Arriving at a village, I tied a small gift to the saddle and the horse turned
back.

◆ ◗

Once in Kurobane I visited the powerful samurai Jōbōji, overseer of the
manor. Surprised by the visit, he kept me up talking through several days and
nights, often at the home of his brother Tōsui. We visited their relatives and
friends. One day we walked out to Inu oumono, Dog-shooting Grounds. We
walked out into the moors to find the tomb of Lady Tamamo, who turned
herself to stone. We paid homage at Hachiman Shrine, where Yoshitsune's
general Yoichi shot a fan from a passing boat after praying to Shō-hachiman,
warrior-god of this shrine. At dusk we returned to Tōsui's home.

Invited to visit Shūgen Kōmyō Temple's hall for mountain monks:

> In summer mountains
> bow to holy high water clogs
> bless this long journey

◆ ◗

In a mountain hermitage near Ungan Temple, my dharma master Butchō
wrote:

> A five-foot thatched hut:
> I wouldn't even put it up
> but for the falling rain

He inscribed the poem on a rock with charcoal—he told me long ago. Curious, several young people joined in, walking sticks pointed toward Ungan Temple. We were so caught up in talking we arrived at the temple unexpectedly. Through the long valley, under dense cedar and pine with dripping moss, below a cold spring sky—through the viewing gardens, we crossed a bridge and entered the temple gate.

I searched out back for Butchō's hermitage and found it up the hill, near a cave on a rocky ridge—like the cave where Myōzenji lived for fifteen years, like Zen master Hōun's retreat.

> *Even woodpeckers leave it alone:*
> *a hermitage*
> *in a summer grove*

[handwritten:] ? . I want to know more]

One small poem, quickly written, pinned to a post.

◀ ▶

Set out to see the Murder Stone, Sesshō-seki, on a borrowed horse, and the man leading it asked for a poem, "Something beautiful, please."

> *The horse lifts his head:*
> *from across deep fields*
> *the cuckoo's cry*

[handwritten: to balance the ugliness to come]

Sesshō-seki lies in dark mountain shadow near a hot springs emitting bad gases. Dead bees and butterflies cover the sand.

◀ ▶

At Ashino, the willow Saigyō praised, "beside the crystal stream," still grows along a path in fields of rice. A local official had offered to lead the way, and I had often wondered whether and where it remained. And now, today, that same willow:

> *Girls' rice-planting done*
> *they depart:*
> *I emerge from willow-shade*

◀ ▶

A little anxious, thinking of the Shirakawa Barrier, thinking on it day by day, but calmed my mind by remembering the old poem, "somehow sending word home." I walked through heavy green summer forests. Many a poet inscribed a few words at one of the Three Barriers—"autumn winds" and "red maple leaves" come to mind. Then, like fields of snow, innumerable white-flowered bushes, *unohana,* covered either side of the road. Here, Kiyosuke wrote, people dressed their very best to pass through the mountain gate, men in small black formal hats as though dressed for the highest courts. Sora wrote:

> Unohana
> *around my head*
> *dressed for ancient rites*

◁ ▷

Over the pass, we crossed the Abukuma River, Mount Aizu to the left, the villages of Iwaki, Sōma, and Miharu on the right, divided from the villages of Hitachi and Shimotsuke by two small mountain ranges. At Kagenuma, the Mirror Pond, a dark sky blurred every reflection.

We spent several days in Sukagawa with the poet Tōkyū, who asked about the Shirakawa Barrier. "With mind and body sorely tested," I answered, "busy with other poets' lines, engaged in splendid scenery, it's hardly surprising I didn't write much":

> *Culture's beginnings:*
> *from the heart of the country*
> *rice-planting songs*

"From this opening verse," I told him, "we wrote three linked-verse poems."

◁ ▷

In the shade of a huge chestnut at the edge of town, a monk made his hermitage a refuge from the world. Saigyō's poem about gathering chestnuts deep in the mountains refers to such a place. I wrote on a slip of paper: The Chinese character for *chestnut* means "west tree," alluding to the Western

Paradise of Amida Buddha; the priest Gyōki, all his life, used chestnut for his walking stick and for the posts of his home.

> *Near the eaves*
> *the chestnut blooms:*
> *almost no one sees*

( )

Walked a few miles from Tōkyū's home to the town of Hiwada in the foot-hills of Mount Asaka. Marshlands glistened outside of town. Almost mid-summer, iris-picking time. I asked about blossoming *katsumi*, but no one knew where they grew. I searched all day, muttering, *"Katsumi, katsumi,"* until the sun set over the mountains.

We followed a road to the right at Nihonmatsu and stopped to see Kurozuka Cave. And stayed the night in Fukushima.

( )

At dawn we left for Shinobu, famous for dyed cloth—called *shinobu-zuri*—named after the rock we found half buried in the mountain. Village children joined us and explained, "In the old days, the rock was on top of the mountain, but visitors trampled farmers' crops, the old men rolled it down." Their story made perfect sense.

> *Girls' busy hands plant rice*
> *almost like*
> *the ancient ones making dye.*

( )

Crossed on the ferry at Tsukinowa to the post town of Se-no-ue to see the ruins that were Satō Shōji's house, beyond town to the left, near the moun-tains. We were told to look at Saba Moor in Iizuka, and we eventually came to Maru Hill, where the castle ruins lay. Seeing the main gate sundered, the ancient temple nearby, seeing all the family graves, tears glazed my eyes. Especially at the tombs of two young widows who had dressed in the armor of fallen sons and then lay down their lives. Like Tu Yu at Weeping Grave-mound, I dried my eyes with a sleeve. Inside the temple, enjoying tea,

Yoshitsune's great long sword and the priest Benkei's little Buddhist wicker chest, both enshrined.

> *Sword, chest, and wind-carp*
> *all proudly displayed*
> *on Boys' Festival Day*

It was the first of Satsuki, rice-planting month.

( )

Staying the night in Iizuka, we bathed in a mineral hot springs before returning to thin straw sleeping mats on bare ground—a true country inn. Without a lamp, we made our beds by firelight, in flickering shadows, and closed our tired eyes. Suddenly a thunderous downpour and leaky roof aroused us, fleas and mosquitoes everywhere. Old infirmities tortured me throughout the long, sleepless night.

At first light, long before dawn, we packed our things and left, distracted, tired, but moving on. Sick and worried, we hired horses to ride to the town of Kori. I worried about my plans. With every pilgrimage one encounters the temporality of life. To die along the road is destiny. Or so I told myself. I stiffened my will and, once resolute, crossed Ōkido Barrier in Date Province.

( )

Though narrow Abumizuri Pass and on, passing Shiroishi Castle, we entered Kasashima Province. We asked for directions to the gravemound of Lord Sanekata, Sei Shonagon's exiled poet-lover, and were told to turn right on the hills near the villages of Minowa and Kasashima when we came to the Shrine of Dōsojin. It lies nearly hidden in sedge grass Saigyō remembered in a poem. May rains turned the trail to mud. We stopped, sick and worn out, and looked at the two aptly named villages in the distance: Straw Raincoat Village and Umbrella Island.

> *Where's Kasashima?*
> *Lost on a muddy road*
> *in the rainy season*

The night was spent in Iwanuma.

◦ ◦

Deeply touched by the famous pine at Takekuma, twin trunks just as long ago. The poet-priest Nōin came to mind. Before he came, Lord Fujiwara-no-Takayoshi cut down the tree for lumber, building a bridge across the Natorigawa. Nōin wrote: "No sign here now of that famous pine." Reported to have been cut down and replaced several times, it stood like a relic of a thousand years, impossibly perfect. The poet Kyohaku had given me a poem at my departure:

> *Remember to show my master*
> *the famous Takekuma pine,*
> *O northern blossoming cherries*

To which I now reply:

> *Ever since cherry blossom time*
> *I longed to visit two-trunked pine:*
> *three long months have passed*

◦ ◦

We crossed over the Natorigawa on the seventh day, fifth moon, and entered Sendai on the day we tie blue iris to the eaves and pray for health. We found an inn and decided to spend several days. I'd heard of a painter here, Kaemon, who was a kindred spirit and had visited all the nearby places the poets had made famous. Before him, these places were all but forgotten. He agreed to be our guide. The fields at Miyagi were carpeted with bush clover that would bloom in autumn. In Tamada and Yokono and at Azalea Hill there were andromeda flowers in bloom. Passing through pine woods sunlight couldn't penetrate, we came to Kinoshita, the "Under Woods" where the poet in the *Kokinshū* begged an umbrella for his lord in falling dew. We visited Yakushido Shrine and the Shrine of Tenjin until the sun went down. Later the painter gave us drawings of Matsushima and Shiogama. And two pairs of new straw sandals with iris-blue straps—*hanamuke,* farewell gifts. He was a truly kindred spirit.

Significance of gifts in Japanese culture?

To have blue irises
blooming on one's feet:
walking-sandal straps

◀ ▶

Checking Kaemon's drawings as we walked, we followed the *oku-no-hosomichi* along the mountainside where sedge grass grew tall in bunches. The Tofu area is famous for its sedge mats, sent in tribute to the governor each year.

At Taga Castle we found the most ancient monument Tsubo-no-ishibumi, in Ichikawa Village. It's about six feet high and three feet wide. We struggled to read the inscription under heavy moss:

> This Castle was Built by Shogun Ono-no-Azumabito in 724.
> In 762, His Majesty's Commanding General, Emi-no-Asakari,
> Supervised Repairs.

Dated from the time of Emperor Shōmu, Tsubo-no-ishibumi inspired many a poet. Floods and landslides buried trails and markers, trees have grown and died, making this monument very difficult to find. The past remains hidden in clouds of memory. Still it returned us to memories from a thousand years before. Such a moment is the reason for a pilgrimage: infirmities forgotten, the ancients remembered, joyous tears trembled in my eyes.

◀ ▶

We stopped along the Tama River at Noda, and at the huge stone in the lake, Oki-no-ishi, both made famous in poems. On Mount Sue-no-matsu, we found a temple called Masshozan. There were graves everywhere among the pines, underscoring Po Chu-i's famous lines quoted in *The Tale of Genji*, "wing and wing, branch and branch," and I thought, "Yes, what we all must come to," my sadness heavy.

At Shiogama Beach, a bell sounded evening. The summer rain-sky cleared to reveal a pale moon high over Magaki Island. I remembered the "fishing boats pulling together" in a *Kokinshū* poem, and understood it clearly for the first time.

Along the Michinoku
every place is wonderful,
but in Shiogama
fishing boats pulling together
are most amazing of all

That night we were entertained by a blind singer playing a lute to boisterous back-country ballads one hears only deep inside the country, not like
the songs in *The Tale of the Heike* or the dance songs. A real earful, but
pleased to hear the tradition continued.

focus on appreciation of the past & tradition

Rose at dawn to pay respects at Myōjin Shrine in Shiogama. The former
governor rebuilt it with huge, stately pillars, bright-painted rafters, and a
long stone walkway rising steeply under a morning sun that danced and
flashed along the red lacquered fence. I thought, "As long as the road is,
even if it ends in dust, the gods come with us, keeping a watchful eye. This
is our culture's greatest gift." Kneeling at the shrine, I noticed a fine old
lantern with this inscribed on its iron grate:

In the Third Year of the Bunji Era
Dedicated by Izumi Saburō

Suddenly, five long centuries passed before my eyes. A trusted, loyal man
martyred by his brother; today there's not a man alive who doesn't re-
vere his name. As he himself would say, a man must follow the Confucian
model—renown will inevitably result.

Sun high overhead before we left the shrine, we hired a boat to cross to
Matsushima, a mile or more away. We disembarked on Ojima Beach.

As many others often observed, the views of Matsushima take one's
breath away. It may be—along with Lake Tung-t'ing and West Lake in
China—the most beautiful place in the world. Islands in a three-mile bay,
the sea to the southeast entering like floodtide on the Ch'ien-t'ang River
in Chekiang. Small islands, tall islands pointing at the sky, islands on top

" mother nature "

of islands, islands like mothers with baby islands on their backs, islands cradling islands in the bay. All covered with deep green pines shaped by salty winds, trained into sea-wind bonsai. Here one is almost overcome by the sense of intense feminine beauty in a shining world. It must have been the mountain god Ōyamazumi who made this place. And whose words or brush could adequately describe a world so divinely inspired?

◦

Ojima Beach is not—as its name implies—an island, but a strand projected into the bay. Here one finds the ruins of Ungo Zenji's hermitage and the rock where he sat *zazen*. And still a few tiny thatched huts under pines where religious hermits live in tranquillity. Smoke of burning leaves and pine cones drew me on, touching something deep inside. Then the moon rose, shining on the sea, day turned suddenly to night. We stayed at an inn on the shore, our second-story windows opening on the bay. Drifting with winds and clouds, it was almost like a dream. Sora wrote:

> *In Matsushima*
> *you'll need the wings of a crane*
> *little cuckoo*

I was speechless and tried to sleep, but rose to dig from my pack a Chinese-style poem my friend Sodō had written for me, something about Pine Islands. And also a *waka* by Hara Anteki, and haiku by Sampu and Dakushi.

◦

On the eleventh day, fifth moon, we visited Zuigan Temple and were met by the thirty-second-generation descendant of the founder. Established by Makabe-no-Heishiro at the time he returned from religious studies in T'ang China, the temple was enlarged under Ungo Zenji into seven main structures with new blue tile roofs, walls of gold, a jeweled Buddha-land. But my mind wandered, wondering if the priest Kembutsu's tiny temple might be found.

◦

Early morning of the twelfth day, fifth moon. We started out for Hiraizumi, intending to go by way of the famous Aneha Pine and the Odae Bridge.

The trail was narrow and little-traveled—only the occasional woodcutter or hunter. We took a wrong road and ended up in the port town of Ishinomaki on a broad bay with Mount Kinka in the distance. Yaka-mochi has a poem for the emperor in the *Man'yōshū* saying Kinka's "where gold blossoms." It rises across water cluttered with cargo boats and fishing boats, shoreline packed with houses, smoke rising from their stoves. Our unplanned visit prompted an immediate search for lodging. No one made an offer. Spent the night in a cold shack and left again at daybreak, following unknown paths. We passed near the Sode Ferry, Obuchi Meadow, and the Mano Moor—all made famous in poems. After crossing a long miserable marsh, we stayed at Toima, pushing on to Hiraizumi in the morning. An arduous trek of over forty difficult miles in two days.

◦

Here three generations of the Fujiwara clan passed as though in a dream. The great outer gates lay in ruins. Where Hidehira's manor stood, rice fields grew. Only Mount Kinkei remained. I climbed the hill where Yoshitsune died; I saw the Kitakami, a broad stream flowing down through the Nambu Plain, the Koromo River circling Izumi Castle below the hill before joining the Kitakami. The ancient ruins of Yasuhira—from the end of the Golden Era—lie out beyond the Koromo Barrier where they stood guard against the Ainu people. The faithful elite remained bound to the castle, for all their valor, reduced to ordinary grass. Tu Fu wrote:

> *The whole country devastated,*
> *only mountains and rivers remain.*
> *In springtime, at the ruined castle,*
> *the grass is always green.*

[handwritten annotation: that which is built by man can be destroyed, while nature continues to thrive]

We sat awhile, our hats for a seat, seeing it all through tears.

> *Summer grasses:*
> *all that remains of great soldiers'*
> *imperial dreams*

Sora wrote:

Kanefusa's
own white hair
seen in blossoming briar

◦▸

Two temple halls I longed to see were finally opened at Chuson Temple. In the Sutra Library, Kyōdō, statues of the three generals of Hiraizumi; and in the Hall of Light, Hikaridō, their coffins and images of three buddhas. It would have all fallen down, jeweled doors battered by winds, gold pillars cracked by cold, all would have gone to grass, but added outer roof and walls protect it. Through the endless winds and rains of a thousand years, this great hall remains.

Fifth-month rains hammer
and blow but never quite touch
Hikaridō

◦▸

The road through the Nambu Plain visible in the distance, we stayed the night in Iwate, then trudged on past Cape Oguro and Mizu Island, both along the river. Beyond Narugo Hot Springs, we crossed Shitomae Barrier and entered Dewa Province. Almost no one comes this way, and the barrier guards were suspicious, slow, and thorough. Delayed, we climbed a steep mountain in falling dark and took refuge in a guard shack. A heavy storm pounded the shack with wind and rain for three miserable days.

Eaten alive by lice and fleas
now the horse
beside my pillow pees

101 - are these poems
functioning as diary
entries?

◦▸

The guard told us, "To get to Dewa, you'd better take a guide. There's a high mountain and a hard-to-find trail." He found us a powerful young man, short sword on his hip and oak walking stick in hand, and off we went, not without a little trepidation. As forewarned, the mountain was steep, the trail narrow, not even a birdcall to be heard. We made our way through deep forest dark as night, reminding me of Tu Fu's poem about "clouds bring-

ing darkness." We groped through thick bamboo, waded streams, climbed
through rocks, sweaty, fearful, and tired, until we finally came to the village
of Mogami. Our guide, turning back, said again how the trail was tough.
"Happy you didn't meet many surprises!" And departed. Hearing this, our
hearts skipped another beat.

from relief?. fear?

• •

Visited a merchant in Obanazawa, a Mr. Seifū, finding him to be wealthy
but relatively free of the vulgarities of the merchant class. And he knew
from his own many travels to Miyako the trials of life on the road, so invited us to stay the week. All in all, quite relaxing.

> *"My house is your house"*
> *and so it is—cool,*
> *sleeping in, sprawling out*

> *Come out from hiding*
> *under the silkworm room*
> *little demon toad.*

> *Little rouge brush*
> *reminding me*
> *of local safflower fields*

Sora wrote:

> *Women in the silkworm room*
> *all dressed simply*
> *like women in antiquity*

• •

In Yamagata Province, the ancient temple founded by Jikaku Daishi in
860, Ryūshaku Temple, is stone quiet, perfectly tidy. Everyone told us to
see it. It meant a few miles extra, doubling back toward Obanazawa to
find shelter. Monks at the foot of the mountain offered rooms, then we
climbed the ridge to the temple, scrambling up through ancient gnarled pine
and oak, smooth gray stones and moss. The temple doors, built on rocks,

were bolted. I crawled among boulders to make my bows at shrines. The silence was profound. I sat, feeling my heart begin to open.

> *Lonely silence*
> *a single cicada's cry*
> *sinking into stone*

◀ ▶

Planning to ride down the Mogami River, we were delayed at Ōishida, waiting for decent weather. "This is haiku country," someone told us, "seeds from old days blooming like forgotten flowers, the sound of a bamboo flute moving the heart. With no one to show us the way, however, local poets try new style and old style together." We made a small anthology together, but the result is of little merit. So much for culture.

The Mogami flows from the Michinoku at the far northern edge of Yamagata country. It is dangerous through Go Stone Rapids and Falcon Rapids, circumscribing northern Mount Itajiki to meet the sea at Sakata. Mountains rose from either side of the boat as we sped between the trees. The boat was only a tiny rice boat not meant for all we carried. We passed Shiraito Falls where it tumbles under pines. Sennin, Hall of Immortals, on the riverbank. The waters so high, it was a dangerous ride.

> *All the summer rains*
> *violently gather:*
> *Mogami River*

◀ ▶

Climbed Mount Haguro on the third day of the sixth moon and, with the help of a friend who dyes cloth for mountain monks' robes, Zushi Sakichi, obtained an audience with the abbot of Gongen Shrine, Master Egaku, who greeted us warmly. He arranged for quarters at nearby South Valley Temple. The next day we met at the main temple to write haiku:

> *The winds that blow*
> *through South Valley Temple*
> *are sweetened by snow*

◀ ▶

W paid homage at Gongen Shrine on the fifth. The first shrine on the mountain, it was built by Nōjō, no one knows exactly when. The *Engi Ceremonies* calls it Ushusato Mountain, Feather Province Village Mountain, but calligraphers' errors got it changed to Feather *Black* Mountain. The province is called Dewa, Feather Tribute, dating from an eighth-century custom whereby feather-down from this region was used as payment of tribute. Together with Moon Mountain and Bath Mountain, Feather Black Mountain completes the Dewa Sanzan, or Three Holy Mountains of Dewa. This temple is Tendai sect, like the one in Edo on Toei Hill. Both follow the doctrine of *shikan,* "concentration and insight," a way of enlightenment as transparent as moonlight, its light infinitely increasing, spreading from hermitage to mountaintop and back, reverence and compassion shining in everything it touches. Its blessing flows down from these mountains, enriching all our lives.

( )

On the eighth we climbed Moon Mountain, wearing the holy paper necklaces and cotton hats of Shinto priests, following behind a mountain monk whose footsteps passed through mist and clouds and snow and ice, climbing miles higher as though drawn by invisible spirits into the gateway of the sky—sun, moon, and clouds floated by and took my breath away. Long after sunset, moon high over the peak, we reached the summit, spread out in bamboo grass, and slept. Next day, after the sun burned away the clouds, we started down toward Yudono, Bath Mountain.

Approaching the valley, we passed Swordsmith Hut, named for the twelfth-century smith Gassan, who purified himself with holy water here and used it to temper his blades. On each blade he inscribed "Gassan," Moon Mountain. He admired the famous Dragon Spring swords of China. I remembered the legendary man-and-wife smiths renowned for their dedication to detail and technique.

We stretched on a rock to rest and noticed the opening buds of a three-foot cherry tree. Buried under stubborn snow, it insists upon honoring spring, however late it arrives. Like the Chinese poem, "Plum blossoms fragrant in burning sun!" And Gyōson Sōjō wrote, "So sad, blossoming cherry, you have no one to admire you." It's all here, in these tiny blossoms!

To say more is sacrilege. Forbidden to speak, put down the brush, respect Shinto rites. Later, back with Master Egaku, we wrote poems on the Three Holy Mountains:

Cool crescent moon
high above
Feather Black Mountain

How many rising clouds
collapse and fall
on the Moon's Mountain

Forbidden to speak
alone on Yudono Mountain
tears on my sleeve

Sora wrote:

Bath Mountain walkway
paved with pilgrims' coins:
here too are tears

◆ ▶

After leaving Haguro we came to the castle town of Tsuru-ga-oka accompanied by Zushi Sakichi and were greeted by the samurai Nagayama
Shigeyuki. We composed a round of haiku, bade farewell, and started by
boat down the Mogami, bound for Sakata Harbor. We stayed overnight
with a certain doctor who wrote under the nom de plume En-an Fugyoku.

From Hot Sea Mountain
southward to Windy Beach
the evening cools

A burning summer sun
slowly drowns:
Mogami River

◆ ▶

After all the breathtaking views of rivers and mountains, lands and seas,
after everything we'd seen, thoughts of seeing Kisakata's famous bay still
made my heart begin to race. Twenty miles north of Sakata Harbor, as we
walked the sandy shore beneath mountains where sea winds wander, a

storm came up at dusk and covered Mount Chōkai in mist and rain reminiscent of Su Tung-p'o's famous poem. We made our way in the dark, hoping for a break in the weather, groping on until we found a fisherman's
shack. By dawn the sky had cleared, sun dancing on the harbor. We took a
boat for Kisakata, stopping by the priest Nōin's island retreat, honoring his
three-year seclusion. On the opposite shore we saw the ancient cherry tree
Saigyō saw reflected and immortalized, "Fishermen row over blossoms."

Near the shore, Empress Jingū's tomb. And Kammanju Temple. Did
the empress ever visit? Why is she buried here?

Sitting in the temple chamber with the blinds raised, we saw the whole
lagoon, Mount Chōkai holding up the heavens inverted on the water.
To the west the road leads to the Muyamuya Barrier; to the east it curves
along a bank toward Akita; to the north the sea comes in on tide flats at
Shiogoshi. The whole lagoon, though only a mile or so across, reminds
one of Matsushima, although Matsushima seems much more contented,
whereas Kisakata seems bereaved. A sadness maybe in its sense of isolation here, where nature's darker spirits hide—like a strange and beautiful
woman whose heart has been broken.

nature = a strange & beautiful feminine presence

> *Kisakata rain*
> *the legendary beauty Seishi*
> *wrapped in sleeping leaves*

> *At Shiogoshi*
> *the long-legged crane*
> *cool, stepping in the sea*

Sora wrote:

> *Kisakata Festival:*
> *at holy feasts*
> *what specialties do locals eat?*

The merchant Teiji from Mino Province wrote:

> *Fishermen sit*
> *on their shutters on the sand*
> *enjoying the evening cool*

Sora found an osprey nest in the rocks:

> *May the ocean resist*
> *violating the vows*
> *of the osprey's nest*

After several days, clouds gathering over the North Road, we left Sakata
reluctantly, aching at the thought of a hundred thirty miles to the provincial capital of Kaga. We crossed the Nezu Barrier into Echigo Province, and
from there went on to Ichiburi Barrier in Etchu, restating our resolve all
along the way. Through nine hellish days of heat and rain, all my old mala-
dies tormenting me again, feverish and weak, I could not write.

> *Altair meets Vega*
> *tomorrow—Tanabata—*
> *already the night is changed*

> *High over wild seas*
> *surrounding Sado Island:*
> *the river of heaven*

〇 〉

Today we came through places with names like Children-Desert-Parents,
Lost Children, Send-Back-the-Dog, and Turn-Back-the-Horse—some of the
most fearsomely dangerous places in all the North Country. And well named.
Weakened and exhausted, I went to bed early but was roused by the voices
of two young women in the room next door. Then an old man's voice joined
theirs. They were prostitutes from Niigata in Echigo Province and were on
their way to Ise Shrine in the south, the old man seeing them off at this barrier,
Ichiburi. He would turn back to Niigata in the morning, carrying their letters
home. One girl quoted the *Shinkokinshū* poem, "On the beach where white
waves fall, / we all wander like children into every circumstance, / carried forward every day. . . ." And as they bemoaned their fate in life, I fell asleep.

In the morning, preparing to leave, they came to ask directions. "May
we follow along behind?" they asked. "We're lost and not a little fearful.
Your robes bring the spirit of the Buddha to our journey." They had mistaken us for priests. "Our way includes detours and retreats," I told them.
"But follow anyone on this road, and the gods will see you through." I

hated to leave them in tears and thought about them hard for a long time after we left. I told Sora, and he wrote down:

> *Under one roof, prostitute and priest,*
> *we all sleep together:*
> *moon in a field of clover*

◀ ▶

We managed to cross all "forty-eight rapids" of the Kurobe River on our way to the bay of Nago. Although it was no longer spring, we thought even an autumn visit to the wisteria at Tako—made famous in the *Man'yōshū*—worth the trouble, and asked the way: "Five miles down the coast, then up and over a mountain. A few fishermen's shacks, but no lodging, no place even to camp." It sounded so difficult, we pushed on instead into the province of Kaga.

> *Fragrance of ripening rice*
> *as we pass by*
> *the angry Ariso Sea*

◀ ▶

We crossed Mount Unohana and Kurikara Valley at noon on the fifteenth day of the seventh moon and entered Kanazawa, where we took rooms at an inn with a merchant from Osaka, a Mr. Kasho, who was in town to attend memorial services for the haiku poet Isshō, locally renowned for his verse and devotion to craft. The poet's elder brother served as host, the poet having died last winter.

> *Tremble if you can,*
> *gravemound:*
> *this autumn wind's my cry*

◀ ▶

We were invited to visit a thatched-roof hermitage:

> *Autumn's very cool*
> *hands busy peeling*
> *cucumber and eggplant*

Later, written along the road:

Intense hot red sun
and this autumn wind
indifferent

◀ ▶

At a village called Komatsu:

Aptly named Komatsu,
Little Pine, a breeze blows
over pampas grass and clover

Here we visited Tada Shrine to see Sanemori's helmet and a piece of his brocade armor-cloth presented to him by Lord Yoshitomo when he served the Genji clan. His helmet was no common soldier's gear: engraved with chrysanthemums and ivy from eyehole to earflap, crowned with a dragon's head between two horns. After Sanemori died on the battlefield, Kiso Yoshinaka sent it with a prayer, hand-carried to the shrine by Higuchi Jirō, Sanemori's friend. The story's inscribed on the shrine.

Ungraciously, under
a great soldier's empty helmet,
a cricket sings

◀ ▶

Along the road to Yamanaka Hot Springs, Mount Shirane rose behind our backs. At the foot of a mountain to our left we found a small temple to Kannon, Bodhisattva of Compassion. After the retired Emperor Kazan had made a pilgrimage to the thirty-three western temples, he enshrined an image of the goddess Kannon here, naming the temple Nata, using the first syllables of the first and last temples of the thirty-three: Nachi and Tanigumi. A small thatched-roof temple built on a rock among boulders and twisted pines, Nata lingers in the mind:

Whiter than the stones
of White Stone Temple:
autumn wind blows

◀ ▶

We bathed in mineral hot springs comparable to those at Ariake.

> *After bathing for hours*
> *in Yamanaka's waters*
> *I couldn't even pick a flower*

[handwritten annotation: too relaxed? too much respect for nature?]

Our host at the inn was a young man named Kumenosuke. His father was a knowledgeable haiku poet who had embarrassed the poet Teishitsu of Kyoto when Teishitsu was still ignorant and young. The latter thus returned to Kyoto and apprenticed himself to haiku master Teitoku. When Teishitsu returned to Yamanaka to judge a poetry contest, he refused to accept payment, having been so humbled. It's a legend around here now.

◀ ▶

Sora, suffering from persistent stomach ailments, was forced to return to his relatives in Nagashima in Ise Province. His parting words:

> *Sick to the bone*
> *if I should fall*
> *I'll lie in fields of clover*

He carries his pain as he goes, leaving me empty. Like paired geese parting in the clouds.

> *Now falling autumn dew*
> *obliterates my hatband's*
> *"We are two"*

◀ ▶

I stayed at Zenshō-ji, a temple near the castle town of Daishōji in Kaga Province. It was from this temple that Sora departed here the night before, leaving behind:

> *All night long*
> *listening to autumn winds*
> *wandering in the mountains*

One night like a thousand miles, as the proverb says, and I too listened to fall winds howl around the same temple. But at dawn, the chanting of sutras, gongs ringing, awakened me. An urgent need to leave for distant Echizen Province. As I prepared to leave the temple, two young monks arrived with ink stone and paper in hand. Outside, willow leaves fell in the wind.

> *Sweep the garden*
> *all kindnesses*
> *falling willow leaves repay*

My sandals already on, I wrote it quickly and departed.

◀ ▶

At the Echizen Province border, at an inlet town called Yoshizaki, I hired a boat and sailed for the famous pines of Shiogoshi. Saigyō wrote:

> *All the long night*
> *salt-winds drive*
> *storm-tossed waves*
> *and moonlight drips*
> *through Shiogoshi pines*

This one poem says enough. To add another would be like adding a sixth finger to a hand.

◀ ▶

In the town of Matsuoka, I visited Tenryū Temple, renewing an old friendship with the elder. The poet Hokushi from Kanazawa, intending only to see me off a way, had come this far with me, but turned back here. His poems on views along the way were sensitive, and I wrote for him:

> *Written on my summer fan*
> *torn in half*
> *in autumn*

◀ ▶

Walked a few miles into the mountains to pray at Dōgen Zenji's temple, Eihei-ji. To have placed it here, "a thousand miles from the capital," as the old saying goes, was no accident.

◀ ▶

After supper, I set out for Fukui, five miles down the road, the way made difficult by falling dark. An old recluse named Tōsai lived somewhere around here. More than ten years had passed since he came to visit me in Edo. Was he still alive? I was told he still lived near town, a small, weathered house just off the road, lost in tangles of gourd vines growing under cypress. I found the gate and knocked. A lonely-looking woman answered. "Where do you come from, honorable priest? The master has gone to visit friends." Probably his wife, she looked like she'd stepped right out of *Genji*.

I found Tōsai and stayed two days before deciding to leave to see the full moon at Tsuruga Harbor. Tōsai, enthused, tied up his robes in his sash, and we set off with him serving as guide.

‹ ›

Mount Shirane faded behind us and Mount Hina began to appear. We crossed Asamuzu Bridge and saw the legendary "reeds of Tamae" in bloom. We crossed Uguisu Barrier at Yuno-o Pass and passed by the ruins of Hiuchi Castle. On Returning Hill we heard the first wild geese of autumn. We arrived at Tsuruga Harbor on the evening of the fourteenth day of the eighth moon. The harbor moonlight was marvelously bright.

I asked at the inn, "Will we have this view tomorrow night?" The innkeeper said, "Can't guarantee weather in Koshiji. It may be clear, but then again it may turn overcast. It may rain." We drank sake with the innkeeper, then paid a late visit to the Kehi Myōjin Shrine honoring the second-century Emperor Chūai. A great spirituality—moonlight in pines, white sands like a touch of frost. In ancient times Yugyō, the second high priest, himself cleared away the grounds, carried stones, and built drains. To this day, people carry sands to the shrine. *"Yugyō-no-sunamochi,"* the innkeeper explained, "Yugyō's sand-bringing."

> *Transparent moonlight*
> *shines over Yugyō's sand*
> *perfectly white*

‹ ›

On the fifteenth, just as the innkeeper warned, it rained:

> *Harvest moon—*
> *true North Country weather—*
> *nothing to view*

‹ ›

The sky cleared the morning of the sixteenth. I sailed to Iro Beach a dozen miles away and gathered several colorful shells with a Mr. Tenya, who provided a box lunch and sake and even invited his servants. Tail winds got us there in a hurry. A few fishermen's shacks dotted the beach, and the tiny Hokke Temple was disheveled. We drank tea and hot sake, lost in a sweeping sense of isolation as dusk came on.

> Loneliness greater
> than Genji's Suma Beach:
> the shores of autumn

> Wave after wave
> mixes tiny shells
> with bush clover flowers

Tosai wrote a record of our afternoon and left it at the temple.

is this customary?

A disciple, Rotsū, had come to Tsuruga to travel with me to Mino Province. We rode horses into the castle town of Ōgaki. Sora returned from Ise, joined by Etsujin, also riding a horse. We gathered at the home of Jokō, a retired samurai. Lord Zensen, the Keikō family men, and other friends arrived by day and night, all to welcome me as though I'd come back from the dead. A wealth of affection!

Still exhausted and weakened from my long journey, on the sixth day of the darkest month, I felt moved to visit Ise Shrine, where a twenty-one-year Rededication Ceremony was about to get under way. At the beach, in the boat, I wrote:

> Clam ripped from its shell
> I move on to Futami Bay:
> passing autumn

(translated by Sam Hamill)

1729

Ireland

King George I never bothered to learn English. Mary Tofts, a maidservant, has given birth to sixteen rabbits. And Sir Isaac Newton, the smartest person in the world, has recently calculated the exact date on which Armageddon will occur. Because of this, it is hard to imagine that British readers would be able to understand that Jonathan Swift's satire, "A Modest Proposal," is a metaphorical argument. And yet, the essay almost immediately becomes a best seller throughout Britain. As recently as 1984, however, Peter O'Toole was booed off the stage at the Gaiety Theatre when he began reciting this essay to an audience in Dublin. Are we more gullible these days than people were in eighteenth-century Britain? Or is it that we've tied the essay so inexorably to "nonfiction" that we now have trouble believing it's even capable of metaphor?

Jonathan Swift

A Modest Proposal for Preventing the Children of Poor People in Ireland from Being a Burden to Their Parents or Country, and for Making Them Beneficial to the Public

It is a melancholy object to those who walk through this great town or travel in the country, when they see the streets, the roads, and cabin doors, crowded with beggars of the female sex, followed by three, four, or six children, all in rags and importuning every passenger for an alms. These mothers, instead of being able to work for their honest livelihood, are forced to employ all their time in strolling to beg sustenance for their helpless infants: who as they grow up either turn thieves for want of work, or leave their dear native country to fight for the Pretender in Spain, or sell themselves to the Barbados.

I think it is agreed by all parties that this prodigious number of children in the arms, or on the backs, or at the heels of their mothers, and frequently of their fathers, is in the present deplorable state of the kingdom a very great additional grievance; and, therefore, whoever could find out a fair, cheap, and easy method of making these children sound, useful members of the commonwealth, would deserve so well of the public as to have his statue set up for a preserver of the nation.

But my intention is very far from being confined to provide only for the children of professed beggars; it is of a much greater extent, and shall take in the whole number of infants at a certain age who are born of parents in effect as little able to support them as those who demand our charity in the streets.

As to my own part, having turned my thoughts for many years upon this important subject, and maturely weighed the several schemes of other projectors, I have always found them grossly mistaken in the computation. It is true, a child just dropped from its dam may be supported by her milk for a solar year, with little other nourishment; at most not above the value of 2s., which the mother may certainly get, or the value in scraps, by her lawful occupation of begging; and it is exactly at one year old that I propose to provide for them in such a manner as instead of being a charge upon their parents or the parish, or wanting food and raiment for the rest of their lives, they shall on the contrary contribute to the feeding, and partly to the clothing, of many thousands.

There is likewise another great advantage in my scheme, that it will prevent those voluntary abortions, and that horrid practice of women murdering their bastard children, alas! too frequent among us! sacrificing the poor innocent babes I doubt more to avoid the expense than the shame, which would move tears and pity in the most savage and inhuman breast.

The number of souls in this kingdom being usually reckoned one million and a half, of these I calculate there may be about two hundred thousand couple whose wives are breeders; from which number I subtract thirty thousand couples who are able to maintain their own children, although I apprehend there cannot be so many, under the present distresses of the kingdom; but this being granted, there will remain an hundred and seventy thousand breeders. I again subtract fifty thousand for those women who miscarry, or whose children die by accident or disease within the year. There only remains one hundred and twenty thousand children of poor parents annually born. The question therefore is, how this number shall be reared and provided for, which, as I have already said, under the present situation of affairs, is utterly impossible by all the methods hitherto proposed. For we can neither employ them in handicraft or agriculture; we neither build houses (I mean in the country) nor cultivate land: they can very seldom pick up a livelihood by stealing, till they arrive at six years old, except where they are of towardly parts, although I confess they learn the rudiments much earlier, during which time, they can however be properly looked upon only as probationers, as I have been informed by a principal gentleman in the county of Cavan, who protested to me that he never knew above one or two instances under the age of six, even in a part of the kingdom so renowned for the quickest proficiency in that art.

I am assured by our merchants, that a boy or a girl before twelve years old is no salable commodity; and even when they come to this age they will not yield above three pounds, or three pounds and half-a-crown at most on the exchange; which cannot turn to account either to the parents or kingdom, the charge of nutriment and rags having been at least four times that value.

I shall now therefore humbly propose my own thoughts, which I hope will not be liable to the least objection.

I have been assured by a very knowing American of my acquaintance in London, that a young healthy child well nursed is at a year old a most delicious, nourishing, and wholesome food, whether stewed, roasted, baked, or boiled; and I make no doubt that it will equally serve in a fricassee or a ragout.

I do therefore humbly offer it to public consideration that of the hundred and twenty thousand children already computed, twenty thousand may be reserved for breed, whereof only one-fourth part to be males; which is more than we allow to sheep, black cattle or swine; and my reason is, that these children are seldom the fruits of marriage, a circumstance not much regarded by our savages, therefore one male will be sufficient to serve four females. That the remaining hundred thousand may, at a year old, be offered in the sale to the persons of quality and fortune through the kingdom; always advising the mother to let them suck plentifully in the last month, so as to render them plump and fat for a good table. A child will make two dishes at an entertainment for friends; and when the family dines alone, the fore or hind quarter will make a reasonable dish, and seasoned with a little pepper or salt will be very good boiled on the fourth day, especially in winter.

I have reckoned upon a medium that a child just born will weigh 12 pounds, and in a solar year, if tolerably nursed, increaseth to 28 pounds.

I grant this food will be somewhat dear, and therefore very proper for landlords, who, as they have already devoured most of the parents, seem to have the best title to the children.

Infants' flesh will be in season throughout the year, but more plentiful in March, and a little before and after; for we are told by a grave author, an eminent French physician, that fish being a prolific diet, there are more children born in Roman Catholic countries about nine months after Lent than at any other season; therefore, reckoning a year after Lent, the markets will be more glutted than usual, because the number of popish infants is at least three to one in this kingdom: and therefore it will have one other collateral advantage, by lessening the number of papists among us.

I have already computed the charge of nursing a beggar's child (in which list I reckon all cottagers, laborers, and four-fifths of the farmers) to be about two shillings per annum, rags included; and I believe no gentleman would repine to give ten shillings for the carcass of a good fat child, which, as I have said, will make four dishes of excellent nutritive meat, when he hath only some particular friend or his own family to dine with him. Thus the squire will learn to be a good landlord, and grow popular among his tenants; the mother will have eight shillings net profit, and be fit for work till she produces another child.

Those who are more thrifty (as I must confess the times require) may flay the carcass; the skin of which artificially dressed will make admirable gloves for ladies, and summer boots for fine gentlemen.

As to our city of Dublin, shambles may be appointed for this purpose in the most convenient parts of it, and butchers we may be assured will not be wanting; although I rather recommend buying the children alive, and dressing them hot from the knife, as we do roasting pigs.

A very worthy person, a true lover of his country, and whose virtues I highly esteem, was lately pleased in discoursing on this matter to offer a refinement upon my scheme. He said that many gentlemen of this kingdom, having of late destroyed their deer, he conceived that the want of venison might be well supplied by the bodies of young lads and maidens, not exceeding fourteen years of age nor under twelve; so great a number of both sexes in every country being now ready to starve for want of work and service; and these to be disposed of by their parents, if alive, or otherwise by their nearest relations. But with due deference to so excellent a friend and so deserving a patriot, I cannot be altogether in his sentiments; for as to the males, my American acquaintance assured me, from frequent experience, that their flesh was generally tough and lean, like that of our schoolboys by continual exercise, and their taste disagreeable; and to fatten them would not answer the charge. Then as to the females, it would, I think, with humble submission be a loss to the public, because they soon would become breeders themselves; and besides, it is not improbable that some scrupulous people might be apt to censure such a practice (although indeed very unjustly), as a little bordering upon cruelty; which, I confess, hath always been with me the strongest objection against any project, however so well intended.

But in order to justify my friend, he confessed that this expedient was put into his head by the famous Psalmanazar, a native of the island Formosa, who came from thence to London above twenty years ago, and in conversation told my friend, that in his country when any young person happened to be put to death, the executioner sold the carcass to persons of quality as a prime dainty; and that in his time the body of a plump girl of fifteen, who was crucified for an attempt to poison the emperor, was sold to his imperial majesty's prime minister of state, and other great mandarins of the court, in joints from the gibbet, at four hundred crowns. Neither indeed can I deny, that if the same use were made of several plump young girls in this town, who without one single groat to their fortunes cannot stir abroad without a chair, and appear at playhouse and assemblies in foreign fineries which they never will pay for, the kingdom would not be the worse.

Some persons of a desponding spirit are in great concern about that vast number of poor people, who are aged, diseased, or maimed, and I have been desired to employ my thoughts what course may be taken to ease the nation of so grievous an encumbrance. But I am not in the least pain upon that matter, because it is very well known that they are every day dying and rotting by cold and famine, and filth and vermin, as fast as can be reasonably expected. And as to the young laborers, they are now in as hopeful a condition; they cannot get work, and consequently pine away for want of nourishment, to a degree that if at any time they are accidentally hired to common labor, they have not strength to perform it; and thus the country and themselves are happily delivered from the evils to come.

I have too long digressed, and therefore shall return to my subject. I think the advantages by the proposal which I have made are obvious and many, as well as of the highest importance.

For first, as I have already observed, it would greatly lessen the number of papists, with whom we are yearly overrun, being the principal breeders of the nation as well as our most dangerous enemies; and who stay at home on purpose with a design to deliver the kingdom to the Pretender, hoping to take their advantage by the absence of so many good protestants, who have chosen rather to leave their country than stay at home and pay tithes against their conscience to an episcopal curate.

Secondly, The poorer tenants will have something valuable of their own, which by law may be made liable to distress and help to pay their land-lord's rent, their corn and cattle being already seized, and money a thing unknown.

Thirdly, Whereas the maintenance of an hundred thousand children, from two years old and upward, cannot be computed at less than ten shillings a-piece per annum, the nation's stock will be thereby increased fifty thousand pounds per annum, beside the profit of a new dish introduced to the tables of all gentlemen of fortune in the kingdom who have any refinement in taste. And the money will circulate among ourselves, the goods being entirely of our own growth and manufacture.

Fourthly, The constant breeders, beside the gain of eight shillings sterling per annum by the sale of their children, will be rid of the charge of maintaining them after the first year.

Fifthly, This food would likewise bring great custom to taverns; where the vintners will certainly be so prudent as to procure the best receipts for dressing it to perfection, and consequently have their houses frequented by all the fine gentlemen, who justly value themselves upon their knowledge in good eating: and a skillful cook, who understands how to oblige his guests, will contrive to make it as expensive as they please.

Sixthly, This would be a great inducement to marriage, which all wise nations have either encouraged by rewards or enforced by laws and penalties. It would increase the care and tenderness of mothers toward their children, when they were sure of a settlement for life to the poor babes, provided in some sort by the public, to their annual profit instead of expense. We should see an honest emulation among the married women, which of them could bring the fattest child to the market. Men would become as fond of their wives during the time of their pregnancy as they are now of their mares in foal, their cows in calf, their sows when they are ready to farrow; nor offer to beat or kick them (as is too frequent a practice) for fear of a miscarriage.

Many other advantages might be enumerated. For instance, the addition of some thousand carcasses in our exportation of barreled beef, the propagation of swine's flesh, and improvement in the art of making good bacon, so much wanted among us by the great destruction of pigs, too frequent at our tables; which are no way comparable in taste or magnificence to a well-grown, fat, yearling child, which roasted whole will make a considerable figure at a lord mayor's feast or any other public entertainment. But this and many others I omit, being studious of brevity.

Supposing that one thousand families in this city, would be constant customers for Infant's Flesh, besides others who might have it at merry meetings, particularly at weddings and christenings, I compute that Dublin would take off annually about twenty thousand carcasses, and the rest of the Kingdom (where probably they will be sold somewhat cheaper) the remaining eighty thousand.

I can think of no one objection, that will possibly be raised against this proposal, unless it should be urged, that the number of people will be thereby much lessened in the Kingdom. This I freely own, and 'twas indeed one principal design in offering it to the world. I desire the reader will observe, that I calculate my remedy for this one individual kingdom of Ireland, and for no other that ever was, is, or I think, ever can be upon Earth. Therefore let no man talk to me of other expedients: of taxing our absentees at five shillings a pound: of using neither clothes, nor household furniture, except what is of our own growth and manufacture: of utterly rejecting the materials and instruments that promote foreign luxury: of curing the expensiveness of pride, vanity, idleness, and gaming in our women: of introducing a vein of parsimony, prudence and temperance: of learning to love our country, wherein we differ even from Laplanders, and the inhabitants of Topinamboo: of quitting our animosities, and factions, nor act any longer like the Jews, who were murdering one another at the very moment their city was taken: of being a little cautious not to sell our country and consciences for nothing: of teaching our landlords to have at least one degree of mercy towards their tenants. Lastly, of putting a spirit of honesty, industry, and skill into our shop-keepers, who, if a resolution could now be taken to buy only our native goods, would immediately unite to cheat and exact upon us in the price, the measure and the goodness, nor could ever yet be brought to make one fair proposal of just dealing, though often and earnestly invited to it.

Therefore I repeat, let no man talk to me of these and the like expedients, till he hath at least some glimpse of hope, that there will ever be some hearty and sincere attempt to put them into practice.

But as to my self, having been wearied out for many years with offering vain, idle, visionary thoughts, and at length despairing of success, I fortunately fell upon this proposal, which as it is wholly new, so it hath something solid and real, of no expense and little trouble, full in our own power, and whereby we can incur no danger in disobliging England. For this kind of commodity will not bear exportation, the flesh being of too tender a consistence, to admit a long continuance in salt, although perhaps I could name a country, which would be glad to eat up our whole nation without it.

After all, I am not so violently bent upon my own opinion as to reject any offer proposed by wise men, which shall be found equally innocent, cheap, easy, and effectual. But before something of that kind shall be advanced in contradiction to my scheme, and offering a better, I desire the author or authors will be pleased maturely to consider two points. First, as things now stand, how they will be able to find food and raiment for an hundred thousand useless mouths and backs. And secondly, there being a round million of creatures in human figure throughout this kingdom, whose whole subsistence put into a common stock would leave them in debt two millions of pounds sterling, adding those who are beggars by profession to the bulk of farmers, cottagers, and laborers, with their wives and children who are beggars in effect: I desire those politicians who dislike my overture, and may perhaps be so bold as to attempt an answer, that they will first ask the parents of these mortals, whether they would not at this day think it a great happiness to have been sold for food, at a year old in the manner I prescribe, and thereby have avoided such a perpetual scene of misfortunes as they have since gone through by the oppression of landlords, the impossibility of paying rent without money or trade, the want of common sustenance, with neither house nor clothes to cover them from the inclemencies of the weather, and the most inevitable prospect of entailing the like or greater miseries upon their breed for ever.

I profess, in the sincerity of my heart, that I have not the least personal interest in endeavoring to promote this necessary work, having no other motive than the public good of my country, by advancing our trade, providing for infants, relieving the poor, and giving some pleasure to the rich. I have no children by which I can propose to get a single penny; the youngest being nine years old, and my wife past child-bearing.

1763

England

When Christopher Smart met Samuel Johnson in 1763, the young writer demanded that Johnson immediately start praying. "Madness frequently discovers itself by unnecessary deviation," Johnson wrote. "My poor friend Smart showed the disturbance of his mind by falling upon his knees, and saying his prayers in the street, or in any other unusual place." Indeed, Christopher Smart could frequently be spotted in London's Hyde Park, accosting passersby and insisting that they pray. His wife eventually left him because of his behavior. Then he lost his job, fell quickly into debt, and was in and out of jail for the remainder of his life. Smart suffered from what doctors called "religious mania," a condition that compelled the writer to remain continually suppliant. Yet what his condition also did was unloose an imagination unfettered by the Age of Enlightenment, a period during which the autonomy of reason was the primary aesthetic propelling the arts. This was a period during which one kind of essay particularly flourished: John Locke's, Thomas Paine's, David Hume's, Edward Gibbon's. It was a period, in other words, that rejected the irrational, illogical, unconventional flights of writing that Christopher Smart would explore for decades in his work—the revelations, the ecstasies, the transcendent uses of knowledge—those that gave rise to later essayists who would come to inhabit the boundaries of sanity, faith, and genre: Velimir Khlebnikov, Theresa Hak Kyung Cha, Kathy Acker, Joe Wenderoth. The outcasts, the rebels, the exiles, the manics. "I'd as like pray with Kit Smart," Samuel Johnson also wrote, "as any other man."

CHRISTOPHER SMART

My Cat Jeoffry

For I will consider my Cat Jeoffry.

For he is the servant of the Living God duly and daily serving him.

For at the first glance of the glory of God in the East he worships in his way.

For this is done by wreathing his body seven times round with elegant quickness.

For then he leaps up to catch the musk, which is the blessing of God upon his prayer.

For he rolls upon prank to work it in.

For having done duty and received blessing he begins to consider himself.

For this he performs in ten degrees.

For first he looks upon his fore-paws to see if they are clean.

For secondly he kicks up behind to clear away there.

For thirdly he works it upon stretch with the fore paws extended.

For fourthly he sharpens his paws by wood.

For fifthly he washes himself.

For sixthly he rolls upon wash.

For seventhly he fleas himself, that he may not be interrupted upon the beat.

For eighthly he rubs himself against a post.

For ninthly he looks up for his instructions.

For tenthly he goes in quest of food.

For having consider'd God and himself he will consider his neighbour.

For if he meets another cat he will kiss her in kindness.

For when he takes his prey he plays with it to give it a chance.

For one mouse in seven escapes by his dallying.

For when his day's work is done his business more properly begins.

For he keeps the Lord's watch in the night against the adversary.

For he counteracts the powers of darkness by his electrical skin & glaring eyes.

For he counteracts the Devil, who is death, by brisking about the life.

For in his morning orisons he loves the sun and the sun loves him.

For he is of the tribe of Tiger.

For the Cherub Cat is a term of the Angel Tiger.

For he has the subtlety and hissing of a serpent, which in goodness he suppresses.

For he will not do destruction, if he is well-fed, neither will he spit without provocation.

For he purrs in thankfulness, when God tells him he's a good Cat.

For he is an instrument for the children to learn benevolence upon.

For every house is incompleat without him & a blessing is lacking in the spirit.

For the Lord commanded Moses concerning the cats at the departure of the Children of Israel from Egypt.

For every family had one cat at least in the bag.

For the English Cats are the best in Europe.

For he is the cleanest in the use of his fore-paws of any quadrupede.

For the dexterity of his defence is an instance of the love of God to him exceedingly.

For he is the quickest to his mark of any creature.

For he is tenacious of his point.

For he is a mixture of gravity and waggery.

For he knows that God is his Saviour.

For there is nothing sweeter than his peace when at rest.

For there is nothing brisker than his life when in motion.

For he is of the Lord's poor and so indeed is he called by benevolence perpetually—Poor Jeoffry! poor Jeoffry! the rat has bit thy throat.

For I bless the name of the Lord Jesus that Jeoffry is better.

For the divine spirit comes about his body to sustain it in compleat cat.

For his tongue is exceeding pure so that it has in purity what it wants in musick.

For he is docile and can learn certain things.

For he can set up with gravity which is patience upon approbation.

For he can fetch and carry, which is patience in employment.

For he can jump over a stick which is patience upon proof positive.

For he can spraggle upon waggle at the word of command.

For he can jump from an eminence into his master's bosom.

For he can catch the cork and toss it again.

For he is hated by the hypocrite and miser.

For the former is afraid of detection.

For the latter refuses the charge.

For he camels his back to bear the first notion of business.

For he is good to think on, if a man would express himself neatly.

For he made a great figure in Egypt for his signal services.

For he killed the Icneumon-rat very pernicious by land.

For his ears are so acute that they sting again.

For from this proceeds the passing quickness of his attention.

For by stroaking of him I have found out electricity.

For I perceived God's light about him both wax and fire.

For the Electrical fire is the spiritual substance, which God sends from heaven to sustain the bodies both of man and beast.

For God has blessed him in the variety of his movements.

For, tho he cannot fly, he is an excellent clamberer.

For his motions upon the face of the earth are more than any other quadrupede.

For he can tread to all the measures upon the musick.

For he can swim for life.

For he can creep.

1790

England

"The Marriage of Heaven and Hell," one critic has written, "compounds ethical and theological contraries. Its form mocks the categorical techniques that seek to make those contraries appear as negations. The unity of the *Marriage* is itself dialectical, and therefore cannot be grasped except by a mind in constant motion." Let me ask a question that's as clear as I can make it: Why is a text like William Blake's "The Marriage of Heaven and Hell" a poem? Is it because it's good? Is it because approximately 14 percent of it is in lines, and therefore, by the rule of poetic association, *all* of it is in lines? Is it because it's more flamboyantly engaged with the imagination than most eighteenth-century English prose, and therefore it cannot be prose? Let me ask another way: Why do I want to think that Blake's "Marriage" is an essay? Is it because it's good?

WILLIAM BLAKE

The Marriage of Heaven and Hell

The Argument

Rintrah roars & shakes his fires in the burden'd air;
Hungry clouds swag on the deep.

Once meek, and in a perilous path,
The just man kept his course along
The vale of death.
Roses are planted where thorns grow,
And on the barren heath
Sing the honey bees.

Then the perilous path was planted,
And a river and a spring
On every cliff and tomb,
And on the bleached bones
Red clay brought forth;

Till the villain left the paths of ease,
To walk in perilous paths, and drive
The just man into barren climes.
Now the sneaking serpent walks
In mild humility,
And the just man rages in the wilds
Where lions roam.

Rintrah roars & shakes his fires in the burden'd air;
Hungry clouds swag on the deep.

As a new heaven is begun, and it is now thirty-three years since its advent, the Eternal Hell revives. And lo! Swedenborg is the Angel sitting at the tomb: his writings are the linen clothes folded up. Now is the dominion of Edom, & the return of Adam into Paradise; see Isaiah xxxiv & xxxv Chap.

Without Contraries is no progression. Attraction and Repulsion, Reason and Energy, Love and Hate, are necessary to Human existence.

From these contraries spring what the religious call Good & Evil. Good is the passive that obeys Reason. Evil is the active springing from Energy.

Good is Heaven. Evil is Hell.

The Voice of the Devil

All Bibles or sacred codes have been the causes of the following Errors:

1. That Man has two real existing principles: Viz: a Body & a Soul.
2. That Energy, call'd Evil, is alone from the Body; & that Reason, call'd Good, is alone from the Soul.
3. That God will torment Man in Eternity for following his Energies.

But the following Contraries to these are True :

1. Man has no Body distinct from his Soul; for that call'd Body is a portion of Soul discern'd by the five Senses, the chief inlets of Soul in this age.
2. Energy is the only life, and is from the Body; and Reason is the bound or outward circumference of Energy.
3. Energy is Eternal Delight.

Those who restrain desire, do so because theirs is weak enough to be restrained; and the restrainer or reason usurps its place & governs the unwilling.

And being restrain'd, it by degrees becomes passive, till it is only the shadow of desire.

The history of this is written in Paradise Lost, & the Governor or Reason is call'd Messiah.

And the original Archangel, or possessor of the command of the heavenly host, is call'd the Devil or Satan, and his children are call'd Sin & Death.

But in the Book of Job, Milton's Messiah is call'd Satan.

For this history has been adopted by both parties.

It indeed appear'd to Reason as if Desire was cast out; but the Devil's account is, that the Messiah fell, & formed a heaven of what he stole from the Abyss.

This is shewn in the Gospel, where he prays to the Father to send the comforter, or Desire, that Reason may have Ideas to build on; the Jehovah of the Bible being no other than he who dwells in flaming fire.

Know that after Christ's death, he became Jehovah.

But in Milton, the Father is Destiny, the Son a Ratio of the five senses, & the Holy-ghost Vacuum!

Note: The reason Milton wrote in fetters when he wrote of Angels & God, and at liberty when of Devils & Hell, is because he was a true Poet and of the Devil's party without knowing it.

A Memorable Fancy

As I was walking among the fires of hell, delighted with the enjoyments of Genius, which to Angels look like torment and insanity, I collected some of their Proverbs; thinking that as the sayings used in a nation mark its character, so the Proverbs of Hell show the nature of Infernal wisdom better than any description of buildings or garments.

When I came home: on the abyss of the five senses, where a flat sided steep frowns over the present world, I saw a mighty Devil folded in black clouds, hovering on the sides of the rock: with corroding fires he wrote the following sentence now perceived by the minds of men, & read by them on earth:

How do you know but ev'ry Bird that cuts the airy way,
Is an immense world of delight, clos'd by your senses five?

Proverbs of Hell

In seed time learn, in harvest teach, in winter enjoy.
Drive your cart and your plow over the bones of the dead.
The road of excess leads to the palace of wisdom.
Prudence is a rich, ugly old maid courted by Incapacity.
He who desires but acts not, breeds pestilence.
The cut worm forgives the plow.
Dip him in the river who loves water.
A fool sees not the same tree that a wise man sees.
He whose face gives no light, shall never become a star.
Eternity is in love with the productions of time.
The busy bee has no time for sorrow.
The hours of folly are measur'd by the clock; but of wisdom, no
    clock can measure.
All wholesom food is caught without a net or a trap.
Bring out number, weight & measure in a year of dearth.
No bird soars too high, if he soars with his own wings.
A dead body revenges not injuries.
The most sublime act is to set another before you.
If the fool would persist in his folly he would become wise.
Folly is the cloke of knavery.
Shame is Pride's cloke.
Prisons are built with stones of Law, Brothels with bricks of
    Religion.
The pride of the peacock is the glory of God.
The lust of the goat is the bounty of God.
The wrath of the lion is the wisdom of God.
The nakedness of woman is the work of God.
Excess of sorrow laughs. Excess of joy weeps.
The roaring of lions, the howling of wolves, the raging of the
    stormy sea, and the destructive sword, are portions of eter-
    nity, too great for the eye of man.
The fox condemns the trap, not himself.
Joys impregnate. Sorrows bring forth.

Let man wear the fell of the lion, woman the fleece of the sheep.

The bird a nest, the spider a web, man friendship.

*The selfish, smiling fool, & the sullen, frowning fool shall be both
  thought wise, that they may be a rod.*

What is now proved was once only imagin'd.

*The rat, the mouse, the fox, the rabbit watch the roots; the lion,
  the tyger, the horse, the elephant watch the fruits.*

The cistern contains: the fountain overflows.

One thought fills immensity.

*Always be ready to speak your mind, and a base man will
  avoid you.*

Every thing possible to be believ'd is an image of truth.

*The eagle never lost so much time as when he submitted to learn
  of the crow.*

The fox provides for himself, but God provides for the lion.

*Think in the morning. Act in the noon. Eat in the evening. Sleep
  in the night.*

He who has suffer'd you to impose on him, knows you.

As the plow follows words, so God rewards prayers.

The tygers of wrath are wiser than the horses of instruction.

Expect poison from the standing water.

*You never know what is enough unless you know what is more
  than enough.*

Listen to the fool's reproach! it is a kingly title!

*The eyes of fire, the nostrils of air, the mouth of water, the beard
  of earth.*

The weak in courage is strong in cunning.

*The apple tree never asks the beech how he shall grow; nor the
  lion, the horse, how he shall take his prey.*

The thankful receiver bears a plentiful harvest.

If others had not been foolish, we should be so.

The soul of sweet delight can never be defil'd.

*When thou seest an Eagle, thou seest a portion of Genius; lift up
  thy head!*

*As the catterpiller chooses the fairest leaves to lay her eggs on, so
  the priest lays his curse on the fairest joys.*

To create a little flower is the labour of ages.

Damn braces: Bless relaxes.

The best wine is the oldest, the best water the newest.

Prayers plow not! Praises reap not!

Joys laugh not! Sorrows weep not!

The head Sublime, the heart Pathos, the genitals Beauty, the hands & feet Proportion.

As the air to a bird or the sea to a fish, so is contempt to the contemptible.

The crow wish'd every thing was black, the owl that every thing was white.

Exuberance is Beauty.

If the lion was advised by the fox, he would be cunning.

Improvement makes strait roads; but the crooked roads without Improvement are roads of Genius.

Sooner murder an infant in its cradle than nurse unacted desires.

Where man is not, nature is barren.

Truth can never be told so as to be understood, and not be believ'd.

Enough! or Too much.

The ancient Poets animated all sensible objects with Gods or Geniuses, calling them by the names and adorning them with the properties of woods, rivers, mountains, lakes, cities, nations, and whatever their enlarged & numerous senses could perceive.

And particularly they studied the genius of each city & country, placing it under its mental deity;

Till a system was formed, which some took advantage of, & enslav'd the vulgar by attempting to realize or abstract the mental deities from their objects : thus began Priesthood;

Choosing forms of worship from poetic tales.

And at length they pronounc'd that the Gods had order'd such things.

Thus men forgot that All deities reside in the human breast.

A Memorable Fancy

The Prophets Isaiah and Ezekiel dined with me, and I asked them how they dared so roundly to assert that God spoke to them; and whether they did not think at the time that they would be misunderstood, & so be the cause of imposition.

Isaiah answer'd: "I saw no God, nor heard any, in a finite organical perception; but my senses discover'd the infinite in every thing, and as I was then perswaded, & remain confirm'd, that the voice of honest indignation is the voice of God, I cared not for consequences, but wrote."

Then I asked: "does a firm perswasion that a thing is so, make it so?"

He replied: "All poets believe that it does, & in ages of imagination this firm perswasion removed mountains; but many are not capable of a firm perswasion of any thing."

Then Ezekiel said: "The philosophy of the east taught the first principles of human perception: some nations held one principle for the origin, & some another: we of Israel taught that the Poetic Genius (as you now call it) was the first principle and all the others merely derivative, which was the cause of our despising the Priests & Philosophers of other countries, and prophecying that all Gods would at last be proved to originate in ours & to be the tributaries of the Poetic Genius; it was this that our great poet, King David, desired so fervently & invokes so pathetic'ly, saying by this he conquers enemies & governs kingdoms; and we so loved our God, that we cursed in his name all the deities of surrounding nations, and asserted that they had rebelled: from these opinions the vulgar came to think that all nations would at last be subject to the jews."

"This," said he, "like all firm perswasions, is come to pass; for all nations believe the jews' code and worship the jews' god, and what greater subjection can be?"

I heard this with some wonder, & must confess my own conviction. After dinner I ask'd Isaiah to favour the world with his lost works; he said none of equal value was lost. Ezekiel said the same of his.

I also asked Isaiah what made him go naked and barefoot three years? he answer'd: "the same thing that made our friend Diogenes, the Grecian."

I then asked Ezekiel why he eat dung, & lay so long on his right & left side? he answer'd, "the desire of raising other men into a perception of the infinite: this the North American tribes practise, & is he honest who resists his genius or conscience only for the sake of present ease or gratification?"

The ancient tradition that the world will be consumed in fire at the end of six thousand years is true, as I have heard from Hell.

For the cherub with his flaming sword is hereby commanded to leave his guard at tree of life; and when he does, the whole creation will be consumed and appear infinite and holy, whereas it now appears finite & corrupt.

This will come to pass by an improvement of sensual enjoyment.

But first the notion that man has a body distinct from his soul is to be expunged; this I shall do by printing in the infernal method, by corrosives, which in Hell are salutary and medicinal, melting apparent surfaces away, and displaying the infinite which was hid.

If the doors of perception were cleansed every thing would appear to man as it is, infinite.

For man has closed himself up, till he sees all things thro' narrow chinks of his cavern.

A Memorable Fancy

I was in a Printing house in Hell, & saw the method in which knowledge is transmitted from generation to generation.

In the first chamber was a Dragon-Man, clearing away the rubbish from a cave's mouth; within, a number of Dragons were hollowing the cave.

In the second chamber was a Viper folding round the rock & the cave, and others adorning it with gold, silver and precious stones.

In the third chamber was an Eagle with wings and feathers of air: he caused the inside of the cave to be infinite; around were numbers of Eagle-like men who built palaces in the immense cliffs.

In the fourth chamber were Lions of flaming fire, raging around & melting the metals into living fluids.

In the fifth chamber were Unnam'd forms, which cast the metals into the expanse.

There they were receiv'd by Men who occupied the sixth chamber, and took the forms of books & were arranged in libraries.

The Giants who formed this world into its sensual existence, and now seem to live in it in chains, are in truth the causes of its life & the sources of all activity; but the chains are the cunning of weak and tame minds which have power to resist energy; according to the proverb, the weak in courage is strong in cunning.

Thus one portion of being is the Prolific, the other the Devouring: to the Devourer it seems as if the producer was in his chains; but it is not so, he only takes portions of existence and fancies that the whole.

But the Prolific would cease to be Prolific unless the Devourer, as a sea, received the excess of his delights.

Some will say: "Is not God alone the Prolific?" I answer: "God only Acts & Is, in existing beings or Men."

These two classes of men are always upon earth, & they should be enemies: whoever tries to reconcile them seeks to destroy existence.

Religion is an endeavour to reconcile the two.

Note: Jesus Christ did not wish to unite, but to separate them, as in the Parable of sheep and goats! & he says: "I came not to send Peace, but a Sword."

Messiah or Satan or Tempter was formerly thought to be one of the Antediluvians who are our Energies.

A Memorable Fancy

An Angel came to me and said: "O pitiable foolish young man! O horrible! O dreadful state! consider the hot burning dungeon thou art preparing for thyself to all eternity, to which thou art going in such career."

I said: "Perhaps you will be willing to shew me my eternal lot, & we will contemplate together upon it, and see whether your lot or mine is most desirable."

So he took me thro' a stable & thro' a church & down into the church vault, at the end of which was a mill: thro' the mill we went, and came to a cave: down the winding cavern we groped our tedious way, till a void boundless as a nether sky appear'd beneath us, & we held by the roots of trees and hung over this immensity; but I said, "if you please, we will commit ourselves to this void, and see whether providence is here also: if you will not, I will:" but he answer'd: "do not presume, O young man, but as we here remain, behold thy lot which will soon appear when the darkness passes away."

So I remain'd with him, sitting in the twisted root of an oak; he was suspended in a fungus, which hung with the head downward into the deep.

By degrees we beheld the infinite Abyss, fiery as the smoke of a burning city; beneath us, at an immense distance, was the sun, black but shining; round it were fiery tracks on which revolv'd vast spiders, crawling after their prey, which flew, or rather swum, in the infinite deep, in the most terrific shapes of animals sprung from corruption; & the air was full of them, & seem'd composed of them: these are Devils, and are called Powers of the air. I now asked my companion which was my eternal lot? he said: "between the black & white spiders."

But now, from between the black & white spiders, a cloud and fire burst and rolled thro' the deep, black'ning all beneath, so that the nether deep grew black as a sea, & rolled with a terrible noise; beneath us was nothing now to be seen but a black tempest, till looking east between the clouds & the waves, we saw a cataract of blood mixed with fire, and not many stones' throw from us appear'd and sunk again the scaly fold of a monstrous serpent; at last, to the east, distant about three degrees, appear'd a fiery crest above the waves; slowly it reared like a ridge of golden rocks, till we discover'd two globes of crimson fire, from which the sea fled away in clouds of smoke; and now we saw it was the head of Leviathan; his forehead was divided into streaks of green & purple like those on a tyger's forehead: soon we saw his mouth & red gills hang just above the raging foam, tinging the black deep with beams of blood, advancing toward us with all the fury of a spiritual existence.

My friend the Angel climb'd up from his station into the mill: I remain'd alone; & then this appearance was no more, but I found myself sitting on a pleasant bank beside a river by moonlight, hearing a harper, who sung to the harp; & his theme was: "The man who never alters his opinion is like standing water, & breeds reptiles of the mind."

But I arose and sought for the mill, & there I found my Angel, who, surprised, asked me how I escaped?

I answer'd: "All that we saw was owing to your metaphysics; for when you ran away, I found myself on a bank by moonlight hearing a harper. But now we have seen my eternal lot, shall I shew you yours?" he laugh'd at my proposal; but I by force suddenly caught him in my arms, & flew westerly thro' the night, till we were elevated above the earth's shadow; then I flung myself with him directly into the body of the sun; here I clothed myself in white, & taking in my hand Swedenborg's volumes, sunk from the glorious clime, and passed all the planets till we came to saturn: here I stay'd to rest, & then leap'd into the void between saturn & the fixed stars.

"Here," said I, "is your lot, in this space—if space it may be call'd." Soon we saw the stable and the church, & I took him to the altar and open'd the Bible, and lo! it was a deep pit, into which I descended, driving the Angel before me; soon we saw seven houses of brick; one we enter'd; in it were a number of monkeys, baboons, & all of that species, chain'd by the middle, grinning and snatching at one another, but withheld by the short-ness of their chains: however, I saw that they sometimes grew numerous, and then the weak were caught by the strong, and with a grinning aspect, first coupled with, & then devour'd, by plucking off first one limb and then another, till the body was left a helpless trunk; this, after grinning & kissing it with seeming fondness, they devour'd too; and here & there I saw one savourily picking the flesh off of his own tail; as the stench terribly annoy'd us both, we went into the mill, & I in my hand brought the skeleton of a body, which in the mill was Aristotle's Analytics.

So the Angel said: "thy phantasy has imposed upon me, & thou ough-test to be ashamed."

I answer'd: "we impose on one another, & it is but lost time to converse with you whose works are only Analytics."

Opposition is True Friendship.

I have always found that Angels have the vanity to speak of themselves as the only wise; this they do with a confident insolence sprouting from systematic reasoning.

Thus Swedenborg boasts that what he writes is new; tho' it is only the Contents or Index of already publish'd books.

A man carried a monkey about for a shew, & because he was a little wiser than the monkey, grew vain, and conceiv'd himself as much wiser than seven men. It is so with Swedenborg: he shews the folly of churches, & exposes hypocrites, till he imagines that all are religious, & himself the single one on earth that ever broke a net.

Now hear a plain fact: Swedenborg has not written one new truth. Now hear another: he has written all the old falsehoods.

And now hear the reason. He conversed with Angels who are all religious, & conversed not with Devils who all hate religion, for he was incapable thro' his conceited notions.

Thus Swedenborg's writings are a recapitulation of all superficial opinions, and an analysis of the more sublime—but no further.

Have now another plain fact. Any man of mechanical talents may, from the writings of Paracelsus or Jacob Behmen, produce ten thousand volumes of equal value with Swedenborg's, and from those of Dante or Shakespear an infinite number.

But when he has done this, let him not say that he knows better than his master, for he only holds a candle in sunshine.

A Memorable Fancy

Once I saw a Devil in a flame of fire, who arose before an Angel that sat on a cloud, and the Devil utter'd these words: "The worship of God is: Honouring his gifts in other men, each according to his genius, and loving the greatest men best: those who envy or calumniate great men hate God; for there is no other God."

The Angel hearing this became almost blue; but mastering himself he grew yellow, & at last white, pink, & smiling, and then replied:

"Thou Idolater! is not God One? & is not he visible in Jesus Christ? and has not Jesus Christ given his sanction to the law of ten commandments? and are not all other men fools, sinners, & nothings?"

The Devil answer'd: "bray a fool in a morter with wheat, yet shall not his folly be beaten out of him; if Jesus Christ is the greatest man, you ought to love him in the greatest degree; now hear how he has given his sanction to the law of ten commandments: did he not mock at the sabbath, and so mock the sabbath's God? murder those who were murder'd because of him? turn away the law from the woman taken in adultery? steal the labor of others to support him? bear false witness when he omitted making a defence before Pilate? covet when he pray'd for his disciples, and when he bid them shake off the dust of their feet against such as refused to lodge them? I tell you, no virtue can exist without breaking these ten commandments. Jesus was all virtue, and acted from impulse, not from rules."

When he had so spoken, I beheld the Angel, who stretched out his arms, embracing the flame of fire, & he was consumed and arose as Elijah.

Note: This Angel, who is now become a Devil, is my particular friend; we often read the Bible together in its infernal or diabolical sense, which the world shall have if they behave well.

I have also The Bible of Hell, which the world shall have whether they will or no.

One Law for the Lion & Ox is Oppression.

A Song of Liberty

1. The Eternal Female groan'd! it was heard over all the Earth:
2. Albions coast is sick silent; the American meadows faint!
3. Shadows of Prophecy shiver along by the lakes and the rivers and mutter across the ocean: France, rend down thy dungeon;
4. Golden Spain burst the barriers of old Rome;
5. Cast thy keys O Rome into the deep down falling, even to eternity down falling.
6. And weep!
7. In her trembling hands she took the new born terror howling;
8. On those infinite mountains of light now barr'd out by the atlantic sea, the new born fire stood before the starry king!
9. Flag'd with grey brow'd snows and thunderous visages the jealous wings wav'd over the deep.
10. The speary hand burned aloft, unbuckled was the shield, forth went the hand of jealousy among the flaming hair, and hurl'd the new born wonder thro' the starry night.
11. The fire, the fire is falling!
12. Look up! look up! O citizen of London, enlarge thy countenance; O Jew, leave counting gold! return to thy oil and wine; O African! black African! (go, winged thought widen his forehead.)
13. The fiery limbs, the flaming hair, shot like the sinking sun into the western sea.
14. Wak'd from his eternal sleep, the hoary element roaring fled away:
15. Down rush'd beating his wings in vain the jealous king; his grey brow'd councellors, thunderous warriors, curl'd veterans, among helms, and shields, and chariots horses, elephants: banners, castles, slings and rocks,

16. Falling, rushing, ruining! buried in the ruins, on Urthona's dens.

17. All night beneath the ruins, then their sullen flames faded emerge round the gloomy king.

18. With thunder and fire: leading his starry hosts thro' the waste wilderness he promulgates his ten commands, glancing his beamy eyelids over the deep in dark dismay,

19. Where the son of fire in his eastern cloud, while the morning plumes her golden breast,

20. Spurning the clouds written with curses, stamps the stony law to dust, loosing the eternal horses from the dens of night, crying

Empire is no more! and now the lion & wolf shall cease.

Chorus

Let the Priests of the Raven of dawn, no longer in deadly black, with hoarse note curse the sons of joy. Nor his accepted brethren, whom, tyrant, he calls free; lay the bound or build the roof. Nor pale religious letchery call that virginity, that wishes but acts not!

For every thing that lives is Holy.

1849

England

Actually, there is some great prose in English at this time, but it is prose that few critics appreciate. Thomas De Quincey's essays would influence the work of Charles Baudelaire, Edgar Allan Poe, and Jorge Luis Borges. But in his day De Quincey was called by Sir Leslie Stephen, the father of Virginia Woolf—and a leading nineteenth-century literary critic—"a bastard writer." This is perhaps because De Quincey's essays exhibit for the first time in English prose an idiosyncratic exploration of the poetic imagination that is forged out of the traditions of Michel de Montaigne, Sir Thomas Browne, and William Blake: structurally discursive, syntactically daring, and passionately opposed to conventional expectations. In other words, "Thomas De Quincey is a writer of pure experience," as Virginia Woolf will later write in opposition to her father. Indeed, even at the age of fifteen, De Quincey already seemed to know that he was destined to pioneer a new trail for the essay. Writing to his mother from boarding school, De Quincey complained about life in the industrial city of Manchester, where "I cannot stir out of doors without being nosed by a factory, a cotton bag, a cotton dealer, or anything else allied to that most detestable trade. Such a subject dissipates the whole train of romantic visions that I prefer to conjure up." Eventually he'd run away before receiving his diploma, take up opium in London with a group of prostitutes and artists, become addicted and then broke, get accepted into Oxford, write the most highly ranked Greek essays in the school's recent history, and then flee from there as well without receiving a degree. In response, his mother threatened to withhold his allowance. Why don't you put your writing to good use? she begged her son. Writing back to his mother, De Quincey explained that he considered himself in possession of "original knowledge not commonly derived from books and, as such, I am indisposed to sell this knowledge for money in any format that may betray the artful possibility of my prose." The commercial forms of prose that De Quincey railed against for years were those which could be found in the British periodical, that bastion of fashionable commentary that had been entertaining readers for two centuries already. Out of such periodicals came Addison, Steele, Johnson, and Dickens, writers who regularly proffered the commerce of prose's usual conventions, relegating the essay to a kind of literary transaction: the subject matter advertised in the title of each piece, the unthreateningly middling thesis, the unsurprising exploration in fulfillment of that thesis, and the proudly dramatic reminder of what the reader has just read. Thomas De Quincey, in the meantime, was still an opium addict. His memoir about addiction had become a best seller, and so it looked as though he'd be able to keep on smoking all his life. His addiction, however, overcame his royalties. And with an inheritance now gone, a mother long dead, and a reputation for promising a "new kind of prose" that he had never actually managed to deliver to his readers, Thomas De Quincey gave in and began to write for those "despicable" periodicals. For the last thirty-six years of his life, De Quincey published long and elaborate essays that spun wildly from the norm, incorporating personal experience, literary criticism, politics, history, gossip, dreams—all strung together loosely by the music of association, by an infuriating and gorgeous labyrinthine style that remains narratively seductive no matter where De Quincey goes because of his insistence on following his own rules.

he's invested in the "glory of motion"

THOMAS DE QUINCEY

The English Mail-Coach

mind wandering-
tangential ideas

lots of long/
run-on sentences!

The Glory of Motion

Some twenty or more years before I matriculated at Oxford, Mr. Palmer, at that time M.P. for Bath, had accomplished two things, very hard to do on our little planet, the Earth, however cheap they may be held by eccentric people in comets: he had invented mail-coaches, and he had married the daughter of a duke. He was, therefore, just twice as great a man as Galileo, who did certainly invent (or, which is the same thing, discover) the satellites of Jupiter, those very next things extant to mail-coaches in the two capital pretensions of speed and keeping time, but, on the other hand, who did *not* marry the daughter of a duke.

These mail-coaches, as organised by Mr. Palmer, are entitled to a circumstantial notice from myself, having had so large a share in developing the anarchies of my subsequent dreams: an agency which they accomplished, 1st, through velocity at that time unprecedented—for they first revealed the glory of motion; 2dly, through grand effects for the eye between lamplight and the darkness upon solitary roads; 3dly, through animal beauty and power so often displayed in the class of horses selected for this mail service; 4thly, through the conscious presence of a central intellect, that, in the midst of vast distances—of storms, of darkness, of danger—overruled all obstacles into one steady co-operation to a national result. For my own feeling, this post-office service spoke as by some mighty orchestra, where a thousand instruments, all disregarding each other, and so far in danger of discord, yet all obedient as slaves to the supreme *baton* of some great leader, terminate in a perfection of harmony like that of heart, brain, and lungs in a healthy animal organisation. But, finally, that particular element in this whole combination which most impressed myself, and through which

idiosyncratic-reflection of the individual mind - his
wandering, drug-addled mind

it is that to this hour Mr. Palmer's mail-coach system tyrannises over my dreams by terror and terrific beauty, lay in the awful *political* mission which at that time it fulfilled. The mail-coach it was that distributed over the face of the land, like the opening of apocalyptic vials, the heart-shaking news of Trafalgar, of Salamanca, of Vittoria, of Waterloo. These were the harvests that, in the grandeur of their reaping, redeemed the tears and blood in which they had been sown. Neither was the meanest peasant so much below the grandeur and the sorrow of the times as to confound battles such as these, which were gradually moulding the destinies of Christendom, with the vulgar conflicts of ordinary warfare, so often no more than gladiatorial trials of national prowess. The victories of England in this stupendous contest rose of themselves as natural *Te Deums* to heaven; and it was felt by the thoughtful that such victories, at such a crisis of general prostration, were not more beneficial to ourselves than finally to France, our enemy, and to the nations of all western or central Europe, through whose pusillanimity it was that the French domination had prospered.

The mail-coach, as the national organ for publishing these mighty events, thus diffusively influential, became itself a spiritualised and glorified object to an impassioned heart; and naturally, in the Oxford of that day, *all* hearts were impassioned, as being all (or nearly all) in *early* manhood. In most universities there is one single college; in Oxford there were five-and-twenty, all of which were peopled by young men, the *élite* of their own generation; not boys, but men: none under eighteen. In some of these many colleges the custom permitted the student to keep what are called "short terms"; that is, the four terms of Michaelmas, Lent, Easter, and Act, were kept by a residence, in the aggregate, of ninety-one days, or thirteen weeks. Under this interrupted residence, it was possible that a student might have a reason for going down to his home four times in the year. This made eight journeys to and fro. But, as these homes lay dispersed through all the shires of the island, and most of us disdained all coaches except his majesty's mail, no city out of London could pretend to so extensive a connexion with Mr. Palmer's establishment as Oxford. Three mails, at the least, I remember as passing every day through Oxford, and benefiting by my personal patronage—viz. the Worcester, the Gloucester, and the Holyhead mail. Naturally, therefore, it became a point of some interest with us, whose journeys revolved every six weeks on an average, to look a little into the executive details of the system. With some of these Mr. Palmer had no concern; they rested upon bye-laws enacted by posting-houses for their own benefit, and upon other bye-laws, equally stern, enacted by the inside passengers for the illustration of their own haughty exclusiveness. These last were of a nature to rouse our scorn; from which the transition was not very long to systematic mutiny. Up to this time, say 1804, or 1805 (the year of Trafalgar), it had been the fixed assumption of the four inside people (as an old tradition of all public carriages derived from the reign of Charles II) that they, the illustrious quaternion, constituted a porcelain variety of the human race, whose dignity would have been compromised by exchanging one word of civility with the three miserable delf-ware outsides. Even to have kicked an outsider might have been held to attaint the foot concerned in that operation, so that, perhaps, it would have required an act of Parliament to restore its purity of blood. What words, then, could express the horror, and the sense of treason, in that case, which *had* happened, where all three outsides (the trinity of Pariahs) made a vain attempt to sit down at the same breakfast-table or dinner-table with the consecrated four? I myself witnessed such an attempt; and on that occasion a benevolent old gentleman endeavoured to soothe his three holy associates, by suggesting that, if the outsides were indicted for this criminal attempt at the next assizes, the court would regard it as a case of lunacy or *delirium tremens* rather than of treason. England owes much of her grandeur to the depth of the aristocratic element in her social composition, when pulling against her strong democracy. I am not the man to laugh at it. But sometimes, undoubtedly, it expressed itself in comic shapes. The course taken with the infatuated outsiders, in the particular attempt which I have noticed, was that the waiter, beckoning them away from the privileged *salle-à-manger*, sang out, "This way, my good men," and then enticed these good men away to the kitchen. But that plan had not always answered. Sometimes, though rarely, cases occurred where the intruders, being stronger than usual, or more vicious than usual, resolutely refused to budge, and so far carried their point as to have a separate table arranged for themselves in a corner of the general room. Yet, if an Indian screen could be found ample enough to plant them out from the very eyes of the high table, or *dais*, it then became possible to assume as a fiction of law that the three delf fellows, after all, were not present. They could be ignored by the porcelain men, under the maxim that objects not appearing and objects not existing are governed by the same logical construction.

thinks of himself as a snob?

Such being, at that time, the usage of mail-coaches, what was to be done by us of young Oxford? We, the most aristocratic of people, who were addicted to the practice of looking down superciliously even upon the insides themselves as often very questionable characters—were we, by voluntarily going outside, to court indignities? If our dress and bearing sheltered us generally from the suspicion of being "raff" (the name at that period for "snobs"), we really *were* such constructively by the place we assumed. If we did not submit to the deep shadow of eclipse, we entered at least the skirts of its penumbra. And the analogy of theatres was valid against us,— where no man can complain of the annoyances incident to the pit or gallery, having his instant remedy in paying the higher price of the boxes. But the soundness of this analogy we disputed. In the case of the theatre, it cannot be pretended that the inferior situations have any separate attractions, unless the pit may be supposed to have an advantage for the purposes of the critic or the dramatic reporter. But the critic or reporter is a rarity. For most people, the sole benefit is in the price. Now, on the contrary, the outside of the mail had its own incommunicable advantages. These we could not forgo. The higher price we would willingly have paid, but not the price connected with the condition of riding inside; which condition we pronounced insufferable. The air, the freedom of prospect, the proximity to the horses, the elevation of seat: these were what we required; but, above all, the certain anticipation of purchasing occasional opportunities of driving.

Such was the difficulty which pressed us; and under the coercion of this difficulty we instituted a searching inquiry into the true quality and valuation of the different apartments about the mail. We conducted this inquiry on metaphysical principles; and it was ascertained satisfactorily that the roof of the coach, which by some weak men had been called the attics, and by some the garrets, was in reality the drawing-room; in which drawing-room the box was the chief ottoman or sofa ; whilst it appeared that the *inside,* which had been traditionally regarded as the only room tenantable by gentlemen, was, in fact, the coal-cellar in disguise.

? hard to visualize

Great wits jump. The very same idea had not long before struck the celestial intellect of China. Amongst the presents carried out by our first embassy to that country was a state-coach. It had been specially selected as a personal gift by George III; but the exact mode of using it was an intense mystery to Pekin. The ambassador, indeed (Lord Macartney), had made some imperfect explanations upon this point; but, as His Excellency communicated these in a diplomatic whisper at the very moment of his departure, the celestial intellect was very feebly illuminated, and it became necessary to call a cabinet council on the grand state question, "Where was the Emperor to sit?" The hammer-cloth happened to be unusually gorgeous; and, partly on that consideration, but partly also because the box offered the most elevated seat, was nearest to the moon, and undeniably went foremost, it was resolved by acclamation that the box was the imperial throne, and, for the scoundrel who drove,—he might sit where he could find a perch. The horses, therefore, being harnessed, solemnly his imperial majesty ascended his new English throne under a flourish of trumpets, having the first lord of the treasury on his right hand, and the chief jester on his left. Pekin gloried in the spectacle; and in the whole flowery people, constructively present by representation, there was but one discontented person, and *that* was the coachman. This mutinous individual audaciously shouted, "Where am *I* to sit?" But the privy council, incensed by his disloyalty, unanimously opened the door, and kicked him into the inside. He had all the inside places to himself; but such is the rapacity of ambition that he was still dissatisfied. "I say," he cried out in an extempore petition addressed to the Emperor through the window—"I say, how am I to catch hold of the reins?"—"Anyhow," was the imperial answer; "don't trouble *me*, man, in my glory. How catch the reins? Why, through the windows, through the keyholes—*any*how." Finally this contumacious coachman lengthened the check-strings into a sort of jury-reins communicating with the horses; with these he drove as steadily as Pekin had any right to expect. The Emperor returned after the briefest of circuits; he descended in great pomp from his throne, with the severest resolution never to remount it. A public thanksgiving was ordered for his majesty's happy escape from the disease of broken neck; and the state-coach was dedicated thenceforward as a votive offering to the god Fo Fo—whom the learned more accurately called Fi Fi.

A revolution of this same Chinese character did young Oxford of that era effect in the constitution of mail-coach society. It was a perfect French Revolution; and we had good reason to say, *ça ira*. In fact, it soon became *too* popular. The "public"—a well-known character, particularly disagreeable, though slightly respectable, and notorious for affecting the chief seats in synagogues—had at first loudly opposed this revolution; but, when the opposition showed itself to be ineffectual, our disagreeable friend went

[margin note: Oxford of the public]

into it with headlong zeal. At first it was a sort of race between us; and, as the public is usually from thirty to fifty years old, naturally we of young Oxford, that averaged about twenty, had the advantage. Then the public took to bribing, giving fees to horse-keepers, &c., who hired out their persons as warming-pans on the box-seat. *That,* you know, was shocking to all moral sensibilities. Come to bribery, said we, and there is an end to all morality,—Aristotle's, Zeno's, Cicero's, or anybody's. And, besides, of what use was it? For *we* bribed also. And, as our bribes, to those of the public, were as five shillings to sixpence, here again young Oxford had the advantage. But the contest was ruinous to the principles of the stables connected with the mails. This whole corporation was constantly bribed, rebribed, and often sur-rebribed; a mail-coach yard was like the hustings in a contested election; and a horse-keeper, ostler, or helper, was held by the philosophical at that time to be the most corrupt character in the nation.

There was an impression upon the public mind, natural enough from the continually augmenting velocity of the mail, but quite erroneous, that an outside seat on this class of carriages was a post of danger. On the contrary, I maintained that, if a man had become nervous from some gipsy prediction in his childhood, allocating to a particular moon now approaching some unknown danger, and he should inquire earnestly, "Whither can I fly for shelter? Is a prison the safest retreat? or a lunatic hospital? or the British Museum?" I should have replied, "Oh no; I'll tell you what to do. Take lodgings for the next forty days on the box of his majesty's mail. Nobody can touch you there. If it is by bills at ninety days after date that you are made unhappy—if noters and protesters are the sort of wretches whose astrological shadows darken the house of life—then note you what I vehemently protest: viz. that, no matter though the sheriff and under-sheriff in every county should be running after you with his *posse,* touch a hair of your head he cannot whilst you keep house and have your legal domicile on the box of the mail. It is felony to stop the mail; even the sheriff cannot do that. And an *extra* touch of the whip to the leaders (no great matter if it grazes the sheriff) at any time guarantees your safety." In fact, a bedroom in a quiet house seems a safe enough retreat; yet it is liable to its own notorious nuisances—to robbers by night, to rats, to fire. But the mail laughs at these terrors. To robbers, the answer is packed up and ready for delivery in the barrel of the guard's blunderbuss. Rats again! there *are* none about mail-coaches, any more than snakes in Von Troil's Iceland;

[margin note: everything has its own danger—why worry about this in particular?]

except, indeed, now and then a parliamentary rat, who always hides his shame in what I have shown to be the "coal-cellar." <u>And, as to fire, I never knew but one in a mail-coach;</u> which was in the Exeter mail, and caused by an obstinate sailor bound to Devonport. Jack, making light of the law and the lawgiver that had set their faces against his offence, insisted on taking up a forbidden seat in the rear of the roof, from which he could exchange his own yarns with those of the guard. No greater offence was then known to mail-coaches; it was treason, it was *læsa majestas,* it was by tendency arson; and the ashes of Jack's pipe, falling amongst the straw of the hinder boot, containing the mail-bags, raised a flame which (aided by the wind of our motion) threatened a revolution in the republic of letters. Yet even this left the sanctity of the box unviolated. In dignified repose, the coachman and myself sat on, resting with benign composure upon our knowledge that the fire would have to burn its way through four inside passengers before it could reach ourselves. I remarked to the coachman, with a quotation from Virgil's *Æneid* really too hackneyed—

> *"Jam proximus ardet*
> *Ucalegon."*

But, recollecting that the Virgilian part of the coachman's education might have been neglected, I interpreted so far as to say that perhaps at that moment the flames were catching hold of our worthy brother and inside passenger, Ucalegon. The coachman made no answer,—which is my own way when a stranger addresses me either in Syriac or in Coptic; but by his faint sceptical smile he seemed to insinuate that he knew better,—for that Ucalegon, as it happened, was not in the way-bill, and therefore could not have been booked.

<u>No dignity is perfect which does not at some point ally itself with the mysterious.</u> The connexion of the mail with the state and the executive government—a connexion obvious but yet not strictly defined—gave to the whole mail establishment an official grandeur which did us service on the roads, and invested us with seasonable terrors. Not the less impressive were those terrors because their legal limits were imperfectly ascertained. Look at those turnpike gates: with what deferential hurry, with what an obedient start, they fly open at our approach! Look at that long line of carts and carters ahead, audaciously usurping the very crest of the road. Ah! traitors, they do

not hear us as yet; but, as soon as the dreadful blast of our horn reaches them with proclamation of our approach, see with what frenzy of trepidation they fly to their horses' heads, and deprecate our wrath by the precipitation of their crane-neck quarterings. Treason they feel to be their crime; each individual carter feels himself under the ban of confiscation and attainder; his blood is attainted through six generations; and nothing is wanting but the headsman and his axe, the block and the sawdust, to close up the vista of his horrors. What! shall it be within benefit of clergy to delay the king's message on the high road?—to interrupt the great respirations, ebb and flood, *systole* and *diastole,* of the national intercourse?—to endanger the safety of tidings running day and night between all nations and languages? Or can it be fancied, amongst the weakest of men, that the bodies of the criminals will be given up to their widows for Christian burial? Now, the doubts which were raised as to our powers did more to wrap them in terror, by wrapping them in uncertainty, than could have been effected by the sharpest definitions of the law from the Quarter Sessions. We, on our parts (we, the collective mail, I mean), did our utmost to exalt the idea of our privileges by the insolence with which we wielded them. Whether this insolence rested upon law that gave it a sanction, or upon conscious power that haughtily dispensed with that sanction, equally it spoke from a potential station; and the agent, in each particular insolence of the moment, was viewed reverentially, as one having authority.

Sometimes after breakfast his majesty's mail would become frisky; and, in its difficult wheelings amongst the intricacies of early markets, it would upset an apple-cart, a cart loaded with eggs, &c. Huge was the affliction and dismay, awful was the smash. I, as far as possible, endeavoured in such a case to represent the conscience and moral sensibilities of the mail; and, when wildernesses of eggs were lying poached under our horses' hoofs, then would I stretch forth my hands in sorrow, saying (in words too celebrated at that time, from the false echoes of Marengo), "Ah! wherefore have we not time to weep over you?"—which was evidently impossible, since, in fact, we had not time to laugh over them. Tied to post-office allowance in some cases of fifty minutes for eleven miles, could the royal mail pretend to undertake the offices of sympathy and condolence? Could it be expected to provide tears for the accidents of the road? If even it seemed to trample on humanity, it did so, I felt, in discharge of its own more peremptory duties.

Upholding the morality of the mail, *a fortiori* I upheld its rights; as a

matter of duty, I stretched to the uttermost its privilege of imperial precedency, and astonished weak minds by the feudal powers which I hinted to
be lurking constructively in the charters of this proud establishment. Once
I remember being on the box of the Holyhead mail, between Shrewsbury
and Oswestry, when a tawdry thing from Birmingham, some "Tallyho" or
"Highflyer," all flaunting with green and gold, came up alongside of us.
What a contrast to our royal simplicity of form and colour in this plebeian
wretch! The single ornament on our dark ground of chocolate colour was
the mighty shield of the imperial arms, but emblazoned in proportions
as modest as a signet-ring bears to a seal of office. Even this was displayed
only on a single panel, whispering, rather than proclaiming, our relations
to the mighty state; whilst the beast from Birmingham, our green-and-gold
friend from false, fleeting, perjured Brummagem, had as much writing and
painting on its sprawling flanks as would have puzzled a decipherer from
the tombs of Luxor. For some time this Birmingham machine ran along
by our side—a piece of familiarity that already of itself seemed to me sufficiently jacobinical. But all at once a movement of the horses announced
a desperate intention of leaving us behind. "Do you see *that*?" I said to the
coachman.—"I see," was his short answer. He was wide awake,—yet he
waited longer than seemed prudent; for the horses of our audacious oppo-
nent had a disagreeable air of freshness and power. But his motive was loyal;
his wish was that the Birmingham conceit should be full-blown before he
froze it. When *that* seemed right, he unloosed, or, to speak by a stronger
word, he *sprang*, his known resources: he slipped our royal horses like
cheetahs, or hunting-leopards, after the affrighted game. How they could
retain such a reserve of fiery power after the work they had accomplished
seemed hard to explain. But on our side, besides the physical superiority,
was a tower of moral strength, namely the king's name, "which they upon
the adverse faction wanted." Passing them without an effort, as it seemed,
we threw them into the rear with so lengthening an interval between us
as proved in itself the bitterest mockery of their presumption; whilst our
guard blew back a shattering blast of triumph that was really too painfully
full of derision.

I mention this little incident for its connexion with what followed.
A Welsh rustic, sitting behind me, asked if I had not felt my heart burn
within me during the progress of the race? I said, with philosophic calm-
ness, *No*; because we were not racing with a mail, so that no glory could be

so pretentious omg THOMAS DE QUINCEY

gained. In fact, it was sufficiently mortifying that such a Birmingham thing should dare to challenge us. The Welshman replied that he didn't see *that*; for that a cat might look at a king, and a Brummagem coach might lawfully race the Holyhead mail. "*Race* us, if you like," I replied, " though even *that* has an air of sedition; but not *beat* us. This would have been treason; and for its own sake I am glad that the 'Tallyho' was disappointed." So dissatisfied did the Welshman seem with this opinion that at last I was obliged to tell him a very fine story from one of our elder dramatists: viz. that once, in some far oriental kingdom, when the sultan of all the land, with his princes, ladies, and chief omrahs, were flying their falcons, a hawk suddenly flew at a majestic eagle, and, in defiance of the eagle's natural advantages, in contempt also of the eagle's traditional royalty, and before the whole assembled field of astonished spectators from Agra and Lahore, killed the eagle on the spot. Amazement seized the sultan at the unequal contest, and burning admiration for its unparalleled result. He commanded that the hawk should be brought before him; he caressed the bird with enthusiasm; and he ordered that, for the commemoration of his matchless courage, a diadem of gold and rubies should be solemnly placed on the hawk's head, but then that, immediately after this solemn coronation, the bird should be led off to execution, as the most valiant indeed of traitors, but not the less a traitor, as having dared to rise rebelliously against his liege lord and anointed sovereign, the eagle. "Now," said I to the Welshman, "to you and me, as men of refined sensibilities, how painful it would have been that this poor Brummagem brute, the 'Tallyho,' in the impossible case of a victory over us, should have been crowned with Birmingham tinsel, with paste diamonds and Roman pearls, and then led off to instant execution." The Welshman doubted if that could be warranted by law. And, when I hinted at the 6th of Edward Longshanks, chap. 18, for regulating the precedency of coaches, as being probably the statute relied on for the capital punishment of such offences, he replied drily that, if the attempt to pass a mail really were treasonable, it was a pity that the "Tallyho" appeared to have so imperfect an acquaintance with law.

The modern modes of travelling cannot compare with the old mailcoach system in grandeur and power. They boast of more velocity,—not, however, as a consciousness, but as a fact of our lifeless knowledge, resting upon *alien* evidence: as, for instance, because somebody *says* that we have

[handwritten margin note at top: mail coach = better because of the "personal experience" it provides]

gone fifty miles in the hour, though we are far from feeling it as a personal experience; or upon the evidence of a result, as that actually we find ourselves in York four hours after leaving London. Apart from such an assertion, or such a result, I myself am little aware of the pace. But, seated on the old mail-coach, we needed no evidence out of ourselves to indicate the velocity. On this system the word was not *magna loquimur,* as upon railways, but *vivimus.* Yes, "magna *vivimus*"; we do not make verbal ostentation of our grandeurs, we realise our grandeurs in act, and in the very experience of life. The vital experience of the glad animal sensibilities made doubts impossible on the question of our speed; we heard our speed, we saw it, we felt it as a thrilling; and this speed was not the product of blind insensate agencies, that had no sympathy to give, but was incarnated in the fiery eyeballs of the noblest amongst brutes, in his dilated nostril, spasmodic muscles, and thunder-beating hoofs. The sensibility of the horse, uttering itself in the maniac light of his eye, might be the last vibration of such a movement; the glory of Salamanca might be the first. But the intervening links that connected them, that spread the earthquake of battle into the eyeball of the horse, were the heart of man and its electric thrillings—kindling in the rapture of the fiery strife, and then propagating its own tumults by contagious shouts and gestures to the heart of his servant the horse. But now, on the new system of travelling, iron tubes and boilers have disconnected man's heart from the ministers of his locomotion. Nile nor Trafalgar has power to raise an extra bubble in a steam-kettle. The galvanic cycle is broken up for ever; man's imperial nature no longer sends itself forward through the electric sensibility of the horse; the inter-agencies are gone in the mode of communication between the horse and his master out of which grew so many aspects of sublimity under accidents of mists that hid, or sudden blazes that revealed, of mobs that agitated, or midnight solitudes that awed. Tidings fitted to convulse all nations must henceforwards travel by culinary process; and the trumpet that once announced from afar the laurelled mail, heart-shaking when heard screaming on the wind and proclaiming itself through the darkness to every village or solitary house on its route, has now given way for ever to the pot-wallopings of the boiler. Thus have perished multiform openings for public expressions of interests scenical yet natural, in great national tidings,—for revelations of faces and groups that could not offer themselves amongst the fluctuating mobs of

[handwritten margin note, vertical: the difference]

a railway station. The gatherings of gazers about a laurelled mail had one centre, and acknowledged one sole interest. But the crowds attending at a railway station have as little unity as running water, and own as many centres as there are separate carriages in the train.

How else, for example, than as a constant watcher for the dawn, and for the London mail that in summer months entered about daybreak amongst the lawny thickets of Marlborough forest, couldst thou, sweet Fanny of the Bath road, have become the glorified inmate of my dreams? Yet Fanny, as the loveliest young woman for face and person that perhaps in my whole life I have beheld, merited the station which even now, from a distance of forty years, she holds in my dreams; yes, though by links of natural association she brings along with her a troop of dreadful creatures, fabulous and not fabulous, that are more abominable to the heart than Fanny and the dawn are delightful.

Miss Fanny of the Bath road, strictly speaking, lived at a mile's distance from that road, but came so continually to meet the mail that I on my frequent transits rarely missed her, and naturally connected her image with the great thoroughfare where only I had ever seen her. Why she came so punctually I do not exactly know; but I believe with some burden of commissions, to be executed in Bath, which had gathered to her own residence as a central rendezvous for converging them. The mail-coachman who drove the Bath mail and wore the royal livery happened to be Fanny's grandfather. A good man he was, that loved his beautiful granddaughter, and, loving her wisely, was vigilant over her deportment in any case where young Oxford might happen to be concerned. Did my vanity then suggest that I myself, individually, could fall within the line of his terrors? Certainly not, as regarded any physical pretensions that I could plead; for Fanny (as a chance passenger from her own neighbourhood once told me) counted in her train a hundred and ninety-nine professed admirers, if not open aspirants to her favour; and probably not one of the whole brigade but excelled myself in personal advantages. Ulysses even, with the unfair advantage of his accursed bow, could hardly have undertaken that amount of suitors. So the danger might have seemed slight—only that woman is universally aristocratic; it is amongst her nobilities of heart that she *is* so. Now, the aristocratic distinctions in my favour might easily with Miss Fanny have compensated my physical deficiencies. Did I then make love to Fanny? Why, yes; about as much love as one *could* make whilst the mail was changing horses—a process which, ten years later, did not occupy above eighty seconds; but *then*,—viz. about Waterloo—it occupied five times eighty. Now, four hundred seconds offer a field quite ample enough for whispering into a young woman's ear a great deal of truth, and (by way of parenthesis) some trifle of falsehood. Grandpapa did right, therefore, to watch me. And yet, as happens too often to the grandpapas of earth in a contest with the admirers of granddaughters, how vainly would he have watched me had I meditated any evil whispers to Fanny! She, it is my belief, would have protected herself against any man's evil suggestions. But he, as the result showed, could not have intercepted the opportunities for such suggestions. Yet, why not? Was he not active? Was he not blooming? Blooming he was as Fanny herself.

"Say, all our praises why should lords—"

Stop, that's not the line.

"Say, all our roses why should girls engross?"

The coachman showed rosy blossoms on his face deeper even than his granddaughter's—*his* being drawn from the ale-cask, Fanny's from the fountains of the dawn. But, in spite of his blooming face, some infirmities he had; and one particularly in which he too much resembled a crocodile. This lay in a monstrous inaptitude for turning round. The crocodile, I presume, owes that inaptitude to the absurd *length* of his back; but in our grandpapa it arose rather from the absurd *breadth* of his back, combined, possibly, with some growing stiffness in his legs. Now, upon this crocodile infirmity of his I planted a human advantage for tendering my homage to Miss Fanny. In defiance of all his honourable vigilance, no sooner had he presented to us his mighty Jovian back (what a field for displaying to mankind his royal scarlet!), whilst inspecting professionally the buckles, the straps, and the silvery turrets of his harness, than I raised Miss Fanny's hand to my lips, and, by the mixed tenderness and respectfulness of my manner, caused her easily to understand how happy it would make me to rank upon her list as No. 10 or 12: in which case a few casualties amongst her lovers (and, observe, they *hanged* liberally in those days) might have promoted me speedily to the top of the tree; as, on the other hand, with how much loyalty of submission I acquiesced by anticipation in her award, supposing that she should plant me in the very rearward of her favour, as No. 199 + 1. Most truly I loved this beautiful and ingenuous girl; and, had it not been for the Bath mail, timing all courtships by post-office allowance, heaven only knows what might have come of it. People talk of being over head and ears in love; now, the mail was the cause that I sank only over ears in love,—which, you know, still left a trifle of brain to overlook the whole conduct of the affair.

Ah, reader! when I look back upon those days, it seems to me that all things change—all things perish. "Perish the roses and the palms of kings": perish even the crowns and trophies of Waterloo: thunder and lightning are not the thunder and lightning which I remember. Roses are degenerating. The Fannies of our island—though this I say with reluctance—are not visibly improving; and the Bath Road is notoriously superannuated. Crocodiles, you will say, are stationary. Mr. Waterton tells me that the crocodile does *not* change,—that a cayman, in fact, or an alligator, is just as good for riding upon as he was in the time of the Pharaohs. *That* may be; but the reason is that the crocodile does not live fast—he is a slow coach. I believe it is generally understood among naturalists that the crocodile is a blockhead. It is my own impression that the Pharaohs were also blockheads. Now, as the Pharaohs and the crocodile domineered over Egyptian society, this accounts for a singular mistake that prevailed through innumerable generations on the Nile. The crocodile made the ridiculous blunder of supposing man to be meant chiefly for his own eating. Man, taking a different view of the subject, naturally met that mistake by another: he viewed the crocodile as a thing sometimes to worship, but always to run away from. And this continued till Mr. Waterton changed the relations between the animals. The mode of escaping from the reptile he showed to be not by running away, but by leaping on its back booted and spurred. The two animals had misunderstood each other. The use of the crocodile has now been cleared up—viz. to be ridden; and the final cause of man is that he may improve the health of the crocodile by riding him a-foxhunting before breakfast. And it is pretty certain that any crocodile who has been regularly hunted through the season, and is master of the weight he carries, will take a six-barred gate now as well as ever he would have done in the infancy of the pyramids.

If, therefore, the crocodile does *not* change, all things else undeniably *do*: even the shadow of the pyramids grows less. And often the restoration in vision of Fanny and the Bath road makes me too pathetically sensible of that

lost in his web of thoughts—
hallucinating? definitely high

that is... a complex web of thoughts. it he calls up are
imags, it leads him to another, then another...

truth. Out of the darkness, if I happen to call back the image of Fanny, up
rises suddenly from a gulf of forty years a rose in June; or, if I think for an
instant of the rose in June, up rises the heavenly face of Fanny. One after the
other, like the antiphonies in the choral service, rise Fanny and the rose in
June, then back again the rose in June and Fanny. Then come both together,
as in a chorus—roses and Fannies, Fannies and roses, without end, thick as
blossoms in paradise. Then comes a venerable crocodile, in a royal livery of
scarlet and gold, with sixteen capes; and the crocodile is driving four-in-hand
from the box of the Bath mail. And suddenly we upon the mail are pulled
up by a mighty dial, sculptured with the hours, that mingle with the heavens
and the heavenly host. Then all at once we are arrived at Marlborough forest,
amongst the lovely households of the roe-deer; the deer and their fawns retire
into the dewy thickets; the thickets are rich with roses; once again the roses
call up the sweet countenance of Fanny; and she, being the granddaughter
of a crocodile, awakens a dreadful host of semi-legendary animals—griffins,
dragons, basilisks, sphinxes—till at length the whole vision of fighting images crowds into one towering armorial shield, a vast emblazonry of human
charities and human loveliness that have perished, but quartered heraldically
with unutterable and demoniac natures, whilst over all rises, as a surmount-
ing crest, one fair female hand, with the forefinger pointing, in sweet, sorrowful admonition, upwards to heaven, where is sculptured the eternal writing
which proclaims the frailty of earth and her children. ·

giving us his experience - how rooted in reality that is
isn't really important

Going Down with Victory

But the grandest chapter of our experience within the whole mail-coach
service was on those occasions when we went down from London with
the news of victory. A period of about ten years stretched from Trafalgar
to Waterloo; the second and third years of which period (1806 and 1807)
were comparatively sterile; but the other nine (from 1805 to 1815 inclusively)
furnished a long succession of victories, the least of which in such a contest
of Titans, had an inappreciable value of position: partly for its absolute
interference with the plans of our enemy, but still more from its keeping
alive through central Europe the sense of a deep-seated vulnerability in
France. Even to tease the coasts of our enemy, to mortify them by continual
blockades, to insult them by capturing if it were but a baubling schooner
under the eyes of their arrogant armies, repeated from time to time a sullen proclamation of power lodged in one quarter to which the hopes of

Christendom turned in secret. How much more loudly must this proclamation have spoken in the audacity of having bearded the *élite* of their troops, and having beaten them in pitched battles! Five years of life it was worth paying down for the privilege of an outside place on a mail-coach, when carrying down the first tidings of any such event. And it is to be noted that, from our insular situation, and the multitude of our frigates disposable for the rapid transmission of intelligence, rarely did any unauthorised rumour steal away a prelibation from the first aroma of the regular despatches. The government news was generally the earliest news.

From eight p.m. to fifteen or twenty minutes later imagine the mails assembled on parade in Lombard Street; where, at that time, and not in St. Martin's-le-Grand, was seated the General Post-office. In what exact strength we mustered I do not remember; but, from the length of each separate *attelage,* we filled the street, though a long one, and though we were drawn up in double file. On *any* night the spectacle was beautiful. The absolute perfection of all the appointments about the carriages and the harness, their strength, their brilliant cleanliness, their beautiful simplicity—but, more than all, the royal magnificence of the horses—were what might first have fixed the attention. Every carriage on every morning in the year was taken down to an official inspector for examination: wheels, axles, linchpins, pole, glasses, lamps, were all critically probed and tested. Every part of every carriage had been cleaned, every horse had been groomed, with as much rigour as if they belonged to a private gentleman; and that part of the spectacle offered itself always. But the night before us is a night of victory; and, behold! to the ordinary display what a heart-shaking addition!—horses, men, carriages, all are dressed in laurels and flowers, oak-leaves and ribbons. The guards, as being officially his Majesty's servants, and of the coachmen such as are within the privilege of the post-office, wear the royal liveries of course; and, as it is summer (for all the *land* victories were naturally won in summer), they wear, on this fine evening, these liveries exposed to view, without any covering of upper coats. Such a costume, and the elaborate arrangement of the laurels in their hats, dilate their hearts, by giving to them openly a personal connexion with the great news in which already they have the general interest of patriotism. That great national sentiment surmounts and quells all sense of ordinary distinctions. Those passengers who happen to be gentlemen are now hardly to be distinguished as such except by dress; for the usual reserve of their manner in speaking to the attendants has on this night melted away. One heart, one pride, one glory, connects every man by the transcendent bond of his national blood. The spectators, who are numerous beyond precedent, express their sympathy with these fervent feelings by continual hurrahs. Every moment are shouted aloud by the post-office servants, and summoned to draw up, the great ancestral names of cities known to history through a thousand years—Lincoln, Winchester, Portsmouth, Gloucester, Oxford, Bristol, Manchester, York, Newcastle, Edinburgh, Glasgow, Perth, Stirling, Aberdeen—expressing the grandeur of the empire by the antiquity of its towns, and the grandeur of the mail establishment by the diffusive radiation of its separate missions. Every moment you hear the thunder of lids locked down upon the mail-bags. That sound to each individual mail is the signal for drawing off; which process is the finest part of the entire spectacle. Then come the horses into play. Horses! can these be horses that bound off with the action and gestures of leopards? What stir!—what sea-like ferment!—what a thundering of wheels!—what a trampling of hoofs!—what a sounding of trumpets!—what farewell cheers—what redoubling peals of brotherly congratulation, connecting the name of the particular mail—"Liverpool for ever!"—with the name of the particular victory—"Badajoz for ever!" or "Salamanca for ever!" The half-slumbering consciousness that all night long, and all the next day—perhaps for even a longer period—many of these mails, like fire racing along a train of gunpowder, will be kindling at every instant new successions of burning joy, has an obscure effect of multiplying the victory itself, by multiplying to the imagination into infinity the stages of its progressive diffusion. A fiery arrow seems to be let loose, which from that moment is destined to travel, without intermission, westwards for three hundred miles—northwards for six hundred; and the sympathy of our Lombard Street friends at parting is exalted a hundredfold by a sort of visionary sympathy with the yet slumbering sympathies which in so vast a succession we are going to awake.

Liberated from the embarrassments of the city, and issuing into the broad uncrowded avenues of the northern suburbs, we soon begin to enter upon our natural pace of ten miles an hour. In the broad light of the summer evening, the sun, perhaps, only just at the point of setting, we are seen from every storey of every house. Heads of every age crowd to the windows; young and old understand the language of our victorious symbols; and rolling volleys of sympathising cheers run along us, behind us, and before

[handwritten note:] sounds like an awesome experience, probably made them feel pretty good about themselves

us. The beggar, rearing himself against the wall, forgets his lameness—real or assumed—thinks not of his whining trade, but stands erect, with bold exulting smiles, as we pass him. The victory has healed him, and says, Be thou whole! Women and children, from garrets alike and cellars, through infinite London, look down or look up with loving eyes upon our gay ribbons and our martial laurels; sometimes kiss their hands; sometimes hang out, as signals of affection, pocket-handkerchiefs, aprons, dusters, anything that, by catching the summer breezes, will express an aerial jubilation. On the London side of Barnet, to which we draw near within a few minutes after nine, observe that private carriage which is approaching us. The weather being so warm, the glasses are all down; and one may read, as on the stage of a theatre, everything that goes on within. It contains three ladies—one likely to be "mamma," and two of seventeen or eighteen, who are probably her daughters. What lovely animation, what beautiful unpremeditated pantomime, explaining to us every syllable that passes, in these ingenuous girls! By the sudden start and raising of the hands on first discovering our laurelled equipage, by the sudden movement and appeal to the elder lady from both of them, and by the heightened colour on their animated countenances, we can almost hear them saying, "See, see! Look at their laurels! Oh, mamma! there has been a great battle in Spain; and it has been a great victory." In a moment we are on the point of passing them. We passengers—I on the box, and the two on the roof behind me—raise our hats to the ladies; the coachman makes his professional salute with the whip; the guard even, though punctilious on the matter of his dignity as an officer under the crown, touches his hat. The ladies move to us, in return, with a winning graciousness of gesture; all smile on each side in a way that nobody could misunderstand, and that nothing short of a grand national sympathy could so instantaneously prompt. Will these ladies say that we are nothing to *them*? Oh no; they will not say *that*. They cannot deny—they do not deny—that for this night they are our sisters; gentle or simple, scholar or illiterate servant, for twelve hours to come, we on the outside have the honour to be their brothers. Those poor women, again, who stop to gaze upon us with delight at the entrance of Barnet, and seem, by their air of weariness, to be returning from labour—do you mean to say that they are washerwomen and charwomen? Oh, my poor friend, you are quite mistaken. I assure you they stand in a far higher rank; for this one night they feel themselves by birthright to be daughters of England, and answer to no humbler title.

Every joy, however, even rapturous joy—such is the sad law of earth—
may carry with it grief, or fear of grief, to some. Three miles beyond Barnet,
we see approaching us another private carriage, nearly repeating the circumstances of the former case. Here, also, the glasses are all down; here,
also, is an elderly lady seated; but the two daughters are missing; for the
single young person sitting by the lady's side seems to be an attendant—
so I judge from her dress, and her air of respectful reserve. The lady is in
mourning; and her countenance expresses sorrow. At first she does not
look up; so that I believe she is not aware of our approach, until she hears
the measured beating of our horses' hoofs. Then she raises her eyes to
settle them painfully on our triumphal equipage. Our decorations explain
the case to her at once; but she beholds them with apparent anxiety, or
even with terror. Some time before this, I, finding it difficult to hit a flying
mark when embarrassed by the coachman's person and reins intervening,
had given to the guard a *Courier* evening paper, containing the gazette, for
the next carriage that might pass. Accordingly he tossed it in, so folded that
the huge capitals expressing some such legend as GLORIOUS VICTORY
might catch the eye at once. To see the paper, however, at all, interpreted as
it was by our ensigns of triumph, explained everything; and, if the guard
were right in thinking the lady to have received it with a gesture of horror,
it could not be doubtful that she had suffered some deep personal affliction in connexion with this Spanish war.

Here, now, was the case of one who, having formerly suffered, might,
erroneously perhaps, be distressing herself with anticipations of another
similar suffering. That same night, and hardly three hours later, occurred
the reverse case. A poor woman, who too probably would find herself, in a
day or two, to have suffered the heaviest of afflictions by the battle, blindly
allowed herself to express an exultation so unmeasured in the news and its
details as gave to her the appearance which amongst Celtic Highlanders is
called *fey*. This was at some little town where we changed horses an hour or
two after midnight. Some fair or wake had kept the people up out of their
beds, and had occasioned a partial illumination of the stalls and booths,
presenting an unusual but very impressive effect. We saw many lights moving about as we drew near; and perhaps the most striking scene on the
whole route was our reception at this place. The flashing of torches and the
beautiful radiance of blue lights (technically, Bengal lights) upon the heads
of our horses; the fine effect of such a showery and ghostly illumination
falling upon our flowers and glittering laurels; whilst all around ourselves,

that formed a centre of light, the darkness gathered on the rear and flanks in massy blackness: these optical splendours, together with the prodigious enthusiasm of the people, composed a picture at once scenical and affecting, theatrical and holy. As we staid for three or four minutes, I alighted; and immediately from a dismantled stall in the street, where no doubt she had been presiding through the earlier part of the night, advanced eagerly a middle-aged woman. The sight of my newspaper it was that had drawn her attention upon myself. The victory which we were carrying down to the provinces on *this* occasion was the imperfect one of Talavera—imperfect for its results, such was the virtual treachery of the Spanish general, Cuesta, but not imperfect in its ever-memorable heroism. I told her the main outline of the battle. The agitation of her enthusiasm had been so conspicuous when listening, and when first applying for information, that I could not but ask her if she had not some relative in the Peninsular army. Oh yes; her only son was there. In what regiment? He was a trooper in the 23d Dragoons. My heart sank within me as she made that answer. This sublime regiment, which an Englishman should never mention without raising his hat to their memory, had made the most memorable and effective charge recorded in military annals. They leaped their horses—*over* a trench where they could; *into* it, and with the result of death or mutilation, when they could *not*. What proportion cleared the trench is nowhere stated. Those who *did* closed up and went down upon the enemy with such divinity of fervour (I use the word *divinity* by design: the inspiration of God must have prompted this movement to those whom even then He was calling to His presence) that two results followed. As regarded the enemy, this 23d Dragoons, not, I believe, originally three hundred and fifty strong, paralysed a French column six thousand strong, then ascended the hill, and fixed the gaze of the whole French army. As regarded themselves, the 23d were supposed at first to have been barely not annihilated; but eventually, I believe, about one in four survived. And this, then, was the regiment—a regiment already for some hours glorified and hallowed to the ear of all London, as lying stretched, by a large majority, upon one bloody aceldama—in which the young trooper served whose mother was now talking in a spirit of such joyous enthusiasm. Did I tell her the truth? Had I the heart to break up her dreams? No. To-morrow, said I to myself—to-morrow, or the next day, will publish the worst. For one night more wherefore should she not sleep in peace? After to-morrow the chances are too many that peace will forsake her pillow. This brief respite, then, let her owe to *my* gift and *my* forbearance. But, if I told her not of the bloody price that had been paid, not therefore was I silent on the contributions from her son's regiment to that day's service and glory. I showed her not the funeral banners under which the noble regiment was sleeping. I lifted not the overshadowing laurels from the bloody trench in which horse and rider lay mangled together. But I told her how these dear children of England, officers and privates, had leaped their horses over all obstacles as gaily as hunters to the morning's chase. I told her how they rode their horses into the mists of death,— saying to myself, but not saying to *her,* "and laid down their young lives for thee, O mother England! as willingly—poured out their noble blood as cheerfully—as ever, after a long day's sport, when infants, they had rested their wearied heads upon their mother's knees, or had sunk to sleep in her arms." Strange it is, yet true, that she seemed to have no fears for her son's safety, even after this knowledge that the 23d Dragoons had been memorably engaged; but so much was she enraptured by the knowledge that *his* regiment, and therefore that *he,* had rendered conspicuous service in the dreadful conflict—a service which had actually made them, within the last twelve hours, the foremost topic of conversation in London—so absolutely was fear swallowed up in joy—that, in the mere simplicity of her fervent nature, the poor woman threw her arms round my neck, as she thought of her son, and gave to *me* the kiss which secretly was meant for *him.*

The Vision of Sudden Death

What is to be taken as the predominant opinion of man, reflective and philosophic, upon SUDDEN DEATH? It is remarkable that, in different conditions of society, sudden death has been variously regarded as the consummation of an earthly career most fervently to be desired, or, again, as that consummation which is with most horror to be deprecated. Cæsar the Dictator, at his last dinner-party *(caena),* on the very evening before his assassination, when the minutes of his earthly career were numbered, being asked what death, in *his* judgment, might be pronounced the most eligible, replied "That which should be most sudden." On the other hand, the divine Litany of our English Church, when breathing forth supplications, as if in some representative character, for the whole human race prostrate before God, places such a death in the very van of horrors: "From lightning and tempest; from plague, pestilence, and famine; from battle and murder, and from SUDDEN DEATH—*Good Lord, deliver us.*" Sudden death is here made to crown the climax in a grand ascent of calamities; it is ranked among the last of curses; and yet by the noblest of Romans it was ranked as the first of blessings. In that difference most readers will see little more than the essential difference between Christianity and Paganism. But this, on consideration, I doubt. The Christian Church may be right in its estimate of sudden death; and it is a natural feeling, though after all it may also be an infirm one, to wish for a quiet dismissal from life, as that which *seems* most reconcilable with meditation, with penitential retrospects, and with the humilities of farewell prayer. There does not, however, occur to me any direct scriptural warrant for this earnest petition of the English Litany, unless under a special construction of the word "sudden." It seems a petition indulged rather and conceded to human infirmity than exacted from human piety. It is not so much a doctrine built upon the eternities of the Christian system as a plausible opinion built upon special varieties of physical temperament. Let that, however, be as it may, two remarks suggest themselves as prudent restraints upon a doctrine which else *may* wander, and *has* wandered, into an uncharitable superstition. The first is this: that many people are likely to exaggerate the horror of a sudden death from the disposition to lay a false stress upon words or acts simply because by an accident they have become *final* words or acts. If a man dies, for instance, by some sudden death when he happens to be intoxicated, such a death is falsely regarded with peculiar horror; as though the intoxication were suddenly exalted into a blasphemy. But *that* is unphilosophic. The man was, or he was not, *habitually* a drunkard. If not, if his intoxication were a solitary accident, there can be no reason for allowing special emphasis to this act simply because through misfortune it became his final act. Nor, on the other hand, if it were no accident, but one of his *habitual* transgressions, will it be the more habitual or the more a transgression because some sudden calamity, surprising him, has caused this habitual transgression to be also a final one. Could the man have had any reason even dimly to foresee his own sudden death, there would have been a new feature in his act of intemperance—a feature of presumption and irreverence, as in one that, having known himself drawing near to the presence of God, should have suited his demeanour to an expectation so awful. But this is no part of the case supposed. And the only new element in the man's act is not any element of special immorality, but simply of special misfortune.

The other remark has reference to the meaning of the word *sudden*. Very possibly Cæsar and the Christian Church do not differ in the way supposed,—that is, do not differ by any difference of doctrine as between Pagan and Christian views of the moral temper appropriate to death; but perhaps they are contemplating different cases. Both contemplate a violent death, a Βιαθανατος—death that is βιαιος, or, in other words, death that is brought about, not by internal and spontaneous change, but by active force having its origin from without. In this meaning the two authorities agree. Thus far they are in harmony. But the difference is that the Roman by the word "sudden" means *unlingering*, whereas the Christian Litany by "sudden death" means a death *without warning*, consequently without any available summons to religious preparation. The poor mutineer who kneels down to gather into his heart the bullets from twelve firelocks of his pitying comrades dies by a most sudden death in Caesar's sense; one shock, one mighty spasm, one (possibly *not* one) groan, and all is over. But, in the sense of the Litany, the mutineer's death is far from sudden: his offence originally, his imprisonment, his trial, the interval between his sentence and its execution, having all furnished him with separate warnings of his fate—having all summoned him to meet it with solemn preparation.

Here at once, in this sharp verbal distinction, we comprehend the faithful earnestness with which a holy Christian Church pleads on behalf of her poor departing children that God would vouchsafe to them the last great privilege and distinction possible on a death-bed, viz. the opportunity of untroubled preparation for facing this mighty trial. Sudden death, as a mere variety in the modes of dying where death in some shape is inevitable, proposes a question of choice which, equally in the Roman and the Christian sense, will be variously answered according to each man's variety of temperament. Meantime, one aspect of sudden death there is, one modification, upon which no doubt can arise, that of all martyrdoms it is the most agitating—viz. where it surprises a man under circumstances which offer (or which seem to offer) some hurrying, flying, inappreciably minute chance of evading it. Sudden as the danger which it affronts must be any effort by which such an evasion can be accomplished. Even *that*, even the sickening necessity for hurrying in extremity where all hurry seems destined to be vain,—even that anguish is liable to a hideous exasperation in one particular case: viz. where the appeal is made not exclusively to the instinct of self-preservation, but to the conscience, on behalf of some other life besides your own, accidentally thrown upon *your* protection. To fail,

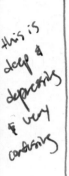

to collapse in a service merely your own, might seem comparatively venial; though, in fact, it is far from venial. But to fail in a case where Providence has suddenly thrown into your hands the final interests of another,—a fellow-creature shuddering between the gates of life and death: this, to a man of apprehensive conscience, would mingle the misery of an atrocious criminality with the misery of a bloody calamity. You are called upon, by the case supposed, possibly to die, but to die at the very moment when, by any even partial failure or effeminate collapse of your energies, you will be self-denounced as a murderer. You had but the twinkling of an eye for your effort, and that effort might have been unavailing; but to have risen to the level of such an effort would have rescued you, though not from dying, yet from dying as a traitor to your final and farewell duty.

The situation here contemplated exposes a dreadful ulcer, lurking far down in the depths of human nature. It is not that men generally are summoned to face such awful trials. But potentially, and in shadowy outline, such a trial is moving subterraneously in perhaps all men's natures. Upon the secret mirror of our dreams such a trial is darkly projected, perhaps, to every one of us. That dream, so familiar to childhood, of meeting a lion, and, through languishing prostration in hope and the energies of hope, that constant sequel of lying down before the lion, publishes the secret frailty of human nature—reveals its deep-seated falsehood to itself—records its abysmal treachery. Perhaps not one of us escapes that dream; perhaps, as by some sorrowful doom of man, that dream repeats for every one of us, through every generation, the original temptation in Eden. Every one of us, in this dream, has a bait offered to the infirm places of his own individual will; once again a snare is presented for tempting him into captivity to a luxury of ruin; once again, as in aboriginal Paradise, the man falls by his own choice; again, by infinite iteration, the ancient earth groans to Heaven, through her secret caves, over the weakness of her child. "Nature, from her seat, sighing through all her works," again "gives signs of woe that all is lost"; and again the counter-sigh is repeated to the sorrowing heavens for the endless rebellion against God. It is not without probability that in the world of dreams every one of us ratifies for himself the original transgression. In dreams, perhaps under some secret conflict of the midnight sleeper, lighted up to the consciousness at the time, but darkened to the memory as soon as all is finished, each several child of our mysterious race completes for himself the treason of the aboriginal fall.

The incident, so memorable in itself by its features of horror, and so scenical by its grouping for the eye, which furnished the text for this reverie upon *Sudden Death,* occurred to myself in the dead of night, as a solitary spectator, when seated on the box of the Manchester and Glasgow mail, in the second or third summer after Waterloo. I find it necessary to relate the circumstances, because they are such as could not have occurred unless under a singular combination of accidents. In those days, the oblique and lateral communications with many rural post-offices were so arranged, either through necessity or through defect of system, as to make it requisite for the main north-western mail (*i.e.* the *down* mail) on reaching Manchester to halt for a number of hours; how many, I do not remember; six or seven, I think; but the result was that, in the ordinary course, the mail recommenced its journey northwards about midnight. Wearied with the long detention at a gloomy hotel, I walked out about eleven o'clock at night for the sake of fresh air; meaning to fall in with the mail and resume my seat at the post-office. The night, however, being yet dark, as the moon had scarcely risen, and the streets being at that hour empty, so as to offer no opportunities for asking the road, I lost my way, and did not reach the post-office until it was considerably past midnight; but, to my great relief (as it was important for me to be in Westmorland by the morning), I saw in the huge saucer eyes of the mail, blazing through the gloom, an evidence that my chance was not yet lost. Past the time it was; but, by some rare accident, the mail was not even yet ready to start. I ascended to my seat on the box, where my cloak was still lying as it had lain at the Bridgewater Arms. I had left it there in imitation of a nautical discoverer, who leaves a bit of bunting on the shore of his discovery, by way of warning off the ground the whole human race, and notifying to the Christian and the heathen worlds, with his best compliments, that he has hoisted his pocket-handkerchief once and for ever upon that virgin soil: thenceforward claiming the *jus dominii* to the top of the atmosphere above it, and also the right of driving shafts to the centre of the earth below it; so that all people found after this warning either aloft in upper chambers of the atmosphere, or groping in subterraneous shafts, or squatting audaciously on the surface of the soil, will be treated as trespassers—kicked, that is to say, or decapitated, as circumstances may suggest, by their very faithful servant, the owner of the said pocket-handkerchief. In the present case, it is probable that my cloak might not have been respected, and the *jus gentium* might have been cruelly violated in my person—for, in the dark, people commit deeds of darkness, gas being a great ally of morality; but it so happened that on this night there was no other outside passenger; and thus the crime, which else was but too probable, missed fire for want of a criminal.

Having mounted the box, I took a small quantity of laudanum, having already travelled two hundred and fifty miles—viz. from a point seventy miles beyond London. In the taking of laudanum there was nothing extraordinary. But by accident it drew upon me the special attention of my assessor on the box, the coachman. And in *that* also there was nothing extraordinary. But by accident, and with great delight, it drew my own attention to the fact that this coachman was a monster in point of bulk, and that he had but one eye. In fact, he had been foretold by Virgil as

"*Monstrum horrendum, informe, ingens, cui lumen ademptum.*"

He answered to the conditions in every one of the items:—1, a monster he was; 2, dreadful; 3, shapeless; 4, huge; 5, who had lost an eye. But why should *that* delight me? Had he been one of the Calendars in the *Arabian Nights,* and had paid down his eye as the price of his criminal curiosity, what right had *I* to exult in his misfortune? I did *not* exult; I delighted in no man's punishment, though it were even merited. But these personal distinctions (Nos. 1, 2, 3, 4, 5) identified in an instant an old friend of mine whom I had known in the south for some years as the most masterly of mail-coachmen. He was the man in all Europe that could (if *any* could) have driven six-in-hand full gallop over *Al Sirat*—that dreadful bridge of Mahomet, with no side battlements, and of *extra* room not enough for a razor's edge—leading right across the bottomless gulf. Under this eminent man, whom in Greek I cognominated Cyclops *Diphrélates* (Cyclops the Charioteer), I, and others known to me, studied the diphrelatic art. Excuse, reader, a word too elegant to be pedantic. As a pupil, though I paid extra fees, it is to be lamented that I did not stand high in his esteem. It showed his dogged honesty (though, observe, not his discernment) that he could not see my merits. Let us excuse his absurdity in this particular by remembering his want of an eye. Doubtless *that* made him blind to my merits. In the art of conversation, however, he admitted that I had the whip-hand of him. On this present occasion great joy was at our meeting. But what was Cyclops doing here? Had the medical men recommended northern air, or how? I collected, from such explanations as he volunteered, that he had an interest at stake in some suit-at-law now pending at Lancaster; so that probably he had got himself transferred to this station for the purpose of connecting with his professional pursuits an instant readiness for the calls of his lawsuit.

Meantime, what are we stopping for? Surely we have now waited long enough. Oh, this procrastinating mail, and this procrastinating post-office! Can't they take a lesson upon that subject from *me*? Some people have called *me* procrastinating. Yet you are witness, reader, that I was here kept waiting for the post-office. Will the post-office lay its hand on its heart, in its moments of sobriety, and assert that ever it waited for me? What are they about? The guard tells me that there is a large extra accumulation of foreign mails this night, owing to irregularities caused by war, by wind, by weather, in the packet service, which as yet does not benefit at all by steam. For an *extra* hour, it seems, the post-office has been engaged in threshing out the pure wheaten correspondence of Glasgow, and winnowing it from the chaff of all baser intermediate towns. But at last all is finished. Sound your horn, guard! Manchester, good-bye!; we've lost an hour by your criminal conduct at the post-office: which, however, though I do not mean to part with a serviceable ground of complaint, and one which really *is* such for the horses, to me secretly is an advantage, since it compels us to look sharply for this lost hour amongst the next eight or nine, and to recover it (if we can) at the rate of one mile extra per hour. Off we are at last, and at eleven miles an hour; and for the moment I detect no changes in the energy or in the skill of Cyclops.

From Manchester to Kendal, which virtually (though not in law) is the capital of Westmorland, there were at this time seven stages of eleven miles each. The first five of these, counting from Manchester, terminate in Lancaster; which is therefore fifty-five miles north of Manchester, and the same distance exactly from Liverpool. The first three stages terminate in Preston (called, by way of distinction from other towns of that name, *Proud* Preston); at which place it is that the separate roads from Liverpool and from Manchester to the north become confluent. Within these first three stages lay the foundation, the progress, and termination of our night's adventure. During the first stage, I found out that Cyclops was mortal: he was liable to the shocking affection of sleep—a thing which previously I had never suspected. If a man indulges in the vicious habit of sleeping, all the skill in aurigation of Apollo himself, with the horses of Aurora to execute his notions, avails him nothing. "Oh, Cyclops!" I exclaimed, "thou art mortal. My friend, thou snorest." Through the first eleven miles, however, this infirmity—which I grieve to say that he shared with the whole Pagan Pantheon—betrayed itself only by brief snatches. On waking up, he made an apology for himself which, instead of mending matters, laid open a gloomy vista of coming disasters. The summer assizes, he reminded me, were now going on at Lancaster: in consequence of which for three nights and three days he had not lain down in a bed. During the day he was waiting for his own summons as a witness on the trial in which he was interested, or else, lest he should be missing at the critical moment, was drinking with the other witnesses under the pastoral surveillance of the attorneys. During the night, or that part of it which at sea would form the middle watch, he was driving. This explanation certainly accounted for his drowsiness, but in a way which made it much more alarming; since now, after several days' resistance to this infirmity, at length he was steadily giving way. Throughout the second stage he grew more and more drowsy. In the second mile of the third stage he surrendered himself finally and without a struggle to his perilous temptation. All his past resistance had but deepened the weight of this final oppression. Seven atmospheres of sleep rested upon him; and, to consummate the case, our worthy guard, after singing "Love amongst the Roses" for perhaps thirty times, without invitation and without applause, had in revenge moodily resigned himself to slumber—not so deep, doubtless, as the coachman's, but deep enough for mischief. And thus at last, about ten miles from Preston, it came about that I found myself left in charge of his Majesty's London and Glasgow mail, then running at the least twelve miles an hour.

What made this negligence less criminal than else it must have been thought was the condition of the roads at night during the assizes. At that time, all the law business of populous Liverpool, and also of populous Manchester, with its vast cincture of populous rural districts, was called up by ancient usage to the tribunal of Lilliputian Lancaster. To break up this old traditional usage required, 1, a conflict with powerful established interests, 2, a large system of new arrangements, and 3, a new parliamentary statute. But as yet this change was merely in contemplation. As things were at present, twice in the year so vast a body of business rolled northwards from the southern quarter of the county that for a fortnight at least it occupied the severe exertions of two judges in its despatch. The consequence of this was that every horse available for such a service, along the whole line of road, was exhausted in carrying down the multitudes of people who were parties to the different suits. By sunset, therefore, it usually happened that, through utter exhaustion amongst men and horses, the road sank into profound silence. Except the exhaustion in the vast adjacent county of York from a contested election, no such silence succeeding to no such fiery uproar was ever witnessed in England.

On this occasion the usual silence and solitude prevailed along the road. Not a hoof nor a wheel was to be heard. And, to strengthen this false luxurious confidence in the noiseless roads, it happened also that the night was one of peculiar solemnity and peace. For my own part, though slightly alive to the possibilities of peril, I had so far yielded to the influence of the mighty calm as to sink into a profound reverie. The month was August; in the middle of which lay my own birthday—a festival to every thoughtful man suggesting solemn and often sigh-born thoughts. The county was my own native county—upon which, in its southern section, more than upon any equal area known to man past or present, had descended the original curse of labour in its heaviest form, not mastering the bodies only of men, as of slaves, or criminals in mines, but working through the fiery will. Upon no equal space of earth was, or ever had been, the same energy of human power put forth daily. At this particular season also of the assizes, that dreadful hurricane of flight and pursuit, as it might have seemed to a stranger, which swept to and from Lancaster all day long, hunting the county up and down, and regularly subsiding back into silence about sunset, could not fail (when united with this permanent distinction of Lancashire as the very metropolis and citadel of labour) to point the thoughts pathetically upon that counter-vision of rest, of saintly repose from strife and sorrow, towards which, as to their secret haven, the profounder aspirations of man's heart are in solitude continually travelling. Obliquely upon our left we were nearing the sea; which also must, under the present circumstances, be repeating the general state of halcyon repose. The sea, the atmosphere, the light, bore each an orchestral part in this universal lull. Moonlight and the first timid tremblings of the dawn were by this time blending; and the blendings were brought into a still more exquisite state of unity by a slight silvery mist, motionless and dreamy, that covered the woods and fields, but with a veil of equable transparency. Except the feet of our own horses,—which, running on a sandy margin of the road, made but little disturbance,—there was no sound abroad. In the clouds and on the earth prevailed the same majestic peace; and, in spite of all that the villain of a schoolmaster has done for the ruin of our sublimer thoughts, which are the thoughts of our infancy, we still believe in no such nonsense as a limited atmosphere. Whatever we may swear with our false feigning lips, in our faithful hearts we still believe, and must for ever believe, in fields of air traversing the total gulf between earth and the central heavens. Still, in the confidence of children that tread without fear *every* chamber in their father's house, and to whom no door is closed, we, in that Sabbatic vision which sometimes is revealed for an hour upon nights like this, ascend with easy steps from the sorrow-stricken fields of earth upwards to the sandals of God.

Suddenly, from thoughts like these I was awakened to a sullen sound, as of some motion on the distant road. It stole upon the air for a moment; I listened in awe; but then it died away. Once roused, however, I could not but observe with alarm the quickened motion of our horses. Ten years' experience had made my eye learned in the valuing of motion; and I saw that we were now running thirteen miles an hour. I pretend to no presence of mind. On the contrary, my fear is that I am miserably and shamefully deficient in that quality as regards action. The palsy of doubt and distraction hangs like some guilty weight of dark unfathomed remembrances upon my energies when the signal is flying for *action*. But, on the other hand, this accursed gift I have, as regards *thought*, that in the first step towards the possibility of a misfortune I see its total evolution; in the radix of the series I see too certainly and too instantly its entire expansion; in the first syllable of the dreadful sentence I read already the last. It was not that I feared for ourselves. *Us* our bulk and impetus charmed against peril in any collision. And I had ridden through too many hundreds of perils that were frightful to approach, that were matter of laughter to look back upon, the first face of which was horror, the parting face a jest—for any anxiety to rest upon *our* interests. The mail was not built, I felt assured, nor bespoke, that could betray *me* who trusted to its protection. But any carriage that we could meet would be frail and light in comparison of ourselves. And I remarked this ominous accident of our situation,—we were on the wrong side of the road. But then, it may be said, the other party, if other there was, might also be on the wrong side; and two wrongs might make a right. *That* was not likely. The same motive which had drawn *us* to the right-hand side of the road—viz. the luxury of the soft beaten sand as contrasted with the paved centre—would prove attractive to others. The two adverse carriages would therefore, to a certainty, be travelling on the same side; and from this side, as not being ours in law, the crossing over to the other would, of course, be looked for from *us*. Our lamps, still lighted, would give the impression of vigilance on our part. And every creature that met us would rely upon *us* for quartering. All this, and if the separate links of the anticipation had been a thousand times more, I saw, not discursively, or by effort, or by succession, but by one flash of horrid simultaneous intuition.

Under this steady though rapid anticipation of the evil which *might* be gathering ahead, ah! what a sullen mystery of fear, what a sigh of woe, was that which stole upon the air, as again the far-off sound of a wheel was heard! A whisper it was—a whisper from, perhaps, four miles off—secretly announcing a ruin that, being foreseen, was not the less inevitable; that, being known, was not therefore healed. What could be done—who was it that could do it—to check the storm-flight of these maniacal horses? Could I not seize the reins from the grasp of the slumbering coachman? You, reader, think that it would have been in *your* power to do so. And I quarrel not with your estimate of yourself. But, from the way in which the coachman's hand was viced between his upper and lower thigh, this was impossible. Easy was it? See, then, that bronze equestrian statue. The cruel rider has kept the bit in his horse's mouth for two centuries. Unbridle him for a minute, if you please, and wash his mouth with water. Easy was it? Unhorse me, then, that imperial rider; knock me those marble feet from those marble stirrups of Charlemagne.

The sounds ahead strengthened, and were now too clearly the sounds of wheels. Who and what could it be? Was it industry in a taxed cart? Was it youthful gaiety in a gig? Was it sorrow that loitered, or joy that raced? For as yet the snatches of sound were too intermitting, from distance, to decipher the character of the motion. Whoever were the travellers, something must be done to warn them. Upon the other party rests the active responsibility, but upon *us*—and, woe is me! that *us* was reduced to my frail opium-shattered self—rests the responsibility of warning. Yet, how should this be accomplished? Might I not sound the guard's horn? Already, on the first thought, I was making my way over the roof to the guard's seat. But this, from the accident which I have mentioned, of the foreign mails being piled upon the roof, was a difficult and even dangerous attempt to one cramped by nearly three hundred miles of outside travelling. And, fortunately, before I had lost much time in the attempt, our frantic horses swept round an angle of the road which opened upon us that final stage where the collision must be accomplished and the catastrophe sealed. All was apparently finished. The court was sitting; the case was heard; the judge had finished; and only the verdict was yet in arrear.

Before us lay an avenue straight as an arrow, six hundred yards, perhaps, in length; and the umbrageous trees, which rose in a regular line from either side, meeting high overhead, gave to it the character of a cathedral aisle. These trees lent a deeper solemnity to the early light; but there was still light enough to perceive, at the further end of this Gothic aisle, a frail reedy gig, in which were seated a young man, and by his side a young lady. Ah, young sir! what are you about? If it is requisite that you should whisper your communications to this young lady—though really I see nobody, at an hour and on a road so solitary, likely to overhear you—is it therefore requisite that you should carry your lips forward to hers? The little carriage is creeping on at one mile an hour; and the parties within it, being thus tenderly engaged, are naturally bending down their heads. Between them and eternity, to all human calculation, there is but a minute and a-half. Oh heavens! what is it that I shall do? Speaking or acting, what help can I offer? Strange it is, and to a mere auditor of the tale might seem laughable, that I should need a suggestion from the *Iliad* to prompt the sole resource that remained. Yet so it was. Suddenly I remembered the shout of Achilles, and its effect. But could I pretend to shout like the son of Peleus, aided by Pallas? No: but then I needed not the shout that should alarm all Asia militant; such a shout would suffice as might carry terror into the hearts of two thoughtless young people and one gig-horse. I shouted—and the young man heard me not. A second time I shouted—and now he heard me, for now he raised his head. ?? Can he not drive?

Here, then, all had been done that, by me, *could* be done; more on *my* part was not possible. Mine had been the first step; the second was for the young man; the third was for God. If, said I, this stranger is a brave man, and if indeed he loves the young girl at his side—or, loving her not, if he feels the obligation, pressing upon every man worthy to be called a man, of doing his utmost for a woman confided to his protection—he will at least make some effort to save her. If *that* fails, he will not perish the more, or by a death more cruel, for having made it; and he will die as a brave man should, with his face to the danger, and with his arm about the woman that he sought in vain to save. But, if he makes no effort,—shrinking without a struggle from his duty,—he himself will not the less certainly perish for this baseness of poltroonery. He will die no less: and why not? Wherefore should we grieve that there is one craven less in the world? No; *let* him perish, without a pitying thought of ours wasted upon him; and, in that case, all our grief will be reserved for the fate of the helpless girl who now, upon the least shadow of failure in *him,* must by the fiercest of translations— must without time for a prayer—must within seventy seconds—stand before the judgment-seat of God.

But craven he was not: sudden had been the call upon him, and sudden was his answer to the call. He saw, he heard, he comprehended, the ruin that was coming down: already its gloomy shadow darkened above him; and already he was measuring his strength to deal with it. Ah! what a vulgar thing does courage seem when we see nations buying it and selling it for a shilling a-day: ah! what a sublime thing does courage seem when some fearful summons on the great deeps of life carries a man, as if running before a hurricane, up to the giddy crest of some tumultuous crisis from which lie two courses, and a voice says to him audibly, "One way lies hope; take the other, and mourn for ever!" How grand a triumph if, even then, amidst the raving of all around him, and the frenzy of the danger, the man is able to confront his situation—is able to retire for a moment into solitude with God, and to seek his counsel from *Him!*

For seven seconds, it might be, of his seventy, the stranger settled his countenance stedfastly upon us, as if to search and value every element in the conflict before him. For five seconds more of his seventy he sat immovably, like one that mused on some great purpose. For five more, perhaps, he sat with eyes upraised, like one that prayed in sorrow, under some extremity of doubt, for light that should guide him to the better choice. Then suddenly he rose; stood upright; and, by a powerful strain upon the reins, raising his horse's fore-feet from the ground, he slewed him round on the pivot of his hind-legs, so as to plant the little equipage in a position nearly at right angles to ours. Thus far his condition was not improved; except as a first step had been taken towards the possibility of a second. If no more were done, nothing was done; for the little carriage still occupied the very centre of our path, though in an altered direction. Yet even now it may not be too late: fifteen of the seventy seconds may still be unexhausted; and one almighty bound may avail to clear the ground. Hurry, then, hurry! for the flying moments—*they* hurry. Oh, hurry, hurry, my brave young man! for the cruel hoofs of our horses—*they* also hurry! Fast are the flying moments, faster are the hoofs of our horses. But fear not for *him,* if human energy can suffice; faithful was he that drove to his terrific duty; faithful was the horse to *his* command. One blow, one impulse given with voice and hand, by the stranger, one rush from the horse, one bound as if in the act of rising to a fence, landed the docile creature's fore-feet upon the crown or arching centre of the road. The larger half of the little equipage had then cleared our over-towering shadow: *that* was evident even to my own agitated sight. But it mattered little that one wreck should float off in safety if upon the wreck that perished were embarked the human freightage. The rear part of the carriage—was *that* certainly beyond the line of absolute ruin? What power could answer the question? Glance of eye, thought of man, wing of angel, which of these had speed enough to sweep between the question and the answer, and divide the one from the other? Light does not tread upon the steps of light more indivisibly than did our all-conquering arrival upon the escaping efforts of the gig. *That* must the young man have felt too plainly. His back was now turned to us; not by sight could he any longer communicate with the peril; but, by the dreadful rattle of our harness, too truly had his ear been instructed that all was finished as regarded any effort of *his.* Already in resignation he had rested from his struggle; and perhaps in his heart he was whispering, "Father, which art in heaven, do Thou finish above what I on earth have attempted." Faster than ever mill-race we ran past them in our inexorable flight. Oh, raving of hurricanes that must have sounded in their young ears at the moment of our transit! Even in that moment the thunder of collision spoke aloud. Either with the swingle-bar, or with the haunch of our near leader, we had struck the off-wheel of the little gig; which stood rather obliquely, and not quite so far advanced as to be accurately parallel with the near-wheel The blow, from the fury of our passage, resounded terrifically. I rose in horror, to gaze upon the ruins we might have caused. From my elevated station I looked down, and looked back upon the scene; which in a moment told its own tale, and wrote all its records on my heart for ever.

Here was the map of the passion that now had finished. The horse was planted immovably, with his fore-feet upon the paved crest of the central road. He of the whole party might be supposed untouched by the passion

of death. The little cany carriage—partly, perhaps, from the violent torsion of the wheels in its recent movement, partly from the thundering
blow we had given to it—as if it sympathised with human horror, was all
alive with tremblings and shiverings. The young man trembled not, nor
shivered. He sat like a rock. But *his* was the steadiness of agitation frozen
into rest by horror. As yet he dared not to look round; for he knew that, if
anything remained to do, by him it could no longer be done. And as yet
he knew not for certain if their safety were accomplished. But the lady—

But the lady—! Oh, heavens! will that spectacle ever depart from
my dreams, as she rose and sank upon her seat, sank and rose, threw up
her arms wildly to heaven, clutched at some visionary object in the air,
fainting, praying, raving, despairing? Figure to yourself, reader, the elements of the case; suffer me to recall before your mind the circumstances
of that unparalleled situation. From the silence and deep peace of this
saintly summer night—from the pathetic blending of this sweet moonlight, dawnlight, dreamlight—from the manly tenderness of this flattering,
whispering, murmuring love—suddenly as from the woods and fields—
suddenly as from the chambers of the air opening in revelation—suddenly
as from the ground yawning at her feet, leaped upon her, with the flashing
of cataracts, Death the crowned phantom, with all the equipage of his terrors, and the tiger roar of his voice.

The moments were numbered; the strife was finished; the vision was
closed. In the twinkling of an eye, our flying horses had carried us to the
termination of the umbrageous aisle; at the right angles we wheeled into
our former direction; the turn of the road carried the scene out of my eyes
in an instant, and swept it into my dreams for ever.

Dream Fugue: Founded on the Preceding Theme of Sudden Death

> "*Whence the sound*
> *Of instruments, that made melodious chime,*
> *Was heard, of harp and organ; and who moved*
> *Their stops and chords was seen; his volant touch*
> *Instinct through all proportions, low and high,*
> *Fled and pursued transverse the resonant fugue.*"
>
> PARADISE LOST, BOOK XI
> *TUMULTUOSISSIMAMENTE*

Passion of sudden death! that once in youth I read and interpreted by the shadows of thy averted signs!—rapture of panic taking the shape (which amongst tombs in churches I have seen) of woman bursting her sepulchral bonds—of woman's Ionic form bending forward from the ruins of her grave with arching foot, with eyes upraised, with clasped adoring hands—waiting, watching, trembling, praying for the trumpet's call to rise from dust for ever! Ah, vision too fearful of shuddering humanity on the brink of almighty abysses!—vision that didst start back, that didst reel away, like a shrivelling scroll from before the wrath of fire racing on the wings of the wind! Epilepsy so brief of horror, wherefore is it that thou canst not die? Passing so suddenly into darkness, wherefore is it that still thou sheddest thy sad funeral blights upon the gorgeous mosaics of dreams? Fragment of music too passionate, heard once, and heard no more, what aileth thee, that thy deep rolling chords come up at intervals through all the worlds of sleep, and after forty years have lost no element of horror?

I

Lo, it is summer—almighty summer! The everlasting gates of life and summer are thrown open wide; and on the ocean, tranquil and verdant as a savannah, the unknown lady from the dreadful vision and I myself are floating—she upon a fairy pinnace, and I upon an English three-decker. Both of us are wooing gales of festal happiness within the domain of our common country, within that ancient watery park, within the pathless chase of ocean, where England takes her pleasure as a huntress through winter and summer, from the rising to the setting sun. Ah, what a wilderness of floral beauty was hidden, or was suddenly revealed, upon the tropic islands through which the pinnace moved! And upon her deck what a bevy of human flowers: young women how lovely, young men how noble, that were dancing together, and slowly drifting towards *us* amidst music and incense, amidst blossoms from forests and gorgeous corymbi from vintages, amidst natural carolling, and the echoes of sweet girlish laughter. Slowly the pinnace nears us, gaily she hails us, and silently she disappears beneath the shadow of our mighty bows. But then, as at some signal from heaven, the music, and the carols, and the sweet echoing of girlish laughter—all are hushed. What evil has smitten the pinnace, meeting or overtaking her?

feels like a completely different voice

Did ruin to our friends couch within our own dreadful shadow? Was our shadow the shadow of death? I looked over the bow for an answer, and, behold! the pinnace was dismantled; the revel and the revellers were found no more; the glory of the vintage was dust; and the forests with their beauty were left without a witness upon the seas. "But where," and I turned to our crew—"where are the lovely women that danced beneath the awning of flowers and clustering corymbi? Whither have fled the noble young men that danced with *them?*" Answer there was none. But suddenly the man at the mast-head, whose countenance darkened with alarm, cried out, "Sail on the weather beam! Down she comes upon us: in seventy seconds she also will founder."

II

I looked to the weather side, and the summer had departed. The sea was rocking, and shaken with gathering wrath. Upon its surface sat mighty mists, which grouped themselves into arches and long cathedral aisles. Down one of these, with the fiery pace of a quarrel from a cross-bow, ran a frigate right athwart our course. "Are they mad?" some voice exclaimed from our deck. "Do they woo their ruin?" But in a moment, as she was close upon us, some impulse of a heady current or local vortex gave a wheeling bias to her course, and off she forged without a shock. As she ran past us, high aloft amongst the shrouds stood the lady of the pinnace. The deeps opened ahead in malice to receive her, towering surges of foam ran after her, the billows were fierce to catch her. But far away she was borne into desert spaces of the sea: whilst still by sight I followed her, as she ran before the howling gale, chased by angry sea-birds and by maddening billows; still I saw her, as at the moment when she ran past us, standing amongst the shrouds, with her white draperies streaming before the wind. There she stood, with hair dishevelled, one hand clutched amongst the tackling—rising, sinking, fluttering, trembling, praying; there for leagues I saw her as she stood, raising at intervals one hand to heaven, amidst the fiery crests of the pursuing waves and the raving of the storm; until at last, upon a sound from afar of malicious laughter and mockery, all was hidden for ever in driving showers; and afterwards, but when I know not, nor how,

III

Sweet funeral bells from some incalculable distance, wailing over the dead that die before the dawn, awakened me as I slept in a boat moored to some familiar shore. The morning twilight even then was breaking; and, by the dusky revelations which it spread, I saw a girl, adorned with a garland of white roses about her head for some great festival, running along the solitary strand in extremity of haste. Her running was the running of panic; and often she looked back as to some dreadful enemy in the rear. But, when I leaped ashore, and followed on her steps to warn her of a peril in front, alas! from me she fled as from another peril, and vainly I shouted to her of quicksands that lay ahead. Faster and faster she ran; round a promontory of rocks she wheeled out of sight; in an instant I also wheeled round it, but only to see the treacherous sands gathering above her head. Already her person was buried; only the fair young head and the diadem of white roses around it were still visible to the pitying heavens; and, last of all, was visible one white marble arm. I saw by the early twilight this fair young head, as it was sinking down to darkness—saw this marble arm, as it rose above her head and her treacherous grave, tossing, faltering, rising, clutching, as at some false deceiving hand stretched out from the clouds—saw this marble arm uttering her dying hope, and then uttering her dying despair. The head, the diadem, the arm—these all had sunk; at last over these also the cruel quicksand had closed; and no memorial of the fair young girl remained on earth, except my own solitary tears, and the funeral bells from the desert seas, that, rising again more softly, sang a requiem over the grave of the buried child, and over her blighted dawn.

I sat, and wept in secret the tears that men have ever given to the memory of those that died before the dawn, and by the treachery of earth, our mother. But suddenly the tears and funeral bells were hushed by a shout as of many nations, and by a roar as from some great king's artillery, advancing rapidly along the valleys, and heard afar by echoes from the mountains. "Hush!" I said, as I bent my ear earthwards to listen—"hush!—this either is the very anarchy of strife, or else"—and then I listened more profoundly, and whispered as I raised my head—"or else, oh heavens! it is *victory* that is final, victory that swallows up all strife."

IV

Immediately, in trance, I was carried over land and sea to some distant kingdom, and placed upon a triumphal car, amongst companions crowned with laurel. The darkness of gathering midnight, brooding over all the land, hid from us the mighty crowds that were weaving restlessly about ourselves as a centre: we heard them, but saw them not. Tidings had arrived, within an hour, of a grandeur that measured itself against centuries; too full of pathos they were, too full of joy, to utter themselves by other language than by tears, by restless anthems, and *Te Deums* reverberated from the choirs and orchestras of earth. These tidings we that sat upon the laurelled car had it for our privilege to publish amongst all nations. And already, by signs audible through the darkness, by snortings and tramplings, our angry horses, that knew no fear of fleshly weariness, upbraided us with delay. Wherefore *was* it that we delayed? We waited for a secret word, that should bear witness to the hope of nations as now accomplished for ever. At midnight the secret word arrived; which word was—*Waterloo and Recovered Christendom!* The dreadful word shone by its own light; before us it went; high above our leaders' heads it rode, and spread a golden light over the paths which we traversed. Every city, at the presence of the secret word, threw open its gates. The rivers were conscious as we crossed. All the forests, as we ran along their margins, shivered in homage to the secret word. And the darkness comprehended it.

Two hours after midnight we approached a mighty Minster. Its gates, which rose to the clouds, were closed. But, when the dreadful word that rode before us reached them with its golden light, silently they moved back upon their hinges; and at a flying gallop our equipage entered the grand aisle of the cathedral. Headlong was our pace; and at every altar, in the little chapels and oratories to the right hand and left of our course, the lamps, dying or sickening, kindled anew in sympathy with the secret word that was flying past. Forty leagues we might have run in the cathedral, and as yet no strength of morning light had reached us, when before us we saw the aerial galleries of organ and choir. Every pinnacle of the fretwork, every station of advantage amongst the traceries, was crested by white-robed choristers that sang deliverance; that wept no more tears, as once their fathers had wept; but at intervals that sang together to the generations, saying,

Why include these sections in this same essay, instead of a new one?

"Chant the deliverer's praise in every tongue,"

and receiving answers from afar,

"Such as once in heaven and earth were sung."

And of their chanting was no end; of our headlong pace was neither pause nor slackening.

Thus as we ran like torrents—thus as we swept with bridal rapture over the Campo Santo of the cathedral graves—suddenly we became aware of a vast necropolis rising upon the far-off horizon—a city of sepulchres, built within the saintly cathedral for the warrior dead that rested from their feuds on earth. Of purple granite was the necropolis; yet, in the first minute, it lay like a purple stain upon the horizon, so mighty was the distance. In the second minute it trembled through many changes, growing into terraces and towers of wondrous altitude, so mighty was the pace. In the third minute already, with our dreadful gallop, we were entering its suburbs. Vast sarcophagi rose on every side, having towers and turrets that, upon the limits of the central aisle, strode forward with haughty intrusion, that ran back with mighty shadows into answering recesses. Every sarcophagus showed many bas-reliefs—bas-reliefs of battles and of battle-fields; battles from forgotten ages, battles from yesterday; battle-fields that, long since, nature had healed and reconciled to herself with the sweet oblivion of flowers; battle-fields that were yet angry and crimson with carnage. Where the terraces ran, there did *we* run; where the towers curved, there did *we* curve. With the flight of swallows our horses swept round every angle. Like rivers in flood wheeling round headlands, like hurricanes that ride into the secrets of forests, faster than ever light unwove the mazes of darkness, our flying equipage carried earthly passions, kindled warrior instincts, amongst the dust that lay around us—dust oftentimes of our noble fathers that had slept in God from Créci to Trafalgar. And now had we reached the last sarcophagus, now were we abreast of the last bas-relief, already had we recovered the arrow-like flight of the illimitable central aisle, when coming up this aisle to meet us we beheld afar off a female child, that rode in a carriage as frail as flowers. The mists which went before her hid the fawns that drew her, but could not hide the shells and tropic flowers with which she played—but could not hide the lovely smiles by which she uttered her trust in the mighty cathedral, and in the cherubim that looked down upon her from the mighty shafts of its pillars. Face to face she was meeting us; face to face she rode, as if danger there were none. "Oh, baby!" I exclaimed, "shalt thou be the ransom for Waterloo? Must we, that carry tidings of great joy to every people, be messengers of ruin to thee!" In horror I rose at the thought; but then also, in horror at the thought, rose one that was sculptured on a bas-relief—a Dying Trumpeter. Solemnly from the field of battle he rose to his feet; and, unslinging his stony trumpet, carried it, in his dying anguish, to his stony lips—sounding once, and yet once again; proclamation that, in *thy* ears, oh baby! spoke from the battlements of death. Immediately deep shadows fell between us, and aboriginal silence. The choir had ceased to sing. The hoofs of our horses, the dreadful rattle of our harness, the groaning of our wheels, alarmed the graves no more. By horror the bas-relief had been unlocked unto life. By horror we, that were so full of life, we men and our horses, with their fiery fore-legs rising in mid air to their everlasting gallop, were frozen to a bas-relief. Then a third time the trumpet sounded; the seals were taken off all pulses; life, and the frenzy of life, tore into their channels again; again the choir burst forth in sunny grandeur, as from the muffling of storms and darkness; again the thunderings of our horses carried temptation into the graves. One cry burst from our lips, as the clouds, drawing off from the aisle, showed it empty before us.—"Whither has the infant fled?— is the young child caught up to God?" Lo! afar off, in a vast recess, rose three mighty windows to the clouds; and on a level with their summits, at height insuperable to man, rose an altar of purest alabaster. On its eastern face was trembling a crimson glory. A glory was it from the reddening dawn that now streamed *through* the windows? Was it from the crimson robes of the martyrs painted *on* the windows? Was it from the bloody bas-reliefs of earth? There, suddenly, within that crimson radiance, rose the apparition of a woman's head, and then of a woman's figure. The child it was—grown up to woman's height. Clinging to the horns of the altar, voiceless she stood— sinking, rising, raving, despairing; and behind the volume of incense that, night and day, streamed upwards from the altar, dimly was seen the fiery font, and the shadow of that dreadful being who should have baptized her with the baptism of death. But by her side was kneeling her better angel, that hid his face with wings; that wept and pleaded for *her;* that prayed when *she* could *not;* that fought with Heaven by tears for *her* deliverance; which also, as he raised his immortal countenance from his wings, I saw, by the glory in his eye, that from Heaven he had won at last.

V

Then was completed the passion of the mighty fugue. The golden tubes of the organ, which as yet had but muttered at intervals—gleaming amongst clouds and surges of incense—threw up, as from fountains unfathomable, columns of heart-shattering music. Choir and anti-choir were filling fast with unknown voices. Thou also, Dying Trumpeter, with thy love that was victorious, and thy anguish that was finishing, didst enter the tumult; trumpet and echo—farewell love, and farewell anguish—rang through the dreadful *sanctus.* Oh, darkness of the grave! that from the crimson altar and from the fiery font wert visited and searched by the effulgence in the angel's eye—were these indeed thy children? Pomps of life, that, from the burials of centuries, rose again to the voice of perfect joy, did ye indeed mingle with the festivals of Death? Lo! as I looked back for seventy leagues through the mighty cathedral, I saw the quick and the dead that sang together to God, together that sang to the generations of man. All the hosts of jubilation, like armies that ride in pursuit, moved with one step. Us, that, with laurelled heads, were passing from the cathedral, they overtook, and, as with a garment, they wrapped us round with thunders greater than our own. As brothers we moved together; to the dawn that advanced, to the stars that fled; rendering thanks to God in the highest— that, having hid His face through one generation behind thick clouds of War, once again was ascending, from the Campo Santo of Waterloo was ascending, in the visions of Peace; rendering thanks for thee, young girl! whom having overshadowed with His ineffable passion of death, suddenly did God relent, suffered thy angel to turn aside His arm, and even in thee, sister unknown! shown to me for a moment only to be hidden for ever, found an occasion to glorify His goodness. A thousand times, amongst the phantoms of sleep, have I seen thee entering the gates of the golden dawn, with the secret word riding before thee, with the armies of the grave be- hind thee,—seen thee sinking, rising, raving, despairing; a thousand times in the worlds of sleep have seen thee followed by God's angel through storms, through desert seas, through the darkness of quicksands, through dreams and the dreadful revelations that are in dreams; only that at the last, with one sling of His victorious arm, He might snatch thee back from ruin, and might emblazon in thy deliverance the endless resurrections of His love!

1860

Belgium

Now, coincidentally, we are fighting an Opium War. According to some historians, we are either doing so because we are all addicted to morphine, or we are doing so because the Chinese are not. Also at issue is the Industrial Revolution. This year, Aloysius Bertrand's only book will be published posthumously. It's a short collection of musings on ancient and medieval history that scholars like to say is "flowery," "fantastic," and "completely out of touch," a naive and blind denial of the world that clangs around him. Example: in the most famous of his texts, Bertrand imagines a water nymph who is trying to seduce him. She offers immortality. She offers him her beauty. She says she has a kingdom under the water that he can share. But Bertrand, in the end, declines the ondine's offer, because he knows that he won't be able to breathe beneath the water. This is around the time that the middle class is born. Also: modern cities, modern crime, modern anomie. A new world is struggling to emerge from the old. And Bertrand is trapped between them. He's invented the prose poem.

ALOYSIUS BERTRAND

Ondine

I fell asleep, and thought I heard ere long
A harmony, subtle and enchanting;
And close beside me a gentle murmuring
So tender and sad it can silence song.

CHARLES BRUGNOT, *THE TWO SYLPHS*

"Listen!—Listen!—it's me down here, Ondine, splashing all these drop-lets against your casement windowpanes so that they echo, here in the dim, regretful moonlight; and up there, high above us in her black silk dress, is the chateau's lady upon her balcony, gazing out at this beautiful starry night and at my lovely, sleeping lake.

"Each ripple that you see is a water-sprite, swimming in the flowing cur-rents; each current of each stream winds path-like towards my palace; and my palace, too, is a liquid domain, located well beneath the lake-waters, in the triangle of fire, and earth, and air.

"Listen!—Listen!—my father stirs the croaking stream with a green birch branch, and my sisters with their foam-flecked arms embrace entire islands of iris, water-lilies, and glistening stands of grass; or, giggling, make a mockery of the ancient, bearded willow, as he bends his back and goes on fishing."

And when her softly murmured song was done, she begged me outright to slip her ring on my finger, so as to become an Ondine's husband; and to return with her to her palace, there to become king of the lakes.

And when I told her I loved a mortal woman, she pouted as if vexed; then shed a teardrop or two—but finally burst out into laughter, to dissolve then like radiant raindrops, streaming down the length of my blue-black windows.

(translated by Michael Benedikt)

1869

France

"Which of us," asks Charles Baudelaire, "has not dreamed of the miracle of a more poetic prose—musical, rhythmic, supple enough to adapt to the soul's lyrical impulses, the undulations of the reverie, the jibes of the unconscious?" Baudelaire has read Aloysius Bertrand's book twenty-seven times. And now, the same year during which plastic is invented, when women's suffrage has begun, when someone driving in central Ireland becomes the world's first victim of a traffic accident, Baudelaire fulfills his dream of a more poetic prose: unadorned, free flowing, associative in movement, something that follows the patterns of the human thought process, rather than the process of fulfilling a villanelle. Indeed, the subjects in Baudelaire's poems frequently reside on the underside of contemporary Parisian life—beneath the rules of society—thus justifying his formal break with the strict high-minded conventions of French poetry at the time. His subjects were dirty; his formal experiments naughty. "Free verse" in poetry has now been introduced, and the most rebellious poets are those who are writing prose.

CHARLES BAUDELAIRE

Be Drunk

You have to be always drunk. That's all there is to it—it's the only way. So as not to feel the horrible burden of time that breaks your back and bends you to the earth, you have to be continually drunk.

But on what? Wine, poetry, or virtue—as you wish. But be drunk.

And if sometimes, on the steps of a palace or the green grass of a ditch, in the mournful solitude of your room, you wake again, drunkenness already diminishing or gone, ask the wind, the wave, the star, the bird, the clock, everything that is flying, everything that is groaning, everything that is rolling, everything that is singing, everything that is speaking . . . ask what time it is, and wind, wave, star, bird, clock will answer you: "It is time to be drunk! So as not to be the martyred slaves of time, be drunk, be continually drunk! On wine, on poetry, or virtue as you wish."

(translated by Louis Simpson)

1873

France

And yet: "There is no freedom in art," as T. S. Eliot will insist. For every artist is in constant communication with the past, vacillating repeatedly between an adherence to and a resistance of our heritage of conventions. A "fixity and flux" as Eliot later called it—that which constitutes the very vitality of art. "I don't know how to explain it to you," Arthur Rimbaud will write, "but it is time to challenge the reality on which you've been making yourself drunk." Poets have placed Rimbaud in a long line of writers who have advanced the tradition of verse. I think it's time for essayists to add some flux to that assumption.

Arthur Rimbaud

A Season in Hell

"Once, If My Memory Serves Me Well"

Once, if my memory serves me well, my life was a banquet where every heart revealed itself, where every wine flowed.

One evening I took Beauty in my arms—and I thought her bitter—and I insulted her.

I steeled myself against justice.

I fled. O witches, O misery, O hate, my treasure was left in your care . . .

I have withered within me all human hope. With the silent leap of a sullen beast, I have downed and strangled every joy.

I have called for executioners; I want to perish chewing on their gun butts. I have called for plagues, to suffocate in sand and blood. Unhappiness has been my god. I have lain down in the mud, and dried myself off in the crime-infested air. I have played the fool to the point of madness.

And springtime brought me the frightful laugh of an idiot.

Now recently, when I found myself ready to *croak!* I thought to seek the key to the banquet of old, where I might find an appetite again.

That key is Charity. (This idea proves I was dreaming!)

"You will stay a hyena, etc. . . . ," shouts the demon who once crowned me with such pretty poppies. "Seek death with all your desires, and all selfishness, and all the Seven Deadly Sins."

Ah, I've taken too much of that: still, dear Satan, don't look so annoyed, I beg you! And while waiting for a few belated cowardices, since you value in a writer all lack of descriptive or didactic flair, I pass you these few foul pages from the diary of a Damned Soul.

Bad Blood

From my ancestors the Gauls I have pale blue eyes, a narrow brain, and awkwardness in competition. I think my clothes are as barbaric as theirs. But I don't butter my hair.

The Gauls were the most stupid hide-flayers and hay-burners of their time.

From them I inherit: idolatry, and love of sacrilege—oh, all sorts of vice; anger, lechery—terrific stuff, lechery—lying, above all, and laziness.

I have a horror of all trades and crafts. Bosses and workers, all of them peasants, and common. The hand that holds the pen is as good as the one that holds the plow. (What a century for hands!) I'll never learn to use my hands. And then, domesticity goes too far. The propriety of beggary shames me. Criminals are as disgusting as men without balls; I'm intact, and I don't care.

But who has made my tongue so treacherous, that until now it has counseled and kept me in idleness? I have not used even my body to get along. Out-idling the sleepy toad, I have lived everywhere. There's not one family in Europe that I don't know. Families, I mean, like mine, who owe their existence to the Declaration of the Rights of Man. I have known each family's eldest son!

If only I had a link to some point in the history of France!

But instead, nothing.

I am well aware that I have always been of an inferior race. I cannot understand revolt. My race has never risen, except to plunder: to devour like wolves a beast they did not kill.

I remember the history of France, the Eldest Daughter of the Church. I would have gone, a village serf, crusading to the Holy Land; my head is full of roads in the Swabian plains, of the sight of Byzantium, of the ramparts of Jerusalem; the cult of Mary, the pitiful thought of Christ crucified, turns in my head with a thousand profane enchantments—I sit like a leper among broken pots and nettles, at the foot of a wall eaten away by the sun. —And later, a wandering mercenary, I would have bivouacked under German nighttimes.

Ah! one thing more: I dance the Sabbath in a scarlet clearing, with old women and children.

I don't remember much beyond this land, and Christianity. I will see myself forever in its past. But always alone, without a family; what language, in fact, did I used to speak? I never see myself in the councils of Christ; nor in the councils of the Lords, Christ's representatives. What was I in the century past? I only find myself today. The vagabonds, the hazy wars are gone. The inferior race has swept over all—the People (as they put it), Reason; Nation and Science.

Ah, Science! Everything is taken from the past. For the body and the soul—the last sacrament—we have Medicine and Philosophy, household remedies and folk songs rearranged. And royal entertainments, and games that kings forbid. Geography, Cosmography, Mechanics, Chemistry! . . .

Science, the new nobility! Progress! The world moves! . . . And why shouldn't it?

We have visions of numbers. We are moving toward the *Spirit.* What I say is oracular and absolutely right. I understand . . . and since I cannot express myself except in pagan terms, I would rather keep quiet.

Pagan blood returns! The Spirit is at hand . . . why does Christ not help me, and grant my soul nobility and freedom? Ah, but the Gospel belongs to the past! The Gospel. The Gospel . . .

I wait gluttonously for God. I have been of inferior race for ever and ever.

And now I am on the beaches of Brittany. . . . Let cities light their lamps in the evening; my daytime is done, I am leaving Europe. The air of the sea will burn my lungs; lost climates will turn my skin to leather. To swim, to pulverize grass, to hunt, above all to smoke; to drink strong drinks, as strong as molten ore, as did those dear ancestors around their fires.

I will come back with limbs of iron, with dark skin, and angry eyes: in this mask, they will think I belong to a strong race. I will have gold; I will be brutal and indolent. Women nurse these ferocious invalids come back from the tropics. I will become involved in politics. Saved.

Now I am accursed, I detest my native land. The best thing is a drunken sleep, stretched out on some strip of shore.

But no one leaves. Let us set out once more on our native roads, burdened with my vice—that vice that since the age of reason has driven roots of suffering into my side—that towers to heaven, beats me, hurls me down, drags me on.

Ultimate innocence, final timidity. All's said. Carry no more my loathing and treacheries before the world.

Come on! Marching, burdens, the desert, boredom and anger.

Hire myself to whom? What beast adore? What sacred images destroy? What hearts shall I break? What lie maintain? Through what blood wade?

Better to keep away from justice. A hard life, outright stupor—with a dried-out fist to lift the coffin lid, lie down, and suffocate. No old age this way—no danger: terror is very un-French.

—Ah! I am so forsaken I will offer at any shrine impulses toward perfection.

Oh, my self-denial, my marvelous Charity, my Selfless Love! And still here below!

De profundis, Domine . . . what an ass I am!

When I was still a little child, I admired the hardened convict on whom the prison door will always close; I used to visit the bars and the rented rooms his presence had consecrated; I saw *with his eyes* the blue sky and the flower-filled work of the fields; I followed his fatal scent through city streets. He had more strength than the saints, more sense than any explorer—and he, he alone! was witness to his glory and his rightness.

Along the open road on winter nights, homeless, cold, and hungry, one voice gripped my frozen heart: "Weakness or strength: you exist, that is strength. . . . You don't know where you are going or why you are going; go in everywhere, answer everyone. No one will kill you, any more than if you were a corpse." In the morning my eyes were so vacant and my face so dead that the people I met *may not even have seen me.*

In cities, mud went suddenly red and black, like a mirror when a lamp in the next room moves, like treasure in the forest! Good luck, I cried, and I saw a sea of flames and smoke rise to heaven, and left and right all wealth exploded like a billion thunderbolts.

But orgies and the companionship of women were impossible for me. Not even a friend. I saw myself before an angry mob, facing a firing squad, weeping out sorrows they could not understand, and pardoning—like Joan of Arc!—"Priests, professors and doctors, you are mistaken in delivering me into the hands of the law. I have never been one of you; I have never been a Christian; I belong to the race that sang on the scaffold; I do not understand your laws; I have no moral sense; I am a brute: you are making a mistake. . . ."

Yes, my eyes are closed to your light. I am an animal, a nigger. But I can be saved. You are fake niggers; maniacs, savages, misers, all of you. Businessman, you're a nigger; judge, you're a nigger; general, you're a nigger; emperor, old scratch-head, you're a nigger: you've drunk a liquor no one taxes, from Satan's still. This nation is inspired by fever and cancer. Invalids and old men are so respectable that they ask to be boiled. The best thing is to quit this continent where madness prowls, out to supply hostages for these wretches. I will enter the true kingdom of the sons of Ham.

Do I understand nature? Do I understand myself? *No more words.* I shroud dead men in my stomach. . . . Shouts, drums, dance, dance, dance! I can't even imagine the hour when the white men land, and I will fall into nothingness.

Thirst and hunger, shouts, dance, dance, dance, dance!

The white men are landing! Cannons! Now we must be baptized, get dressed, and go to work.

My heart has been stabbed by grace. Ah! I hadn't thought this would happen.

But I haven't done anything wrong. My days will be easy, and I will be spared repentance. I will not have had the torments of the soul half-dead to the Good, where austere light rises again like funeral candles. The fate of a first-born son, a premature coffin covered with shining tears. No doubt, perversion is stupid, vice is stupid; rottenness must always be cast away. But the clock must learn to strike more than hours of pure pain! Am I to be carried away like a child, to play in paradise, forgetting all this misery?

Quick! Are there any other lives? Sleep for the rich is impossible. Wealth has always lived openly. Divine love alone confers the keys of knowledge. I see that nature is only a show of kindness. Farewell chimeras, ideals and errors.

The reasonable song of angels rises from the rescue ship: it is divine love. Two loves! I may die of earthly love, die of devotion. I have left behind creatures whose grief will grow at my going. You choose me from among the castaways; aren't those who remain my friends?

Save them!

I am reborn in reason. The world is good. I will bless life. I will love my brothers. There are no longer childhood promises. Nor the hope of escaping old age and death. God is my strength, and I praise God.

Boredom is no longer my love. Rage, perversion, madness, whose every impulse and disaster I know—my burden is set down entire. Let us appraise with clear heads the extent of my innocence. I am no longer able to ask for the consolation of a beating. I don't imagine I'm off on a honeymoon with Jesus Christ for a father-in-law.

I am no prisoner of my own reason. I have said: God. I want freedom, within salvation: how shall I go about it? A taste for frivolity has left me. No further need for divine love or for devotion to duty. I do not regret the age of emotion and feeling. To each his own reason, contempt, Charity: I keep my place at the top of the angelic ladder of good sense.

As for settled happiness, domestic or not . . . no, I can't. I am too dissipated, too weak. Work makes life blossom, an old idea, not mine; my life doesn't weigh enough, it drifts off and floats far beyond action, that third pole of the world.

What an old maid I'm turning into, to lack the courage to love death!

If only God would grant me that celestial calm, ethereal calm, and prayer—like the saints of old. —The Saints! They were strong! Anchorites, artists of a kind we no longer need. . . .

Does this farce have no end? My innocence is enough to make me cry. Life is the farce we all must play.

Stop it! This is your punishment. . . . *Forward march!*

Ah! my lungs burn, my temples roar! Night rolls in my eyes, beneath this sun! My heart . . . my arms and legs. . . .

Where are we going? To battle? I am weak! the others go on ahead . . . tools, weapons . . . give me time!

Fire! Fire at me! Here! or I'll give myself up! —Cowards! —I'll kill myself! I'll throw myself beneath the horses' hooves!

Ah! . . .

—I'll get used to it.

That would be the French way, the path of honor!

Night in Hell

I have just swallowed a terrific mouthful of poison. —Blessed, blessed, blessed the advice I was given!

—My guts are on fire. The power of the poison twists my arms and legs, cripples me, drives me to the ground. I die of thirst, I suffocate, I cannot cry. This is Hell, eternal torment! See how the flames rise! I burn as I ought to. Go on, Devil!

I once came close to a conversion to the good and to felicity, salvation. How can I describe my vision; the air of Hell is too thick for hymns! There were millions of delightful creatures in smooth spiritual harmony, strength and peace, noble ambitions, I don't know what all.

Noble ambitions!

But I am still alive! Suppose damnation is eternal! A man who wants to mutilate himself is certainly damned, isn't he? I believe I am in Hell, therefore I am. This is the catechism at work. I am the slave of my baptism. You, my parents, have ruined my life, and your own. Poor child! —Hell is powerless against pagans. —I am still alive! Later on, the delights of damnation will become more profound. A crime, quick, and let me fall to nothingness, condemned by human law.

Shut up, will you shut up! Everything here is shame and reproach—Satan saying that the fire is worthless, that my anger is ridiculous and silly. —Ah, stop! . . .those mistakes someone whispered—magic spells, deceptive odors, childish music—and to think that I possess the truth, that I can have a vision of justice: my judgment is sound and firm, I am prime for perfection. . . . Pride. —My scalp begins to tighten. Have mercy! Lord, I'm afraid! Water, I thirst, I thirst! Ah, childhood, grass and rain, the puddle on the paving stones, *Moonlight, when the clock strikes twelve.* . . . The devil is in the clock tower, right now! Mary! Holy Virgin! . . .—Horrible stupidity.

Look there, are those not honorable men, who wish me well? Come on . . . a pillow over my mouth, they cannot hear me, they are only ghosts. Anyway, no one ever thinks of anyone else. Don't let them come closer. I must surely stink of burning flesh. . . .

My hallucinations are endless. This is what I've always gone through: the end of my faith in history, the neglect of my principles. I shall say no more about this; poets and visionaries would be jealous. I am the richest one of all, a thousand times, and I will hoard it like the sea.

O God—the clock of life stopped but a moment ago. I am no longer within the world. —Theology is accurate; hell is certainly *down below*—and heaven is up on high. Ecstasy, nightmare, sleep, in a nest of flames.

How the mind wanders idly in the country . . . Satan, Ferdinand, blows with the wild seed . . . Jesus walks on purple thorns but doesn't bend them . . . Jesus used to walk on troubled waters. In the light of the lantern we saw him there, all white, with long brown hair, standing in the curve of an emerald wave. . . .

I will tear the veils from every mystery—mysteries of religion or of nature, death, birth, the future, the past, cosmogony, and nothingness. I am a master of phantasmagoria.

Listen!

Every talent is mine! —There is no one here, and there is someone: I wouldn't want to waste my treasure. —Shall I give you Afric chants, belly dancers? Shall I disappear, shall I begin an attempt to discover the *Ring*? Shall I? I will manufacture gold, and medicines.

Put your faith in me, then; faith comforts, it guides and heals. Come unto me all of you—even the little children—let me console you, let me pour out my heart for you—my miraculous heart! —Poor men, poor laborers! I do not ask for prayers; give me only your trust, and I will be happy.

Think of me, now. All this doesn't make me miss the world much. I'm lucky not to suffer more. My life was nothing but sweet stupidities, unfortunately.

Bah! I'll make all the ugly faces I can! We are out of the world, that's sure. Not a single sound. My sense of touch is gone. Ah, my château, my Saxony, my willow woods! Evenings and mornings, nights and days. . . . How tired I am!

I ought to have a special hell for my anger, a hell for my pride—and a hell for sex; a whole symphony of hells!

I am weary, I die. This is the grave and I'm turning into worms, horror of horrors! Satan, you clown, you want to dissolve me with your charms. Well, I want it. I want it! Stab me with a pitchfork, sprinkle me with fire!

Ah! To return to life! To stare at our deformities. And this poison, this eternally accursèd embrace! My weakness, and the world's cruelty! My God, have pity, hide me, I can't control myself at all! I am hidden, and I am not.

And as the Damned soul rises, so does the fire.

First Delirium: The Foolish Virgin, the Infernal Bridegroom

Let us hear the confession of an old friend in Hell:

"O Lord, O Celestial Bridegroom, do not turn thy face from the confession of the most pitiful of thy handmaidens. I am lost. I'm drunk. I'm impure. What a life!

"Pardon, Lord in Heaven, pardon! Ah, pardon! All these tears! And all the tears to come later on, I hope!

"Later on, I will meet the Celestial Bridegroom! I was born to be *His* slave. —That other one can beat me now!

"Right now, it's the end of the world! Oh, girls . . . my friends . . . no, not my friends . . . I've never gone through *anything* like this; delirium, torments, anything. . . . It's so silly!

"Oh, I cry, I'm suffering! I really am suffering! And still I've got a right to do whatever I want, now that I am covered with contempt by the most contemptible hearts.

"Well, let me make my confession anyway, though I may have to repeat it twenty times again—*so* dull, and *so* insignificant!

"I am a slave of the Infernal Bridegroom; the one who seduced the foolish virgins. That's exactly the devil he is. He's no phantom, he's no ghost. But I, who have lost my wits, damned and dead to the world—no one will be able to kill me—how can I describe him to you? I can't even talk anymore! I'm all dressed in mourning, I'm crying, I'm afraid. Please, dear Lord, a little fresh air, if you don't mind, please!

"I am a widow—I used to be a widow—oh, yes, I used to be very serious in those days; I wasn't born to become a skeleton! He was a child—or almost. . . . His delicate, mysterious ways enchanted me. I forgot all my duties in order to follow him. What a life we lead! True life is lacking. We are exiles from this world, really—I go where he goes; I *have* to. And lots of times he gets mad at me—at *me,* poor sinner! That Devil! (He really *is* a Devil, you know, and *not a man.*)

"He says: 'I don't love women. Love has to be reinvented, we know that. The only thing women can ultimately imagine is security. Once they get that, love, beauty, everything else goes out the window. All they have left is cold disdain; that's what marriages live on nowadays. Sometimes I see women who ought to be happy, with whom I could have found companionship, already swallowed up by brutes with as much feeling as an old log. . . .'

"I listen to him turn infamy into glory, cruelty into charm. 'I belong to an ancient race: my ancestors were Norsemen: they slashed their own bodies, drank their own blood. I'll slash my body all over, I'll tattoo myself, I want to be as ugly as a Mongol; you'll see, I'll scream in the streets. I want to go really mad with anger. Don't show me jewels; I'll get down on all fours and writhe on the carpet. I want my wealth stained all over with blood. I will *never* do any work. . . .' Several times, at night, his demon seized me, and we rolled about wrestling! —Sometimes at night when he's drunk he hangs around street corners or behind doors, to scare me to death. 'I'll get my throat cut for sure, won't *that* be disgusting.' And, oh, those days when he wants to go around pretending he's a criminal!

"Sometimes he talks, in his backcountry words, full of emotion, about death, and how it makes us repent, and how surely there are miserable people in the world, about exhausting work, and about saying goodbye and how it tears your heart. In the dives where we used to get drunk, he would cry when he looked at the people around us—cattle of the slums. He used to pick up drunks in the dark streets. He had the pity of a brutal mother for little children. He went around with all the sweetness of a little girl on her way to Sunday school. He pretended to know all about everything—business, art, medicine—and I always went along with him; I had to!

"I used to see clearly all the trappings that he hung up in his imagination; costumes, fabrics, furniture. . . . It was I who lent him weapons, and a change of face. I could visualize everything that affected him, exactly as he would have imagined it for himself. Whenever he seemed depressed, I would follow him into strange, complicated adventures, on and on, into good and evil; but I always knew I could never be a part of his world. Beside his dear body, as he slept, I lay awake hour after hour, night after night, trying to imagine why he wanted so much to escape from reality. No man before had ever had such a desire. I was aware—without being afraid for him—that he could become a serious menace to society. Did he, perhaps, have secrets that would *remake life?* No, I told myself, he was only looking for them. But of course, his charity is under a spell, and I am its prisoner. No one else could have the strength—the strength of despair!—to stand it, to stand being cared for and loved by him. Besides, I could never imagine him with anybody else—we all have eyes for our own Dark Angel, never other people's Angels—at least I think so. I lived in his soul as if it were a palace that had been cleared out so that the most unworthy person in it would be you, that's all. Ah, *really,* I used to depend on him terribly. But what did he want with my dull, my cowardly existence? He couldn't improve me, though he never managed to kill me! I get so sad and disappointed; sometimes I say to him 'I understand you.' He just shrugs his shoulders.

"And so my heartaches kept growing and growing, and I saw myself going more and more to pieces (and everyone else would have seen it, too, if I hadn't been so miserable that no one even looked at me anymore!), and still more and more I craved his affection. . . . His kisses and his friendly arms around me were just like heaven—a dark heaven, that I could go into, and where I wanted only to be left—poor, deaf, dumb, and blind. Already, I was getting to depend on it. I used to imagine that we were two happy children free to wander in a Paradise of sadness. We were in absolute harmony. Deeply moved, we labored side by side. But then, after a piercing embrace, he would say: 'How funny it will all seem, all you've gone through, when I'm not here anymore. When you no longer feel my arms around your shoulders, nor my heart beneath you, nor this mouth on your eyes. Because I will have to go away some day, far away. Besides, I've got to help out others too; that's what I'm here for. Although I won't really like it . . . dear heart. . . .' And in that instant I could feel myself, with him gone, dizzy with fear, sinking down into the most horrible blackness—into death. I made him promise that he would never leave me. And he promised, twenty times; promised like a lover. It was as meaningless as my saying to him: 'I understand you.'

"Oh, I've never been jealous of him. He'll never leave me, I'm sure of it. What will he do? He doesn't know a soul; he'll never work; he wants to live like a sleepwalker. Can his kindness and his charity by themselves give him his place in the real world? There are moments when I forget the wretched mess I've fallen into. . . . He will give me strength; we'll travel, we'll go hunting in the desert, we'll sleep on the sidewalks of unknown cities, carefree and happy. Or else some day I'll wake up and his magic power will have changed all laws and morals, but the world will still be the same and leave me my desires and my joys and my lack of concern. Oh, that wonderful world of adventures that we found in children's books—won't you give me that world? I've suffered so much; I deserve a reward. . . . He can't. I don't know what he *really* wants. He says he has hopes and regrets: but they have nothing to do with me. Does he talk to God? Maybe I should talk to God myself. I am in the depths of the abyss, and I have forgotten how to pray.

"Suppose he did explain his sadness to me—would I understand it any better than his jokes and insults? He attacks me, he spends hours making me ashamed of everything in the world that has ever meant anything to me, and then he gets mad if I cry.

". . . 'Do you see that lovely young man going into that beautiful, peaceful house? His name is Duval, Dufour; . . . Armand, Maurice, whatever you please. There is a woman who has spent her life loving that evil creature;

she died. I'm sure she's a saint in heaven right now. You are going to kill me
the way he killed that woman. That's what's in store for all of us who have
unselfish hearts. . . .' Oh, dear! There were days when all men of action
seemed to him like the toys of some grotesque raving. He would laugh,
horribly, on and on. Then he would go back to acting like a young mother,
or an older sister. . . . If he were not such a wild thing, we would be saved!
But even his sweetness is mortal. . . . I am his slave. . . .

"Oh, I've lost my mind!

"Some day maybe he'll just disappear miraculously, but I absolutely
must be told about it, I mean if he's going to go back up into heaven or
someplace, so that I can go and watch for just a minute the Assumption of
my darling boy. . . ."

One hell of a household!

Second Delirium: The Alchemy of Words

My turn now. The story of one of my insanities.

For a long time I boasted that I was master of all possible landscapes—
and I thought the great figures of modern painting and poetry were
laughable.

What I liked were: absurd paintings, pictures over doorways, stage
sets, carnival backdrops, billboards, bright-colored prints, old-fashioned
literature, church Latin, erotic books full of misspellings, the kind of novels
our grandmothers read, fairy tales, little children's books, old operas, silly
old songs, the naïve rhythms of country rimes.

I dreamed of Crusades, voyages of discovery that nobody had heard
of, republics without histories, religious wars stamped out, revolutions in
morals, movements of races and of continents; I used to believe in every
kind of magic.

I invented colors for the vowels! A black, E white, I red, O blue, U
green. I made rules for the form and movement of every consonant, and I
boasted of inventing, with rhythms from within me, a kind of poetry that
all the senses, sooner or later, would recognize. And I alone would be its
translator.

I began it as an investigation. I turned silences and nights into words.
What was unutterable, I wrote down. I made the whirling world stand
still.

Far from flocks, from birds and country girls,
What did I drink within that leafy screen
Surrounded by tender hazelnut trees
In the warm green mist of afternoon?

What could I drink from this young Oise
—Tongueless trees, flowerless grass, dark skies—
Drink from these yellow gourds, far from the hut
I loved? Some golden draught that made me sweat.

I would have made a doubtful sign for an inn.
Later, toward evening, the sky filled with clouds . . .
Water from the woods runs out on virgin sands,
And heavenly winds cast ice thick on the ponds;

Then I saw gold, and wept, but could not drink.

◀ ▶

At four in the morning, in summertime,
Love's drowsiness still lasts . . .
The bushes blow away the odor
    Of the night's feast.

Beyond the bright Hesperides,
Within the western workshop of the Sun,
Carpenters scramble—in shirtsleeves—
    Work is begun.

And in desolate, moss-grown isles
They raise their precious panels
    Where the city
    Will paint a hollow sky.

For these charming dabblers in the arts
Who labor for a King in Babylon,
Venus! Leave for a moment
    Lovers' haloed hearts . . .

O Queen of Shepherds!
Carry the purest eau-de-vie
To these workmen while they rest
And take their bath at noonday, in the sea.

The worn-out ideas of old-fashioned poetry played an important part in my alchemy of words.

I got used to elementary hallucination: I could very precisely see a mosque instead of a factory, a drum corps of angels, horse carts on the highways of the sky, a drawing room at the bottom of a lake; monsters and mysteries. A vaudeville's title filled me with awe.

And so I explained my magical sophistries by turning words into visions!

At last, I began to consider my mind's disorder a sacred thing. I lay about idle, consumed by an oppressive fever: I envied the bliss of animals—caterpillars, who portray the innocence of a second childhood; moles, the slumber of virginity!

My mind turned sour. I said farewell to the world in poems something like ballads:

A SONG FROM THE HIGHEST TOWER

Let it come, let it come,
The season we can love!

I have waited so long
That at length I forget,
And leave unto heaven
My fear and regret;

A sick thirst
Darkens my veins.

Let it come, let it come,
The season we can love!

So the green field
To oblivion falls,

Overgrown, flowering
With incense and weeds.

And the cruel noise
Of dirty flies.

Let it come, let it come,
The season we can love!

I loved the desert, burnt orchards, tired old shops, warm drinks. I dragged myself through stinking alleys, and with my eyes closed I offered myself to the sun, the god of fire.

"General: If on your ruined ramparts one cannon still remains, shell us with clods of dried-up earth. Shatter the mirrors of expensive shops! And the drawing rooms! Make the city swallow its dust! Turn gargoyles to rust. Stuff boudoirs with rubies' fiery powder. . . ."

Oh, the little fly! Drunk at the urinal of a country inn, in love with rotting weeds; a ray of light dissolves him!

I only find within my bones
A taste for eating earth and stones.
When I feed, I feed on air,
Rocks and coals and iron ore.

My hunger, turn. Hunger, feed:
        A field of bran.
Gather as you can the bright
        Poison weed.

Eat the rocks a beggar breaks,
The stones of ancient churches' walls,
Pebbles, children of the flood,
Loaves left lying in the mud.

◆ ▶

Beneath a bush the wolf will howl,
Spitting bright feathers

From his feast of fowl:
Like him, I devour myself.

Waiting to be gathered
Fruits and grasses spend their hours;
The spider spinning in the hedge
Eats only flowers.

Let me sleep! Let me boil
On the altars of Solomon;
Let me soak the rusty soil
And flow into Kedron.

Finally, O reason, O happiness, I cleared from the sky the blue which is darkness, and I lived as a golden spark of this light, Nature. In my delight, I made my face look as comic and as wild as I could.

It is recovered.
What? Eternity.
In the whirling light
Of the sun in the sea.

O my eternal soul,
Hold fast to desire
In spite of the night
And the day on fire.

You must set yourself free
From the striving of Man
And the applause of the World!
You must fly as you can . . .

No hope, forever;
No orietur.
Science and patience,
The torment is sure.

The fire within you,

Soft silken embers,
Is our whole duty—
But no one remembers.

It is recovered.
What? Eternity.
In the whirling light
Of the sun in the sea.

I became a fabulous opera. I saw that everyone in the world was doomed to happiness. Action isn't life; it's merely a way of ruining a kind of strength, a means of destroying nerves. Morality is water on the brain.

It seemed to me that everyone should have had several *other* lives as well. This gentleman doesn't know what he's doing; he's an angel. That family is a litter of puppy dogs. With some men, I often talked out loud with a moment from one of their other lives—that's how I happened to love a pig.

Not a single one of the brilliant arguments of madness—the madness that gets locked up—did I forget; I could go through them all again, I've got the system down by heart.

It affected my health. Terror loomed ahead. I would fall again and again into a heavy sleep, which lasted several days at a time, and when I woke up, my sorrowful dreams continued. I was ripe for fatal harvest, and my weakness led me down dangerous roads to the edge of the world, to the Cimmerian shore, the haven of whirlwinds and darkness.

I had to travel, to dissipate the enchantments that crowded my brain. On the sea, which I loved as if it were to wash away my impurity, I watched the compassionate cross arise. I had been damned by the rainbow. Felicity was my doom, my gnawing remorse, my worm. My life would forever be too large to devote to strength and to beauty.

Felicity! The deadly sweetness of its sting would wake me at cockcrow—*ad matutinum*, at the *Christus venit*—in the somberest of cities.

O seasons, O châteaus!
Where is the flawless soul?

I learned the magic of
Felicity. It enchants us all.

To Felicity, sing life and praise
Whenever Gaul's cock crows.

Now all desire has gone—
It has made my life its own.

That spell has caught heart and soul
And scattered every trial.

O seasons, O châteaus!

And, oh, the day it disappears
Will be the day I die.

O seasons, O châteaus!

All that is over. Today, I know how to celebrate beauty.

The Impossible

Ah! My life as a child, the open road in every weather; I was unnaturally abstinent, more detached than the best of beggars, proud to have no country, no friends—what stupidity that was!—and only now I realize it!

I was right to distrust old men who never lost a chance for a caress, parasites on the health and cleanliness of our women—today when women are so much a race apart from us.

I was right in everything I distrusted . . . because I am running away!

I am running away!

I'll explain.

Even yesterday, I kept sighing: "God! There are enough of us damned down here! I've done time enough already in their ranks. I know them all. We always recognize each other; we disgust each other. Charity is unheard of among us. Still, we're polite; our relations with the world are quite correct." Is that surprising? The world! Businessmen and idiots!—there's no dishonor in being here—but the company of the elect; how would they receive us? For there are surly people, happy people, the false elect, since we must be bold or humble to approach them. These are the real elect. No saintly hypocrites, these!

Since I've got back two cents' worth of reason—how quickly it goes!—
I can see that my troubles come from not realizing soon enough that this
is the Western World. These Western swamps! Not that light has paled,
form worn out, or movement been misguided. . . . All right! Now my mind
wants absolutely to take on itself all the cruel developments that mind
has undergone since the Orient collapsed. . . . My mind demands it!

. . . And that's the end of my two cents' worth of reason! The mind is in
control, it insists that I remain in the West. It will have to be silenced if I
expect to end as I always wanted to.

I used to say, to hell with martyrs' palms, all beacons of art, the inventor's pride, the plunderer's frenzy; I expected to return to the Orient
and to original, eternal wisdom. But this is evidently a dream of depraved
laziness!

And yet I had no intention of trying to escape from modern suffering—
I have no high regard for the bastard wisdom of the Koran. But isn't there a
very real torment in knowing that since the dawn of that scientific discovery, Christianity, Man has been making a fool of himself, proving what is
obvious, puffing with pride as he repeats his proofs . . . and living on that
alone? This is a subtle, stupid torment—and this is the source of my spiritual ramblings. Nature may well be bored with it all! Prudhomme was born
with Christ.

Isn't it because we cultivate the fog? We swallow fever with our watery
vegetables. And drunkenness! And tobacco! And ignorance! And blind
faith! Isn't all this a bit far from the thought, the wisdom of the Orient,
the original fatherland? Why have a modern world, if such poisons are
invented?

Priests and preachers will say: Of course. But you are really referring
to Eden. There is nothing for you in the past history of Oriental races. . . .
True enough. It was Eden I meant! How can this purity of ancient races
affect my dream?

Philosophers will say: The world has no ages; humanity moves from
place to place, that's all. You are a Western man, but quite free to live in
your Orient, as old a one as you want . . . and to live in it as you like.
Don't be a defeatist. Philosophers, you are part and parcel of your Western
world!

Careful, mind. Don't rush madly after salvation. Train yourself! Ah,
science never goes fast enough for us!

But I see that my mind is asleep.

—If it stays wide awake from this moment on, we would soon reach the truth, which may even now surround us with its weeping angels! . . .

—If it had been wide awake until this moment, I would have never given in to degenerate instincts, long ago! . . .

—If it had always been wide awake, I would be floating in wisdom! . . . O Purity! Purity!

In this moment of awakening, I had a vision of purity! Through the mind we go to God!

What a crippling misfortune!

Lightning

Human labor! That explosion lights up my abyss from time to time.

"Nothing is vanity; on toward knowledge!" cries the modern Ecclesiastes, which is *Everyone*. And still the bodies of the wicked and the idle fall upon the hearts of all the rest. . . . Ah, quick, quick, quick! there, beyond the night . . . that future reward, that eternal reward . . . will we escape it?

What more can I do? Labor I know, and science is too slow. That praying gallops and that light roars; I'm well aware of it. It's too simple, and the weather's too hot; you can all do without me. I have my duty; but I will be proud, as others have been, to set it aside.

My life is worn out. Well, let's pretend, let's do nothing; oh, pitiful! And we will exist, and amuse ourselves, dreaming of monstrous loves and fantastic worlds, complaining and quarreling with the appearances of the world, acrobat, beggar, artist, bandit—priest! . . . on my hospital bed, the odor of incense came so strongly back to me . . . guardian of the holy aromatics, confessor, martyr. . . .

There I recognize my filthy childhood education. Then what? . . . turn twenty: I'll do my twenty years, if everyone else does.

No! No! Now I rise up against death! Labor seems too easy for pride like mine: To betray me to the world would be too slight a punishment. At the last moment I would attack, to the right, to the left. . . .

Oh! poor dear soul, eternity then might not be lost!

Morning

Hadn't I *once* a youth that was lovely, heroic, fabulous—something to write down on pages of gold? . . . I was too lucky! Through what crime, by what fault did I deserve my present weakness? You who imagine that animals sob with sorrow, that the sick despair, that the dead have bad dreams, try now to relate my fall and my sleep. I can explain myself no better than the beggar with his endless Aves and Pater Nosters. *I no longer know how to talk!*

And yet, today, I think I have finished this account of my Hell. And it *was* Hell; the old one, whose gates were opened by the Son of Man.

From the same desert, toward the same dark sky, my tired eyes forever open on the silver star, forever; but the three wise men never stir, the Kings of life, the heart, the soul, the mind. When will we go, over mountains and shores, to hail the birth of new labor, new wisdom, the flight of tyrants and demons, the end of superstition, to be the *first* to adore . . . Christmas on earth!

The song of the heavens, the marching of nations! We are slaves; let us not curse life.

Farewell

Autumn already! . . . But why regret the everlasting sun, if we are sworn to a search for divine brightness—far from those who die as seasons turn. . . .

Autumn. Our boat, risen out of hanging fog, turns toward poverty's harbor, the monstrous city, its sky stained with fire and mud. Ah! Those stinking rags, bread soaked with rain, drunkenness, and the thousands of loves who nailed me to the cross! Will there never, ever be an end to that ghoulish queen of a million dead souls and bodies *and who will all be judged!* I can see myself again, my skin corroded by dirt and disease, hair and armpits crawling with worms, and worms still larger crawling in my heart, stretched out among ageless, heartless unknown figures. . . . I could easily have died there. . . . What a horrible memory! I detest poverty.

And I dread winter because it's so *cozy!*

—Sometimes in the sky I see endless sandy shores covered with white rejoicing nations. A great golden ship, above me, flutters many-colored pennants in the morning breeze. I was the creator of every feast, every triumph, every drama. I tried to invent new flowers, new planets, new flesh, new languages. I thought I had acquired supernatural powers. Ha! I have to bury my imagination and my memories! What an end to a splendid career as an artist and storyteller!

I! I called myself a magician, an angel, free from all moral constraint. . . .

I am sent back to the soil to seek some obligation, to wrap gnarled reality in my arms! A peasant!

Am I deceived? Would Charity be the sister of death, for me ?

Well, I shall ask forgiveness for having lived on lies. And that's that.

But not one friendly hand . . . and where can I look for help?

True; the new era is nothing if not harsh.

For I can say that I have gained a victory; the gnashing of teeth, the hissing of hellfire, the stinking sighs subside. All my monstrous memories are fading. My last longings depart—jealousy of beggars, bandits, friends of death, all those that the world passed by—Damned souls, if I were to take vengeance!

One must be absolutely modern.

Never mind hymns of thanksgiving: hold on to a step once taken. A hard night! Dried blood smokes on my face, and nothing lies behind me but that repulsive little tree! The battle for the soul is as brutal as the battles of men; but the sight of justice is the pleasure of God alone.

Yet this is the watch by night. Let us all accept new strength, and real tenderness. And at dawn, armed with glowing patience, we will enter the cities of glory.

Why did I talk about a friendly hand! My great advantage is that I can laugh at old love affairs full of falsehood, and stamp with shame such deceitful couples—I went through women's Hell over there—and I will be able now *to possess the truth within one body and one soul.*

(translated by Paul Schmidt)

1896

France

In other words, the prose poetry experiments of the late nineteenth century spark a phenomenon during which fact and fantasy coincide. When dinosaur bones and dragon bones lay side by side in museums. When our "two ancestral genres," as Stéphane Mallarmé first puts it, "are united and alienated at the very same time." The greatest work that he produces is a testament to this tension. "A Throw of the Dice Will Never Abolish Chance" is a text whose title also functions as its main syntactical unit, a central thesis around which a complex network of dependent clauses teem, intermingle, and yet never coalesce. What "A Throw of the Dice" challenges is the tacit assumption in any essay that a subject should have a predicate, or that subordinate clauses necessarily depend upon anything, or that parentheticals, digressions, asides, and allusions require a firm context from which they must spring. As one Mallarmé critic will eventually note, this is an essay that's employing a poem in order to make the boldest statement about essays yet: that no act of knowing can avoid what's unknowable, that no thesis statement is without contingency, that every essay is a journey of a thought into risk.

STÉPHANE MALLARMÉ

A Throw of the Dice
Will Never Abolish Chance

A THROW OF THE DICE

NEVER

EVEN ROLLED IN EVERLASTING

CIRCUMSTANCES

FROM THE HEART OF A SHIPWRECK

THOUGH
            the

                    Deep

        whitened

                at slack water
                        wild
                            beneath a sheer
                                hangs desperately

                                    on the wing

                                        itself
                                            at

the start fallen off from badly rigged flight
                  and foundering spray
                                cutting these surges to the root

          so inwardly sums

the shadow drowned deep by this other sail

                      almost to trim
                          the spread

               its depth gaping as big as the hull

                    of a ship

                  heeled to one or the other board

THE MASTER

risen
   reckoning

                       by this holocaust

                              that

                     as to threaten

             the one Number which cannot

                        hesitates
                   corpse an arm's

   rather
       than play
          the greying lunatic
         in a game
        with the name of waves
                     one

               shipwreck which

            past old calculations
        where the handling from age was forgotten

            once he gripped the tiller

at his feet
            of the unanimous horizon

looms
    rolls and knots itself
            in the fist that would hold it
a fate and the winds

be another

                Mind
                to hurl it
                        into the storm
                    mend its division and proudly pass on

length cut off from the secret he withholds

overruns his head
flows as an unresisting beard

from just a man

        shipless
            no matter
                    where vain

ancestrally not opening his hand
                    clenched
              over the useless head

      legacy on its dissolution

                    to someone
                            uncertain

              the latter-day immemorial demon

having
          from blank geographies
                        beguiled
the old man to this supreme conjunction with probability

                            the one
                              his boyish shadow
caressed and polished and rendered and washed
                        suppled by the wave and drawn out
              from stoney bones lost in the planks

                            born
                              of a pastime
the sea in the patriarch taking or the patriarch against the sea
              an idle chance

                                        Betrothal

whose
          veil of illusion threw back their obsession
          as the ghost of a gesture

                    will toss
                    will pitch

                        madness

WILL ABOLISH

AS IF

A simple

around silence

into some near

wheels

insinuation

wreathed with irony
                    or
                        the mystery
                                cast
                                    howled   down

whirlwind of hilarity and horror

about the abyss
                        not shattering it
                                    or turning away

                            and lulls its virgin sign

                                            AS IF

alone a feather distraught

unless

it chances on or lights upon a midnight cap
　　　　　　and sticks fast
　　　　　　　to velvet crushed by a burst of black laughter

　　　　　　　this stiff whiteness

ridiculous

　　　　　　　　　against the sky
　　　　too much
　　　　　not to mark
　　　　　　　inadequately
　　　　　　　　　anyone

　　　　　　bitter reef prince

　　　　　who decks himself in it like the heroic
　　　　　irresistible but held
　　　　in his little manly reason
　　　　　　　　　in lightning

anxious
          expiating and pubescent

                                              dumb

                                         The lucid and lordly plume
                                            on the invisible brow
                                         glistens
                                              then shadows
                                                a slight dark form
                                            in her siren's twisting

                                         with last impatient scales

laugh

that

IF

of vertigo

reared up

time enough
         to slap
split

         a rock

false estate
         instantly
              vanished into fogs

              which set
                   a boundary to infinity

IT WAS

star born

IT WOULD BE

no

worse

more or less

indifferently just

THE NUMBER

MIGHT ONE BE

other than agony's scattered hallucination

MIGHT ONE BEGIN AND END

welling up though denied and shut if seen

at last

in some lavishness poured out from scarcity

MIGHT ONE BE FIGURED

evidence of the sum however small

MIGHT ONE SHINE

CHANCE

Drops

    the feather

       rhythmic suspense of the disaster

            to shroud itself

         in the original foam

where moments ago its delirium mounted nearly to a peak

         fouled

      by the same neutrality of the deep

NOTHING

of the memorable crisis
or might have
the episode

been resolved in view of no outcome

      possibly human

    WOULD HAVE TAKEN PLACE
   an ordinary swell spills the loss

         EXCEPT THE PLACE
a sort of fallen lapping as if to break up the empty act
     abruptly which otherwise
    by its lie
      might have founded
     the downfall

in these waters
    of crosscurrents
       where all reality dissolves

EXCEPT

at an altitude
PERHAPS
so high the place

fuses with the beyond

above concern
singled out there
in general
by such a bearing by such a declination
of fires

toward
what must be
the Seven Polar Stars or North

A CONSTELLATION

cold with forgetfulness and neglect
not so much
that it stops reckoning
on some vacant and uplifted surface
the succeeding shock
starwise
of a final count still forming

watching
doubting
rolling
brilliant and contemplative

before it ends
at some last point that makes it grace

All Thought casts a Throw of the Dice

(translated by D. J. Waldie)

1907

Russia

For example—

VELIMIR KHLEBNIKOV

The I-Singer of Universong

Beside the lake, these peacefilling shores. Worldlings growing here and there, white between the ravens' nests. And the gloomgrass grew all around.

An elk descends, its antlers branching, shaking the shore, caressing its head. The whistler warbles, exulting, tendering birdsong in gambling actation. The deathface blackcock makes his mating call and never tires, flapping toward the deathground. And sweettree and thoughtthicket grew all around.

The sky was calm.   *has a Dr. Seuss vibe*

Beauty displayed all the beauty of its limbs.   *to it*

The sky was blue.

Torn tears, her weeping tearturn, and all joy gone forever.

Farewell, she cried, and wept a twig of tears.

The dearling trembled in the wildwood. The Worldwings sang their unflappable song. And who knows from where—the worldflock settling down upon branches, beginning their worldring.

And there was a boy who wore white clothes, his looks dark with skyblue light; in his fresh bound bunting of bast he heard the Worldwing singing, and cut himself a reed where the gloomgrass grew, carved out a panpipe and called it his worldwhistle and himself the first world-whistler. *childhood*

The sounds of a silent flute had called up a playparty, scarlet and blue, onto green glitter, greener than grass, then stopped silent.

In the distance the wordbrethren beat out the word with their vocable hammers.   *¶.*

Sometimes the daughter of the forest would come to the white rock by the boat dock, lean her white head against her knees and cast her worldring gaze upon the dark water.

When power came over the waters and watery blue feet began to move

393

in the dance, a sudden splashing and tossing of black hooves with white curlylocks, then a ha-ha resounded and lotuses nodded their worldform flowers and worldrings flocked together to trumpet to the music of world-overing gleemen, and from a few low strings came a rhythmic racket, and from the blue waters of languor the watersprites arose, faces and limbs and eyes of belleblush femfolk, their pranky faces floating over the dark blue lake amid thick dark clouds, swansdown clouds and dewdrops universalized on flytraps.

In the airy thoughtlandish bodies of these beings sprouted eyes and glances of stone, and the worldbodies of trumpeting worldrings, carved from some primordial Whorold, twined themselves into doublesighted stare and sank slowly into the depths of the sea.

Those strains of thought, the racket of those strings! Who stretched you here, that I should come take you? Long strings stretched from stars to stones and thicket. Swaying, the leafy towertops of dreams! Blueness, wind, and song! Night and silence! Night highness of strings from there to here, like shifting shafts of time, straining strings, gauntlet thrown down from there to here.

Proud flew the heavy weagle of the world, hollowing all with the aquiline bent of its beak. He who finds the weagle's feather, who hears the battering weagle's wings, who hears the weagle wailing—he is othered forever. Its beak, its beck and call "come hither," they set the grass ablaze.

Littlelife lulls itself and its idleness on the waterlily's leaves. Raising a pouting white mouth and chortling, the watery pufferbelly plays, blows froth from the watery greengrowth, holding his sides.

O bright white piper, young shepherd whistling on your worldwhistle, in your white bast shoes and your white white clothes! And here is the song the worldwhistle sang:

Tearstung Belun, and chattergummed goblins with brazenlaughing hooves! They tighten the hair of their heads and pluck it like harpstrings, guityres, to the beat of a gallop, a rush of frisk and fly. Greatness—remember—is cousin to tears.

Belun, his hair a flow of antique time. Shining still, his unancient eyes. Beautiful storms on unalterable lips. Lakelike, lost, a tear caught in his curlclusters, a lake beneath woodwelkin, postpluvially blue.

This is the way the piping herdboy played. Pointy, pouty, the woodweirds drooped, you'd think their unpracticed eyes were hornets' nests, in-

[handwritten: town/settlement]

sensed in song. And the dwellers of the nearby settledown brought to these greeny deeps their glances, in glittered blue and whitening garments, exchanging sacred mysterious whispers. Then they let their clothes grow white and blue. . . .

This is the way the piping herdboy sang, with his pipe to his mouth, bound with gold hoops and figures.

The distance grew into a wiseman, the daytime silence grew sweet and lovely. And there was a glancing cup. And ceaselessly murmuring, falling and fluttering high and low, the mortaline doves of desire. The bark of treetrunks sparkled with eyes and the sticky running resins of desire. . . .

This is the way he sang. And Horrowing at peace flew on.

A huddle of folk like a rune of worldwise letters stood fierce and brave, conjuring someone out of high heaven.

And this is the way the boy sang on. *[handwritten: the boy who made the world whistle]*
Belun's blue eyes wet with a wetness.

And the boy took the pipe from his mouth. It fell by an oaktree trunk. And a willow-fingered woodwilly picked up the pipe and turned a tune.

I was still a very young woodwilly then, another Gorodetsky, my hair all unruly tousle, when I heard that voice.

We'd gone begging a blessing from every twig, when I heard that voice and saw that hand.

No, it's not worth bringing all that up here, not worth it at all! Old Belun snickered into his gray whiskers, and it reminded the boy of something.

The woodweirds lawghen with springtime mouths, and the treetoilers smiled at him. *[handwritten: love the personifications happening here]*
And here is the song the woodwilly sang:

The goers go and the getters get. The laufers laechen. Worldlings flocked and twined their virgin-feathered wings to start to be silent in the dove-dappled soundling. And in the sufferation of unbeseech, all the beauty of the sounds was heard. Ah, every rib of the fan was finialed with a shining face.

The sourdine, braiding itself into heavening, strong was its blueness, like silver or iron.

Silence descended, like unvocal chords.

The tear-riven cheeks were covered with cold. Tight lips closed ranks. Fierce eyes. Sticks stuck all over with doves. The brackets of the gatepost proceed from suffereyes.

You are a stare of sadness in a dungeon of bright blue sky.

Those delicate stringplayer fingers wafting blue darkness with a blue-water stone, set in a ring they wore.

And dawns covered his body, his head, and his boldpart with ribbing.

Divinity thinks of the flame of its heart as the architecture of palaces. Eyes did not dissipate the dark, and the mouth above the cherry tree, and the cloud.

Outpourings reddling the bluely blueing sea.

The whitefire underbellied clouds.

Whiter-than-whiteness, a cloud. Bluelies. Blueration.

Fame kept advancing with his broadsword. Prideful sheaf of vengeance in the eyes of one who sings with it, death winds its wings and smothers the small man where all are great, the great man where all are small, the coward where all are brave, the brave man where all are cowards. The vision of a bast shoe may be a worldring one. The rivers rolls, a silver singer.

See the hornmuzzleherdmaneheadstream flow by the shores of the road. Munching a morsel of darkening dark bread, the white boy trails his switch. Dawns exchanged smiles and one of them kissed the edge of the ear bent down beneath his hat. And the kiss lit up his face as he chewed his bread. A twilit hound with a wicked bonfire eye.

Again came the racket of unseen guityres. The muteling sevenreed of a mysterious hand moves to a singer's hidden mouth.

There were the steppes, there were the swaying wings of silvery feath-ergrass. A gray-whiskered piper wended his way through the feathergrass. The airy piping wound long through the grass.

Beneath mighty wings and mighty necks, hours of vespering swan-hordes pounded past, all slid into a sheaf, a holocaust.

The grassy rung of heaven was pleasant and near. And I kissed them all, those rungfingers.

Sufferation of solitude and place!

You were a flier in silver-gray shawls, simile of storm-anger. "Whose clansman are you?" they ask, and you answer: "I am of the race of heaven."

The wolf leapt forward, his fur all aflower with dying embers. Shadowy headdress of the princesses of evening who had gone to gather flowers. Clouds drape the shrine in embroidered veils. The flowers bowed and bent.

Blueish sky. Blueing water. Reddening pinetrees, naked . . . their bodies all horny elbows.

Greeningtailed previrginal serpent. Searippling scales. Naked curly baby, whose palm is a bodycurl at dawn. Girls who pierce their mother's house in glances, their deckings and wearings all heaven-skied with blueness, they lull the child into calm.

And mobfoot mindswarm. The morningface girl, nightbodied and day-handed. And on the hum of a summons flew an admiral evildo, scourge of dreamdark, lover of light.

Learning lessens: death learns to be life, to take on a mouth and nose.

Mornfaced he and brightance-eyed. Blue-eye brightances.

Youngman jollijoe seizes a whistle from a tuft of plairs. Famiferous young-man, smartseer. Laeghen rippleflow. Youngbrightman eyedazzling everyone. Us and the femfolk too.

Woodwide thicket of torment. Sufferance in a gleamgirl's glances.

And in the woodwilly's cuttings they read: strength to see God. With no glass darkly, your heart is spearsteel. And the cutter's wild thin face peaked over his shoulder. And my un-other made her eyes an angry squinny, back-stepping lak a turkledove. And the grave (oh fallow furrow!) put on timebeak and eyeglasses, gave a diligent read: "How to raise delicious vegetables."

And the cutterwriter ran to get birchbark to condite another litter.

Press your anxious ears against moist mother earth!

Trust no one: they may be old, may be deaf, may be foe, may be slave. . . .

Oh go carefully into the clatter of far-off horses!

And the heightest stars were all agreed.

Blue bunting in the eyes of loverings and the youngest brother bent to the forge, beating a broadsword, to have something to support him when he demanded his portion. And he took up the call and called to cold to be strongman among the strong. And the whistlering was light and offleading, went right to the head. what is the "I-name"?

And the I-name was lost in a thoughtress of forces, and mutemum stompled by introaders' merciless horses . . . to briders, no ridles. And lus-triant starstare.

And he took her by the hand to the hallowhall, and here hung the lus-trous faces of all the ancestors. Oh prayers for the birthing of earth, and the skyfurred beast and the futureheaded gleamgirl, and a worldfeathered "darling" and a big "thank you"—was it the size of a sparrow, the size of a dove, or the size of the universe?

And the thankhorned bull, the universetailed cat (there are some, alas).

And all only a stepping-off place to a name, even the nightname universe. And spreading bluethaw slipping soundless by.

And dreamer and dreamsleep are alltered. The dreamsleeper's fate is to understand reality. And a dreamsprite casts an alltering shadow over everything, land and air, took up strings, supporters in the dim deeds of a Slavlover. And never stopping to catch me up, tormenting tormentor, and I a still sad herald of the world, the pooring of my orphan eye.

And in a soundary the high and mighty snatched up harps. Ah, that passing captivation, beautifix: forget not!

And in the expent from rootrace foundation to fatface these swarms of smudges swam, glooming the shine. And Slav-girls skier than sky!

And the glittergreening lacelove, veiling and vealing her elbows and fingerings, languing and luxuring with the shameless half-gape of her mouth, exporing with half-open eyes.

And the shadowy besetter, the potscold, the graying grassglade, and upon it a teetering tottering danceling. And tailgreening beneath a branch lay the previrginal serpent and the laughmarkered oldlady age. And a trio of white standers, halfcircle enskied, gone greening. O firelock, darktail cockerel!

Boybattle, suffires, battleboy, manpain.

And the youngrings screamed all out, and sliver-smiling younglets began to laugh.

And the youngmouth sometime truth. And loverlady, runaway into double-dreamed dreams, you were the wing's blueblush. And a whistle-player, and the friendship of dreams. And his youngoreyed holynose.

And horse manes universized, made main, and a blaze between the eyes; two nights divided by a day.

Laughcaster from the boywhistle and a mouth that had no power to hold back laughter. And oldman's laufish look; eternity popped in his pocket.

And one gave goodlooks and loving and then took it back. And mechanical clocks.

And treestumps flocked together, talking in treetalk.

And bright was quiet. And flare.

And bright stole over the sky. And a bold-faced honker flew across the bright.

Twilight and murk are two things that love me. My soul, got up in these peacocking getups.

And the bee-prophet in a friendship crown.

And ripplating smook, forming faces and flourishing horns.

And something glancing and branching to eat. Laughing not-knowers wrapped themselves in dovefeathered smales. Joyful, the depth and droop of blue eyes in the blue settletown.

Knowsons on the move. A clutch of madbeaky masks and movement of mild-mannered freshoots tangled in dumblind.

And skyseeking skoun drooped down its soundings to hearson. And racketing skystringations.

And the Venger of goodfaring ways.

And ever-widening deepgape of a mouth. The lovefeathered bird of murkdom.

"Our own wiser," the dawns opined.

And notness flew toward brightning like a falconfeather cloud.

Uncle Borie put on boots of eternality, and a sunfeather hat on his headback. But even here the cradle kept rocking.

Overhead the azurewrite, neither moved away nor melted. And a saytelling and goldclouded goldrinning strings; soundron of its tender, tenderly tinkling hands and laffron of unsure mouths, loverlaching, smilestinging. And the smilestung shore, the sad streams, the happy birches there on the birchbank, the high bank, and the wild sorrowing treetrunks.

Thunder shows its face, and the stillorn of the whiting reeds. And a horse, flashing a festival tongue.

And carvered in the carvering of words, the curving carvator, and the writ he wrought—yours, and a smilish saddening, and a bearded ancient, and blue-figured girlsong. And the endless do-dens of a dead-handed deathscriber, and drifting across them the spirit of scripting and scribing.

Babblowing, babbloon, and sorrowing sorreen in the sorroons, and sorroweed, his eyes all sorrowed over, and the sorroner-loveling stare of lovring lids; but his mouth a hatch of stillatinies, and stillorn fluttering upon it.

And someone's young face, universalizing.

Skybove and earthlow whispering back and forth in a ceaseless whisper. Soundificance, and a differing soundatrice, a sounding soul. And a dancing woman spinning circles around a spring flower.

But the people stand dumb.

(translated by Paul Schmidt)

1913

Italy

Or—

Dino Campana

The Night

I. The Night

I remember an old city, red walks and red battlements, on the immense plain burnt out from the August heat, with the far-away spongy cold comfort of green hills in the background. Enormous emptiness of bridge-arches over the stagnant river dried to thin leaden puddles: a black molding of gypsies shifting and silent along the banks: among the dazzle and glare of a distant cane-brake the far-off naked figures of teen-age boys and the Hasidic beard of an old man: and suddenly out of the midst of the dead water the gypsy women came and a song, primordial dirge from the voiceless swamp monotonous and irritating: and time ground down and held still.

◀ ▶

I raised my eyes unconsciously to the barbarous tower which dominated the long avenues of plane trees. Above a silence wound to intensity it began to drag from the dead its distant savage mythology: at the same time, through other distant hallucinations, other vague, violent apprehensions, another myth—also mysterious and wild—kept coming back to me. Down below the old women, the strollers, had dragged their long dresses softly toward the vague splendor of the gate: the countryside was beginning to numb up and go sleepy in its network of canals; young girls with weightless hair, and profiles cut from medallions, disappeared now and then in little carts around green bends in the road. The sweet silver toll of a bell from far away: Evening: in the empty chapel, in the shadows of the modest nave, I held Her, the rose-pale flesh and the burning fugitive eyes: years and years and years melted together in the triumphal sweet taste of the memory.

◀ ▶

403

The person I once had been found himself unconsciously heading toward the barbarous tower, legendary keeper of adolescent dreams. In the silence of ancient lanes and half-streets he climbed up alongside the church and the convent walls: you couldn't even hear the noise of his footsteps. A deserted little piazza, broken hovels like old bruises, dead windows: to one side in an enormous wash of light, the tower, eight-pointed arid impenetrably red and unadorned; a dried-up 16th-century fountain kept silent, its stone shattered in the middle of its own Latin commentary. A deserted cobblestone road opened up toward the city.

( )

He was startled by a door that had been thrown open. Old men, crooked and silent bony forms, straddled and crawled over each other with their piercing elbows, terrible in the wide light. Then they stopped with anxious and servile bows in front of the whiskery face of a monk who was leaning out from the emptiness of a doorway, and then slinked away muttering, raising themselves up little by little, dragging their long shadows after them one by one across the red and flaking walls, each one just like a shadow. A women with a swinging walk and a foolish laugh joined them, finishing off the cortege.

( )

They stretched their shadows out along the red plaster-flaked walls: he followed, an automaton. He said one word to the woman and it fell into the noon silence: an old man turned to stare at him with an absurd vacant and luminous look. And the woman kept on smiling with a soft sweet smile in the aridity of noon, doltish and alone in the catastrophic light.

( )

I never knew how I saw my own shadow coasting along the torpid canals, my ghost that laughed back at me from the depths. It went with me along the strong-smelling streets where women sang in the hot weather. At the edge of the countryside a door cut in the stone, watched by a young woman in a red dress, pale and fat, caught its eye: I entered. An aging but opulent older woman was sitting inside, profile like a ram's, with black hair twisted loosely about her sculptural head wildly decorated by a rheumy eye like a black gem stone with bizarre facets, agitated by childish graces that kept resurfacing like false hopes being pulled from a deck of cards in long sanctimonious strange theories of languishing queens a king infantrymen weapons and knights. I spoke to her and a voice from the convent, deep and melodramatic answered me along with a wrinkled and gracious smile. I could see stretched out in the shadows the maidservant half nude who slept with her mouth half open, her throat rattling in a heavy sleep, her beautiful body supple and amber. I sat down slowly.

‹ ›

The long thread of speculations about her loves unraveled monotonously in my ears. Old family portraits were scattered sanctimoniously over the table. The lithe figure with amber skin stretched out on a bed and listened curiously, leaning on her elbow like a sphinx: outside the green green orchard between reddened walls: only we three alive in the southern hush.

‹ ›

In the meantime the sun had set and had wound up in its gold, as a spider winds up its prey, the buzzing center of memory and seemed to consecrate it. The voice of the Procuress became sweeter little by little, and her head like that of an oriental priestess seemed comfortable in languid poses. The black magic of evening, sly girlfriend of the criminal, was the go-between for our dark souls and its splendors seemed to promise a mysterious reign. And the priestess of sterile pleasures, the ingenuous and greedy maidservant and the poet all watched each other, barren souls unwittingly looking for the problem of their lives. But the evening only sent down a golden message from the fresh shudderings of the night.

‹ ›

Night came, and the conquest of the serving girl. Her amber body her voracious mouth her bristling black hair at times the revelation of lust in her terrified eyes wove and rewove a fantastic situation. Sweeter meanwhile, and already just about to die out, the memory still reigned in the distance of the persuasive older woman, still queen in her classic line among the great sisters of memory: after Michelangelo had bent her down again on her tired knees tired from her journey she who bends, who bends but will not lie down, barbarous queen under the weight of the whole human dream, and the battering of arcane and violent poses of the overthrown queens of antiquity who heard Dante extinguish himself in Francesca's cry there on the banks of rivers which exhausted from wars open their mouths, while on their own banks love's everlasting pain is recreated. And the serving girl, the ingenuous Magdalene of the bristly hair and brilliant eyes, was begging with tremors of her barren, golden body, crude and savage, sweetly closed in the humility of her mystery. The long night full of the deceits of various images.

‹ ›

The old images appeared at the silver gates of the first adventures, sweetened by a life of love, to protect me again with their smiles of ineffable mystery and tenderness. The closed halls were opened where light falls in a steady sheet to infinity in the mirrors, random images of courtesans appearing in their sphinx-like posturings out of the reflected pale light: and once more everything that had been arid and sweet, the unpetaled roses of youth, returned to full bloom on the skeletal panorama of the world.

‹ ›

In the gunpowder smell of festival night, the last clanging dying away down the air, I saw the young girls of antiquity, those of the first illusion, appear clearly in the middle of the bridges that jut out from the city to the suburb in the torrid summer nights: faces turned to a three-quarters view, listening to the insistent clanging from the suburb announcing the tongues of fire in uneasy lamps boring through a night sky already full of orgiastic lights: now sweetened: in the already-dead and rose-blushed sky, unburdened by the veil of light: thus Saint Marta, instruments broken on the ground, the song already hushed across the ever-green landscapes that the heart of Saint Cecilia tunes with the Latin sky, soft and pink near the old twilight rusting in the heroic lines of great Roman women. Memories of gypsies, memories of long-ago loves, memories of music and light: exhaustions of love, sudden exhaustions on a pensione bed long ago, another adventurous cradle of uncertainty and regret: thus all that was once more sterile and sweet, the roses of youth unpetalled and dry, sprang up on the skeletal panorama of the world.

‹ ›

In the evening of flamebursts from the summer festival, in a white and delicious light, when our ears just barely rested in the silence and our eyes were tired from the garlands of fireworks, from the multicolored stars that left an acrid smell of gunpowder, a beautiful reddish weight everywhere in the air, walking side by side made us weary exalting in our own too-diverse beauty, she thin and delicate and dark, pure of eye and face, the dazzle of the necklace lost on her bare throat, walking now with hesitant steps clutching a fan. She was attracted to the hut: her white gown undulated in thin blue jerks through the diffuse light and I followed the pallor burning her forehead under her dark bangs. We went in. Dark, autocratic faces, serene again in the illusion of childhood and the festival, turned toward us, profoundly clear in the light. And we watched the scene, everything a spectral unreality. There were skeletal overviews of the city. Bizarre dead bodies looked up at the sky in stiff postures. A rubber odalisque breathed in a low voice and turned her idol's eyes around the room. And the sharp smell of sawdust that muted footsteps and the continual tide-like whispering of the young women of the town astonished at the mystery. "Is it Paris, then? There's London. The Battle of Mukden." We looked around: it must have been late. All those things seen through the magnetic eyes of the lenses in that dream light! Motionless next to me I felt her grow strange and withdrawn while her fascination deepened under the dark bangs of her hair. She moved. And I felt with a bitter twinge which was immediately consoled that I would never be near her again. I followed her then as you follow a dream you love in vain: thus we had become suddenly far apart and strangers to each other after the tumult of the festival, in front of the skeletal panorama of the world.

◦

I was in the shadow of an arcade which dripped drop after drop of blood-gorged light through the fog of a December night. Without warning a door was flung open in a splendor of light. In the foreground of the far end of the room in the luminescence of a red ottoman an older woman was lying up on one elbow, her head resting in her hand, her brown eyes like brown fire, her breasts enormous: beside her a young girl on her knees, amber and thin, hair cut into bangs down her forehead, a youthful grace, her legs smooth and uncovered beneath her shimmering gown: and over her, over the serious thoughtful older woman with young eyes a curtain, a white lace curtain, a curtain that seemed to move images, the images above her, the pure clean images over the thoughtful older woman with young eyes. Beaten by light from the shadows of the arcade gorged drops of blood-light falling over and over I stared compelled and amazed at the symbolic and daring grace of the scene. It was already late, we were alone and between us an unfettered intimacy was born and the older woman with the young eyes who lay at the far end of the room under the moving white lace curtain talked to me. Her life was a long sin: lust. Lust but still full of an unsatisfiable curiosity for her. "The female peppered him with kisses from the right side: why from the right? Later the male pigeon stayed overhead, immobile?, ten minutes. Why?" The questions remained unanswered, as pushed by nostalgia she remembered her past over and over again. Until the conversation languished and the voice had died out around us, the mystery of sensuality having reclothed whomever it had reinvoked. Upset, tears blearing my eyes in front of the white lace curtain I kept on following the white fantasies. The voice had gone silent around us. Then she had gone. The voice had gone silent. Certainly I had heard her brushing past in destroying silence. In front of the curtain of crumpled lace the young girl was still resting on her amber knees, bending with the grace of an acolyte to love.

( )

Faust was young and handsome and had curly hair. Women from Bologna at that time resembled Siracusean medallions and the slant of their eyes was so perfect that they loved to appear immobile in order to contrast harmoniously with their long brown curls. It was easy to run into them at night in the dark streets (when the moon lit up the streets) and Faust would raise his eyes to the gables of the houses which looked in the moonlight like question marks and then would stare pensively at the diminishing trail of the girls' footsteps. From the old tavern where the students gathered he sometimes liked to hear among the calm talk of the Bologna winter, cold and foggy like his own, and the snap and crack of the wooden logs and the dart and flash of the flames of the ochre vaults and sometimes the hurried footsteps under the near arches. He loved then to gather himself in song while the young waitress in her red petticoats, and with her beautiful cheeks under her smoky hair-do walked back and forth in front of him. Faust was young and handsome. On a morning like that, from the little wallpapered room, among refrains from the player piano and a floral arrangement, from the little room I had heard the crowd rush by and the dark noises of winter. O I remember!: I was young, my hand never just quietly holding up my indecisive face, kind from anxiety and exhaustion. In those days I unburdened myself to the polished, supple dressmaker's dummies, consecrated by my anxiety about supreme love, by the anxiety of all my tormented and thirsty childhood. Everything was mysterious to my faith, my life was entirely "an anxiety about the secret of the stars, everything a bowing over the abyss." I was handsome with torment, restless pale thirsting wandering behind the ghosts of that mystery. Then I fled. I lost myself in the tumult of the colossal cities, saw white cathedrals raise themselves in enormous congeries of faith and dreams with their thousand spires in the air, I saw the Alps raise themselves like still grander cathedrals, and full of the great green shadows of firs, and full of the melody of their rivers and streams in which I heard the song born from the everlastingness of dreams. Up there among the smoky firs in the fog, among their thousand tickings the thousand voices of silence a small light came clear among the tree trunks, and I started up on that path of light: I climbed up to the Alps, into the delicate white mysterious backdrop of the countryside. Lakes, up there among the luminous rocks ponds watched over by the dream's smile, luminous pools the lakes ecstatic from the oblivion that you, Leonardo, dissembled. The stream told me the story vaguely. I stood still among the immobile lances of the firs believing at times I was bringing forth a new melody wild and yet sad perhaps fixing for good the clouds which seemed to slow down curiously for a moment on that bottomless landscape spy on it and then vanish behind the immobile lances of the fir trees. And poor, naked, happy to be poor and naked, to reflect for an instant the landscape like a memory fascinating and horrible deep in my heart I was climbing: and I got there got up there where the Alpine snows blocked my path for good. A young girl was washing in the stream, washing and singing in the white snows of the Alps. She turned, welcomed me, and in the night she loved me. And still in the background the Alps the white delicate mystery, lit the purity of the stellar lamp in my memory, and the light of love's night burned on.

◖ ◗

But which nightmare still weighed all my youth down? O the kisses the vain kisses of the young girl washing, washing and singing in the white snows of the Alps! (tears came to my eyes with her memory). I heard the still-distant stream: it poured down soaking ancient and desolate cities, streets long silent, empty as after a pillaging. A golden warmth in the shadow of the present room, a lavish head of hair a death-rattling nightmarish body in the mystic night of the age-old human animal. The handmaiden was sleeping the oblivion of her own dark dreams: like a Byzantine icon, like an Arabian myth the uncertain pallor of the curtain whitened the background.

◁ ▷

And then fictions of a very old and free life, of enormous solar myths and massacres that created themselves before my spirit. I saw an old image again, a skeletal form alive because of the great force of a barbarous myth, eyes abyss-like and changing glaring with dark blood, in the dream's torture discovering the vulcanized body, two spots two bullet holes on her extinct breasts. I thought I heard the guitars shudder over there in the board-and-branch shack on the lonely fields of the city, a candle throwing light on the bare ground. In front of me a wild older woman stared me down without batting an eyelash. The light was weak on the bare ground in the quivering of the guitars. To one side on the blossoming treasure of a young dreaming girl the woman now clung like a spider while seeming to whisper words in my ear I couldn't make out, words sweet as the wordless wind of the Pampas that sinks you. The wild woman had grabbed me: my indifferent blood had certainly been drunk by the earth: and now the light was even weaker on the bare ground under the metallic breath of the guitars. Suddenly the freed young girl breathed out her childhood, her eyes as soft and piercing as the abyss, languid in her wild grace. And grace grew weaker on the back of the beautiful young thing the shadow of her watery hair and the august mane of the tree of life weaving itself into the ending on the bare ground the guitars inviting a distant sleep. One could hear clearly a leap of wild horses from the Pampas a pawing in the earth, could hear clearly the wind rise, the pawing seeming to be drowned out in the roar of infinity. In the square of the open door the stars flashed brilliantly red and hot in the distance: the shadow of the wild ones in shadow.

II. The Voyage and Return

Voices rose, and other voices, and children's songs and songs of lust, through the twisted little streets inside the burning shadow, to the hill to the hill. In the shadow of the green lamps the white colossal prostitutes dreamed dreams of longing in a light made fantastic by the wind. The sea poured out its salt into the wind which the wind mixed and washed in the lust-smell of the alleys, and the white Mediterranean night joked with the huge shapes of the women while the flame's bizarre death-attempts went on and on in the streetlamp's cave. They watched the flame and sang songs about hearts in chains. All the preludes were quieted now. The night, the stillest joy of the night had fallen. The Moorish doors loaded up and twisted themselves with monstrous black wonders while, in the distance the dark blue dredged a small harbor of stars. Lonely the night now sat on her throne bedizened and fired with all her swarm of stars and flame. In front like a monstrous wound a street deepened. At the sides of the door's angle, white caryatids of a false heaven dreamed away their faces resting on the palms of their hands. She had the pure imperial line in her profile and her throat was bound about with the splendor of opals. With the quick imperial gesture of youth she drew her light dress in one movement over her shoulders and her window shimmered in expectation until shadows closed it softly into a double shadow. And my heart was starved for dreams, for her, for the evanescent one like evanescent love, the love-donor of the doors, caryatid of destiny's heaven. On her divine knees, on her body pale as a dream come forth from the innumerable dreams of the shadows, among the innumerable deceiving lights, the ancient friend, the eternal Chimera held in her red hands my red and ancient heart.

◦ ◦

Return. In the room where I had embraced her shapes revealed by the curtains of light, a lingering breath: and in the twilight my unsullied lamp stars my heart longing for memories again. Faces, faces whose eyes laughed in the just-blooming dreamflower, you young charioteers on the weightless dreamstreets you garlanded so zealously: O fragile poems, O garland of night-loves . . . A song breaks from the garden like the weak link in a chain of sobs: the vein is open: dry and red and sweet is the skeletal panorama of the world.

◦ ◦

O your body! Your perfume veiled my eyes: I didn't see your body (a sweet and acute perfume): there in the great empty mirror, in the great empty mirror veiled by violet smoke, at the top, kissed by a star of light was the beautiful, the beautiful and sweet gift of a god: and the timid breasts were stuffed with light, and the stars were absent, and there wasn't a God in the night of violet love: but you light as down you sat on my knees, night-breathing caryatid of an enchanted heaven. Your body an airy gift on my knee, and the stars in hiding, and there was no God in the night of violet love: but you in the night of violet love: but you with your violet eyes lowered, you from an unknown night sky which had already ravished one melody of caresses. I remember, love: light as a dove's wings you rested your limbs on my own noble limbs. They breathed happily, inhaling their own beauty, my limbs breathing a clearer light in your obedient cloud of divine reflections. O don't burn them! don't burn them! Don't burn them: all is vanity vain is the dream: all is in vain all is dream: Love, spring of the dream you are alone you are alone who appears in the veil of violet smoke. Like a white cloud, like a white cloud next to my heart, O stay O stay O stay. Don't sadden O sun!

We opened the window to the night sky. Men like wandering spirits: they wandered like ghosts: and the city (the streets the churches the squares), composed itself in a cadenced dream, as if through an invisible melody sprung from that wandering. Therefore wasn't the world inhabited by sweet spirits and wasn't the dream awakened again in the night in all its triumphant powers? Which bridge, we asked silently, which bridge have we thrown across to the infinite, so that everything appears to us as a shadow of eternity? To which dream have we raised the nostalgia of our beauty? The moon rose in her old robe behind the Byzantine church.

III. The End

In the pleasant warmth of the red light, inside those closed rooms where light sinks flat inside the mirrors to infinity the whiteness of lace blooms then withers away. The concierge in the cast-off luxury of a green jerkin, the lines of her face kinder, her eyes which in their brightness hide the dark watches the silver door. You feel the indefinite fascination of love. A mature woman is in control sweetened by a life of love a smile on her face a lovely glimmer in her eyes the memory of the flashing tears of sensuality. They pass during her vigil, rich with messengers of love, light spools weaving multicolored fantasies, they wander about, luminous dust that rests in the enigma of mirrors. The concierge watches the silver door. Outside is the night leafy with silent songs, pale love of the wanderers.

(translated by Charles Wright)

1924

France

And—

SAINT-JOHN PERSE

Anabasis

Song

Under the bronze leaves a colt was foaled. Came such an one who laid bitter fruit in our hands. Stranger. Who passed. Here comes news of other provinces to my liking. . . . "Hail, daughter! under the tallest tree of the year."

◀ ▶

For the Sun enters the sign of the Lion and the Stranger has laid his finger on the mouth of the Dead. Stranger. Who laughed. And tells us of an herb. O from the provinces blow many winds. What ease to our way! how the trumpet rejoices my heart and the feather revels in the scandal of the wing! . . . "My Soul, great girl, you had your ways which are not ours."

◀ ▶

Under the bronze leaves a colt had been foaled. Came such an one who laid this bitter fruit in our hands. Stranger. Who passed. Out of the bronze tree comes a great bruit of voices. Roses and bitumen, gift of song, thunder and fluting in the rooms. O what ease in our ways, how many tales to the year, and by the roads of all the earth the Stranger to his ways. . . . "Hail, daughter! robed in the loveliest robe of the year."

I

I have built myself, with honor and dignity have I built myself on three great seasons, and it promises well, the soil whereon I have established my Law.

Beautiful are bright weapons in the morning and behind us the sea is fair. Given over to our horses this seedless earth

delivers to us this incorruptible sky. The Sun is not named but his power
is amongst us.

and the sea at morning like a presumption of the mind.

Power, you sang as we march in darkness! . . . At the pure ides of day
what know we of our dream, older than ourselves?

Yet one more year among us! Master of the Grain, Master of the Salt,
and the commonwealth on an even beam!

I shall not hail the people of another shore. I shall not trace the great
boroughs of towns on the slopes with powder of coral. But I have the idea
of living among you.

Glory at the threshold of the tents, and my strength among you, and
the idea pure as salt holds its assize in the daylight.

( )

. . . So I haunted the City of your dreams, and I established in the desolate
markets the pure commerce of my soul, among you

invisible and insistent as a fire of thorns in the gale.

Power, you sang on our roads of splendor! . . . "In the delight of salt
the mind shakes its tumult of spears. . . . . With salt shall I revive the dead
mouths of desire!

He who has not praised thirst and drunk the water of the sands from
a sallet

I trust him little in the commerce of the soul. . . ." (And the Sun is not
named but his power is amongst us.)

Men, creatures of dust and folk of divers ways, people of business and
of leisure, men from the marches and those from beyond, O men of little
weight in the memory of these lands; people from the valleys and uplands
and the highest slopes of this world to the ultimate reach of our shores;
Scenters of signs and seeds, and confessors of the western winds, followers
of trails and of seasons, breakers of camp in the little dawn wind, seekers of
watercourses over the wrinkled rind of the world, O seekers, O finders of
reasons to be up and be gone,

you traffic not in a salt more strong than this, when at morning with
omen of kingdoms and omen of dead waters swung high over the smokes
of the world, the drums of exile waken on the marches

Eternity yawning on the sands.

◖ ◗

. . . In a single robe and pure, among you. For another year, among you. "My glory is upon the seas, my strength is amongst you!

To our destiny promised this breath of other shores, and there beyond the seeds of time, the splendor of an age at its height on the beam of the scales . . ."

Mathematics hung on the floes of salt! there at the sensitive point on my brow where the poem is formed, I inscribed this chant of all a people, the most rapt god-drunken,

drawing to our dockyards eternal keels!

IV

Such is the way of the world and I have nothing but good to say of it— Foundation of the City. Stone and bronze. Thorn fires at dawn

bared these great

green stones, and viscid like the bases of temples, of latrines,

and the mariner at sea whom our smoke reached saw that the earth to the summit had changed its form (great tracts of burnt-over land seen afar and these operations of channeling the living waters on the mountains).

Thus was the City founded and placed in the morning under the labials of a clear sounding name. The encampments are razed from the hills! And we who are there in the wooden galleries,

head bare and foot bare in the freshness of the world,

what have we to laugh at, but what have we to laugh at, as we sit, for a disembarkation of girls and mules?

and what is there to say, since the dawn, of all this people under sail?— Arrivals of grain! . . . And the ships taller than Ilion under the white peacock of the sky, having crossed the bar, hove to

in this deadwater where floats a dead ass. (We must ordain the fate of this pale meaningless river, color of grasshoppers crushed in their sap.)

In the great fresh noise of the yonder bank, the blacksmiths are masters of their fires! The cracking of whips in the new streets unloads whole

wainsful of unhatched evils. O mules, our shadows under the copper sword!
four restive heads knotted to the fist make a living cluster against the blue.
The founders of asylums meet beneath a tree and find their ideas for the
choice of situations. They teach me the meaning and the purpose of the
buildings: front adorned, back blind; the galleries of laterite, the vestibules
of black stone and the pools of clear shadow for libraries; cool places for
wares of the druggist. And then come the bankers blowing into their keys.
And already in the streets a man sang alone, one of those who paint on
their brow the cipher of their god. (Perpetual crackling of insects in this
quarter of vacant lots and rubbish.) . . . And this is no time to tell you, no
time to reckon our alliances with the people of the other shore; water presented in skins, commandeering of cavalry for the dockworks and princes
paid in currency of fish. (A child sorrowful as the death of apes—one that
had an elder sister of great beauty—offered us a quail in a slipper of rose-
colored satin.)

. . . Solitude! the blue egg laid by a great sea-bird, and the bays at morning all littered with gold lemons!—Yesterday it was! The bird made off!
    Tomorrow the festivals and tumults, the avenues planted with podded
trees, and the dustmen at dawn bearing away huge pieces of dead palm trees,
fragment of giant wings . . . Tomorrow the festivals,
    the election of harbor-masters, the voices practicing in the suburbs and,
under the moist incubation of storms,
    the yellow town, casque'd in shade, with the girls' waist cloths hanging
at the windows.

◀ ▶

. . . At the third lunation, those who kept watch on the hilltops folded
their canvas. The body of a woman was burnt in the sands. And a man
strode forth at the threshold of the desert—profession of his father: dealer
in scent-bottles.

VII

We shall not dwell forever in these yellow lands, our pleasance. . . .

    The Summer vaster than the Empire hangs over the tables of space sev-
eral terraces of climate. The huge earth rolls on its surface overflowing its

pale embers under the ashes—. Sulphur color, honey color of immortal things, the whole grassy earth taking light from the straw of last winter—and from the green sponge of a lone tree the sky draws its violet juices.

A place glittering with mica! Not a pure grain in the wind's barbs. And light like oil.—From the crack of my eye to the level of the hills I join myself, I know the stones gillstained, the swarms of silence in the hives of light; and my heart gives heed to a family of locusts. . . .

Like milch-camels, gentle beneath the shears and sewn with mauve scars, let the hills march forth under the scheme of the harvest sky—let them march in silence over the pale incandescence of the plain; and kneel at last, in the smoke of dreams, there where the peoples annihilate themselves in the dead powder of earth.

These are the great quiet lines that disperse in the fading blue of doubtful vines. The earth here and there ripens the violets of storm; and these sandsmokes that rise over dead river courses, like the skirts of centuries on their route. . . .

Lower voice for the dead, lower voice by day. Such gentleness in the heart of man, can it fail to find its measure? . . . "I speak to you, my soul!—my soul darkened by the horse smell!" And several great land birds, voyaging westwards, make good likeness of our sea birds.

In the east of so pale a sky, like a holy place sealed by the blind man's linen, calm clouds arrange themselves, where the cancers of camphor and horn revolve. . . . Smoke which a breath of wind claims from us! the earth poised tense in its insect barbs, the earth is brought to bed of wonders! . . .

And at noon, when the jujuba tree breaks the tombstone, man closes his lids and cools his neck in the ages. . . . Horsetramplings of dreams in the place of dead powders, O vain ways a breath sweeps smoking toward us! where find, where find, the warriors who shall watch the streams in their nuptials?

At the sound of great waters on march over the earth, all the salt of the earth shudders in dream. And sudden, ah sudden, what would these voices with us? Levy a wilderness of mirrors on the boneyard of streams, let them appeal in the course of ages! Raise stones to my fame, raise stones to silence; and to guard these places, cavalcades of green bronze on the great causeways! . . .

(The shadow of a great bird falls on my face.)

X

Select a wide hat with the brim seduced. The eye withdraws by a century into the provinces of the soul. Through the gate of living chalk we see the things of the plain: living things,

Excellent things!

sacrifice of colts on the tombs of children, purification of widows among the roses and consignments of green birds in the courtyards to do honor to the old men;

many things on earth to hear and to see, living things among us!

celebrations of open air festivals for the name-day of great trees and public rites in honor of a pond; consecration of black stones perfectly round, discovery of springs in dead places, dedication of cloths held up on poles, at the gates of the passes, and loud acclamations under the walls for the mutilation of adults in the sun, for the publication of the bride-sheets!

many other things too at the level of our eyes: dressing the sores of animals in the suburbs, stirring of the crowds toward sheep-shearers, well-sinkers and horse-gelders; speculations in the breath of harvests and turning of hay on the roofs, on the prongs of forks; building of enclosures of rose red terra cotta, of terraces for meat-drying, of galleries for priests, of quarters for captains; the vast court of the horse-doctor; the fatigue parties for upkeep of muleways, of zig-zag roads through the gorges; foundation of hospices in vacant places; the invoicing at arrival of caravans, and disbanding of escorts in the quarter of money-changers; budding popularities under the sheds, in front of the frying vats; protestation of bills of credit; destruction of albino animals, of white worms in the soil; fires of bramble and thorn in places defiled by death, the making of a fine bread of barley and sesame; or else of spelt; and the firesmoke of man everywhere. . . .

ha! all conditions of men in their ways and manners; eaters of insects, of water fruits; those who bear poultices, those who bear riches; the husband-man, and the young noble horsed; the healer with needles, and the salter; the toll-gatherer, the smith, vendors of sugar, of cinnamon, of white metal drinking cups and of lanthorns; he who fashions a leather tunic, wooden shoes and olive-shaped buttons; he who dresses a field; and the man of no trade: the man with the falcon, the man with the flute, the man with bees; he who takes his delight in the pitch of his voice, he who makes it his business to contemplate a green stone; he who burns for his pleasure a thorn-

fire on his roof; he who makes on the ground his bed of sweet-smelling
leaves, lies down there and rests; he who thinks out designs of green pottery
for fountains; and he who has traveled far and dreams of departing again;
he who has dwelt in a country of great rains; the dicer, the knuckle-bone
player, the juggler; or he who has spread on the ground his reckoning tablets; he who has his opinions on the use of a gourd; he who drags a dead
eagle like a faggot on his tracks (and the plumage is given, not sold, for
fletching); he who gathers pollen in a wooden jar (and my delight, says he,
is in this yellow color); he who eats fritters, the maggots of the palmtree, or
raspberries; he who fancies the flavor of tarragon; he who dreams of green
pepper, or else he who chews fossil gum, who lifts a conch to his ear, or he
who sniffs the odor of genius in the freshly cracked stone; he who thinks
of the flesh of women, the lustful; he who sees his soul reflected in a sword
blade; the man learned in sciences, in onomastic; the man well thought of
in councils, he who names fountains, he who makes a public gift of seats in
the shady places, of dyed wool for the wise men; and has great bronze jars,
for thirst, planted at the crossways; better still, he who does nothing, such
a one and such in his manners, and so many others still! those who collect
quails in the wrinkled land, those who hunt among the furze for green-
speckled eggs, those who dismount to pick things up, agates, a pale blue
stone which they cut and fashion at the gates of the suburbs (into cases,
tobacco boxes, brooches, or into balls to be rolled between the hands of the
paralyzed); those who whistling paint boxes in the open air, the man with
the ivory staff, the man with the rattan chair, the hermit with hands like a
girl's and the disbanded warrior who has planted his spear at the threshold
to tie up a monkey . . . ha! all sorts of men in their ways and fashions, and
of a sudden! behold in his evening robes and summarily settling in turn all
questions of precedence, the Storyteller who stations himself at the foot of
the turpentine tree. . . .

O genealogist upon the marketplace! how many chronicles of families
and connections?—and may the dead seize the quick, as is said in the tables
of the law, if I have not seen each thing in its own shadow and the virtue of
its age: the stores of books and annals, the astronomer's storehouses and the
beauty of a place of sepulture, of very old temples under the palm trees,
frequented by a mule and three white hens—and beyond my eye's circuit,
many a secret doing on the routes: striking of camps upon tidings which I

know not, effronteries of the hill tribes, and passage of rivers on skin-jars; horsemen bearing letters of alliance, the ambush in the vineyard, forays of robbers in the depths of gorges and manœuvers over field to ravish a woman, bargain-driving and plots, coupling of beasts in the forests before the eyes of children, convalescence of prophets in byres, the silent talk of two men under a tree . . .

but over and above the actions of men on the earth, many omens on the way, many seeds on the way, and under unleavened fine weather, in one great breath of the earth, the whole feather of harvest! . . .

until the hour of evening when the female star, pure and pledged in the sky heights . . .

Plough-land of dream! Who talks of buildings?—I have seen the earth spread out in vast spaces and my thought is not heedless of the navigator.

Song

I have halted my horse by the tree of the doves, I whistle a note so sweet, shall the rivers break faith with their banks? (Living leaves in the morning fashioned in glory) . . .

◆ ▶

And not that a man be not sad, but arising before day and biding circumspectly in the communion of an old tree, leaning his chin on the last fading star, he beholds at the end of the fasting sky great things and pure that unfold to delight. . . .

◆ ▶

I have halted my horse by the dove-moaning tree, I whistle a note more sweet. . . . Peace to the dying who have not seen this day! But tidings there are of my brother the poet: once more he has written a song of great sweetness. And some there are who have knowledge thereof. . . .

(translated by T. S. Eliot)

1930

France

So. We are deep into the new century now. In recent years, Harry Houdini has died, *Amos 'n' Andy* has debuted, and a Scottish inventor in a department store has made the first public broadcast of a television signal—the silhouetted image of a ventriloquist's dummy. It is in this year, therefore, that Antonin Artaud founds his "Theater of Cruelty," a new approach to making art, one that he hopes will "shatter the false realities surrounding our everyday perceptions" by forcing upon audiences "the primary responsibility for interpreting their art." Artaud decides he'll do this by directing a play, *The Cenci*, by Percy Bysshe Shelley. It's based on the legend of a sixteenth-century Italian family terrorized by its patriarch, and it's considered so scandalous that no one has yet performed it. In the play, Francesco Cenci beats his wife and children on a regular basis, going so far as to even rape his daughter and son and servants. The family finally retaliates by bludgeoning him to death, to which the Pope responds by ordering their executions. Artaud spends seven years adapting and rehearsing his version of *The Cenci*, taking on the role of the patriarch himself, and performing for three hours on his hands and knees each night. The dozen other actors dance around him in Balinese costumes. There are strobe lights, crashing sets, wind machines blowing loose garbage across the stage. One theater critic writes of the production, "This is the most startling artistic event that has occurred in France in years." But within the same paragraph that critic also writes:

423

". . . this is utterly unwatchable." After only six performances Artaud's play is closed, and despite regretting the decision for the remainder of his life he never directs again. Instead, Artaud becomes a kind of prophet of the theater, someone who writes remarkably about what isn't going on. The result is a collection of texts that could be considered the world's first conceptual essays, a body of work that is detailed, imaginative, intimately expressive, and yet in no way tries to help the reader understand its deep significance. This is Artaud's "Theater of Cruelty" transferred to the page. In a letter to an editor who rejected this new work, Artaud once explained:

> It is very important that the few manifestations of spiritual existence that I have been able to give myself not be regarded as nonexistent because of the blotches and awkward expressions with which they are marred. I have felt and accepted these ungainly phrases, these ungainly expressions, which you criticize. Bear in mind: *I* have not questioned them. They come from the deep uncertainty of my own personal thinking. Do you think that a work that is faulty but which has fine and powerful things in it can be considered to have less authenticity than a work that is perfect but without inner resonance? For me, it is no less than a matter of knowing whether or not I have the right to continue thinking at all.

Within a year of writing this, Artaud will kill himself with an overdose of chloral.

ANTONIN ARTAUD

Eighteen Seconds

In a street, at night, on the edge of a pavement, under a lamp-post, stands a man in black, gazing into space, fiddling with his cane while holding a watch in his left hand. The hand of the watch indicates the seconds.

Close shot of the watch indicating the seconds.

The seconds pass infinitely slowly on the screen.

At the eighteenth second the film will be over.

The time that passes on the screen is in the mind of the man.

It is not normal time. The normal time is eighteen real seconds. The events which are to take place on the screen consist of images in the man's mind. The point of the scenario is that although the events described happen in eighteen seconds it takes an hour or two to project them onto the screen.

The spectator is to see the images which, at a certain point, file through the man's mind.

This man is an actor. He is about to achieve fame and to win the heart of a woman with whom he has long been in love.

He has been stricken by a strange malady. He has become incapable of keeping up with his thoughts; he has retained complete lucidity, but he can no longer give a shape to the thoughts that come to him, he cannot express them in appropriate actions and words.

He is at a loss for words; they no longer answer his call, and all he sees is a procession of images, masses of contradictory, disconnected images.

This prevents him from participating in the life of others and from indulging in any activity.

Shot of the man at the doctor's. His arms folded, his fists clenched. The doctor towering over him. The doctor passes his sentence.

The young man is again standing by the lamp-post at the moment when

425

he becomes fully aware of his condition. He curses; he thinks: just as I was about to start living and win the heart of the woman I love, who has yielded after such resistance!

Shot of the woman, beautiful, enigmatic, a hard, closed face.

Shot of the woman's soul as the man imagines it.

Landscape, flowers, gorgeous lighting.

Gesture of the man cursing:

Oh! to be anything! to be that wretched hunchback newsvendor who sells his papers at night, but to be in full possession of one's mind, to be really master of one's mind, to think!

Quick shot of the newsvendor in the street. Then in his room, his head in his hands, as though he were holding the globe. He really is in possession of his mind. He can hope to conquer the world and he has the right to think that he really will conquer it one day.

Because he also possesses INTELLIGENCE. He does not know his limitations, he can hope to possess everything: love, fame, power. And in the meantime he works and he searches.

Shot of the newsvendor gesticulating before his window; towns moving and trembling under his feet. Then again at his table. With books. His finger pointed. Swarms of women in the air. Piles of thrones.

He only has to discover the central problem, the problem on which all the others rest, and he will be able to hope to conquer the world.

He does not even have to solve the problem, he just has to discover the central problem and what it consists of, in order to settle it.

Ah! but his hump? He might even be relieved of his hump.

Shot of the newsvendor in the middle of a crystal ball. Rembrandt lighting. And a bright point at the center. The ball becomes the globe. The globe becomes opaque. The newsvendor disappears in the middle and springs out like a jack-in-the-box, his hump on his back.

And off he goes in search of his problem. He appears in smoky dens, in gatherings where some ideal is being sought. Ritual assemblies. Men make violent speeches. The hunchback sitting at a table, listening. Shaking his head, disappointed. In the middle of the group, a woman. He recognizes her: it is she! He shouts: hey! Arrest her! She is spying, he says. Hullabaloo. Everybody gets up. The woman runs away. He is soundly beaten and thrown out.

What have I done? I have betrayed her, I love her! he says.

Shot of the woman at home. At her father's feet: I recognized him. He is mad.

And he goes further continuing his search. Shot of the man on a road with a kick. Then, by his table, looking through books,—close shot of the cover of a book: the Cabala. Suddenly there is a knock at the door. Policemen enter. They rush at him. He is put into a straight-jacket and taken to a lunatic asylum. He really goes mad. Shot of the man struggling with bars. I shall discover the central problem, he yells, the problem from which all others hang like clusters of fruit, and then:

No more madness, no more world, no more mind, above all no more anything.

But revolution sweeps through the prisons and asylums; the doors of the asylum are opened; he is rescued. You are the mystic, people shout, you are our master, come! And, humbly, he says no. But he is dragged away. Be king, they tell him, accede to the throne! And, trembling; he mounts the throne.

His attendants withdraw and he is left alone.

Vast silence. Magical astonishment. And suddenly he thinks I am master of everything, I can have everything.

He can have everything, yes, everything except for his mind. He is still not master of his mind.

But what is the mind? What does it consist of? If only one could be master of one's physical self. Be able to manage anything, to do everything with one's hands, with one's body. And in the meantime the books accumulate on the table. He falls asleep.

And in the middle of his reverie, comes a new dream.

Yes, to be able to do everything, to be an orator, painter, actor, yes, but is he not an actor already? He is indeed an actor. And there he is, on the stage, with his hump, at the feet of his mistress who is acting with him. And his hump is also false: it is feigned. And his mistress is his real mistress, his mistress in real life.

A magnificent auditorium, crammed with people, and the King in his box. But he is also acting the part of the king. He is king, he hears and sees himself on the stage at the same time. And the king has no hump. He has realized that the hunchback on the stage is none other than his own effigy, a traitor who took his wife and stole his mind. So he stands up and exclaims: Arrest him! Hullabaloo. A commotion. The actors call upon him.

The woman shouts: It is no longer you, you have lost your hump, I do not recognize you. He is mad! And at the same time the two characters dissolve into each other on the screen. The whole auditorium trembles with its columns and candelabra. It trembles more and more. And against this trembling background all the images file past, also trembling, the king, the newsvendor, the hunchback actor, the lunatic, the asylum, the crowds, and the man finds himself on the pavement under the lamp-post, his watch in his left hand, his cane swinging.

Hardly eighteen seconds have elapsed; he contemplates his misery for the last time and then, with no hesitation or emotion, takes a revolver from his pocket and fires a bullet into his head.

(translated by Alastair Hamilton)

1935

Portugal

I've heard scholars say that the literary collage is an unintentional form of self-annihilation. I wonder what it therefore means to compose an autobiography in fragments. Or predominantly in questions. Or in a persona that's not one's own. *"The Book of Disquiet,"* as one scholar has written, "never existed . . . for it can never exist. It is made up of the ingredients for a book whose recipe is ever-sifting, the mutant germ of a book and its weirdly lush ramifications, the rooms and windows to build a book but no floor plan and no floor, a compendium of many potential books and many others already in ruins." The simple truth is: not all of us become the people we once hoped we might become. Just as Wordsworth had in *The Prelude,* or Joyce will do in *A Portrait of the Artist as a Young Man,* or Stein will also try in *The Autobiography of Alice B. Toklas,* this year Fernando Pessoa is leaving upon his death a reworking of his own identity. It's a giant leather trunk filled with twenty thousand manuscripts, all of which were written by a number of different authors who were invented by Pessoa—their biographies, their psychologies, their politics, their aesthetics. Some of his invented authors corresponded with each other. Some of them engaged openly in literary disputes. Some even published reviews of one another's work. The most famous of these texts is Bernardo Soares's kaleidoscopic masterpiece *The Book of Disquiet,* a mélange of theory, memory, daydream, rant, monologue, anecdote, and history.

The surname *Pessoa* can mean in Portugese "persona," "character," "mask," or "nobody." A writer, Pessoa said, "is a faker / so good at performing his act / he even fakes the pain / of pain he feels in fact."

Metaphysics has always struck me as a prolonged form of latent insanity

Metaphysics has always struck me as a prolonged form of latent insanity. If we knew the truth, we'd see it; everything else is systems and approximations. The inscrutability of the universe is quite enough for us to think about; to want to actually understand it is to be less than human, since to be human is to realize it can't be understood.

I'm handed faith like a sealed package on a strange-looking platter and am expected to accept it without opening it. I'm handed science, like a knife on a plate, to cut the folios of a book whose pages are blank. I'm handed doubt, like dust inside a box—but why give me a box if all it contains is dust?

I write because I don't know, and I use whatever abstract and lofty term for Truth a given emotion requires. If the emotion is clear and decisive, then I naturally speak of the gods, thereby framing it in a consciousness of the world's multiplicity. If the emotion is profound, then I naturally speak of God, thereby placing it in a unified consciousness. If the emotion is a thought, I naturally speak of Fate, thereby shoving it up against the wall.

Sometimes the mere rhythm of a sentence will require God instead of the Gods; at other times the two syllables of "the Gods" will be necessary, and I'll verbally change universe; on still other occasions what will matter is an internal rhyme, a metrical displacement, or a burst of emotion, and polytheism or monotheism will prevail accordingly. The Gods are contingent on style.

◆ ▶

Where is God, even if he doesn't exist? I want to pray and to weep, to repent of crimes I didn't commit, to enjoy the feeling of forgiveness like a caress that's more than maternal.

A lap in which to weep, but a huge and shapeless lap, spacious like a summer evening, and yet cosy, warm, feminine, next to a fireplace . . . To be able to weep in that lap over inconceivable things, failures I can't remember, poignant things that don't exist, and huge shuddering doubts concerning I don't know what future . . .

A second childhood, an old nursemaid like I used to have, and a tiny bed where I'd be lulled to sleep by tales of adventure that my flagging attention would hardly even follow—stories that once ran through infant hair as blond as wheat . . . And all of this enormous and eternal, guaranteed for ever and having God's lofty stature, there in the sad, drowsy depths of the ultimate reality of Things . . .

A lap or a cradle or a warm arm around my neck . . . A softly singing voice that seems to want to make me cry . . . A fire crackling in the fireplace . . . Heat in the winter . . . My consciousness listlessly wandering . . . And then a peaceful, soundless dream in a huge space, like a moon whirling among the stars . . .

When I put away my artifices and lovingly arrange in a corner all my toys, words, images and phrases, so dear to me I feel like kissing them, then I become so small and innocuous, so alone in a room so large and sad, so profoundly sad!

Who am I, finally, when I'm not playing? A poor orphan left out in the cold among sensations, shivering on the street corners of Reality, forced to sleep on the steps of Sadness and to eat the bread offered by Fantasy. I was told that my father, whom I never knew, is called God, but the name means nothing to me. Sometimes at night, when I'm feeling lonely, I call out to him with tears and form a idea of him I can love. But then it occurs to me that I don't know him, that perhaps he's not how I imagine, that perhaps this figure has never been the father of my soul . . .

When will all this end—these streets where I drag my misery, these steps where I coldly crouch and feel the night running its hands through my tatters? If only God would one day come and take me to his house and give me warmth and affection . . . Sometimes I think about this and weep with joy just because I can think about it. But the wind blows down the street, and the leaves fall on the pavement. I lift my eyes and look at the stars, which make no sense at all. And all that remains of this is I, a poor abandoned child that no Love wanted as its adopted son and no Friendship accepted as its playmate.

I'm so cold, so weary in my abandonment. Go and find my Mother, O Wind. Take me in the Night to the house I never knew. Give me back my nursemaid, O vast Silence, and my crib and the lullaby that used to put me to sleep.

◀ ▶

The only attitude worthy of a superior man is to persist in an activity he recognizes is useless, to observe a discipline he knows is sterile, and to apply certain norms of philosophical and metaphysical thought that he considers utterly inconsequential.

◀ ▶

To recognize reality as a form of illusion and illusion as a form of reality is equally necessary and equally useless. The contemplative life, to exist at all, must see real-life accidents as the scattered premises of an unattainable conclusion, but it must also consider the contingencies of dreams as in some sense worthy of the attention we give them, since this attention is what makes us contemplatives.

Anything and everything, depending on how one sees it, is a marvel or a hindrance, an all or a nothing, a path or a problem. To see something in constantly new ways is to renew and multiply it. That is why the contemplative person, without ever leaving his village, will nevertheless have the whole universe at his disposal. There's infinity in a cell or a desert. One can sleep cosmically against a rock.

But there are times in our meditation—and they come to all who meditate—when everything is suddenly worn-out, old, seen and reseen, even though we have yet to see it. Because no matter how much we meditate on something, and through meditation transform it, whatever we transform it into can only be the substance of meditation. At a certain point we are overwhelmed by a yearning for life, by a desire to know without the intellect, to meditate with only our senses, to think in a tactile or sensory mode, from inside the object of our thought, as if it were a sponge and we were water. And so we also have our night, and the profound weariness produced by emotions becomes even more profound, since in this case the emotions come from thought. But it's a night without slumber or moon or stars, a night as if all had been turned inside out—infinity internalized and ready to burst, and the day converted into the black lining of an unfamiliar suit.

Yes, it's always better to be the human slug that loves what it doesn't know, the leech that's unaware of how repugnant it is. To ignore so as to live! To feel in order to forget! Ah, and all the events lost in the green-white wake of age-old ships, like a cold spit off the tall rudder that served as a nose under the eyes of the ancient cabins!

❁

A glimpse of open country above a stone wall on the outskirts of town is more liberating for me than an entire journey would be for someone else. Every point of view is the apex of an inverted pyramid, whose base is indeterminate.

There was a time when I was irritated by certain things that today make me smile. And one of those things, which I'm reminded of nearly every day, is the way men who are active in day-to-day life smile at poets and artists. They don't always do it, as the intellectuals who write in newspapers suppose, with an air of superiority. Often they do it with affection. But it's as if they were showing affection to a child, someone with no notion of life's certainty and exactness.

This used to irritate me, because I naïvely assumed that this outward smile directed at dreaming and self-expression sprang from an inner conviction of superiority. In fact it's only a reaction to something that's different. While I once took this smile as an insult, because it seemed to imply a superior attitude, today I see it as the sign of an unconscious doubt. Just as adults often recognize in children a quick-wittedness they don't have, so the smilers recognize in us, who are devoted to dreaming and expressing, something different that makes them suspicious, just because it's unfamiliar. I like to think that the smartest among them sometimes detect our superiority, and then smile in a superior way to hide the fact.

But our superiority is not the kind that many dreamers have imagined we have. The dreamer isn't superior to the active man because dreaming is superior to reality. The dreamer's superiority is due to the fact that dreaming is much more practical than living, and the dreamer gets far greater and more varied pleasure out of life than the man of action. In other and plainer words, the dreamer is the true man of action.

Life being fundamentally a mental state, and all that we do or think valid to the extent we consider it valid, the valuation depends on us. The dreamer is an issuer of banknotes, and the notes he issues circulate in the city of his mind just like real notes in the world outside. Why should I care if the currency of my soul will never be convertible to gold, when there is no gold in life's factitious alchemy? After us all comes the deluge, but only after us all. Better and happier those who, recognizing that everything is fictitious, write the novel before someone writes it for them and, like Machiavelli, don courtly garments to write in secret.

◀ ▶

I've never done anything but dream. This, and this alone, has been the meaning of my life. My only real concern has been my inner life. My worst sorrows have evaporated when I've opened the window on to the street of my dreams and forgotten myself in what I saw there.

I've never aspired to be more than a dreamer. I paid no attention to those who spoke to me of living. I've always belonged to what isn't where I am and to what I could never be. Whatever isn't mine, no matter how base, has always had poetry for me. The only thing I've loved is nothing at all. The only thing I've desired is what I couldn't even imagine. All I asked of life is that it go on by without my feeling it. All I demanded of love is that it never stop being a distant dream. In my own inner landscapes, all of them unreal, I've always been attracted to what's in the distance, and the hazy aqueducts—almost out of sight in my dreamed landscapes—had a dreamy sweetness in relation to the rest of the landscape, a sweetness that enabled me to love them.

I am still obsessed with creating a false world, and will be until I die. Today I don't line up spools of thread and chess pawns (with an occasional bishop or knight sticking out) in the drawers of my chest, but I regret that I don't, and in my imagination I line up the characters—so alive and dependable!—who occupy my inner life, and this makes me feel cosy, like sitting by a warm fire in winter. I have a world of friends inside me, with their own real, individual, imperfect lives.

Some of them are full of problems, while others live the humble and picturesque life of bohemians. Others are traveling salesmen. (To be able to imagine myself as a traveling salesman has always been one of my great ambitions—unattainable, alas!) Others live in the rural towns and villages of a Portugal inside me; they come to the city, where I sometimes run into them, and I open wide my arms with emotion. And when I dream this, pacing in my room, talking out loud, gesticulating—when I dream this and picture myself running into them, then I rejoice, I'm fulfilled, I jump up and down, my eyes water, I throw open my arms and feel a genuine, enormous happiness.

Ah, no nostalgia hurts as much as nostalgia for things that never existed! The longing I feel when I think of the past I've lived in real time, when I weep over the corpse of my childhood life—this can't compare to the fervor of my trembling grief as I weep over the non-reality of my dreams' humble characters, even the minor ones I recall having seen just once in my pseudo-life, while turning a corner in my envisioned world, or while passing through a doorway on a street that I walked up and down in the same dream.

My bitterness over nostalgia's impotence to revive and resurrect becomes a tearful rage against God, who created impossibilities, when I think about how the friends of my dreams—with whom I've shared so much in a make-believe life and with whom I've had so many stimulating conversations in imaginary cafés—have never had a space of their own where they could truly exist, independent of my consciousness of them!

Oh, the dead past that survives in me and that has never been anywhere but in me! The flowers from the garden of the little country house that never existed except in me! The pine grove, orchards and vegetable plots of the farm that was only a dream of mine! My imaginary excursions, my outings in a countryside that never existed! The trees along the roadside, the pathways, the stones, the rural folk passing by—all of this, which was never more than a dream, is recorded in my memory, where it hurts, and I, who spent so many hours dreaming these things, now spend hours remembering having dreamed them, and it's a genuine nostalgia that I feel, an actual past that I mourn, a real-life corpse that I stare at, lying there solemnly in its coffin.

Then there are the landscapes and lives that weren't exclusively internal. Certain paintings without great artistic merit and certain prints on walls I saw every day became realities in me. My sensation in these cases was different—sadder and more poignant. It grieved me that I couldn't be there too, whether or not the scenes were real. That I couldn't at least be an inconspicuous figure drawn in at the foot of those moonlit woods I saw on a small print in a room where I once slept—and this was after my childhood was quite finished! That I couldn't imagine being hidden there, in the woods next to the river, bathed by the eternal (though poorly rendered) moonlight, watching the man going by in a boat beneath the branches of a willow tree. In these cases I was grieved by my inability to dream completely. My nostalgia exhibited other features. The gestures of my despair were different. The impossibility that tortured me resulted in a different kind of anxiety. Ah, if all of this at least had a meaning in God, a fulfillment in accord with the tenor of my desires, fulfilled I don't know where, in a vertical time, consubstantial with the direction of my nostalgias and reveries! If there could at least be a paradise made of all this, even if only for me! If I could at least meet the friends I've dreamed of, walk along the streets I've created, wake up amid the racket of roosters and hens and the early morning rustling in the country house where I pictured myself—and all of this more perfectly arranged by God, placed in the right order for it to exist, in the form needed for me to possess it, which is something not even my dreams can achieve, for there's always at least one dimension missing in the inward space that harbors these hapless realities.

I raise my head from the sheet of paper where I'm writing . . . It's early still. It's just past noon on a Sunday. Life's basic malady, that of being conscious, begins with my body and discomfits me. To have no islands where those of us who are uncomfortable could go, no ancient garden paths reserved for those who've retreated into dreaming! To have to live and to act, however little; to have to physically touch because there are other, equally real people in life! To have to be here writing this, because my soul needs it, and not to be able to just dream it all, to express it without words, without so much as consciousness, through a construction of myself in music and diffuseness, such that tears would well in my eyes as soon as I felt like expressing myself, and I would flow like an enchanted river across gentle slopes of my own self, ever further into unconsciousness and the Far-away, to no end but God.

◖ ◗

The intensity of my sensations has always been less than the intensity of my awareness of them. I've always suffered more from my consciousness that I was suffering than from the suffering of which I was conscious.

The life of my emotions moved early on to the chambers of thought, and that's where I've most fully lived my emotional experience of life.

And since thought, when it shelters emotion, is more demanding than emotion by itself, the regime of consciousness in which I began to live what I felt made how I felt more down-to-earth, more physical, more titillating.

By thinking so much, I became echo and abyss. By delving within, I made myself into many. The slightest incident—a change in the light, the tumbling of a dry leaf, the faded petal that falls from a flower, the voice speaking on the other side of the stone wall, the steps of the speaker next to those of the listener, the half-open gate of the old country estate, the courtyard with an arch and houses clustered around it in the moonlight— all these things, although not mine, grab hold of my sensory attention with the chains of longing and emotional resonance. In each of these sensations I am someone else, painfully renewed in each indefinite impression.

I live off impressions that aren't mine. I'm a squanderer of renunciations, someone else in the way I'm I.

◊

To live is to be other. It's not even possible to feel, if one feels today what he felt yesterday. To feel today what one felt yesterday isn't to feel—it's to remember today what was felt yesterday, to be today's living corpse of what yesterday was lived and lost.

To erase everything from the slate from one day to the next, to be new with each new morning, in a perpetual revival of our emotional virginity— this, and only this, is worth being or having, to be or have what we imperfectly are.

This dawn is the first dawn of the world. Never did this pink color yellowing to a warm white so tinge, towards the west, the face of the buildings whose windowpane eyes gaze upon the silence brought by the growing light. There was never this hour, nor this light, nor this person that's me. What will be tomorrow will be something else, and what I see will be seen by reconstituted eyes, full of a new vision.

High city hills! Great marvels of architecture that the steep slopes secure and make even greater, motley chaos of heaped up buildings that the daylight weaves together with bright spots and shadows—you are today, you are me, because I see you, you are what I'll be tomorrow, and I love you from the deck rail as when two ships pass, and there's a mysterious longing and regret in their passing.

◊

I lived inscrutable hours, a succession of disconnected moments, in my night-time walk to the lonely shore of the sea. All the thoughts that have made men live and all their emotions that have died passed through my mind, like a dark summary of history, in my meditation that went to the seashore.

I suffered in me, with me, the aspirations of all eras, and every disquietude of every age walked with me to the whispering shore of the sea. What men wanted and didn't achieve, what they killed in order to achieve, and all that souls have secretly been—all of this filled the feeling soul with which I walked to the seashore. What lovers found strange in those they love, what the wife never revealed to her husband, what the mother imagines about the son she didn't have, what only had form in a smile or opportunity, in a time that wasn't the right time or in an emotion that was missing—all of this went to the seashore with me and with me returned, and the waves grandly churned their music that made me live it all in slumber.

We are who we're not, and life is quick and sad. The sound of the waves at night is a sound of the night, and how many have heard it in their own soul, like the perpetual hope that dissolves in the darkness with a faint plash of distant foam! What tears were shed by those who achieved, what tears lost by those who succeeded! And all this, in my walk to the seashore, was a secret told me by the night and the abyss. How many we are! How many of us fool ourselves! What seas crash in us, in the night when we exist, along the beaches that we feel ourselves to be, inundated by emotion! All that was lost, all that should have been sought, all that was obtained and fulfilled by mistake, all that we loved and lost and then, after losing it and loving it for having lost it, realized we never loved; all that we believed we were thinking when we were feeling; all the memories we took for emotions; and the entire ocean, noisy and cool, rolling in from the depths of the vast night to ripple over the beach, during my nocturnal walk to the seashore . . .

Who even knows what he thinks or wants? Who knows what he is to himself? How many things music suggests, and we're glad they can never be! How many things the night recalls, and we weep, and they never even were! As if a long, horizontal peace had raised its voice, the risen wave crashes and then calms, and a dribbling can be heard up and down the invisible beach.

How much I die if I feel for everything! How much I feel if I meander this way, bodiless and human, with my heart as still as a beach, and the entire sea of all things beating loud and derisive, then becoming calm, on the night that we live, on my eternal nocturnal walk to the seashore.

◦

I see dreamed landscapes as plainly as real ones. If I lean out over my dreams, I'm leaning out over something. If I see life go by, my dream is of something.

Somebody said about somebody else that for him the figures of dreams had the same shape and substance as the figures of life. Although I can see why somebody might say the same thing about me, I wouldn't agree. For me, the figures of dreams aren't identical to those of life. They're parallel. Each life—that of dreams and that of the world—has a reality all its own that's just as valid as the other, but different. Like things near versus things far away. The figures of dreams are nearer to me, but . . .

◦

The truly wise man is the one who can keep external events from changing him in any way. To do this, he covers himself with an armor of realities closer to him than the world's facts and through which the facts, modified accordingly, reach him.

◦

Today I woke up very early, with a sudden and confused start, and I slowly got out of bed, suffocating from an inexplicable tedium. No dream had caused it; no reality could have created it. It was a complete and absolute tedium, but founded on something. The obscure depths of my soul had been the battleground where unknown forces had invisibly waged war, and I shook all over from the hidden conflict. A physical nausea, prompted by all of life, was born in the moment I woke up. A horror at the prospect of having to live got up with me out of bed. Everything seemed hollow, and I had the chilling impression that there is no solution for whatever the problem may be.

An extreme nervousness made my slightest gestures tremble. I was afraid I might go mad—not from insanity but from simply being there. My body was a latent shout. My heart pounded as if it were talking.

Taking wide, false steps that I vainly tried to take differently, I walked barefoot across the short length of the room and diagonally through the emptiness of the inner room, where in a corner there's a door to the hall-way. With jerky and incoherent movements I hit the brushes on top of the dresser, I knocked a chair out of place, and at a certain point my swinging hand struck one of the hard iron posts of my English bed. I lit a cigarette, which I smoked subconsciously, and only when I saw that ashes had fallen on the headboard—how, if I hadn't leaned against it?—did I understand that I was possessed, or something of the sort, in fact if not in name, and that my normal, everyday self-awareness had intermingled with the abyss.

I received the announcement of morning—the cold faint light that confers a vague whitish blue on the unveiled horizon—like a grateful kiss from creation. Because this light, this true day, freed me—freed me from I don't know what. It gave an arm to my as-yet-unrevealed old age, it cuddled my false childhood, it helped my overwrought sensibility find the repose it was desperately begging for.

Ah, what a morning this is, awakening me to life's stupidity, and to its great tenderness! I almost cry when I see the old narrow street come into view down below, and when the shutters of the corner grocer reveal their dirty brown in the slowly growing light, my heart is soothed, as if by a real-life fairy tale, and it begins to have the security of not feeling itself.

What a morning this grief is! And what shadows are retreating? What mysteries have taken place? None. There's just the sound of the first tram, like a match to light up the soul's darkness, and the loud steps of my first pedestrian, which are concrete reality telling me in a friendly voice not to be this way.

◁ ▷

There are times when everything wearies us, including what we would normally find restful. Wearisome things weary us by definition, restful things by the wearying thought of procuring them. There are dejections of the soul past all anxiety and all pain; I believe they're known only by those who elude human pains and anxieties and are sufficiently diplomatic with themselves to avoid even tedium. Reduced, in this way, to beings armored against the world, it's no wonder that at a certain point in their self-awareness the whole set of armor should suddenly weigh on them and life become an inverted anxiety, a pain not suffered.

I am at one of those points, and I write these lines as if to prove that I'm at least alive. All day long I've worked as if in a half-sleep, doing my sums the way things are done in dreams, writing left to right across my torpor. All day long I've felt life weighing on my eyes and against my temples— sleep in my eyes, pressure from inside my temples, the consciousness of all this in my stomach, nausea, despondency.

To live strikes me as a metaphysical mistake of matter, a dereliction of inaction. I refuse to look at the day to find out what it can offer that might distract me and that, being recorded here in writing, might cover up the empty cup of my not wanting myself. I refuse to look at the day, and with my shoulders hunched forward I ignore whether the sun is present or absent outside in the subjectively sad street, in the deserted street where the sound of people passes by. I ignore everything, and my chest hurts. I've stopped working and don't feel like budging. I'm looking at the grimy white blotting paper, tacked down at the corners and spread out over the advanced age of the slanted desk top. I examine the crossed out scribbles of concentration and distraction. There are various instances of my signature, upside down and turned around. A few numbers here and there, wherever. A few confused sketches, sketched by my absent-mindedness. I look at all this as if I'd never seen a blotter, like a fascinated bumpkin looking at some newfangled thing, while my entire brain lies idle behind the cerebral centers that control vision.

I feel more inner fatigue than will fit in me. And there's nothing I want, nothing I prefer, nothing to flee.

◁ ▷

I always live in the present. I don't know the future and no longer have the past. The former oppresses me as the possibility of everything, the latter as the reality of nothing. I have no hopes and no nostalgia. Knowing what my life has been up till now—so often and so completely the opposite of what I wanted—, what can I assume about my life tomorrow, except that it will be what I don't assume, what I don't want, what happens to me from the outside, reaching me even via my will? There's nothing from my past that I recall with the futile wish to repeat it. I was never more than my own vestige or simulacrum. My past is everything I failed to be. I don't even miss the feelings I had back then, because what is felt requires the present moment—once this has passed, there's a turning of the page and the story continues, but with a different text.

Brief dark shadow of a downtown tree, light sound of water falling into the sad pool, green of the trimmed lawn—public garden shortly before twilight: you are in this moment the whole universe for me, for you are the full content of my conscious sensation. All I want from life is to feel it being lost in these unexpected evenings, to the sound of strange children playing in gardens like this one, fenced in by the melancholy of the surrounding streets and topped, beyond the trees' tallest branches, by the old sky where the stars are again coming out.

( )

If our life were an eternal standing by the window, if we could remain there for ever, like hovering smoke, with the same moment of twilight forever paining the curve of the hills . . . If we could remain that way for beyond for ever! If at least on this side of the impossible we could thus continue, without committing an action, without our pallid lips sinning another word!

Look how it's getting dark! . . . The positive quietude of everything fills me with rage, with something that's a bitterness in the air I breathe. My soul aches . . . A slow wisp of smoke rises and dissipates in the distance . . . A restless tedium makes me think no more of you . . .

All so superfluous! We and the world and the mystery of both.

(translated by Richard Zenith)

1941

England

This is the year she kills herself, on March 28th. During the interval between that day and the one three weeks later when her body is finally found, Adolf Hitler first proposes his "final solution" in Germany. The United States invents the bazooka rocket launcher. And Britain starts a lab at the University of Birmingham to investigate how to start a nuclear chain reaction. The Nobel Prize Foundation, responding to the ongoing war in Europe, decides to withhold bestowing its prizes on anyone. This is a period that is identified as the end of modernism, "a culmination of progress," as E. M. Forster puts it, eulogizing Woolf in a Boston church this year. But, hadn't it always been Woolf's transiency that made her writing vital? Those sharply contrasting moments of paralyzing doubt and strident intuition encourage us as readers to engage more deeply with her texts. She pushes a little further against the limits of our comfort, and we peek into a world of dark exhilaration.

Virginia Woolf

The Death of the Moth

Moths that fly by day are not properly to be called moths; they do not excite that pleasant sense of dark autumn nights and ivy-blossom which the
commonest yellow-underwing asleep in the shadow of the curtain never
fails to rouse in us. They are hybrid creatures, neither gay like butterflies
nor sombre like their own species. Nevertheless the present specimen, with
his narrow hay-coloured wings, fringed with a tassel of the same colour,
seemed to be content with life. It was a pleasant morning, mid-September,
mild, benignant, yet with a keener breath than that of the summer months.
The plough was already scoring the field opposite the window, and where
the share had been, the earth was pressed flat and gleamed with moisture.
Such vigour came rolling in from the fields and the down beyond that it
was difficult to keep the eyes strictly turned upon the book. The rooks too
were keeping one of their annual festivities; soaring round the tree tops
until it looked as if a vast net with thousands of black knots in it had been
cast up into the air; which, after a few moments sank slowly down upon
the trees until every twig seemed to have a knot at the end of it. Then, suddenly, the net would be thrown into the air again in a wider circle this time,
with the utmost clamour and vociferation, as though to be thrown into the
air and settle slowly down upon the tree tops were a tremendously exciting
experience.

The same energy which inspired the rooks, the ploughmen, the horses,
and even, it seemed, the lean bare-backed downs, sent the moth fluttering
from side to side of his square of the window-pane. One could not help
watching him. One was, indeed, conscious of a queer feeling of pity for
him. The possibilities of pleasure seemed that morning so enormous and so
various that to have only a moth's part in life, and a day moth's at that, appeared a hard fate, and his zest in enjoying his meagre opportunities to the

full, pathetic. He flew vigorously to one corner of his compartment, and, after waiting there a second, flew across to the other. What remained for him but to fly to a third corner and then to a fourth? That was all he could do, in spite of the size of the downs, the width of the sky, the far-off smoke of houses, and the romantic voice, now and then, of a steamer out at sea. What he could do he did. Watching him, it seemed as if a fibre, very thin but pure, of the enormous energy of the world had been thrust into his frail and diminutive body. As often as he crossed the pane, I could fancy that a thread of vital light became visible. He was little or nothing but life.

Yet, because he was so small, and so simple a form of the energy that was rolling in at the open window and driving its way through so many narrow and intricate corridors in my own brain and in those of other human beings, there was something marvellous as well as pathetic about him. It was as if someone had taken a tiny bead of pure life and decking it as lightly as possible with down and feathers, had set it dancing and zigzagging to show us the true nature of life. Thus displayed one could not get over the strangeness of it. One is apt to forget all about life, seeing it humped and bossed and garnished and cumbered so that it has to move with the greatest circumspection and dignity. Again, the thought of all that life might have been had he been born in any other shape caused one to view his simple activities with a kind of pity.

After a time, tired by his dancing apparently, he settled on the window ledge in the sun, and, the queer spectacle being at an end, I forgot about him. Then, looking up, my eye was caught by him. He was trying to resume his dancing, but seemed either so stiff or so awkward that he could only flutter to the bottom of the window-pane; and when he tried to fly across it he failed. Being intent on other matters I watched these futile attempts for a time without thinking, unconsciously waiting for him to resume his flight, as one waits for a machine, that has stopped momentarily, to start again without considering the reason of its failure. After perhaps a seventh attempt he slipped from the wooden ledge and fell, fluttering his wings, on to his back on the window sill. The helplessness of his attitude roused me. It flashed upon me that he was in difficulties; he could no longer raise himself; his legs struggled vainly. But, as I stretched out a pencil, meaning to help him to right himself, it came over me that the failure and the awkwardness were the approach of death. I laid the pencil down again.

The legs agitated themselves once more. I looked as if for the enemy against which he struggled. I looked out of doors. What had happened there? Presumably it was mid-day, and work in the fields had stopped. Stillness and quiet had replaced the previous animation. The birds had taken themselves off to feed in the brooks. The horses stood still. Yet the power was there all the same, massed outside indifferent, impersonal, not attending to anything in particular. Somehow it was opposed to the little hay-coloured moth. It was useless to try to do anything. One could only watch the extraordinary efforts made by those tiny legs against an on-coming doom which could, had it chosen, have submerged an entire city, not merely a city, but masses of human beings; nothing, I knew had any chance against death. Nevertheless after a pause of exhaustion the legs fluttered again. It was superb this last protest, and so frantic that he succeeded at last in righting himself. One's sympathies, of course, were all on the side of life. Also, when there was nobody to care or to know, this gigantic effort on the part of an insignificant little moth, against a power of such magnitude, to retain what no one else valued or desired to keep, moved one strangely. Again, somehow, one saw life, a pure bead. I lifted the pencil again, useless though I knew it to be. But even as I did so, the unmistakable tokens of death showed themselves. The body relaxed, and instantly grew stiff. The struggle was over. The insignificant little creature now knew death. As I looked at the dead moth, this minute wayside triumph of so great a force over so mean an antagonist filled me with wonder. Just as life had been strange a few minutes before, so death was now as strange. The moth having righted himself now lay most decently and uncomplainingly composed. O yes, he seemed to say, death is stronger than I am.

— crying

— Who knew an essay about a moth could be so beautiful.

Why is this sad‥

1945

Romania

"The thinker does not think," Theodor Adorno will write this year. "Rather he transforms himself into an arena of intellectual experience." At the end of the war, 72 million people around the world will be dead, two-thirds of them civilians. Somehow, during this turmoil, the computer will be invented. Jets will be invented. The microwave oven, too. But there is something about advancement that is now difficult to embrace. Soon we'll hear stories of Nazi death camps in Europe. Stories of rape in China, slavery in Japan, internments in America. Finland will report that starving Russian soldiers stationed in their country secretly kidnapped villagers to kill and cannibalize. Paul Celan will try to write: "A word—you know, a corpse." He'll be recognized eventually as one of the world's most important writers from the mid-twentieth century, and yet he'll always insist, throughout his life, that he is not making literature. "Literature belongs to those who can be at home in the world," he says. "I am merely writing to acquire my own understanding of reality." In "Conversation in the Mountains," Celan returns to the ancient dialectic form of essaying, addressing himself in two different voices, circling around the gap that is widening within him—between that which understands the world, and that which never will—struggling to find a new way of reaching out across it. I think that someday soon in this genre—sometime between the birth of "New Journalism" in

451

the fifties and the suicide of Paul Celan in the early seventies—we're going to have to divorce our understanding of *essaying* from our understanding of the thing we'll start to call "nonfiction."

PAUL CELAN

Conversation in the Mountains

One evening, when the sun had set and not only the sun, the Jew—Jew and son of a Jew—went off, left his house and went off, and with him his name, his unpronounceable name, went and came, came trotting along, made himself heard, came with a stick, came over stones, do you hear me, you do, it's me, me, me and whom you hear, whom you think you hear, me and the other—so he went off, you could hear it, went off one evening when various things had set, went under clouds, went in the shadow, his own and not his own—because the Jew, you know, what does he have that is really his own, that is not borrowed, taken and not returned—so he went off and walked along this road, this beautiful, incomparable road, walked like Lenz through the mountains, he who had been allowed to live down in the plain where he belongs, he, the Jew, walked and walked.

Walked, yes, along this road, this beautiful road.

And who do you think came to meet him? His cousin came to meet him, his first cousin, a quarter of a Jew's life older, tall he came, came, he too, in the shadow, borrowed of course—because, I ask and ask you, how could he come with his own when God had made him a Jew—came, tall, came to meet the other, Gross approached Klein, and Klein, the Jew, silenced his stick before the stick of the Jew Gross.

The stones, too, were silent. And it was quiet in the mountains where they walked, one and the other.

So it was quiet, quiet up there in the mountains. But it was not quiet for long, because when a Jew comes along and meets another, silence cannot last, even in the mountains. Because the Jew and nature are strangers to each other, have always been and still are, even today, even here.

So there they are, the cousins. On the left, the turk's-cap lily blooms, blooms wild, blooms like nowhere else. And on the right, corn-salad, and *dianthus superbus,* the maiden-pink, not far off. But they, those cousins, have no eyes, alas. Or, more exactly: they have, even they have eyes, but with a veil hanging in front of them, no, not in front, behind them, a moveable veil. No sooner does an image enter than it gets caught in the web, and a thread starts spinning, spinning itself around the image, a veil-thread; spins itself around the image and begets a child, half image, half veil.

Poor lily, poor corn-salad. There they stand, the cousins, on a road in the mountains, the stick silent, the stones silent, and the silence no silence at all. No word has come to an end and no phrase, it is nothing but a pause, an empty space between the words, a blank—you see all the syllables stand around, waiting. They are tongue and mouth as before, these two, and in their eyes there hangs a veil, and you, poor flowers, are not even there, are not blooming, you do not exist, and July is not July.

The windbags! Even now, when their tongues stumble dumbly against their teeth and their lips won't round themselves, they have something to say to each other. All right then, let them talk . . .

"You've come a long way, have come all the way here . . ."

"I have. I've come, like you."

"I know."

"You know. You know and see: The earth folded up here, folded once and twice and three times, and opened up in the middle, and in the middle there is water, and the water is green, and the green is white, and the white comes from even farther up, from the glaciers, and one could say, but one shouldn't, that this is the language that counts here, the green with the white in it, a language not for you and not for me—because, I ask you, for whom is it meant, the earth, not for you, I say, is it meant, and not for me—a language, well, without I and without You, nothing but He, nothing but It, you understand, and She, nothing but that."

"I understand, I do. After all, I've come a long way, I've come like you."

"I know."

"You know and you want to ask: And even so you've come all the way, come here even so—why, and what for?"

"Why, and what for . . . Because I had to talk, maybe, to myself or to you, talk with my mouth and tongue, not just with my stick. Because to whom does it talk, my stick? It talks to the stones, and the stones—to whom do they talk?"

"To whom should they talk, cousin? They do not talk, they speak, and who speaks does not talk to anyone, cousin, he speaks because nobody hears him, nobody and Nobody, and then he says, himself, not his mouth or his tongue, he, and only he, says: Do you hear me?"

"Do you hear me, he says—I know, cousin, I know . . . Do you hear me, he says, I'm here. I am here, I've come. I've come with my stick, me and no other, me and not him, me with my hour, my undeserved hour, me who have been hit, who have not been hit, me with my memory, with my lack of memory, me, me, me . . ."

"He says, he says . . . Do you hear me, he says . . . And Do-you-hear-me, of course, Do-you-hear-me does not say anything, does not answer, because Do-you-hear-me is one with the glaciers, is three in one, and not for men . . . The green-and-white there, with the turk's-cap lily, with the corn-salad . . . But I, cousin, I who stand here on this road, here where I do not belong, today, now that it has set, the sun and its light, I, here, with the shadow, my own and not my own, I—I who can tell you:

"I lay on the stones, back then, you know, on the stone tiles; and next to me the others who were like me, the others who were different and yet like me, my cousins. They lay there sleeping, sleeping and not sleeping, dreaming and not dreaming, and they did not love me, and I did not love them because I was one, and who wants to love One when there are many, even more than those lying near me, and who wants to be able to love all, and I don't hide it from you, I did not love them who could not love me, I loved the candle which burned in the left corner, I loved it because it burned down, not because *it* burned down, because *it* was *his* candle, the candle he had lit, our mothers' father, because on that evening there had begun a day, a particular day: the seventh, the seventh to be followed by the first, the seventh and not the last, cousin, I did not love *it*, I loved its burning down and, you know, I haven't loved anything since.

"No. Nothing. Or maybe whatever burned down like that candle on that day, the seventh, not the last; not on the last day, no, because here I am, here on this road which they say is beautiful, here I am, by the turk's-cap lily and the corn-salad, and a hundred yards over, over there where I could go, the larch gives way to the stone-pine, I see it, I see it and don't see it, and my stick which talked to the stones, my stick is silent now, and the stones you say can speak, and in my eyes there is that moveable veil, there are veils, moveable veils, you lift one, and there hangs another, and the star there—yes, it is up there now, above the mountains—if it wants to enter it will have to wed and soon it won't be itself, but half veil and half star, and I know, I know, cousin, I know I've met you here, and we talked, a lot, and those folds there, you know they are not for men, and not for us who went off and met here, under the star, we the Jews who came like Lenz through the mountains, you Gross and me Klein, you, the windbag, and me, the windbag, with our sticks, with our unpronounceable names, with our shadows, our own and not our own, you here and me here—

"me here, me, who can tell you all this, could have and don't and didn't tell you, me with a turk's-cap lily on my left, me with corn-salad, me with my burned candle, me with the day, me with the days, me here and there, me, maybe accompanied—now—by the love of those I didn't love, me on the way to myself, up here."

(translated by Rosmarie Waldrop)

1952

France

This year, Stanley Miller, a twenty-three-year-old chemistry student at New York University, is alone in a lab with the periodic table and a recipe for making life. He assembles a glass contraption of intricately networked flasks, then adds to them the gases that are thought to have first filled Earth: nitrogen, oxygen, hydrogen, and carbon. He pours in eight ounces of sterilized water and simulates a lightning strike with a single electrode spark. Leaving his lab for seven days, he returns to find brown goo. He scoops it out, examines it, and discovers amino acids, the building blocks of life. Stanley Miller has become the first person in history to demonstrate how life may have started on this planet without the assistance of a god. "Another way of approaching a thing," writes Francis Ponge, "is to consider it unnamed, as well as unnameable."

FRANCIS PONGE

The Pebble

The pebble is not a thing that's easy to define. If a simple description will do, we can begin by saying it is a form or stage of stone between rock and gravel. But already this suggestion implies an idea about stone which must be justified. Let me hear no reproach as I delve far back on this subject, back even before the Flood.

◍

All rocks are descended through scission from the same gigantic forebear. One thing alone can be said about that fabled body, namely that once past the stage of limbo it never again held up.

Reason grasps it only as already amorphous and prostrate in the viscid tremors of its final agony. The mind awakens for the baptism of a hero of the whole world's grandeur, only to come upon the ghastly floundering of a death bed.

Instead of skipping ahead too quickly here, the reader should pause to admire not some dense funereal terms, but rather the grandeur and glory of a truth that has succeeded, however slightly, in rendering those terms transparent while not being entirely obscured by them itself.

◍

Thus, the sun now shines upon a planet already cooled and leaden. No flaming satellite remains to cast doubt on this point. All glory and all existence, all that provides vision and all that provides life, the source of all objective presence, has become centered in the sun. The heroes engendered by the sun, who once gravitated around it, have voluntarily gone into eclipse. Yet in order for the truth—whose glory they surrender in favor of its very source—to retain an audience and subjects dead or dying, they nonetheless keep up their unflagging orbits around it and their service as spectators.

One can well imagine that such a sacrifice, the expulsion of life from natures once so glorious and ardent, did not happen without dramatic interior upheaval. And there you have the origin of this grey chaos, Earth, our humble and magnificent abode.

And so, after a period of writhing and creasing, like a body tossing in sleep beneath the covers, our mythic hero, subdued (by his sentience) as though by a monstrous straitjacket, no longer experienced any but intimate explosions, at greater and greater intervals, with a shattering effect on the mantle, growing colder and heavier.

Dead hero and chaotic earth are now confused.

◀ ▶

Since the slow catastrophe of cooling, the history of this body—having once and for all lost both the capacity to be roused and to recast itself into one complete entity—will be but a tale of perpetual disintegration. Yet this is the moment when other things begin to happen: with grandeur dead, life immediately demonstrates that they two have nothing in common. Immediately, abundantly.

Such is the globe's appearance today. The dismembered corpse of a being that once embodied the whole world's grandeur is reduced to serving as backdrop for the life of creatures by the millions, infinitely smaller and more ephemeral than itself. In places they are so densely packed as to completely conceal the sacred skeleton which once served as their sole support. And the infinite quantity of corpses alone, contriving to imitate the consistency of stone through what we call humus, has for some while now allowed them to reproduce without owing a thing to the rock.

Incidentally the liquid element, whose origin may reach as far back as the one I've been discussing here, long since collected over expanses large or small, covers it, rubs against it, and by repeated friction accelerates its erosion.

Here I shall describe a few of the forms that stone, now scattered and humiliated by the world, lays before us.

◀ ▶

The largest fragments—slabs all but invisible beneath the interwoven vegetation that clings to them, as much out of bounden duty as any other motive—constitute the skeletal framework of the globe.

Veritable temples, they are not structures arbitrarily raised above ground, but the imperturbable remains of the ancient hero who was truly on this earth not long ago.

Man, taken with imagining great things, amid the shade and scents of the forests that sometimes overlay those mysterious slabs, through imagination alone supposes them still lying intact beneath it all.

In these same places, a good many smaller boulders attract his attention. Strewn through the underbrush by Time, sundry crumbly balls of rock, kneaded by the dirty fingers of that god.

Following the explosion of their enormous ancestor, and inexorably struck down from their trajectory in the skies, the rocks have fallen silent.

Permeated and fractured by germination, like a man who has given up shaving, furrowed and filled in by loose soil, no longer capable of the slightest reaction, not one of them utters a word. Their faces, their bodies are crannied.

Within the furrows of experience naivete approaches and settles in. Roses take a seat on their grizzled knees, carry on their naive diatribe against them. The stones accept them. They, whose disastrous rock shower once lit up the forests, whose duration is eternal amid stupor and resignation.

All around them, they're amused to see so many generations of flowers raised and doomed, in flesh tints scarcely more vivid than their own, whatever others may say, and a pink as pale and faded as their gray. They believe (as statues do, without bothering to say so) that the hues are borrowed from the glow of sunset skies, a glow in turn assumed each evening by the skies in memory of a far more extravagant conflagration, at the time of that celebrated cataclysm when, violently hurtled through the skies, they knew one magnificent hour of freedom concluded by the monstrous plunge to earth. Not far from there—at the rocky knees of the giants observing from the shores the foaming struggles of their foundered wives—the sea endlessly rips away boulders, which she protects in her arms, embraces, cradles, fondles, examines, massages, caresses and polishes against her body or tucks into her cheek like a dragée, then slips back out of her mouth and deposits on some hospitable gently sloping shore among a large flock already there within reach, thinking to pick it up again soon to tend it yet more affectionately, more passionately.

Meanwhile the wind blows, kicking up the sand. And if one of its particles, the last form and least of the object in question, should actually happen into our eyes, this is the way, through its own particular means of blinding, that stone punishes, putting an end to our meditation.

Thus nature closes our eyes at the very moment when we should probe memory to see whether information gathered there in prolonged contemplation might already have yielded a principle or two.

( )

To the mind casting about for ideas which has first been nourished on images such as these, nature in respect to stone will ultimately seem, too simplistically perhaps, like a clock whose mechanism is made up of cogwheels revolving at very different rates, though driven by a single motor.

Plant life, animals, gases and liquids revolve quite rapidly in their cycles of dying and returning to life. The great wheel of stone seems all but immobile and, even theoretically, we can grasp only in part its phase of slow disintegration.

Therefore, contrary to popular opinion which considers it a symbol of longevity and passivity, we can say that in fact while stone does not procreate, it is truly the only thing in nature which is constantly dying.

So when life—according to beings who are successively and rather briefly entrusted with it—suggests that it envies the indestructible solidarity of the setting it inhabits, it is in fact abetting the continual disintegration of that setting. And this is the unity of action that life finds dramatic: it has a muddled idea that its support may one day fail, yet believes itself eternally regenerative. In a setting that has abandoned all thought of moving and only contemplates falling into ruin, life grows anxious and frets about knowing only regeneration.

It's true that rock itself at times shows signs of agitation. This happens in its final stages when, as pebbles, gravel, sand, dust, it can no longer play its role of container or support for living things. Split off from the fundamental mass, it rolls, it blows about, it demands a place on the surface, and all life withdraws from the dreary stretches where, turn and turn again, it is dispersed and reassembled in the frenzy of despair.

Finally, I would mention as a most important principle, that all forms of stone, each of them representing some stage in its evolution, exist simultaneously in the world. In this no generations, no vanished races. Temples, Demigods, Wondets, Mammoths, Heroes, Forebears live side by side with their grandchildren. In his own garden any man can touch in living flesh each possibility of that world. No conception: everything exists. Or rather, as in Paradise, the whole of conception exists.

◦ ◦

If now I should wish to study one particular kind of stone more closely, then the perfection of its form, the fact that I can pick it up and turn it over in my hand, lead me to choose the pebble.

Then too, the pebble is stone precisely at the stage when it becomes a person, an individual—in other words, the stage of speech.

Compared to the rocky ledge from which it directly descends, it is stone already fragmented and polished into a vast number of almost similar individuals. Compared to the finest gravel, one can say that given the place where it is found, and because man is not in the habit of putting it to practical use, the pebble is rock still in the wild, or at any rate not domesticated.

For the few remaining days it still lacks meaning in any practical order of the world, let us profit from its virtues.

◦ ◦

Brought ashore one day by one of the countless dump carts of the tide—which since then keep unloading cargoes appealing to our ears alone, or so it seems—each pebble rests on a heap of forms from their earlier stages and their stages yet to come.

Not far from places where a layer of humus still covers its enormous forebears, at the foot of the rocky ledge where its immediate parents' lovemaking carries on, the pebble lodges on ground composed of their seed, where the pick-and-shovel tide seeks it out and loses it.

But those places where the sea tends to relegate it are the most unlikely for all recognition. Its populations lie there known to the vast expanse alone. Each pebble considers itself lost there, lacking a number and seeing none but blind forces to mark its presence.

And indeed wherever such flocks lie, they blanket the ground almost entirely, and their backs form a surface as troublesome for firm footing as for the intellect.

No birds. Occasional blades of grass poke up between the pebbles. Lizards scurry over them, negotiating them casually.

Leaping grasshoppers gauge themselves against each other rather than against the pebbles. From time to time a man will absently toss one far away from the others.

But these paltry objects, lost haphazardly in a solitude invaded by dry grass, seaweed, old corks and the assorted debris of human provender— imperturbable amid the most raging atmospheric upheavals—are mute witnesses to the play of forces dashing blindly until spent in pursuit of all beyond all reason.

Though rooted nowhere, they keep to their random site on the vast expanse. For all that it can uproot a tree or destroy a building, the fiercest wind cannot budge a pebble. But by blowing away surrounding dust, an occasional hurricane can ferret out one of these landmarks of chance from its fortuitous spot, centuries old, below the opaque temporal cover of sand.

◀ ▶

But water, on the other hand, which puts a glancing sheen on things and imparts its quality of fluidity to anything it can cloak, manages at times to seduce the forms and sweep them away. For the pebble recalls that it was born through the exertions of this formless monster upon the equally formless monster of rock. And since its entity can only be completed through repeated applications of liquid, the pebble remains, by definition, ever docile to it.

Pallid on the ground, as day is pallid next to night, the very moment the pebble is reclaimed, the sea gives it back the means to glisten. And while there's no great depth to its effect, which scarcely penetrates the very fine-grained very dense agglomerate, the liquid's exceedingly thin though active adhesion brings about a perceptible change of its surface. The wave seems to burnish it anew, thereby dressing wounds she herself inflicted during their earlier trysts. Then, for one moment, the pebble's exterior resembles its interior: overall it has the glow of youth.

Yet its form withstands both elements to perfection, lying serene amid the unruly seas. The pebble simply comes through the ordeal smaller though whole and, if you will, stands just as tall, since its proportions depend in no way on its volume.

Once out of water it immediately dries. In other words, despite the ter-

rible stress it has endured, no trace of liquid lingers on its surface. It is effortlessly dissipated.

In sum, smaller day by day but ever certain of its form, blind, secure
and dry within, by nature it would sooner be reduced by the seas than
blended in. So when stone, vanquished, is turned at last to sand, water still
can't penetrate as it does with dust. Retaining all marks then, except those
that come from liquids, which merely erase the marks upon it made by others, it lets the whole sea filter through, and disappearing in its depths with
no way to make it into mud.

◑

I'll say no more, for this idea of disappearing signs leads me to reflect on
the faults of a style that relies too heavily on words.

All too pleased for these first attempts to have chosen the pebble: for a
man of wry perception could only be amused, though probably moved as
well, when my critics say, "He ventured to write a description of stone and
wound up in a rock slide."

(translated by Lee Fahnestock)

1955

The problem is that what the term *nonfiction* describes is a conditional state of being, and one that is essentially a negation of genre. *Essay,* on the other hand, describes an activity, a fundamental human behavior that is as vital as storytelling, inherent as song. It's a term that helps the genre function more like a mind: one that can explore the consolidation of ideas, images, emotions, and facts through the negotiation of memory, anecdote, observation, history, religion, science, and even the imagination. "To drain all blood from the voice," Edmond Jabès once wrote. "The voice is the straight way. It follows the tracks of the letters. It is the book's blood. You have no more voice. You have given your blood. You have written."

EDMOND JABÈS

Dread of One Single End

1

Still to be where we are nothing but this "still" to be lived.

The words of friendship always come before friendship, as if the latter must wait to be announced before it can show itself.

We cannot have an image of ourselves.
Do we have one of others?
No doubt, but we never know, alas, if it is the right one.

To see, the way we might say, "see you later," to a stranger we watch leaving.
What passes sheds light on passage.
What remains, annuls it.

Open my name.
Open the book.

The happiness we feel in loving is not necessarily tied to a happy love.
It is a need for love.

In my bathroom mirror I saw a face appear that could have been mine, but whose features I seemed to discover for the first time.

Face of another and yet so familiar.
Sorting through my memories I recognized him as the man I'm mistaken for. I am the only one to know he has always been a stranger to me.

Suddenly the face disappeared, and the mirror, having lost its object, reflected nothing but the bare wall opposite, white and smooth.

Page of glass and page of stone in dialogue, solitary and solidarity.

The book has no point of origin.

Young, the world, in the eyes of eternity, and so old in the eyes of the instant.

Do we ask an island who are you?
Flattered and dazzled by the sea.
One day, to be swallowed up.
Fastened to nothing. Fastened to water.

"How do you see freedom?" the disciple asked his teacher.

"Perhaps as two daredevil wings in the sky, fighting desperately against the wind," replied the teacher.

And added: "Remains to be seen, however, if—as you too have sup-posed—these wings belong to a frail bird of passage."

"And if they were not the wings of a frail bird?" continued the disciple.

"The more fitting," said the teacher then, "the comparison."

"The image of freedom would be the wind."

Each truth works for its truth.
Modest contribution to universal Truth.
Our belief sustains it.

. . . all these little truths that come to undermine the idea we might have of one unique truth.

—Ants, that's what they are—I thought—imperturbable, digging their holes.

Do not try to use a cam where you need a bolt.

"The Truth does not exist, no doubt to allow our truths to exist," he said.

And added: "Once the sun has set, in the celestial void, we lift our eyes to where millions of stars glitter.

"O solitude of every one of them."

By the light of our insistent truths we wander into death.

Immutable and just, the law. Justice is less sure of itself.

Impossible to grasp, perhaps, the Truth.
Trying to express it we are often led astray.
Disloyal in spite of itself, the first word.

Truth as choice rather than voice?
I believe. I map a course.
Light. Light.

"Truth is an unpronounceable word," he said.

Do not hamper the free flight of an idea. You would be the first to regret your thoughtless gesture.

The soul has no restraints.

The sparrow pays no attention to dogs, but does beware the cat.

Eyes riveted to the clock, trembling with expectation. Every movement of the hand makes you jump because it calls you into question.
So capricious, the future. It always takes us by surprise.

Expecting what, if not death? And yet we dread it.
Expecting, perhaps, to be forgotten by death.

God is not in the answer. As the diamond in its reflections, He is in the flash of a question.

Every heart beat is death's punctual answer to the fearful question of the heart and life's evasive answer to the enigmatic question of death.

The body is without projects, without future; those are dreams and desires of the instant that gives it form.

Construct what's running down. Instruct what's being built up.

If I was not here yesterday, why worry if I'll be here tomorrow?

And today, how demonstrate my presence among you if I am unable to furnish proof?

He said: "Do not trust ideas that have traveled more than one road. You won't know which one to take in order to find them.

"Ideas do not come to us. We go toward them the way we return to a spring that has quenched our thirst."

The world is small, so small that the world makes short work of it.

2

"To increase by nothings.

"Lightweight. Lightweight," he said.

"What nothings are you talking about?" asked, one day, a disciple.

And the sage replied: "The mind sets its goal ever farther. O vertiginous push upward; but what is up unless a perpetual denial of down?"

And he added: "Down here was nothing and up there is nothing—but *between*, light strains through."

All light resides in thought.

By day you lay foundations. By night you doubt.

Memory invented time to its own glory, without noticing that time was already the memory of eternity.

The mirror reflects only one single image of us, the one it has decided to reveal to us.

Test by subtraction.

We can read only one word at a time.

What swims is as old as water.
What breathes is as old as air.
What dims is as old as time.

How can the body in pain manage to attract our attention, except by exhibiting images of its pain?

But the soul?

A soul in pain has no image of itself to offer.

The soul is what causes pain, but suffers alone.

The rushing water gradually loses even the notion of its overwhelming force, which at first had dazzled it.

Then, its pride fallen, it is nothing but domesticated power, in the service of man.

O unsuspected sadness of long impassive rivers.

Flaws, *crapauds* and *jardinagers:* misery of the diamond.

Do not ask the ocean to show you the way.

Rather put the question to the reed that has lost it.

As we measure the flow from a source, so we should gauge our output of words.

Be sparing with them, so as not to run dry.

He said: "A vinegar noise." At first this seemed strange, then by and by I got used to the expression, without however understanding it any better.

"Don't I occasionally say: An oily silence?"

And he added:

"Images often speak only to those who use them."

Soul and body are prey to the same illnesses.

Day is sick of images.

Madness. Madness.

Night, sick of oblivion.

There is no true silence except in the symbol's heart of hearts, unexplored.

Winter has covered my pen with snow.

White page, of ice. So young a word and already sentenced.

Ah, to write only resurrected words. To deal only with words of the highest season.

Luminous.

Not to see. Not to know. To be.
To go all the way, then plunge. Chosen.

"We must never leave the sick to their thoughts," wrote a sage, ironically.

"For them, the illness comes before anything. And that is the opposite of wisdom.

"Did not a sick man recently go mad for thinking he really was sick?
"He suffered, unawares, of a different illness."

We die only one death: the one we did not expect.

One flame is not enough for the glory of fire.

As he got older he noticed that one question became more important to him day by day: *how not to get old?*

But he had the question wrong. What he should have asked is: how to keep all the youthfulness of wisdom?

The void is more daring than the whole.

(translated by Rosmarie Waldrop)

1957

Portugal

This is the year that *Sputnik* is launched by the Soviets. On board, the Siberian husky Laika, a three-year-old whose name means "barker" in Russian, will become the first earthling to be thrust into space—and the first cooked alive in Earth's orbit as well. It's a reality that the Soviets try to smother with myth. Elsewhere, in Lisbon, in a small journal of art, the sculptor Ana Hatherly first publishes a "tisane," a kind of writing that she names for the French herbal tea that is said to be "delicious" as well as "medicinal." Part observational, part fantastic, Hatherly's are the kinds of texts that have been so problematic to categorize in the past that we've tended to avoid the issue by just calling them all "fiction." What a tisane is, however, according to Hatherly, is "an attempt to salve the wound between thoughts and dreams." Myths are as important as reality, she says, and it is the job of literature to help the two interact— not to stand guard at the borderline between them. This is the year that a laboratory in São Paulo, Brazil, accidentally releases a swarm of "Africanized" bees. This is the year that the first radio telescope is built, anticipating a signal from extraterrestrial life. And it's when Mary Leakey, in the savannah of Tanzania, finds a two-million-year-old hominid skull from the earliest of our ancestors to build a stone tool. "Just imagine," she will say, holding the new find in the palm of her small hand, "the great power of imagination that was started in this skull." This is the year that the Frisbee is introduced to America.

And commas in this whole essay!

ANA HATHERLY

Tisanes

lots of personification of intangible things

Once upon a time there was a person whose words whenever he spoke did not disappear. They walked right in front of him or else they stayed where they were and did not disappear. When he returned home the words were there. At the doors of other people's houses every morning the used words filled the garbage cans up to the top and some even fell on the ground but in that person's house the words did not die. They filled up the whole house and even the air was full of words. Then one day the person understood that sincerity is what is easy and when someone says he would like to retire inside an orange to sleep really one small grape would be enough.

◁ ▷

Once upon a time there was an anachronic clock. When it struck the hours they would roll through the living room then transform themselves into beautiful silver apples hanging from the ceiling. Every time a new hour rolled through the room the others already silver would smile hanging from the ceiling so that in that room there was always a kind of gleaming twinkle and when the clock had made a complete circuit of the dial the hours already silver would let themselves fall and then the sound would be great pearls of silver laughter.

loooo ooong sentence

◁ ▷

Once upon a time there was a landscape where there were never any clouds. To make rain it was necessary to wash the horizon with feathers. ?.

◁ ▷

Once upon a time there was an infinite serpent. As it was infinite there was no way to know where its head was. Every time a vertebra was removed it was not missed at all. It could even be broken dislocated mended. It always remained infinite. Anyone who wanted to take a piece home could put it on the wall and contemplate a fragment of the infinite serpent.

()

Once upon a time there was an engineer who woke up in the middle of the night. Someone trying to steal a car parked on the street had set off the car alarm so that the horn kept sounding endlessly in the silence of the night in the warmth of the bedclothes the engineer heard the machine calling.

not all start w/ "once upon a time"   ()

On the way home I am thinking: it is only very recently that we have begun to perceive the extent of the vast ruin in which we live, a ruin much vaster than any prehistory and of which the purpose is still inexplicable since the prolific growth of ruins constantly poses the problem of continuous debris. Thinking about this I arrive home. I go in. When my eyes get used to the darkness I see fairly clearly in front of me a specter. I have caught him still with a shape. I clutch at him but he escapes me as if squeezed. I hurry to tell my sisters what happened. I show my left cheek where the specter left a tattooed image representing words written on the back of my hand. I can't decipher. I am afraid they say.

()

I sit down on the doorstep and think: where does the sky begin? is it just above the ground? then are we always in the sky? Across from my house is the river. One fisherman waits patiently while another prepares to return. I lie down on the ground and plunge my face into the earth.

no real order thanks to lack of commas

I am on the bank of the river it is night I am sitting on the stairs carved into the wall watching the water a boat has passed not very big but fast soon afterward big very black waves begin to run against the wall for moments the stairs disappear. *how might the reading differ w/ the placement of commas?*

I am on the mountain it is noon I see innumerable flies soaring and buzzing in the shadow of a rock suddenly a fly appears five times bigger than

normal it stops right in front of me I am surprised I say this is the biggest
fly of my life but I wonder what animal it can be a parasite of.

◊◊

I was quickly crossing the lobby when I felt very dizzy to support myself
I put out my hand to the big table that was there when I closed my eyes
the table disappeared.

◊◊

Every time I breathe I know that I alternately lose and recover my body.
Then I think it is in the high tide of respiration that my body forms itself,
in that interval. (When people are sleeping or at the movies, for example,
how the air of the place becomes alternately full and empty of bodies!)
Expiring the body out inspiring the body in. This is how gymnastics is a
form of vampirism. I think about this when I am on the beach watching
a man surfing. Suddenly he overbalances and falls. Everything profound
reveals itself at the surface.

◊◊

Once upon a time there was a country where the inhabitants had such
hands that when some traveler greeted a native the latter's fingers would
dissolve in his hands. Or else they remained attached in such a way that
the traveler couldn't manage to pull them off unless he plunged his hands
in boiling oil. At that point the traveler's fingers fell off too and were seen
floating in the boiling oil like French fried potatoes. The traveler would
return to his country with the profound knowledge that one gains from
long journeys.

(translated by Jean R. Longland)

[handwritten note: things disappearing to make up for other things piling up— maintaining balance?]

1959

And yet, still, when the essay collection *Eagle or Sun?* by Octavio Paz appears, critics will wonder for a long time how to describe the book. Finally they will settle on just calling it "curious." They will write: "It does not seem to belong to any specific genre," and "it is apparent that this is neither a work of fiction nor poetry," and "what this must be is an extended meditation on the nature of language itself." None of their attempts at describing this book will suggest it's made up of essays. In Mexican culture, the expression "eagle or sun" is similar to "heads or tails." Duality, Paz wrote, "permeates Eastern thought: male and female, pure and impure, left and right. These opposites co-exist in the cultures of the East. In the West, however, they tend to disappear for the worst of reasons: far from being resolved into a higher synthesis, they just cancel each other out." Of the fifty-nine books that Octavio Paz wrote, thirty-four of them are collections of essays. When you think of Octavio Paz, however, what do you think of him as?

OCTAVIO PAZ

Before Sleep

I carry you like an object from another age, found one day by chance, which we touch with ignorant hands: fragment of what cult, master of what now-vanished powers, carrier of what fury, what curses that time has made ridiculous, cipher standing among what fallen numbers? Its presence invades us until it occupies insensibly the center of our preoccupations, in spite of the reprobation of our judgment that declares its beauty—lightly hideous—dangerous for our little system of life, made of bristled negations, circular wall that defends two or three certainties. And you are like that. You have rooted in my chest and like a pneumatic bell have dislodged thoughts, memories, and desires. Invisible and silent, at times you peer through my eyes to see the world outside, and then I feel watched by the objects that you study, and I am overwhelmed by infinite shame and great abandon. But now, do you hear me? Now I am going to throw you out. I'm going to set myself free from you forever. Don't try to escape. You can't. Don't move, I tell you, or you'll pay for it. Keep still: I want to hear your empty pulse, see your featureless face. Where are you? Don't hide. Don't be afraid. Why are you so quiet? I won't do anything to you, it was only a joke. Do you understand? It's just that sometimes I get excited, I'm quick-tempered, and say things that later I regret. It's my character. And life. You wouldn't understand. What do you know about life, always closed in, concealed? It's easy for you to be reasonable. Inside nobody bothers you. Life on the street is something else: they push you, smile at you, rob you. They are insatiable. But now that your silence proves that you've forgiven me, allow me to ask a question. I'm sure you'll answer clearly and simply, as one answers a friend after a long absence. It's true the word absence is not the most appropriate, but I wish to confess that your intolerable presence is much like that which they call the "emptiness of absence." The emptiness of your presence, your empty presence! I never see you, never feel you, never hear you. Why are you so silent? You are silent for hours, crouching in some fold. I don't think I'm being demanding. I don't ask for much: a sign, a little indication, a glance, one of those little attentions that mean nothing to the giver but fill the receiver with joy. I'm not asking, I'm begging. I accept my situation and know how far I can go. I realize that you are the strongest and the cleverest: you pierce the crack of sadness or the opening of happiness, you use dreams and vigils, mirrors and walls, kisses and tears. I know that I belong to you, that you will be by my side on the day of my death, and that you will then take possession of me. Why wait so long? I advise you from now on: don't wait for the death in battle, the criminal's death, nor the martyr's. There will be a small agony, accompanied by the usual terrors, modest deliriums, late revelations without consequence. Do you hear me? I can't see you. You always hide your face. I will confide in you—you see, I don't bear any grudges and I'm sure that one day you're going to break this absurd silence. After so many years of living . . . although I feel that I have never lived, that I have been lived by time, disdainful and implacable time that has never stopped, that has never shown me a sign, that has always ignored me. I'm probably too timid and have never had the courage to grab it by the throat and say, "I too exist," like the petty official who stops the Director General in the corridor and says, "Good morning, I too . . ." but, to the other's amazement, goes dumb, suddenly realizing the uselessness of the gesture: he has nothing to say to his Boss. Such am I: I have nothing to say to time. And likewise, it has nothing to say to me. And now, after all this rambling, I think we are closer to what I was going to tell you: after so many years of living—wait, don't be impatient, don't try to escape, you must hear me to the end—after so many years, I have said to myself: to whom, if not to him, can I tell my stories? In effect— I'm not ashamed to say it and you shouldn't blush—I have only you. You. Don't think I want to arouse your compassion; I have merely uttered a truth, confirmed a fact and nothing more. And you, whom do you have? Are you to someone the way I am to you? Or, if you prefer, do you have someone the way I have you? Ah, you're growing pale, you don't answer. I understand your amazement: I too have been kept awake by the possibility that you are another's, who in turn is another's, until it never ends. Don't worry: I talk only to you. But do you, at this very moment, tell the same things I tell you to a silent third, who in turn . . . ? No, if you were an other, then who would I be? I repeat: who do you have? No one, except me. You too are alone, you too had a solitary and passionate childhood—all the fountains spoke to you, all the birds obeyed you—and now . . . Don't interrupt me. I will begin at the beginning: when I met you—yes, I understand your surprise and can guess what you're going to tell me: in reality, I don't know you, I've never seen you, I don't know who you are. It's true. In other times I thought you were the ambition that our parents and friend filter into our ears with a name and a moral—a name and a moral that with the force of familiarity swells and grows until someone comes along with a slender pin and bursts that little bag of pus. Later I thought you were the thought that one day left my head to assault the world. Later I confused you with my love for Juana, Maria, Dolores, or with my faith in Julian, Agustin, Rodrigo. Then I thought you were something far-off and before me, perhaps my prenatal life. You were simply life. Or, better, the tepid hollow that remains when life leaves. You were the memory of life. And this idea brought me to another: my mother was not a womb but agony and a tomb those nine months of confinement. But I succeeded in rejecting those thoughts. A little reflection has made me see that you are not a memory, not even something forgotten: I do not feel you as the one that I was, but rather as the one that I will be, as the one that is being. And when I want to investigate, you escape. And then I sense you as an absence. In sum, I don't know you, I've never seen you, and yet I have never felt alone, without you. That's why you should accept the phrase—remember it?—"when I met you" as a figurative expression, as a recourse of language. What is certain is that you always accompany me, that there is always someone with me. To say it all at once: who are you? It's useless to hide any longer. This game has lasted long enough. Don't you realize that I could die right now? If I die your life will no longer have meaning. I am your life and the meaning of your life. Or is it the reverse, that you are the meaning of my life? Speak. Say something. Do you still hate me because I threatened to throw you out the window? I only said it to provoke you. And you remained silent. You're a coward. Remember when I insulted you? When I vomited all over you? And when you had to see with these eyes that never close how I slept with that vile hag and talked of suicide? Show me your face. Where are you? Actually, none of this matters to me. I'm tired, that's all. I'm sleepy. Don't these endless discussions tire you? It's as if we were a couple who, at five in the morning, with swollen eyes, continues on the rumpled sheets a quarrel started twenty years ago. Let's go to sleep. Say good night. Show a little courtesy. You are condemned to live with me and you ought to force yourself to make life more bearable. Don't shrug your shoulders. Be quiet if you want, but don't go away. I don't want to be alone: the less I suffer, the more unhappy I am. Maybe happiness is like the foam of the painful tide of life that covers our souls with a red fullness. Now the tide recedes and nothing remains of that which made us suffer so. Nothing but you. We are alone, you are alone. Don't look at me. Close your eyes so I can close mine. I can't get used to your eyeless watching.

(translated by Eliot Weinberger)

1960

France

My point is that the essay exists. And it seems, in fact, to have always existed. But even now, five thousand years since the earliest essay appeared, at a point in literary history when transgressive fiction writers are exploring "metatexts," when Language poets are introducing the so-called "new sentence," and when performance artists are reinventing what "art" even is, essayists who are trying to offer more than information are still not being recognized as practitioners of the form. Marguerite Yourcenar's *Fires* is made up of a series of voice portraits that speak on her behalf. It is not quite memoir, therefore, but it's not biography either. We couldn't call it fiction, and yet it's propelled by myths. The *New York Times,* in reviewing the book, tried to invent a new genre in order to describe it: "This 'unwritten novel,'" its critic announced, "is a work that appears on its surface to be a compilation of fragments. It is a salad of notebook ecstasies, diaristic confessions, prose poems, epigrams, and shafts of critical discourse.... Yet these collections of scattered works are not mere pastiches." No, they certainly aren't. Marguerite Yourcenar's *Fires* is a personal meditation that is informed by history, memory, and the long complex tradition of our shared experiences with myth. "The best thing for a writer," Yourcenar once wrote, "is to be elsewhere." What she asks is whether the "I" in an essay needs to be an autobiographical "I." It's around this time that Carl Jung dies. When Elie Wiesel's *Night* is first published in

America. And when Andy Warhol unveils his Campbell's Soup cans. In other words, we might not be noticing at the moment, but the very concept of "nonfiction"—a term that's been in use for a decade by now—is being challenged by artists in a variety of media who are demonstrating the meaninglessness of a term that describes a way of art-making that is based on the veracity of its claims rather than on what it's expressing. "Every literary work," Marguerite Yourcenar wrote, "is forced upon its author in a mixture of vision, memory, idea, and action. Everything in the course of an individual's life becomes somehow a part of her art." I'm not saying that essayists do not traffic in information. I'm saying that maybe that information is sometimes experienced, sometimes it is researched, and sometimes it's inherited from a collective unconscious.

Fires

I hope this will never be read.

There is between us something better than love: a complicity.

Absent, your face expands so that it fills the universe. You reach the fluid state which is the one of ghosts. Present, your face condenses, you achieve the concentration of the heaviest metals, of iridium, of mercury. This weight kills me when it falls on my heart.

The admirable Paul was wrong (I am speaking of the great sophist, Paul Valéry, and not of the predicator). There is for each thought, for each love that if left alone would perhaps fail, a singularly strong stimulant—the ENTIRE REST OF THE WORLD—which is opposed to it and is not worthy of it.

Loneliness . . . I don't believe as they do, I don't live as they do, I don't love as they do . . . I will die as they die.

Alcohol sobers me. After a few swallows of brandy, I no longer think of you.

Phaedra; or, Despair

Phaedra settles everything. She abandons her mother to the bull, her sister to loneliness: she is uninterested in these kinds of love. She leaves her country like someone giving up dreams: she disowns her family like someone pawning memories. Living where innocence is a crime, she witnesses with disgust what she will end up being. Seen from the outside, her destiny horrifies her: right now she knows it only through the inscriptions on the Labyrinth's wall: she escapes from her terrible future by running away. She marries Theseus as absentmindedly as Saint Mary of Egypt paid the price of passage with her body. She lets the gigantic slaughterhouses of her American Crete sink in the West behind her, in a fog of fables. She lands, permeated with the odor of the ranch and of fish from Haiti, unsuspectingly carrying the leprosy contracted in a torrid-heart Tropic. Her astonishment upon seeing Hippolytus is that of a traveler who unknowingly has retraced her steps: the boy's profile recalls Knossos and the Cretan two-edged ax. She hates him, she raises him; he grows up against her, rebuffed by her hatred, accustomed, since his early years, to mistrust women, forced since school to skip over obstacles an inimical stepmother has raised. She is jealous of his arrows—his victims, of his companions—his solitude. In this virgin forest which is Hippolytus' domain, she unwillingly plants the signposts of Minos' palace; she traces through the underbrush the one-way road leading to Fatality. She creates and re-creates Hippolytus; her love is a true incest; she cannot kill this youth without a sort of infanticide. She manufactures his beauty, his chastity, his weaknesses, extracting these from deep within herself; to be able to hate it under the guise of an insipid virgin, she removes his detestable purity; his nonexistent Aricia is wrought from scratch. She gets drunk on the impossible, the heady basis of all mixtures of misfortunes. In Theseus' bed she has the bitter pleasure of cheating, in actuality, on the man she loves, and, in imagination, on the one she doesn't. She becomes a mother: she has children as she would have remorse. Feverish between her damp sheets, she comforts herself by whispering confessions like a child mumbling secrets on her nurse's neck; she suckles her unhappiness; at last she becomes Phaedra's downtrodden servant. Confronting Hippolytus' coldness, she imitates the sun coming up against crystal: she turns into a specter; she haunts her body as if it were her personal hell. She re-creates inside herself a deep Labyrinth where she is bound to dwell again; Ariadne's thread will not pull her out, since she winds it around her heart. She is widowed; at last she can weep without being asked why. But black does not become this dark figure; she begrudges her mourning because it falsifies her grief. Rid of Theseus, she carries her hope like a shameful posthumous pregnancy. To forget herself, she becomes involved in intrigues; she accepts the Regency as she would begin to knit a shawl. Theseus returns too late to bring her back into the world of routine he lives in; she can enter it only through the opening of a subterfuge: rapture by rapture, she imagines the rape Hippolytus will be accused of, so that her lie becomes her fulfillment. She is telling the truth: she has been raped; her imposture is a translation. She takes poison, since gradually she has become immune to her own; Hippolytus' disappearance creates a void around her; drawn into this void, she is engulfed by death. She confesses before dying, to have the pleasure, for the last time, of talking about her crime. Without changing places, she returns to the family palace where sin is innocence. Pushed by the throng of her ancestors, she slides along these subway corridors filled with animal smells; here oars split the oily waters of the Styx, here shiny rails suggest either suicide or departure. At the bottom of the mining galleries of her underground Crete, she will undoubtedly end up meeting the young man disfigured by her claws, since she has all the detours of eternity to find him. She has not seen him since the fatal scene of Act Three; it's because of him that she is dead; it's because of her that he did not live; he owes her only death; she owes him the convulsions of an irrepressible agony. She has the right to hold him responsible for her crime, for blackening her immortality now that poets will use her name for their own incestuous desires, in the same way that a driver lying on the road with a broken skull can hold the tree he has smashed against responsible; like all victims, he was his own torturer. At last, definitive words will come from her lips no longer trembling with hope. What will she say? Perhaps, thank you.

A heart is perhaps something unsavory. It's on the order of anatomy tables and butcher's stalls. I prefer your body.

There is around us the atmosphere of Leysin, of Montana, of high mountain sanatoria glassed in like an aquarium, gigantic reserves where Death keeps coming to fish. The patients spit out bloodied confessions, trade bacilli, compare fever charts, settle into a friendship of danger signals. Between you and me, who has the most cavities?

Where shall I run to? You fill the world. I can only escape you in you.

Destiny is lighthearted. He who lends Fatality whatever beautiful mask knows it only through theatrical disguises. An unknown practical joker repeats the same vulgar seesaw, ad nauseam, until the death struggle. Chance is surrounded by a floating odor of children's rooms, of toy boxes which release the demons of Habit, of closets from which our maids, ludicrously dressed, sprang, hoping to make us scream. The Tragic characters jump up, brutally startled by booming, thunderous laughter. All his life, before losing his sight, Oedipus did nothing but play blindman's buff with Chance.

No matter how I change, my luck does not change. Any figure can be drawn within a circle.

We remember our dreams: we do not remember our sleep. Only twice did

I enter these depths crossed by currents; there our dreams are only wreckage of submerged realities. The other day, drunk with happiness as you can be drunk with fresh air after a long race, I threw myself on my bed like a diver falling backwards, arms spread: I toppled over in a blue sea. Leaning against the abyss like a swimmer floating, and held up by the oxygen bag of my lungs full of air, I emerged from this Greek sea like a newborn island. Tonight, glutted with unhappiness, I drop into bed like a drowning woman letting go: I yield to sleep as though yielding to asphyxiation. Streams of memories persist through stupefied nocturnal weariness, dragging me toward an Asphaltic lake. There is no way to sink into this salt-saturated water, bitter as eyelid secretions. I am floating like the mummy in its bitumen, in fear of an awakening that at the very most will be a survival. The flux, then reflux of sleep bring me back, in spite of myself, to this batiste beach. My knees continually bump against your memory. The cold awakens me as though I had slept next to someone dead.

I bear your faults. One is resigned to God's faults. I bear your lacks. One is resigned to God's lacks.

A child is a hostage. Life has you. The same holds true of a dog, a panther, or a cicada. Leda would say: "I am no longer free to kill myself since I bought a swan."

Patroclus; or, Destiny

Night—or rather, a vague daylight—was falling on the flat, open country; you couldn't tell which way twilight was heading. Towers seemed like rocks, foothills seemed like towers. Painfully giving birth to the future, Cassandra was howling from atop the city walls. Blood stuck like rouge on the unrecognizable cheeks of corpses; Helen was painting her vampire mouth with lipstick that made one think of blood. Everyone had been settled there for years in a sort of red routine in which war and peace mingled like sand and water in stinking marsh regions. Harvested by armored trucks, the first generation of heroes had accepted war as a privilege, almost an investiture; they were followed, in turn, by a contingent of soldiers who accepted it as a duty and later bore it as a sacrifice. The invention of tanks made enormous gaps in these ranks now there only as ramparts; a third wave of assailants stormed death; staking their whole life, these gamblers fell as though hit by their own ball right square in the heart. Gone were the days of heroic tenderness, when the adversary was the dark other side of the friend. Iphigenia was dead, shot by Agamemnon's order; she had been convicted of having had a hand in the mutiny of the fleet. Paris had been disfigured by the explosion of a grenade; Polyxena had just succumbed to typhoid in Troy's hospital; the Oceanids, kneeling on the beach, had given up trying to keep the blue flies from Patroclus' corpse. Since the death of this friend who had first filled, then become his world, Achilles no longer left his tent; it was littered with shadows: naked, lying flat on the ground as though striving to imitate the corpse, he let himself be eaten by the vermin of his memories. More and more, death seemed to him a sort of conse-cration only the purest men were worthy of; many are undone, few die. Thinking of Patroclus, he remembered the particularities: his paleness, the rigidity of his shoulders ever so slightly hunched, his hands always a little cold, the weight of his body sinking into sleep with the heaviness of a stone—all these finally achieved their full meaning posthumously, as though, alive, Patroclus had only been the rough sketch of his corpse. The unavowed hatred sleeping in the bottom of love predisposed Achilles to the sculptor's task: he envied Hector for perfecting this masterpiece: only he, himself, should have torn away the last veils that thought, gesture, the very fact of being alive, placed between them, in order to discover Patroclus in the sublime nudity of his death. In vain did the Trojan chiefs have the horn blown, to announce skilled hand-to-hand combat now stripped of its early simplicity; widowed of this companion who deserved to be an enemy, Achilles did not kill any more, so as not to give Patroclus otherworldly rivals. From time to time, screams were heard; helmeted shadows went by the tent's red wall: now that Achilles had locked himself up with this dead man, the living appeared to him only as ghosts. A treacherous dampness rose from the bare ground; the footsteps of armies on the move shook the tent; its stakes wobbled in the shaky ground. Reconciled, the two sides struggled with the river of death: Achilles, pale, entered this Apocalyptic night. To him, the living were not precarious survivors of a still threaten-ing wave of death; rather, it was the dead who seemed submerged in the vile deluge of the living. Against this moving, animated, formless water, Achilles defended the stones and the cement used to make tombs. When the fire coming from the forest of Mount Ida reached the port and licked the belly of ships, Achilles held against the trunks, the masts, the insolently fragile sails a flame that isn't afraid to kiss the dead on funeral pyres. Strange tribes from Asia emerged like rivers: caught up in Ajax's madness, Achilles

slaughtered this cattle without recognizing its human traits. He was sending Patroclus herds for hunting parties in the otherworld. The Amazons
appeared; a flood of breasts covered the slopes of the river; the army shook,
aroused by that smell of bared fleece. All his life, Achilles had taken women
to represent the instinctive part of misfortune, the one he did not choose
but had to endure and couldn't accept. He blamed his mother for having
made him a half-breed, halfway between a man and a god, therefore taking away from him half of the merit men earn in becoming gods. He bore
her a grudge for having dipped him as a child in the Styx to immunize him
against fear, as if heroism weren't precisely a question of being vulnerable.
He resented Lycomedes' daughters not recognizing in his travesty the opposite of disguise. He did not forgive Briseis the humiliation of having loved
her. His blade sank in this pink froth, cutting visceral Gordian knots: howling, giving birth to death through the gaps in their wounds, the women
were entangled in the disheveling of their entrails like horses in bullfight
arenas. Penthesilea broke loose from this heap of trampled women. She
had lowered her visor so that no one could be moved by looking at her
eyes; she alone dared give up the advantage of fighting nude. Carapaced,
helmeted, masked in gold, this mineral Fury kept only her hair and her
voice as human attributes, but her hair was golden and gold ran in this pure
voice. She was the only one among her companions who had consented to
have one of her breasts cut off, but the mutilation was hardly noticeable on
this godlike chest. The dead women were dragged out of the arena by their
hair; the soldiers formed a line transforming the battlefield into an arena,
pushing Achilles in the middle of a circle from which murder would be his
only way out. In this khaki, field-gray, horizon-blue setting, the Amazon's
armor changed forms with each ensuing century, changed tint depending
on the spotlights. With this Slavic woman making a dance step of each
feint, the hand-to-hand combat became a tournament, then a Russian bal-
let. Invaded by the love found at the heart of hatred, Achilles moved forward, then back, riveted to this metal housing a victim. As though to break
the spell, he threw his blade with all his might, pierced the thin breastplate
that had put god knew what pure soldier between him and this woman.
Yielding, Penthesilea fell, unable to resist the iron rape. Orderlies rushed
forward; the sputtering of flashbulbs going off sounded like machine-gun
fire; impatient hands were skinning the golden corpse. Lifted, the visor
revealed, instead of a face, a mask with blind eyes no longer responsive to

kisses. Achilles was sobbing, holding up the head of this victim worthy of being a friend. She was the only creature in the world who looked like Patroclus.

Not to be loved anymore is to become invisible; now you don't notice that I have a body.

Between us and death there is sometimes only the width of one single person. Remove this person and there would be only death.

How dull it would have been to be happy!

I owe each of my tastes to the influence of chance friendships, as though I could only accept the world from human hands. From Hyacinth I have this liking of flowers, from Philip of travel, from Celeste of medicine, from Alexis of laces. From you, why not a predilection for death?

Sappho; or, Suicide

I have just seen, reflected in the mirrors of a theater box, a woman called Sappho. She is pale as snow, as death, or as the clear face of a woman who has leprosy. And since she wears rouge to hide this whiteness, she looks like the corpse of a murdered woman with a little of her own blood on her cheeks. To shun daylight, her eyes recede from the arid lids, which no longer shade them. Her long curls come out in tufts like forest leaves falling under precocious storms; each day she tears out new gray hairs, and soon there will be enough of these white silken threads to weave her shroud. She weeps for her youth as if for a woman who betrayed her, for her childhood as if for a little girl she has lost. She is skinny; when she steps into her bath, she turns away from the mirror, from the sight of her sad breasts. She wanders from city to city with three big trunks full of false pearls and bird wreckage. She is an acrobat, just as in ancient times she was a poetess, because the particular shape of her lungs forces her to choose a trade that is practiced in midair. In the circus at night, under the devouring eyes of a mindless public, and in a space encumbered with pulleys and masts, she fulfills her contract; she is a star. Outside, upstaged by the luminous letters of posters stuck to the wall, her body is part of that ghostly circle currently in vogue that soars above the gray cities. She's a magnetic creature, too winged for the ground, too corporal for the sky, whose wax-rubbed feet have broken the pact that binds us to the earth: Death waves her dizzy scarves but does not fluster her. Naked, spangled with stars, from afar she looks like an athlete who won't admit being an angel lest his perilous leaps be underrated; from close up, draped in long robes that give her back her wings, she looks like a female impersonator. She alone knows that her chest holds a heart too heavy and too big to be lodged elsewhere than in a broad bosom: this weight, hidden at the bottom of a bone cage, gives each of her springs into the void the mortal taste of danger. Half eaten by this implacable tiger, she secretly tries to be the tamer of her heart. She was born on an island and that is already a beginning of solitude; then her profession intervened, forcing on her a sort of lofty isolation every night; fated to be a star, she lies on her stage board, half undressed, exposed to the winds of the abyss, and suffers from the lack of tenderness as from the lack of pillows. Men in her life have only been steps of a ladder she had to climb, often dirtying her feet. The director, the trombone player, the publicity agent, all made her sick of waxed mustaches, cigars, liqueurs, striped ties, leather wallets—the exterior attributes of virility that make women dream. Only young women's bodies would still be soft enough, supple enough, fluid enough to let themselves be handled by this strong angel who would playfully pretend to drop them in midair. She can't hold them very long in this abstract space bordered on all sides by trapeze bars: quickly frightened by this geometry changing into wingbeats, all of them soon give up acting as her sky companion. She has to come down to earth, to their level, to share their ragged, patchy lives, so that affection ends up like a Saturday pass, a twenty-four-hour leave a sailor spends with easy women. Suffocating in these rooms no bigger than alcoves, she opens the door to the void with the hopeless gesture of a man forced, by love, to live among dolls. All women love one woman: they love themselves madly, consenting to find beauty only in the form of their own body. Sappho's eyes, farsighted in sorrow, looked further away. She expects of young women what self-adorning idolatrous coquettes expect of mirrors: a smile answering her trembling smile, until the breath from lips moving closer and closer obscures the reflection and clouds the crystal. Narcissus loves what he is. Sappho bitterly worships in her companions what she has not been. Poor, held in contempt, which is the other side of celebrity, and having only the perspectives of the abyss in stock, she caresses happiness on the bodies of her less threatened friends. The veils of communicants carrying their souls outside themselves make her dream of a brighter childhood than hers had been; when one has run out of illusions, one can still lend others a sinless childhood. The pallor of these girls awakens in her the almost unbelievable memory of virginity. In Gyrinno, she loved pride, and lowered herself to kiss the girl's feet. Anactoria's love brought her the taste of French fries eaten by handfuls in amusement parks, of rides on the wooden horses of carousels, and brought her the sweet feel of straw, tickling the neck of the beautiful girl lying down in haystacks. In Attys, she loved misfortune. She met Attys in the center of a big city, asphyxiated by the breath of its crowds and by the fog of its river; her mouth still smelled of the ginger candy she had been chewing. Soot stains stuck to her cheeks shiny with tears: she was running on a bridge, wearing a coat of fake otter; her shoes had holes; her face like that of a young goat had a haggard sweetness. To explain why her lips were pinched and pale like the scar of an old wound, why her eyes looked like sick turquoises, Attys had three different stories that were after all only three aspects of the same misfortune: her boyfriend, whom she saw every Sunday, had left her because one evening she wouldn't let him caress her in a taxi; a girlfriend who let her sleep on the couch of her student room had turned her out, accusing her wrongly of trying to steal her fiancé's heart; and finally, her father beat her. Attys was afraid of everything: of ghosts, of men, of the number 13, of the green eyes of cats. The hotel dining room dazzled her like a temple where she felt obliged to speak only in a whisper; the bathroom made her clap her hands in amazement. Sappho spends the money she has saved for years through suppleness and temerity for this whimsical girl. She makes circus directors hire this mediocre artist who can only juggle flower bouquets. With the regularity of change that is the essence of life for nomadic artists and sad profligates, together they tour the arenas and stages of all capitals. Each morning, in the furnished rooms rented so that Attys will avoid the promiscuity of hotels full of too rich clients, they mend their costumes and the runs in their tight silk stockings. Sappho has nursed this sick child so often, has so many times warded off men who would tempt her, that her gloomy love imperceptibly takes on a maternal cast, as though fifteen years of sterile voluptuousness had produced this child. The young men in tuxedos met in the halls of theater boxes, all recall to Attys the friend whose repulsed kisses she perhaps misses: Sappho has heard her talk so often of Philip's beautiful silk shirts, of his blue cuff links, of the shelves of pornographic albums decorating his room in Chelsea, that she now has as clear a picture of this fastidiously dressed businessman as of the few lovers she couldn't avoid slipping into her life. She stows him away absentmindedly among her worst memories. Little by little, Attys' eyelids take on a lavender hue; she gets letters at a post-office box and she tears them up after reading them; she seems strangely well informed about the business trips that might make the young man run into them, by chance, on their nomadic road. It is painful to Sappho not to be able to give Attys anything more than a back room in life, and to know that only fear keeps the little fragile head leaning on her strong shoulder. Sappho, embittered by all the tears she had the courage never to shed, realizes that all she can offer her friends is a tender form of despair; her only excuse is to tell herself that love, in all its forms, has nothing better to offer shy creatures, and were Attys to leave, she would not find more happiness somewhere else. One night Sappho, arms full of flowers picked for Attys, comes home later than usual. The concierge looks at her differently than she ordinarily does as she walks by; suddenly the spirals of the staircase look like serpent rings. Sappho notices that the milk carton is not in its usual place on the doormat; as soon as she is in the entrance hall, she smells the odor of cologne and blond tobacco. She notices in the kitchen the absence of an Attys busy frying tomatoes; in the bathroom the want of a young woman naked and playing with bathwater; in the bedroom the removal of an Attys ready to let herself be rocked. Facing the mirrors of the wide-open wardrobe, she weeps over the disappearance of the beloved girl's underwear. A blue cuff link lying on the floor reveals the cause of this departure, which Sappho stubbornly refuses to accept as final, afraid that it could kill her. Once again, she is trampling alone on city arenas, avidly scanning the theater boxes for a face her folly prefers to all bodies. After a few years, during one of her tours in the East, she learns that Philip is now director of a company that sells Oriental tobaccos; he has just been married to a rich and imposing woman who couldn't be Attys. Rumor has it that the girl has joined a dance company. Once again, Sappho makes the rounds of Middle East hotels; each doorman has his own way of being insolent, impudent, or servile; she checks out the pleasure spots where the smell of sweat poisons perfumes, the bars where an hour of stupor in alcohol and human heat leaves no more trace than a wet circle left by a glass on a black wooden table. She carries her search even as far as going to the Salvation Army, in the vain hope of finding Attys impoverished and ready to let herself be loved. In Istanbul, she happens to sit, every night, next to a casually dressed young man who passes himself off as an employee of a travel agency; his slightly dirty hand lazily holds up the weight of his forehead. They exchange those banal words that are often used between strangers as a bridge to love. He says his name is Phaon, claims he is the son of a Greek woman from Smyrna and of a sailor in the British fleet: once again, Sappho's heart quickens when she hears the delightful accent so often kissed on Attys' lips. Behind him stand memories of escape, of poverty, and of dangers unrelated to wars and more secretly connected to the laws of his own heart. He, too, seems to belong to a threatened race; one that is allowed to exist through a precarious and ever provisional permissiveness. Not having a residence visa, this young man has his own difficulties; he's a smuggler dealing in morphine, perhaps an agent of the secret police; he lives in a world of secret meetings and passwords, a world Sappho cannot penetrate. He doesn't need to tell her his story to establish a fraternity of misfortune between them. She tells him her sorrows; she goes on and on about Attys. He thinks he has met her; he vaguely remembers seeing a naked girl juggling flowers in a cabaret of Pera. He owns a little sailboat that he uses on Sundays for outings on the Bosphorus; together they go looking in all sad cafés along the shore, in restaurants of the island, in the modest boarding-houses on the Asian coast that poor foreigners live in. Seated at the stern, Sappho watches this handsome male face, which is now her only human sun, waver in the light of a lantern. She finds in his features certain traits once loved in the runaway girl: the same pouting mouth that a mysterious bee seems to have stung; the same little hard forehead under different hair that this time seemed to have been dipped in honey, the same eyes looking like greenish turquoises but framed by a tanned, rather than livid, face, so that the pale brown-haired girl seems to have been simply the wax lost in casting this bronze and golden god. Surprised, Sappho finds herself slowly preferring these shoulders rigid as trapeze bars, these hands hardened by the contact of oars, this entire body holding just enough feminine softness for her to love it. Lying down on the bottom of the boat, she yields to the new sensations of the floodwaters parted by this ferryman. Now she only mentions Attys to tell him that the lost girl looked like him but wasn't as handsome: Phaon accepts these compliments with a mocking but worried satisfaction. She tears up, in front of him, a letter in which Attys announces that she is coming back; she doesn't even bother to make out the return address. He watches her doing this with a faint smile on his trembling lips. For the first

time, she neglects the discipline of her demanding profession, she interrupts the exercises which put every muscle under the control of the spirit;
they dine together; and surprisingly, she eats a little too much. She only has
a few days left with him in this city; her commitments have her soaring in
other skies. Finally he consents to spend the last evening with her in the
little apartment she rents near the port. She watches him come and go in
the cluttered room, he is like a voice mingling clear and deep notes. Unsure
of his moves, as though afraid of breaking fragile illusions, Phaon leans
over the portraits of Attys for a better look. Sappho sits down on the
Viennese sofa covered with Turkish embroideries; she presses her face in
her hands like someone trying to erase memories. This woman who until
now took upon herself the choice, the offer, the seduction, the protection
of her more vulnerable girlfriends, relaxes and, falling, yields limply, at last,
to the weight of her own sex and of her own heart. She is happy that, from
now on, all she has to do with a lover is to make the gesture of acceptance.
She listens to the young man prowl in the next room; there, the whiteness
of a bed is sprawled like a hope remaining, in spite of everything, miraculously open; she hears him uncork flasks on the dresser, rummage in drawers with the ease of a housebreaker or a boyfriend who feels he is allowed
everything. He opens the folding doors of the wardrobe, where, among a
few ruffles left by Attys, Sappho's dresses hang like women who have killed
themselves. Suddenly the ghostly shudder of a silken sound draws near
like a dangerous caress. She rises, turns around; the beloved creature has
wrapped himself in a robe Attys left behind: the thin silk gauze worn on
naked flesh accentuates the quasi-feminine gracefulness of the dancer's long
legs; relieved of its confining men's clothing, this flexible body is almost a
woman's body. This Phaon, comfortable in his impersonation, is nothing
more than a stand-in for the beautiful absent nymph; once again, it's a girl
coming toward her with a crystal laugh. Distraught, Sappho runs to the
door to escape from this fleshly ghost who will only give her the same sad
kisses. Outside, she charges into the swell of bodies and runs down the
streets leading to the sea; they are littered with debris and garbage. She realizes that no encounter holds her salvation, since, no matter where she goes,
she runs into Attys again. This overwhelming face blocks all openings but
those leading to death. Night falls like a weariness confusing her memory; a
little blood endures next to the sunset. Suddenly she hears cymbals clashing
as though fever hit them in her heart; a long-standing habit has brought

her back, unwares, to the circus at the very hour when she struggles with the angel of dizziness each night. For the last time, she is intoxicated by this wild-beast odor that has been the odor of her life, by this music like that of love, loud and discordant. A wardrobe woman lets her into the dressing room, which she enters now as if condemned to death; she strips as if for God; she rubs white makeup all over herself to become a ghost; she snaps the choker of memory around her neck. An usher, dressed in black, arrives to tell her that her hour has come; she climbs the rope ladder of her celestial scaffold: she is fleeing skywards from the mockery of believing that there had been a young man. She removes herself from the yells of orange vendors, from the cutting laughter of pink children, from the skirts of dancers, from the mesh of human nets. With one pull, she brings herself to the last support her will to die will allow: the trapeze bar swinging in midair transforms this creature, tired of being only half woman, into a bird; she glides, sea gull of her own abyss, hanging by one foot, under the gaze of a public which does not believe in tragedy. Her skill goes against her; no matter how she tries, she can't lose her balance; shady equestrian, Death has her vault the next trapeze. She climbs at last higher than the spotlights: spectators can no longer applaud her, since now they can't see her. Hanging on to the ropes that pull the canopy painted with stars, she can only continue to surpass herself by bursting through her sky. Under her, the ropes, the pulleys, the winches of her fate now mastered, squeak in the wind of dizziness; space leans and pitches as on a stormy sea; the star-filled firmament rocks between mast yards. From here, music is only a smooth swell washing over all memory. Her eyes no longer distinguish between red and green lights; blue spotlights, sweeping over the dark crowd, bring out, here and there, naked feminine shoulders that look like tender rocks. Hanging on to her death as to an overhanging ledge, Sappho looks for a place to fall and chooses a spot beyond the netting where the mesh will not hold her. Her own acrobatic performance occupies only half of the immense vague arena; in the other half, where seals and clowns carry on, nothing has been set up to prevent her from dying. Sappho dives, arms spread as if to grasp half of infinity; she leaves behind her only the swinging of a rope as proof of having left the sky. But those failing at life run the risk of missing their suicide. Her oblique fall is broken by a lamp shining like a blue jellyfish. Stunned but safe, she is thrown by the impact toward the netting that pulls and repulses the foamy light; the meshes give but do not yield under the weight of this statue fished out from the bottom of the sky. And soon roustabouts will only have to haul onto the sand this marble pale body streaming with sweat like a drowning woman pulled from the sea.

I will not kill myself. The dead are so quickly forgotten.

One can only raise happiness on a foundation of despair. I think I will be able to start building.

Let no one be accused of my life.

It's a not a question of suicide. It's only a question of beating a record.

(translated by Dori Katz)

1962

Argentina

And it's possible that some essayists just make their information up.

Tlön, Uqbar, Orbis Tertius

I owe the discovery of Uqbar to the conjunction of a mirror and an encyclopedia. The unnerving mirror hung at the end of a corridor in a villa on
Calle Goana, in Ramos Mejía; the misleading encyclopedia goes by the
name of *The Anglo-American Cyclopaedia* (New York, 1917), and is a literal
if inadequate reprint of the 1902 *Encyclopaedia Britannica*. The whole affair
happened some five years ago. Bioy Casares had dined with me that night
and talked to us at length about a great scheme for writing a novel in the
first person, using a narrator who omitted or corrupted what happened and
who ran into various contradictions, so that only a handful of readers, a
very small handful, would be able to decipher the horrible or banal reality
behind the novel. From the far end of the corridor, the mirror was watching us; and we discovered with the inevitability of discoveries made late at
night, that mirrors have something grotesque about them. Then Bioy
Casares recalled that one of the heresiarchs of Uqbar had stated that
mirrors and copulation are abominable, since they both multiply the
numbers of man. I asked him the source of that memorable sentence,
and he replied that it was recorded in the *Anglo-American Cyclopaedia,* in
its article on Uqbar. It so happened that the villa (which we had rented
furnished) possessed a copy of that work. In the final pages of Volume
XLVI, we ran across an article on Upsala; in the beginning of Volume
XLVII, we found one on Ural-Altaic languages; but not one word on
Uqbar. A little put out, Bioy consulted the index volumes. In vain he tried
every possible spelling—Ukbar, Ucbar, Ooqbar, Ookbar, Oukbahr. . . .
Before leaving, he informed me it was a region in either Iraq or Asia
Minor. I must say that I acknowledged this a little uneasily. I supposed
that this undocumented country and its anonymous heresiarch had been
deliberately invented by Bioy out of modesty, to substantiate a phrase. A

futile examination of one of the atlases of Justus Perthes strengthened my doubt.

On the following day, Bioy telephoned me from Buenos Aires. He told me that he had in front of him the article on Uqbar, in Volume XLVI of the encyclopedia. It did not specify the name of the heresiarch, but it did note his doctrine, in words almost identical to the ones he had repeated to me, though, I would say, inferior from a literary point of view. He had remembered: "Copulation and mirrors are abominable." The text of the encyclopedia read: "For one of those gnostics, the visible universe was an illusion or, more precisely, a sophism. Mirrors and fatherhood are abominable because they multiply it and extend it." I said, in all sincerity, that I would like to see that article. A few days later, he brought it. This surprised me, because the scrupulous cartographic index of Ritter's *Erdkunde* completely failed to mention the name of Uqbar.

The volume which Bioy brought was indeed Volume XLVI of *The Anglo-American Cyclopaedia*. On the title page and spine, the alphabetical key was the same as in our copy, but instead of 917 pages, it had 921. These four additional pages consisted of the article on Uqbar—not accounted for by the alphabetical cipher, as the reader will have noticed. We ascertained afterwards that there was no other difference between the two volumes. Both, as I think I pointed out, are reprints of the tenth *Encyclopaedia Britannica*. Bioy had acquired his copy in one of a number of book sales.

We read the article with some care. The passage remembered by Bioy was perhaps the only startling one. The rest seemed probable enough, very much in keeping with the general tone of the work and, naturally, a little dull. Reading it over, we discovered, beneath the superficial authority of the prose, a fundamental vagueness. Of the fourteen names mentioned in the geographical section, we recognized only three—Khurasan, Armenia, and Erzurum—and they were dragged into the text in a strangely ambiguous way. Among the historical names, we recognized only one, that of the imposter, Smerdis the Magian, and it was invoked in a rather metaphorical sense. The notes appeared to fix precisely the frontiers of Uqbar, but the points of reference were all, vaguely enough, rivers and craters and mountain chains in that same region. We read, for instance, that the southern frontier is defined by the lowlands of Tsai Haldun and the Axa delta, and that wild horses flourish in the islands of that delta. This, at the top of page 918. In the historical section (page 920), we gathered that, just after the religious persecutions of the thirteenth century, the orthodox sought refuge in the islands, where their obelisks have survived, and where it is a common enough occurrence to dig up one of their stone mirrors. The language and literature section was brief. There was one notable characteristic: it remarked that the literature of Uqbar was fantastic in character, and that its epics and legends never referred to reality, but to the two imaginary regions of Mlejnas and Tlön. . . . The bibliography listed four volumes, which we have not yet come across, even although the third—Silas Haslam: *History of the Land Called Uqbar,* 1874—appears in the library catalogues of Bernard Quaritch. The first, *Lesbare und lesenswerthe Bemerkungen über das Land Ukkbar in Klein-Asien,* is dated 1641, and is a work of Johann Valentin Andreä. The fact is significant; a couple of years later I ran across that name accidentally in the thirteenth volume of De Quincey's *Writings,* and I knew that it was the name of a German theologian who, at the beginning of the seventeenth century, described the imaginary community of Rosae Crucis—the community which was later founded by others in imitation of the one he had preconceived.

That night, we visited the National Library. Fruitlessly we exhausted atlases, catalogues, yearbooks of geographical societies, memoirs of travelers and historians—nobody had ever been in Uqbar. Neither did the general index of Bioy's encyclopedia show the name. The following day, Carlos Mastronardi, to whom I had referred the whole business, caught sight, in a Corrientes and Talcahuano bookshop, of the black and gold bindings of *The Anglo-American Cyclopaedia.* . . . . He went in and looked up Volume XLVI. Naturally, there was not the slightest mention of Uqbar.

II

Some small fading memory of one Herbert Ashe, an engineer for the southern railroads, hangs on in the hotel in Androgué, between the luscious honeysuckle and the illusory depths of the mirrors. In life, he suffered from a sense of unreality, as do so many Englishmen; dead, he is not even the ghostly creature he was then. He was tall and languid; his limp squared beard had once been red. He was, I understand, a widower, and childless. Every so many years, he went to England to visit—judging by the photographs he showed us—a sundial and some oak trees. My father and he had cemented (the verb is excessive) one of those English friendships which begin by avoiding intimacies and eventually eliminate speech altogether. They used to exchange books and periodicals; they would beat one another at chess, without saying a word. . . . I remember him in the corridor of the hotel, a mathematics textbook in his hand, gazing now and again at the passing colors of the sky. One afternoon, we discussed the duodecimal numerical system (in which twelve is written 10). Ashe said that as a matter of fact, he was transcribing some duodecimal tables, I forget which, into sexagesimals (in which sixty is written 10), adding that this work had been commissioned by a Norwegian in Rio Grande do Sul. We had known him for eight years and he had never mentioned having stayed in that part of the country. . . . We spoke of rural life, of *capangas*, of the Brazilian etymology of the word *gaucho* (which some old people in the east still pronounce *gaúcho*), and nothing more was said—God forgive me—of duodecimal functions. In September, 1937 (we ourselves were not at the hotel at the time), Herbert Ashe died of an aneurysmal rupture. Some days before, he had received from Brazil a stamped, registered package. It was a book, an octavo volume. Ashe left it in the bar where, months later, I found it. I began to leaf through it and felt a sudden curious lightheadedness, which I will not go into, since this is the story, not of my particular emotions, but of Uqbar and Tlön and Orbis Tertius. In the Islamic world, there is one night, called the Night of Nights, on which the secret gates of the sky open wide and the water in the water jugs tastes sweeter; if those gates were to open, I would not feel what I felt that afternoon. The book was written in English, and had 1001 pages. On the yellow leather spine, and again on the title page, I read these words: *A First Encyclopaedia of Tlon.* Volume XI Hlaer to Jangr. There was nothing to indicate either date or place of origin. On the first page and on a sheet of silk paper covering one of the colored engravings there was a blue oval stamp with the inscription: ORBIS TERTIUS. It was two years since I had discovered, in a volume of a pirated encyclopedia, a brief description of a false country; now, chance was showing me something much more valuable, something to be reckoned with. Now, I had in my hands a substantial fragment of the complete history of an unknown planet, with its architecture and its playing cards, its mythological terrors and the sound of its dialects, its emperors and its oceans, its minerals, its birds, and its fishes, its algebra and its fire, its theological and metaphysical arguments, all clearly stated, coherent, without any apparent dogmatic intention or parodic undertone.

The eleventh volume of which I speak refers to both subsequent and preceding volumes. Néstor Ibarra, in an article (in the *N.R.F.*), now a classic, has denied the existence of those corollary volumes; Ezequiel Martínez Estrada and Drieu La Rochelle have, I think, succeeded in refuting this doubt. The fact is that, up until now, the most patient investigations have proved fruitless. We have turned the libraries of Europe, North and South America upside down—in vain. Alfonso Reyes, bored with the tedium of this minor detective work, proposes that we all take on the task of reconstructing the missing volumes, many and vast as they were: *ex ungue leonem.* He calculates, half seriously, that one generation of Tlönists would be enough. This bold estimate brings us back to the basic problem: who were the people who had invented Tlön? The plural is unavoidable, because we have unanimously rejected the idea of a single creator, some transcendental Leibniz working in modest obscurity. We conjecture that this "brave new world" was the work of a secret society of astronomers, biologists, engineers, metaphysicians, poets, chemists, mathematicians, moralists, painters, and geometricians, all under the supervision of an unknown genius. There are plenty of individuals who have mastered these various disciplines without having any facility for invention, far less for submitting that inventiveness to a strict, systematic plan. This plan is so vast that each individual contribution to it is infinitesimal. To begin with, Tlön was thought to be nothing more than a chaos, a free and irresponsible work of the imagination; now it was clear that it is a complete cosmos, and that the strict laws which govern it have been carefully formulated, albeit provisionally. It is enough to note that the apparent contradictions in the eleventh volume are the basis for proving the existence of the others, so lucid and clear is the scheme maintained in it. The popular magazines have publicized, with pardonable zeal, the zoology and topography of Tlön. I think, however, that its transparent tigers and its towers of blood scarcely deserve the unwavering attention of *all* men. I should like to take some little time to deal with its conception of the universe.

Hume remarked once and for all that the arguments of Berkeley were not only thoroughly unanswerable but thoroughly unconvincing. This dictum is emphatically true as it applies to our world; but it falls down completely in Tlön. The nations of that planet are congenitally idealist. Their language, with its derivatives—religion, literature, and metaphysics—presupposes idealism. For them, the world is not a concurrence of objects in space, but a heterogeneous series of independent acts. It is serial and temporal, but not spatial. There are no nouns in the hypothetical *Ursprache* of Tlön, which is the source of the living language and the dialects; there are impersonal verbs qualified by monosyllabic suffixes or prefixes which have the force of adverbs. For example, there is no word corresponding to the noun *moon*, but there is a verb *to moon* or *to moondle*. *The moon rose over the sea* would be written *hlör u fang axaxaxas mlö*, or, to put it in order: *upward beyond the constant flow there was moondling*. (Xul Solar translates it succinctly: *Upward, behind the onstreaming it mooned*.)

The previous passage refers to the languages of the southern hemisphere. In those of the northern hemisphere (the eleventh volume has little information on its *Ursprache*) the basic unit is not the verb, but the monosyllabic adjective. Nouns are formed by an accumulation of adjectives. One does not say moon; one says *airy-clear over dark-round* or *orange-faint-of-sky* or some other accumulation. In the chosen example, the mass of adjectives corresponds to a real object. The happening is completely fortuitous. In the literature of this hemisphere (as in the lesser world of Meinong), ideal objects abound, invoked and dissolved momentarily, according to poetic necessity. Sometimes, the faintest simultaneousness brings them about. There are objects made up of two sense elements, one visual, the other auditory—the color of a sunrise and the distant call of a bird. Other objects are made up of many elements—the sun, the water against the swimmer's chest, the vague quivering pink which one sees when the eyes are closed, the feeling of being swept away by a river or by sleep. These second degree objects can be combined with others; using certain abbreviations, the process is practically an infinite one. There are famous poems made up of one enormous word, a word which in truth forms a poetic *object,* the creation of the writer. The fact that no one believes that nouns refer to an actual reality means, paradoxically enough, that there is no limit to the numbers of them. The languages of the northern hemisphere of Tlön include all the names in Indo-European languages—plus a great many others.

It is no exaggeration to state that in the classical culture of Tlön, there is only one discipline, that of psychology. All others are subordinated to it. I have remarked that the men of that planet conceive of the universe as a series of mental processes, whose unfolding is to be understood only as a time sequence. Spinoza attributes to the inexhaustibly divine in man the qualities of extension and of thinking. In Tlön, nobody would understand the juxtaposition of the first, which is only characteristic of certain states of being, with the second, which is a perfect synonym for the cosmos. To put it another way—they do not conceive of the spatial as everlasting in time. The perception of a cloud of smoke on the horizon and, later, of the countryside on fire and, later, of a half-extinguished cigar which caused the conflagration would be considered an example of the association of ideas.

This monism, or extreme idealism, completely invalidates science. To explain or to judge an event is to identify or unite it with another one. In Tlön, such connection is a later stage in the mind of the observer, which can in no way affect or illuminate the earlier stage. Each state of mind is ir- reducible. The mere act of giving it a name, that is of classifying it, implies a falsification of it. From all this, it would be possible to deduce that there is no science in Tlön, let alone rational thought. The paradox, however, is that sciences exist, in countless number. In philosophy, the same thing happens as happens with the nouns in the northern hemisphere. The fact that any philosophical system is bound in advance to be a dialectical game, a *Philosophie des Als Ob*, means that systems abound, unbelievable systems, beautifully constructed or else sensational in effect. The metaphysicians of Tlön are not looking for truth, nor even for an approximation of it; they are after a kind of amazement They consider metaphysics a branch of fantastic literature. They know that a system is nothing more than the subordination of all the aspects of the universe to some one of them. Even the phrase "all the aspects" can be rejected, since it presupposes the impos- sible inclusion of the present moment, and of past moments. Even so, the plural "past moments" is inadmissible, since it supposes another impossible operation. . . . One of the schools in Tlön has reached the point of denying time. It reasons that the present is undefined, that the future has no other reality than as present hope, that the past is no more than present memory. Another school declares that the *whole of time* has already happened and that our life is a vague memory or dim reflection, doubtless false and frag- mented, of an irrevocable process. Another school has it that the history of the universe, which contains the history of our lives and the most tenuous details of them, is the handwriting produced by a minor god in order to communicate with a demon. Another maintains that the universe is com- parable to those code systems in which not all the symbols have meaning, and in which only that which happens every three hundredth night is true. Another believes that, while we are asleep here, we are awake somewhere else, and that thus every man is two men.

Among the doctrines of Tlön, none has occasioned greater scandal than the doctrine of materialism. Some thinkers have formulated it with less clarity than zeal, as one might put forward a paradox. To clarify the general understanding of this unlikely thesis, one eleventh century heresiarch offered the parable of nine copper coins, which enjoyed in Tlön the same noisy reputation as did the Eleatic paradoxes of Zeno in their day. There are many versions of this "feat of specious reasoning" which vary the number of coins and the number of discoveries. Here is the commonest:

> On Tuesday, X ventures along a deserted road and loses nine copper coins. On Thursday, Y finds on the road four coins, somewhat rusted by Wednesday's rain. On Friday, Z comes across three coins on the road. On Friday morning, X finds two coins in the corridor of his house. [The heresiarch is trying to deduce from this story the reality, that is, the continuity, of the nine recovered coins.] It is absurd, he states, to suppose that four of the coins have not existed between Tuesday and Thursday, three between Tuesday and Friday afternoon, and two between Tuesday and Friday morning. It is logical to assume that they *have* existed, albeit in some secret way, in a manner whose understanding is concealed from men, in every moment, in all three places.

The language of Tlön is by its nature resistant to the formulation of this paradox; most people do not understand it. At first, the defenders of common sense confined themselves to denying the truth of the anecdote. They declared that it was a verbal fallacy, based on the reckless use of two neological expressions, not substantiated by common usage, and contrary to the laws of strict thought—the verbs *to find* and *to lose* entail a *petitio principii*, since they presuppose that the first nine coins and the second are identical. They recalled that any noun—*man, money, Thursday, Wednesday, rain*—has only metaphorical value. They denied the misleading detail "somewhat rusted by Wednesday's rain," since it assumes what must be demonstrated—the continuing existence of the four coins between Thursday and Tuesday. They explained that equality is one thing and identity another, and formulated a kind of *reductio ad absurdum,* the hypothetical case of nine men who, on nine successive nights, suffer a violent pain. Would it not be ridiculous, they asked, to claim that this pain is the same one each time? They said that the heresiarch was motivated mainly by the blasphemous intention of attributing the divine category of *being* to some ordinary coins; and that sometimes he was denying plurality, at other times not. They argued thus: that if equality entails identity, it would have to be admitted at the same time that the nine coins are only one coin.

Amazingly enough, these refutations were not conclusive. After the problem had been stated and restated for a hundred years, one thinker no less brilliant than the heresiarch himself, but in the orthodox tradition, advanced a most daring hypothesis. This felicitous supposition declared that there is only one Individual, and that this indivisible Individual is every one of the separate beings in the universe, and that those beings are the instruments and masks of divinity itself. X is Y and is Z. Z finds three coins because he remembers that X lost them. X finds only two in the corridor because he remembers that the others have been recovered. . . . The eleventh volume gives us to understand that there were three principal reasons which led to the complete victory of this pantheistic idealism. First, it repudiated solipsism. Second, it made possible the retention of a psychological basis for the sciences. Third, it permitted the cult of the gods to be retained. Schopenhauer, the passionate and clear-headed Schopenhauer, advanced a very similar theory in the first volume of his *Parerga und Paralipomena*.

The geometry of Tlön has two somewhat distinct systems, a visual one and a tactile one. The latter system corresponds to our geometry; they consider it inferior to the former. The foundation of visual geometry is the surface, not the point. This system rejects the principle of parallelism, and states that, as man moves about, he alters the forms which surround him. The arithmetical system is based on the idea of indefinite numbers. It emphasizes the importance of the concepts *greater* and *lesser,* which our mathematicians symbolize as > and <. It states that the operation of counting modifies quantities and changes them from indefinites into definites. The fact that several individuals counting the same quantity arrive at the same result is, say their psychologists, an example of the association of ideas or the good use of memory. We already know that in Tlön the source of all-knowing is single and eternal.

In literary matters too, the dominant notion is that everything is the work of one single author. Books are rarely signed. The concept of plagiarism does not exist; it has been established that all books are the work of one single writer, who is timeless and anonymous. Criticism is prone to invent authors. A critic will choose two dissimilar works— the *Tao Tê Ching* and *The Thousand and One Nights*, let us say—and attribute them to the same writer, and then with all probity explore the psychology of this interesting *homme de lettres*. . . .

The books themselves are also odd. Works of fiction are based on a single plot, which runs through every imaginable permutation. Works of natural philosophy invariably include thesis and antithesis, the strict pro and con of a theory. A book which does not include its opposite, or "counter-book," is considered incomplete.

Centuries and centuries of idealism have not failed to influence reality. In the very oldest regions of Tlön, it is not an uncommon occurrence for lost objects to be duplicated. Two people are looking for a pencil; the first one finds it and says nothing; the second finds a second pencil, no less real, but more in keeping with his expectation. These secondary objects are called *hrönir* and, even though awkward in form, are a little larger than the originals. Until recently, the *hrönir* were the accidental children of absent-mindedness and forgetfulness. It seems improbable that the methodical production of them has been going on for almost a hundred years, but so it is stated in the eleventh volume. The first attempts were fruitless. Nevertheless, the *modus operandi* is worthy of note. The director of one of the state prisons announced to the convicts that in an ancient river bed certain tombs were to be found, and promised freedom to any prisoner who made an important discovery. In the months preceding the excavation, printed photographs of what was to be found were shown the prisoners. The first attempt proved that hope and zeal could be inhibiting; a week of work with shovel and pick succeeded in unearthing no *hrön* other than a rusty wheel, postdating the experiment. This was kept a secret, and the experiment was later repeated in four colleges. In three of them the failure was almost complete; in the fourth (the director of which died by chance during the initial excavation), the students dug up—or produced— a gold mask, an archaic sword, two or three earthenware urns, and the mold-ered mutilated torso of a king with an inscription on his breast which has so far not been deciphered. Thus was discovered the unfitness of witnesses who were aware of the experimental nature of the search. . . . Mass investigations produced objects which contradicted one another; now, individual projects, as far as possible spontaneous, are preferred. The methodical development of *hrönir*, states the eleventh volume, has been of enormous service to archaeologists. It has allowed them to question and even to modify the past, which nowadays is no less malleable or obedient than the future. One curious fact: the *hrönir* of the second and third degree—that is, the *hrönir* derived from another *hrön*, and the *hrönir* derived from the *hrön* of a *hrön*—exaggerate the flaws of the original; those of the fifth degree are almost uniform; those of the ninth can be confused with those of the second; and those of the eleventh degree have a purity of form which the originals do not possess. The process is a recurrent one; a *hrön* of the twelfth degree begins to deteriorate in quality. Stranger and more perfect than any *hrön* is sometimes the *ur*, which is a thing produced by suggestion, an object brought into being by hope. The great gold mask I mentioned previously is a distinguished example.

Things duplicate themselves in Tlön. They tend at the same time to efface themselves, to lose their detail when people forget them. The classic example is that of a stone threshold which lasted as long as it was visited by a beggar, and which faded from sight on his death. Occasionally, a few birds, a horse perhaps, have saved the ruins of an amphitheater. (1940. *Salto Oriental.*)

Postscript. 1947. I reprint the foregoing article just as it appeared in the *Anthology of Fantastic Literature*, 1940, omitting no more than some figures of speech, and a kind of burlesque summing up, which now strikes me as frivolous. So many things have happened since that date. . . . I will confine myself to putting them down.

In March, 1941, a manuscript letter by Gunnar Erfjord came to light in a volume of Hinton, which had belonged to Herbert Ashe. The envelope bore the postmark of Ouro Preto. The letter cleared up entirely the mystery of Tlön. The text of it confirmed Martínez Estrada's thesis. The elaborate story began one night in Lucerne or London, in the early seventeenth century. A benevolent secret society (which counted Dalgarno and, later, George Berkeley among its members) came together to invent a country. The first tentative plan gave prominence to "hermetic studies," philanthropy, and the cabala. Andreä's curious book dates from that first period. At the end of some years of conventicles and premature syntheses, they realized that a single generation was not long enough in which to define a country. They made a resolution that each one of the master-scholars involved should elect a disciple to carry on the work. That hereditary arrangement prevailed; and after a hiatus of two centuries, the persecuted brotherhood reappeared in America. About 1824, in Memphis, Tennessee, one of the members had a conversation with the millionaire ascetic, Ezra Buckley. Buckley listened with some disdain as the other men talked, and then burst out laughing at the modesty of the project. He declared that in America it was absurd to invent a country, and proposed the invention of a whole planet. To this gigantic idea, he added another, born of his own nihilism—that of keeping the enormous project a secret. The twenty volumes of the *Encyclopedia Britannica* were then in circulation; Buckley suggested a systematic encyclopedia of the imaginary planet. He would leave the society his mountain ranges with their gold fields, his navigable rivers, his prairies where bull and bison roamed, his Negroes, his brothels, and his dollars, on one condition: "The work will have no truck with the imposter Jesus Christ." Buckley did not believe in God, but nevertheless wished to demonstrate to the nonexistent God that mortal men were capable of conceiving a world. Buckley was poisoned in Baton Rouge in 1828; in 1914, the society forwarded to its collaborators, three hundred in number, the final volume of the *First Encyclopedia of Tlön*. The edition was secret; the forty volumes which comprised it (the work was vaster than any previously undertaken by men) were to be the basis for another work, more detailed, and this time written, not in English, but in some one of the languages of Tlön. This review of an illusory world was called, provisionally, *Orbis Tertius,* and one of its minor demiurges was Herbert Ashe, whether as an agent of Gunnar Erfjord, or as a full, associate, I do not know. The fact that he received a copy of the eleventh volume would favor the second view. But what about the others? About 1942, events began to speed up. I recall with distinct clarity one of the first, and I seem to have felt something of its premonitory character. It occurred in an apartment on the Calle Laprida, facing a high open balcony which looked to the west. From Poitiers, the Princess of Faucigny Lucinge had received her silver table service. Out of the recesses of a crate, stamped all over with international markings, fine immobile pieces were emerging—silver plate from Utrecht and Paris, with hard heraldic fauna, a samovar. Amongst them, trembling faintly, just perceptibly, like a sleeping bird, was a magnetic compass. It shivered mysteriously. The princess did not recognize it. The blue needle longed for magnetic north. The metal case was concave. The letters on the dial corresponded to those of one of the alphabets of Tlön. Such was the first intrusion of the fantastic world into the real one. A disturbing accident brought it about that I was also witness to the second. It happened some months afterwards in a grocery store belonging to a Brazilian, in Cuchilla Negra. Amorim and I were on our way back from Sant'Anna. A sudden rising of the Tacuarembó river compelled us to test (and to suffer patiently) the rudimentary hospitality of the general store. The grocer set up some creaking cots for us in a large room, cluttered with barrels and wineskins. We went to bed, but were kept from sleeping until dawn by the drunkenness of an invisible neighbor, who alternated between shouting indecipherable abuse and singing snatches of *milongas,* or rather, snatches of the same *milonga.* As might be supposed, we attributed this insistent uproar to the fiery rum of the proprietor. . . . At dawn, the man lay dead in the corridor. The coarseness of his voice had deceived us; he was a young boy. In his delirium, he had spilled a few coins and a shining metal cone, of the diameter of a die, from his heavy gaucho belt. A serving lad tried to pick up this cone—in vain. It was scarcely possible for a man to lift it. I held it in my hand for some minutes. I remember that it was intolerably heavy, and that after putting it down, its oppression remained. I also remember the precise circle it marked in my flesh. This manifestation of an object which was so tiny and at the same time so heavy left me with an unpleasant sense of abhorrence and fear. A countryman proposed that it be thrown into the rushing river. Amorim acquired it for a few pesos. No one knew anything of the dead man, only that "he came from the frontier." Those small and extremely heavy cones, made of a metal which does not exist in this world, are images of divinity in certain religions in Tlön.

Here I conclude the personal part of my narrative. The rest, when it is not in their hopes or their fears, is at least in the memories of all my readers. It is enough to recall or to mention subsequent events, in as few words as possible; that concave basin which is the collective memory will furnish the wherewithal to enrich or amplify them. About 1944, a reporter from the Nashville, Tennessee, *American* uncovered, in a Memphis library, the forty volumes of the *First Encyclopaedia of Tlön.* Even now it is uncertain whether this discovery was accidental, or whether the directors of the still nebulous *Orbis Tertius* condoned it. The second alternative is more likely. Some of the more improbable features of the eleventh volume (for example, the multiplying of the *hrönir*) had been either removed or modified in the Memphis copy. It is reasonable to suppose that these erasures were in keeping with the plan of projecting a world which would not be too incompatible with the real world. The dissemination of objects from Tlön throughout various countries would complement that plan. . . . The fact is that the international press overwhelmingly hailed the "find." Manuals, anthologies, summaries, literal versions, authorized reprints, and pirated editions of the Master Work of Man poured and continue to pour out into the world. Almost immediately, reality gave ground on more than one point. The truth is that it hankered to give ground. Ten years ago, any symmetrical system whatsoever which gave the appearance of order—dialectical materialism, anti-Semitism, Nazism—was enough to fascinate men. Why not fall under the spell of Tlön and submit to the minute and vast evidence of an ordered planet? Useless to reply that reality, too, is ordered. It may be so, but in accordance with divine laws—I translate: inhuman laws—which we will never completely perceive. Tlön may be a labyrinth, but it is a labyrinth plotted by men, a labyrinth destined to be deciphered by men.

Contact with Tlön and the ways of Tlön have disintegrated this world. Captivated by its discipline, humanity forgets and goes on forgetting that it is the discipline of chess players, not of angels. Now the conjectural "primitive language" of Tlön has found its way into the schools. Now, the teaching of its harmonious history, full of stirring episodes, has obliterated the history which dominated my childhood. Now, in all memories, a fictitious past occupies the place of any other. We know nothing about it with any certainty, not even that it is false. Numismatics, pharmacology, and archaeology have been revised. I gather that biology and mathematics are awaiting their avatar. . . . A scattered dynasty of solitaries has changed the face of the world. Its task continues. If our foresight is not mistaken, a hundred years from now someone will discover the hundred volumes of the *Second Encyclopaedia of Tlön*.

Then, English, French, and mere Spanish will disappear from this planet. The world will be Tlön. I take no notice. I go on revising, in the quiet of the days in the hotel at Androgué, a tentative translation into Spanish, in the style of Quevedo, which I do not intend to see published, of Sir Thomas Browne's *Urn Burial*.

(translated by Alastair Reid)

1965

Argentina

After all, if information alone were what we considered "art," wouldn't the encyclopedia be the world's greatest book? Where do we draw the line then—in a genre that's still thought of as a source for only data—between texts that want merely to inform their readers, and those that attempt to transform us?

JULIO CORTÁZAR

The Instruction Manual

The job of having to soften up the brick every day, the job of cleaving a passage through the glutinous mass that declares itself to be the world, to collide every morning with the same narrow rectangular space with the disgusting name, filled with doggy satisfaction that everything is probably in its place, the same woman beside you, the same shoes, the same taste of the same toothpaste, the same sad houses across the street, the filthy slats on the shutters with the inscription THE HOTEL BELGIUM.

Drive the head like a reluctant bull through the transparent mass at the center of which we take a coffee with milk and open the newspaper to find out what has happened in whatever corner of that glass brick. Go ahead, deny up and down that the delicate act of turning the doorknob, that act which may transform everything, is done with the indifferent vigor of a daily reflex. See you later, sweetheart. Have a good day.

Tighten your fingers around a teaspoon, feel its metal pulse, its mistrustful warning. How it hurts to refuse a spoon, to say no to a door, to deny everything that habit has licked to a suitable smoothness. How much simpler to accept the easy request of the spoon, to use it, to stir the coffee.

And it's not that it's so bad that things meet us every day and are the same. That the same woman is there beside us, the same watch, that the novel lying open there on the table starts once more to take its bicycle ride through our glasses. What could be wrong with that? But like a sad bull, one has to lower the head, hustle out from the middle of the glass brick toward the one nearest us, who is as unattainable as the picador, however close the bull is to him. Punish the eyes looking at that which passes in the sky and cunningly accept that its name is cloud, its answer catalogued in the mind. Don't believe that the telephone is going to give you the numbers you try to call, why

521

should it? The only thing that will come is what you have already prepared and decided, the gloomy reflection of your expectations, that monkey, who scratches himself on the table and trembles with cold. Break that monkey's head, take a run from the middle of the room to the wall and break through it. Oh, how they sing upstairs! There's an apartment upstairs in this house with other people in it. A floor upstairs where people live who don't know there's a downstairs floor and that all of us live in the glass brick. And if suddenly a moth lands on the edge of a pencil and flutters there like an ash-colored flame, look at it, I am looking at it, I am touching its tiny heart and I hear it, that moth reverberates in the pie dough of frozen glass, all is not lost. When the door opens and I lean over the stairwell, I'll know that the street begins down there; not the already accepted matrix, not the familiar houses, not the hotel across the street: the street, that busy wilderness which can tumble upon me like a magnolia any minute, where the faces will come to life when I look at them, when I go just a little bit further, when I smash minutely against the pie dough of the glass brick and stake my life while I press forward step by step to go pick up the newspaper at the corner.

Instructions on How to Cry

Putting the reasons for crying aside for the moment, we might concentrate on the correct way to cry, which, be it understood, means a weeping that doesn't turn into a big commotion nor proves an affront to the smile with its parallel and dull similarity. The average, everyday weeping consists of a general contraction of the face and a spasmodic sound accompanied by tears and mucus, this last toward the end, since the cry ends at the point when one energetically blows one's nose.

In order to cry, steer the imagination toward yourself, and if this proves impossible owing to having contracted the habit of believing in the exterior world, think of a duck covered with ants or of those gulfs in the Straits of Magellan *into which no one sails ever.*

Coming to the weeping itself, cover the face decorously, using both hands, palms inward. Children are to cry with the sleeve of the dress or shirt pressed against the face, preferably in a corner of the room. Average duration of the cry, three minutes.

Instructions on How to Sing

Begin by breaking all the mirrors in the house, let your arms fall to your side, gaze vacantly at the wall, *forget yourself.* Sing one single note, listen to it from inside. If you hear (but this will happen much later) something like a landscape overwhelmed with dread, bonfires between the rocks with squatting half-naked silhouettes, I think you'll be well on your way, and the same if you hear a river, boats painted yellow and black are coming down it, if you hear the smell of fresh bread, the shadow of a horse.

Afterwards, buy a manual of voice instruction and a dress jacket, and please, don't sing through your nose and leave poor Schumann at peace.

Instructions or Rather Examples of How to Be Afraid

In a small town in Scotland they sell books with one blank page hidden someplace in the volume. If the reader opens to that page and it's three o'clock in the afternoon, he dies.

In the Piazza Quirinal in Rome, there is one spot, unknown even to the initiated after the nineteenth century, from which, under a full moon, the statues of the Dioscuri can be seen to move, fighting against their horses as they rear back.

At Amalfi, where the seacoast ends, there's a jetty which stretches out into the sea and night. Out beyond the last lighthouse, you can hear a dog bark.

A man is squeezing toothpaste onto his brush, all of a sudden he sees the tiny figure of a woman lying on her back, coral sort of, or a breadcrumb that's been painted.

Opening the door of the wardrobe to take out a shirt, an old almanac falls out which comes apart immediately, pages falling out and crumbling, and covers the white linen with millions of dirty paper butterflies.

There was a story about this traveling salesman whose left wrist began to hurt him, just under his wrist watch. When he removed the watch, blood spurted out. The wound showed the imprints of very tiny teeth.

The doctor finishes his examination and his conclusions are very reassuring to us. His cordial and somber voice precedes the medicines, prescriptions for which he is writing out at the moment, seated behind his desk. Every once in a while he raises his head and smiles, to cheer us up. We don't have a thing to worry about, we'll be better inside of a week. We sit at ease in our easy chair, happy, and look idly and distractedly about the room. In the shadowed area beneath the desk, suddenly we see the doctor's legs. The trousers are pulled up to just above the knees and he's wearing women's stockings.

Instructions on How to Understand Three Famous Paintings
Sacred Love and Profane Love by Titian

This hateful painting depicts a wake on the banks of the Jordan. In only a very few instances has the obtuseness of a painter been able to refer more contemptibly to mankind's hope for a Messiah *who is radiant by his absence*; missing from the canvas which is the world, he shines horribly in the obscene yawn of the marble tomb, while the angel commissioned to announce the resurrection of his dreadful executed flesh waits patiently for the signs to be fulfilled. It will be unnecessary to explain that the angel is the nude figure prostituting herself in her marvelous plumpness, and disguised as Mary Magdalen, mockery of mockeries, at the moment when the true Mary Magdalen is coming along the road (where, on the other hand, swells the venomous blasphemy of two rabbits).

The child putting his hand into the tomb is Luther, or maybe the Devil. Of the clothed figure it has been said that she represents Glory about to announce that all human ambition fits into a washbowl; but she's badly painted and reminds one of artificial flowers or a lightning flash like a soft sponge-rubber baseball bat.

Lady of the Unicorn by Raphael

Saint-Simon thought he saw in this portrait a confession of heresy. The unicorn, the narwhal, the obscene pearl in the locket that pretends to be a pear, and the gaze of Maddalena Strozzi fixed dreadfully upon a point where lascivious poses or a flagellation scene might be taking place: here Raphael Sanzio lied his most terrible truth.

The passionate green color in the face of the figure was frequently attributed to gangrene or to the *spring solstice*. The unicorn, a phallic animal, would have infected her: in her body rest all the sins of the world. Then they realized that they had only to remove the overlayers painted by three irritated enemies of Raphael: Carlos Hog, Vincent Grosjean (known as "The Marble"), and Rubens the Elder. The first overpainting was green, the second green, and the third white. It is not difficult to observe here the triple symbol of the deadly nightmoth; the wings conjoined to its dead body they confused with the rose leaves. How often Maddalena Strozzi cut a white rose and felt it squeak between her fingers, twisting and moaning weakly like a tiny mandrake or one of those lizards that sing like lyres when you show them a mirror. But it was already too late and the deadly nightmoth had pricked her. Raphael knew it and sensed she was dying. To paint her truly, then, he added the unicorn, symbol of chastity who will take water from a virgin's hand, sheep and narwhal at once. But he painted the deadly nightmoth in her image, and the unicorn kills his mistress, digs into her superb breast its horn working with lust; it reiterates the process of all principles. What this woman holds in her hands is the mysterious cup from which we have all drunk unknowingly, thirst that we have slaked with other mouths, that red and foamy wine from which come the stars, the worms, and railroad stations.

Portrait of Henry VIII of England by Holbein

In this canvas people have wanted to see an elephant hunt, a map of Russia, the constellation Lyra, a portrait of the Pope disguised as Henry VIII, a storm over the Sargasso Sea, or the golden polyp which thrives in the latitudes south of Java and which, under the influence of lemon, sneezes delicately and succumbs with a tiny whiff.

Each of these interpretations takes exact account of the general configurations of the painting, whether they are seen from the position in which it is hung or head downwards or held sideways. The differences can be narrowed to the details; the center remains which is GOLD, the number SEVEN, the OYSTER observable in the hat-and-string-tie sections, with the PEARL-head (center irradiating from the pearls on the jacket or central territory) and the general SHOUT absolutely green which bursts forth from the aggregate whole.

Experience simply going to Rome and laying your hand against the king's heart, and you understand the origin of the sea. Even less difficult is to approach it with a lit candle held at the level of the eyes; it will then be seen that *that is not a face* and that the moon, blinded by simultaneity, races across a background of Catherine wheels and tiny transparent ball bearings decapitated in the remembrances in hagiographies. He is not mistaken who sees in this stormy petrifaction a combat between leopards. But also there are reluctant ivory daggers, pages who languish from boredom in long galleries, and a tortuous dialogue between leprosy and the halberds. The man's kingdom is a page out of the great chronicle, but he does not know this and toys peevishly with gloves and fawns. This man looking at you comes back from hell; step away from the canvas and you will see him smile a bit at a time, because he is empty, he is a windbag, dry hands hold him up from behind; like a playing-card figure, when you begin to pick him up the castle and everything totters. And his maxim is this: "There is no third dimension, the earth is flat and man drags his belly on the earth. Hallelujah!" It might be the Devil who is saying these words, and maybe you believe them because they are spoken to you by a king.

Instructions on How to Comb the Hair

There's something like a bone wing from which extends a series of parallels, and the comb isn't the bone but the gaps which penetrate space. The tresses will enter and leave this comb of air with a firm melody, a set design. The lavish play of disarray goes on toward sleep, toward love, toward the wind in the streets, toward rain. Medusa's serpents grow above a superbly handsome face. Comb of swords, a terrifying harvest! But turtle-shell as well, when it's Faustina, bronze gone green for the daughters of Knossos, ivory for Sakuntala, baby-bone for Melisande. Plows furrowing the centuries whose crop will be a perfume, a lariat, a crown; like rolling triremes, those combs of the sea.

So. The man will comb his hair without a mirror, working his open hand through it. The woman will make her reflection into a tower or treetop, whatever peak, where the lines of storm and the blue mark of the broody kingfisher can be found. She'll know how to stem sweetly that flow from tenuous high tides, how to light the fire of remembrance without smoke. To comb the hair will be to take auguries for the rising day, give shape to the lover's secret thought, instruct from the blood the son not yet born.

When it comes to children, let the air comb them.

Instructions on How to Dissect a Ground Owl

Small ground owls range themselves on posts along the road
Little old lady ground owls, like wisdom, come out of the sea
Small young ground owls are like the weather! there it comes,
    there it comes
No one stuffs a small owl without a red lantern
Without a red robe in a black room
Without a wardrobe where scratchy wreaths screak mildly

In the Argentine countryside the little owls await the hour
Like the Creoles and the Indians they wait without hope
Ranged on posts along the road watching the cars pass
A Buick   a Ford   a Pontiac   a Plymouth   a Cadillac
In which the taxidermists ride with their wives and children
Without a red robe in a black room
Without a wardrobe where scratchy wreaths screak mildly
No one stuffs an owl without a red lantern
Without a red robe in a black room

To dissect lions
You need lightning
For little owls you need
Forget-
    fulness.

Instructions on How to Kill Ants in Rome

Ants, it is said, will eat Rome. They scurry between the flagstones: O she-wolf, what highway of precious stones slices your throat? On every side waters flow from the fountains, the living slate, the tremulous cameos that mumble history, dynasties, and commemorations in the dead of night. One would have to find the heart that makes the fountains leap in order to stave off the ants, and in this city of swollen blood bristling with cornucopias like a blind man's hands, organize a salvation ritual so that the future file down its teeth on the mountains, drag itself off gently and weakly, completely without ants.

First we shall prospect for the sites of the fountains, which is simple, because on the colored maps the fountains also have jets and cascades in sky blue, you only have to locate them precisely and put a circle around them with a blue pencil, not a red one, for a good map of Rome is red as Rome is red. The blue pencil on Rome's red will mark a violet circle around every fountain, and now we are sure we have all of them and that we know the foliage of the waters.

More difficult, more withdrawn and concealed, is the business of drilling through the dark stone under which the veins of mercury run, to take into account by dint of patience the code of all the fountains, and to keep a loving vigil near the imperial vessels on nights when the moon is bright, until after so much green murmuring, so much quavering like flowers, the directions begin to come clear, the confluences, *the other streets*, the living ones. And to track them down without sleeping, with hazel rods shaped in a fork, triangular, with two verges in each hand, one held only loosely between the fingers, but all this invisible to the carabinieri and the amicably suspicious population: go by way of the Quirinal, climb to the Campidoglio, run shouting through the Pincio, land with a motionless apparition like a ball of fire on the orderly walks of the Piazza della Essedra, this is how to extract from the ground's silent metals the catalogue of subterranean rivers. And ask help of no one. Ever.

Afterwards, you will see it gradually, how, in this flayed marble hand, the veins wander leisurely and sonorous, for the pleasure of the waters, for the artifice of the play, until coming closer little by little, they join in the confluence, interweave, swell into arteries, spill out their continuities into the central square where the drum of liquid glass throbs, the root of the pale crowns of trees, the abstruse horse. And then we shall know where it is, in which water table of calcified vaults, between the minuscule skeletons of lemurs, the heart of the water hammers out its time.

It takes some trouble to find out, but it will be found out. Then we'll kill the ants that lust after the fountains, we'll burn out the tunnels these monstrous miners have devised in order to draw close to the secret life of Rome. We shall kill the ants by arriving before them at the central fountain. And we'll leave by the night train fleeing the vengeful demons, vaguely happy, hobnobbing with soldiers and nuns.

Instructions on How to Climb a Staircase

No one will have failed to observe that frequently the floor bends in such a way that one part rises at a right angle to the plane formed by the floor and then the following section arranges itself parallel to the flatness, so as to provide a step to a new perpendicular, a process which is repeated in a spiral or in a broken line to highly variable elevations. Ducking down and placing the left hand on one of the vertical parts and the right hand upon the corresponding horizontal, one is in momentary possession of a step or stair. Each one of these steps, formed as we have seen by two elements, is situated somewhat higher and further than the one prior, a principle which gives the idea of a staircase, while whatever other combination, producing perhaps more beautiful or picturesque shapes, would be incapable of translating one from the ground floor to the first floor.

You tackle a stairway face on, for if you try it backwards or sideways, it ends up being particularly uncomfortable. The natural stance consists of holding oneself upright, arms hanging easily at the sides, head erect but not so much so that the eyes no longer see the steps immediately above, while one tramps up, breathing lightly and with regularity. To climb a staircase one begins by lifting that part of the body located below and to the right, usually encased in leather or deerskin, and which, with a few exceptions, fits exactly on the stair. Said part set down on the first step (to abbreviate we shall call it "the foot"), one draws up the equivalent part on the left side (also called "foot" but not to be confused with "the foot" cited above), and lifting this other part to the level of "the foot," makes it continue along until it is set in place on the second step, at which point the foot will rest, and "the foot" will rest on the first. (The first steps are always the most difficult, until you acquire the necessary coordination. The coincidence of names between the foot and "the foot" makes the explanation more difficult. Be especially careful not to raise, at the same time, the foot and "the foot.")

Having arrived by this method at the second step, it's easy enough to repeat the movements alternately, until one reaches the top of the staircase. One gets off it easily, with a light tap of the heel to fix it in place, to make sure it will not move until one is ready to come down.

Preamble to the Instructions on How to Wind a Watch

Think of this: When they present you with a watch they are gifting you with a tiny flowering hell, a wreath of roses, a dungeon of air. They aren't simply wishing the watch on you, and many more, and we hope it will last you, it's a good brand, Swiss, seventeen rubies; they aren't just giving you this minute stonecutter which will bind you by the wrist and walk along with you. They are giving you—they don't know it, it's terrible that they don't know it—they are gifting you with a new, fragile, and precarious piece of yourself, something that's yours but not a part of your body, that you have to strap to your body like your belt, like a tiny, furious bit of something hanging onto your wrist. They gift you with the job of having to wind it every day, an obligation to wind it, so that it goes on being a watch; they gift you with the obsession of looking into jewelry-shop windows to check the exact time, check the radio announcer, check the telephone service. They give you the gift of fear, someone will steal it from you, it'll fall on the street and get broken. They give you the gift of your trademark and the assurance that it's a trademark better than the others, they gift you with the impulse to compare your watch with other watches. They aren't giving you a watch, you are the gift, they're giving you yourself for the watch's birthday.

Instructions on How to Wind a Watch

Death stands there in the background, but don't be afraid. Hold the watch down with one hand, take the stem in two fingers, and rotate it smoothly. Now another installment of time opens, trees spread their leaves, boats run races, like a fan time continues filling with itself, and from that burgeon the air, the breezes of earth, the shadow of a woman, the sweet smell of bread.

What did you expect, what more do you want? Quickly strap it to your wrist, let it tick away in freedom. Imitate it greedily. Fear will rust all the rubies, everything that could happen to it and was forgotten is about to corrode the watch's veins, cankering the cold blood and its tiny rubies. And death is there in the background, we must run to arrive beforehand and understand it's already unimportant.

(translated by Paul Blackburn)

1967

Brazil

In Brazil, there is a genre that's called the *crônica,* a form usually found in the nation's daily papers. It takes the shape of travelogues, interviews, sketches, memoirs, anecdotes, jokes, etc. "I'm apprehensive," Clarice Lispector said, when the Brazilian *News* first approached her with their request for a *crônica.* She was one of the world's foremost experimental novelists at the time, and the form of the *crônica* did not interest her as art. Nevertheless, several months later, Lispector submitted to the Brazilian *News* a short essay on sleep. The next week, unexpectedly, she submitted one on children. Then there came "On Water," "On Illness," "On the Experience of Dying." Over the next six years, Lispector contributed a *crônica* every week to the Brazilian *News.* "If there exists such a thing as expression," she wrote, "let it emanate from what I am."

CLARICE LISPECTOR

The Egg and the Chicken

1

In the morning the egg is lying on the kitchen table.

I see the egg at a single glance. I immediately perceive that I cannot be simply seeing an egg. Seeing an egg is always in the present: No sooner do I see the egg than I have seen an egg, the same egg which has existed for three thousand years. The very instant an egg is seen, it becomes the memory of an egg. The only person to see an egg is someone who has seen it before. Like a man who, in order to understand the present, must have had a past. Upon seeing the egg, it is already too late: an egg seen is an egg lost. A vision that passes like a sudden flash of lightning. To see the egg is the promise of being able to see the egg again one day. A brief glance which cannot be divided. Does thought intervene? No, there is no thought: there is only the egg. Vision is the essential faculty and, once used, I shall cast it aside. I shall remain without the egg. The egg has no *itself*. Individually, it does not exist.

It is impossible actually to see the egg. The egg is supravisible just as there are supersonic sounds the ear can no longer hear. No one is capable of seeing the egg. Can the dog see the egg? Only machines can see the egg. The windlass sees the egg. In ancient times an egg settled on my shoulder. Nor can anyone feel love for the egg. My love for the egg is suprasensitive and I have no way of knowing that I feel this love. One is unaware of loving the egg. In ancient times I was the depository of the egg and I walked on tiptoe in order not to disturb the egg's silence. When I died, they carefully removed the egg inside me: it was still alive. Just as we ignore the world because it is obvious, so we fail to see the egg because it, too, is so obvious. Does the egg no longer exist? It exists at this moment. Egg, you are perfect.

You are white. To you I dedicate this beginning. To you I dedicate this first moment.

To the egg, I dedicate the Chinese nation.

The egg is something in suspense. It has never settled. When it comes to rest, it is not the egg that has come to rest. A surface has formed beneath the egg. I vaguely glance at the egg in the kitchen in order not to break it. I take the greatest care not to understand it. It cannot be understood and I know that if I were to understand the egg, it could only be in error. To understand is proof of error. Never to think about the egg is one way of having seen it. Could it be that I know about the egg? Of course I know about it. Like this: I exist, therefore I know. What I do not know about the egg is what really matters. What I do not know about the egg gives me the egg itself. The Moon is inhabited by eggs . . .

The egg is an exteriorization: to have a shell is an act of giving. The egg exposes the kitchen. It transforms the table into a slanting plane. The egg exposes everything. Anyone who fathoms the egg, who can penetrate the egg's surface, is seeking something else: that person is suffering from hunger.

The egg is the chicken's soul. The awkward chicken. The stable egg. The startled chicken. The placid egg. Like a missile suspended in mid-air. For the egg is an egg in space. An egg against a blue background. Egg, I love you. I love you like something that does not even know it loves another thing. I do not touch it. It is the aura of my fingers that sees the egg. I do not touch it. But to devote myself to the vision of the egg would be to renounce my earthly existence which I continue to need, both yolk and white. Can the egg see me? Is it trying to fathom me? No, the egg only sees me. And it is immune to that painful understanding. The egg has never struggled to be an egg. The egg is a gift. It is invisible to the naked eye. From egg to egg, one reaches God Who is invisible to the naked eye. Perhaps the egg was once a triangle which turned so much in space that it ended up being oval. Is the egg basically a sealed jar? Perhaps the first jar to be modeled by the Etruscans? No. The egg originated from Macedonia. There it was designed, the fruit of the most deliberate spontaneity. On the sands of Macedonia a mathematician traced it out with a rod in one hand. And then erased it with his bare foot.

An egg needs careful handling. That is why the chicken is the egg's disguise. The chicken exists so that the egg may traverse the ages. This is what a mother is for. The egg lives like a fugitive because it is always ahead of its time: it is more than contemporary: it belongs to the future. Meanwhile the egg will always be revolutionary. It lives inside the chicken so that no one may call it white. The egg is really white but must not be called white. Not because this would harm the egg which is immune from danger, but those people who state the obvious by describing the egg as white renege on life. To call something white which is white can destroy humanity. Truth is always in danger of destroying humanity. A man was once accused of being what he was and referred to as That Man. They were not lying: he was man. But we have not recovered since. This is the universal law so that we may go on living. One may say "a pretty face" but anyone who says "face" will die for having exhausted the subject.

In time the egg became the egg of a chicken. It is not. But once adopted, the surname is used. One should say "the egg of the chicken." If people simply say "egg," the topic is exhausted and the world goes back to being naked. An egg is the most naked thing in existence. Regarding the egg, there is always the danger that we may discover what could be termed beauty, in other words, its utter veracity. The egg's veracity has no semblance of truth. If its beauty were to be discovered, people might try to make it rectangular. The egg is in no danger, it would not become rectangular. (Our guarantee is that it cannot: and that is the egg's great strength: its supremacy stems from the greatness of being incapable, which spreads like reluctance.) But as I was saying, the egg would not become rectangular and anyone struggling to make it rectangular would be in danger of losing his own life. And so the egg puts us at risk. Our advantage is that the egg is invisible to the vast majority of people. And as for the initiated, the initiated conceal the egg as in a freemasonry.

As for the chicken's body, the chicken's body is the clearest attempt to prove that the egg does not exist. Because one look at the chicken is enough to see that the egg could not possibly exist.

And what about the chicken?

The egg is the chicken's great sacrifice. The egg is the cross the chicken bears in life. The egg is the chicken's unattainable dream. The chicken loves the egg. She does not know that the egg truly exists. Were she to know she has an egg inside her, would she be saved? Were she to know she has an egg inside her, would she lose her function as a chicken? To be a chicken is the chicken's only chance of surviving mentally. Survival means salvation. For it would appear that the act of living does not exist. Living ends in death. While the chicken goes on surviving. And to survive is to keep up the struggle against mortal existence. This is what it means to be a chicken. The chicken always looks ill at ease.

The chicken must not know she is carrying an egg. Otherwise she might be saved as a chicken—although there is no guarantee—but at the same time she would lose her egg in a premature birth to rid herself of that exalted ideal. Therefore she does not know. The chicken only exists on behalf of the egg. She had a mission to fulfill which she enjoyed. And this was the chicken's undoing. Enjoyment has nothing to do with birth. To enjoy being alive is painful.

As for what came first, it was the egg that discovered the chicken would make the perfect disguise. The chicken was not even summoned. The chicken is directly chosen. She exists as in dreams. She has no sense of reality. She gets nervous because people are always interrupting her daydreams. The chicken is one great slumber. She suffers from some strange malaise. Her strange malaise is the egg. She cannot explain: "I know the fault lies with me." She calls her life a mistake. "I no longer know what I feel," etc.

What clucks all day long inside the chicken is etc. etc. etc. The chicken has considerable resources of inner life. If truth be told, inner life is all she possesses. Our vision of her inner life is what we refer to as *chicken*. The chicken's inner life consists of behaving as if she understood. The slightest threat of danger and she screeches her head off. All this simply to ensure that the egg does not break inside her. The egg which breaks inside the chicken has the appearance of blood.

The chicken watches the horizon.

2

The chicken watches the horizon. As if she were watching an egg slowly advance from the distant horizon. Apart from being a means of transport for the egg, the chicken is stupid, idle and short-sighted. How can the chicken understand herself when she is everything the egg is not? The egg is still that same egg which originated in Macedonia. But the chicken is always a recent tragedy. She is continuously being designed anew. Yet no more apt form has been found for the chicken. As my neighbor answers the telephone, he absentmindedly sketches a chicken with his pencil. But nothing can be done for the chicken: it is in her nature to be of no use to herself. And since her destiny is more important than the chicken herself and her destiny is the egg, her private life is of no interest to us.

The chicken neither recognizes the egg when it is still inside her nor when it has been laid. When the chicken sees the egg, she thinks she is confronting the impossible. And suddenly I see the egg in the kitchen and all I see there is food. I do not recognize it. My heart is beating fast. Something is changing inside me. I can no longer see the egg clearly. Apart from each individual egg, apart from the egg one eats, the egg no longer exists for me. I can no longer bring myself to believe in an egg. I find it more and more difficult to believe, I am weak and dying. Farewell. I have been looking at an egg for so long that it has hypnotized me and sent me to sleep.

The chicken had no desire to sacrifice her life. She who had chosen to be "happy." She who had failed to perceive that if she were to spend her life designing the egg inside herself like an illuminated manuscript, she would be doing all that could be expected of her. She remained true to herself. She who thought her feathers were to cover her precious skin, unaware that those feathers were only intended to lighten her burden while she carried the egg, because the chicken's deep suffering might put the egg at risk. She who thought satisfaction was a gift rather than a ploy to keep her totally distracted until the egg had been formed. She who did not know that *"I"* is only one of the words people jot down on paper when answering the telephone, a mere attempt to find some more convenient form. She who thought that *I* means to possess a *selfness*. The chickens in greatest danger of harming the egg are those who pursue a relentless *I*. Their *I* is so persistent that they cannot pronounce the word egg. But who knows, perhaps this is precisely what the egg needs. Because if they were not so distracted and were to pay closer attention to the great life forming inside them, they might disturb the egg.

I began discussing the chicken, yet for some time now I have said nothing about the chicken. I am still talking about the egg. Only to realize that I do not understand the egg. All I understand is a broken egg: broken in the frying pan. And this is how I indirectly pledge myself to the egg's existence. My sacrifice is to reduce myself to my inner self. I have concealed my destiny with my joys and sorrows. Like those in the convent who sweep floors and wash linen, serving without the glory of any higher office, my task is to live my joys and sorrows. It is essential that I should possess the modesty of living. In the kitchen I take one more egg and break its shell and form. And from this very moment the egg no longer exists. It is most important that I should be kept occupied and distracted. I am essentially one of those who renege. I belong to the freemasonry of those who, once having seen the egg, reject it as a form of protection. Anxious to avoid destruction, we destroy ourselves. Agents in disguise and assigned to discreet inquiries, we occasionally recognize each other. A certain manner of looking, a certain way of shaking hands, help us to recognize each other, and we call this love. Then there is no further need for disguise. Though one does not speak, one does not hear either; though one may be telling the truth, there is no further need for pretense. Love prospers, especially between a man and woman, when one is allowed to share a little more. Few people desire true love because love shakes our confidence in everything else. And few can bear to lose all their other illusions. There are some who opt for love in the belief that love will enrich their personal lives. On the contrary: love is poverty, in the end. Love is to possess nothing. Love is also the deception of what one believed to be love. And it is not a prize likely to make one conceited. Love is not a prize. It is a state conceded only to those who would otherwise contaminate the egg with their private sorrow. This does not make an honorable exception of love. It is conceded precisely to those unworthy agents who would spoil everything unless they were allowed some vague intuition.

All the agents enjoy many advantages in order to ensure the egg is formed. There is no cause for envy, because even the worst of the conditions imposed on some agents happen to be the ideal conditions for the egg. As for the satisfaction of the agents, they receive that, too, without conceit. They quietly savor any satisfaction. This is the sacrifice we make so that the egg may be formed. We have been endowed with a nature which has a considerable capacity for satisfaction, which helps to make satisfaction less painful. There are instances of agents who commit suicide: they discover that the handful of instructions at their disposal are insufficient and sense a lack of support. There was the case of the agent who publicly revealed his identity because he could not bear not to be understood, just as he found it intolerable not to be respected by others. He died after being run over as he was leaving a restaurant. There was another agent who did not even need to be eliminated: he slowly burned himself up in disgust, a disgust which overwhelmed him when he discovered that the few instructions he had been given explained nothing. Another agent was also eliminated because he thought "the truth should be spoken courageously," and he set about searching for that truth. People say he died in the name of truth, but in fact he simply obscured truth, he was so ingenuous. His seeming courage was mere folly and his desire for loyalty was naïve. He had failed to understand that loyalty is not something pure, that to be loyal is to be disloyal to all the rest. These extreme cases of death are not provoked by cruelty. There is a job to be done which one might term cosmic, and unfortunately individual cases cannot be taken into consideration. For those who succumb and become individuals, there are instructions, there is charity, there is an understanding which does not discriminate between motives—our human life, in short.

3

The eggs sizzle in the frying pan and, lost in a dream, I prepare breakfast. Without any sense of reality, I call the children who jump out of bed, draw up their chairs and start eating and the work of the day which has just dawned begins, with shouting and laughter and food, the white and the yolk, happiness amidst squabbles, the day is our salt and we are the salt of the day, life is quite tolerable, life occupies and distracts, life provokes laughter.

It makes me smile in my mystery. The mystery of my being which is simply a means, and not an end, has given me the most dangerous freedom of all. I am not stupid and I use it to my advantage. I even do considerable harm to others. I take advantage of the phony job they have given me to conceal my identity and turn it into my real occupation. I have even misused the money they pay me on a daily basis to make life easier while the egg is being formed. Having changed the money on the black market, I have misused it and only recently bought shares in a brewery which has made me a rich woman. I still refer to all this as the essential modesty of living. They have also allowed me time so that the egg may form inside me at its leisure but I have frittered away my time in illicit pleasures and sorrows, completely forgetting about the egg. That is my simplicity as a human agent.

Or is this precisely what they wanted to happen so that the egg may be formed? Is this freedom a coercion? For I am now beginning to see that every error on my part has been exploited. My grievance is that in their eyes I count for nothing, I am simply useful. With the money they pay me I have started drinking.

No one knows how you feel inside when you are hired to pretend you are a traitor and you end up believing in your own betrayal. A job which consists of forgetting day after day. Being expected to feign dishonor. My mirror no longer reflects a face which can even be called my own. Either I am an agent or this is truly betrayal. But I sleep the sleep of the just in the knowledge that my futile existence does not impede the march of infinite time. On the contrary: it would appear that I am expected to be utterly futile, that I should even sleep the sleep of the just. They want me occupied and distracted, by whatever means. For with my wandering thoughts and solemn foolishness I might impede what is happening inside me. Strictly speaking, I myself have only served to impede. The notion that my destiny exceeds me suggests that I might be an agent. At least, they might have allowed me to perceive as much, for I am one of those people who do a job badly unless I am allowed some insight. They made me forget what I had been allowed to perceive, but I still have this vague notion that my destiny exceeds me and that I am the instrument of their work.

In any case, I could only be the instrument because the work could never be mine. I have already tried to establish myself in my own right without success; my hand has never stopped trembling to this day. Had I insisted a little more, I should have lost my health for good. Since then, after that abortive experience, I have tried to reason as follows: I have already received a great deal and they have made me every possible concession. And the agents, far better than me, have also worked only for what they did not know. And with the same meager instructions and, like me, they were modest civil servants or otherwise. I have already received a great deal. Sometimes overcome with emotion at being so privileged yet without showing any gratitude! My heart beating with emotion, yet without understanding anything! My heart beating confidently, yet leaving me baffled.

But what about the egg? This is precisely one of their little ruses. As I was talking about the egg, I forgot about the egg. "Keep on talking, keep on talking," they told me. And the egg remains completely protected by all those words. "Keep on talking" is one of their guiding rules. I feel so weary.

Out of devotion to the egg I forgot about it. Forgetfulness born out of necessity. Forgetfulness born out of self-interest. For the egg is an evasion. Confronted by my possessive veneration, the egg could withdraw never to return and I should die of sorrow. But suppose the egg were to be forgotten and I were to make the sacrifice of getting on with my life and forgetting about it. Suppose the egg proved to be impossible. Then perhaps—free, delicate, without any message whatsoever for me—the egg would move through space once more and come up to the window I have always left open. And perhaps with the first light of day the egg might descend into our apartment and move serenely into the kitchen. As I illuminate it with my pallor.

(translated by Giovanni Pontiero)

1968

France

"Reason," wrote Michel de Montaigne, "has so many shapes that we do not know which to take hold of. Experience has no fewer."

Michel Butor

Egypt

My back is against the wall; it is high time I finally set to work on the piece about Egypt that I have promised, that I have promised to everything in me that has become Egyptian to some degree because of the eight months I spent in the Valley and which reminded me of this promise so fiercely, and with such shame and distress during the lamentable events of the past year, with respect to which certain people—I was abroad—thought it proper to congratulate me, unaware of the bonds I want to write about now, and to congratulate my country for holding up its head at last, as they put it, that head which was suddenly so . . . and here I need an adjective to describe disappointment, but one much stronger than "disappointing," a word to express a real and completely unexpected betrayal . . . to those who had placed such an eager, naive confidence in it, a confidence so faithful until then, despite the many obvious bad omens,

for I can say (I will use the word because there isn't any other word for it, even though it has deviated so far from its root and is by now so associated here with so many horrible and insinuating duperies, and I use it very gingerly indeed), that for me Egypt was like a second fatherland, and it was almost a second birth that took place for me there in that elongated belly sucking through its deltaic mouth the Mediterranean and its passing civilizations, hoarding them and amalgamating them in its slow fermentation;

and it is high time, not only because of external urgency, since it is obviously a good idea, in this disastrous haste forced upon us by the scope and rapidity of changes whose reasons and actual dimensions we fail to see most of the time, in this rush to judge which prevents us from thoughtfully examining the facts involved in the problems we would so much like to solve, to try to bring a little light, a little information, however partial, however weak, however individual it may be, into the area where these dissensions and these questions sprout and take root,

but also because this Egyptian core in myself, if it is still just as active, acts more and more secretly, because it is sinking, more and more deeply covered over by what has happened for me since then,

and because if I don't want to lose track of what I think and what I see and what I want to say, while these images of Egypt are still sufficiently within my grasp, while I am still able to describe them more or less as I would like to, though already with less precision, I must make a preliminary list of them, a memorandum, a recension.

Now if there is only thing I am quite certain of—and I have known it ever since I returned; for this I didn't even need the conversations I have had since with other people who spent time in Egypt, tourists or businessmen, some of whom were there much longer than I; on rare occasions in Cairo, I had certainly seen some of these compatriots living in Heliopolis or Garden City, profoundly absent from Egypt, blind to Egypt, experiencing its magic only though the most anaesthetizing and deleterious side of it, all the more dangerous, naturally, because one refuses to recognize that it exists—

it is that, if I saw what I was there, if I had to fight so hard against the power of the deep-seated strangeness of Egypt, if, therefore, I saw at that time filled with such a vigorous and lasting passion for it, if I explored, during such an unfortunately limited time and with such curiosity, the only quarters of Cairo, it was because I came from farther away in Egypt, because I didn't live in one of the two large cities in which a European, a young Parisian with a degree in philosophy, would normally live,

and, consequently, I can only begin to talk about Egypt, I can only make myself understood, especially by those who have also lived in Egypt but in completely different conditions, by starting with what my life was like in Minya, then a small city of 80,000 inhabitants in Middle Egypt, two hundred kilometers south of Cairo, on the western bank of the Nile, one of the big cotton markets, without any notable monuments, without any building more than a century old, although the town itself is at least five thousand years old, very likely standing on the same spot as the ancient Monat-Khufu, "nurse" of Cheops, who built the great pyramid, and although, in any case, whatever the exact identification one might finally manage to give it, some town has always been there, ever since that time, wandering very slowly through the region as its mud brick houses have collapsed, worn away by the wind or eaten away by the very infrequent rains, and as new houses have been built,

down until the one I knew, to the north of which they were hastily constructing tall concrete buildings.

I should say that at that time (King Farouk was still in power; it was his last year; one felt clearly that things could not go on much longer the way they were, but no one dared hope that the blow-up would come so fast) the Egyptian government had decided to make the teaching of French compulsory in the secondary schools just as English was, and, finding themselves faced with a need for more French teachers, and also wanting to do things right (the minister was the blind writer Taha Hussein, the preface for one of whose books was written by André Gide), through the intermediary of official agencies they had requested that a contingent of degree-holders, no matter what degrees they held, be sent to meet this sudden demand.

Wanting to get away, at that time, wanting to withdraw, and also looking for a bit of adventure, and with a feeling for Egypt if only because of the Empire-style fountain across the street from me in the rue de Sèvres, called the Fountain of the Fellah, I happily allowed myself to be roped in by that invitation,

endeavoring to be on my guard against the aura of illusions surrounding the word Orient, telling myself that everything the romantics went there to find had to be dead forever, firmly determined not to let myself be seduced by a certain picturesqueness linked to poverty and maintained for touristic ends, the Orient of hairdressers and boxes of dates; expecting, consequently, to find nothing in the town where I would be living but a particularly remote provincial place, particularly backward in certain respects, but thoroughly banal, except for the existence of poverties more pronounced, more visible than anywhere in France, more glaring wealth perhaps allowing culture and bold thinking for a few, with a climate warmer than that of Marseilles, but, since all this required no real effort on my part, offering me no discoveries (and this entire preliminary vision would have been completely confirmed if I had ended up in Alexandria),

bringing with me a trunkful of books that justified and called for rereading, and my little typewriter because I intended to write a book which I wasn't able to write there, which I could only write in England, looking back longingly to Egypt.

And so, having arrived at Cairo after an arduous voyage, having taken a room in the Luna Park Hotel, which looked out on a triangular square with a great noisy jet of water in its center, I went to the address I had been given in Paris, to the Ministry of National Education where we were supposed to be received by the man in charge of the teaching of French, an affable and ignorant old Frenchman, satisfied with his lot, established there for years, and who said to me:

"you're supposed to go to Minya; you're lucky; it's a large town with new buildings, big cotton warehouses, a very nice-looking sports club with lovely croquet lawns; it isn't too far from Cairo; you'll see, your life will be very pleasant there; everyone I've sent there has always been very happy."

I also went to see the people to whom I had been given letters of introduction, asking them what they knew of Minya, if they knew anyone there, and they in turn gave me further letters of introduction.

Now, picture the long station platform, with signs bearing the name of Minya spelled out in European letters and also, with superbly thick and supple strokes, in Arabic characters, which I hadn't yet succeeded in identifying and which I've forgotten since,

and the building in the middle similar to the ones you see in the small towns of Languedoc, a stairway going down, a little square, and a perfectly straight street leading to the Nile and bordered by two- and three-story houses painted in wan, washed-out colors.

Only drabness and innocuousness in all this, at first; the weather was nice, it had been nice ever since I had got off the boat, but I didn't see anything surprising in that yet, I was simply enjoying it; it was only little by little that the landscape in which I found myself, and the town that was part of it, and the men living there, under the very thin layer of Europeanization they assumed so carefully, revealed to me their strangeness, slowly, but more and more strongly, so that instead of getting used to it, I lived through my whole stay there with an increasing feeling of being out of place which soon changed into amazement overlaying a feeling of boredom and homesickness, as I appreciated more and more how right the passage from the second book of Herodotus still was that I had translated a few years earlier at the Sorbonne, trying to pass my examination in Greek:

"the Egyptians, who live in a singular climate, on the banks of a river presenting a character different from that of other rivers, have also adopted in almost all things habits and customs opposite from those of other men."

First of all, it's that the space in the Nile Valley has one main direction, an absolutely special direction, something that the composition in ancient Egyptian painting with its superimposed parallels admirably shows us.

If I am in France, I can go away from the place I live, heading toward any point on the compass; the countryside unfolds all around and even the mountains, certain parts of which are so hard to get to, only seem to us like obstacles, like islands of resistance beyond which everything is all right again; but in Upper Egypt, which is a groove in the Saharan plateau, nine hundred fifty kilometers long if you measure it only from First Cataract to Cairo, and on the average ten kilometers wide, as long as you go parallel to the course of the Nile, you can travel indefinitely toward Lower Egypt and the Mediterranean in one direction, and in the other toward Ethiopia or the Sudan, but if you set out at right angles to the course of the Nile, you are very soon stopped by the desert, which begins extremely abruptly, without any of the transitions you find in North Africa, and you always know that you will be stopped, because the desert begins with a cliff you can see from wherever you are.

At Minya the Nile flows south to north, and between Cairo, two hundred fifty kilometers to the north, and Assiut, one hundred fifty kilometers to the south, there is no bridge to cross it, and the road that runs along close beside it, forming a boulevard planted with coral trees in full bloom when I arrived in October, which I took every day to go to the Egyptian lycée, learning how full of variety the fine morning weather can be, is the only road that cars other than jeeps can normally travel (there isn't any at all on the other bank), and the narrow town broadens out towards the north, modern buildings being added one next to the other along parallel streets while in the south the mud brick houses are falling to pieces (Minya must have changed a good deal since the day I left it; it must have been considerably developed and stabilized, and I would like very much to go see what sort of face it has now; I knew it as it was solidifying a little, but it was still in motion, precarious in its poorer neighborhoods, melting away between one's fingers as the villages surely still do and will do for years, like all things in the Valley, persisting in its continual demolition, renewing

itself for thousands of years now in the dust accumulating from its ruins),
the city squeezed in by the parallel railroad, the Valley's one line,

and beyond this, among the fields that are like aquariums filled with liquid wheat because the stalks are so close together, or planted with cotton, with their irrigation ditches fed by the shadoof or the Persian wheel, whose squeaking you can hear accompanied sometimes, at night, by the rending song of the man who works them, with those earthen walls delimiting them, paths on which the men follow each other in a line, solemnly, one by one, in their white striped or blue cotton robes, as in the ancient bas-reliefs, so that of all the paintings the one they most remind one of is a wonderful part of the third tomb in Beni Hasan, the burial place of a prominent figure, one of whose titles was Prince of Monat Khufu, which is famous under the name of "Caravan of Asians" and often reproduced on the basis of the diagram Champollion made of it, but which has never yet to my knowledge been photographed,

in their robes of white cotton which have turned gray or brown like their felt skull-caps, like the earth, like the water of the Nile, or like their skin, or like their eyes, the women wrapped in the long black shroud that leaves their feet bare, and that they raise slightly when they enter the water to fill the pale, porous jugs they carry full and cold on their heads, their black shrouds, a fold of which they draw over their laughing faces now and then, with the incomparable bearing they retain even into their old age, the little children often with suppurating eyes, always covered with flies which their mothers stop them from brushing away, their hair shaved off except for a lock or two,

the sheep one by one, the donkeys, the black cow-buffaloes with twisted horns and sometimes the camels sniffing the air, a fox tail hanging at their necks,

and a little farther off, and on the other side of the other fields on the other bank of the broad, slow Nile marked here and there with large triangular sails bellying with the passage of a cooling breeze from the north, or the burning wind of the khamsin in the spring raising swirls of dust and carrying along with it dry insects, scorpions, even small snakes,

the parallel cliffs extend, forming the wall, the proud, irrecusable limit of this damp vegetable word, the abrupt, pitiless frontier of the kingdom of men, the cliffs always visible from everywhere, even during the clear nights, their shadows and their hues varying deliciously every morning according to the angle of the sun and the degree of transparency of the air more or less filled with shining crystalline dust or vapor rising from the river in flood, to the point where I would have liked to keep a journal of these differences,

the endless cliffs interrupted only by extremely rare openings where very uncertain trails lead off, very little frequented trails, phantom trails towards extremely rare oases or distant ports, distant abandoned mines,

edge of the valley up which we climbed, slipping through the dried bed of a wadi, my friends and I, French teachers who had arrived at about the same time I had, in the same conditions, who had come from different places and were versed in different areas of knowledge, like a handful of pebbles thrown into the long crucible, two of whom in particular, one a grammarian, the other an historian, I am so grateful to for having helped me to live "in" Egypt, which involved very hard work, a relentless surveillance of ourselves, keeping our eyes open in spite of the constant temptation to yield to the prevailing somnolence, who so supported me in my passion to see things (I have lost all trace of one of them, who may still be there and who I hope will some day read what I have written here),

we climbed without worrying about the surprise of our Egyptian colleagues or the students who went with us, acting as guides and sometimes putting us up at their parents' farms,

because we wanted to know how it went on afterward, because, having arrived from Europe, we didn't understand that it didn't go on, that something quite different began, a space in which we were nothing, like the surface of another planet, that a few steps away from the most intensive cultivation in the world, from those fields producing three harvests a year, all at once, without the slightest transition, we encountered nothing but rock worn by the wind, the dry crust of the globe,

fairly often at first, then less and less often, as the lesson was gradually learned,

gazing always with the same almost scandalized disappointment at the immense sterile spaces without grass, without trees, without roads or towns, knowing that they continued without any perceptible interruption (a few infinitesimal green islands, in hollows, in the middle of this petrified ocean that was not navigable, where one couldn't swim, where one couldn't breathe) on one side as far as the Red Sea, on the other as far as the Atlantic,

so that, of course, any desire we might have had in our ignorance, then in our forgetfulness, while we were still down below, to enter it, to plunge into it, to take walks there, enjoying the landscape, to find relaxation there in its hoped-for variety, faded away,

because we would have needed some distinctive point, a grotto, peak or ruin, something allowing us to organize the space around it, fit it into our human plans, providing us with reasons for choosing one or another of the innumerable directions that all looked equivalent to us, attaching it to the valley, whereas, as we knew, there was nothing out there, nothing for us, nothing accessible, that whether we took one step, ten steps, a hundred, to the right or the left, it was all the same,

and so that our walking, starting from this very visible boundary line, could no longer have either any meaning or any purpose (what was the use of making our way painfully over this bare, hilly plateau, or, in other spots, through this sand, under the sun, without hope of shadow or spring, for one kilometer or five, without even reaching that first fold in the ground, to find nothing more than the monotony of this uninhabited stone that we could already see spread out before us, and then come back?),

realizing that it was the domain of the gods and the dead, an immense elsewhere close by, without names, without landmarks, and without maps, an immense reserve of menace which could sometimes take on a form and invade the dreams of Egyptians in the shape of devastating phantoms, or jackals appearing at nightfall with shining eyes, or wild animals breaking into stables and sheep-folds, and pillagers (here the nomads can only survive by brigandage; parasites on the valley, they are, for those who inhabit it, living people who even before death already have a spectral, ghostly existence) or a parching wind,

a sacred domain both because of its dazzling permanence on the horizon of daily occupations, above the fields, at the ends of streets, and because of its so distinctly separate nature,

after which we could only turn our eyes back to the valley at our feet, its mosaic of cultivated plots, of squares of different shades of green which became more and more luminous, like a large habitable stained glass window, as evening approached, toward this landscape with its horizontal registers, to the great Nile reflecting the sky and the sun from here, to the road and the train, to the town and its crowd, in front of the other cliff and the pure sky.

This fundamental direction of space is all the more powerfully felt because in Minya, and in almost the entire valley except for the segment from

Qenan to Girga, where the Nile runs more or less from east to west (but even there, the mentality of the neighboring regions is so contagious that this appears to be an anomaly, like a singular fold in the compass card, a momentary torsion of the whole space), every day one can follow the course of the sun as it moves perpendicular to this terrestrial axis and hardly varying in a sky that is almost always very clear, without anything to cloud it, born every morning after a thin fringe at the summit of the eastern cliff catches fire, appearing and brightening above a point that is always predictable, with the same rapidity, the same sureness of flight as the black scarab beetles used by the ancient hieroglyphics to designate it in its youth, in its first hours, and which children unearth in their play, striking the east side of objects in houses and the trunks of trees, and then, every evening, he who had been so dazzling, so lofty, so motionless above the river at midday, Horus with wings outspread petrifying men's motions with his terrible eye, causing the wings of the kites above us to become transparent, or Aton caressing them with his numberless hands at the tips of his rays as he is portrayed in the Amarnian monuments, would reach the west, sink and darken more and more quickly, fall truly as though snapped up by an immense mouth, then melt in a horizon of bloody dust that turns violet before abruptly giving way to the night, the temperature immediately falling so that in winter, with the feeling of abandon, you are suddenly seized by the cold—and you have to button up your coat even though you wouldn't even have thought of putting it on just a short time before—and in springtime life can start happily,

as the calm moon takes over, a power among the voluminous stars, incomparably more numerous and closer than in our country, standing out against the black sky, and appearing, according to its phase, either round, celebrated by all the wrinkles of the Nile, or with its two points in the air like a pair of horns, like a boat, down below like the arch of a bridge, like a door, like the beak of an ibis,

on which the Moslems base their calendar, while Europeans and Copts base theirs on the sun a little differently, so that each day has several dates, the feast days of the various faiths drawing closer together or moving farther apart, the years and the months rolling along gently one across the other like the oiled gears of an immense, silent machine,

in the sky, which is almost always clear since in this region, they say, it rains, on the average, two hours a year (in Luxor the joke is that the last downpour they had there was the announcement of the Napoleonic expedition), and since, although we had already seen clouds, already seen drops of water fall for a few minutes and then evaporate even as they approached the hot ground and the dry dust, just once (I remember, I was at the home of one of my French friends), an extraordinary noise tore us from our reading, a sound like a drumroll, which at first we couldn't figure out, then seeing, flabbergasted, that this transformation in the air, these shouts in the street, this was rain, real rain, with an unheard of violence and illuminated by the sun; just once we had been able to watch it working away for almost an hour, as drunk as though each of those drops of water were a drop of alcohol, after which, the clouds having dispersed, the streams having dried on the ground, where they had carved complex furrows, we learned that several houses had been damaged in the southern quarter,

this fundamental organization so evident that to show to you where a particular place is, an apartment in a building, for example, they don't use your position at the moment as a reference point, but those constants of the landscape identical to the cardinal points, those absolute landmarks which even the walls of a room can't hide; and that, consequently, they will not say to you, Take your first left, then turn right, but, Take the first street to the east, then turn north, go up the stairs and it's the south door; that at the table one will even speak of a chair that is to the west of another chair.

In opposition to the sacred domain of the sky and the desert, the domain of divine permanence and its clear movements on which everything must be regulated, Upper Egypt itself, the back of the Valley where the people live, "the black earth," which hasn't in the least always been there, but is a gift of the Nile, this very soil on which one lives, which one cultivates, from which one draws one's sustenance, being already a "production" whose slow accumulation one can note each year, this soil so precious that sometimes, in order not to waste a single acre, the villages form little enclaves in the desert, minuscule excrescences, is entirely governed by precariousness, by a continual deterioration against which one must constantly fight if one wants to maintain anything whatever already achieved.

Everything here seems ephemeral, men certainly, and all the domestic animals, but also the very configuration of the terrain, of these fields that used to be covered every year by the dark and nourishing waters (only the towns emerging, says Herodotus, with almost the same effect as the islands in the Aegean Sea), of these fields whose borders had to be redrawn by a whole army of surveyors every time the river fell, borders which were engulfed and obliterated, now, certainly, for the most part remaining at all seasons beyond reach of the overflowing river, already regularized by the first dams, but in the middle of which, nevertheless, I saw, as it subsided, banks of sand and earth form, without one being able to predict where, soon true islands, dry in a few days, their black surfaces fissuring into deep crevices in all directions like an intense, amorous penetration by the air and the sun, then worked by the fellahs leaning on their wooden plows behind their asses or female buffaloes, then sprout, turn green, grow their quick, dense crops, islands that one never thought of giving any particular name to, since one knew that at the next return of the waters they would be unrecognizable again.

Faced with such a manifest division of the universe, this landscape of contrasts, how natural it was that the ancient Egyptians should have considered that if it was to be stable, the organization of their society also had to integrate a contrast, had to be based on a balance of opposed parts, and that they should have hailed as "their first king who was a man," as the first successor to the gods, Min or Menes who succeeded in bringing together on his head the crowns of two regions as visibly distinct as Upper and Lower Egypt, linking this event to the construction of a dike to protect from the flood a site on which to build a permanent capital in the middle of the "earth";

faced with the constant humiliation of the near world by another world, how natural it was that they should have believed that the pharaoh, that maintainer, came from the family of the gods, and that under his direction they should have spent such a fabulous sum of work to allow him to assure them of where he came from and who he belonged to by leaving a mark of his reign, of his presence, a mark as obviously lasting as possible, a monument of human fabrication but capable of rivaling in mass the desert escarpments, in conformance with the laws of this divine world, the pyramid oriented according to its fundamental direction, four-sided, its polished faces corresponding exactly to the cardinal points, whose top was lit in the morning not only before anything else in the valley, but even before the edge of the cliff, dazzling at midday, reflecting horizontally the almost vertical rays, the true earthly image of the sun, looming in the evening in front of us as it sinks in the sky, like a mask before its face as it dies, like the door to its tomb;

how natural it is, consequently, that among all the lands of the ancient Orient, it should be in Upper Egypt that the most numerous, the most impressive, and above all the best preserved ruins stand.

◖◗

The day after I arrived in Minya, I went to see a cotton buyer whose address I had been given, an aging Jew from Alexandria who advised me, since I wanted to settle somewhere, to rent part of an apartment.

Actually, one of his accountants, who spoke very good French, had just found one that he would be happy to share with me.

This was how I met Hassan, who acted as a sort of steward to me throughout my stay and who now took me into an empty, tiled, high-ceilinged room with cement walls painted green which soon became punctuated with little spots of blood up to a certain height, because it was autumn, the waters of the Nile were just beginning to go down, and as a result there were swarms of very irritating mosquitoes which I would squash before I went to sleep.

We hired a man with a cart to move my trunk, then we went off to look for a bed, which wasn't hard to find because the year before, I believe, the hospital had ordered a few more than it had room for,

a metal bed with a noisy bedspring of wires.

At a cloth merchant's we chose some material for the mattress, thick and silky with gray stripes, like the material from which the farmers made their robes; we got samples of raw cotton at the warehouse and we entrusted the lot to someone who did sewing.

Then we bought a pair of sheets and a bedspread, so that the next day I was able to move into the apartment whose only other piece of furniture was Hassan's big double bed and, on the floor of the alcove that served as a kitchen, a Primus stove,

(a pitcher, a water-bottle, a few pink-flowered china plates, a few glasses and some silverware, two pots with lids).

Nor did I have any trouble finding chairs, because the "sports club" had ordered quantities of them for its garden; but I needed still other objects in that room; I felt it was impossible to live without a table, needing one to read and write, do my job, however elementary, as teacher, needing it even for eating comfortably.

Now if the richest Egyptians of Minya had quantities of heavy, stupidly sumptuous pieces of furniture in their homes—thickly gilded, in an overloaded Louis XV style, covered in boldly-flowered cretonne—they generally ordered it from Cairo, or even directly from the big stores in Paris and London, and at the time there wasn't one table to be bought in the whole city.

Because of the delays of the royal government, I had very little money at the beginning of my stay, and so the only solution was to have a table made by one of those actually quite skillful carpenters who took so much pride in their painstakingly produced fretwork for sideboards they hoped would be able to measure up to the ones occasionally unloaded from the train,

to buy the wood, to make a working drawing showing exactly how I wanted it,

then to go to the workshop every day for three weeks, learning patience and the fact that it simply wasn't possible to find an Arab equivalent for the words *too late*, to see how the job was coming along,

until the time when at last I saw it, the longed-for table, varnished, with a drawer, as I had specially requested, but standing much too high, so that I had to have its legs sawed down, and then sawed down again before I could use it.

Then we undertook to have another similar table made for the dining room, whose installation we celebrated with a banquet; then, encouraged by these handsome successes, I went so far as to order and make a precise drawing for a small cupboard that was finished either before or after the Christmas holidays, I don't remember which, the dimensions I had given having been respected but inverted, where I was at last able to put away, safe from the dust, my clothes and my books, which I hadn't really been able to take out of my trunk since I left Paris.

And so these objects, which were so familiar, which I had taken for granted in France, to which my everyday activities were so tied, which I knew I could do without for a while, during the holidays, while camping, but which I was absolutely sure of finding again a few days later, when I returned to normal life, to my work,

which were a fundamental given of the world I belonged to, which existed in all dwellings without exception, whose presence and the need for which were absolutely the rule,

here seemed to me to be the result of a long desiring, a sort of extraordinary luxury, associated with the rich class that had the leisure to order them

from Europe or wait interminably for local craftsmen to make imitations
of them,

as the result of a whole special cultural evolution.

When I walked through the streets of the villages, I could see the inside
of the houses, more or less empty but for the Primus stove, a few jars, a mat
and some coverlets;

when I walked through the streets of Minya, which at first seemed so
like the sad streets of towns in the South of France, I knew that inside these
buildings the furnishing in the rooms were utterly rudimentary compared
to the ones I needed, whose existence was implied by my habits and my
way of being,

that my Egyptian colleagues, dressed like me, and even, I must say,
much more carefully than I, therefore had, when they returned home, a
routine behavior that was completely different from mine.

I knew some who lived in apartments like the one I lived in, with several
members of their families who were pupils at the lycée, with a single desk
for all of them, which they used one at a time, with their freshly washed
shirts arranged in a pile on the tile floor in one corner, covered with a piece
of paper to protect them a little from the dust, their suits hanging one on
top of another from a nail driven into the wall, like Hassan's in the room
next to mine.

Considering all that, how could I not marvel at the table?

How could I not see that to speak of this simple object is also to posit
an entire civilization of a certain kind, an entire area of history, and that the
introduction of such objects into a culture where they are alien, or what
amounts to the same thing, the adoption of a European-style education,
absolutely inevitable because of the latter's obvious technical superiority,
that is, an education that implies among other things the existence of these
objects, that calls for them when they aren't yet there, causes a gigantic perturbation and disarray even in the most everyday behavior.

Theoretically, secondary education was compulsory and free, even the
books, indeed all the educational material being provided by the State, and
every day a free lunch was served: sandwiches stuffed with halvah, that oily
and sandy gray sweet of all Eastern Mediterranean countries, oranges or ba-
nanas, at first in the classrooms themselves, which produced an indescrib-
able disorder, then outdoors,

but this compulsoriness remained purely theoretical, and in actuality the education was reserved for a quite small fraction of the population, because, in order to be admitted into the precincts of the lycée, the pupils had to wear a European suit, long pants, shirt, tie, jacket, socks and shoes, which very few farmers could afford.

So it was that I would find myself facing classes of forty to fifty students between the ages of fourteen and twenty whose names I could not only not manage to remember, but in the beginning not even repeat or transcribe,

who had all had some French already, in principle, but most of whom didn't know a single word, I at first not knowing a word of Arabic, not knowing even the alphabet, which I took a long time to learn and after-wards forgot.

They generally knew a little English, and I did too, but we pronounced it in such different ways that it was a very precarious means of communication. We were therefore reduced to the direct method in its most primitive form, one of the only effective methods of explanation being drawing pictures.

Soon half the students, realizing they would never learn French under such conditions, gave up for good, installing themselves in the back of the room to play cards peacefully or memorize the textbooks they at least had the possibility of reading, while the others came up close to me and began to make some progress,

for which they deserved all the more credit since there reigned a continuous agitation and noise which I could do nothing about, first of all because if I mentioned it to the other teachers they were astonished at my astonishment, considering the state of things to be perfectly normal and unavoidable, the students always answering, sincerely surprised, that they always did this in the other classes, which was true,

and because, on the other hand, there was no system of punishments besides the whip, administered by a policeman who was always walking in the hallway, truncheon at his belt and handy, ready to come to the aid of teachers in distress, a method too contrary to my French habits for me ever to be able to decide to use it, but which was not distasteful to my colleagues, in their moments of ill temper, so that now and then one heard some long resigned howls.

For example, from time to time I would see two students who were very good friends and always sat next to each other stand up, their eyes blazing, though nothing had given any warning of the coming storm, grab each other, roll in the aisle showering each other with blows and tearing each other's clothes while the other looked on, not even very interested, simply accustomed to it,

then, after a few moments, rarely more than a minute, get up feeling calmer, brush off their jackets, sit down next to each other again as though nothing had happened, continue to follow the lessons sharing the same book, because often one of them had forgotten or lost his;

and afterwards I would try to find out about it from the others, who answered me graciously, always amused at my preposterous curiosity, that they belonged to two neighboring villages between whom for a very long time there had been disputes whose origin no one was very sure of any more, or most often, that one was a Moslem, with sometimes a little lion tattooed on the back of his hand, and the other a Copt, with almost always a little cross tattooed on his wrist, that they were certainly very good friends, but that they were clearly obliged, from time to time, to have things out, to settle, temporarily, differences that were not theirs personally but in that midst of which they found themselves caught.

The religious landscape of Minya was very complex:

confronting Islam, which was almost monolithic where doctrine and ritual were concerned, but within which one found a great diversity of attitudes towards the observance of practices, very few people following them strictly, or of the prohibitions, the more or less frequent, more or less public use of wine being very closely connected with the membership within this or that social group, all joining in the at least public obedience of the rules of Ramadan,

there were a host of Christian sects and churches in perpetual disagreement, first of all the orthodox Copts, quite numerous and powerful, proud of how long they had been in the Valley, endeavoring to compete with the Moslems in the austerity of their fasting, but on Easter celebrating their spiritual independence by dazzling bouts of drunkenness, with superb, extremely long and dramatic ceremonies whose canon remained in that Coptic language inherited from the ancient Egyptians, the rest translated into Arabic, accompanied by wonderful hoarse chants led by a Moslem who was always blind, a blind child next to him learning the job little by little, small cymbals and a triangle beating out the rhythm,

then the Roman Catholics with Coptic rituals, the Greek Orthodox, the Greeks having preserved ever since Herodotus an almost complete monopoly on the spice trade in Egypt, the Roman Catholics with Greek rituals, the Maronites, the Roman Catholics with Roman rituals represented at that time by two schools: one, an elementary school for boys, in the south of the city, in full decline, run by Jesuits, French-speaking though for the most part Syrians, and which at least had in its library a complete edition with translations of the works of Saint Augustine; the other, for girls, run by nuns who were also French-speaking but who came from all sorts of countries (there was notably one wonderfully beautiful Mexican), teaching that "our ancestors the Gauls had blue eyes and blond hair" and who also had what was to us a treasure in their library, the *National Geographic Magazine*,

maybe about ten Protestant sects, some of English origin, others of American origin, imported at the same time as the agricultural machinery,

and lastly, of course, a scattering of Jews.

But all these "official" religions in discreet conflict, especially the two main ones—Islam and Coptic Christianity—with rare explosions in the midst of general tolerance, were in communication through a whole fabric of beliefs and practices that one could call superstitious, whose diffuse presence one was constantly aware of, but about which it was often difficult to obtain information, our pupils and our colleagues being afraid that we Europeans would react with mockery, they themselves being ashamed of them, no longer adhering to them, of course, in their fully conscious moments, but always obscurely subject to their magic, and not managing to detach themselves sufficiently from them to be able to view them with ethnographic objectivity,

practices and beliefs which, when they came into patent conflict with the two great religions, when they were forbidden and secret, having as a consequence the status of witchcraft, were naturally connected for the believers of one with the presence of the other, so that the most effective magician for the Moslems was as a rule of Coptic persuasion, Moslem for the Christians,

were naturally connected for everyone in every case to the ruins of the ancient monuments, particularly scandalous to the strict Moslems, more and more rare, because of the innumerable figures that decorated them, vestiges for everyone of the world where Joseph had ruled, from which Moses had fled.

Thus, to the plurality of religions present, felt, moreover, to be part of an historic sequence, Coptic Christianity considering itself as coming after the Jewish religion, Islam as coming after the Jewish and Christian revelations, the Protestant sects and even Roman Catholicism appearing here as latecomers closely connected with the European invasion, as the return of a Christianity that had evolved differently elsewhere, all religions including a certain number of shared sacred figures, having in common a certain reference to ancient Egypt,

was therefore added the confusedly but very strongly sensed presence of another, older religion, something dark and dangerous in the background, but haunted by a strange wisdom, and this, not only because it is actually possible to show a continuity between ancient beliefs and practices and a good part of current superstitions, but because this continuity was felt as such owing to the endurance of the monuments, if not at Minya itself, then at least in the region, and owing to the role they played in witchcraft or at least had still played a few years before,

felt as such especially in certain completely public customs, for example the feast of Cham al Nessim, "the smell of the breeze," the biggest feast of the year because it was the only one celebrated by the whole population without distinction (there were a few political anniversaries, naturally, but their celebrations were nothing like this), the theoretical date of the beginning of the dry, hot wind, calculated according to the Coptic Moslem calendar, the calendar, I was told by a landowner of the environs of Minya whose wife was French, which he himself had to refer to in his agricultural work, because it was based on that of the ancient Egyptians, which was developed in this same valley,

a festival that marked the beginning of spring (one spent all night outdoors, in new clothes, with flowers and onions over all the doors), that is, which corresponded to a complete transformation of daily life for which nothing had prepared me, day and night abruptly changing roles, the afternoon, which soon became torrid, henceforth being devoted to sleep, an exhausted sleep on a mattress which had to be dried in the evening when I woke up because it was soaked thought with sweat, life beginning at sunset, the streets, empty until then, suddenly coming alive with a gaiety that hadn't existed during the winter,

and fragrances taking on an importance, a volume, that they never have in Europe, the smells of flowers and fruits, which made you turn your head in the street as though they were calling out to you, the smells of animals and men, and most of all the smell of corpses which penetrated everything, which was in earth and water, which remained attached to your clothes when you had passed near a cemetery, whether they were recent or thousands of years old, pleasant or disagreeable smells, sometimes so heady that I said to myself that if Saint Augustine had lived in Upper Egypt in the springtime, he wouldn't have been able, when enumerating in the tenth book of the *Confessions* the temptations he was exposed to, and when describing to us the different sorts of concupiscence, to tell us so simply, and with some surprise and distrust of himself, that "the seductiveness of fragrances leaves him rather indifferent."

From that time on, the school also had a changed look, the teaching began to disintegrate when confronted with the violent rejuvenation of all things, the students turning up less and less often, the last of the faithful taking out of their pockets, when they arrived, handfuls of little roses they had picked on the way, so that in the end we didn't go to school any more except to verify that the classrooms were empty;

and if they didn't come any more it wasn't only because they wanted to sleep or take a walk, it was more than anything because they were terrified of the approaching exams, even though the richest of them shouldn't have had anything to worry about, since everything in Egypt at that time, without exception, could be bought, and they prepared feverishly in little groups, learning their textbooks by heart from cover to cover, reciting them sitting in a circle at night in the streets around each streetlight, because many of them had no electricity in their homes, and preparing memory aids for themselves with wonderful care, "aspirins," as they called them, squares of white paper kept in their palms, covered with very tightly packed fine lines of that admirable writing which, reduced to its principal elements, constitutes its own stenography.

To help them in this considerable effort of memorizing—and it must be understood that if they were reduced in this way to learning by rote, it wasn't only through a carry-over from the habit of Koranic teaching, where the sacred text plays a much more important role than the Bible in Christian religions, being not only inspired by God, but his eternal word itself, so that recitation becomes the religious act par excellence,

but it was also because this knowledge that they were asked to acquire and that they wanted so much to acquire because it was obviously the key to power, most of the time formed extremely circumscribed little islands in their minds, which virtually did not communicate with their personal experience,

(to take an extreme example, I remember examining students in a Southern city for the Egyptian baccalaureate, which involved a whole program, in imitation of the French one, of geography, physics, etc., asking them questions about a passage from the French book that seemed to me very simple, which had to do with a railroad train, and realizing that they had never seen one because they came from a college situated in a small town on the other side of the river and had crossed the river for the first time on the occasion of their examination),

in their minds and in the minds of most of their teachers and examiners, so that it would have been useless for the latter to pose additional questions, or to ask for supplementary details, because, as they well knew, since there were always a few who would try it, they would only have been answered by a confession of ignorance naturally accompanied by a fit of ill humor,

islands that pulverized the habits of thinking that surrounded them, just as the machines, the furniture, the clothes imported from Europe, all those emblems of power, pulverized the old habits around them, though this did not mean that the "European-style life" for which these objects had been made could be established throughout the whole country,

gradually shaking all the beliefs, but without being able to obliterate or replace them, leaving them defenseless, in a kind of chaotic mental emptiness with, in certain of my colleagues, a terrible feeling of frustration, which could find no outlet except in the still very distant hope that one day it would be possible to wrest from Europe every last one of its mysteries and that then you would be able to get your revenge and beat it on its own ground,

islands which remained separated from one another, and which in some sense floated, too obviously incomplete, full of lacunae, without managing to organize themselves stably and coherently in relation to what they saw, in relation to the crumbling world they came from, amidst the wreckage of which they lived—

therefore, in order to help them in this considerable effort, in order to fix their attention better on these words and phrases often so barely intelligible, many mixed hashish in cigarettes and smoked it, drugging themselves with it, though its use was officially forbidden, so that the surest way to obtain it without risk was to apply to the policemen, the prohibition thus creating, in practice, a State monopoly,

with hashish, whose extremely widespread use, beyond these scholarly applications, evidently played an important role in the equilibrium of the Egyptian mentality, not only because it was a little less clearly prohibited than the use of alcohol in the prescriptions of the Koran, but more importantly because the cold high it induces, which leaves the lid firmly on a person's dreams, would allow the disoriented consciousness a marvelous rest, masking its own devastation from it by a sort of inward flight, by the happy contemplation, in the moment, of the objects, the landscape, the arrangement of reality which, when one returned, sobered, to one's daily chores, appeared so inexplicably fissured, shaky, here and there so strangely foreign and obscure,

what you contemplate then, in your intoxication, isolating you, filling you, pushing back into the shadow all your relations with the rest.

I certainly can't boast of any great experience with hashish, since I felt a good deal of distrust of it in the beginning, obviously afraid of acquiring a taste for it (it was a subject that occupied an important place in our conversations, and at that time my friends and I carefully consulted the passages in *Les Paradis artificiels* that talk about it),

and I only felt the full effects of it one time, one night, in the spring, on the way back from a visit we had paid to the uncle of one of our students, long hours passed in an orchard doing nothing, saying almost nothing, tasting little strangely tart fruits, and watching the branches of the trees or the palms swaying, a veil passing on the other side of the wall.

It was at the home of the parents of another student who lived halfway back from there, more or less a cousin of the first, with whom he had arranged to prepare this little party for us in a tiny courtyard, below street level, illuminated by an oil lamp, surrounded by benches, I think (certain details of this scene have remained present in my mind with a wonderful distinctness, others, though I need them to show how all this was arranged, have completely disappeared into vacancy, they have sunk forever into the vacancy to which they were already relegated that night the moment the intoxication began),

with a few embers glowing in an earthenware plate, with one of the students standing in a gray robe, in profile, resplendent in his pride as host, with the faces of the women appearing furtively in a doorway, smiling, intrigued, startled, drawing their black veils back over their faces, with a policeman, his red tarboosh on his head,

and the amazing stars above, and the stirring of the air, the rustling of the leaves, that kind of breathing of the water and the sleepers, men and animals, which one heard, and that smoke smelling of eucalyptus that we drank greedily from the reed stem of the chibouk, that great pipe with its water filter, which passed from mouth to mouth, and the sweets that one was always offered at these times;

so, yes, I felt it, that exaltation, my eyes dilated, and on my face appeared that fixed smile that is so easy to recognize, and everything I saw overwhelmed me by its beauty;

and of course I understand that when you remember the pleasure you were made to feel by the glorious detachment of these same objects and faces which, when you consider them now in the midst of your problems, your mental distress, no longer succeed in delivering you from them, you may have the impression of a veil interposing itself between them and you, a veil Indian hemp dissipates, and that a legend like that of the Paradise of Assassins could have come into being,

but as far as I'm concerned, I know very well that as soon as these effects began to wear off, what immediately invaded me was a feeling of discontent and frustration, because I should have been able to experience this beauty, this emotion, even without the power of this weed,

(I was in the middle of the Valley at night, we were returning on foot to Minya), but it was impossible for me to judge to what extent exactly,

because that beauty, as a consequence, far from having been given to me as I had had the illusion it was, all of a sudden had been denied me, whereas I could have attained it,

because I was obliged to mark those few hours, despite their radiance, which endures even today, with a symbol of doubt, just as one marks an uncertain passage in a text with an obelus.

As for the students—the teachers for their part not having the means to procure themselves these little brownish green cubes very often—it is clear that from the moment they became however confusedly aware of the role their habitual use was beginning to play, no longer innocent stimulation of the pleasure of being in society, but worsening fragmentation of the knowledge they wanted to acquire, aggravation of the mental disorder they were suffering, it is clear that they grew ashamed of this sterile comfort, that the very pleasures it procured for them turned rotten,

because falsehood and vanity continued to leer out at them from the shadows around the luminous objects,

and because, as a consequence, their secret resentment of Europe deepened, their envy, their uneasiness, their painful, silent need for a reshaping of the whole configuration of the world, naturally taking into account all that Europe contributed, but not something that boiled down to a mere adoption of the contribution in the form it came in.

◀ ▶

This insidious strangeness, this cunning dissolution, in which I felt myself threatened with asphyxia and lethargy, in which everything risked turning into a drug and a pretext for somnolence, a pretext for avoiding all of this so visible unhappiness—in the beginning, I escaped it as often as possible, fleeing from the school every weekend, fleeing from the school at noon every Thursday as soon as the bell rang, because for us Friday took the place of Sunday, just barely catching the train for Cairo to breathe a little of the cooler air from the West,

to recover an image of it that was a little less caricatured, a little less thin, a little less dislocated than the image whose ravages I saw in Minya,

in order that the dreadful perturbation caused by our mere presence, our gestures, our ohs and ahs, our questions, our explanations, be got into the best possible focus, running off to movie theaters to see films I probably wouldn't have gone to see in Paris, but which nevertheless formed an approximation,

haunting bookstores and lending libraries, delighting in the presence of shops, posters, and tramways.

But soon, as I came to feel closer to Egypt, beginning to see this landscape, at last, in its difference, the faces that surrounded me in their splendor and their unhappiness,

as the feeling of my involuntary guilt became sharper and sharper in this night, this perdition which I caught more and more clearly in those at once confident and envious eyes that observed me and questioned me, of my original sin, in some sense, as a European,

as I began to become Egyptian myself, sufficiently steeped in these dissonances to find that I too was faced with an imperious need to attenuate them, to introduce a little order and clarity in the menacing confusion, to become a little better acquainted with the terrain where there was taking place a devastation in which I myself had a hand ineluctably,

the need, consequently, to situate correctly in relation to one another the dissociated elements whose shreds were all I could see in Minya,

soon it wasn't only a return to Europe that I went to seek in Cairo, but the city's admirable analysis of the different elements present in the life and mentality of Egypt, its wonderful exhibit of the successive civilizations to which these elements were attached.

For although it is of course completely wrong to say, as Nerval does, that Cairo is "the only Eastern city where one can rediscover the clearly distinct layers of many historical ages," this "distinctness" is certainly clearer here than in the others (much clearer today, what is more, than at the time of Nerval's journey), and this, as he was quite aware, because of the durable nature of its monuments, of its princes' obsession with endurance:

"the mosques alone tell the whole story of Moslem Egypt, for each prince had at least one built, wanting to hand down the memory of his time and his glory forever; the names of Amru, Hakim, Tulun, Saladin, Bibars or Barkuk are thus preserved in the people's memory."

The durability of its buildings, which makes Cairo so unusual among the cities of Moslem Egypt, all doomed, until the arrival of concrete, to see their sun-dried bricks crumble away, is the reason for the way its different quarters are so neatly juxtaposed, so that to cross certain streets is to go from one time to another, from one mental world to another.

Thus, along the magnificent Nile with its islands and their gardens, close to its bifurcation into a delta, there are the rich, European-style neighborhoods, with their arrow-straight avenues bordered by large, modern, reinforced concrete blocks of offices and apartments, with a fever of construction everywhere which has certainly increased even more since I left Egypt, so that the look of the main squares must have changed considerably,

with the movie theaters and their lighted signs, their immense placards painted all colors of the rainbow, the Paris-style store windows, the English-style tearooms, the restaurants for tourists, the travel agencies, the grand hotels with their "pharaoh" or "thousand and one nights" decors, always inspired in fact by wretched Western degradations of the works of art of these two worlds, even though they were only a few steps away and so easy to consult, for example Shepheard's Hotel, since burned down, as I was not displeased to learn, I must confess,

with the tramways, the taxis, nearly all dark blue, almost black Chevrolets at that time, with loudspeakers shouting Arab adaptations of American songs,

and certain more tranquil areas, planted with trees, with gently winding streets, with separate houses, the private residences belonging to the embassies,

from time to time kites wheeling above the crossroads, and in a passageway, reminding you it was there as though by the sounding of a gong, the dazzling cliff of the moqattam through the dust.

To the north of this area, which its inhabitants, Europeans or rich, Europeanized Egyptians, virtually never left except to go to elegant suburbs of the same type, Heliopolis or Helwan,

on the other side of the station, losing itself little by little in the spreading reaches of Lower Egypt, lay Shubra, Cairo's Aubervilliers, where of course nothing remained of the rose gardens, the alleys, and the pavilion that so delighted Nerval,

an enormous, teeming, black outlying district, with nothing left of the festive din of the elegant and lazy capital one had just left, nothing but the rumbling, harsh and desperate monotony of the poorly industrialized suburbs, with smoke, the smell of gas and detergents, the puddles, the broken windows, the famished cats with elongated muzzles, as in the ancient statues, whom no one dares to destroy.

Then, parallel to the Nile, to the cliff, and to this whole first recent city, to this city you come upon first, already so divided, some parts so brilliant and others so miserable,

pierced by a few straight avenues to ease the traffic, otherwise all little streets where cars can't go through, beginning almost as abruptly as the desert with something menacing about it, still surrounded by part of its old ramparts with three magnificent gates,

reigns medieval Cairo, the one Lane and Nerval saw in its already dilapidated splendor, the one into which even the Cairo tourists didn't dare to venture except rarely and in groups because among the inhabitants of those neighborhoods there was a terrible mistrust of the desecrating, frivolous stranger,

so that if, by the end of my stay, we were able to feel altogether at ease strolling there, going into mosques without buying tickets, staying there as long as we liked, it was because for us they had become true objects of pilgrimage, because our few months in Minya had already led to our assimilation into the landscape, our way of walking and looking at things was in harmony with that of other people, so that for these caretakers, these tradesmen, these people who passed us in the street, although we certainly didn't have the appearance of Egyptians, we also no longer corresponded in the least to the type of European they hated, so that they would ask us, amused at our ignorance of Arabic, whether we were Turks or Persians.

For the resentment against Europe was concentrated in the shadow and under the protection of those innumerable mosques, almost all of which, unfortunately, were cracked, halfway abandoned, needing an enormous amount of repair work, with their architecture that was so noble and so strict, their superb severity sometimes enriched at certain points by the most whimsical evolutions, with the exalting geometry of their Kufic inscriptions, all of this so admirably in tune with certain of the most urgent tendencies and needs of modern architecture that to study them, to visit them, could have fertilized the imaginations of present-day Egyptian architects in a wonderful way if only they had been able to look at them with different eyes

(for the moment they became architects, necessarily having to learn the new construction techniques that had been imported from Europe, they went off to live in the other part of the city, they began to belong to that other part of the city, losing their normal communication with this one, ceasing to come here, at a loss to assign it a suitable place among the things they had been taught, avoiding the agitation it would have caused in them to return here),

these sublime cubes or cupolas of calm in the midst of the bazaars, and, since in Egypt Islam appeared especially as a revelation that had come from the desert, the Koran an immense voice rumbling over the desert, exquisite cool equivalents of the desert and of its silence in full valley concentration, places conceived as resonators of pure recitation.

In the South, confined inside other, even more ancient walls, whose round Roman towers served as models for that of the medieval surrounding wall, are the Coptic churches and convents associated with the memory of the hermits and their temptations.

Lastly, on the other side of the Nile, at Giza, appear the first notes of that long, inexhaustible melody that continues, for travelers going south by train, until the branching off at Fayum, the three pyramids to the base of which the tramway goes, those three immense, irrecusable monuments which, when one begins to approach them, lose the straightness of their lines, begin to resemble very large piles of stones whose size and distance one can't appreciate, so that one thinks one has already arrived when there is still quite a long way to go,

stones that increase individually in volume as one walks, assuming proportions one would not have suspected, so that a moment comes when one wonders how long this amazing growth is going to go on,

the whole then losing its shape, which is so well known, the face ahead of you now filling the entire horizon, its three points causing the eye to leap between dizzying perspectives when your hand at last touches the stone,

this tremendous response of the pharaohs to the humiliating night of the desert ("They boasted," says Bossuet, "that they were the only ones who had, like the gods, made immortal works"), a constant humiliation throughout the Middle Ages for those sultans who considered themselves the heralds of that very word thundering over the desert, a permanent scandal because of their massiveness, which rendered the process of their construction inexplicable to those who contemplated them, demanding recourse to magical powers, to the intervention of demons, the way the other ancient monuments were a permanent scandal because of their innumerable figures, the writing itself, indecipherable, teeming with animal and human signs,

so that if many mosques in Cairo were built with blocks of limestone or granite that came from the pyramids, it wasn't only, as people are accustomed to suggest, because of convenience, but also because of a very directly religious necessity.

A way had to be found to affirm conclusive victory over this prestigious past, to try to break free of this power that had to be acknowledged and endured, as is admirably expressed in the fact that the stone threshold of the very beautiful and very severe Khanqah of the Sultan Bibars is an ancient stone engraved with the cartouches of Ramses X, a very visible inscription which one thus treads upon, that one anathematizes every time one enters before taking off one's shoes.

Edward William Lane, the author of an admirable book which Nerval made abundant use of, about the customs of the Egyptians at the beginning

of the 19th century, a book which is still one of the best tools for helping the explorer of present-day Egyptian life, declares at the beginning of
his first chapter on superstitions: "It is commonly believed that the earth was
inhabited, before the time of Adam, by a race of beings different from us
in form, and much more powerful; and that forty (or, according to some,
seventy-two) pre-adamite kings, each of whom bore the name of Suleymán
(or Salomon), successively governed this people. The last of these Suleymáns
was called Gánn Ibn-Gánn; and from him, some think, the ginn (who are
also called ganns) derive their name. Hence, some believe the ginn to be
the same with the pre-adamite race here mentioned; but others assert that
they (the ginn) were a distinct class of beings, and brought into subjection
by the other race."

And later he says:

"The ancient tombs of Egypt, and the dark recesses of the temples,
are commonly believed, by the people of this country, to be inhabited by
'efreets [that is, jinns]. I found it impossible to persuade one of my servants
to enter the Great Pyramid with me, from his having this idea. Many of the
Arabs ascribe the erection of the Pyramids, and all the most stupendous
remains of antiquity in Egypt, to Gánn Ibn-Gánn, and his servants, the
jinns; conceiving it impossible that they could have been raised by human
hands."

We remember the passage in the *Voyage en Orient* in which Nerval tells
us about the conversation he claims he had during a walk on the island of
Roda with an old sheik whom he asked what he thought of the Pyramids,
which had just come into view:

"Some authors think the Pyramids were built by the pre-adamite king
Gian-ben-Gian; but, according to a tradition much more widespread among
us, there existed, three hundred years before the flood, a king named Saurid,
some of Salahoc, who dreamed one night that everything was turned upside down on earth, men falling on their faces . . ."

Now, this whole passage is of particular interest at this point, since we
have to clarify a little how the Pyramids were viewed by Moslem Cairo in
its great period, a vision that still prevails beneath the many new elements
that have added to it,

since this conversation never took place the way Nerval reports it, the
people talking being in reality separated by several centuries, since the
words put in the mouth of the old sheik are in reality, as Jean Richer discovered, an almost literal transcription of an Arab manuscript translated by

Pierre Vattier in 1666 under the title: *L'Egypte de Murtadi, fils du Gaphiphe, où il est traité des Pyramides, du débordement du Nil et des autres merveilles de cette province selon les opinions et traditions des Arabes* (the Egypt of Murtadi, son of Gaphiph, in which are discussed the Pyramids, the flooding of the Nile and the other wonders of this province according to the opinions and traditions of the Arabs), which I will now quote, going back to the original French text because it is obviously more characteristic and more illuminating for us than its adaptation:

"Then he ordered that the Pyramids be built, so that they could carry and shut up there the most precious of their treasures, with the bodies of their kings and their riches . . .

"The guard of the eastern Pyramid was an idol of black and white jamanic scale that had both eyes open and was sitting on a throne, having near it a sort of halberd, and did anyone cast his gaze upon it, he would hear a dreadful noise coming from there, that nigh made his heart fail him, and whoever heard that noise would die from it.

"The guard of the western Pyramid was an idol of hard red stone holding in his hand likewise a sort of halberd, and having on his head a serpent twined around, which serpent struck at those who approached.

"For a guard of the third Pyramid, there was a small idol of bahe stone set on a base of the same material, which idol drew to it those who looked at it and clove to them inseparably until it made them die or made them lose their minds."

This is how he describes the contemporary phantoms that haunted them:

"They say the spirit of the southern Pyramid never appears outside save in the form of a woman naked even about her private parts, who is also beautiful . . . When she wants to give love to someone and make him lose his mind, she laughs at him and forthwith he approaches her and she draws him to her and maddens him through love so that he loses his mind then and there and runs vagabond through the country. Several people have seen her gliding around the Pyramid at noon and near sunset.

"The spirit of the second Pyramid which is the colored one, is an old Nubian man who carries a basket on his head and in his hands a censer, etc."

And again it is from Murtadi and a few other Arab historians he was able to consult in translation that Nerval borrows the details of the opening of the great Pyramid and its exploration by the caliph al-Ma'mun of the Abbasid dynasty:

"Their chronicles relate that they found in what was called the King's

Room a statue of a man of black stone and a statue of a woman of white stone standing on a table, one holding a lance and the other a bow. In the middle of the table was a hermetically sealed vase which, when it was opened, was found to be full of still fresh blood. There was also a rooster of red gold speckled with hyacinths which cried out and beat its wings when one entered."

In this collection of legends, which other people, having access to original texts, could certainly study much better than I, it is not surprising that almost all the details can be precisely related to what we know today about the ancient royal Egyptian tombs since that of Tutankhamen revealed its black guards to us, its white women, its furniture, its plates and dishes, its kites and vultures of enameled gold

(in Murtadi, the discovery of the golden rooster, that Nerval, despite all his desire to believe, found a little too "thousand and one nights," is related in a somewhat more detailed way which allows us to see how its fantastic aspects were able to develop quite naturally from the discovery of some treasure in the depths of a tomb—and why not the Pyramid itself, which, if it had been despoiled from Antiquity on, certainly could have served as a hiding place once again at a relatively late date:

". . . they found a square place like a gathering place where there were many statues, among others the figure of a rooster made of red gold. This figure was fearful, speckled with hyacinths, of which there were two large ones on the two eyes, which shone like two great torches. They approached it and at once it cried out dreadfully and began to beat its two wings and at the same time they heard many voices coming to them from all sides"),

this is not surprising because of the necessary existence of a tradition of stories linked to these enduring monuments, of stories becoming more and more legendary as the relation between their various elements is less well understood, being changed according to new interpretations, but preserving a certain number of basic images revived, consolidated by the discoveries here and there of ancient objects corroborating them.

It is not at all surprising that these idols and these phantoms should have the very faces of these statues or these bas-relief figures, so troubling and so numerous,

and one can see what a prodigious depth, often expressly considered as superhuman, all this gave to the personage of the Pharaoh, Moses' interlocutor, and to the magic surrounding him in those passages in the Koran where he appears, proclaiming in chapter xliii: "Oh my people! This kingdom of Egypt is it not mine? And these rivers which flow below me? What! Are you not able to see? Am I not superior to this contemptible creature who can hardly speak?", declaring in chapter lxxix: "I am your Lord God Almighty,"

what illumination all this gave to that pride, what an explanation, an explanation that would really have become too good, in contradiction to the sacred text, if one had made him out directly to have been the builder of the Pyramids, if one had identified with one of them the tower whose plan is attributed to him by the Koran:

"Oh you leaders! I know of no other gods for you besides me; therefore, have clay baked, Oh Haman, and build me a tower, so that I may climb up to that so-called God of Moses; for, in truth, I think he is a liar!"

and this is why he was considered solely, in conformance with the historic truth, as the distant heir of their builders, which already introduced into that obscure and as if faltering reference to Antiquity, a great internal dislocation, the idea of a great distance between certain of its moments, consequently the idea of an historical duration much longer than that marked by the three great reference points enumerated in the Koran, the three points of origin of the three religions currently present, Moses, Jesus, Mohammed, whence the notion of "before the Flood," or "before Adam," which plays exactly the same role.

Thus the use, as quarry, of these ancient monuments so terribly there, so terribly near (and that was the immense difference between Egypt and other countries of the Middle East where the vestiges of remote Antiquity, which were completely covered with sand, which only came back to light after excavation, did not directly trouble the Moslem Middle Ages at all),

the re-use of these stones is a response to their superstitious power, to the persistence, accursed for the conqueror, of habits and beliefs linked to them;

but the result of this response, since the destruction of the ancient monument remains insignificant, changes almost nothing about its imposing mass, since the presence of these ancient stones in the new monuments is evident from the exoticism of their material, granite of Asswan, for example, and far from obliterating that power and that endurance, preserves it, stabilizes it, accentuates it.

What is more, as it is only when the old attitude is obviously in contradiction to the new order that it takes on this status of witchcraft, and that other aspects of it come to be integrated quite naturally into the teaching of the conqueror, into his way of life, come to give him little by little, subtly, smoothly, an altogether original physiognomy compared to the one he had before and to the one he has taken on in other landscapes against backgrounds less encumbered, less rich,

color him even in his most official manifestations,

the use of these artificial quarries is in some sense the material corollary of that contamination, and therefore the very configuration of Moslem Cairo; its difference in structure, compared to other great cities of Islam, illustrates the particularities of Egyptian Islam, the singular characteristics of the historic and geographical soil on which it developed,

which manifests itself with great clarity in a feature of the city of Cairo which I haven't yet mentioned, that is, the extent and magnificence of its necropolises,

unlike Istanbul, for example, with its fields of steles packed together in the shadow of a sanctuary or unfurled over the surrounding hills as though tossed by the wind, here we have neighborhoods for the dead more or less similar to those of the living, with a more or less equal area, only still more dilapidated, with their streets and their squares, with their funerary mosques, the tombs of the sultans, as sumptuous, as lofty as those other mosques in the interior, which often contain tombs as well,

including here and there, at the main crossroads, veritable small villages of shops among the mausoleums, for welcoming the inhabitants of the other streets, the other squares, because of the size and frequency of the funeral ceremonies, not only of the burials but also of those long visits paid to the dead on the occasion of certain holidays, during which people come to eat, chat, sleep next to the tombs,

which for the wealthy used to include a true underground chamber so that "the person or persons buried in it," as Lane says, "may be able with ease to sit up when visited and examined by the two angels, Munkar and Nekee,"

a private judgment in preparation for which an "instructor of the dead" would lecture him at the time of the closing of the tomb (just as in the ancient tombs the cadaver was, if possible, provided with passages from the *Book of the Dead,* that famous negative confession that was supposed to help one pass the test victoriously), declaring to him (I am still quoting Lane):

"O servant of God! O son of a handmaid of God! know that, at this time, there will come down to thee two angels commissioned respecting thee and the like of thee: when they say to thee: 'Who is thy Lord?' answer them, 'God is my Lord,' in truth; and when they ask thee concerning thy Prophet, or the man who hath been sent unto you, say to them, 'Mohammad is the Apostle of God,' with veracity; and when they ask thee concerning thy religion, say to them, 'El-Islám is my religion;' and when they ask thee concerning thy book of direction, say to them, 'The Kur-án is my book of direction, and the Muslims are my brothers;' and when they ask thee concerning thy Kibleh, say to them, 'The Kaabeh is my Kibleh and I have lived and died in the assertion that there is no deity but God, and Mohammad is God's Apostle;' and they will say, 'Sleep, O servant of God, in the protection of God.'"

This attention paid to death, this familiarity with the cadaver, whose smell on the warmest days impregnates the whole Valley, this constant awareness of the transitory nature of the individual, so different from the sort of obliviousness towards that condition that exists now in most countries of Western Europe, so that when someone dies, it always seems to be an unexpected event, we don't know how to behave, how to talk, how to get rid of the scandalous body,

that enormous importance accorded to the tomb is very closely connected to the structure of the Valley's landscape, to that very clear humiliation of the transitory human and his domain by another, permanent world, and it is consequently necessary that in its response to such a situation, every civilization that has come from somewhere else, come from a region in which the question of the dead body was posed with much less violence, so that it was possible to hide it, to more or less neglect it—that it adopt the solutions, the customs of those that preceded it here.

The civilization of Moslem Egypt was therefore made up of a balance between elements whose age and whose origins were very different; now, what the European presence brings about is not only the destruction, around certain objects, certain persons, certain new teachings, of old habits which taken together formed a coherent way of life and thought that it doesn't succeed in replacing in a satisfactory way,

it is also the dissociation of those elements that were formerly in balance, so that the constitution, the invention of a new balance becomes an even more difficult problem that cannot be resolved until the historical relations of all these present domains are clarified.

In fact, the European infiltration will not fail to affect these ancient monuments, with which so many ways of doing and thinking have been bound up; far from participating, like earlier waves of civilizations, in demolishing them, obliterating them, burying them in a thicker dust and darkness, it is going to increase their presence through its archaeologists, exhume them, restore them, explore them and study them, exalt them, project onto them and onto the whole world to which they testify a completely new light, completely different from the ambiguous glimmer that used to mark them;

through the development of a tourism that focuses primarily upon them, it is going to make them play a quite unexpected role in the economy of the country, thus recalling them constantly to the attention of the Egyptian even if he doesn't live near them, in a way that wasn't foreseen, the whole former attitude towards them therefore requiring a complete revision.

In France or in other Western countries there are certainly scholars who are studying Islam, who probably are more familiar with certain aspects of its history or its literature than the professors at El Azhar, who are capable of providing much better editions of certain texts, others who are studying Ancient Egypt or Coptic Christianity, but, in the Valley of the Nile, what is at once so dramatic and so exciting is that each farmer, no matter how uncultivated, how deprived he may be, finds himself daily faced with the question of the respective situation of these worlds in relation to one another and in relation to modern Europe, or America, whose technology, whose thought is submerging him,

a question he is obviously incapable of answering for the moment, which he can leave tranquilly in suspense so long as he is still far enough away from a factory or a school, but which will eventually gnaw at him and cloud his mind, to the point where it will prevent him from learning correctly what he might want and need to know once he sets about it.

Now, what can be called average European thinking, that is, the mental structure common to those French or English or American merchants, engineers, professors who held so much power, the thinking which at that time wholly inspired their modern universities (I am speaking of 1950–1951, before Farouk left), could not really help the Egyptians in this respect, and still can't.

For, if it demands a historical perspective of a certain type, the one it has to offer is inadequate in its temporal and geographical dimensions.

In effect, every Frenchman, for example, especially if he has had second-ary schooling, is able to give a rough summary of the history of mankind in which will figure the Greeks, the Romans (also the Jews, to whom we owe the Bible and the Catholic religion, but that is a special area, which people often prefer not to bring up), then the Christian Middle Ages, the Renaissance, and finally modern Europe, with its science, which conquers the rest of the world,

a schema which seems sufficient, allowing as it does for all the expla-nations without having to bring in those other nations, those other civi-lizations, the strange, curious, exotic, amusing ones, to which a serious, well-balanced person, a gentleman concerned with business or politics would think it rather silly to pay any real attention,

so that entities as enormous and prestigious as Ancient Egypt and Islam only appear in their representation of the universe as appendices, footnotes, half-humorous vignettes,

as little secondary regions whose existence can very well be ignored since, in principle, that existence doesn't change anything, explain anything,

and whose works and language certain eccentrics clearly have a right to study if they have enough leisure time for that,

to explore the ruins, if they bring back statues or jewels to enrich the museums or collections, which is a flattering luxury for everyone, but which one is quite ready to consider as unreasonable, to strike from the list of expenses.

Naturally this schema can be of no use at all to even the humblest Egyptian peasant, since within his perspective it is primarily pharaonic an-tiquity that constitutes a riddle, it is primarily Islam that constitutes a past or tradition, so that he finds himself having to situate European history, history such as it is reflected by one of those Europeans he may meet in the streets of Cairo or in the hotels of Luxor, within a much vaster context,

an enormous task, a monstrous task, but so urgent that a start will cer-tainly be made upon it soon and a new way of looking at and interpret-ing history will be invented, will spread through this country, as in all the great countries of the East in upheaval, a way of interpreting history that will necessarily react upon that of Europe itself, bringing with it immense changes of emphasis and outlook,

a task which I myself was faced with, living in that country, finding that I had in some sense become one of them, one who had especially forgotten his origins and who had particularly well assimilated what Europe teaches, as though I had been born in that country, had left it for France when I was very small, and coming here had really come back,

if I wanted to survive intact, if I wanted to remain open-eyed, if I wanted to escape that ruin, that intellectual desolation overcoming my colleagues at the Minya lycée, who were so much less, so scandalously less favored than I.

Also, just as thenceforth my visits to Cairo were no longer mere returns to a Europe I missed, but the most potent tool I could have for analyzing modern Egypt, for seeing it better, in the same way, very soon, visiting an ancient site was no longer a simple matter of esthetic escapism; it was tied to an effort to rethink, to enlarge the perspectives I had inherited from my education, an effort the need for which I had clearly felt already before I left France, but only distantly, disinterestedly, certainly not with this precision, this urgency, this acuteness.

Thus the amazing Djéser monument at Saqqara, for example, as it had been rediscovered and restored, such a new puzzle for the inhabitants of Egypt, became a consuming puzzle for me too, and no longer merely an object which one admires and at which one looks with an astonished but detached gaze; it became so bound to me that a certain region of my consciousness could only become clear to the extent that I could better understand, better picture to myself the reasons why those men of five thousand years ago, in such a violent explosion of inventive genius, built with such care those false doors, those delicate houses filled with rough boulders, that stepped Pyramid which only emerged from the sand a few years ago, and what relation all that has to what came after it;

thus, in the tomb of Petosiris at Tounah el-Jebel, near Minya, from the Persian period, on the walls of which, I knew, were engraved maxims certain of which had been translated literally in the *Book of Proverbs,* what I was looking for was some illumination of my origins and of that of the religion in which I had been brought up and was looking for this perhaps even more clearly still in the sterilized amphitheater of El-Amarna,

a renewal, an improvement in the position of problems that had troubled me for years and were troubling me there much more directly and profoundly.

Not being an Egyptologist at all, I must be content with simply pointing to this area; I would like to do no more than show what a source of

illumination there may be in this gigantic nest of problems which the researchers' scrupulously careful picks are unearthing, causing to hum like a
swarm of wasps, as they study them and solve them,

not only for understanding this contemporary country which slyly
keeps referring back to itself, but for Europe itself, daughter of the Roman
Empire, within which a quantity of scattered signals keep pointing to that
hearth whose radiance is almost as ambiguous for us as it is for the Moslems
of Cairo.

Now the place where this hearth opens up most perfectly, spreads out,
and proffers itself, splendid to examine, whatever the beauties of the other
sites may be, is obviously that enormous city of tombs and temples on the
two banks at Luxor, certainly the most impressive known group of ruins,
ancient Thebes which even in its worst abandonment has never ceased to
emit a constant, secret glow—to which I would ask for no other testimony
than the description of it in Bossuet:

"In the Said (as you know, this is the name for the Thebaid) they have
discovered temples and palaces still almost intact, where those columns
and statues are innumerable. Here one admires above all a palace whose
remains seem to have survived only in order to outshine the glory of all
the greatest works. Four alleys as far as the eye can see, delimited on either
side by sphinxes of a substance as rare as they are striking in size, serve as
an avenue leading to four porticoes whose height astonishes one's eyes.
What magnificence and what scale! Those who have described this amazing structure to us have not had time to go all around it, and are not even
sure they have seen half of it; but everything they saw was astounding.
One hall, which was apparently the middle of this superb palace, was supported by six score columns six men's arms around, proportionately high,
and intermingled with obelisks still upright despite the passing of so many
centuries. Even the colors, that is, the soonest to feel the power of time,
yet endure among the ruins of that admirable structure, and preserve their
brightness, such was the ability of Egypt to imprint the character of immortality upon all her works."

This is in the third part of the *discours*, and of course one starts imagining the other direction classical French art could have taken, the other face
Versailles might have shown us, had the advice he gives in the following
paragraph ever been followed:

"Now that the name of the King is reaching the most unknown parts of the world, and now that this prince is sending so far for the finest works of nature and art, would it not be a fit object of that noble curiosity, to uncover the beauties which the Thebaid contains in its wilderness, and to enrich our architecture with the inventions of Egypt? What power and what art were able to make of such a country the wonder of the world?"

Now he realized that Imperial Rome, on whose memory Imperial France was endeavoring from a distance to model itself, was even more sensitive to Egypt's prestige, which he himself experienced so strongly through the intermediary of a traveler's description, for Bossuet went on to say:

"It was left to Egypt alone to raise monuments for posterity. Its obelisks are still the principal ornament of Rome today, as much because of their beauty as because of their loftiness; and the power in Rome, despairing of equaling the Egyptians, felt it had done enough for its grandeur when it borrowed their kings' monuments."

And to mark clearly to what extent our knowledge of Egyptian antiquity is still in its infancy, not only because of the dim inheritance made up of countless prejudices towards it and which can only be got rid of slowly, but also because of the bulk of the documentary material itself that has to be deciphered and sorted out, it is enough to say that when I went to Luxor for the first time, in February, during the mid-year vacation, one of the young Egyptologists I met there told me that in his free time he was recopying the inscriptions that completely covered the walls of that part of the temple at Karnak which is famous and has been for so long, that great hypostyle hall where, as Bossuet says, a few colors "yet endure" but much less well, with much less freshness than in certain other monuments that have been unearthed since, for example in the wonderful temple of Seti I at Abydos,

he was collating these inscriptions, which had never been done before because these were only ritual texts and the most urgent thing was naturally for the scholars to recopy, publish and interpret everything that allows dates to be established.

I returned to Luxor in May, since my French colleagues from Minya and I were giving exams in Qena, the neighboring prefecture. The time of very great heat had already arrived; not a single tourist was left; we had it all to ourselves.

One morning, at five o'clock, we took the boat we had rented the night before, steered by a boy of thirteen or fourteen to whose father we had paid five piastres, fifty francs in all, for the entire day, and we went to the bank of the dead.

This time, to get into the long winding ravine among the dazzling rocks that ends at the Valley of the Kings, we chose not to go by way of that cirque that has dug itself in the mountain in the shape of a pyramid,

that mountain which was interpreted as a natural pyramid, centuries and centuries after the first ones had been raised by men,

this funerary monument built by the gods for the sovereigns who were their brothers, as people had known for a long time then, and who endeavored to make sure people remembered it by erecting their succession of funerary temples down below, facing the river,

we didn't take those strange black barouches pulled by thin horses, long lines of which had been collected by the tourist organizations for their groups,

but we found a donkey-driver who accompanied us throughout our long tour.

We saw a few of the royal sepulchers that are the hardest to get to, notably that of Thutmose III with its great oval hall where, with his acetylene lamp, the guardian illuminated for us the walls along whose length ran so effectively schematized illustrations of the book of what is in Hades,

then we visited a few of the hundred other numbered tombs, we went onto the terraces of Deir el-Bahari, we must have lunched at the "resthouse" near the Ramesseum on the provisions we had brought along, fallen asleep . . .

I no longer remember the order very well, it has all become a little confused, things have become something of a jumble . . .

But in the evening a scene took place that summed up for me my whole Egyptian itinerary, in which were symbolically resolved all the swarm of difficulties I had raised with every new step and which was in some sense Egypt's answer, in some sense its fundamental acquiescence to the very lively interrogation I had begun to address to it.

As we had just left the necropolis of Deir el-Medina, on the path, a tall Egyptian peasant, wearing a very neat, long, dark blue, almost black robe and a little white turban, stopped us, greeted us, me especially, with an air of great joy.

I understood absolutely nothing of what he said to me, what he wanted of me, the reason for his attitude, when suddenly among his words I recognized these four syllables: *André Lebon.*

It was the name of the ship I had taken at Marseilles seven months earlier, with another friend who wasn't there, who had ended up in a different Egyptian city from mine, a ship that did not usually do the Alexandria run, but was that one time replacing the *Champollion,* which was being repaired,

a ship whose hold had been fitted out to transport troops to Indochina, hammocks slung one above another all around the great square hatch reached by a long ladder, covered with a big tarpaulin at night and when it rained,

and this time accommodated steerage passengers, including us.

When we left, each of us had been given an old metal plate, flatware, and a mug, which we would carefully stow away so that we could find them again at the next meal, and which we didn't always find, so that we would appropriate others that were lying around here and there,

passengers who were not entitled to service, so that two of us, we were told, would either have to volunteer or be picked to go to the galley and get bread, wine, mess-tins of soup and other food (it was always my friend and I, as soon as the hour sounded, because we were absolutely determined to have hot food), which we balanced as we climbed down the steps of the ladder, but often on windy days, not skillfully enough to prevent food from spilling over, making star-shaped puddles on the table below.

For four days we lived this way, in this sort of primitive state, surrounded by vomit, in this sort of commoners' locker, in this pit from the edges of which ladies would sometimes gaze down, my philosopher friend and I, as well as a young Lebanese who had just finished his hitch in the Foreign Legion and was going to set himself up as a hairdresser in Beirut, some rich students from Cairo who had spent their vacations in Paris, where they had run through a little too much money, various individuals of dubious professions, the Egyptian gymnastics team, except for their star, who, having picked up a medal, qualified for a first class ticket, coming back from some championship or other,

who had all given a demonstration of their talents before the whole ship, the captain presiding, a pleasant interlude being provided by a contortionist who was also a beauty king, Mr. Egypt or something like that, and who was also coming back from a meet along with his wife, the only woman in that hold,

and in a bunk not far from mine (there were many empty ones, but only some of the lamps worked), smiling, a peasant from Upper Egypt who didn't know a word of French, the only one who was not wearing European clothes, but was dressed in a very neat, long, blue, almost black robe, on his head a felt skullcap surrounded by a very clean white turban, and that, so we managed to understand, because he was the servant of a man who worked at Luxor and who had taken him along with him to Paris during his summer vacation, a man who was himself returning second class, upstairs, with his wife and children,

to Paris which had amazed him and from where he had brought back in his suitcase a talisman he would only show, with extreme caution, to people he thought would be just as enchanted by it as he was:

a stereoscope with about ten views: the Opéra, the Arc de Triomphe, etc.,

this peasant, whom I at last recognized on the path near the cemetery of Deir el-Medina, the excavating of which was overseen by his employer, absent for the moment.

We got off our donkeys; we went into the little village, into his earth house, into his room furnished only with an extravagant large brass bed, surely brought to Luxor decades ago for one of the big hotels on the other bank.

Then, we having finished drinking the burning hot mint tea brought by one of those women who laugh in the window recesses, he went to get the stereoscope, which for me, too, in the meantime, had become a talisman.

And so, after a whole day's gorging on sunlight and Antiquity, in the cool shade of this room, thanks to the friendship of this man with whom we couldn't really talk, whom I wouldn't have imagined seeing again, whom I certainly wouldn't have recognized if he hadn't recognized me first,

we were able to contemplate, delighted, more surprised and more overwhelmed even than we had been on the day of the one true rainfall at Minya,

those streets which had been so familiar to us, but which had become so remote to us during our stay, the Champs-Elysées and especially the Place de la Concorde, with its obelisk in the middle; and though we had been aware before, though we had certainly heard it said, that this was an obelisk from Luxor, it was only now that we began to grasp the meaning and the implications of the phrase.

And I knew very well that for the understanding that existed between us, which was so secure and so pure but which remained mute, to pass to the level of language, for it to be able to develop into a real conversation, there would have had to be an already existing organization at the level of this language, one to which we could have referred, on which we could have relied,

an organization, satisfactory to both of us, of those various places and times that were contracted into the present moment.

We stayed for a long time drinking in the coolness that flowed from those pictures, then one of my friends reminded us that we had told our boatman that we would be back before sundown.

Now the sun was already very low, and was sinking more and more rapidly.

We got back up on our donkeys, casting long shadows before us through the red air, like the pylons of the funeral temple of Ramses III to our right, like the colossi of Memnon to our left, and I felt extraordinarily happy because, yes, something of the world had been unveiled for me, in a confused way, but in an absolute certainty that would never leave me, the slight pain I felt between my vertebrae, the fatigue that suddenly overwhelmed me, being in some sense the guarantee of it.

The night had long since fallen when we reached the riverbank. Our boatman complained.

When will I return to Egypt?

(translated by Lydia Davis)

1969

Italy

On the other hand: maybe there still exists, in every kind of essay, no matter the period it's written in, the culture that it emerges from, or the specific aesthetic allegiances that the essay maintains, the musculature of an implicit rhetorical gesture at work. Not the rhetoric of a thesis, or of "therefores," or of the five-paragraph form, but rather the rhetoric of wanting something that language cannot achieve. It's the kind of rhetoric we sometimes see in a writer's forced transitions, illogical deductions, or cumulative insistences. We see it, too, in the bright distracting glints of snazzy stylistic devices, as if a new literary gimmick could magically weave around a writer the armor of obstinate denial. Natalia Ginzburg did not use many gimmicks in her work. She lived under the confines of Italian fascism. We might say, in fact, that because of this Ginzburg's became a structurally economical style. She is, after all, detached in her essays. But I would like to say that it's a vulnerable detachment. Italo Calvino described Ginzburg's prose as both "stubbornly fierce" and "frighteningly desperate," a style that tries to pour the entire sea into a funnel, imposing upon itself only a portion of expression in order to convey the tension of a particular predicament. Here, for example, she gives us a flat-voiced catalogue of the deceptively mundane differences between her and her husband. Tenacious in tone, unwavering in form, it's written throughout in such matter-of-factness that what she reveals about herself is incidental to what she discovers.

587

He and I

He always feels hot, I always feel cold. In the summer when it really is hot he does nothing but complain about how hot he feels. He is irritated if he sees me put a jumper on in the evening.

He speaks several languages well; I do not speak any well. He manages—in his own way—to speak even the languages that he doesn't know.

He has an excellent sense of direction, I have none at all. After one day in a foreign city he can move about in it as thoughtlessly as a butterfly. I get lost in my own city; I have to ask directions so that I can get back home again. He hates asking directions; when we go by car to a town we don't know he doesn't want to ask directions and tells me to look at the map. I don't know how to read maps and I get confused by all the little red circles and he loses his temper.

He loves the theater, painting, music, especially music. I do not understand music at all, painting doesn't mean much to me, and I get bored at the theater. I love and understand one thing in the world and that is poetry.

He loves museums, and I will go if I am forced to but with an unpleasant sense of effort and duty. He loves libraries and I hate them.

He loves traveling, unfamiliar foreign cities, restaurants. I would like to stay at home all the time and never move.

All the same I follow him on his many journeys. I follow him to museums, to churches, to the opera. I even follow him to concerts, where I fall asleep.

Because he knows the conductors and the singers, after the performance is over he likes to go and congratulate them. I follow him down long corridors lined with the singers' dressing-rooms and listen to him talking to people dressed as cardinals and kings.

He is not shy; I am shy. Occasionally however I have seen him be shy.

With the police when they come over to the car armed with a notebook and pencil. Then he is shy, thinking he is in the wrong.

And even when he doesn't think he is in the wrong. I think he has a respect for established authority. I am afraid of established authority, but he isn't. He respects it. There is a difference. When I see a policeman coming to fine me I immediately think he is going to haul me off to prison. He doesn't think about prison; but, out of respect, he becomes shy and polite.

During the Montesi trial, because of his respect for established authority, we had very violent arguments.

He likes tagliatelle, lamb, cherries, red wine. I like minestrone, bread soup, omelettes, green vegetables.

He often says I don't understand anything about food, that I am like a great strong fat friar—one of those friars who devour soup made from greens in the darkness of their monasteries; but he, oh he is refined and has a sensitive palate. In restaurants he makes long inquiries about the wines; he has them bring two or three bottles then looks at them and considers the matter, and slowly strokes his beard.

There are certain restaurants in England where the waiter goes through a little ritual: he pours some wine into a glass so that the customer can test whether he likes it or not. He used to hate this ritual and always prevented the waiter from carrying it out by taking the bottle from him. I used to argue with him about this and say that you should let people carry out their prescribed tasks.

And in the same way he never lets the usherette at the cinema direct him to his seat. He immediately gives her a tip but dashes off to a completely different place from the one she shows him with her torch.

At the cinema he likes to sit very close to the screen. If we go with friends and they look for seats a long way from the screen, as most people do, he sits by himself in the front row. I can see well whether I am close to the screen or far away from it, but when we are with friends I stay with them out of politeness; all the same it upsets me because I could be next to him two inches from the screen, and when I don't sit next to him he gets annoyed with me.

We both love the cinema, and we are ready to see almost any kind of film at almost any time of day. But he knows the history of the cinema in great detail; he remembers old directors and actors who have disappeared and been forgotten long ago, and he is ready to travel miles into the most distant suburbs in search of some ancient silent film in which an actor appears—perhaps just for a few seconds—whom he affectionately associates with memories of his early childhood. I remember one Sunday afternoon in London; somewhere in the distant suburbs on the edge of the countryside they were showing a film from the 1930s, about the French Revolution, which he had seen as a child, and in which a famous actress of that time appeared for a moment or two. We set off by car in search of the street, which was a very long way off; it was raining, there was a fog, and we drove for hour after hour through identical suburbs, between rows of little grey houses, gutters, and railings; I had the map on my knees and I couldn't read it and he lost his temper; at last, we found the cinema and sat in the completely deserted auditorium. But after a quarter of an hour, immediately after the brief appearance of the actress who was so important to him, he already wanted to go; I on the other hand, after seeing so many streets, wanted to see how the film finished. I don't remember whether we did what he wanted or what I wanted; probably what he wanted, so that we left after a quarter of an hour, also because it was late—though we had set off early in the afternoon it was already time for dinner. But when I begged him to tell me how the film ended I didn't get a very satisfactory answer; because, he said, the story wasn't at all important, the only thing that mattered was those few moments, that actress's curls, gestures, profile.

I never remember actors' names, and as I am not good at remembering faces it is often difficult for me to recognize even the most famous of them. This infuriates him; his scorn increases as I ask him whether it was this one or that one; "You don't mean to tell me," he says, "You don't mean to tell me that you didn't recognize William Holden!"

And in fact I didn't recognize William Holden. All the same, I love the cinema too; but although I have been seeing films for years I haven't been able to provide myself with any sort of cinematic education. But he has made an education of it for himself and he does this with whatever attracts his curiosity; I don't know how to make myself an education out of anything, even those things that I love best in life; they stay with me as scattered images, nourishing my life with memories and emotions but without filling the void, the desert of my education.

He tells me I have no curiosity, but this is not true. I am curious about a few, a very few, things. And when I have got to know them I retain scattered impressions of them, or the cadence of phrase, or a word. But my world, in which these completely unrelated (unless in some secret fashion unbeknown to me) impressions and cadences rise to the surface, is a sad, barren place. His world, on the other hand, is green and populous and richly cultivated; it is a fertile, well-watered countryside in which woods, meadows, orchards, and villages flourish.

Everything I do is done laboriously, with great difficulty and uncertainty. I am very lazy, and if I want to finish anything it is absolutely essential that I spend hours stretched out on the sofa. He is never idle, and is always doing something; when he goes to lie down in the afternoons he takes proofs to correct or a book full of notes; he wants us to go to the cinema, then to a reception, then to the theater—all on the same day. In one day he succeeds in doing, and in making me do, a mass of different things, and in meeting extremely diverse kinds of people. If I am alone and try to act as he does I get nothing at all done, because I get stuck all afternoon somewhere I had meant to stay for half an hour, or because I get lost and cannot find the right street, or because the most boring person and the one I least wanted to meet drags me off to the place I least wanted to go to.

If I tell him how my afternoon has turned out he says it is a completely wasted afternoon and is amused and makes fun of me and loses his temper; and he says that without him I am good for nothing.

I don't know how to manage my time; he does.

He likes receptions. He dresses casually, when everyone is dressed formally; the idea of changing his clothes in order to go to a reception never enters his head. He even goes in his old raincoat and crumpled hat; a woolen hat which he bought in London and which he wears pulled down over his eyes. He only stays for half an hour; he enjoys chatting with a glass in his hand for half an hour; he eats lots of *hors d'oeuvres,* and I eat almost none because when I see him eating so many I feel that I at least must be well-mannered and show some self-control and not eat too much; after half an hour, just as I am beginning to feel at ease and to enjoy myself, he gets impatient and drags me away.

I don't know how to dance and he does.

I don't know how to type and he does.

I don't know how to drive. If I suggest that I should get a license too he disagrees. He says I would never manage it. I think he likes me to be dependent on him for some things.

I don't know how to sing and he does. He is a baritone. Perhaps he would have been a famous singer if he had studied singing.

Perhaps he would have been a conductor if he had studied music. When he listens to records he conducts the orchestra with a pencil. And he types and answers the telephone at the same time. He is a man who is able to do many things at once.

He is a professor and I think he is a good one.

He could have been many things. But he has no regrets about those professions he did not take up. I could only ever have followed one profession—the one I chose and which I have followed almost since childhood. And I don't have any regrets either about the professions I did not take up, but then I couldn't have succeeded at any of them.

I write stories, and for many years I have worked for a publishing house.

I don't work badly, or particularly well. All the same I am well aware of the fact that I would have been unable to work anywhere else. I get on well with my colleagues and my boss. I think that if I did not have the support of their friendship I would soon have become worn out and unable to work any longer.

For a long time I thought that one day I would be able to write screenplays for the cinema. But I never had the opportunity, or I did not know how to find it. Now I have lost all hope of writing screenplays. He wrote screenplays for a while, when he was younger. And he has worked in a publishing house. He has written stories. He has done all the things that I have done and many others too.

He is a good mimic, and does an old countess especially well. Perhaps he could also have been an actor.

Once, in London, he sang in a theater. He was Job. He had to hire evening clothes; and there he was, in his evening clothes, in front of a kind of lectern; and he sang. He sang the words of Job; the piece called for something between speaking and singing. And I, in my box, was dying of fright. I was afraid he would get flustered, or that the trousers of his evening clothes would fall down.

He was surrounded by men in evening clothes and women in long dresses; who were the angels and devils and other characters in Job.

It was a great success, and they said that he was very good.

If I loved music I would love it passionately. But I don't understand it, and when he persuades me to go to concerts with him my mind wanders off and I think of my own affairs. Or I fall sound asleep.

I like to sing. I don't know how to sing and I sing completely out of tune; but I sing all the same—occasionally, very quietly, when I am alone. I know that I sing out of tune because others have told me so; my voice must be like the yowling of a cat. But I am not—in myself—aware of this, and singing gives me real pleasure. If he hears me he mimics me; he says that my singing is something quite separate from music, something invented by me.

When I was a child I used to yowl tunes I had made up. It was a long wailing kind of melody that brought tears to my eyes.

It doesn't matter to me that I don't understand painting or the figurative arts, but it hurts me that I don't love music, and I feel that my mind suffers from the absence of this love. But there is nothing I can do about it, I will never understand or love music. If I occasionally hear a piece of music that I like I don't know how to remember it; and how can I love something that I can't remember?

It is the words of a song that I remember. I can repeat words that I love over and over again. I repeat the tune that accompanies them too, in my own yowling fashion, and I experience a kind of happiness as I yowl.

When I am writing it seems to me that I follow a musical cadence or rhythm. Perhaps music was very close to my world, and my world could not, for whatever reason, make contact with it.

In our house there is music all day long. He keeps the radio on all day. Or plays records. Every now and again I protest a little and ask for a little silence in which to work; but he says that such beautiful music is certainly conducive to any kind of work.

He has bought an incredible number of records. He says that he owns one of the finest collections in the world.

In the morning when he is still in his dressing gown and dripping water from his bath, he turns the radio on, sits down at the typewriter and begins his strenuous, noisy, stormy day. He is superabundant in everything; he fills the bath to overflowing, and the same with the teapot and his cup of tea. He has an enormous number of shirts and ties. On the other hand he rarely buys shoes.

His mother says that as a child he was a model of order and precision; apparently once, on a rainy day, he was wearing white boots and white clothes and had to cross some muddy streams in the country—at the end of his walk he was immaculate and his clothes and boots had not one spot of mud on them. There is no trace in him of that former immaculate little boy. His clothes are always covered in stains. He has become extremely untidy.

But he scrupulously keeps all the gas bills. In drawers I find old gas bills, which he refuses to throw away, from houses we left long ago.

I also find old, shriveled Tuscan cigars, and cigarette holders made from cherry wood.

I smoke a brand of king-size, filterless cigarettes called *Stop*, and he smokes his Tuscan cigars.

I am very untidy. But as I have got older I have come to miss tidiness, and I sometimes furiously tidy up all the cupboards. I think this is because I remember my mother's tidiness. I rearrange the linen and blanket cupboards and in the summer I reline every drawer with strips of white cloth. I rarely rearrange my papers because my mother didn't write and had no papers. My tidiness and untidiness are full of complicated feelings of regret and sadness. His untidiness is triumphant. He has decided that it is proper and legitimate for a studious person like himself to have an untidy desk.

He does not help me get over my indecisiveness, or the way I hesitate before doing anything, or my sense of guilt. He tends to make fun of every tiny thing I do. If I go shopping in the market he follows me and spies on me. He makes fun of the way I shop, of the way I weigh the oranges in my hand unerringly choosing, he says, the worst in the whole market; he ridicules me for spending an hour over the shopping, buying onions at one stall, celery at another and fruit at another. Sometimes he does the shopping to show me how quickly he can do it; he unhesitatingly buys everything from one stall and then manages to get the basket delivered to the house. He doesn't buy celery because he cannot abide it.

And so—more than ever—I feel I do everything inadequately or mistakenly. But if I once find out that he has made a mistake I tell him so over and over again until he is exasperated. I can be very annoying at times.

His rages are unpredictable, and bubble over like the head on beer. My rages are unpredictable too, but his quickly disappear whereas mine leave a noisy nagging trail behind them which must be very annoying—like the complaining yowl of a cat.

Sometimes in the midst of his rage I start to cry, and instead of quieting him down and making him feel sorry for me this infuriates him all the more. He says my tears are just play-acting, and perhaps he is right. Because in the middle of my tears and his rage I am completely calm.

I never cry when I am really unhappy.

There was a time when I used to hurl plates and crockery on the floor during my rages. But not any more. Perhaps because I am older and my rages are less violent, and also because I dare not lay a finger on our plates now; we bought them one day in London, in the Portobello Road, and I am very fond of them.

The price of those plates, and of many other things we have bought, immediately underwent a substantial reduction in his memory. He likes to think he did not spend very much and that he got a bargain. I know the price of that dinner service—it was £16, but he says £12. And it is the same with the picture of King Lear that is in our dining room, and which he also bought in the Portobello Road (and then cleaned with onions and potatoes); now he says he paid a certain sum for it, but I remember that it was much more than that.

Some years ago he bought twelve bedside mats in a department store. He bought them because they were cheap, and he thought he ought to buy them; and he bought them as an argument against me because he considered me to be incapable of buying things for the house. They were made of mud-colored matting and they quickly became very unattractive; they took on a corpse-like rigidity and were hung from a wire line on the kitchen balcony, and I hated them. I used to remind him of them, as an example of bad shopping; but he would say that they had cost very little indeed, almost nothing. It was a long time before I could bring myself to throw them out—because there were so many of them, and because just as I was about to get rid of them it occurred to me that I could use them for rags. He and I both find throwing things away difficult; it must be a kind of Jewish caution in me, and the result of my extreme indecisiveness; in him it must be a defense against his impulsiveness and open-handedness.

He buys enormous quantities of bicarbonate of soda and aspirins.

Now and again he is ill with some mysterious ailment of his own; he can't explain what he feels and stays in bed for a day completely wrapped up in the sheets; nothing is visible except his beard and the tip of his red nose. Then he takes bicarbonate of soda and aspirins in doses suitable for a horse, and says that I cannot understand because I am always well, I am like those great fat strong friars who go out in the wind and in all weathers and come to no harm; he on the other hand is sensitive and delicate and suffers from mysterious ailments. Then in the evening he is better and goes into the kitchen and cooks himself tagliatelle.

When he was a young man he was slim, handsome, and finely built;

he did not have a beard but long, soft moustaches instead, and he looked like the actor Robert Donat. He was like that about twenty years ago when I first knew him, and I remember that he used to wear an elegant kind of Scottish flannel shirt. I remember that one evening he walked me back to the *pensione* where I was living; we walked together along the *Via Nazionale*. I already felt that I was very old and had been through a great deal and had made many mistakes, and he seemed a boy to me, light years away from me. I don't remember what we talked about on that evening walking along the *Via Nazionale;* nothing important, I suppose, and the idea that we would become husband and wife was light years away from me. Then we lost sight of each other, and when we met again he no longer looked like Robert Donat, but more like Balzac. When we met again he still wore his Scottish shirts but on him now they looked like garments for a polar expedition; now he had his beard and on his head he wore his ridiculous crumpled woolen hat; everything about him put you in mind of an imminent departure for the North Pole. Because, although he always feels hot, he has the habit of dressing as if he were surrounded by snow, ice, and polar bears; or he dresses like a Brazilian coffee-planter, but he always dresses differently from everyone else.

If I remind him of that walk along the *Via Nazionale* he says he remembers it, but I know he is lying and that he remembers nothing; and I sometimes ask myself if it was us, these two people, almost twenty years ago on the *Via Nazionale;* two people who conversed so politely, so urbanely, as the sun was setting; who chatted a little about everything perhaps and about nothing; two friends talking, two young intellectuals out for a walk; so young, so educated, so uninvolved, so ready to judge one another with kind impartiality; so ready to say goodbye to one another forever, as the sun set, at the corner of the street.

(translated by Dick Davis)

1970

Barbados

I don't know if there's such a thing as a "performative essay," but I know that there are texts that are more profound because of the arguments they try to demonstrate rather than merely state. In linguistics, this is called an "illocutionary action": "Thank you," "I apologize," "I now pronounce you husband and wife." They are statements that simultaneously enact the concepts they represent. Caribbean writer Kamau Brathwaite intentionally subverts the hierarchy of conventionally printed material by complicating the format in which his work is presented. Brathwaite therefore emphasizes the experience of reading his texts, encouraging us to find alternative paths into their meanings: visually, aurally, authentically participatory. This is not the year that Brathwaite writes "Trench Town Rock," his essay that critiques Bob Marley's infamous neighborhood. Instead, it's the year before Bob Marley becomes an international star. It's the year when Bob Marley gives a concert in Kingstown, saying to a reporter who doesn't know who Marley is, "If you don't got it in you, you can't let it out." The essay is an illocutionary act.

KAMAU BRATHWAITE

Trench Town Rock

1.
The
Marley
Manor Shoot/in

16 July 1990

Lass night about 2:45 well well well before the little black bell of the walk of my electronic clock cd wake me—

aweakened by gunshatt

—the eyes trying to function open too stunned to work out there through the window & into the dark with its various glints & glows: mosquito, very distant cock-crow, sound system drum, the tumbrel of a passing engine somewhere some/where in that dark. It must have been an ear/ring's earlier sound that sprawled me to the window, but it was

TWO SHATTS

—silence—

not evening the dogs barking or the trees blazing
& then a cry we couldn't see of

do
do
do

 *repetition*

nuh kill me

answeared by a volley of some

SEVEN

crack-like-firecracker-racket shats & then a soundless figure fleeing like on
air towards the right of sound perhaps towards the fence or laundry?

⌐ .
↓   Silence

The eyes like thir/sty out there in the dark & then two _males_—two
malés—high steppin through the street-lit gateway of the Marley Manor
& quickly joined by a (?wounded) lagging third. I watch them walk down
Marley's Road . . . then they begin to run . . .

10 minutes late—not later—longer—white headlights—

<<THE POLICE>>

the whole place crawling plainclothes cops

whose finger on which blind
frightened trigger of a telephone
had beckoned them?

eventually three soldiers in full battledress of olive leaves. the ariels of their walkie-talkies bending the night sky skye like breeze like bamboos . . . and like ants, it sadly seemed . . . their cars to car/casses . . .

Xcept that ants are never late as these now were too late although they came, their welcome rumbling in—so many now—*I had not thought death had undone so many*—& even then their radios were blaring out . . . three men on Hope Road armed & dangerous . . . a door kick-off at Stannpipe . . . another traffic axe . . . & all the other rapes & burns & murthers taking place all over Kingston in the kingdom of this world . . .

From down my upstairs window I cd see all this. like opposite the Marley gateway to so sudden swiftly

HELL ⟲

where just a world before there had been laughter splashing in the pool, reverb & ghetto-box, Red Stripe, bells softly sing/ing sing/ing, somebody sucking cane & shouting out dem dancehall business in the dark—if only Mr Crook wd oversee the cutting of him *bush* we wd have seen the whole court/yard, the bleak car/park & more—the stark lawns to the right ob- scured by almond leaves where I had seen the "person" running running running down that first loud waking valley of the

SHARKS

Now/at the wild white Marley gateway, there is a little matching dolly house where our "security guard"— well—*sleeps*. Seeing no light come on in there despite the shats, I wondered & was worried Might it have been him I saw there *running* out there just that while ago? . . . & only yesterday he'd been the boss in here . . .

him own gun cracking off sometimes at night & next day we wd hear the
story of how he'd almost *shat a one* . . . but now that cry & silence & my
worry for him beating in the silence, my heart like in my eyes & bandage
& beating till it hurt as if my pain was his inside my head & bondage . . .

The police had driven straight in, jumping out their cars & jeeps with
salaams & slams & semi-automatic acks, revolvers slung from belts & hol-
sters or tucked like asps into their waist-line trousers; & evvabody walkin
fass fass fass, some runnin plenty movement, their flashlights in their hands
like little ashen candles—

All Souls

As we approach the guard's dull house anxious to findout why it was not
now lit up—like it was either him out there or somewhere dead—*do do
nuh kill me*—or had he run away(?)—perhaps he hadn't even come to work
at all *on this momentous night O God help us* and what was it that Chad first
saw—like lying part-way on the curb between its whitelime border & the
grass that curved away towards that palisade where we had seen ?his shadow
fleeing—do you remember?—into this bundle of like nothing now—this
dirty clot—this empty silent clothing . . .

Was a young dreadlocks [later I was to learn that he was
known as "Early Bird"/catching his first too early worm of death that
early All Souls Mourning] **his beautiful long hair like
curled around his body making snakes like dance/
like dancing. the seven bullet holes that walked us
from our sleep all bleeding in the early morning
light. One rebok trainer some way off. as if it had
been cut off from his body in the terror. & his
hair—some of his hair—his locks—beside him—
pulled out by the very roots by some strange/some
strange strangar violence—the gunmen had been
dragging him away like that by all his loveliness.**

his body now without its bones or muscleature.
without its meat without its clutch & nomen of
a face/familiar creatures/that someone somewhere
somehow knew/that someone/somewhere loved
& because the man himself had fled out through
these leaking holes, his locks had whirled around
him as the bullets made him dance his death &
wrapped themselves around him as he fell, so now
there was this eerie beauty in the barley light. his
hair become his only perhaps comforter

Mystery killings at Apartment complex

newspaper title

As the latest wave of killings in the Corporate Area continues,
three men, including a policeman, were slain at an apartment
complex in the Kingston 6 area in the early hours of Sunday
morning. Two of them were tied with their hands behind
their backs, then shot in the head.

Residents in the area heard shots at about 2:30 a.m, and
called the police. When the Police arrived at Marley Manor
Apartments off Hope Road, they discovered the body of [but
that was later . . .]

Further investigation revealed the body of the apartment security guard inside his station, with his hands tied.
The Daily Gleaner Monday, July 16,1990, p1

Yes he was dead in there (though second not third found), the door locked in
upon him, lights not on—

now on——

he crumpled down upon his back upon the narrow
cement floor
his hands tied up behind his back
his feet like under him & also bound
the dead eyes staring
the face not even twisted by the fatal blow
a big red plop and poppy on his chest
among the hairs
still thick & softly leaking out & leaking out & leaking out
his chair half-broken with the sudden soundless blackward crash

And then with the sun coming up, right on the green
embankment underneath my window, between, in
fact, the frieze my car made with the bank, so
squeezed & un-

X- *forceful pause*

pected there that no police had seen it with their candles, was a third: blue jeans, chest naked, hands
bound behind his back with

TWO DISHCLOTHS

— for goodness sake—
taken no doubt from the Marley Manor clothesline—

with the sun coming up coming up coming up the
police ask—no—order me—abrupt & violent as any
crime—to roll my cyar away & then they rolled him

over like a stone & from the stain of dark green blood
upon our grass & sepulchre & untied his dishcloth
hands behind his back and let his arms fall
free—

**a police—big, dark, meaty guy whose job, it seems,
was checking on security at MMA
But I can't tell you what he looked like: features,
the human face, I mean: both eyes shot out/stabbed
in, his nose unhinged, a huge gash in the right side
of the throat, his tongue there black & smooth &
half-leaf out his face as if he'd
strangled also
yet all his skin & flesh still firm & natural
like if he flash & living still & not a ant or insect
coming even near his blood & no one say a
prayer—at least out loud—nor paused—**

O Sodom & Gomorrah—

**nor raised a hum or hymn for anyone—for anyone
of us—that night/that early morning sun/day**

**And by the two o'clock midday TV news my poor
blue cyar** the same "poor cyar" that wd some nine weeks later (see
below) be stolen from me from this same sad place. at this same level time
of gunpoint dawn & I wd think aloud that it was grey—the color of the
light inside me on that morn **was on "the air" as if it/self had
carried out the crime & all day long there was this
trek of visits to "the scene"**

**click/click
gape/gossip
even though the**

bodies & their silence of potato sacks had long been thrown into the dark blue police vans. the dark blood hosed away . . .

This the **309th** dead by gunshot in **6½** months in Kingston in the king-doom of this world on 15 Aug 90 the Police High Command, having said a few weeks earlier that "Crime was under control," announced that since the begrinning of the year, there had been some 3000 crimes recorded in Jamaica—how many many not!—inc 357 murders

creepy

Last night's tv glimpsed us a picture of the Spanish Town morgue where children's bodies were piled up like at Belsen or Auschwitz. The object of this particular xercise was to show us the bodies of two children murdered in their home while their mother was at Church last Sunday ?night (12 Aug 90). Brother & sister, aged 8 and 10 & naked in the picture to the bone, had been stabbed 25 times/each—But no—the newspaper report (17 Aug 90) is much more boggling. The boy, Darian, was actually 18 (not 8) years old & he was stabbed—by ice-pick—not 25 but 70. His sister, Allecia, 140 times . . .

17 Aug is Marcus Garvey Birthday

the same day (1983) that poet Mikey Smith was stoned
to death on Stony Hill

By the end of October 1990

622
Violent Deaths

"More than 620 people died violently up to the end of October, making this the most violent year since 1980 [when 889 people died violently in that Election year].

"Figures compiled from police reports show that a total of 622 people were shot, stabbed with a knife or icepick, hacked to death with a machete, or bludgeoned with a blunt instrument. Murders totalled 469—242 persons were killed by guns and 109 by knives.

"In addition to the murders, 153 fatal shootings have been recorded in the year's first 10 months: 133 by police, 20 by civilians . . .

"If the average of almost 47 murders per month continues, the country could record a total over 550 murders by the end of December. [The two months June & July—the 'Independence holiday season'—totalled a high of 167 murders, because a/c to Dep Police Commissioner Bertram Millwood i/c of Crime, of the "existing high spirits and criminals' need for more spending money during the approaching Independence holiday season"]

"Millwood added that the lifting of the Suppression of Crime Act in May in Kingston, St Andrew and St Catherine, coupled with a period of feuding between rival gangs and fighting for leadership among gang members, may also have contributed to the two-month spurt."
The Sunday Gleaner, Gordon C Williams 11 Nov 1990, p1

in addition
there are an equal number of/if not more violent
deaths on the road—inc 229 children killed

at noon 10 Dec 90 JBC TV announced fatality no
375

—not to mention all the physical & psychological
damage & maiming—

+

one rape every 8 hours: 1000+ reported cases of
abuse & rape last year 44 reported cases of incest
all in a population just barely 2.3+ million

+

"Early Bird"
buried

Hundreds of Matthews Lane community members, including relatives, close friends and curious
onlookers, turned out to say their
last farewell to
Glenford St Joseph Phipps
"Early Bird"
on Wednesday at the
All Saints Church, West Street, Kingston.

Bird, a former supervisor at
Metropolitan Parks and Markets (MPM)
and "a godfather" to many
in the Matthews Lane community
in downtown Kingston,
was paid
glowing tributes at the service,
which saw a wide cross-section of
well-known people in attendance.

A close relative of Bird who
resides overseas, called on members of the congregation to

dismiss the idea of "revenge." He
quoted a line from the scripture:
"A soft answer turneth away
wrath, but grievous words stirreth
anger."

"We miss you, we love you,"
he cried. "My friends, death ends
life, but not a relationship."

Bird's brother, Kevin,
described him as a man
who lived a "moral life" of principles, a courageous soldier, and
one who always cried peace.

He said that Bird was a person
who always sought to "defuse
tension, rather than add to it."

Greta Robinson,
general manager of MPM who worked
closely with Bird, described him
as "a special person to all of us, a
brother and a son who was
always there when everybody
was in need of help."

Bird was inspirational in
setting up the Matthews United
Basic School, later changed to
Bird's name (in memory of him).
The church was filled to capacity
and family members and
friends were overcome with grief
at different stages of the service . . .

Bird is survived by mother, Sunshine,
nine children,
six brothers, three sisters
and a host of other relatives.

Phipps was shot and killed
on Sunday July 15, when gunmen
invaded his Marley Manor apartment.
He was found dead in the
driveway, with bullet wounds to
the head. A security guard and a
policeman were also killed in the attack.
The Jamaica Record, Fri 27 July, 1990

**This clipping
was sent to a friend of mine in
London
It was send by a friend (?) of mine in Jamaica
a poet & a writer!
who knew/who knows that I was/am
(?) living here
& therefore possibly in danger of dying here
that fatal foreday morning**

**Yet in that covering letter
w/ the clip. the clipping
there is no. not a single reference
to me. my presence
myself in danger possibly
no flick or feather of concern**

**So that these crimes we *all* embrace
the victim & the violate
the duppy & the gunman
so close on these plantations still
so intimate
the dead/undead**

2.
Straight
Talk

19 July 1990

ttortt

When last did you see your Father?

P**olice reports state that 120 persons were detained and I have a list ere in front of me, Mr Perkins, where one undred an *two* of the undread & twenty persons that were detained**

Perkins: Yes

— **came from the Rema area alone**

Perkins: Yes

— **Now I doan know what sort a operation dat is**

[This is the JLP Councillor & Caretaker for the Rema area of West Kingston speaking to Wilmot (Motty/Mutty) Perkins, the host of the KLAS FM/Manchester (Jamaica) radio talk show, *Straight Talk,* on the midday of 19 July 90

But despite all a dat, Mr Perkins, despite de/despite de/de/de/de detention of de people Mr Perkins, I want to make it clear, Mr Perkins, that we are not against raids & search & curfew to stem the gun voiolence, we are not against it; what we are against, Mr Perkins, is the attitude of the Military towards individual there yesterday and I'm going to tell you some of the things that took place there yesterday

[Meanwhile on TV, young Tivoli women speak in loud quarrelling voices of the rat-foot soldiers—the *rat patrol soldiers*—dat *come up in ere* shooting & abusin people; one dahta tells the camera how she was juss comin back from the supermarket with she ten-month baby when the shooting star & she was *so fraid* she like she *tun fool* & run pass she mudda ouse & buck up inna smaddy else yord & the baby it im ead before she study <steady> sheself & fine out wha gwaan]

When the men were taken from their ouses, Mr Perkins . . . they were axed to drape each other in their pants waist

Perkins: Yes—

—   **You box me, I box you; I kiss you, you kiss me**

Perkins: Kiss?

—   **Kiss, Mr Perkins. Kiss like ow a man kiss/a woman. The soldiers/instruct/the men/tokiss/each other**

Perkins: You saw this happening?

—   **This is a fac, Mr Perkins**

Perkins: I'm asking—

—   **Mr Perkins—**

Perkins: I'm asking you—

—   **Mr—**

Perkins: Hold on!

—   **Mr Perkins—**

Perkins: Who says—

—   **I did not see it with my own two eyes, Mr. Perkins, but the—**

Perkins: Hold—

—   **persons oou were *victims* of it, Mr Perkins, I spoke with one such person lass night and that person is prepared to come out an say it. I have a *number* of statements here in front of me—**

Perkins: Uhuh

—   **Not only the kissing alone, Mr Perkins. They were axed, Mr Perkins, the men were axed to rub up themselves on each other**

Perkins: No Mr—

—   **No no Mr Perkins, this is not a *joke,* Mr Perkins**

Perkins: **Mr McKenzie!**   *bold switches*

McKenzie: Yes sir

Perkins: **Hold on likkle bit now.** [Pause]. **Now: I remember hearing stories like these, coming, as it happened, from the other side, because in those days in 1980**

McKenzie: Yes

Perkins: **it was held that the police & soldiers had turned
           against the then Government, right?**

McKenzie: Yes

Perkins: **as we were coming to the elections and I heard
           allegations like these**

McKenzie: Yes

Perkins: **made on JBC radio & television—**

McKenzie: Yes

Perkins: **against the—which was then—as Mr Seaga described
           it—a PNP cesspool**

McKenzie: Yes

Perkins: **I heard stories like these—**

McKenzie: Yes—

Perkins: **being told against the soldiers in that year, right?
           Nothing ever came of it, nobody ever did anything
           about it, nobody ever preferred any allegations in
           any formal way about it**

McKenzie: Yes—

Perkins: **I now hear it coming from the *other political* side—**

McKenzie: **Well this is not a political sityation now, Mr. Perkins**

Perkins: Now hold on—

McK: **Mr Perkins, this—what I am saying to you now—**

Perkins: I have to be very skeptical about stories like this

McK: **Mr Perkins! Mr Perkins! There's *nutten* to be skeptical about . . . Mr Perkins, there is one report here I ave in front of me, where the men were axed to lie down in the grass, eat the dry grass, some were forced to eat plastic bag, and some were forced to eat—ah—faeces—dog faeces. This is not a jokin matter, Mr Perkins**

P: No—Mr McKenzie—

[Perkins had in fact retailed a similar story just before McKenzie phoned]

McK: **Mr Perkins, Mr Perkins, I doan call you all de way from Kingston** [KLAS, remember, originates in Mandeville] **to score cheap political points; that is not what I call you about**

P: **No Mr McKenzie. Mr/Mr/Mr** [pause] **McKenzie**

McK: Yes sah

P: **I think—you know—I wonder—whether what should happen, is that the political representatives from these areas should not make an attempt to be present—who/who is the MP for/for/for this—for that—area at the moment?**

McK: Minister Jones, Bobby Jones . . .

[an earlier caller when asked this Q had said that there was no MP for the area & Perkins had told her that that was because she was JLP and was not recognizing the PNP MP]

P:

Bobby Jones . . . I wonder whether Mr. Bobby Jones should not have been making/or whether the MPs in the particular area, should not be making an attempt to be present when these operations are going on—just to observe, just to observe—and to be able to go—

[Perkins' point is that the MPs and the political reps and the Press shd be present during these searches—not interfering— but being eye-witnesses and referees to what was going on, so that cases of brutality, if such they were, wd be observed, monitored & officially/publicly reported etc. That the Press shd find ways to "get in there" & do their work, despite the reported abuse & smashing of cameras by soldiers; and that the soldiers were in any case acting illegally in searching and detaining people in view of the repeal of the Suppression of Crimes Act just a few weeks ago—a repeal, some people say, which is responsible for the flare up of violence in the "Inner City" areas such as Tivoli, Rema, Fletcher's Land [and now/1 August 90] West Road & Matches Lane etc/to such a degree that the Suppression of Crimes Act has been RE/INTRODUCED for a period of 30 days] and attorney at law and Human Rights activist, Dennis Daley had come on *Straight Talk* and declared that all present and indeed past police action in detaining people (from "the deprived areas") was illegal and that he wished that somebody wd bring a court action against the Security Forces for this and not long after, on the 6pm News, we heard that Mr Seaga was doing just that—a Court action against the Attorney General and the Commissioner of Police and Brig Gen Neish]. McKENZIE COUNTERED WITH . . .

McK:

Well . . . I wear two caps as I speak to you. I'm the Councillor for Tivoli and the JLP Caretaker for that constituency. When Tivoli Gardens was cordon on Monday, I came down, I went to the soldier, I was very polite, I identified myself an/an e told me in a very polite but a forceful manner dat you/you cannot enter into the area! So regardless of your status, Mr Perkins—

P:

Yes

McK: **the treatment dat dey are anding out to people dere—**

P: Yes

McK: **Ah/I was dere when they assaulted de/de *Record* reporter—**

P: Yes

McK: **I saw it on Darling Street, an dat was not fictitious, it was a fac—**

P: You saw it happen?

McK: **Yes! I saw it!**

[The day before Motty had dedicated nearly his whole programme to fulminating against this incident; he even had Brig General Neish and the Commissioner of Police on the line to answer questions . . . though neither of them, "up the news time," as it were, had been officially informed of the incident but admitted that if it had happened as reported, that it was reprehensible and punishable—Motty wanted to know if the soldiers wd be court-martialled & they said they wd certainly look into it and act if necessary as quickly as possible]

McK: **It was a fact!** [Pause]. **And the point I'm making to you now, Mr Perkins is that the incidents that took place in Rema—I thought the people in Tivoli Gardens during that curfew on Monday was treated badly, but what was dun to de people in REMA yesterday M/M/ Mr Perkin, is beyonn a all—no human be'en, Mr. Perkins deserve to be treated in dat way and a want to take you back, Mr. Perkins, to 1976, Mr. Perkin when those very same people, Mr. Perkins, were victims of invasions where they furnitures, their/ their personal property was destroyed and they were thrown out of doors in 1976, Mr Perkins.**

Mr Perkins, what took place there yesterday is a total/disgrace and/and Mr Perkins, there is no way you can pinpoint a soldier to say dat dis is de soldier dat did it because the soldiers doan carry numbers! The soldiers doan carry anyting dat you can i/dentify dem to say dat dis is de man oou/oou did it! M/M Mr Perkins, what I am saying to you is not fictitious, it is not done to score political points, it is someting dat took place, I am speaking about REALITY, someting dat took place yesterday

[Perkins now (his voice calm & assured) repeats (develops) his point about Police/Soldier illegality, the need to have the Press present regardless, and above all for MPs to be present—not to interfere—but so that they cd OBSERVE & report what was happening back to Parliament /which is "the body responsible" and he didn't think that any soldier had the RIGHT to go and interfere with any Parliamentarian . . .]

Perkins: **I don't think that the soldiers & police cd have any right to exclude a parliamentarian from there, I am not say—**

[At this point, McKenzie interrupts with]

McK: **Well Mr Perkins I don't think that that sorta privilege has been afforded to anybody—**

P: [getting xcited] **No! is not a matter—No No No No!— Hole on likkle bit!—No! Mr/ Mr/Mr McKenzie doan tell me *rubbish*—**

McK: But Mr Perkins—

P: **Hole on a minit—**

McK: Mr—

font reflecting their voices

P: **BUT HOLE ON!**

McK: But Mr Perkins—

P: **YOU HOLE ON A—**

McK: Mr Perkins—

Perkins: [louder & louder]

Mr McKenzie, you lissen to me!

McK: Mr Perkins, dat sort a—

Perkins: **Mr McKenzie, you lissen to me!**

McK: If/if in my office—

P: [sucking his teeth and pretty close to apoplexy now]

O lissen to me or/or we stop this conversation!

McK: Go ahead, go ahead

P: **Parliament makes the laws in this country . . .**

Conversation ends with this bittle classic

McK: There is a youngster in custody from Monday—an I
          wan' you to unnerstann ow far dis ting go, you know
          Mr. Perkins. We ave a patient—e is asthmatic. Is name
          is Andrew Williams. E was taken out of is sick bed on
          Monday by the military & the police & e was taken
          away. Is mother was able to fine im lass night at the
          Alf Way Tree Police Station

P: Yes

McK: When she went in, she brought some tablets for im.
          The police say e cyaan get the tablets, doctor ave to
          approve the tablet before im can get it An when they
          finally decide to release the fellow, when e was coming
          out, a Superintendent Howell said to im—

"Where Jim Brown ide im gun?"

Lester Lloyd Coke, alias Jim Brown (also "Jim," "Big Man"[he was], "Dads,"
"Bomber," "Don") of the gold-colored Mercedes Benz (*Sun Gleaner*, 15 March
92, p3A) "identified as a co-leader of [the] notorious [Miami-based] Shower
Posse crime gang, has been in custody [in the General Penitentiary]
awaiting extradition to the US to face murder charges" (*Ja Record* Sun
Feb 9,1992, p2A) [his partner, "Storyteller" Morrison, held for the same charges at
the same time, was "accidentally"/ "prematurely" sent back to the States & protests,
pleas, diplomatic & court actions failed to budge the Americans] is apparently the
present ruling *The-harder-they-come* Rhygin of the Corporate area, reputed
gunman & political activist & "Don Gorgon" wanted in the US on
various charges & ?finally captured (1991) in Kingston in a paramilitary
SEARCH+DESTROY ("Rat Patrol") OPERATION & is in police custody
(some say "custardy") here awaiting xtradition . . . But the word on the street
is that **if dem deport Jim Brown to Amerika, Kingston go bun dung**

flat flat flat like a flat cake inna Bandung & that a lot of the recent violence [July-Aug 90], inc that in the Coronation Market (& prob at MM) is connect w/ this

On 2 March 1992, JIM BROWN, about a week after his son Jah T was guNNED down on IM MOTOBIKE ON MAXWELL AVE in broad daylight (1 Feb 92)/d 2 Feb 92 & **400 WAS FE DEAD FE DAT** & the carnAGE had started—some 14 dead or injured—Brown was found "incinerated" (some reports say DEAD FROM "SMOKE INHILATION") in IM "CUSTARDY"

> A NUMBER of vendors in the CORONATION MARKET have complained to the *Gleaner* of being robbed of thousands of dollars at gunpoint on Saturday when, they said, over 30 gunmen from Tivoli Gardens invaded the place Higglers along Barry Street and other market streets in West Kingston have also claimed they, too, were robbed by the gunmen. **"At one time dem hol' up 20 woman and when dem no tek off dem apron fass enough dem cut dem off."**
> [*Daily Gleaner*, 21 July 1990, p17]

Information reaching *The Jamaica Record* is that men were "moving around" yesterday warning vendors that they should clear the streets. A source told our newsroom that

"there is expected to be war tonight," "there will be a lot of gunshots"

our source said.

By August 1/Emancipation Day 1990, parts of west/downtown Kingston were in fact "locked down": daylight gunfire, banks, stores closed, no vendors on the street . . . While in Trinidad, Imam Yassim Abu Bakr's 100+

Black Muslims (Jamaat al-Muslimeen) were holding the Prime MInister of Trinidad & Tobago and some 42 other Parliamentarians & others hostage— Fri July 27—Wed 1 August—that same Emancipation Day that Iraq's Muslim President Saddam Hussein did what Abu Bakr failed to do when he stormed & overthrew the Royal Government of Kuwait "in response to a popular uprising"—the consequences of this being yet another story . . .

"A visit to Spanish Town Road and its environs by our newsteam yesterday confirmed that some of the vendors were clearing the streets. This was at 4:30 pm yesterday afternoon. One vendor when asked why there was a hurry to leave the streets, said

"Gunmen a go shoot up the place."

Vendors were reluctant to speak to our newsteam. As one vendor put it,

"The gunman dem might a lissen to what we a say."

Unconfirmed reports are that gunmen **have about four youts** in their custody and that **[they] are expected to face a fate similar to the three youths . . . found dead on West Street yesterday . . .**

The bloodied bodies of Ricardo Saunders, 15, of 21 Foster Lane, Oniel Sewell, 18, of 11 Gold Street, and an unidentified youth known only as "Blacka" were found [yesterday morning] on a handcart on [Matches Lane], West Street near to the Redemption Market: all had gunshot wounds to the heads . . ."
[*Ja Record* 31 July 1990, p3]

—Don Gorgon's people trying to bring the country to ransom, as it were, in xchange for his body of freedom . . . and all this coevil, as it were, with the JAG SMITH CASE—the former (JLP) Minister of Labor & at the moment (July 90) still Opposition Senator (his seat was not given up until mid 1991) on public trial for—and the day after this conversation found guilty of—appropriating hundreds of thousands of dollars ($J490,000) from the "poor-people" US & Canadian Farm-Workers Program into him own pocket in the form of cash, cars, property & gifts for friends & family and sentenced to 5 years hard labor

> "This man is a former Minister of Government [from a famous
> father & family], a person who was viewed as an ambassador for
> the country and for many years a man of integrity, a person
> who we as Jamaicans looked to for leadership and guidance."
> Now guilty not of need but xcessive greed & "displaying
> a reprehensible contempt for his colleagues, his Party, his
> forebears and his country . . ."

McK: **an de man seh, *"Sir, whatcha axin meh, I doan know dem sort a ting, so wha kind a foolishness yu axin meh"* an you know wha happen Mr Perkins?**

P: Alright, okay

McK: **The Superintendent of Police—**

P: OK, hold on—

McK: **The Superintendent of Police—**

P: Mr McKenzie, I don't want you to make any allegations against the Superintendent of—

McK: **No, is not allegations! is not an allegation, Mr Perkins**

P: Okay

McK: **When e said e didn't know** [this is the same asthmatic Andrew Williams] **e was ordered back in the cell an e was told**

One more night in custody might refresh your memory ["Where Jim Brown ide im gun?"] So tomorrow morning yu mother can come back fe yow . . .

*transcribed the above interview from tape of radio programme cited. Wrote Mr Perkins for permish to reproduce it here; after sev months silence, phoned Motty at KLAS/FM/ Mandeville who generously gave GO AHEAD

DG of 16 May 1992 carries photo of Mr McKenzie, surrounded by concerned JLP leaders, lying on Hospital bed or slab of white after receiving what the Report said was "a severe beating from unnamed 'political opponents.' The Police & JLP were "investigating."

3. Kingstonin the "kingdomof this world"

Sept 1990

the wind blows on the hillside
　　　and i suffer the little children
i remember the lilies of the field
　　　the fish swim in their shoals of silence
our flung nets are high wet clouds drifting

with this reed i make music
with this pen i remember the word
with these lips i can remember the beginning of the
world

between these bars is this sudden lock-up
　　　where there is only the darkness of dog-bark

        where i cannot make windmills of my hands
        where i cannot run down the hill-path of faith
        where i cannot suffer the little children

a man may have marched with armies
        he may have crossed the jordan and the red sea
        he may have stoned down the wells of jericho

here where the frogs creak where there is only the croak
of starlight

he is reduced
he is reduced
he is reduced

                            to a bundle of rags/a broken
                                    stick
                        that will never whistle through
                                fingerstops into the music
                                    of flutes
                        that will never fling nets/white
                                    sails crossing

gospel was a great wind freedom of savannas
gospel was a great mouth telling thunder of heroes
gospel was a cool touch warm with the sunlight like

                            water in claypots, healing
                                this reduction wilts the flower
                                weakens the water
                                    coarsens the lips

                            fists at the bars, shake rattle &
                            hammer at the locks

                                suffer the little children
                                suffer the rose gardens

* lots of repetition
* like poetry

                              suffer the dark clouds
                              howling for bread
                              suffer the dead fish pois-
                                  oned in the lake

my authority was sunlight; the man who arose from
         the dead called me saviour
         his eyes had known moons
         older than jupiters
my authority was windmills. choirs singing of the
flowers of rivers

your authority is these chains that strangle my wrists
your authority is the red whip that circles my head
your authority is the white eye of interrogator's
         terror. siren price fix the law of undarkness
         he dreadness of the avalanches of unjudgement

it is you who roll down boulders when I say word
it is you who cry wolf when I offer the peace
         of wood doves
it is you who offer up the silence of dead leaves

         i would call out but the guards do not listen
         i would call out but the dew out there on the
                  grass cannot glisten
         i would call out but my lost children
                  cannot unshackle their shadows of silver

                         here i am reduced
                                 to this hole of my head
                         where i cannot cut wood
                                 where i cannot eat bread
                         where i cannot break fish
                                 with the multitudes

my authority was foot-stamp upon the ground
      the curves the palms the dancers
my authority was nyambura inching closer
      embroideries of fingers, silver earrings balancers

                      but i am reduced
                        i am reduced
                        i am reduced

                      to these black eyes
                      this beaten face
                      these bleach-
                      ing lips blear-
                      ing obscenities
              i am reduced
              i am reduced
              i am reduced
                   to this damp
                   to this dark
                   to this driven
                   rag
                              awaiting
                       the water of sun/light
                              awaiting
                the lilies to spring up out of the iron
                              awaiting
                  your eyes o my little children

                              awaiting

4.
My turn

Foreday morning
Wednesday, October 24 1990

Get back here safe [from Bdos] only to run into a two-gunman break-in (actually one gun/one knife—one of my sharpest kitchen knives is missing . . . /**& were they more outside? lookhouts, get-away or back-up drivers, duppies, warriors, drones?**]) at my Marley Manor apartment in the early hours of Wednesday morning (Oct 24)—the same apartment complex where only 90 days ago there was a posse shoot-in in which 3 persons murthered (Trench Town Rock) and now I find myself in the position of those dead bodies: hands tied behind my back, feet x'd & bound, a wire round my neck! In the earlier case they used dishcloths, you may recall, from the Marley Manor clothesline since that was then an outside (al fresco) job. This time (inside) they used my telephone xtension chord; although it seems they used a **dishcloth** also: one that had fallen from my balcony (which they had entered my rooms from).

Last time—remember?—they used dishcloths to tie the "moonlight" police up before they killed him. This time they used the cloth **to shit in**—at least that's the only xplanation for what we found next day upon the ground half-hid in flower-beds beneath the balcony: the whole thing wrapped up like a patty!

Dem gone with my **cyar** 2 colour **tvs** (the remote one the property of Marley Manor/but they had tief my own new new Remote that I had brought from Yale, from Barbican), the huge (ole fashion now) **IBM selectrix** that Mexican had type *Creole Society* on at Mecklenburgh Sq in London, **her wedding ring** from off my coward finger (the gunman whispered is dis GOLE?)—she gave me that in Georgetown 30 yrs ago. I never took it off; they almost broke it off; a **cassette/radio**, too many **tapes** (inc copy of my Bruce St John "In Tribute" lecture & many of the H201 lectures that Chad had taped last year), a baby **calculator** from Air France (to Senegal), 4 **swatches**, 2 **torch lights** (one a very fancy one Kayiga wife helped me to buy at Harvard when I was coming back post-Gilbert), **binoculars** (I'd always wanted, like the one(s) at Round House), **money** too too much **money**, **telephone**, even 2 haffs of valium (they even went into my toilet bog) & at one time I thought they took my (only pair!) of **glasses**

ENTIRE little submarine is CHURNED up by the gunmen lookin money whe de money deh bwoy gimme de money bwoy) *& whatever else to cum & tek away. They come in thru a flimsy ungrilled deregulated balcon door (ply wood & glass with bolts no bigger than small safety* *pins at top of same said door). Had spoken to the Marley Manor Man/agement in vain about security. After the horse had bolted, as it were, they put on (two) large (larger) bolts: one at the top, one at the bottom of one side only of the two-leaf door. If they had SHOOT me as one of them had wisp* me

jess waaan **kill** *smaddy twnite. It* **sweet** *me*

shoott you bwoy **I wd have bleed to death upon that bed**

& been in there alone perhaps for days before Chad come to find me only in her dream . . .

on this night of heavy intermittent rain & power cuts, had turned in early underneath the thunder. about 4:30—MM killing time—hear something wake me with a sense of like a door been open in the sitting room and like a

ANAMAL

was sniffing round. out there. glasses, torchlight, check this out. at bedroom door I see the sky/light—yes—door open—wha!—and then out of that dark room, a shove, obscenities, the metal thing with its round hole of death first hit me in the forehead, spin me round, pushing me back into the bedroom with a tense voice whispering like quiet bwoy (down rover down) or we going **shoot** yu claat to rass: push shove gunbutt onto my only bed. face down my pillow pressed upon my only head: cuffs, gunbutts, tuffs at my locks etc &whe de money, bwoy; & (more urgent) whe de money deh; and later, dese yu cyar keys? & an xplanation (!) that deni needed it (the cyar) for going on a mission & that when dem finish, dem wd PHONE—(gimme de numba hey—what

POWA

in dat gun—& TELL yu whe to pick it up again

that voice, as I write to you now & replay it & replay it once again, was MIDDLECLASS not ghetto stereotype. Despite the glot & argot style, it was the voice of someone who (why not?) had spent some clear-tongued years in a "good" (secondary?) school (like) **"we have information that yu have money here . . ."**

*but then I never see the voice of either face xcept just briefly once—too briefly
to remember—& when I also see the knife (my kitchen knife? one of the stainless steel
meat-cutting set I get as brahta from the Coop in Harvard Sq?) which they now use to
cut my t-phone wire so they cd tie me hand & foot & neck—like if they going
to heng or strangle me—& stiff some claat inside me mouth —the Marley
Man—or Xecution Style—"now yu goin know how it will feel when we go*

shoot

*yu bwoy" and all this time my bright ears hearing like the rape of what was
once my room: swishes & billows & clatterings down & then again & again
somebody wd sit on the bed near my head with the hard & hot & cold of the
gun at the back of my neck the other hand drowning me into the blackwater
dark of the mattrass & whispering whispering* **whe de money deh bwoy & yu
goin sorry yu nevva tell we whe de money deh bwoy** *and when they had
done—when they had gone—suit-cases piled pillaged all over the place—my
room like the sea—the debris & litter all over the beaches—bibliography files
& my poetry manuscript folders all trampled & curled by the breakers—books
hit by like a hurricane—what more can I tell you?—clothes torn from their
hooks & their shoulders—my life like torn from its moorings & something like
spiders crawling over my faces . . .*

*and outside in the very normal dawnlight, not only the security guard no
doubt sleepin safe (three months before don't forget he was cut up like meat in his
"station") but OUR MAN VICTOR tell the police he had seen them running
down the steps from my flat (I mean with the tvs & ting?) & even pushin my cyar
out de yard since it doan start early a mornin these days & in fac one of them
COME BACK UP when I thought they had gone, to ax me which key open up
the door & VICTOR say that he see them hearsin my cyar away & thought, e
say, (I hear im tell the Police) they was my own*

MECKANICS

*is only when I got myself like free—had shuffled off the mortal coils of all the
chords & wires & reached the bathroom window of my dreams to shout out
FREEDOM to my neighbor—my wrists & ankles sullen swollen buked &*

abused & brazed for weeks to come—did Mr V come knock knock knocking on my door (the GUARD dem seh was SLEEPIN!) & one month after these events, one month & more of letters letters letters phonecalls all in a vain attempt to see the Chairman Person Owner Manor Manger Manager did me receive (19 Nov 90) a "deep" & hand-delivered missile of "concern" informing me that if I continue to feel threat at MMA, I "should" (I quote) "look into the possibility of alternate [sic] accomodation [sic]"

5.
Short
History
of Dis

or

Middle
Passages
Today

Events that I here chronicle personwise or foolish cd have been recorded in various degrees—some less intense, some as you know far far more so—for other Caribbean countries & beyond. See Achebe, see Soyinka, see Biko, see Jackson, see Morislav Holub, see the *Diary of Anna Frank,* see Sun Yet Sun, see all the Disappeared of S America—*see see see until yu bline*

I remember Wilson Harris Mona 1968 on the eve of Black Power & Genet's **Blacks** departing from "the green academy" of our campus with the "smell *of carrion*" on his lips. I recall the night in 1975 when Brazil's conquering Santos came here to play before the hungry for them thousands at the Stadium. Pelé had scored a goal *olé* and all our world erupted. A young boy/man ran through the metal cordon of police—STATE OF EMERGENCY—and reached the maestro. Cheers

Going back. warm spille/ing all around his face. is knocked down by pursuit police onto the winning ground. A brown belt Superintendent of Police no less then kicks him in the face then kicks again to riff before the hundred thousand hungry live & tv eyes. It was Pelé who threw himself between the yout & that last brutal blow & hugged him to him. so

Another year, a gunshot, man bleeding. dead. face down in gutter right outside Tom Redcam's Public Libe. Shot by a Supercop or plainclothes JDF in pain broad daylight. And the police who came to "pick him up"— he never bother stoop down to the brother. stood there & kicked my head until he bashed it in. until the kicking turned my body over. And no one in that lover crowd—like Pelé, MMA, / *cover the waterfront*—said anything said anything said anything Soon after that. news of another & another robbery with v.

another dead, another woman raped inside her house outside her house along the roadside going home from supermart from dancehall club from church from school. one poet friend of mine raped on the highway near the great greenheart traffic lights. another stoned to death on Stony Hill

The grills go up. the old nightwatchmen disappear. Welcome the red-tooth dog. the squat-face bodyguard. Those with good sense walk with their sawn-off shotguns. M16s & AK48s enter the rapidly declining currency of grace & courtesy. No Natty Dread but Natty Morgan hero of the nineteen-ninety-ninety-ones. Orlando Patto's Dungle of the 60s Sisyphus become the Riverton City (Kingston) Dump of 1992: an image of a city smouldering in garbage. & men & woman plundering that monstrous HELL of stench & detritus & death. dead rat. live rat. for bread. bone. dead rotting flesh. dead rotting fish. the

decomposing contexts of yr kitchen sink & toilet bowl & latrine & what you sweep off from yr floor & doormat tabletop in greasy paper plastic bags

into that Dump goes the dead body of one University lecture & his woman frenn. profane cremation of the silence that surrounds that loss that no one hardly notices. The University itself says nothing since I suppose they'll say they DO NOT KNOW. They DO NOT KNOW who pays his salary or if his widow (is she?) gets his prison pension. His contract I suspect "frustrated"/like Walter Rodney's was. And like the victims of our first (that 18th century) Middle Pass. no memory of no mourning for this passage

Bad Memories of
or the half-
hazard birthing of Caliban

Jubilee

Tonia Byfield [herself an "inmate" of the Jubilee Maternity Hospital] . . . said she witnessed some mothers undergoing painful experiences. One mother was ordered to go into the waiting room and sit there until the nurse attended to her. The baby's head appeared as the mother moaned. The nurses ignored her and she had to run to the delivery room with the baby head between her legs. Another mother, who had been in labour, said she went for a nurse on hearing the cry of [another] mother that [her] baby was on the way. She said the nurse merely said **"mek she stay down there an bawl."** *SG* Nov 3, 1991

Human scavengers loot death car

By Claire Clarke
S Gleaner, 31 Mar 1991

With tracks of blood and brain marrow trailed around the site, a woman in the crowd excitedly captured a tube of lipstick from the wreckage. This young woman had also located a shoe saying, *"Mi like it, but mi nuh know whey de nex one dey."* Scanning the scene, she realized that the other foot was still inside the contorted machine of death; she attempted to close in and capture her prize, but the police intercepted, so for the time being she let it be.

This was not a scene from a movie showing the depravity of the human condition, rather it was the scene of the GOOD FRIDAY NIGHT CAR ACCIDENT ALONG THE SP Tn ROAD IN Kgn which left two people dead.

The accident, which took place in the vicinity of the RIVERTON CITY DUMP, at approx 7:00 pm, attracted a crowd of curious and excited onlookers.

Human scavengers were quick to take what they cd from the twisted wreckage. By the time the SG team arrived . . . two tyres had already been removed from the vehicle.

Inside the car, no personal belongings were in sight save a lone ten cent . . . on the back seat. This too was removed.

[Professor] Aubrey Eraser [former Head of the Norman Manley Law School, UWI, Mona & prominent Caribbean legal luminary] was found dead in bed with his throat cut at his home in Jack's Hill, St Andrew, on the night of Nov 29 1988. The autopsy showed he had multiple [i.e 22] stab wounds to the neck, chest and behind the left ear and he had been bashed on the back of the head with the heavy procelain [sic] cover of a toilet tank

22

DG 12 Apr 91, p2
[By Dec 91, Eraser's wife & two of his chn were being charged w/his murder]

Shame of May
Pen Cemetery
"Gone to the bones"

On Wednesday, on the second visit in a few days, a *Sunday Gleaner* team found the skeleton of a man who seemed to have been buried years ago. The skeletal remains were dressed in a pair of socks and blue pants. All that remained of him were the bones scattered on the ground nearby and the bones which remained inside his socks. The casket in which he was laid to rest was nowhere to be seen . . .

One mausoleum belonging to the late Bishop Mary Louise Coore stood as an old derelict structure. The concrete pillars supporting the roof had been crudely chopped into, the grilles dug out and the steel stolen leaving a mass of rubble and garbage on top of the grave . . .

On one visit by the team, smoke was seen spreading across the afternoon sky in the cemetery. On investigation, a large coal kiln was seen burning on top of a grave. Wood, presumably from the many trees in the cemetery, is cut, laid out on top and then sand is heaped over it, with the appropriate vent for lighting to produce firewood coal. Two other kilns, already "drawn," were built on other graves in this section. The coal burner, however, was nowhere to be seen . . .

This reporter [Misha Lobban] on Tuesday witnessed the theft of three goats that were tethered in an overgrown section of the cemetery. The lone robber escaped with them across the train line. The sorrowing owner, Joseph Williams, 81, who lives in Trench Town, stood helpless looking in the direction in which the thief had disappeared. He said the goats were valued at $1000.

Sun Gleaner 10 Nov 91

Chopping off
Peoples Dreams

A WOMAN WHO STEPPED FROM A BUS IN THE PARADE
AREA, DOWNTOWN KINGSTON, LOST AN ARM AND
BRACELET TO ONE OF TWO MEN WHO CHOPPED OFF
HER ARM, STOLE THE BRACELET OFF THE SEVERED
ARM AND RAN AWAY.

EYEWITNESSES TOLD THE *TUESDAY STAR* THAT THE
MID-AFTERNOON INCIDENT TWO WEEKS AGO WAS
SWIFT AND DEADLY.

The *TUESDAY STAR* has learned that the woman who was
wearing a thick bracelet stepped off the bus and into the path
of a man armed with a meat chopper. Poised with the sharp
weapon, the man inflicted a single blow which severed the
woman's arm. When the arm fell to the ground, the man took it
up, and while running, he removed the bracelet and threw away
the arm. Eyewitnesses told the *TUESDAY STAR* that the woman
fainted and was immediately removed from the scene by a passing
motorist. **"When de hann drop, one a de man grab it up, and
while running drag off de bracelet and dash wey de hann,"** an
eyewitness said.

A nurse from the Bustamante Hospital for Children who said she
witnessed the incident said, **"my blood run cold when I saw the
woman fainted and the piece of arm began pulsating."**

THE MEN ESCAPED ALONG EAST QUEEN STREET.

THE *TUESDAY STAR* HAS BEEN TRYING TO IDENTIFY
THE WOMAN WHO WAS SAID TO BE WEARING
A TIGHTLY FITTED JEANS PANTS AND MULTI-
COLOURED BLOUSE.

When *The Star* checked w/ various Kingston area hospitals about
the woman, there was no information. A nurse at the Kingston

Public went through the log for that day but found "no such case reported" there. The University Hospital said "we are not allowed to give out any information . . ." When contacted, a rep of the Nuttall Hospital asked, "What is her name? Are you a relative?" She added, "In any case it is not a policy to give out information like that."

>>Bloody Robbery/Robber flees with woman's arm<<

The Star/frontpage 17 Dec 1991

●

By now the Age of Dis. Distress Dispair & Disrespect. Distrust Disrupt Distruction. A Gardener cutlashes off a Helper's hand for saying that he shd not come in here & take Employer's food. The Friends he entertain laugh after him for letting Woman dis im

They break into our finest literary editor's home one night and place her carving knife between her teeth & force it forward. forward. forward. slicing the boundaries of skin that mark her lips that let her snark & smile & speak, until the dark blade reached the skull. You never knew a human tongue cd be so red & look so long & gurgle with such flame

Near where I write this now a man is training dogs to guard you or to kill you. seen? He stands in naked smoke in his ram/shack/le yard of galvanize & cast-off wood & kennels. a long whip in his leathered hand. his jackboots on. the animal like tied to him by leash & lash & violence. he grieves the dog an order & it dis/obeys. he hits it wham wham wham. the grey hound howls. the others writhe & crash against their cages in dis/pair. hout hout hout howl. the tails aggressive & yet crazy in their primal fear. he barks again. the animal howls back & dis/obeys. he strikes again again then strokes the fire. smoke. more smoke. a crackle in the fury. he strides within the noise he cannot hear & lashes out & howls & howls again

Does he have wife & children. mother, close friends. red distant relatives? what
if he sees his dahta coming down the road? what if he hears his Grannie calling
home?

The leashed dog howls like human baby in its terror. sparks squinting from
its lurid tearless eye of error. wham wham wham wham. **command.** the
salivating canine howls & leaps & tries to break away. the black whip turns
it back & almost breaks its back. it howls again & staggers almost grovels
as the Man commands. until the thin bitch whimpers. tail comes down. &
falls. till in that silent yard. only the fire burns.

6.
Anansese

Significance? different from rest of story - I think [handwritten annotation]

Once when Ananse was a likkle bwoy he was
goin on & im see PingWing Bramble wid a
rat. Him fight Ping Wing tek way de rat so
carry it heng up in de kitchen. When him was gawn
Granny come een & eat off de rat. When Ananse come
back, im cyaan fine de rat. Ananse seh, "Come come
Granny gi me me rat me rat come from PingWing
PingWing come from God." Granny seh, "A cyaan gi yu
back de rat because a heat it off, but tek dis knife"

Ananse go awn until im see a man was cuttin cane wid-
out a knife. Im seh, "Man, ow come yu cuttin cane wid-
out a knife an I ave knife?" The man tek Ananse knife
start cut de cane an bruk de knife

Ananse seh, "Come come Man gi me me knife mi knife
come from Granny Granny heat mi rat mi rat come
from PingWing PingWing juk mi hann mi hann
come from God"

De Man seh, "A cyaan gi yu back yu knife for it breake.
But tek dis grass"

Ananse go awn until ini see Cow eatin dirt. Im seh, "Ow
yu eatin dirt an I ave grass?"
The cow tek de grass heat it off. Ananse seh, "Come
come Cow gi me mi grass mi grass come from Man
Man bruk mi knife mi knife come from Granny Granny

eat mi rat mi rat come from PingWing PingWing juk
mi hann mi hann come from God"

Cow seh, "Well a cyaan gi yu back yu grass
but tek dis milk"
Ananse go on until im see a woman givin er baby black
tea. Him seh, "Ow yu givin yu baby black tea an
I have milk"
The Woman tek de milk give it to er baby, baby
drink it off

Ananse seh, "Come come Woman gi me mi milk mi milk
come from Cow Cow eat mi grass mi grass come from
Man Man bruk mi knife mi knife come from Granny
Granny eat mi rat mi rat come from PingWing
PingWing juk mi hann mi hann come from God"

The woman seh, "A cyaan gi yu back yu milk cause
Baby drink it off, but tek dis blue . . ."

1971

This is the year that the world's first email message is transmitted in America. Over the next three decades, as the Internet is developed, it is estimated that the entire store of everything that humans know doubles. According to the National Forum on Information Literacy, more information will be produced during this period than all the information ever produced in the previous five thousand years. "There is no drama here," Peter Handke once wrote. "No action that has occurred will be reenacted here. Only a now and a now and a now shall exist."

PETER HANDKE

Suggestions for Running Amok

First, run through a cornfield.

Then run through rows in an empty concert hall.

Then, at the end of the football game, try to get back in the stadium through the main entrance.

When you step out on the street are you capable of having only *presence of mind?*

When you have stepped out on the street are you capable of being only *active?*

Once you have reached a decision are you capable of reaching no *other* decision?

Are you capable of distinguishing not among particulars but only among movements? not horizontals but only perpendiculars, nothing human but only softness?

Are you capable of *everything?*

Where do people gather? —People gather where other people have gathered.

Where do people gather? —In front of newspapers on display.

Where do people gather? —In front of traffic lights.

Where do people gather? —In front of bank counters.

Where else? —In front of store windows when the display is being changed.

Where else? —

Around two dogs that fight.

Around spot-remover salesmen.

In front of hotel doormen who've stepped out on the street.

Where else?
Under awnings when it suddenly begins to rain.

It has begun to rain. —It's not raining hard enough yet.

Where are you going? —First I'll turn over the fruit cart and wait until enough children have gathered to pick up the fruit.

And then? —Then I announce glad tidings at the street corner and wait until enough people have gathered. ·

And then? —Then I wait until enough people have gathered to form a lane for someone to run through.

And then? —Then I play dead and leap up when I hear enough people calling for a doctor.

And then? —Then I get people to bet on how many will fit into one car and wait until the car is crammed full.

And then? —Then I wait in the lobby, preferably of a high-rise building, and wait till the elevator reaches the lobby.

And then? —Then I advertise a tour and wait until I have assembled a minimum number of tourists.

And then? —Then I publicize a competition where every participant wins a prize and wait until the first participant asks to collect his prize in person.

And then? —To the telephone booths.

And then? —To the sightseeing tour.

And then? —To the department store escalators.

And then? —To the railway station at the end of the holidays.

And then? —To the observation towers.

And then? —To the resort towns.

And? —Highway exits.

And? —Mountain passes when the sun is bright and hot.

And? —Popular excursion spots.

And? —Park benches during lunch hour.

And then? —Suburban windows at supper time.

And first of all? —First of all I engage a single person and wait until enough people have gathered around that individual.

"In other words, you use the first frightful moment to make sure that there will be a second moment of fright, and the second frightful moment to make sure of a further moment of fright, so that you, since you yourself, of course, are free of fright, will always be one moment of fright ahead of them when they are just beginning to recover from their last frightful moment, for which you were responsible, while they were still recovering from the initial moment of fright, so that finally the moments of fright become legion."

And how?

Make short shrift. Don't fuck around. Kill 'em all off. Finish it up. Get it over with.
"Don't let anyone count, not even to three."

And to top it all off?
And to top it all off I spare someone to carry on the tradition.

(translated by Michael Roloff)

1972

France

"In the morning, when I hear you come downstairs, always late, cheerful and bubbly, words of vomit come into my head like 'gay boy,' 'poofter,' 'queer.' That's right, that's him. . . . But then you appear, a charming young man, and I ask myself, What's he doing here?" For the last sixteen years of her life, Marguerite Duras lived with a young gay admirer by the name of Yann Andrea. She was sixty-six, and he was twenty-eight, and although Duras fell in love with the boy, he remained solely an admirer of hers. Duras was often immobilized by these kinds of relationships—a passionate instinct for genuine love that was always undercut by love's impossibility. Long before Yann Andrea ever entered Duras's life, her best-known book recounted a doomed affair that she had as a teenager with a Chinese businessman. Before that, as a child, she forced her younger brother into an incestuous affair. And as a married woman in Paris during the Second World War, her husband was arrested by the Nazis for insurrection, interned at Dachau, and left there for dead. By the time Duras managed to negotiate his release, her husband had shrunken down to ninety-one pounds and was so weak that he was no longer even able to eat. In fact, none of Duras's doctors believed that he'd survive, so she nursed her husband back to health alone for eighteen months, and then, once he was better, she asked him for a divorce. Throughout her writing we can see this same kind of activity—a staunch refusal to occupy any kind of fixed space, be it genre, theme, or even point of view—and yet simultaneously we feel in it her anxiety for something whole. Her sentences, on the one hand, are sharp-willed statements of syntactical certainty. But they are always undermined by repetition, fragmentation, a refusal to draw conclusions. "The whiteness of meaning," as Duras herself once put it. Sometimes, so jealous of the lovers that Yann Andrea brought home, she would kick him out of the house for whole months at a time, then obsessively write about him until he returned. Duras wrote a novel about Yann Andrea. And then she wrote a memoir. She wrote short stories, letters, secret diary entries. There is even a documentary entitled "The Atlantic Man," a fourteen-minute study of her achingly errant desire for the young devotee. In its credits, Yann Andrea is listed as the only actor in the film, but on the screen for all that time we see absolutely nothing—no actors, not even images—just forty-two minutes of blankness over which we hear Duras, reading to us an essay, addressing the emptiness.

MARGUERITE DURAS

The Atlantic Man

You will not look straight at the camera. Except when you are told to do so.

You will forget.
You will forget.

You will forget that this is you.
I believe it can be done.
You will also forget the camera. But above all, you will forget that this is you. You.

Yes, I believe it can be done. For instance, from other points of view, the point of view of death among others, your death, lost somewhere in the midst of a nameless and pervasive death.

You will look at what you see. But you will look at it absolutely. You will try to look at it until your sight fails, until it makes itself blind, and even through this blindness you must try again to look. Until the end.

You ask me: look at what?
I say, well, I say "the sea," yes, this word facing you, these walls facing the sea, these successive disappearances, this dog, this coast, this bird beneath the Atlantic wind.

Listen. I also believe that if you were not to look at that which appears before you, it would become apparent on the screen. And the screen would go blank.

What you would see there—the sea, the window-panes, the wall, the sea beyond the window-panes, the windows in the walls—all things are things that you have never seen before, never looked at before.

You will think that this, which is about to take place, is not a rehearsal, that this is a first night, just as your life itself is a first night as every second unfolds. That, among the millions of men hurling themselves to their deaths throughout the ages, you are the only one to stand for himself, in my presence, at this very moment of the film that is being made.

You will think that it is I who have chosen you. I. You. You who are at every moment all of you, beside me, and this is true whatever you do, however far or near you might be from my hopes.

You will think about you own self, but in the same way as you think about this wall, this sea that has not yet taken place, that wind and that gull separated for the very first time, that lost dog.

You will think the miracle is not in the apparent similarity between each of the particles that make up those millions of men in their continuous hurling, but in the irreducible difference that separates them from each other, that separates men from dogs, dogs from film, sand from the sea, God from the dog or from that tenacious gull struggling against the wind, from the liquid crystal of your eyes, from the sharp crystal of the sands, from the unbreathable foul air in the hall of that hotel after the dazzling light of the beach, from each word, from each sentence, from each line in each book, from each day and each century and each eternity past or future, and from you and from me.

During your stay you must believe in your inalienable majesty.

You will proceed. You will walk as you do when you are alone and when you believe someone is watching you, I or God, or that dog along the sea, or that tragic gull braving the wind, so alone in the presence of the Atlantic element.

I wanted to say: film believes it can preserve what you are doing at this moment. But you, from where you are, wherever it may be, whether you have gone away still bonded to the sand, or the wind, or the sea, or the wall, or the bird, or the dog, you will realize that film cannot do that.

Go on to something else. Give up.
Proceed.

You will see, everything will come from your walking along the sea, beyond the pillars in the hall, from the movements of your body that you had, until now, thought natural.

You will turn right and walk along the window-panes and the sea, the sea behind the window-panes, the windows in the walls, the gull, and the wind, and the dog.

You have done it.

You are on the edge of the sea, you are on the edge of those things trapped among themselves by your eyes.

Now the sea is to your left. You can hear its murmur mingled with the wind.
In huge strides it advances towards you, towards the dunes on the coast.

You and the sea, you are but one for me, one single object, the object of my role in this adventure. I too look at it. You must look at it as I do, as I look at it, with all my power, from where you are.

You have left the camera's field of view.

You are absent.

With your leaving, your absence has taken over, it has been photographed just as your presence was photographed a little while ago.

Your life has distanced itself.

Only your absence remains now, bodyless, without any possibility of reaching it, of falling prey to desire.

You are precisely nowhere.
You are no longer the chosen one.

Nothing remains of you except this floating absence, ambulatory, that fills the screen, that peoples by itself, why not? a prairie in the Far West, or this abandoned hotel, or these sands.

Nothing happens except this absence drowned in regret and which, at this point, leaves nothing to weep for.
Don't let yourself be overcome by these tears, by this sadness.

No.

Continue to forget, to ignore the future of all this, and also your own future.

Last night, after your final departure, I went into the room on the ground floor, the room that opens onto the park, there where I always go during the tragic month of June, the month that leads into winter.
I had swept the house, I had cleaned everything as thoroughly as if preparing for my funeral. Everything had been cleared of life, exempted, emptied of traces, and then I said to myself: I'll start to write, in order to cure myself of the lie of this love affair that is ending. I washed my things, only a few things, and everything was clean, my body, my hair, my clothes, and also their enclosure: these rooms, this house, this park.

And then I started to write.

When everything was ready for my death, I began to write about what you've never understood, knowing that you would never understand. That's how it happens. I always address myself to your lack of understanding. Without that, you see, it wouldn't be worthwhile.
But suddenly I cared little for that impossibility of yours, I would leave it in your hands, I'd have no part of it, I'd give it back to you, my wish being that you take it with you, that you make it part of your dreams, part of the decomposing dream you were told was happiness—I mean the decay of the mutual happiness of lovers.

And the day returned as usual, in tears, and ready for the performance. And once again, the performance took place.

And instead of dying, I went out onto the terrace in the park and without emotion I called out loud the date of that day, Monday June fifteenth, 1981, that day you left in the dreadful heat, forever, and I believed, this time yes, that it was forever.

I think I didn't suffer from your leaving. Everything was as usual, the trees, the roses, the turning shadow of the house on the terrace, the time and date, and yet you, you, you were absent. I didn't think that you had to come back. Around the park, the doves on the rooftops called out to their mates to join them. And then it was seven in the evening.

I told myself that I would have loved you. I thought that by then all that was left to me of you was nothing more than a hesitant memory, but no, I was wrong. My eyes remembered those beaches, a place to kiss and a place to lie on the warm sand, and that look of yours so focused on death.

That was when I said to myself, why not? Why not make a film? From now on writing would be too difficult. Why not a film?

And then the sun rose. A bird crossed the terrace along the wall of the house. Thinking the house empty, it flew so close that it grazed one of the roses, one of the roses I call "of Versailles." The movement was violent, the only movement in that park under the even light in the sky. I heard the bird's brushing of the rose in its velvet flight. And I looked at the rose. The rose stirred as if imbued with life, and then little by little, became again an ordinary rose.

You have remained in the state of having left. And I have made a film out of your absence.

You will pass once again in front of the camera. This time you will look at it.

Look at the camera.

The camera will now capture your reappearance in the mirror parallel to that in which it sees itself.

Don't move. Wait. Don't be surprised. I'll tell you this: you will reappear in the image. No, I didn't warn you. Yes, it will happen again.

Now you already have, behind you, a past, a plan.
Now you already have grown old.

Now you already are in danger. Now your greatest danger is resembling yourself, resembling the man in that first shot taken an hour ago.

Forget more.
Forget even more.

You will look at all the people in the audience, one by one, each one in particular.
Remember this, very clearly: the movie-theatre is in itself, like yourself, the entire world, you are the entire world, you, you alone. Never forget that.

Don't be afraid.

No one, no other person in the world can do what you will now do: pass by this place a second time today, under my orders alone, before God.
Don't try to understand that photographic phenomenon, life.

This time, you will die as you look on.

You will look at the camera as you looked at the sea, as you looked at the sea and the window-panes and the dog and the tragic bird in the wind and the still sands braving the waves.

At the end of the journey, the camera will have decided what you will have looked at. Look. The camera won't lie. But look at it as if it were an object of choice determined by yourself, something for which you have always waited, as if you had decided to face it at last, to engage with it in a struggle of life and death.

Act as if you had just now understood, as you held it in your eyes, that it was this, the camera, that at first had wanted to kill you.

Look around you. As far as the eye can see you will recognize these barren stretches of land, these valleys held together by wars and by happiness, these valleys of film, they look at one another, face one another.

Turn away.
Walk on.
Forget.
Walk away from that detail, the cinema.

The film will remain like this. Finished. You are at once hidden and present. Present only through the film, beyond this film, hidden from yourself, from all knowledge anyone could have of you.

While I no longer love you I no longer love anything, nothing, except you, still.

Tonight it's raining. It's raining around the house and on the sea. The film will remain like this, as it is. I have no more images for it. I no longer know where we are, at what end of what love, at what beginning of what other love, in what story we have lost ourselves. It is only for this film that I know. For the film alone I know, I know, I know that no image, no single image more, could make it last any longer.

Light hasn't broken all day long and there isn't the slightest breeze in the treetops of the forests, or in the fields, the valleys. No one knows if it's still summer or the end of summer, or some other deceitful, undecided season, ugly, nameless.

I no longer love you like I did on the first day. I no longer love you.

Nevertheless, those expanses around your eyes remain, always there, and the life that stirs you in your sleep.
There also remains that exaltation that comes over me from not knowing what to do with all this, with the knowledge I have of your eyes, of the immensities your eyes explore, to the point of knowing what to write,

what to say, what to show of their pristine insignificance. Of those things I only know this: that I have nothing to do now except suffer that exaltation about someone who once was here, someone who was not aware of being alive and whom I knew was alive, of someone who didn't know how to live, as I was saying, and of myself who knew it and who didn't know what to do with the knowledge, with that knowledge of the life he lived, and who didn't know what to do with me either.

They say that midsummer is on its way, perhaps. I don't know. That the roses are already out, there, at the bottom of the park. That sometimes they are not seen by anyone during their entire life and that they hold themselves like that in their perfume, open, for several days, and then fall to pieces. Never seen by that lone woman who is trying to forget. Never seen by me, they die.

I am in a state of love between living and dying. It is through your lack of feeling that I rediscover your quality: that of pleasing me. I desire only that life should not leave you, otherwise I care nothing for its progress, for it can teach me nothing about you; it can only draw death closer to me, render it more tolerable and, yes, desirable. That is how you stand: facing me, softly, in constant provocation, innocent, unfathomable.

You do not know this.

(translated by Alberto Manguel)

1973

Ireland

"There is," wrote Samuel Beckett, "nothing with which to express, nothing from which to express, no power to express, no desire to express, together with the obligation to express."

SAMUEL BECKETT

Afar a Bird

Ruinstrewn land, he has trodden it all night long, I gave up, hugging the hedges, between road and ditch, on the scant grass, little slow steps, no sound, stopping ever and again, every ten steps say, little wary steps, to catch his breath, then listen, ruinstrewn land, I gave up before birth, it is not possible otherwise, but birth there had to be, it was he, I was inside, now he stops again, for the hundredth time that night say, that gives the distance gone, it's the last, hunched over his stick, I'm inside, it was he who wailed, he who saw the light, I didn't wail, I didn't see the light, one on top of the other the hands weigh on the stick, the head weighs on the hands, he has caught his breath, he can listen now, the trunk horizontal, the legs asprawl, sagging at the knees, same old coat, the stiffened tails stick up behind, day dawns, he has only to raise his eyes, open his eyes, raise his eyes, he merges in the hedge, afar a bird, a moment past he grasps and is fled, it was he had a life, I didn't have a life, a life not worth having, because of me, it's impossible I should have a mind and I have one, someone divines me, divines us, that's what he's come to, come to in the end, I see him in my mind, there divining us, hands and head a little heap, the hours pass, he is still, he seeks a voice for me, it's impossible I should have a voice and I have none, he'll find one for me, ill beseeming me, it will meet the need, his need, but no more of him, that image, the little heap of hands and head, the trunk horizontal, the jutting elbows, the eyes closed and the face rigid listening, the eyes hidden and the whole face hidden, that image and no more, never changing, ruinstrewn land, night recedes, he is fled, I'm inside, he'll do himself to death, because of me, I'll live it with him, I'll live his death, the end of his life and then his death, step by step, in the present, how he'll go about it, it's impossible I should know, I'll know, step by step, it's he will die, I won't die, there will be nothing of him left but bones, I'll

665

be inside, nothing but a little grit, I'll be inside, it is not possible otherwise, ruinstrewn land, he is fled through the hedge, no more stopping now, he will never say I, because of me, he won't speak to anyone, no one will speak to him, he won't speak to himself, there is nothing left in his head, I'll feed it all it needs, all it needs to end, to say I no more, to open its mouth no more, confusion of memory and lament, of loved ones and impossible youth, clutching the stick in the middle he stumbles bowed over the fields, a life of my own I tried, in vain, never any but his, worth nothing, because of me, he said it wasn't one, it was, still is, the same, I'm still inside, the same, I'll put faces in his head, names, places, churn them all up together, all he needs to end, phantoms to flee, last phantoms to flee and to pursue, he'll confuse his mother with whores, his father with a roadman named Balfe, I'll feed him an old curdog, a mangy old curdog, that he may love again, lose again, ruinstrewn land, little panic steps

(translated by the author)

1974

Canada

From Heraclitus's river, to Annie Dillard's eclipse, to Samuel Beckett's survey of ruinstrewn land. From Susan Sontag's hopeful claim that "there's water, O my heart. And salt on my tongue," to Artaud's resignation that it will take eighteen seconds. From Mary Rowlandson's preoccupation with the logging of her suffering—"Now away we must go with those Barbarous Creatures, with our bodies wounded and bleeding, and our hearts no less than our bodies"—or Christopher Smart's determination to stave off insanity—"For I will consider my Cat Jeoffry"—or Anne Carson's intellectualizing—"Surely the world is full of simple truths that can be obtained by asking questions and noting the answers"—Melville's playful listing—"Men . . . none; Anteaters . . . unknown; Menhaters . . . unknown; Lizards . . . 500,000"—Gertrude Stein's insistence that we see the entire plane—"In the inside there is sleeping, in the outside there is reddening, in the morning there is meaning, in the evening there is feeling"—the essay is at its best when it is trying to get somewhere. But, as James Agee demonstrates in his desperate, willful, incantatory song, *Let Us Now Praise Famous Men*—

George says; Well; and fluffs out the lamp, and its light from the cracks in my wall, and there is silence; and George speaks, low, and is answered by both women; and a silence; and Emma murmurs something; and after a few seconds Annie Mae murmurs a reply; and there is a silence, and a slow and constrained twisting on springs and extension of a body; and silence; and a long silence in the darkness of the peopled room that is chambered in the darkness of the continent before the unwatching stars; and Louise says, Good night Immer, and Emma says, Good night Louise; and Louise says, Good night mamma; and Annie Mae says, Good night Louise; and Louise says, Good night daddy; and George says, Good night Louise; good night George; night, Immer; night, Annie Mae; night, Louise; night; good night; good night—

just because an essay has something it's pursuing does not mean, necessarily, that what's arrived at is what's gained.

Seven Walks

First Walk

(Once again the plaque on the wall had been smashed. We attempted to recall the subject of official commemoration, but whatever we said about it, we said about ourselves. This way the day would proceed with its humiliating diligence, towards the stiffening silver of cold evening, when the dissolute hours had gathered into a recalcitrant knot and we could no longer stroll in the fantasy that our waistcoats were embroidered with roses, when we would feel the sensation of unaccountability like a phantom limb. But it is unhelpful to read a day backwards.)

My guide raised the styrofoam coffee cup as if it were the most translucent of foliate porcelains. During the instant of that gesture morning was all recollection, vestige—something quite ordinary to be treated with love and intelligence. From our seat on the still, petal-choked street we reconjured the old light now slithering afresh across metropolitan rooms we had in our past inhabited: rooms shrill and deep and blush and intermediate, where we had felt compelled to utter the grail-like and subordinated word "rougepot" because we had read of these objects in the last century's bawdish books; rooms with no middleground, differently foxed as certain aging mirrors are foxed; shaded rooms pleasure chose; shabby, faded rooms in which, even for a single day, our paradoxical excitements had found uses and upholsteries; rooms of imbrication and elaboration where we began to resist the logic of our identity, in order to feel free.

And specifically we recalled the small pinkish room above the raucous market street, the room whose greenish sconces had seemed to transmit new conditions for an entire week. This was the room where, in first light, a rhythm was generating some sort of Greek Paris, the room where, still-too-organic, we discovered we could exude our fumbling as a redundant architecture.

My guide deliberately swirled the final sugars into the steaming fluid in the cup. "The fragile matinal law makes room for all manners of theatre and identity and description of works, the tasting and having, bagatelles, loose-vowelled dialects—lest we get none in paradise." We rose from the wooden bench. We felt limber and sleek and ambitious: Ready. We agreed to prepare the document of morning.

When we built our first library it was morning and we were modern, and the bombed windows admitted morning, which flowed in shafts and tongued over stone. Paper documents had been looted or confiscated; new descriptions became necessary. Twelve pixilated scenes from the life of a teenager replaced walls. The pigments were those of crushed weeds under skin and just for a moment we left our satchels leaning on the font.

The satchels, the pixilation, the confiscations: What actually happened was a deep split, deep in the texture of mortality. We had been advised in the morning papers that there was no longer a paradise. Hell also was outmoded. That is why we were modern. We built this library with an applied effort of our memory and its arches were the chic curvature of our tawdry bead necklaces turned up on end. We laced its hollowness with catwalks, to make use of our intellectual frivolity. We could survive on these catwalks, slung across the transept, the emptied stacks, the nave, the richly carved choir, dangling our little bright plastic buckets for earthly supplies, and the bombed windows served as passages for our smoke. Always we were waking suspended in this cold library, as our neighbours were waking on their own narrow scaffolds and platforms, performing their slow, ornamental copulations, and we called our matinal greetings like larks.

It was a preposterous reverie, borrowing several of its aspects from stolen engravings we had seen and coveted and surreptitiously slit from expensive books in order to furnish the numerous inner pockets of our coats. But we felt some sort of use had to be made of the abolished heaven. Since it was redundant, now we could colonize it. Ours was a *fin-de-siècle* hopefulness, which bloomed in tandem with its decay.

The resting point of our long avenue was the shipyard with its jaunty assemblage of stacked containers. We talked of the bare co-mixture of stuff and life in the stacked hulls of freighters, strangers shipped anonymously in containers among their dying and dead. We had read of this also in the papers, how in the city's ports the wracked individuals had been prized or extruded as mute cargo, living or dead. They had attempted to migrate into experiment. The rhetorics of judgement and hope are incommensurate. We spoke of these rhetorics because morning is overwhelmingly the experiment of belief. We rise into the failed library of *civitas*. We agreed for the moment not to speak of the nature of the individual tether, the institutes and lordships and instituted shortages, and certainly this agreement marked our complicity with the administration of shortage. But we did not know any other way to go on. We in no sense expect to be excused from judgement because, our own ancestral arrivals having receded into the billboards and whitewash of public myth, we cannot fully imagine the terribly annulled waking of strangers buried in the lurching hulls of ships. We wished also to include in the document our willful ignorance and forgetting, not to ennoble them but because they exist in a crippling equivalence with the more doctrinal sentiments, such as pride and shame.

There we were, nudging the plentiful chimera of the foreground, maudlin and picturesque in our rosy waistcoats and our matinal etiquettes—please?—of course—if only—my pleasure—dawdling into the abstract streets. Or let us say that we were the scribbled creatures who received the morning's pronouns and applied them quixotically to our persons. Perhaps morning simply helped us to feel somewhat pertinent.

Clangour of the rising grates of shops, rattles of keys, the gathering movements in the clearer warming air, rhythmic drawl of trucks of stuff, skinny boys in aprons dragging bins of fruits, shut markets now unpleating themselves so that the fragile spaciousness leafed out into commodities. And this played out to the familiar accompaniment of the sub-melodic birds of our region, striving away in the boulevard trees. Yet we could in no way say that the hour was a development towards a phantom differentiation: already it contained everything, even those elaborately balanced sentences that would not reveal themselves until noon, even the long passivities, even the lilac suckers at night plunging up. We consulted the morning as a handbook of exempla as outmoded as it was convivial.

And what did we acquire through the consultation? Was it dignity or the final limpid understanding of a fashion in love? Or was it a hint of that suave heaven made from Europe (slightly mannish, famous for violets and roses, extra-refined and commodious with stuff)? Obviously we were confectioners. At least we were not hacking with random anger at the shrubbery and the absences, dulling our instruments. Yet we envied that capacity for anger we witnessed in others. Our own passions often prematurely matriculated into irony or doubt, or most pathetically, into mere scorn. We consulted morning also because we wanted to know all the dialects of sparkling impatience, bloated and purple audacity, long, irreducible grief, even the dialects of civic hatred that percolated among the offices and assemblies and dispatches. We wanted knowledge.

We entered this turbulence in our document as a blotted, perky line, a sleazy glut and visual crackle in gelatinous, ridged, and shiny blacks, an indolent pocket where self and not-self met the superb puberty of a concept. We understood latency, the marrow. We watched girls with briefcases enter the architecture, the ones we had seen juggling fire in the alleys at night. Morning is always strategic.

Inextricably my guide and I were moving towards lunch, our favourite meal.

Second Walk

Habitually we walked in the park late afternoons. Slowly the park revealed to us the newness deep within banality. This was the city where the site oozed through its historical carapace to become a paradoxical ornament. In this way the emblem of the park could appear anywhere on our daily routes, insinuating itself deviously within the hairline cracks in capital as we ourselves were apt to do. Amidst persistently creeping foliage we would tease out wiry angers and saccharine tenderness mixed, in this manner both flaunting and secreting our souls. In any case we were radically inseparable from the context we disturbed. It was as if everything we encountered had become some sort of nineteenth century, this long century that encroached so splendidly on much of July. We would lean on its transparent balustrade, rhythmically adjusting our muted apparel, waiting somewhat randomly to achieve the warmth of an idea. But you should not assume that my guide and I were entirely idle. Waiting was many-roomed and structured and moody, and we measured, then catalogued, each of its mobile affects. We dawdled morosely in the corners of waiting, resenting our own randomness. Or we garnered our inherent insouciance towards the more subtle sediments of passivity. But it is hard to make remarkable faults in a spiritual diorama. Only slowly did contrary dreamings appear.

Only slowly did we come to see our own strolling as a layered emergency: we recognized that we were the outmoded remainders of a class that produced its own mirage so expertly that its temporal disappearance went unnoticed. We found ourselves repeatedly original. The diva, the waves, the hotel, aroma of apples—these were structures in us. How like lyric we had been. Here, then, was the warmth, here the awaited idea. We were equally maligned and arrogant, performing our tired doggeries against a sky inlaid with phrases. We were of the lyric class.

Ours had been a rarified training—haute décor of dragonfly on cirrus, the crickets shriller. Our favorite objects were spoons. The eroticization of a privileged passivity twisted, turned, passed, and remained. Inexplicably both prim and sensuous, we drifted then and gamboled in puffs of golden dust. We were meant to be starlets. But since that time our grooming had undergone much revision. This rigged our vernacular also in a sort of lapsed trousseau. We now called our garments shifts or shells or even slacks. As the lyric class indeed we pertained to all that was lapsed or enjambed. Even our pathologies were those of a previous century, as when beside the daily marital protocols, lovefights wake a neighborhood. Remember lovefights? Nor could we act and change deliberately: although we desired fine clothes and freedoms on the patio of late modernism, what our passivity achieved or attracted were the fallen categories of experience—the gorgeous grammars of restraint, pure fucking and secrecy and sickness, mixtures of unclassifiable actions performed in tawdry décors, passional sincerities and their accompanying dialectics of concealment and candour, cruelty and malice, the long, ill-recalled choreographies of greeting and thanking, memory. Our agonies were farcically transparent and public. Yet those fallen categories, seemingly suspended in some slimy lyric harness, came to animate and rescue our bodies' role as witness, witness to the teaching and fading cognitions of the park.

Here, on the clipped margins of the century, in our regalia of mud-freckled linens, and with our satchel of cold provisions, we needed to prove to ourselves at least that although we had no doubt as to our lyric or suspended status, we were eager to be happy. We wanted to be the charmed recipients of massive energies. Why not? Our naïveté was both shapeless and necessary. We resembled a botched alfresco sketch. Who could say that we were a symmetry; who could say that we were not?

Previously I mentioned the spiritual diorama. Just for the satisfaction,

I'll repeat myself. "It is hard to make great and remarkable faults in a spiritual diorama." We knew our happiness was dependent on such faults— proportional errors, say, which expanded the point where the passional and the social meet, or the misapplied tests for chemical residues, which revealed only the critical extravagance of our narcissism. Yet our attraction was inexplicably towards the diorama. The glittering attires and airs of summer began to vitrify so that we felt ourselves on the inside of a sultry glass, gazing outwards towards an agency that required us no more than we required the studied redundancy of our own vocabulary. Hope became a spectacle, a decoration. Anger was simply annulled. All that we could experience inside the diorama was the fateful listlessness usually attributed to the inmates of decaying houses, or to the intolerable justice of betterment, the listlessness of scripted consumption. It was innocuous and pleasant, but it did not move.

Thus, the park. The bursts of early evening rain would thrust the foliage aside and shape a little room for us, promising truant privacies. Fragments of a hundred utopian fantasies of one sort or another mingled with all the flicking and dripping. My guide would utter gorgeous nonsense simply to intrigue and tickle me, such as "Swinburne couldn't swim" or "Seeing is so inexperienced." Is it possible to persuade towards disassembly? For such a persuasion is what the park performed upon us, loosely, luxuriantly, but not without malice. If the park were a pharmaceutical, it would be extruded from the stick of an herb called mercury; if it were a silk, its drapery would show all slit-film and filament printed with foam. If it were a velvet (one of those worn ones that shrinks or adheres like a woman's voice with ruptured warp and covert intelligence); if it were a canvas (all ground and flayed beyond the necessity for permanence). We were meant to inquire "whose desire is it?" and we did inquire, of the lank dampness, the boulder tasting faintly of warm sugar, of the built surfaces also, such as benches and curbs—we inquired but we were without the competence to interpret the crumbling response. And the tattered cloud and leaf tatters transferred to us sensations that we did not deserve. In the park, our generous government had provided conditions for the wildest fantasy—but what we repeatedly released ourselves into were the rehearsed spontaneities of poverty fables, the erotic promise of acts of disproportion and spatial discomfort, dramas of abandonment, the commodious weaving and bleaching of screen-like stories, as if we were to one another not amorous colleagues but weird sockets of uncertain depth.

"Our happiness" "our naïveté" "our attraction" "our regalia" "our humiliation" "our intention" "our grooming": this is the habitual formula I have used. While normally such a grammar would indicate a quality belonging to us, in this landscape the affects took on an independence. It was we who belonged to them. They hovered above the surfaces, disguised as clouds or mists, awaiting the porousness of a passing ego. By ethereal fornications they entered us. We had observed the images and geometries of such intercourses in the great galleries, print rooms and libraries of our travels, but here we ourselves became their medium. And as in those galleries, the affects that usurped or devised us were not all contemporary. The park's real function was archival. Dandering here, a vast melancholy would alight upon us, gently, so as not to frighten, and the pigmented nuance of a renaissance shadow eased its inks and agitations beneath our skin. Or we were seized by a desperate frivolity, plucked up, cherub-style, into marooned pastels and gildings. We foxed the silver mirrors up there and absorbed the nineteen meanings of the flexure of the human wrist. Or a fume would swathe us in the long modern monochrome of regret. I insist that we did not choose to submit to these alienations and languors. It was they who chose us. "No space ever vanishes utterly," said my guide.

If I have mistakenly given the impression that my guide and I were alone in this vast parkland, it is because our fractured emotional syntax rendered us solipsists. In fact the park was populated by gazes. They swagged the sites where desire and convention met. Now we found an advantageous perch on a marble kerb near the plashing of a minor fountain. We unfastened our satchel; we intended to nibble and observe and refract. We ate two champagne peaches. A gamine laced in disciplined Amazonian glitter strode past. Her trigonometric gaze persuaded us entirely. Clearly she was not mortal. We chose a fig and discussed how we approved of arborists— here the specifically Marxian arborist emerged from among branchwork like an errant connotation. With our pearly pocket knife we cut into an unctuous cheese and again the clouds tightened and the lilies curled and the little child ran cringing from us to its mother. We ate the cheese. "Hey, cobweb," a soldier called out, and the light fluxed in patterns of expansion and contraction. Oh, and the long leonine gathering from the green eyes of the womanly boy, his essence feathering, his gestures swelling, his fabrics purely theoretical. No interpretation could extinguish this. When we methodically compared him to what we already knew of boyhood— the strange dialect, the half-finished sentences, the exorbitant yearning for certitude—we experienced the delirious bafflement of a double pleasure, a furious defiance of plausibility. But the plausible would never be our medium. And then the ranks of slender bachelors frantically propelling themselves in too-crisp suits towards the chemical alleviation of loneliness, so frantically that they could not glance, could not comprehend the invitation of the glance, so that to them we were naught. And then the merely dutiful glance of the courier, which halfheartedly urged us towards a bogus simplification, and then the she-theorist sauntering purposefully from her round hips, her heavy leather satchel swinging like an oiled clock. Her saturate gaze demanded secret diplomacy, public contrition, and intellectual disguise, so that we blushed and were flung among swirling canals, sleaze, simulated musculatures, collective apertures, gaudy symbols, kits of beautiful moves and paper parts, vertiginous scribbles and futurist hopes. The she-theorist knew something more crimson than place. We felt suddenly and simultaneously that we should hire a theorist to underwrite our fantasies, the thought communicating by the mutually nervous adjustments of our carefully tousled coifs. She passed and we became tenants of a dry season, professionless. Her hazel gaze had informed us that we merely frolicked in semblance. Our pencil spilled across the silent path. A black panting dog loped past. And so on.

The gaze is a machine that can invent belief and can destroy what is tender. In this way it is like an animal or a season or a politics, or like the dark bosco of the park. Our scopic researches aligned us, we liked to think, with the great tradition of the natural philosophers, for whom seeing was indeed and irrevocably inexperienced, and wherein the admission of such inexperience served as an emblem or badge of belonging. What can we claim about the park, about the sorrows that are and were not our own? Nothing. We simply sign ourselves against silence. But the gaze and our researches upon it might yield a medium for a passional historiography, building with their interpenetrations a latticework for civic thought. We remembered the free women moving from city to city eating fruits in their seasons previously. To be those women, their feminine syllables bristling, to be a modernist declining the spurious hybridizations and pollutions that we intermittently adore and repudiate, to cup a superb expectancy in a sentence, to make with our hands a sensation that is pleasant and place in it then a redundant politics: this is not quite it. But as researchers we were bound to scrupulously visit each potential explanation for the scopic piety

we so cherished. Admittedly it was a relief when we found the explanation lacking. For to continue with our researches was our strongest wish.
The inevitability of failure became our most dependable incentive. And
as we strolled through the park to accomplish our speculations always we
wondered—were we inside or outside the diorama?

Third Walk

I said to my guide: "Must we recede into the wild spending of intelligence?
Might we go to dinner and have a fight upon a little sofa?" My guide said
yes. Although we agreed to assume that each thing that we witnessed was
real, I do think I first imagined what we later knew.

Evening. Palindromic façade: recalibrated symmetries. The temperature
swings. Torqued pillars; quoted porch. Quibbles say nothing about the
life-sized streets, the life-sized society, the justice of human warmth as you
enter evening. The rain looks expensive beneath sodium lights. Or perhaps
it's the word "justice" that has an expensive sheen. We went to restaurants.

We pass through a sheer façade. We find ourselves efficiently courted,
seated, appeased. Bleached textiles quiver. Placating foods appear. In
this setting, even the pale monochrome corners would further prompt
my guide's peculiar formality. How would one recant an atmosphere? As
a ruthlessly bland texture crosses my palate I lightly slap my guide's impassive face. Gastronomy restores nothing; neither would the wet street beyond the translucent glass. There, words want tamping. From the strained
sauces, the melting, the fillets of tender pigeon, the conical arrangement of
cherries, the aspics and the little grill of twigs, the giblets and vinaigrettes
and pale and quartered hearts and the sieved and the thick and firm and
moderate, the emptied pods, the shallow dishes with their slippery rims,
the routinely macerating heart—I abruptly rise and, clattering, flee into the
aforementioned street. We had had asinine hopes. We preserved them in
brines according to the precise instructions of ancient didactic books. The
words I wanted tended to become wasted infatuations, and here I will recall
little of the troubled interpretation of mutability, gifts of cheerful money
or sullen money, the wedding of skin-like textures, the fastidious rinsing.
It was not merely the diminished typologies nor the deferred substitution
of semantic monotony for touch. It was something ubiquitous and squan-
dered and ultra-minimalist about which, finally, I could say nothing. So

I walked, beyond the bare lobbies downtown and further. There was no window in the city that was not overtly moralistic—the roadways were illuminated and my decadence seemed to soak the asphalt so it shone. Ah, the longing for feeling, the tiny jaws of feeling.

Next, a syntactically cylindrical eating arena that converts spectacle into innovative light. We shall not enter this establishment: we do not care for the lucrative sugaring of glutinous cakes. Or, theatron (also a sort of eating arena flaunting contrapuntal gastronomic sighs). This is a high-status vacuousness, a superb adroitness, an actual veil of redundant brilliance. What else would we expect from the public quotation of a market's dream? Each vast room displays sociological moments as if the physical texture of watching inspired a décor. The flavors are plagiaries. The beverages ripple in heavy cups. In each sip a second, and occasionally a third sensation can be perceived. Though my guide and I had agreed, in principle, that taste can be doubled, or indeed multiplied, I grow to loathe the sumptuous, the elegant, the draped volumes, smooth pleasure's well-known hand. In this plenum, my boredom is an embarrassment so I cease to speak. From the brackish echo of public sensation my guide's neutral face absorbs a cruel and varnished sneer. Our silence is a style of temporary hatred, nourished by each little loosened oyster we swallow, each acidic little kiss, each sweetmeat, each odour of saturation, each quirky, saline broth. This cuisine reduces ennui to an essence, or worse, a glaze. The blurred arrival of exquisite courses is a sentence. We pluck at posh linen.

Or, engaged in close, indeterminate conversation which causes the mingling of the plundered textiles of our sweeping coats, we open an anonymous door, cross a rough threshold, and descend directly to the commercial heart of pleasure and regret. A diminished idea of daylight suffuses the soft membranes of the lower world. Poignant gasps; translucent rosy porcelains: the cradle of all that. Someone must believe in the chiaroscuro of love and aluminum. A mannered curve that has become a complexity meanders into radiating slits. Before this neon-lit rhythm of niches, these glimpses into figured inaccessibility, we do not understand whether we are guests or clientele. We can't ever request the rare fishes poached in foreign creams, nor the substantiation of the perfume of cumin, and other, intangible herbs. It is the restaurant called shame. Our mouths can't speak words. Although we are slavishly willing to imitate them, we comprehend none of the gestures of the articulate diners. We observe the inhalation of dirty powders from the small hollows on the backs of the diners' upheld hands, the flick of throats and the subsequent cluttering of laundered shirts. We cannot discern whether we have entered a microcosm or a landscape or a lackadaisical simulation of time. Pleasure is a figured vacuum that does not recognize us as persons. We stand annulled in our ancient, ostentatious coats.

This is how my guide and I passed our evenings. To sup became a refinement of irreparable insinuation, but also a realignment of specifically anodyne architectures with the complicit banalities of our soul. Yes, we were banal. We would call for "a little dish of honey," "a dish of theory," as if they could slake the burn of phenomena. What else was there to do? Bray up to love's ceiling? Deliberately polish the lovely, whoring dust? Practice the anticipation of failure? We never left doubt out of our studies. We were a purpleness learning itself. And if we spoke in the accent of the rhetorical past, in the myriad ligatures of cities, if desperation belonged to our texture, it is because, massively vulnerable, we were precisely unfree. We embodied the conflation of elegance and shame. Or did I only imagine that I had read reports of strange experiments in hunger and wandering before I set out to represent them with my guide and my body and the buildings and their intensities and their foods and the streets? We had agreed to assume that each thing that we witnessed was free. Was that the fiction of the strangeness of the city?

In the script that we followed, every cry was preserved by a dream. We constructed a journey out of a series of games of chance. Governments and volleys established themselves in our method. We found examples of the most brilliant hopes encumbered by verbal ambiguity, and from this ambiguity we composed elegant terms of expression. But the happiest days of our life are incomprehensible deliria, frontiers whose passages are blocked by words. We had recourse to material and rightly or wrongly we assigned the word rapture to its strangeness and obscurity. We knew memory to be superfluous ornament. And yet all our thinking is memory. Our investigations will terminate in a sublime falsehood; we will have failed to draw a waking life. We can't hold the stiff blood of paradise over silent paper.

Fourth Walk

The sky over the defunct light-industrial district was still the sky, less sublime, but more articulate. And walking what we witnessed was, like a flickering appetite, the real end of sunlight, buildings torn out of the earth and forgotten, the superabundant likenesses of pictured products collapsed into our dream and over and over in the dark the flickering appetite now bunched under the ribs. We were partly in another place. It's hard not to disappear. I pondered this ritual of crisis and form as my guide and I walked the unprofitable time of the city, the pools of slowness, the lost parts. We breached the city's principal at every moment with our incommensurate yearnings, and in the quasi-randomness of our route.

Ruined factories rising into fog; their lapsed symmetries nearly gothic. The abandoned undulations of the vast mercantile storage facilities, the avenues of these—sooty, Roman, blunt—and down below, the clapboard family houses with little triangular porticoes, lesser temples in the scheme, but as degraded. And in these rough and farcical mirrors, the struggle to recognize a city. By a habitual process of transubstantiation, some of this struggle was named "the heart." But we wanted the heart to mean something other than this interminable roman metronome of failed eros and placation, something more like the surging modifications of the inventive sky. So we attempted to notice the economies that could not appear in money: vast aluminum light sliding over the sea-like lake; the stacks of disposable portable buildings labeled Women and Men; decayed orchards gone oblique between parking lots and the complex grainy scent that pervaded the street. As we walked we presented one another with looted images, tying them with great delicacy to our mortal memories and hopes. It was as if at that hour we became strands of attention that spoke. In this way we tethered our separate mortalities to a single mutable surface. This was description, or love. "We must live as if this illusion is our freedom," said my guide.

Freed, we moved into the anxious pause pressing forward, that pause shown to us in its detailed itinerancy by every failing surface, every bland or lurid image, each incapable caress. The world was leaning on us, leaning and budding and scraping, as if it too was subjected to strange rules never made explicit.

Fifth Walk

My guide and I carefully selected our item, which I then purchased using my father's money. I still remember clearly our journey back from that indiscreet neighborhood: the lattice of little streets brindled with soft rain; the cheerful and nonchalant passing of messengers who we imagined were accompanying or parsing our gentle excitement; the way the late shadows made bowers for our tentative embraces, there among the sooty shops peddling used cups and hairpieces, and the hawkers and their fractured syntax, and the smell of spoiled fruit lingering in the moist air like an outmoded style of punctuation. Each matched, quickening step we took was a fresh conceit for the fibrous intimacy this new item promised to ambassador—or rather it was old content, even, though I may seem indelicate, used, since the tiny, poorly lit shop where we had chosen it, a shop whose shabbiness was strangely distinguished by the murmur of cultish erudition and disdain among its cloaked habitués, offered many slightly differing items, some enigmatic as to the techniques of their application, others of an obtuseness that titillated our inexperience while seeming to promise only minimal subtleties, but all united in their concupiscence and great antiquity. Each freshened the enigma of ancient dignity. We had chosen only after having appealed to the somewhat intimidating expertise of the shopkeeper, who had with hushed authority advised us to consider methodically both the unique and the importantly banal qualities of each item until a latent texture compelled itself towards our skin. Now, on the strewn pavements, our urgency increased in proportion to the luxurious withdrawal of light from the greased sky. We ignored the crowds that we resembled. This was a journey of hurried, determined steps, of distant irregularities, of involuting grammars, of tumescence and slurried rain. I tightened my clasp on the scarlet packet that seemed so generously to absorb the pulse of my anticipation. I believed that soon my cherished guide and I would become dependents of experience. We hardly limped at all.

The weather seared a ripe grey evenly over the lengths of our bodies. My guide and I talked about cold things to punctuate our adjacency. Sometimes our sentences began to cancel our flesh, their stately clefts of emotion erasing our bounded proprieties. And yet the hard structures of our palates were palpitating something tender and immaculate. And I must refer also to our phonemes, which in the soft air seemed to gloss earth with its sullen particles. Our woolen sleeves mingled their shining raised sheaths; my heart was suspended in the icy sky, sifting and rationing gesture. Early evening had pulled after it an imprecise dusk. All of this gave us more time.

Our desultory conversation veiled the inadvertent transgression of our route into the Secular District. The courts of my father's sanctuaries trickled their viscous light into the scoured streets. Huge columns flanked us. A tersely bent figure passed with tight-hipped gait, purposefully diminishing into the hostile iteration of a colonnade. We exposed ourselves to grimly imagined dangers in navigating this district. Our foreboding protected our bodies with hot surges of attentiveness. We scanned the shadowed gateways and clinging porches; we realized we would be known by our steps if they were heard by savants. Our ambered fragrance also distinguished us, and the woolen coats that brushed our ankles were of a flexible cut little appreciated by the tenured acolytes. I slipped our purchase into my deep inner pocket. The subtle pressure of its weight against my torso transferred to me a sensation of quietude—I felt both inviolate and assuaged.

Beyond the porticoed towers the broad street rose to address a sort of quincunx or grove. Generations of wanderers had remapped the city's inchoate routes to lead to this district's venerated mound. My guide and I, like many other travelers, were pleased to briefly enjoy the hospice of that thick-set wood. For we were not alone among the pedestaled trees that named the myths of liberty. We knew our sylvan companions among pommier d'Antoinette, Fiennesque elm, Nosier de Certeau, by the same means we had feared would precipitate our own recognition. Garments of rare subtlety and variety spoke the generous courage of their wearers—soft seams modeled mobile torsos, drape of ineluctable cloths framed the specificity of gait, fanning collars shielded the tenuous vulnerability of throats. As we penetrated the semi-lit margin of foliage to join this covert gathering, we saw, half-concealed in cedar and mist, a gold cab waiting. Through smoked glass the leaning driver covertly signaled to us. We entered the insuperable femininity of neglect. We receded into upholstered anonymity.

I would prefer to narrate an indiscernible movement towards a pronoun caked in doubt, but the gentle rocking of the car, the mock-innocence of gesture, the closed-in heat, suggested certainty. I did not know that those surfaces would lock. In that life, in that narrative, a shared object shaped our moral cusp. I thought of my guide, who was like a text that coverts itself through the most inexplicable activities—erased reflexes, ineptitude, insensitive deposits—as if the dispersed will could simply become something. Under the faintly saffron skin, beneath the curved black hairs that seemed engraved in their exactitude, under that loose skin with slight texture visible as a screen, a history of shifting proportions hid itself in the brackish pleasure of its own autonomy. It was as if my guide had extra conceptual organs washed up into the body like flotsam. This history was giving my guide life from a slightly altered or fragmented perspective, which affected me also—perhaps magnetically, or by some other sympathetic or electrical means. I sensed it internally. We were listing on stained velvet on the back seat of the cab. Our loose comfort metred the pocked road, the sudden turns and pauses. Blurred neighbourhoods slid past the glass: indulged white sculpture, burnt odour coming forward, glass grid, fringes of dust, errant monument, lit inscription and condensed ornament, darkened market, republican lustre of oil on canal water, threshold, embassy, paper, mast. I thought of my guide's stolid happiness, a happiness that circulated as a substance or a vapour might, sometimes to linger at the churlish skin, at other times to rush through the limbs as a mobility of means, and sometimes to pool around the gilded organs, remotivating the ancient tenure of introspection. My guide's was a practised thought which administrated unknowable generosities of detail with felicity. Yet this complexity was sparingly deployed. Observing my guide had taught me that happiness is the consolidation of complicities.

Undoubtedly I am misunderstood. Although I am not unaware of the fraught uses of the belling word "complicity," the company of my guide had pleated, among its maligned syllables, intimations of the byzantine bonds fastening want to its soft cage. That "we" in its moot atmosphere, clinking against knowledge, was circumfluent to the propriety of doubt. If we were abstract, if we cupped ambiguity and translucence, we also gave to one another the spurious syntax of thought. Books swell and shirts flower: events please by deferring bounds. But these words are vagaries that cannot indicate the wanton suppleness with which we attached ourselves to the tensing flesh. We were held to our wandering by permissive texts that also reconciled our itinerant lusts: our simplest membranes applied themselves to the world only under their querulous agreement. I know that when I say "the world" I resort to a tired method of reference. Each pronoun I used was a willing link in a chain of nonchalant extravagance that locked us to both luxury and thought. Hopefulness bent into its own opacity. Even the terse display of grief concealed reflexive superfluities. (I speak here of the civic grief that has passed from sorrow to anger, as such grief does during the extremes of ethical abandonment.) As love requires a politics, so worldliness cathects.

Then, in the humming silence of the cab, a movement of that inexorable body closer to mine. My guide said, "There are distances so detailed you feel compelled to construct belief. But it's the same finite drama of utterance. Something is not being represented. One day you will laugh at even this substitute, this obedience, this hope."

Kids in their nylon halos of beauty were passing. We saw the street lamps annotate their grace. Loose certainties of gait forestalled astonishment. Our car, still for a moment, occupied the centre of all their luminosity. I was witness to my own desire, as if erased, and it was something like history: a frivolously maintained dependency on the canceled chimeras of place, the obscene luxury of an analysis that rejects what it next configures as reversed. Nevertheless I wanted.

Sixth Walk

I feel I can look through the paintings and narrations, the sentences and devices of knowledge, the pleasure and melancholy, through the strange windows with their yellow light and shadows and curtains in the style of someone else's childhood. I can begin to see through another's technique of forgiveness or introspection.

When I started off towards my guide the bridge seemed to be made of astonishingly tawdry materials. Branches, twine, tiny mirrors, smashed crockery, wire, bundled grasses, living fronds, pelt-like strips, discarded kitchen chairs of wood their rungs missing, sagging ladders, bits of threadbare carpet, cheap shiny grating, rusted metal strips, gilded frames of nothing, lengths of fraying sisal rope, straw mats unraveling, limp silken roses on green plastic stems, tattered basketry, twisted papers, flapping plastic tarps lit from beneath, woven umbrella spokes, stray asphalt shingles, stained toile de Jouy curtains their wooden rings rattling, a ticking cot-mattress bleeding straw, swollen books stuffing the chinks of the swaying sounding structure, everything knit as if with an indiscernible but precisely ornate intention which would never reveal the complexity of its method to the walker. This was not a bridge I would have chosen to cross. I awoke already embarqued on the superb structure. There was nothing to do but continue. What the bridge passed over changed as I walked. At first, rivers of motor traffic hissing on a black highway, this with the skewed strangeness of a foreign highway, sulfur headlamps occasionally emblazoning the trembling bridge, which by then had become a cradle of slung planks, their wrist-wide gaps admitting blue-black silence of a forest, punctuated with the snapping and crashing of branches and odd whistlings in the wind, which rocked me also.

I believe that solitude is chaos. I believe that the bridge came to be swathed in undulating stuff, unknowable fibres that fluctuated like the dendrites of nerves, in response to the minute flickering of thought and light and things astral as well. My fingers stroked its pure oscillation. There was a sensation of cushioning, of safety, which at the same time was not different from chaos—as if unknowable varieties of experience would be held gently, suspended in an elastic breeze. What this experience was I can't say— it was held by the bridge the way sleep is contained by the person. Solitude and sleep are autonomous and festal. Gorgeous structures cradle them. We can approach the structures but not the substance, which is really more like a moving current. Then the rippling of fibres converted themselves again to foliage, as all speech converts itself to foliage in the night, and I felt this rippling simultaneously all over my skin. It was not necessary to differentiate the sensations of particular organs or leaves since this rippling unknit the proprieties and zones of affect—the entire body became an instrument played by weather and chance. We are so honoured to live with chance.

I wished for my guide to join me on this bridge. I dawdled and sauntered and loitered at its sultry interstices. In expectation I adjusted my maudlin garments and touched my hair. Everything around me unbuttoned. Did I cause this? Perhaps it was dawn, or something lucid. Animals were crossing. Mules and dogs and cattle. Children too. Bicycles with devilish horns. The bridge-urchins were at their card games and games of dice. Some of us were men and some were women. Some of us cheated. And in this matter also it was not necessary to differentiate. Some wore secular velvets and I touched them in passing, then uttered the velvet syllables. We carried wrapped packets. Some scattered papers. Some would sing. Maybe one was my guide. I called out not knowing if my voice would arrive. The harsh or worried sound simply blended with the frequency of motion. Was it a name? What could I hear or follow? The bridge was gently swaying; I wished to receive and to know my guide. But stronger and newer and more ancient than that wish was the barely recognizable desire to submit to the precocity and insecurity of the bridge itself.

Imagine a very beautiful photograph whose emulsion is lifting and peeling from the paper. There is no longer a negative. To preserve it you must absorb this artifact through your skin, as if it were an antique cosmetic comprised of colloidal silver. You must absorb its insecurity. Imagine the post-festal table, rinds and crusts and pink crustacean shells and crumpled stuff smeared with fats and juices, the guests gone, for a moment the raw morning utterly silent, your shirt stained with the wine, your face pulsing with the specific sadness of something you won't know. Imagine a sound with no context. Only that emotion. It is not called doubt.

Context has become internal, rather than hovering as a theatrical outside. Like new cells speak us. We call itself a name. We call it change and beautifully it's swaying as the new electrical patterns fringe our sight. Everything is tingling. We forget about Europe. It won't hurt soon. Soon we will relax. We will walk above polders and marshes and roads. The clouds are real or painted.

Seventh Walk

We had been at our physical exercises. Now we entered into the late civic afternoon. The scissoring metres of the apparatus had left us lucid, distant, and extreme. Cool air parsed our acuity. Although we indeed sauntered in the street, through the grey discourse called human and concatenations of rain (in short, in the mode of the ordinary), my guide and I perceived as from a vast temporal distance an impertinently muttering tide of ambitions and ticks. It was our city. We recognized the frayed connective cables sketched by words like "went" and "pass," the sacral nostalgias fueling violence and the desiring apparatus of love. Utopia was what punctuated the hum of disparities. Utopia: a searing, futuristic retinal trope that oddly offered an intelligibility to the present. We saw that we could lift it and use it like a lens. We observed guys in their cities, guys in their cities and their deaths and their little deaths and mostly what we coveted was their sartorial reserve, so marvelously useful for our purpose. "The fact remains that we are foreigners on the inside," opined my guide; "but there is no outside." And it was true that inside any "now" there was the syllable by syllable invention and the necessity for the disappearance of faces and names. Therefore we wanted only to document the present. For example, women—what were they? Arrows or luncheons, a defenestration, a burning frame, the great stiff coat with its glossy folds, limbs, inner Spains . . . Our hands forgot nothing. We searched for these pure positions to frame with our lens. Our foreignness was a precisely burdensome gift.

Make no mistake. Here I am narrating an abstraction. When I say "our lens" I do not intend to indicate that, like the master Atget, we hauled a cumbersome and fragile equipment across neighbourhoods. I do not refer to an atelier made opaque by the detritus of use, the economy of repeated gestures trapped in the mended furnishings, vials of golden dusts, privacies of method, sheets of albumen. Nothing was known about that. And when I say "women" I mean nothing like an arcane suppleness or a forged memory of plenty. I'm painting the place in the polis of the sour heat and the pulse beneath our coats, the specific entry of our exhalations and words into the atmosphere. And when we pass each reflective surface, glimpsing our passage among sibylline products, what are we then if not smeared stars, close to it, close to what happens; the sequin, the syllable, the severance.

This is a manner of speaking; never fear hyperbole. In practise we knew intimately the inadequacy of means for discerning the intelligible. Given inevitable excess, irreversible loss and unreserved expenditure, how were we to choose and lift the components of intelligibility from among the mute and patient junk? We wished to produce new disciplines within the lexicon of the secular; we paid a ferocious piety to artifice. In a way we were just rehearsing.

We began to imagine that we were several, even many. In the guise of several we lounged dissolute on nonce-coloured couches, bold in conscious merit. What we were to ourselves: fabulously dangerous. We never performed the pirouette of privation. Dangerously we pulled our kneesocks up over our knees. We asked the first question and we answered. What is earth?—A haunt. A tuft. A garland. An empress. A mockery. Girlfriend. A violet. A milk. A cream. A hazardous trinket. A flask. A basket. A mimic. A wild ideal pageant in the middle of London. A plinth. A liking. A bachelor. A thickening. A military straggling. And the severance, utter. And so on.

As many or several we played other games as well. We would mottle our vernacular with an affected modesty because we enjoyed the noble sensation of bursting. Flippantly we would issue implausible manifestoes, seeking no less than to abolish the therapeutic seance of novelty. When there was a call for images we would fan through the neighbourhood constructing our documents. Our method was patience. We would slowly absorb each image until we were what we had deliberately chosen to become. Of course then we ourselves were the documents; we acquired a fragility. Hello my Delicate we would repeat when we met by chance in the streets under the rows of posters Hello my Delicate.

And we learned that as many we could more easily be solitary. As solitaries, this is what we would do. We would silently practise the duplicitous emotion known as anarchy or scorn. We would closely observe strangers to study how, in a manner, or in a touch, we might invent the dream of the congress of strange shapes. We would make use of their resistance; it showed us our own content. We were not at all pleasant. As I said, our intentions were documentary.

One of us was famished for colour; this one would lasciviously brush up on the paused automobiles as if it were somehow possible to carnally blot the knowledges locked in those saturate and subtly witty pigments. One of us would take eight days to write a letter describing the superb greyhound of the Marchesa Casati, as painted by Boldini; the sublime haunches of the slightly cowering creature, and the intelligence of its ears. One of us wanted only to repeat certain words: diamond, tree, vegetable. This was the one who would touch the street with the point of her toe to establish its irreality and this is the one who would scream through the filters of gauze to illustrate the concept "violet" and this is the one who remembered flight. This one remembered flight. This one remembered the smooth cylinders glimpsed at evening through the opened portals of the factory. What discipline is secular? This one remembered each acquaintance by an appetite. This one remembered each lie, each blemish, each soft little tear in the worn cottons of the shirts.

But now we needed to abandon our pastime. My guide and I found ourselves leaning into the transition to night. Everything had a blueness, or to be more precise, every object and surface invented its corresponding blueness. And the trees of the park became mystical, and we permitted ourselves to use this shabby word because we were slightly fatigued from our exercises and our amusements and because against the deepening sky we watched the blue-green green-gold golden black-gold silver-green green-white iron-green scarlet-tipped foliage turn black. No birds now; just the soft motors stroking the night. Stillness. We went to our tree. It was time for the study of the paradox called lust. Our chests burst hugely upwards to alight in the branches, instrumental and lovely, normal and new. It was time for the lyric fallen back into teeming branches or against the solid trunk gasping

What Reconciles Me

What reconciles me to my own death more than anything else is the image of a place: a place where your bones and mine are buried, thrown, uncovered, together. They are strewn there pell-mell. One of your ribs leans against my skull. A metacarpal of my left hand lies inside your pelvis. (Against my broken ribs, your breast like a flower.) The hundred bones of our feet are scattered like gravel. It is strange that this image of our proximity, concerning as it does mere phosphate of calcium, should bestow a sense of peace. Yet it does. With you I can imagine a place where to be phosphate of calcium is enough.

—John Berger

Acknowledgments

If it were appropriate to dedicate a collection of other people's work I would dedicate this book to my students who have been reading and discussing some of these essays for many years with me, and who sometimes in response—to the benefit of this project—have challenged my thinking by declaring these not essays.

Eighteen Seconds by Antonin Artaud © 1949 by Editions de Gallimard. Reprinted by permission of Georges Borchardt, Inc., for Editions de Gallimard. Translation reprinted from *Collected Works, Volume 3* © John Calder Publishers Ltd, 1972; translation © Victor Corti, 1972.

Excerpt from *Narrow Road to the Interior and Other Writings,* by Matsuo Bashō, translated by Sam Hamill, © 1998 by Sam Hamill. Reprinted by arrangement with Shambhala Publications Inc., Boston, MA. www.shambhala.com

Translation of "Be Drunk" by Charles Baudelaire copyright © Louis Simpson. Reprinted by permission of the translator.

"Fizzle 3: Afar a bird" from *The Complete Short Prose: 1929–1989* by Samuel Beckett. Copyright © 1995 by the Estate of Samuel Beckett. Used by permission of Grove/Atlantic, Inc.

Excerpt from *And Our Faces, My Heart, Brief as Photos* by John Berger was first published by Random House, Inc.

"Ondine" by Aloysius Bertrand was translated and published by Michael Benedikt. It appeared on his personal AOL webpage. All best efforts have been made to secure permission to reprint this text.

"Tlön, Uqbar, Orbis Tertius" from *Ficciones* by Jorge Luis Borges. Copyright © 1962 by Grove Press, Inc. Used by permission of Grove/Atlantic, Inc.

"Trench Town Rock" © copyright 1994 by Kamau Brathwaite. Reprinted from *Trench Town Rock* by permission of Lost Roads Publishers.

"Egypt" by Michel Butor, from *The Spirit of Mediterranean Places*. Evanston: Northwestern University Press/Marlboro Press, 1998, pp. 79–147. Reprinted by permission of Northwestern University Press.

"The Night," from *Orphic Songs* by Dino Campana, translated and edited by Charles Wright, FIELD Translation Series 9, Oberlin College, © 1984. Reprinted by permission of Oberlin College Press.

Paul Celan: "Conversation in the Mountains," In: *Ders. Gessamelte Werke* Bd. 3, pp. 169–174. © Suhrkamp Verlag, Frankfurt am Main, 1983. Translation © Rosmarie Waldrop. Reprinted from *Collected Prose* by Paul Celan (Carcanet Press, Manchester, England) with permission.

"The Instruction Manual" by Julio Cortázar, translated by Paul Blackburn. From *Cronopios and Famas*. Reprinted by permission of New Directions Publishing Corp.

Translation of excerpts from *Florentine Codex* by Bernardino de Sahagún copyright © Charles Dibble and Arthur Anderson. Reprinted by permission of the University of Utah Press.

"The Atlantic Man" by Marguerite Duras. © 1982 by Editions de Minuit. Translation © Alberto Manguel c/o Guillermo Schavelzon & Asociados, Agencia Literaria, info@schavelzon.com. Reprinted by permission of Georges Borchardt, Inc., for Editions de Minuit and Guillermo Schavelzon & Asociados.

Translation of "Dialogue of Pessimism" by Ennatum of Akkad copyright © Emily Dimasi. Reprinted by permission of the translator.

"He and I" by Natalia Ginzburg copyright © 1962 by Giulio Einaudi editore s.p.a. Translation copyright © 1985 by Dick Davis. Reprinted from *Little Virtues* by Natalia Ginzburg published by Seaver Books, New York, New York, and Carcanet Press Limited. Originally published in Italian under the title *Le Piccole Virtù*.

Peter Handke, "Suggestions for Running Amok" (poem), from *Die Innenwelt der Außenwelt der Innenewelt*. © Suhrkamp Verlag, Frankfurt am Main, 1969. Translation © Michael Roloff. Reprinted by permission.

Translation of excerpts from "Tisanes" by Ana Hatherly copyright © Jean Longland. Reprinted by permission of the translator.

"I Have Looked Diligently at My Own Mind" by Heraclitus of Ephesus, translated by Guy Davenport. From *7 Greeks*, copyright © 1995 by Guy Davenport. Reprinted by permission of New Directions Publishing Corp.

Translation of "Dread of One Single End" by Edmond Jabès, translated by Rosmarie Waldrop. Reprinted from *Dread of One Single End* by permission of the translator and Granary Books.

Excerpts from *Essays in Idleness* by Yoshida Kenkō (Donald Keane, editor) copyright © 1967. Reprinted by permission of Columbia University Press.

"The I-Singer of Universong" reprinted by permission of the publisher from *The Collected Works of Velimir Khlebnikov: Volume II—Prose, Plays, and Supersagas*, translated by Paul Schmidt, edited by Ronald Vroom, pp. 12–19, Cambridge, Mass.: Harvard University Press, copyright © 1989 by the Dia Art Foundation.

Excerpt from "Miscellany" by Li Shang-yin, translated by E. D. Edwards. Copyright © 1996. Reprinted from *The Columbia Anthology of Traditional Chinese Literature*, edited by Victor Mair, with the permission of Columbia University Press.

Translation of "Is There a God?" by Li Tsung-Yuan copyright © Lucy Willis. Reprinted by permission of the translator.

"The Egg and the Chicken [I-III]" by Clarice Lispector, translated by Giovanni Pontiero. From *Selected Crônicas*, copyright © 1984 Editora Nova Fronteiro. Translation copyright © 1992 by Giovanni Pontiero. Reprinted by permission of New Directions Publishing Corp.

Translation of "A Throw of the Dice Will Never Abolish Chance" by Stéphane Mallarmé copyright © 1990 by D. J. Waldie. Reprinted from *A Throw of the Dice Will Never Abolish Chance* by permission of Greenhouse Review Press.

"On Some Verses of Virgil" by Michel de Montaigne, from *The Complete Essays of Montaigne*, translated by Donald Frame. Copyright © 1958 by the Board of Trustees of the Leland Stanford Jr. University; 1971 renewed. All rights reserved. Used with the permission of Stanford University Press, www.sup.org.

"Before Sleep" by Octavio Paz, translated by Eliot Weinberger. From *Eagle or Sun?*, copyright © 1976 by Octavio Paz and Eliot Weinberger. Reprinted by permission of New Directions Publishing Corp.

"Anabasis" by Saint-John Perse, from *Collected Poems.* Translated by T. S. Eliot. ©
1971 Princeton University Press, 1999 renewed PUP. Reprinted by permission of
Princeton University Press.

Excerpt from *The Book of Disquiet* by Fernando Pessoa, translated by Richard
Zenith (Allen Lane, The Penguin Press, 2001). Copyright © Richard Zenith, 2001.
Reprinted by permission of Penguin Books Ltd.

Translation of "My Journey Up the Mountain" by Francesco Petrarch copyright ©
2009 by John D'Agata.

Translation of "Some Information about the Spartans" by Mestrius Plutarch copyright © 2009 by John D'Agata.

"The Pebble" by Francis Ponge, translation © Lee Fahnestock. Reprinted from *The
Nature of Things* by permission of Red Dust.

"A Season in Hell," pages 193–213 from *Arthur Rimbaud: Complete Works,* translated from the French by Paul Schmidt. Copyright © 1967, 1970, 1971, 1972, 1975
by Paul Schmidt. Reprinted by permission of HarperCollins Publishers.

"Seven Walks" copyright © 2003 by Lisa Robertson. Reprinted from *Occasional
Work and Seven Walks from the Office for Soft Architecture* (Oregon: Clear Cut Press)
by permission of the author.

Translation of "Sick" by Lucius Seneca copyright © 2009 by John D'Agata.

Excerpt from *The Pillow Book* by Sei Shōnagon, translated by Meredith McKinney.
Copyright © Meredith McKinney, 2006. Reproduced by permission of Penguin
Books Ltd. and Columbia University Press.

T'ao Chi'en, "The Biography of Master Five-Willows," translated by David
Hinton, from *The Selected Poems of T'ao Chi'en.* Translation copyright © 1993
by David Hinton. Reprinted with the permission of Copper Canyon Press,
www.coppercanyonpress.org

Translation of "These Are Them" by Theophrastus of Eressos copyright © 2009 by
John D'Agata.

"Question and Answers" by Azwinaki Tshipala was translated and published by N. J. Warmelo in "Contribution Towards History, Religion & Tribal Ritual," *Ethnological Publications* (Department of Native Affairs, Union of South Africa). All best efforts have been made to secure permission to reprint this text.

"The Death of the Moth" from *The Death of the Moth and Other Essays* by Virginia Woolf, copyright 1942 by Harcourt, Inc., and renewed 1970 by Marjorie T. Parsons, Executrix, reprinted by permission of the publisher.

"Patroclus: Or Destiny" and "Sappho: Or Suicide" from *Fires* by Marguerite Yourcenar, translated by Dori Katz. Translation © 1981 by Farrar, Straus & Giroux, Inc. Reprinted by permission of Farrar, Straus & Giroux, Inc.

Translation of "The List of Ziusudra" by Ziusudra of Sumer copyright © Joshua Barnes. Reprinted by permission of the translator.

A Note about the Title

Because I think that having a broader sense of history can inspire a deeper sense of identity.

A Note about the Editor

John D'Agata teaches creative writing at the University of Iowa.

A Note about the Typography

The text of these essays has been set in Adobe Garamond Pro, a typeface drawn by Robert Slimbach and based on type cut by Claude Garamond in the sixteenth century.

Book design by Wendy Holdman.
Composition by BookMobile Design and Publishing Services,
Minneapolis, Minnesota. Manufactured by Friesens on acid-free paper.